The first edition of this book appeared in German in 1985, and set a new agenda for the study of medieval literary theory. Rather than seeing vernacular writers' reflections on their art, such as are found in prologues, epilogues and interpolations in literary texts, as merely deriving from established Latin traditions, Walter Haug shows that they marked the gradual emancipation of an independent vernacular poetics that went hand in hand with changing narrative forms. While focussing primarily on medieval German writers, Haug also takes into account French literature of the same period, and the principles underlying his argument are equally relevant to medieval literature in English or any other European language. This ground-breaking study is now available in English for the first time.

CAMBRIDGE STUDIES IN MEDIEVAL LITERATURE 29

Vernacular Literary Theory in the Middle Ages

CAMBRIDGE STUDIES IN MEDIEVAL LITERATURE

General Editor: Professor Alastair Minnis, Professor of Medieval Literature,
University of York

Editorial Board
Professor Piero Boitani (Professor of English, Rome)
Professor Patrick Boyde, FBA (Serena Professor of Italian, Cambridge)
Professor John Burrow, FBA (Winterstoke Professor of English, Bristol)
Professor Alan Deyermond, FBA (Professor of Hispanic Studies, London)
Professor Peter Dronke, FBA (Professor of Medieval Latin Literature, Cambridge)
Dr Tony Hunt (St Peter's College, Oxford)
Professor Nigel Palmer (Professor of German Medieval Studies, Oxford)
Professor Winthrop Wetherbee (Professor of English, Cornell)

This series of critical books seeks to cover the whole area of literature written in the major medieval languages – the main European vernaculars, and medieval Latin and Greek – during the period *c.* 1100–*c.* 1500. Its chief aim is to publish and stimulate fresh scholarship and criticism on medieval literature, special emphasis being placed on understanding major works of poetry, prose and drama in relation to the contemporary culture and learning which fostered them.

A complete list of titles in the series is given at the end of this volume

Vernacular Literary Theory in the Middle Ages

The German tradition, 800–1300, in its European context

WALTER HAUG

Translated by Joanna M. Catling

CAMBRIDGE UNIVERSITY PRESS

Published by the Press Syndicate of the University of Cambridge
The Pitt Building, Trumpington Street, Cambridge CB2 1RP
40 West 20th Street, New York, NY 10011–4211, USA
10 Stamford Road, Oakleigh, Melbourne 3166, Australia

Originally published in German as *Literaturtheorie im deutschen Mittelalter. Von den Anfängen bis zum Ende des 13. Jahrhunderts. Eine Einführung*, by Wissenschaftliche Buchgesellschaft, Darmstadt, West Germany, 1985; 2nd edition, *Literaturtheorie im deutschen Mittelalter. Von den Anfängen bis zum Ende des 13. Jahrhunderts, überarbeitete und erweiterte Auflage*, 1992; © Wissenschaftliche Buchgesellschaft, Darmstadt, West Germany, 1985, 1992.

First published in English by Cambridge University Press 1997 as *Vernacular Literary Theory in the Middle Ages: The German tradition, 800–1300, in its European context*

The translation of this work has been sponsored by Inter Nationes, Bonn.

English translation © Cambridge University Press 1997

Printed in the United Kingdom at the University Press, Cambridge

A catalogue record for this book is available from the British Library

Library of Congress cataloguing in publication data

Haug, Walter, 1927–
[Literaturtheorie im deutschen Mittelalter. English]
Vernacular Literary Theory in the Middle Ages / Walter Haug;
translated by Joanna M. Catling.
p.   cm. – (Cambridge Studies in Medieval Literature; v. 29)
Includes bibliographical references and index.
ISBN 0 521 34197 3 (hardback)
1. German literature – Middle High German, 1050–1500 – History and
criticism.   2. Aesthetics, Medieval.   I. Title.   II. Series.
PT179.H3813   1997
809'.02 – dc20   96–6228 CIP

ISBN 0 521 34197 3 hardback

The genuinely great work of art vibrates and 'moves' still from the artist's ability to proceed from one order of life to another.

Claudio Guillén

Contents

List of contents

Translator's preface

Walter Haug writes, in his preface to the English edition of this book, of 'perseverance' (*Beharrlichkeit*) – a term which may also be translated as insistence, persistence or steadfastness. I have to thank him for *his* demonstration of all three qualities, which must have been sorely tried while waiting for the book to appear in English. He refers to the unexpected complexities of translation, an enterprise to which he has shown unprecedented commitment and involvement at all stages, particularly the earlier ones.

Few translators, I imagine, are afforded the privilege of discussing their work with the author in such depth and at such length. Translation is always a process of compromise and decision-making; the author will testify that this process was not always easy – nor were the eventual solutions always arrived at lightly.

As a result of this collaboration, this volume is in effect a new edition and an adaptation as much as a translation; this process inevitably is much more time-consuming than a so-called straightforward translation, but the finished product is – I trust – immeasurably the richer for it. I have in all cases striven to remain faithful to the original while making the text – necessarily a highly specialized one – as accessible as possible to an English-speaking readership.

As one with a traditional training in *Germanistik* but (initially) minimal experience of medieval literature and thought – and indeed of theology – much of the material covered in this volume was unfamiliar to me when I started work on the project. (Such is, of course, the translator's lot!) I am grateful for the challenge it presented, the opportunity to become familiar with new areas and patterns of thought and the opportunity to learn which this provided.

Nigel Palmer's translations of the quotations in Old and Middle High German, Old French and Latin have all been made afresh from the original texts, consulting the translations provided in the German edition and the author's discussion of them in context but not slavishly following the reading offered there. They are 'authorized' in that all points of difference have been talked through with Walter Haug and resolved.

This book has accompanied me on many moves, both professional and geographical (my own *Wanderjahre*, in fact), and to these circumstances – the vagaries of the changing academic climate in Britain over the last decade and a half, which led to the creation of a new generation of 'wandering scholars' – may be ascribed in some measure the delay in its publication. It is with a sense of relief and accomplishment, but also with a certain nostalgia, that I view the completion of this project; I wish to take this opportunity to thank all the friends and colleagues in various universities who have offered both support and expert advice. In particular I should like to thank Nigel Palmer in Oxford, who first suggested the possibility of this translation and whose insights and explanations have been of invaluable assistance; my sister, for early comments; Kate Brett at Cambridge University Press for her indefatigable support; Caroline Mason in Durham, for proofreading and commenting on an earlier draft of the manuscript – not to mention unwavering moral support and encouragement; and Anthony Vivis and colleagues at the University of East Anglia for generous comments and suggestions on the final stages. My principal thanks however are due to Walter Haug himself, both for his generous hospitality in Tübingen on numerous occasions and for his co-operation and collaboration, patience in answering queries, perseverance – and many fruitful and interesting discussions.

It seems appropriate that this long-standing project should finally reach completion at the University of East Anglia – now home to the British Centre for Literary Translation – and in Norwich, whence many years ago I set out on my own academic wanderings.

J. M. Catling
Norwich

Preface to the English edition

This work first appeared in German in 1985.[1] As the first attempt to reconstruct a literary theory for the German literature of the Middle Ages from the specific statements of the authors and the theoretical implications in the works themselves, it sparked off a lively discussion about medieval literary theory. A number of universities started to hold seminars on the subject, often at the request of the students. Numerous reviews of the work have now appeared.[2] Their main criticisms fell into two categories: fundamental objections to certain aspects – in particular to the use of the terms 'fictionality' and 'literary autonomy' in the context of medieval literature;[3] and detailed criticism of particular points. When a second edition was proposed in 1992,[4] I was grateful for the opportunity to answer these criticisms and include more precise explanations and corrections where appropriate. I was also able, up to a point, to take recent research into account in the revised edition; in particular, to incorporate insights from Joachim Heinzle's new edition of Wolfram's *Willehalm*[5] and from Georg Steer's research on the prologue to *Lucidarius*.[6] Meanwhile, A. J. Minnis kindly suggested including a translation of the book in the Cambridge University Press series Cambridge Studies in Medieval Literature. I should like to express my sincere thanks for this opportunity to present my work to English-speaking readers. Jo Catling agreed to undertake the translation, while Nigel Palmer has

[1] Walter Haug, *Literaturtheorie im deutschen Mittelalter. Von den Anfängen bis zum Ende des 13. Jahrhunderts. Eine Einführung*, Darmstadt, 1985.
[2] The more extensive of these reviews have been included in the bibliography (secondary literature). See entries under Cieslik; Curschmann; Dick; W. Freytag; Heinzle; Huber; Krywalski; Lofmark; Marigold; Spitz; Voorwinden; and Wehrli.
[3] Heinzle, 'Entdeckung der Fiktionalität', 62–3; Huber, 'Literaturtheorie', 63ff.
[4] Walter Haug, *Literaturtheorie im deutschen Mittelalter*. Second revised and expanded edition, Darmstadt, 1992
[5] Joachim Heinzle (ed.), *Wolfram von Eschenbach. Willehalm*, Frankfurt am Main, 1991.
[6] Steer, 'Der deutsche *Lucidarius*'.

provided new translations of the quotations and generously brought his expert knowledge of the field to bear on the whole project. This resulted in an intensive and fruitful process of collaboration lasting several years from which I learned a great deal; the translator's queries repeatedly led me to reformulate various points of my argument more precisely, while Nigel Palmer suggested many improvements and offered support and advice. I was able to incorporate many of these insights into the second German edition. Even so, producing an English version of this book turned out to be an enterprise whose complexities I completely underestimated when we first embarked upon this project. One of the main difficulties from my point of view was that the English language is apparently much less flexible in its use of theoretical terminology than German, which has a far greater range of critical terms at its disposal – not least through the availability of *Fremdwörter* (loan-words). As a result, much of the text had to be paraphrased or reformulated, so as to ensure a coherent and consistent style. Occasionally some neologisms were felt to be necessary, and in a few instances a German term was left in the original – either when no English equivalent was readily available, or when repeated paraphrasing would have created awkwardness or clumsiness of expression. Jo Catling has shown enormous patience in this process of repeated reformulation while striving for the best means to express my line of argument in English, while Nigel Palmer has kept a critical eye on the whole project. I should like to thank them both for their time and trouble. Without their unstinting perseverance this project could not have been brought to a successful conclusion.

W. Haug
Tübingen

Introductory remarks

Medieval studies, especially in Germany, had some difficulty in assimilating the work of Ernst Robert Curtius. His work, which placed medieval literature in the wider context of the classical cultural tradition after the débâcle of 1945, opened up new perspectives and directions for medieval studies which were to prove difficult to resist. At the same time, this wider European perspective presented a challenge to medievalists which was, ultimately, bound to encounter resistance in the form of a defence of the specific characteristics of the Romance and Germanic literatures of the Middle Ages.

Since then, however, the critical focus has shifted, with a great deal of emphasis once more being placed on the traditional nature of medieval literature. This traditional aspect has been defined as a supra-personal set of rules for a vernacular *écriture* which is continually redeployed in a fixed number of structural 'types'. Paul Zumthor has suggested that the essential competence of medieval poets lay in their use of traditional elements.[1] However, this merely gives a new twist to old aesthetic controversies – artificial construct versus experience, adherence to a model versus direct expression of experience, conventionality versus originality. Despite the fact that it has long been agreed that these alternatives are not necessarily diametrically opposed – no more so than, say, synchronic and diachronic approaches in linguistics – most attempts to escape from this kind of dualistic approach seem to become ever more deeply enmeshed in it. Thus whether one wishes to demonstrate an original use of traditional elements, or the constant element within individual variations, this dualism recurs as a rigid principle which comes to dominate method and approach. Even those critics whose arguments have a broader base, and conceive of literature, in Claudio Guillén's terms, as a

---

[1] Zumthor, *Essai de poétique médiévale*, pp. 79ff.

1

system interacting with other systems, tend to locate its function in the shifting relationship between continuity and change. In other words, however complex the relationship between tradition and innovation may appear in the historical process as a whole, there is still a tendency to fall back on the familiar dialectic pattern when seeking to define the motive forces behind history – which in turn becomes all the more dependent on this dialectic concept, since it also tends to set the criteria by which it is judged. This applies even when one is aware that the aesthetic forms and devices employed are essentially ambivalent, so that form is alternately perceived as a guarantee of continuity and as a means of striking out into new territory, and change is understood at some times as liberation, and at others as a loss of self-confidence and identity. No intrinsic correlation exists between structures and their functions – a hermeneutic axiom which Hugo Kuhn, in particular, never tired of recalling.[2]

The plethora of positions in which this traditional dualism manifests itself today may be seen as a justification of the many and varied new approaches of recent decades, while at the same time compelling them to do justice to this almost Protean variety. This is as true – to name only two outstanding examples – of Hans Robert Jauss' reception aesthetics, which sought by the subtlest of means to reveal innovations and departures from the 'horizon' of a given literary tradition, as it is of Karl Bertau's book *Deutsche Literatur im europäischen Mittelalter* ('German Literature in the European Middle Ages'), in which he undertook to assess the critical potential of a given piece of literature against its political and social context. Both however leave open the crucial question as to how the aesthetic value of a literary challenge (or 'provocation') is manifested. Its value surely must lie in the achieving of a form for such a challenge – either directly or by implication – or, failing this, in reflecting the problematic nature of such an undertaking in the very disjointed and hybrid nature of its form.

The opposition between tradition and innovation thus seems to result in an infinite number of potential variations. However, it should be borne in mind that this opposition is based on a specific understanding of history, which is itself a function of the historical process. Regardless of the views of those who favour the dialectic argument, therefore, one should take very seriously the possibility of

---

[2] Most recently in 'Versuch über das 15. Jahrhundert in der deutschen Literatur', in Kuhn, *Liebe und Gesellschaft*, p. 151.

an alternative approach to history which is not vitiated by any dualistic pattern: the Middle Ages in particular were familiar with a mode of thought based on a concept of history as hierarchical progression, resulting in static symmetrical patterns rather than a dynamic, or dialectic, pattern of conflict and resolution.[3] A specific technique, typological exegesis, was evolved for this purpose: in other words, an interpretation of history according to which change is understood as a process in which one historical event supersedes and surpasses events which precede it: in which, essentially, the past – carried forward without undergoing any dialectical process of transformation – is confirmed and, once fulfilled, transcended. The only new event in history recognized by typological exegesis is the New Testament *vis à vis* the Old. This new event, simultaneously incorporating and cancelling out the whole of previous history, also affects the perception of the future, since after Christ's act of redemption, essentially nothing new can occur. Once this stage has been reached, the intervening period before the Last Judgement admits of only two possibilities: fulfilment or damnation.

The next stage of the argument, however, is rather more speculative: is it possible to see in typology a model or way of thinking which, outside the context of the relation between the Old and New Testaments, could come to govern all processes of transformation and development, including the establishment of a literary tradition? In other words, might one interpret the intertextual relations within medieval literature as a form of typology applied to the poetological sphere?

Be that as it may, if one assumes that the typological model had a decisive influence on the medieval concept of history, this in turn places a new, heuristic emphasis on the dialectical approach, since it raises the question as to whether this mode of thinking came to be applicable in the Middle Ages, and if so, when and where. Under what conditions and in what form was it possible for the dialectic view of history to take over from the older, hierarchical model, resulting in the latter being abandoned? At what point, then, did new events come to be perceived not as a fulfilment of the past, but as an antithesis to what had gone before, so that history came to be seen as an open-ended, continuing process?

These are the questions which led me to undertake this – perhaps

---

[3] 'Gradualism' is the simplified term by which this phenomenon is known. See Robertson, *A Preface to Chaucer*, pp. 10ff.

rash – attempt to write a history of literary theory in the German Middle Ages. Nowhere else are conventionality and self-conscious reflection so intricately interwoven as they are in the poetic reflections of the vernacular poets, sometimes clashing violently, like the opposing elements of fire and water, at other times merely combining into a tepid blend of traditional components. This seemingly unpromising material should demonstrate better than most not only how historical events have been plotted on a kind of literary-theoretical frame of reference, but also how this act of location was itself conceived of as a historical act. To put this more plainly: by a careful examination of those passages that contain poetological reflections, and in which the conventional elements appear at their most conventional, it should be possible to discover to what extent, and under what conditions, the medieval poet was in a position to articulate – and reflect upon – the pre-set forms of argument for describing poetic activity, and to examine critically how far these forms were applicable to the specific theme of a given work. Such reflection however also reveals the extent of the gulf between form and function.

The present study represents an attempt to make good a long-standing omission. Apart from occasional isolated attempts, previous writers have in the main shrunk from this task: first, the fact that the key passages in which ideas on literary theory might reasonably be sought – prologues, epilogues, literary excursuses – consisted almost entirely of traditional topoi meant that any suggestion that individual theoretical positions might be formulated here had to be treated with the utmost caution; secondly, the suggestion that a connection might exist between these statements and the subject matter of the works in question flew in the face of the rules of rhetoric. This is why up to now studies of medieval literary theory have generally been content to do no more than identify and classify the various topoi, drawing conclusions about the general lines of development on the basis of such historical statistics.[4] It was thus virtually inevitable that the usual pattern of decline, from the Middle High German *Blütezeit* to the

---

[4] The most comprehensive work on the German Middle Ages is Boesch, *Die Kunstanschauung in der mittelhochdeutschen Dichtung*. Viëtor, 'Die Kunstanschauung der höfischen Epigonen', Burger, *Die Kunstauffassung der frühen Meistersinger* and Tschirch, 'Das Selbstverständnis des mittelalterlichen deutschen Dichters' take a narrower and/or more schematic view. Even more recent works, which show an awareness of the pitfalls of such a technique, end up in practice with a mere catalogue of topoi – a prime example being Kobbe, 'Funktion und Gestalt des Prologs'.

post-classical epigones, should come to be accepted as the prevailing view.

In contrast to this approach, I have tried in what follows to present each theoretical statement in the context of the work in which it belongs, while at the same time giving the background to its tradition and viewing it against the light of this background. To some extent this necessarily means contravening the critical convention whereby the medieval prologue is held to be a discrete literary entity, independent of the work it precedes, to be treated solely in the context of its own separate tradition. This study starts from the assumption that prologues and other theoretical passages should, despite the fact that they consist of traditional elements, be interpreted in the context of their concrete historical function, that is to say, both with regard to their place in the tradition, and in the specific context of the work in question.

The fact that this new approach forms the basis for the present study means that the interpretations which follow are by definition of an experimental nature. The study is thus subject to certain limitations; it cannot compete with previous comprehensive accounts, since it cannot hope to accommodate all the available material. Instead, I have selected, quoted and analysed those theoretical passages which seem to me to mark decisive steps in the development outlined above, in which the pre-set forms of the medieval understanding of the world and history become increasingly receptive to the alternative view of an open dialectic process.

There will of course be those who disagree with the examples I have selected. Many readers will no doubt find something has been omitted which it might have been fruitful to include. The study thus cannot claim to be comprehensive on any count. On the other hand, my inclusion of Chrétien de Troyes' prologues, and the French discussion about the use of prose, scarcely needs justification in a study of literary theory in Germany: as is well known, at certain epochs developments in German-speaking areas can only be understood by reference to, and contrast with, events in the contemporary literary scene in France.

The present study naturally draws on the results of a wide range of earlier research, without which this undertaking would have been inconceivable: these secondary works are listed in the bibliography, and the footnotes to each chapter indicate where I am indebted to

5

each. Taken as a whole, however, this investigation seeks to open up new directions and to offer a new view of a landscape which, though already familiar in many details, appears markedly different when viewed from this new perspective.

Finally, I wish to avert a possible misconception: the impression that this study, starting from a discussion of literary theory, might ultimately seem to be claiming to be a literary history of the German Middle Ages. Any such pretensions would clearly be seriously misplaced, in that, first, only those works are considered in which explicitly theoretical statements are to be found, and secondly, the problems of literary history which emerge from the works in question are only discussed in so far as they are of relevance to the theoretical issues in question. This history of literary theory, then, can at most be seen as a companion volume to a literary history, and in this sense, despite the pioneering spirit which informs its method and the new ground it covers, the claims it makes remain necessarily modest.

The background: Christian aesthetics versus classical rhetoric

I

So far as we know, no vernacular writer of the Middle Ages wrote a treatise on poetics. The medieval poetics are all written in Latin and accordingly belong to that cultural tradition, derived as they are from classical theories of poetry.

However, a substantial number of vernacular poets had been educated in the Latin classical tradition, indeed all of them – disregarding the native oral tradition to which we have no immediate access – are dependent on it, at least indirectly. It may thus reasonably be assumed that they were not entirely unreceptive, in their vernacular compositions, to the poetic theories – or at least the techniques – provided by the Latin theorists. Closer examination reveals that vernacular writing not only put to practical use what the Latin handbooks had to offer in the way of poetic techniques and material, but also that, on those occasions when the vernacular was used to reflect on the place and function of poetry, traditional Latin forms of argument were employed. Such reflections were included in prologues and epilogues, as well as in isolated literary excursuses inserted into the narrative sequence.

Does this, then, imply that an inquiry into the theoretical premises and implications of medieval vernacular literature should confine itself to determining the extent of the legacy of Latin traditions of poetics? This approach has formed the basis of many fruitful investigations. The results of such inquiry are well documented; it is not the aim of this study to present them anew or to expand upon them. On the contrary, the aim here is to re-examine the scope and implications of this traditional approach and to draw attention to those aspects which have, in the past, on the whole been neglected, in particular the extent to which vernacular writers, working with and against the

7

Latin tradition of poetics, attempt to formulate the specific position and function of their works in theoretical terms.

To begin with, it may be useful to offer the following brief résumé of previous research and approaches.

One of the chief sources of Latin poetic theory is classical rhetoric. The connections between the two traditions are so manifest that the tendency has been to concentrate on them almost exclusively, resulting in an analysis of medieval literature solely from the perspective of rhetorical techniques. There can be no doubt that a whole series of such techniques pertaining to the courtroom could fruitfully be applied to the relationship between the poet and his audience. This was, in fact, already common practice in antiquity: forensic rhetoric had strategies at its disposal which could be adapted, in a poetic context, in order to establish the optimum relationship between poet and audience; the means employed in judicial proceedings to engage the interest of the listeners, and to persuade them of the case represented, could also be used to win favour with the audience of a literary work.

Ever since the *Rhetorica ad Herennium* and Cicero's *De inventione*, the guiding principles in poetic theory had been determined by the four set factors which constitute a legal trial, namely the orator; the opponent; the audience or judges; and the disputed case. The interrelationship of these factors determines the form taken by the argument. The more the case speaks for itself, the less need there is for rhetoric; the weaker it is, the more the orator's rhetorical skill is called upon. The highest art of the orator thus consists in securing victory for even the most hopeless of cases.[1]

The individual strategies employed to obtain the attention of the audience relate to the four set factors listed above.

(1) Presentation of the speaker: the latter may refer to his own merits and previous achievements, or alternatively set out his unworthiness and lack of ability with regard to the difficult task before him, even begging forgiveness for his lack of rhetorical gifts, etc. Such

---

[1] On classical rhetoric, see Eisenhut, *Einführung in die antike Rhetorik*. The following works offer a general view of the history of medieval rhetoric or poetics: Faral, *Les Arts poétiques du XIIᵉ et du XIIIᵉ siècle*; Baldwin, *Medieval Rhetoric and Poetic*; McKeon, 'Rhetoric in the Middle Ages'; Murphy, *Rhetoric in the Middle Ages*; Kennedy, *Classical Rhetoric and its Christian and Secular Tradition*; Klopsch, *Einführung in die Dichtungslehren des lateinischen Mittelalters*; Lutz, *Rhetorica divina*, pp. 15ff. Medieval sources of rhetorical theory are collected in Szklenar, *Magister Nicolaus de Dybin*, pp. 5ff.; cf. also Minnis and Scott, *Medieval Literary Theory and Criticism*. See also the bibliographies in Murphy, *Medieval Rhetoric*, and Jamison and Dyck, *Rhetorik – Topik – Argumentation*.

'humility formulae' flatter the listeners and are designed to gain their indulgence.

(2) Denigration of opponents: the speaker may seek to create antipathy towards the latter, e.g. by disparaging their actions and way of life.

(3) Referring to the audience, the speaker may credit them with great powers of discernment, stressing with what interest their decision is awaited. He may appeal to their superior judgement and/or request their assistance.

(4) Referring to the case itself, interest may be aroused by representing the case as one of vital importance, or by promising something surprising or novel. Furthermore, the position adopted may be reinforced by reference to current usage or proven practice.

The application of these strategies of forensic argument to literature meant that the courtroom situation could be taken as a model for the dialogue between author and public. Since the task of establishing a relationship with the audience was in the first instance allocated to the prologue, the four arguments outlined above reappear, suitably adapted, in those parts of poetic treatises concerned with prologue theory, where the arguments are listed as so-called commonplaces or topoi, which may be employed when it comes to establishing contact with the audience.[2] Thus here also we find, respectively, (1) either confident references to the speaker's own abilities, or, conversely, emphasis on the poet's own lack of ability so as to appeal to the audience's sympathy; (2) attacks on opponents, whether they be colleagues – or rivals – who are accused of not having presented the material properly, or the malevolent critics who seek to denigrate a good cause. Furthermore, (3) a wide variety of direct appeals to the audience may be found, making use of the most diverse forms of flattery; a recurrent feature is the compelling argument that only those who are truly clever and perceptive will be able to comprehend the work fully. Finally, (4) when the argument proceeds from the facts themselves, the same strategies can be found as are used in judicial oratory, with references to the importance, novelty, and the surprising – or indeed the traditional – features of the case, all of

---

[2] On this adaptation of forensic topoi in poetic theory and practice, see Curtius, *Europäische Literatur und lateinisches Mittelalter*, pp. 71ff.; Arbusow, *Colores rhetorici*, pp. 97ff.; Lausberg, *Handbuch der literarischen Rhetorik*, cols. 263–88; Brinkmann, 'Der Prolog im Mittelalter'.

which are supported by reference to authorities or guaranteed by the authenticity of the facts.

The adaptation of rhetorical argument by poetic theory lends a peculiarly schematic character to the literary prologue. Even before literary historians became aware of these connections, the stereotypical nature of the various prologue elements had been noted, and these had been collated and classified accordingly. This also revealed the considerable degree of consistency and universal application of these elements, recurring as they did in a wide variety of linguistic and historical contexts. It was also noted that on the whole epilogues drew upon the same set formulae; the epilogue was probably derived to a large extent from the prologue.[3] However, early examinations of these stereotypes – by Lange, Ritter, Halpersohn and Iwand, for example – tended to be limited to mere collections of the relevant material.[4]

Ernst Robert Curtius was the first to bring a new approach to the subject, by opening up a diachronic view of literary topoi. This not only paved the way for a new, theoretical interest in the topos as such, but also made it an important instrument in the study of cultural history, indeed of cultural criticism. On the one hand, Curtius stressed the classical origins of topoi and conventional stock literary devices. On the other hand, prologue topoi provided him with crucial evidence for the idea of a tradition of classical poetic theory and practice continuing unbroken from antiquity into the Middle Ages, and thence into the modern period.

This re-appraisal was widely acclaimed and adopted by other scholars in the field; existing material was re-assessed in accordance with the new perspective, and the investigation of literary topoi gave rise to a large number of monographs on the traditions and adaptations of literary formulae that took into account not only medieval Latin writing, but the vernacular corpus as well.[5] Meanwhile, the role

---

[3] Sayce, 'Prolog, Epilog und das Problem des Erzählers', 65–6. The motifs are largely interchangeable: Kobbe, 'Funktion und Gestalt des Prologs', 415.

[4] This method – a tabulated list of motifs – still persists today: e.g. Kobbe, 'Funktion und Gestalt des Prologs'; Jaeger, *Prologue Tradition*; Schmolke-Hasselmann, 'Untersuchungen zur Typik'. Its use is justified by Kobbe, 'Funktion und Gestalt des Prologs', 416ff. The slim volume by Schreiber, *Studien zum Prolog*, has little to offer.

[5] See the following surveys of topos research, with further references: Pöggeler, 'Dichtungstheorie und Toposforschung'; Veit, 'Toposforschung'; Jehn, *Toposforschung*; Baeumer, *Toposforschung*; for a broader survey, see Bornscheuer, 'Bemerkungen zur Toposforschung' and *Topik*; Breuer and Schanze, *Topik*.

played by school grammars and poetics in transmitting this tradition became increasingly apparent.[6]

However, as these critical efforts became more fruitful, so the question as to how far medieval literature should after all be regarded as a mere imitation of poetic forms and formulae laid down in antiquity became increasingly pressing. Prologue topoi, in particular, came to be recognized as an area of extreme conventionality. If these topoi really represented nothing more than a stock of techniques designed to influence reception, seeking to manipulate audience response, then to expect such prologues to provide the key to specifically medieval theories of literature – let alone to the literary theories and practice of individual poets – seemed at best misguided.

Curtius' extremely conventional interpretation of topos traditions encountered criticism from the outset. One of the most significant contributions to the debate of cliché versus individuality comes from Helmut Beumann;[7] topos research could have avoided many a false trail had his achievements been appreciated sooner.

Beumann presented his critique of Curtius in the form of an analysis of Einhard's prologue to his *Vita Caroli Magni*, in which he established that the prologue does not contain a single original idea, but rather consists solely of a mere sequence of current topoi. He notes the following: first, the *brevitas* formula – the author's assurance that he will be concise, since he has no wish to bore the audience; in other words, the *fastidium* topos. This is then followed by praise of his contemporaries – an application of the *memoria* topos: what is worthy of recollection must not be allowed to fall prey to oblivion. Then comes the modesty topos: the claim that one's own skill is unequal to the demands of the subject; this leads to a justification of the work from the point of view of the subject matter, and so on: an

---

6   The following monographs appeared before Curtius' work: Ehrismann, *Studien über Rudolf von Ems*; Sawicki, *Gottfried von Straßburg*. Salmon, 'Über den Beitrag des grammatischen Unterrichts', and Kelly, 'Theory of composition' and 'Topical invention in medieval French literature' are indebted to Faral, *Les Arts poétiques du XIIe et du XIIIe siècle*. For Middle Dutch, see Oostrom, *Lantsloot vander Haghedochte*, pp. 183ff.

7   Beumann, 'Topos und Gedankenfuge bei Einhard'; cf. also Beumann, 'Der Schriftsteller und seine Kritiker'. For critiques of Curtius see further Hugo Kuhn, 'Zum neuen Bild vom Mittelalter', 530ff.; Zumthor, *Essai de poétique médiévale*, pp. 51ff.; Szklenar, *Magister Nicolaus de Dybin*, p. 5, note 13. For a discussion of the particular significance of the rhetorical tradition in vernacular literature, see Wehrli, *Literatur im deutschen Mittelalter*, pp. 114–15. Schultz, 'Classical rhetoric', presents a radically different view.

accumulation, then, of conventional arguments handed down from antiquity in the rhetorical tradition. Nevertheless this prologue is, as Beumann shows, absolutely specific, in that Einhard makes use of the topoi to mount a veiled attack on certain ecclesiastical circles at the court who, after Charlemagne's death, took steps to prevent any further cultivation of classical secular literature. Thus it may be seen that traditional elements can be combined to produce highly individual and situation-specific utterances; the masking effect, by which these can be concealed under the disguise of conventional topoi, may serve as an additional attraction here. Topoi may thus be seen not merely as the constant elements of tradition, but also as variables which may be used both in a traditional and in an individual manner; indeed it is precisely from this tension that a particularly subtle intellectual argument arises. Individuality is expressed here to a large extent – and this is true for the Middle Ages in general – in the specific use made of traditional elements. This has long gone unrecognized, obscured either by a search for originality in the modern sense – involving a misinterpretation of the use of topoi – or, as a reaction against this, by an exclusive concentration on traditional elements, with the result that the observer remains unaware of the wealth of nuance possible in the poet's variation and modification of traditional elements.

With regard to exordial topoi, Hennig Brinkmann's important study of 1964[8] attempts to discover the specific form of the medieval prologue. He argues that although the Middle Ages were content to adopt the classical rhetorical patterns of argument in their prologues, in so doing they schematized the construction of the prologue and supplied a theoretical basis for this new scheme. According to Brinkmann, the medieval prologue consists of two parts, the first of which serves in a general way to establish contact between poet and audience. The opening of this 'dialogue' tends to consist of a truism common to both parties (author and public), i.e. a proverb or *sententia* which forms, so to speak, the basis of the understanding on which the rest of the argument may be built up; exempla too may be used for this purpose. The second part then offers an introduction to the work, setting out the source and subject matter and outlining the external circumstances which gave rise to the work. Brinkmann claims to have found Latin theoretical terms for these two parts of the

---

[8]   Brinkmann, 'Prolog im Mittelalter', 85ff.

prologue: John of Garland refers to them as *prooemium* and *prologus*, Konrad of Hirsau as *prologus praeter rem* and *prologus ante rem* respectively.[9] In addition, the form of the prologue varies according to genre: in the *exordium* to the lives of saints, a prayer often takes the place of the initial establishment of contact with the audience. Brinkmann goes on to interpret a series of prologues according to this scheme and this approach has met with widespread acceptance.

Actual poetic practice, however, was far less schematic than Brinkmann's study might suggest. This was quickly pointed out with some force, and Brinkmann himself found occasion to comment on it.[10] Nevertheless, as far as the theory is concerned, Brinkmann's thesis was long accepted uncritically, until Samuel Jaffe, in his reassessment of 1978, came to the conclusion that Brinkmann had not interpreted the relevant texts of John of Garland and Konrad of Hirsau with sufficient accuracy.[11] Neither, in fact, refers to the separate parts of the prologue; instead, the terms used refer to different prologue types. Thus a theoretical basis for the bipartite division of the medieval prologue, as understood by Brinkmann, has never been established, nor can it be seen as obligatory in practice. Of course, there can be no denying a widespread tendency in medieval prologues to establish a dialogue with the audience on a general level, before going on to introduce the subject matter; however, this is such a natural process that it would surely have presented itself to each author in turn as the occasion arose, and in any case is in no way peculiar to the Middle Ages. Thus the opposite view is almost of greater interest: namely the question as to where – and why – this division of the prologue into two distinct stages was *not* of importance, in other words whether this came about because the introduction was reduced to one part, or whether the different aspects of the prologue were so intertwined as to render a bipartite structure impracticable.

Bearing in mind these reservations, however, Brinkmann's scheme is still a useful methodological tool. Any criticism should be not of the approach – which leaves scope for improvement and refinement – but of a principle for which Brinkmann's study of prologue strategies is but one example. The fundamental question here is the

---

[9] On the difficult question of terminology, see Hirdt, 'Untersuchungen zum Eingang', 84ff.
[10] Brinkmann, 'Prolog im Mittelalter', 90. For a critique which makes especial reference to the differences between genres, see Kobbe, 'Funktion und Gestalt des Prologs', 414–15; Naumann, 'Ein- und Ausgänge frühmittelhochdeutscher Gedichte', pp. 56–7.
[11] Cf. also Schultz, 'Classical rhetoric', 12–13, on this.

understanding of the relationship between the prologue and the main body of the work. Even if one agrees with Beumann in recognizing the potential for an individual arrangement of the *prologus praeter rem*, there remains a general consensus that it is not permissible to connect this part of the prologue with the subject matter of the work itself.[12] This idea of an autonomous *prologus praeter rem* should be retained in principle; on a higher level, however, it no longer applies; a true understanding of the relationship between the poet and the implied audience is not possible unless the idea of an autonomous *prologus praeter rem* is called into question. In other words, a literary interpretation must necessarily look beyond a narrow definition of rhetorical prologue strategies. It has all too rarely been taken into account that the introduction to a narrative work does not, unlike forensic rhetoric, necessarily choose to present a case in the most apt strategic fashion possible – rather, it seeks to prime the response of the audience in accordance with the author's intentions for the work. There are, of course, a large number of merely conventional introductions, which aim to do no more than capture the attention or goodwill of the audience; the more general tendency is, however, for the literary prologue to discuss the meaning a work is intended to convey, reflecting the possibilities and limitations of this process, and raising the question as to its status and justification. The further a prologue goes along these lines, the more the traditional strategies tend to become merely incidental, unless they are adapted to the new purpose. Although the rhetorical background of the medieval epic prologue cannot be ignored, it should be remembered that the literary situation differs in essence from the courtroom situation of the rhetoricians, precisely on account of the hermeneutic process involved in literary communication. The function of the prologue should thus be considered from a different perspective, namely whether, or to what extent, it is able to articulate the specific conditions of the hermeneutic act, in addition to reflecting upon itself in the context of this act. However, this level of poetic self-consciousness cannot ultimately be discussed in isolation from its thematic context.[13]

---

12 Cf. Veit, 'Toposforschung', 132; Finster, *Zur Theorie und Technik*, p. 140 refers to poetic theories which explicitly postulate a division between the prologue and the subject of the work.

13 Naumann, 'Vorstudien'; Kobbe, 'Funktion und Gestalt des Prologs'; Hirdt, 'Untersuchungen', and Singer, 'Der Eingang von Strickers *Karl dem Großen*', have gone furthest in this direction with their considerations of prologue theory.

II

The constant series of attempts to reduce the narrative literature of the Middle Ages to its traditional elements, and to embed these in the continuity of Western cultural tradition, have without doubt put a timely end to an older way of thinking which was all too modern in its individualistic observations. In the process, however, not only have the specifically medieval forms of individualization – the selection and combination of particular topical elements, innovation with regard to the situation, and so on – become lost to view in many cases; but also too little attention has been paid to the possibility of breaks with and renewals of tradition, unless from the negative viewpoint of a general lowering of cultural standards. Thus the fundamental transformation effected by the impact of Christianity on classical poetic theory, which formed the particular focus of Erich Auerbach's research, was largely ignored by Curtius. It might reasonably be expected that someone would have subsequently taken the trouble to investigate whether these two contrasting positions were complementary or mutually exclusive, yet while Curtius, like Auerbach, encountered criticism – some of it harsh – as far as the present author can ascertain there has been no attempt to reconcile the thesis of continuity with the thesis of discontinuity, nor even to explain how two such diametrically opposed approaches could have come about.

Pursuing this problem further, one discovers that the conflict is rooted in the historical circumstances of the material itself. These can best be presented from Auerbach's starting position: the more early Christianity was taken up by the educated classes, the more contradictory did its relationship to the classical cultural tradition appear. Rhetoric, the key element of classical education, became a critical touchstone. Augustine asked, in *De doctrina christiana*, whether it was permissible to employ the rhetorical strategies offered by classical poetics and rhetorical practice in a Christian sermon. His answer is emphatically affirmative, for, he states, it would be absurd to leave the weapons of eloquence in the hands of the agents of falsehood while withholding them from the advocates of truth.[14] This was intended less as a programmatic statement than as an apology for current practice, since the Christians had, naturally enough, made use of

---

[14] *De doctrina christiana* IV, ii; cf. Norden, *Die antike Kunstprosa*, pp. 679ff.

secular rhetorical techniques from the outset, and not merely in sermons. Christians too found it necessary to write and speak according to the expectations of an educated audience; rhetorical skill was called for in both speech and writing. There is evidence that sermons were applauded if particularly felicitous figures of speech captured the imagination of the audience.[15]

However, this is only one aspect of the problem. Although it was not possible to ignore classical – and thus profane – stylistic techniques, the underlying principles were nevertheless vigorously called into question. Again it was Augustine who formulated the counter-arguments in particularly striking fashion.

The key doctrine of classical aesthetics was the theory of the different levels of style. These refer to the hierarchical arrangement of subject matter. Thus Cicero, in the *Orator*, distinguishes three distinct kinds of subject to which the three levels of style correspond:[16] trivial or base, ordinary, and exalted subjects, with corresponding 'plain', 'middle' and 'grand' styles. Everyday matters such as financial transactions, comic incidents, intimate or obscene matters should be treated as 'low' subjects in a plain, unsophisticated style. At the opposite extreme are significant events or grand human emotions; the representation of these calls for the highest possible formal art. The range of the 'middle' style occupies an intermediate position. Thus the classical theory of style is based on a strict correlation between the status of the subject and the level of stylistic expression, or in more general terms, between content and form.

This principle of a hierarchical series of correspondences between the world and its linguistic expression necessarily appeared questionable from a Christian viewpoint. St Augustine takes issue with Cicero as follows:[17]

> ea parua dicuntur, ubi de rebus pecuniariis iudicandum est, ea magna, ubi de salute ac de capite hominum, ea uero, ubi nihil horum iudicandum est ... sed tantummodo ut delectetur auditor, inter utrumque quasi media et ob hoc modica ... dixerunt ... In istis autem nostris, quandoquidem omnia, maxime quae de loco superiore populis dicimus, ad hominum salutem nec temporariam, sed aeternam referre debemus ... omnia sunt magna, quae dicimus, usque adeo, ut nec de ipsis pecuniariis rebus uel acquirendis uel amittendis parua uideri debeant, quae doctor ecclesiasticus dicit, siue sit illa magna siue parua pecunia. Neque emim parua est iustitia,

---

[15] Auerbach, 'Sermo humilis', p. 28.   [16] *Orator*, 69ff., esp. 100–1.   [17] CCSL 32.

quam profecto et in parua pecunia custodire debemus, dicente domino: Qui in minimo fidelis est, et in magno fidelis est ...

Nisi forte quoniam calix aquae frigidae res minima atque uilissima est, ideo minimum aliquid atque uilissimum dominus ait, quod eum, qui dederit discipulo eius, non perdet mercedem suam, aut uero quando iste doctor in ecclesia facit inde sermonem, paruum aliquid debet existimare se dicere et ideo non temperate, non granditer, sed submisse sibi esse dicendum. (*De doctrina christiana* IV, xviii, 4–9, 12–21, 58–63)

[Those matters are called plain where monetary affairs are dealt with, those where a man's well-being and life are at stake are called grand, but where no such matters are to be considered ... but rather the listener is to be entertained, the subject matter is considered to be intermediate and is therefore called ordinary ... But for us, since everything has to relate to man's eternal rather than his temporary well-being, especially what we say to the people from the pulpit, all the words we speak are grand, so that not even those things which a doctor of the church says about money and the loss or gain thereof can be considered plain, irrespective of whether a small or large amount is concerned. Nor is that judiciousness which we are obliged to observe with regard to small amounts of money a plain matter, for the Lord says: He who is faithful in a very little is faithful also in much [Luke 16,10] ...

Or rather, just because a cup of cold water is something trifling and worthless, was the Lord speaking of something trifling and worthless when he said that he who gives such a cup to one of his disciples shall not go unrewarded? [Matt 10,42] Or when the preacher bases a sermon on that passage in church, must he consider that he is saying something plain and that he should therefore speak not in a middle or grand but in a low style?]

Thus from the Christian viewpoint there is no objective hierarchy of subject matter. Even the most everyday and most apparently humble objects may, for the Christian, shed their baseness and become exalted when viewed from the perspective of the Redemption. The classical theory of different levels of style is, therefore, not applicable. The different levels of style become independent of content, and may thus be altered at will, so that a mixing of styles becomes possible. However, Christianity took the matter one step further in calling for a markedly anti-classical principle of style.[18] The

---

[18] Auerbach, 'Sermo humilis', 29ff.; cf. also Auerbach, 'Sacrae Scripturae'.

chief reason for this was the necessity of defending the plain style of the Bible against the scorn of the educated. The argument ran as follows: in the Bible, the greatest mysteries are clothed in the plainest language, for they were revealed not to scholars, but to simple peasants and fishermen. This interplay of the highest and the most lowly levels has its exact correspondence in the process of redemption itself. Lowly and yet exalted, at once *humilis* and *sublimis*: this *is* the mystery of God become man; and this, according to the above theory, is reflected in the style in which the divine revelation was made. In antiquity, *humilis* and *sublimis* had been seen as irreconcilably opposed concepts, both of content and form. Now both were united in the Incarnation: *humilitas* acquired new dignity in the paradox of *peraltissima humilitas*, and at the same time became an aesthetic principle, all by way of a challenge to the arrogance of the educated heathens. The conscious paradox of the Christian revelation – the birth of God in a stable – had an exact parallel in the unacceptably primitive style of its biblical representation. The avowed absurdity of evangelist doctrine was thus seen as inextricably bound up with a reverence for the plain words of the Bible.

What Augustine juxtaposes in this way – on the one hand a recommendation not to dispense with the literary and rhetorical means placed at the disposal of Christianity by the classical cultural tradition, and on the other a programmatic *volte-face* to the new aesthetics of the *sermo humilis* – is only a more intense form of the contradiction fundamental to the Christian attitude to the Word and the World which becomes manifest early on in both literary and theoretical documents of the new religion.[19] On the one hand, attempts to present the articles of Christian faith as the greatest good and thus in the highest artistic form, based on the classical educational and literary tradition, result in the genre of biblical epic, repeatedly attempting to re-cast the plain language of the Bible in verse;[20] nor was there any shortage of attempts to establish, by means of a quest for rhetorical devices, the artistic merit of the Bible as it stood.[21] On the other hand, this was countered by the conviction that no

---

[19] In its extreme form, the contradiction may result in conflict: Jerome is a prime example, cf. Eiswirth, *Hieronymus' Stellung zur Literatur und Kunst*. Ellspermann, *The Attitude of the Early Christian Latin Writers*, gives an overview of Augustine's various positions; cf. also Hagendahl, *Latin Fathers and the Classics*.

[20] Kartschoke, *Bibeldichtung*; Herzog, *Die Bibelepik der lateinischen Spätantike*.

[21] Curtius, *Europäische Literatur und lateinisches Mittelalter*, p. 50.

significance should be attached to the formal aspects of the work; content should enjoy absolute precedence over form.[22] *Simplicitas* and *rusticitas* become guarantors of sincerity.[23]

This contradiction also occurs in Christian philosophies of language; here, too, the theoretical foundations were laid by Augustine.[24] In *De magistro* and *De doctrina christiana*, he draws a fundamental distinction between *res* and *signum*. Doctrine is, he says, always essentially concerned with objects and signs, since the object of the teaching is *things*, but the knowledge of them is transmitted by means of *signs*. Objects differ from signs, in that they do not of themselves signify; yet objects may take on a signifying function, just as the basis for the sign is drawn from the material world. Thus the written and phonetic sign *bos* signifies a particular animal, but the latter may in itself be a sign for something different, in this case one of the Evangelists. Augustine refers to the primary signs as *signa propria*. If the signified is itself a sign, he speaks of *signa translata*. We learn, he says, only by means of words; and yet we learn nothing by words alone. Words may deceive, they may be false or intended in a different sense from that in which we understand them. The true understanding of the *res* can only be accomplished in the thought process of the recipient; that is, the signs are meaningless without the process of interpretation. Even the words of the Holy Scriptures belong to the realm of signs; here too the truth must be sought behind the signs, and here too it is possible that meanings are obscure or figurative. Indeed, God deliberately shrouded his words in obscurity in order to stimulate our thought. If signs thus have a part to play in the cognitive process, this at the same time implies that they are ultimately superseded within this same process. Thus they are at one and the same time of value and worthless. Likewise, if the things of this world can function as signs – *signa translata* – then the same applies to the material world as such. Natural phenomena and the events of history

---

[22] On the tradition of this topos, see Beumann, 'Der Schriftsteller und seine Kritiker', 505; Strunk, *Kunst und Glaube*, pp. 16, 23, 92.

[23] On the *rusticitas* topos, see Curtius, *Europäische Literatur und lateinisches Mittelalter*, p. 602; Lausberg, *Handbuch der literarischen Rhetorik*, col. 275β; Thraede, *Studien zur Sprache und Stil des Prudentius*, pp. 61–2; Strunk, *Kunst und Glaube*, p. 47; Herkommer, *Überlieferungsgeschichte der 'Sächsischen Weltchronik'*, pp. 218ff.

[24] On what follows, see Brinkmann: 'Die Zeichenhaftigkeit der Sprache', 'Die Sprache als Zeichen im Mittelalter', and *Mittelalterliche Hermeneutik*, pp. 21ff; Coseriu, *Die Geschichte der Sprachphilosophie*; Huber, 'Wort sint der dinge zeichen'; Maierù, '"Signum" dans la culture médiévale', esp. pp. 55ff.

ultimately act as a stimulus towards recognition of the one Truth which underlies them and which is alone significant.[25]

Yet this is only one aspect. Augustine's dual semiotic system implies a linguistic model of representation; words are the signifiers of things, and the order of the world is reproduced in the logic of semantics and grammar.[26] Of course, this only conveys the primary or literal meaning; however, language may be seen as representing the world – God's handiwork – and the beauty of the linguistic form may in this way be able to reflect the beauty of creation.[27] Inasmuch as language, reflecting the divine glory of the world, necessarily becomes a panegyric, an elevated style is justified. On the other hand, in so far as the world represented by means of language is in turn only a symbol for a higher truth beyond it, language is only a means to an end, a stage which, like the *signa translata*, must be transcended in the hermeneutic process. Thus the allegorical exegesis of language transforms human experience by implying the presence of a transcendental dimension: worldly experience is transformed with regard to the imperative of salvation.

By virtue of this two-tier Christian representational model, then, language becomes an appropriate medium for the fundamental contradiction underlying Christian aesthetics: representing the cosmos as it does, language is able to add its note of praise to the 'cosmic liturgy' by means of the beauty of its form. However, as an expression of the merely transitory nature of creation, it is empty, a mere dead letter which has to be quickened – i.e. filled with significance – by means of interpretation, in order that it may be lived and experienced to the full.[28]

---

[25] Ohly, 'Vom geistigen Sinn des Wortes'; Spitz, *Die Metaphorik des geistigen Schriftsinns*.

[26] In the philosophy of language, especially from the twelfth century onwards, there exists a continuing, and extremely complex, dialogue between Platonic and Aristotelian approaches: cf. Jolivet, 'Eléments pour une étude des rapports'.

[27] On the idea of grammar as an imitation of nature, see John of Salisbury, *Metalogicon* I, XVII (PL 198, col. 847).

[28] On Christian aesthetics, see Bruyne, *Etudes d'esthétique médiévale*, esp. vol. I, pp. 339ff., vol. III, pp. 3ff.; Haug, 'Transzendenz und Utopie'. Huber, in his review of *Literaturtheorie*, 62, makes the point that this conflict should not be exaggerated, since the Middle Ages resolved such contradictions on an 'ontological and epistemological level and in terms of universal history'; what prevails, according to him, is 'a principle of harmony'; this with particular reference to the Augustinian idea of beauty. While I do not doubt that such a striving for harmony is important, harmony cannot be said to 'prevail', since, as it is continually called into question by the fundamental conflict referred to above, it must continually be striven for anew. The present study, by contrast, focusses on precisely this alternation between the attaining and subsequent questioning of apparent states of harmony.

What, then, is the ultimate basis of this contradiction which runs through Christian ideas of education, poetics and philosophy of language? Doubtless it is to be found in the fundamental and ultimately insoluble duality of the Christian experience of salvation: seen from the perspective of resurrection and redemption, the world appears sanctified; humanity has realized that the spirit of God has left its mark on everything which exists, and so the beauty of the universe is a reflection of the absolute beauty of God, and the meaning of earthly phenomena with regard to salvation is revealed to humanity in direct proportion to the degree to which the human soul is illuminated by the Holy Spirit. Language, with all its formal potential, is given to human beings in order that they may represent and praise the beauty of earthly reality. Against all this, however, is set the other dimension, in which the world is viewed from the perspective of the Passion. This draws attention to the radical discrepancy between the secular and divine spheres, and can only seek expression in baseness, in the consciousness of sin and in absolute humility. The image of the Son of God on the Cross signifies the destruction of any possibility of mediation between this world and the transcendental one. There exists ultimately only the conciliatory gesture of Grace, which requires of humanity an acknowledgement of its own worthlessness. Seen from this perspective, human language is doomed to failure, since its function is essentially one of mediation: high-flown rhetoric, the elevated style, is suspected of lies and deception. A representation of what is most noble in the plainest terms, even by means of ugliness, appears more appropriate to the inadequacy of human expression than an ultimately tenuous analogy between earthly and absolute beauty.[29] The two viewpoints alternately contradict and complement each other. Paradoxically, in the end the one is only justified and meaningful when seen against the background of the other, the Passion in the context of the Resurrection, and *vice versa*.

The history of Christian aesthetics is the history of this contradiction. It recurs time and time again, modified according to changes in the language and the development of its stylistic potential. At the same time, this process is reflected on a theoretical level in the history

---

[29] On this problem, see Balthasar, *Herrlichkeit*, passim, esp. vol. I, pp. 35ff., 42ff., vol. III/I, pp. 285ff; Helmut Kuhn, 'Literaturgeschichte als Geschichtsphilosophie'; Jauss, 'Die klassische ... Rechtfertigung des Häßlichen' and the discussion 'Gibt es eine christliche Ästhetik?' in Jauss, *Die nicht mehr schönen Künste. Grenzphänomene*, pp. 583ff.

of the key patterns of argument and critical analysis, which alter their meaning according to the constantly changing cultural and linguistic background.

A consequence of the Christian assimilation of the classical theory of the levels of style was that certain topoi came to be seen in a different light in the new situation; this particularly applies to those 'modesty topoi' which had the rhetorical function of putting the audience in an indulgent frame of mind, by means of the speaker's deliberate deprecation of his own abilities. These topoi, which had traditionally served to provide the introductory flourishes to works which then gave the lie to such clichés by even more brilliant rhetoric, now of necessity acquired a new importance, since, in a Christian context, the professing of a plain style may stem from genuine *humilitas*, rather than necessarily implying an affected incompetence. Similarly, the programmatic rhetorical claim on the part of the author, that his art cannot do justice to the greatness and importance of the subject matter, becomes, from the Christian viewpoint, profoundly true. Finally, the argument that the subject justifies the undertaking, even if the form remains inadequate, becomes the expression of a standpoint which has to be taken absolutely seriously.[30]

Even here, however, the emphasis necessarily varies according to the extent to which language has become debased in the transition from antiquity to the Middle Ages.[31] If the Latin language is perceived as having 'run to seed', finally degenerating into the various Romance dialects, then the claim of *rusticitas* can only be seen as an act of intellectual humility in a limited sense, since it may in fact accompany a genuine lack of ability. Thus the traditional patterns of topical argumentation continue, despite the cultural upheavals which separate the Middle Ages from antiquity, although naturally they undergo considerable modification in the process; and if it is ultimately claimed that it is permissible to write and speak in the language of the uneducated because, according to the biblical example, the highest revelations were made to ordinary people, this merely indicates that Augustine's aesthetics have been used to legitimize the use of the vernacular. It is precisely at the moment when an awareness of being incapable of achieving the high – or even the correct – Latin form is reached, that the vernacular nettle is finally grasped and the use of the 'barbaric' language justified by reference to Christian *humilitas*;

[30] Strunk, *Kunst und Glaube*, pp. 116–17, 128–9.
[31] Auerbach, 'Lateinische Prosa des frühen Mittelalters'.

doubts, and the criticism of others, are forestalled with the argument of the precedence of content over form. Gregory of Tours, for example, re-formulates the old topos of plain style thus:[32] he asks why he should have scruples about his uneducated, coarse mode of expression when Christ himself, in order to denounce the vanity of worldly wisdom, preached not to rhetoricians but to fishermen, not to philosophers but to peasants.

However, such a pronounced profession of *rusticitas* comes into conflict with the constantly renewed attempts to achieve a high style on another count, as is evinced by the fact that the classical theory of levels of style finds its way into medieval treatises on poetics almost despite Augustine.[33]

A history of Christian literary theory must thus on the one hand take as its starting point both the fundamental conflict between a concept of language and literature which acknowledges the 'high style' as the appropriate mode of expression for its elevated subject matter, and the counter-position which continues to stress the fundamental inadequacy of human expression in the face of divine revelation. On the other hand, this conflict must continually be reviewed in the light of the historical conditions which determine its specific characteristics at any given moment.

The tension between these two contradictory positions, an essential characteristic of Christian aesthetics, is still an implicit feature of theoretical arguments in the medieval prologue, and one which, regardless of variations in rhetorical topoi, continues to resurface in the recurring reflections on the problem of how literature is to represent and convey meaning. The main emphasis here is no longer on the strategies of persuasion, but rather on seeking to establish what constitutes the truth of poetry. This process derives, in the first instance, from an awareness of the problematic nature of the relationship between human language and the divine Word. That is to say, in the face of the essentially inadequate human potential for knowledge and expression, poetic truth could only be made legitimate by reference to divine inspiration. Not only does this justify the imitation of the beauty of the universe by high poetic style, it also serves to defend a disregard for style in favour of the subject itself. In either

---

[32] Beumann, 'Gregor von Tours und der Sermo Rusticus'; Vollmann, 'Gregor IV'.
[33] Cf. Quadlbauer, *Die antike Theorie der genera dicendi*, for a comprehensive account of the whole range of variations and modifications.

case, it is divine inspiration which informs the hermeneutic act of literary representation: the revelation of eternal truth in earthly phenomena is inevitably dependent on the intervention of the Holy Spirit. In the process, this fundamental dichotomy is highlighted once more, in that poetry expresses the idea that on the one hand truth is present in earthly phenomena, that earthly light may be seen as a reflection of the divine light, and consequently that humanity may approach the divine by means of human language, while on the other hand the hermeneutic poetic act, offering as it does only meanings and interpretations of the truth, reveals the profound gap between creation and its Creator. Even if redemption is immanent in the experience of earthly beauty, this beauty itself is, in turn, only a metaphor for the Absolute. Thus the hermeneutic act is at once an assurance of salvation and at the same time, in the implicit awareness that, in its function of mediator, it can only fail, a challenging reminder of the Last Things. The function of Christian writing thus alternates between hymnic praise and desperate admonition, between the transfiguration of the world and the denial of it.

This state of affairs holds absolute sway until well into the twelfth century. Then, however, against the background of this theoretical scheme, literature – in the sense of fiction – is discovered as an independent medium of human experience. This in turn leads to a crucial question: how far could this discovery be formulated in the theoretical language of the prevailing aesthetics, and how far was it able to develop an appropriate poetic self-consciousness? Meanwhile, the traditional dichotomy survives through the centuries in various guises; it reappears in secular form in the aesthetic conflict between art understood as provocation and art seen as affirmation, and continues today in the debate about the 'aesthetics of negativity'.[34]

---

[34] Jauss, *Ästhetische Erfahrung und literarische Hermeneutik*, pp. 37ff.; cf. Holub, *Reception Theory*, pp. 53ff.

2

The problem of the vernacular: Otfrid von Weissenburg and the beginnings of literary theory in Old High German

I

The cultural background to early medieval Western literature is characterized by the juxtaposition of two contrasting traditions. On the one hand, there is the heritage of classical and Christian culture, only accessible directly to those with a knowledge of Latin, i.e. those with a clerical education, and on the other, the native vernacular oral tradition. Since the clergy could, on the basis of this Latin tradition, claim exclusive rights to education, the indigenous tradition, with no such advantages, was left with only the sphere of ignorance, indeed of untruth and anti-Christianity. However much the centuries-old tradition of clerical invective against the vernacular oral tradition may be seen as a series of set exercises, these latter nevertheless testify to the continuing potency of the vernacular tradition. Even ecclesiastical circles are by no means immune: a prime example of this is Alcuin's letter of 797, issuing a warning to the bishop of Lindisfarne: 'God's word should be read during the meals for the priests: it is proper to listen to the reader there, not the harpist; the sermons of the church fathers, not heathen songs. What does Ingeld have to do with Christ? The house is narrow, and there is no room for both.'[1]

---

[1] *MGH, Epist. Merov. et Carol. aevi* IV, no. 124: 'Verba dei legantur in sacerdotali convivio. Ibi decet lectorem audire, non citharistam, sermones patrum, non carmina gentilium. Quid Hiniellus cum Christo? Angusta est domus utrosque tenere non poterit.' Ingeld is the protagonist of a tragic-heroic lay. In the ninth century, Benedictus Levita complains that on Sundays time is passed with 'vanae fabulae', 'locutiones' or 'cantationes' (*Capitularium Collectio*, PL 97, col. 772). In the tenth century Regino of Prüm makes a similar complaint (*De synodalibus* I, 216, ed. H. Wasserschleben, 1940). In the eleventh century, Meinhard of Bamberg's letters testify to the extent to which even such high-ranking clergy as Bishop Gunther of Bamberg concerned themselves with indigenous heroic lays; cf. Erdmann, 'Fabulae curiales' and 'Gunther von Bamberg als Heldendichter'. Further examples from the eleventh century are furnished by Williram's paraphrase of the Song of Solomon, 128 (ed. J. Seemüller, 1878), and the prologue to the *Annolied*: see below, chapter 3, pp. 60–1. Further documents are provided for the twelfth century in the prologue to the *Kaiserchronik*

This conflict with the native oral tradition overlaps to some extent with the Church's campaign against secular classical literature, although the conditions – and indeed the strategies employed – are essentially different, as will be demonstrated later.[2]

The first theoretical utterances on vernacular literature are thus polemical statements on the part of clerical writers, who dismiss the native oral tradition as mendacious, and therefore a corrupting influence. This tradition is by its very nature spontaneous and unselfconscious, as the few remnants which have come down to us confirm. Its justification lies in its very traditionality; its validity is never questioned by its proponents, since it represents the expression of their cultural and historical consciousness. Any apparently reflective or theoretical statements which do occur turn out to be stock phrases: affirmations of the genre, and cues for the start of the performance proper, for example exordial phrases, 'I know' and 'I have heard' phrases, imperatives, e.g: *Ik gihorta ðat seggen*; *Dat gafregin ih*; *Uns ist geseit*; *merket*; *vernemet*; *swîget*, etc.[3]

Only under extraordinary external circumstances does an oral tradition – or part of it – come to be set down in writing. In Western culture in the early Middle Ages there was even less occasion for this, in that Latin covered all the usual functions which required written expression, namely certain forms of administration, religion, and science.

It was thus not possible for a vernacular written literature to evolve directly out of the oral tradition, as it were from below; instead, the breakthrough in the cultural barrier separating the two media had to come from above. Language provided a first opening, since translation from classical Latin became increasingly necessary as distinct vernacular idioms developed in Romance-speaking regions: in Germanic areas Latin was in any case a foreign language which had to be learned, so that the vernacular inevitably played a part in the teaching process. For this reason, our earliest written evidence of German takes the form of glosses in Latin manuscripts, followed by vocabularies and inter-linear translations; that is to say, the oldest vernacular writing is nothing more than a translation aid, with no function outside its subservient role to Latin. Its use therefore does not require

---

and in the epilogue to *Das himmlische Jerusalem*: see chapter 3, pp. 67–8, and p. 60, note 17, respectively. Cf. also Jones, *Prologue and Epilogue*, pp. 28, 43ff.

2 See chapter 4 below, pp. 75–6.

3 Hövelmann, 'Die Eingangsformel in germanischer Dichtung'; for the French heroic lays, see Gsteiger, 'Note sur les préambules des chansons de geste'.

justification, and so no theoretical reflections of any kind are to be expected.

The relationship between Latin and German really begins to develop when it comes to the need for instructing those with no knowledge of Latin in the contents of the Latin Christian tradition – if only in the most elementary form. In order that the Christian faith could be conveyed in the vernacular, it was first necessary to create an adequate terminology, so as to circumvent the necessity of adopting Greek or Latin loan words. This led to the development of an early Old High German religious language. The process of loan formation which gave rise to it may be reconstructed; a particularly striking example is the displacement, in southern Germany in the eighth century, of ancient terms for the emotions – presumably charged with heathen overtones – by a series of new Christian ones : e.g. *dulten* for *dolēn*, *zwīvalōn* for *zwehōn*, *klagōn* for *wuofen*, *sih frawen* for *gifehan*. These are artificial verbal derivations from nouns or adjectives: from *dult* (cf. modern German *Geduld*, 'patience'), *zwīval* (*Zweifel*, 'doubt'), *klaga* (*Klage*, 'complaint' or 'lament') and *frao* (*froh*, 'glad') respectively.[4] This kind of interference with the semantics of a language can only be the result of a deliberate programme which, as here, aims to transform the vernacular into a fitting vehicle for the Christian message. It is difficult to determine how far this can be held responsible, in the first instance, for the creation of an experimental – and necessarily provocative – specialized language, the more so as there is very little concrete historical evidence as to the intentions which may have informed it; it is thus impossible to gauge accurately the relative proportion of deliberate advances versus gradual change.

This situation alters as soon as the earliest German translation literature becomes available. This consists of German renderings of fundamental catechetic texts such as the Lord's Prayer, the Creed, and confessional formulae, all of them essential for the conversion of the broad mass of the population to Christianity. Initially, these may have been isolated experiments; in the second half of the eighth century, however, they culminated in the educational reforms introduced by Charlemagne. He integrated older educational ideas into a general programme so as to guarantee familiarity with a corpus of elementary Christian texts. To prepare the ground for this, it seems he also

4   Eggers, *Sprachgeschichte*, vol. I, pp. 154ff., with further literature.

arranged for the collation and standardization of the basic ecclesiastical texts. The *Admonitio generalis* of 789, in particular, sets out and justifies his aims, and may be regarded as his true manifesto. Admittedly he does not refer directly to the vernacular, but there can be no doubt as to its significance for the practical execution of his programme.[5]

However, Charlemagne was not content merely to make provision for the dissemination of the elementary texts in everyday ecclesiastical use, thus indirectly encouraging their translation into German; he also arranged for the creation of a corpus of Old High German model translations. The texts in question are sophisticated – they include, *inter alia*, Isidore of Seville's treatise *De fide catholica*, the Gospel according to Saint Matthew, and a sermon by St Augustine – and the German versions are of the highest linguistic quality. All are preserved only in fragmentary form; while little is known of the circumstances of their production, there can be little doubt that they originated at court, since it is unlikely that the kind of erudite élite which the quality of these renderings presupposes would have been present in any other context.[6]

What was attempted in these model translations far exceeds the ambitions of the *Admonitio generalis*. The vernacular is here no longer limited to the practical and pedagogical function of transmitting the Latin tradition; rather, German is intended to become equal in rank to Latin, as a medium for the Word of God and a vehicle for the theological and philosophical tradition. How far Charlemagne's educational programme envisaged a specifically German cultural element must remain a matter for speculation: while there is some evidence of a Frankish consciousness on the part of the emperor, there is dispute as to whether he ever caused indigenous heroic lays to be recorded, since the 'barbara et antiquissima carmina' which, according to a note on the part of his biographer Einhard, he caused to be collected cannot with absolute certainty be identified as vernacular texts.[7]

One of the striking features of this model corpus of translations is the set of orthographical rules devised for the purpose. This represents a bold attempt to create a systematic orthography appropriate to

5 Baesecke, 'Die Karlische Renaissance und das deutsche Schrifttum'; Bischoff, *Karl der Große*; Bertau, *Deutsche Literatur im europäischen Mittelalter*, vol. I, pp. 42ff.
6 Matzel, *Untersuchungen zur Verfasserschaft*, esp. pp. 469ff.
7 Meissburger, 'Zum sogenannten Heldenliederbuch Karls des Großen'.

the German language, which in turn presupposes phonological and grammatical studies which, likewise, are only conceivable in a court environment.[8]

All in all, then, this creation of a corpus of model translations is revealed as an astonishing undertaking, from which one might expect a clear theoretical programme to have developed. That this did not occur may be due to the fact that such a venture overtaxed the cultural resources of the time, and thus failed to achieve any lasting success. With the death of Charlemagne in 814, the educational programme he had devised also collapsed. The translation of catechetic texts into German continued, it is true, but the set of model translations was to have scarcely any influence on the further development of German literature.

II

Another impetus, albeit of an essentially different nature, towards the creation of a German literary culture was to come from the eastern part of the Carolingian empire, particularly during the reign of Louis the German (840–76), with the creation of biblical epics in Old Saxon and Old High German – that is, not translations, but literary creations in their own right. On the one hand, there are the Old Saxon *Heliand* and *Genesis*, on the other Otfrid's Rhenish-Franconian *Evangelienbuch*. One of the dedications of Otfrid's work which has survived is addressed to Louis the German, while the *praefatio* to the *Heliand* records that the work was commissioned by 'Ludouuicus piissimus Augustus'. This may in fact be another reference to Louis the German, rather than to Louis the Pious.[9] Be that as it may, these biblical epics are now increasingly considered as expressions of a developing German cultural consciousness in the East Franconian part of the empire; further evidence for this in part dates back to the time of Louis the Pious.[10]

Otfrid, a monk in the abbey of Weissenburg (Wissembourg) in Alsace, wrote his *Evangelienbuch* in the seventh decade of the ninth

---

8 Matzel, *Untersuchungen zur Verfasserschaft*, pp. 513ff., connects this with Einhard's remark that Charlemagne had commissioned a 'grammatica patrii sermonis'.

9 Haubrichs, 'Die Praefatio des *Heliand*', and *Die Anfänge*, p. 338; for another view, see Taeger, '*Heliand*', cols. 958–9.

10 Schlosser, 'Literaturtheorie bei Otfried von Weißenburg', pp. 391ff.; Haubrichs, 'Eine prosopographische Skizze zu Otfrid', pp. 406ff., and *Die Anfänge*, pp. 324ff.; Rexroth, 'Volkssprache und werdendes Volksbewußtsein'.

century. It is a free rendering of the life of Christ which combines and harmonizes the accounts of the four Evangelists. It was an unusual undertaking, inasmuch as it represented the first instance of a written composition in verse in Old High German, corresponding to the Anglo-Saxon and Old Saxon biblical epics. However, whereas the Anglo-Saxon and Old Saxon versions make use of alliteration, Otfrid introduces end-rhyme to German narrative literature.[11]

Otfrid was well aware of the boldness of his experiment. Feeling it necessary to justify it, he composed the first literary theory for a vernacular work. These theoretical statements preface the work in two forms; first in the form of a Latin dedication to Liutbert, archbishop of Cologne, to whom he submits his *Evangelienbuch* for approval; and secondly in German verse, in the first chapter of the work itself, under the Latin heading 'Cur scriptor hunc librum theotisce dicta-verit': 'Why the writer composed this book in the German language'.

How, then, did Otfrid justify his undertaking? How far was he able to make use of traditional forms of argument, and how far did he devise a new theory to correspond to the new situation?

Let us first consider the letter to Liutbert.[12] Setting aside the introductory and concluding passages, in which Otfrid seeks approval for his work from his superior, the letter deals with three main points: first, the occasion and purpose of the poem; secondly, the method of composition, amounting to an explanation of its structure; and thirdly, the problem of language, i.e. the question as to how far the German vernacular is a fitting instrument for such an undertaking.

1. Justification and aims of the poem

Otfrid, so he claims, intends to write a German gospel harmony, or *Evangelienharmonie*. Models for this existed within the Latin tradition, particularly the *Diatessaron* by the Syrian writer Tatian; this had already been translated into German under the guidance of Hrabanus Maurus, abbot of Fulda between 822 and 842. It was, however, an unsophisticated rendering which laboriously followed the Latin. Since Otfrid had studied in Fulda, it seems likely that he would have known of it.[13]

---

[11] See Ernst, '*Liber Evangeliorum*', pp. 350ff., on the question of the historical beginnings of German rhymed poetry.
[12] Vollmann-Profe, *Kommentar*, pp. 28ff. She also gives a comprehensive account of earlier literature. On the tradition of the 'letter prologue', see W. Freytag, 'Otfrieds Briefvorrede'.
[13] Haubrichs, 'Otfrid', 405, and 'Althochdeutsch'.

Otfrid was, so he tells us, encouraged to compose the work by his fellow monks and a certain – unidentifiable – *matrona* by the name of Judith. The 'commission motif' is a common prologue topos.[14] The aim of the work is, according to Otfrid, to replace the pagan songs – which were distracting the monks from their holy way of life – by a German poem based on the Gospels. This outburst against profane poetry is part of the established tradition of ecclesiastical criticism of secular literature mentioned above.[15] He further complains that the world is flooded with classical secular literature – Virgil, Ovid, Lucan. However, he does not mean to denigrate these so much as encourage the creation of an equally valid Frankish literature.[16] The modesty formula which follows also fits into the traditional scheme: Otfrid claims to have taken on the work – encouraged by his friends, as suggested – despite the fact that he lacked the necessary qualifications for it.[17] Then a second justification is offered; anyone who has difficulty in understanding Latin should at least be given the opportunity of getting to know the Gospels in German. Even this reference to the better understanding which can be gained from a vernacular account is itself another topos.[18] In short, all the explanations as to the occasion and purpose of the poem may be seen within this traditional context: no individual and original note is as yet discernible.

2. Method and composition

Otfrid proceeds in his Gospel narrative, as he tells us, by combining the texts of the four Gospels in the first and last sections of his book.

---

[14] Vollmann-Profe, *Kommentar*, pp. 35–6, with further literature; cf. also Arbusow, *Colores rhetorici*, p. 98; Lausberg, *Handbuch*, col. 275α; Beumann, 'Schriftsteller', 505; Simon, 'Untersuchungen', I, 59ff.; Jones, *Prologue and Epilogue*, pp. 21–2.; Wilkerson, 'Form and function of the prologue', pp. 115ff. In addition to the secular 'commission' topos, the classical idea of the divine vocation of the poet also found its way into medieval vernacular literature; for example, Bede's account of Caedmon's calling, and the verse prologue to the *Heliand*: see Schirmer, 'Antike Traditionen'; Haubrichs, *Die Anfänge*, p. 333.

[15] See note 1 above; cf. also Ernst, '*Liber Evangeliorum*', pp. 138ff.

[16] Cf. Vollmann-Profe, *Kommentar*, p. 39.

[17] On the 'modesty' or 'humility formula' and the protestation of lack of ability often associated with the 'commission' topos, see Schwietering, 'Demutsformel', pp. 170ff.; Curtius, *Europäische Literatur und lateinisches Mittelalter*, pp. 93ff., 590, 602, 604; Arbusow, *Colores rhetorici*, pp. 97–8, 105; Simon, 'Untersuchungen', I, 108ff.; Beumann, 'Der Schriftsteller und seine Kritiker'; Thraede, 'Untersuchungen', esp. II; Kobbe, 'Funktion und Gestalt des Prologs', pp. 442–3.; Wilkerson, 'Form and function of the prologue', pp. 103ff.; Vollmann-Profe, *Kommentar*, p. 35.

[18] Gregory of Tours cites it as a common opinion in the preface to his *Historia Francorum* (ed. R. Buchner, 1955, p. 2, lines 16f.).

In the central section, so as not to tire his audience, as he says, he has dealt with the material more freely, summing up the central portion of Christ's life – the miracles, the parables, Christ's teaching and so on – 'as they came into his head'. Moreover, he divides his work into five books – a symbolic number: the five books are intended to correspond to the five human senses. These five senses, with their inherent sinfulness, are in turn to be resolved in and cancelled out by the sacred number four of the Gospels. In other words, the imperfect five of the sinful senses is transfigured when applied to the perfect four of the Gospels. The symbolism of the numbers four and five is traditional, but its use in this context seems to be, as far as one can ascertain, Otfrid's own idea.[19]

3. The problem of the vernacular

Otfrid perceives himself as faced with great difficulties in attempting to write in German. This is, he says, because the Franks, unlike the Ancients, had failed to develop a literature of their own, preferring to write in Greek or Latin; if they ever did attempt to use German, then they wrote it incorrectly. Because they had neglected their own language in this fashion, it was not a pliant tool like Latin, but coarse, *inculta*, only with difficulty submitting itself to a poetic form – *indisciplinabilis*. This comparison with a Latin model is carried surprisingly far in what follows, at any rate by modern standards. For example, Otfrid complains that he was not always able to render a masculine noun in the biblical text with a German masculine, or match a Latin feminine with the same in German. Furthermore, the German often compelled him to use a singular where the Latin employs a plural, and so on. He appears to find the fact that German is not amenable to Latin verse forms particularly grave. Despite these criticisms of the limited potential of the German language, however, Otfrid did not make any attempt to force it to comply with Latin grammatical structures; on the contrary, he defends the autonomy of the German language in all its idiosyncrasies, referring specifically to everyday usage. What is important, then, is not merely Otfrid's realization that the German vernacular was no match for the strict rules and poetic possibilities of the Latin language, but that, in spite of this, he places himself firmly on the side of the vernacular, in the hope

---

[19] Vollmann-Profe, *Kommentar*, p. 45, with further bibliography on number symbolism.

of being able to cultivate it to such an extent that it might do justice to the task demanded of it.

Thus Otfrid is concerned, in so far as this is possible, with the development of an elevated style; he does not argue from the perspective of the *sermo humilis*, but instead takes as his models the early Christian epics in hexameters by Juvencus, Arator and Prudentius,[20] concluding as follows: 'It is fitting that the human race should praise the Creator of all things, since he gave them speech in order that they might sing his praises. And they should indeed do this in any way possible, however imperfect their language, for what matters to God is not the smooth flattery of a polished style, nor mere lip service, but the piety of individual thoughts and the effort each has made.'

It is not easy to determine the full significance of this last sentence, since once again Otfrid is making use of a series of traditional elements.[21] It might merely represent a further safeguard, a means of taking the wind out of the sails of potential critics. On the other hand, the sentence may also be understood as lifting the discussion on to a higher plane, putting all that has gone before into perspective. In that case the form would, ultimately, be of secondary significance; only the praise of God would count.

The tension between striving for an elevated style on the one hand, and the diminishing importance of formal elements in the light of the higher demands of the praise of God on the other, also forms the true theme of the theoretical introduction in German. Initially, Otfrid repeats some of the reflections from his letter to Liutbert. However, the radical extent of this contradiction between ethics and aesthetics, still only implicit in the latter, is now revealed:

> Was líuto filu in flíze,   in managemo ágaleize,
>   sie thaz in scríp gicleiptin,   thaz sie iro námon breittin;
> Sie thés in io gilícho   flizzun gúallicho,
>   in búachon giméinti   thio iro chúanheiti.
> (*Evangelienbuch*, I,1,1–4)

[Many peoples have undertaken with great persistence to set something out in writing so that their name might become known; it was ever their noble endeavour that the bravery of their people should be set forth in writing.]

---

[20] This applies only as a general principle, and not in the sense of direct imitation; cf. Rupp, 'Otfrid'.

[21] Vollmann-Profe, *Kommentar*, pp. 69–70, on lines 115–21.

First of all Otfrid makes retrospective use of the *memoria* topos to refer to Latin writings, that is, those works of classical literature to which he had already referred in the letter to Liutbert. In what follows, particular emphasis is given to the exemplary character of their form:

> Tharána dátun sie ouh thaz dúam: óugdun iro wísduam
> ougdun iro cleini   in thes tihtonnes reini.
> (*Evangelienbuch*, I,1,5–6)

> [Thereby they have also won fame themselves: they have demonstrated their wisdom, they have demonstrated their skill in the flawlessness of their poetry.]

The words *duam* and *wisduam*, fame and wisdom, should probably be interpreted not so much in a general sense as in a specifically poetic one: the poets in question have achieved fame through their art. The term *cleini* may be read as the German equivalent of *subtilitas* – a rhetorical term for a highly polished style, also used in the letter to Liutbert,[22] while *reini* implies perfection in the sense of grammatical accuracy.[23]

> Iz ist ál thuruh nót   so kléino girédinot
> (iz dúnkal eigun fúntan,   zisámane gibúntan),
> (*Evangelienbuch*, I,1,7–8)

> [The language is fashioned so intricately to a particular end – they selected difficult figures and combined them.]

Otfrid is here clearly translating Latin rhetorical terms into German.[24] The word *funtan* (from 'to find') has to be defined by comparison with *inventio*; in rhetorical terms, *inventio* means the selection and skilful use of rhetorical topoi. The term *dunkal* (literally 'dark') expresses the degree of difficulty of the rhetorical figures employed. The 'combining' may be seen as referring to the skilful and artistic combination of rhetorical devices.

What is being praised here is thus the highly artificial use of formal and figurative techniques in the 'difficult' rhetorical style, the *ornatus difficilis*. The terms *ornare* and *decorare* – both also used in the letter to Liutbert – refer to rhetorical ornament. The argument thus expressly follows the theory of levels of style: the elevated rhetorical style of classical poetry now appears as an exemplary norm for German poetry also.

---

22 Ibid., p. 92.   23 Ibid., pp. 93–4.
24 Ibid., pp. 95ff. for a detailed account of what follows.

Sie ouh in thíu gisagetin,   thaz then thio búah nirsmáhetin,
   joh wól er sih firwésti   then lésan iz gilústi.
(*Evangelienbuch*, I,1,9–10)

[They also wrote so that people wanting to read their work would gain in understanding and not hold it in contempt.]

Underlying this idea is the classical notion of rhetorical education, according to which the use of the elevated style led to a development of the spirit, indeed of the whole personality. The contrast between low or plain style, which is of little moral value, and the high art of rhetoric, which is able to transmit wisdom, is conveyed in Old High German by the juxtaposition of *irsmahen* ('to disdain') and *firwizzan* ('to approve').

The following lines explain precisely who was meant by *liuto filu* ('many people') in the opening line:

Zi thiu mág man ouh ginóto   mánagero thíoto
   hiar námon nu gizéllen   joh súntar ginénnen.
Sar Kríachi joh Románi   iz máchont so gizámi,
   iz machont sie al girústit,   so thíh es wola lústit;
Sie máchont iz so réhtaz   joh so fílu sléhtaz,
   iz ist gifúagit al in éin   selp so hélphantes béin.
(*Evangelienbuch*, I,1,11–16)

[It is possible to cite individually the names of many such peoples. Above all the Greeks and Romans write so aptly, they write so ornately, that it gives pleasure; they write so correctly and so perfectly that their work is all of a piece, just like ivory.]

The word *girustit* in line 14 clearly corresponds to the Latin *ornatus*, and thus represents a further translation into German of a central rhetorical term. This artistry of expression is closely linked with formal precision. The comparison with ivory has not yet been adequately explained: it may be that what is meant is ivory inlay work, or carved ivory tablets.[25]

Thie dáti man giscríbe: theist mannes lúst zi líbe;
   nim góuma thera díhta: thaz húrsgit thina dráhta.
Ist iz prósun slihti: thaz drénkit thih in ríhti;
   odo métres kléini: theist góuma filu réini.
(*Evangelienbuch*, I,1,17–20)

[25] Ibid., pp. 104–6.

[That deeds should be written down is a life-long delight; occupy yourself with such literature, that enlivens the spirit. If it has the plainness of prose, that will refresh you with its directness; if it has the ornateness of metrical verse, that is a pure feast.]

This adds a new twist to the topos of the preservation of human deeds in writing: human endeavour is fulfilled in literature, while literature in turn acts as a spur to human ambition. Poetry thus supplies both pleasure and direction: it provides an opportunity for human perfectibility to be realized.

The following lines then pay particular attention to the metrical art of the classical poets. Otfrid stresses that they knew how to obey the metrical rules successfully; the feet (*fuazi*) and stresses (*ziti*) are perfectly correct. Even the Scriptures were re-cast in this elevated metrical form; thus, as in the letter to Liutbert, Otfrid includes Latin Christian literature in this consideration. This brings him back to the question of whether the German language, which he has termed *inculta* and *indisciplinabilis*, is able to live up to such high standards. What kind of possibilities are there for literary style in Frankish?

> Nu es fílu manno inthíhit   in sína zungun scríbit,
>   joh ílit, er gigáhe,   thaz sínaz io gihóhe:
> Wánana sculun Fránkon   éinon thaz biwánkon,
>   ni sie in frénkisgon bigínnen,   sie gotes lób singen?
> (*Evangelienbuch*, I,1,31–4)

[Since many men now undertake to write in their own language and are quick to set about exalting their own causes, why should the Franks alone refrain and fail to sing God's praises in Frankish?]

This rhetorical question seems to echo the end of the letter to Liutbert; everyone should sing God's praises, regardless of how perfectly or imperfectly they are able to do so. However, Otfrid is not prepared simply to leave it at that: he presents the idea from a new angle. The two following lines, the subject of much critical discussion, are crucial to a correct understanding of Otfrid's literary theory:

> Níst si so gisúngan,   mit régulu bithuúngan:
>   si hábet thoh thia ríhti   in scóneru slíhti.
> (*Evangelienbuch*, I,1,35–6)

[It (= the Frankish language) has not been used like this in poetry, it has not been subjected to rules, and yet it has in its plain beauty a certain directness.]

A literal interpretation of these two lines gives rise to an apparently confusing contradiction; although Frankish does not comply with grammatical and metrical rules in the same way that Latin or Greek does, nevertheless it has an order of its own and is thus beautiful and perfect. This contradiction only makes sense if one follows Gisela Vollmann-Profe in seeing in it a pointer to the ethical reinterpretation of the formal poetic arguments which takes place in what follows.[26] Thus by line 1,36 the subject is no longer poetry, but rather the obeying of rules of quite another kind:

> Íli thu zi nóte, theiz scóno thoh gilute,
>   joh gótes wizod thánne tharána scono hélle;
> Tház tharana sínge, iz scóno man ginenne;
>   in themo firstántnisse wir giháltan sin giwísse; . .
> (*Evangelienbuch*, I,1,37–40)

[Take great pains to see that it nonetheless sounds beautiful and that God's law resounds beautifully in this language; that whatever is sung in it may be called beautiful; that we may enjoy certain understanding of this.]

Otfrid appeals to his audience and urges them to compose beautiful poetry. This can only be meant in a figurative, not in a literal sense. Giving expression to God's law in Frankish means a realization of God's Word in one's own life. Thus the concern here is not with the word as a linguistic form but with the Word experienced in living, the Word as a form of Life.

This complex interplay of literal and figurative levels is explained in what follows:

> Thaz laz thir wesan súazi: so mézent iz thie fúazi,
>   zít joh thiu régula; so ist gótes selbes brédiga.
> Wil thú thes wola dráhton, thu métar wolles áhton,
>   in thína zungun wirken dúam joh sconu vérs wolles dúan:
> Il io gótes willen állo ziti irfúllen,
>   so scribent gótes thegana in frénkisgon thie regula;
> In gótes gibotes súazi laz gángan thine fúazi,
>   ni laz thir zít thes ingán: theist sconi férs sar gidán;
> Díhto io thaz si nóti theso séhs ziti,
>   thaz thú thih so girústes, in theru síbuntun giréstes.
> (*Evangelienbuch*, I,1,41–50)

[Take that to heart, that is how it is measured by feet, time and the

---

[26] Ibid., pp. 120ff.

rule; such is God's own Word. If you endeavour to observe the metre, to win fame in your own language and to compose fine verses, try to fulfil God's will at all times. In this way God's warriors will 'write' according to the rules in Frankish. Let your feet wander in the sweetness of God's command, do not let the time slip away: in that way a fine verse is composed in a moment. Strive to compose verses through the six ages ('times') in order so to prepare yourself that in the seventh you may rest.]

With this Otfrid concludes his extended play on the metaphors of life and literature:[27] if one strives earnestly to live according to the Word, all the rules will be perfectly followed, feet, rhythm and metre all be in order. Thus poetry, in the profoundest sense, means living in accordance with God's commandments; what counts is not the poetic representation of the Word of God, but its realization through deeds. In the light of this premise the poetic terms *fuazi, zit, regula, girustit* are taken up and re-interpreted; instead of metrical feet we have the feet that follow God's commandments; metrical time becomes real time, which in God's service one may not allow to slip away; the *sehs ziti*, in the sense of six ages of man or epochs of world history, represent the span of earthly existence, while *girusten* ('to prepare'), previously used in the rhetorical sense as an equivalent of *ornare*, here means preparation for the seventh age, eternity.

Otfrid emphasizes once again in the following lines that all questions of form and style are secondary to the immediacy of the Word of God as transmitted by the Evangelists. This embraces everything: *suazi, nuzzi* and *wizzi* ('sweetness', 'benefit', 'understanding': 1,55), that is to say *delectare* and *prodesse* – both now to be understood as Truth, in a higher sense. It is *himilis gimacha*, 'a thing of Heaven', i.e. the very Word of God (1,51–6). Thus Otfrid ultimately side-steps the issue of literary mediation, focussing on the inspired words of the Gospel by which truth presents itself. Now he is able to reformulate the question previously raised in verse 1,33:

> Ziu sculun Fránkon, so ih quád,   zi thiu éinen wesan úngimah,
>   thie líut es wiht ni duáltun,   thie wir hiar óba zaltun?
> (*Evangelienbuch*, I,1,57–8)

[Why should the Franks alone, as I have said, be incapable of this, when the peoples that we mentioned above did not delay at all in this matter?]

---

[27] Polenz, 'Otfrids Wortspiel'.

After this question there follows a eulogy of the Franks. In terms of both wealth and bravery they are equal to the Greeks and Romans. Their alleged Trojan descent is offered as legitimation of the circumstance that the world rule of the Ancients has been passed down to them. No one is a match for the Franks, since they are God's chosen people; everything they do, they do with his accord.[28] Thus Otfrid wishes to write his *Evangelienbuch* in Frankish in order that God may be praised in this language too, and so that even those who know no other language may also receive his Word.

Otfrid's statements on literary theory are a prime example of the way in which traditional topos elements may be combined into a highly individual utterance. Of particular interest is the way in which individual arguments are juxtaposed, interacting on different levels. For example, the 'humility topos', professing the poet's inadequacy for the task, figures in the letter to Liutbert as the usual *captatio benevolentiae*; it then reappears in the context of the unpolished nature of the author's vernacular idiom, i.e. it turns into the *rusticitas* topos. Otfrid is dealing with a language which – at least at its contemporary stage of development – is indeed incapable of attaining the heights of classical rhetoric. At the same time he is transferring to the Frankish dialect an argument which initially applied to the Vulgar Latin idioms of Romance; though as Frankish, unlike the Romance languages, is not derived from Latin, this argument makes little sense when applied to German. In any case, Otfrid then departs from this argument in insisting that the grammatical autonomy of German be respected; although this might seem obvious, it is clear that – if one thinks, for example, of the practice of interlinear word-for-word translations – such respect was not necessarily observed in practice. Thus the *rusticitas* topos is turned around into a proclamation of the autonomy of the German language. Otfrid's reservations as to the fitness of the language in the end only apply to the fact that there is still no grammar and no adequate system of orthography. Yet this problem, too, is superseded in the transition from the aesthetic dimension, poetry, to the ethical dimension, life. This act of transcendence is itself justified by the unique historical importance which the Franks have attained.

However, this ethical and political change of perspective in no way

---

[28] Otfrid is not completely alone in this political and religious encomium of the Franks; a parallel may be found in the 'longer prologue' of the *Lex Salica*. Cf. Vollmann-Profe, *Kommentar*, pp. 140–1.

implies that the role of poetry is of secondary importance. Otfrid's poem is not only praise of God in a justifiable – indeed necessary – if imperfect form: it also fulfils an important role in the process of transformation of the divine Word into a Christian way of life. The biblical narrative culminates in the allegorical interpretations which Otfrid adds to the accounts of the Evangelists, and which point the way to the practical application of God's Word. Otfrid's work not only introduced allegorical exegesis into the vernacular – or at any rate in a literary form, since one may assume that it was current practice in vernacular sermons – but in addition put it into a particular perspective which is not without implications for poetic theory. Thus it is ultimately the use of allegory which provides a means of circumventing the problem of form, creating a bridge between the meaning, which is inherent in the word, and life, which transforms this meaning into reality.[29]

Otfrid singled out one central prologue motif from the discussion of poetics in his chapter I,1 in order to give it separate treatment in its own right in I,2: the *invocatio Dei*. With its typical characteristics it has, since Juvencus, come to form a traditional opening or climax to introductions to religious works.[30] Since Otfrid has already dealt with the question of the problematic nature of human language – the appropriateness of its form in relation to the content – his *invocatio* can take the form of a virtually unbroken hymn of praise. Poetry is a gift from God and at the same time a grateful and laudatory response to this grace:

> Fíngar thínan   dua anan múnd minan,
>   theni ouh hánt thina   in thia zúngun mina,
> Thaz ih lób thinaz   si lútentaz,
>   giburt súnes thines,   drúhtines mines ...
> (*Evangelienbuch*, I,2,3–6)

---

[29] Two studies on Otfrid's use of allegorical exegesis may be cited as examples: Ernst, 'Magiergeschichte', and Ertzdorff, 'Die Hochzeit zu Kana', alongside Hartmann, 'Die sprachliche Form der Allegorese', on the technique. The interplay between narrative, reflection and meditation is part of the late-Classical/Christian tradition of aesthetics of edification, the principles of which were established by Herzog: *Die Bibelepik der lateinischen Spätantike* and 'Exegese – Erbauung – Delectatio'.

[30] On the *invocatio Dei*, and its relationship to the Classical invocation of the Muses, see Charland, *Artes predicandi*, p. 125; Thraede, 'Untersuchungen', vol. II, 129; Barmeyer, *Die Musen*, pp. 97ff.; Strunk, *Kunst und Glaube*, pp. 29, 37; Kartschoke, *Bibeldichtung*, pp. 56ff.; Jaeger, *Prologue Tradition*, pp. 3ff.; Vollmann-Profe, *Kommentar*, pp. 150–1, with bibliography; Wehrli, *Literatur im deutschen Mittelalter*, pp. 108ff.

[Put your finger to my lips, extend your hand to touch my tongue, so that I may proclaim your praise, the birth of your Son, my Lord ...]

Al gizúngilo thaz íst –   thu drúhtin éin es alles bíst;
    wéltis thu thes líutes   joh alles wóroltthiotes.
Mit thíneru giwélti   sie dati al spréchenti,
    joh sálida in gilúngun   thiu wórt in iro zúngun;
Thaz síe thin io gihógetin,   in éwon iamer lóbotin,
    jóh sie thih irknátin   inti thíonost thinaz dátin.
(*Evangelienbuch*, I,2,33–8)

[Of all languages in existence – you alone are Lord of them all; you have power over men and over all mankind. With your power you gave them all the gift of language and that blessedness that they received words in their own languages, so that they might ever remember you, for all time praise you in eternity, and that they might know you and serve you.]

The poet's word, indeed human language as such, is thus completely absorbed and fulfilled in the service of God. The distance between Creator and created is overcome by virtue of God's grace: if a human individual, touched by divine inspiration, is moved to speak, then this expression takes the form of praise and thanks. Only in one place is there an echo of the problems which dominated chapter I,1:

Thaz ... in themo wáhen   thiu wórt ni missifáhen;
(*Evangelienbuch*, I,2,15–16)

[(Prevent) the words from erring on account of the beautiful form.]

Yet even this is included in the prayer. The all-embracing perspective is that of absolute faith in salvation.

III

Otfrid's *Evangelienbuch* must have existed in a considerable number of manuscripts; it was still being copied in the tenth century.[31] Despite this, it failed to give rise to an immediate and lasting tradition of vernacular German literature. Admittedly, some half dozen shorter Old High German poems have survived from the ninth and tenth centuries, some of which may be supposed to follow Otfrid's new, metrical form. However, the tradition dried up at the beginning of the tenth century, or to be more precise it only continued at the level of

---

[31] Herbst, 'Neue Wolfenbüttler Fragmente'; Kleiber, *Untersuchungen*.

simple catechetic texts. Not until the middle of the eleventh century did a German literary culture become established, which would eventually, under very different conditions, give rise to a continuous tradition. In this gap of some hundred and fifty years, however, one unique work stands out, by Notker III of St Gall, though once again this represents a new beginning and an isolated advance without lasting successors.

Notker III, who was given the epithet Teutonicus because of his devotion to the German language, came from a family of Thurgau nobles, to whom the abbey of St Gall is indebted for a series of noteworthy figures, among them Ekkehart I – Notker's uncle, the presumed author of the *Waltharius* – and Notker's most important pupil, Ekkehart IV, the author of the *Casus Sancti Galli*. The latter dedicated an epitaph in hexameters to his teacher upon Notker's death in 1022, in which he also mentions that Notker was the first to write in the barbarian tongue and make this palatable, and all this out of love for his pupils.[32] If this is not to be dismissed as excessive veneration of a teacher, we are once again faced with an awareness of literary innovation; that is to say that in St Gall in the year 1000 there was no longer any knowledge of the Old High German literature of the eighth and ninth centuries: this in spite of the fact that a copy of Otfrid's *Evangelienbuch*, and probably also of the Old High German version of Tatian's *Diatessaron*, must have been housed in the library there.[33] However, such scepticism must be put aside, for Notker himself expresses the matter in similar terms in his famous letter to Bishop Hugh of Sitten, in which he sets out what one may regard as his literary manifesto.[34]

The bishop of Sitten (Sion) had apparently called on Notker to devote himself more intensively to the liberal arts. Notker rejects this suggestion, saying that he too would have wished to do this, but his duties as a teacher lay in another direction: 'I have renounced those arts in which you desire that I should immerse myself, and I may not pursue them other than as teaching aids (*instrumenta*). It is religious books which should principally be read in the schools, but it is of

---

[32] *Liber benedictionum Ekkeharts IV.* (ed. J. Egli, 1909), pp. 230ff.
[33] On the gaps in the tradition during the development of Old High German literature, cf. Werner Schröder, *Grenzen und Möglichkeiten*; for a different point of view, see Sonder-egger, 'Tendenzen'.
[34] Hellgardt, 'Notkers Brief an Hugo von Sitten'; Werner Schröder, 'Zum Verhältnis von Lateinisch und Deutsch', pp. 430ff.

course not possible to achieve complete understanding of these without having studied the others first.'[35] This, then is yet another formulation of the old question of the status of secular classical literature within the context of a clerical education. In keeping with tradition, Notker can only allocate it a secondary teaching role. He continues: 'Since I wished that our pupils might have access to these works, I ventured to take an unprecedented step, namely, I attempted to translate Latin writings into our language and at the same time ... to elucidate them.'[36]

This sheds light on the nature of this literature: it consists of school translations with detailed commentaries in which, proceeding sentence by sentence and clause by clause, German and Latin are interspersed in a curious fashion. What was seen as so unusual about this enterprise thus becomes clear: the fact that the translation consisted not only of passages from the Bible or ecclesiastical texts in everyday use, but also, and particularly, of pagan classical literature. In his letter to the bishop of Sitten, Notker makes a list of the translations he has undertaken for the St Gall school. It begins with Boethius' *Consolatio Philosophiae*, followed by *Cato*, i.e. the *Disticha Catonis*, a well-known didactic collection of epigrams from the third century AD; Virgil's *Bucolica*, one of Terence's comedies, the *Nuptiae Philologiae et Mercurii* by Martianus Capella, the standard work on the seven liberal arts; two works by Aristotle, and more besides. Nor, on the religious side, should a rendering of the Psalms into German be overlooked.

This body of translations displays an astonishing degree of breadth and variety. Since at this time, there not only existed nothing comparable in the vernacular, but virtually no German literature at all, it is scarcely surprising that such an undertaking should appear unusual in the extreme. It is for this reason, perhaps, that Notker continues his letter to the bishop with the suggestion that, when he sends him his books, he may well initially recoil from the translations as from something quite extraordinary; but gradually they will seem more acceptable, and he, Hugh, will then be in a better position to read and understand them, since one can grasp things faster in one's mother tongue, whereas in a foreign language one understands the same matter only in part, if at all. Here the familiar topos of a better understanding in the vernacular reappears; however, its significance in

---

[35] Hellgardt, 'Notkers Brief an Hugo von Sitten', p. 172, lines 10ff.
[36] Ibid., lines 13ff.

this context is quite different from that in Otfrid's work. Far from the perspective of the theoretician speaking with the authority of a long tradition of theoretical discussion behind him, we find, in Notker, the practitioner enlarging upon an essentially pedagogic standpoint. Nor, unlike Otfrid, is he in the position of seeking to lay the foundations for a German art of poetry, but instead merely has to justify the use of the vernacular for teaching purposes. He is concerned not with the creation of an autonomous German literature, but with the use of the vernacular in pursuit of a better understanding of the Latin texts. Nothing could make this more plain than the mixture of German and Latin in Notker's prose as he continually wrestles with the meaning of the Latin text, even coining new German words in his avid search for equivalents.[37]

This corpus of translations represented the personal achievement of a great scholar and teacher, based as it was on a completely different premiss from the earlier attempts to establish a German tradition of writing. Like these, however, it achieved no lasting success. Unlike the attempts made under Charlemagne and Louis the German, it did not form part of a conscious cultural-political programme. The Ottonian age, by contrast, had, with its idea of the 'Römisches Reich Deutscher Nation', set its sights on a universal empire. The German language, compared to Latin, was clearly of little interest, and attempts to establish it could only take root locally, on the basis of monastic teaching.

The lack of any political emphasis in Notker's educational programme is illustrated by his prologue to the translation of Boethius.[38] He takes as his starting point the theory of the succession of empires. He states that St Paul claimed that the world would end with the collapse of the Roman Empire, and the Day of Judgement would be at hand. Meanwhile, however, the Roman Empire had indeed been destroyed, while the Goths, the Franks and the Saxons had succeeded each other as rulers. Yet this succession is not taken as an opportunity for expanding upon the idea of *translatio*; Notker goes no further than to confirm that the end of the Roman Empire has in fact taken place. His primary purpose is to draw the reader's attention to the imminence of the Last Judgement. The context is thus not the theory of the four empires, but rather the concept of history put forward by Orosius and Augustine, who located mankind in a non-political sense

---

[37] Cf. Bertau, *Deutsche Literatur im europäischen Mittelalter*, vol. I, pp. 98ff.
[38] Ostberg, '*Prologi* reconsidered'.

between the *civitas dei* and the *civitas diaboli*. One may also view the theme of the *Consolatio* from this perspective: the scene in which Philosophy offers consolation to Boethius, in prison under threat of death, was intended to be applied generally to the situation of mankind before the Last Things. In alluding to the *translatio* idea and yet – contrary to official Ottonian ideology – failing to draw any historical and theoretical conclusions from it, this prologue may also be taken as a deliberately anti-political statement within the context of a specifically monastic cultural perspective.

3

Literature, allegory and salvation: theoretical positions in Early Middle High German

Whereas the three earliest attempts to establish a German literature – Charlemagne's programme of translations, the ninth-century biblical epics, and Notker's school texts – though all of a high standard and accompanied by corresponding theoretical reflections, remained without lasting success and influence, in the second half of the eleventh century there arose a new literature in German which, although in many respects less ambitious than its predecessors, was to achieve lasting continuity. It is of a fundamentally different nature and starts from a completely different premiss, arising not from cultural and political impulses directed from above, but from a need which has a much broader and deeper literary-sociological basis. Accordingly, this new literature displays a broad spectrum of types with a corresponding diversity of functions, encompassing both the *Heilsgeschichte* – the history of the human race from the Fall to the Incarnation, Redemption and the Last Judgement – and secular history, Bible translations and hagiographical works, dogmatic instruction and allegorical interpretation; hymns to the Virgin, prayers, admonitory sermons and lamentations, natural science and geography.[1] On the one hand, this wide variety arises from an increasingly urgent demand for education on the part of the laity, originating in the contest between spiritual and secular power in the investiture controversy of the eleventh century, which led to an increased self-awareness among the secular ruling class. On the other hand, this new literature bears witness to the attempts of the clergy to meet this demand. The search for a way of living which would satisfy the practical requirements of earthly existence while yet leading to the

---

[1] Hugo Kuhn, 'Gestalten und Lebenskräfte'; Wehrli, *Geschichte der deutschen Literatur*, pp. 117ff.

salvation of the soul demanded a positive response, and this was offered in the form of a more open attitude to nature and history – which were at the same time subjected to allegorical interpretation.[2] As a consequence, the old controversy about what constituted an appropriate Christian attitude towards nature and history was re-opened in the vernacular. The new positive attitude to nature and history was justified by the immanence of the divine within them; it was now permissible to take the secular world into account, since it was felt that the message of salvation was inscribed in it. However, inasmuch as the merely symbolic nature of earthly phenomena indicated the extent of the distance separating humanity from the absolute, the need for transcending earthly matters was still apparent.

Thus both elements, the joyful experience of divine immanence, and the necessity of transcending earthly phenomena in order to approach the divine, coexist side by side in Early Middle High German literature; indeed, they are inextricably interwoven. Accordingly, two theoretical tendencies may be discerned, which, under certain historical conditions, ultimately diverge to the point where they appear to be in direct conflict with each other. On the one hand, there is the vernacular continuation of the early Christian tradition, with its perception of poetry as being in harmony with God's creation. The spirit of God, which informs all creation, may also permeate the human spirit in such a way as to enable the latter to perceive and appreciate the presence of the divine in nature and history, and to express this insight in terms of praise. Traditionally, the key motif is the invocation of God the Creator or of the Holy Spirit, combined with a plea for inspiration in the process of the representation and interpretation of the world.[3] On the other hand, this re-interpretation, and the shift in perspective it implies, appears as a challenge, in that the metaphorical, symbolic nature of the world is a measure of its incompleteness. Completion or fulfilment can only be effected by overcoming worldly matters, by conversion in the face of the impending Last Judgement. The direct contemplation of the divine is replaced by a more distant view, seeing instead of the

---

[2]   On the use of allegorical exegesis in the early medieval period, see Jantsch, *Studien zum Symbolischen* and H. Freytag, *Die Theorie der allegorischen Schriftdeutung*. The opposite process to the allegorical interpretation of history and the world is the realization of the biblical metaphor of the *miles christianus* in the Christian knight or crusader; cf. Wang, *Der 'Miles Christianus'*, pp. 21ff.

[3]   Egert, *The Holy Spirit in German Literature*; Wilkerson, 'Form and function of the prologue', pp. 59ff. Cf. chapter 2, p. 40 above.

presence of the divine mere signs and exempla, accompanied by the relentless admonition to surrender to the Absolute. The theoretical reflections, taking up the traditional arguments, accordingly move between these two poles.[4]

A series of prologues, especially those which precede early Middle High German biblical epics, illustrate the first position – the immanence of the divine in nature – particularly clearly, for example the introduction to the *Lob Salomons*:

> Inclita lux mundi,
> du dir habis in dinir kundi
> erdin undi lufti
> unde alli himilcrefti,
> du sendi mir zi mundi,
> daz ich eddilichin deil muzzi kundin
> di gebi vili sconi,
> di du deti Salomoni,
> di manicfaltin wisheit:
> ubir dich mendit du cristinheit. (*Lob Salomons*, 1–10)

> [*Glorious light of the world*, you comprehend the earth, the air and all powers of the heavens, place in my mouth the ability to make known in some measure that most splendid gift of manifold wisdom which you granted Solomon; Christendom rejoices in you.]

This prologue may be seen as a summary of the early Christian conception of poetry according to which God's spirit, as it flows out into the world, may also work on the poet so that the latter may comprehend the world as the work of God, as another book, alongside the Bible, through which God speaks to humanity. The *invocatio* is addressed to the Creator, who is apostrophized as light. The *lux mundi* is a metaphor for God's *kunde*, his act of knowing, by which the whole universe exists and becomes meaningful so that it can be understood and interpreted in human works. The poet is therefore asking for the gift of the word, and thus for the possibility of encountering the reality of the divine Word in the world.

This idea and its context reappear in different forms from the time of Juvencus onwards; it has already been noted in Otfrid. Seen in this context, the full meaning of the individual elements, presented in a fragmentary fashion by the author of the *Lob Salomons*, becomes

---

[4] In addition to the works mentioned in note 3, see Gerhaher, *Der Prolog des Annoliedes*; Ochs, *Wolframs 'Willehalm'-Eingang*; and Naumann, 'Ein- und Ausgänge', for sources, motifs, and references to traditions.

apparent; they act as a kind of shorthand by which the whole complex of thought may be evoked.

The subject of the poem is King Solomon, or rather the gifts of wisdom which he received from God. The building of the temple and the encounter with the Queen of Sheba are singled out for description. At the end, the poem focusses on the allegorical interpretation of the king and the *Regina Austri*, according to which these Old Testament characters prefigure Christ and the Church. The term *kunden*, in line 6, referring back to the divine *kunde*, thus signifies more than a mere poetic putting-into-words; what is at issue is the revelation of the hidden meaning of nature and history.

The topos of the invocation of God and the plea for inspiration is abbreviated still further in the prologue to the *Wiener Genesis*. Here it is reduced to one conditional clause: 'ich wil iu eine rede fore tuon. / ube mir got der guote geruochet, senten zuo muote / daz ich chunne reden ...' ('I wish to offer this poem to you / if the gracious God is pleased to grant me the power of language ...'; 1–3). The *Exodus*, by contrast, elaborates on the motif; indeed the poet here asks God for help with the translation:

> dû gib mir dînen wîstûm,
> daz ich muge wandilôn
> mit tûtiskeme munde
> der latînisken zungen. (*Exodus*, 17–20)

[Grant me your wisdom, that I may transform into German what is written in Latin.]

Here the plea for the gift of language is concentrated into the image of God unlocking the power of speech by opening the mouth:

> nû sende mir sanctum
> spiritum paraclitum,
> der mîn gebende lôse,
> sô wil ich gerne chôsen;
> der heilige geist dîn
> ordene die rede mîn. (*Exodus*, 29–34)

[Send to me now that *Comforter which is the Holy Spirit*, that he may undo my bonds, then I will gladly speak. May your Holy Spirit give order to my words.]

This is based on the text of the psalm 'Domine, labia mea aperies' ('O Lord open Thou my lips': Psalm 50,17 (Vulgate)), which is cited verbatim in other works, e.g. at the beginning of the *Vorauer Sündenklage*.[5] The episode of Balaam's ass (Numbers 22,27f.) is often cited as an example in this context. The argument runs thus: if God can imbue even a dumb animal with the gift of language, how much more so then a human being. This example, used as an introductory topos, may be found, for instance, in the prologue to *Brandan*:

> Ein herre der was ûz Trierlant.
> vornemet alle wie er vant
> vil manige gotes tougen.
> Crist erlûhte mînes herzen ougen,
> und rihte mîn gemûte.
> der heilige geist durch sîne gûte,
> der einer eselinne
> gab sô getâne sinne
> daz sie menschlîchen sprach
> dô sie den engel vor ir sach
> mit einem vûerigen swerte,
> dô sie sich sô hin kêrte, –
> daz tet sie hern Balam kunt, –
> der got entslieze ouch mînen munt,
> der ir verlêch sulhe craft
> daz sie wart sus redehaft. (*Van sente Brandan*, 1–16)

[There was once a lord from the land of Trier (for 'Trierlant', read Ireland). You must all hear how he discovered many of God's secret wonders. May Christ illuminate the eyes of my heart and direct my thoughts. The Holy Spirit in His grace, who granted such intelligence to an ass that it spoke like a human being when it saw the angel standing before it with a fiery sword and turned aside, and told its master Balaam what it had seen, may this God who granted the ass the ability to speak likewise unlock my mouth.]

The use of the Balaam exemplum in prologues likewise dates back to the time of the church fathers: it is used by Paulinus of Nola. It then mainly occurs in prologues to the lives of the saints.[6] In Early

---

5   Cf. Otfrid 2,3, pp. 40–1 above. The motif continues to be employed for a long period; cf. Boesch, *Die Kunstanschauung in der mittelhochdeutschen Literatur*, pp. 114–15.; Kartschoke (ed.), *Wolfram von Eschenbach, 'Willehalm'*, pp. 269–70 (note on 2,23ff.).

6   References may be found in Heinzel (ed.), *Heinrich von Melk*, pp. 146–7, notes 460–3; Ernst, '*Liber Evangeliorum*', pp. 53–4, note 172. Der Stricker is still using the exemplum in his prologue to *Karl der Große* (lines 92ff.), cf. Singer, 'Der Eingang von Strickers *Karl*', 81.

Middle High German literature it is further cited by Der Wilde Mann in the introduction to *Veronica*, and in the *Anegenge*.

In the prologue to *Brandan*, the characteristic parallel between the presence of the divine in the world and the workings of God in the human spirit recurs: with this inspiration the chosen one is capable of apprehending the creation as a book of divine wonders. Admittedly, Brandan's voyage is far from being a straightforward contemplation and interpretation of the world; rather, it is a voyage of discovery to particular divine wonders which are selected precisely on account of their miraculous quality. Initially, Brandan was unwilling to believe that God was capable of creating as many wonders as had been reported: finally, however – and this is the result of his voyage – he has to acknowledge that God's miracles far exceed what human experience is able to comprehend.[7]

This version of Brandan's voyage – set down around 1150 in the central Franconian region – thus represents an important advance on the traditional prologue concept, with its implied parallel between the world imbued with the spirit of God and human knowledge given by God. Here, this parallel itself becomes the theme of the work, in that it is called into question, only to turn into a mere matter of quantity: could God really have created so many incredible wonders? This altered emphasis, though, suggests a move towards an alternative, contrastive concept, inasmuch as it underlines the discrepancy between the human and the divine spirit. Brandan's voyage takes him to the Promised Land, but he returns to Ireland to relate his tale; only then may he enter paradise. The way through God's wonders in this world thus leads to the recognition that the human individual, with all the potential of human understanding, simply cannot comprehend the greatness of God; all human experience of the world becomes as nothing in the experience of this difference or discrepancy. With this insight Brandan's life has reached its goal and its fulfilment.

Before considering this contrasting type, one more prologue may be cited. The prologue to *Sankt Veit* presents the correspondence between the divine and human spheres in a particularly attractive and cogent fashion:

> Cheiser aller chunige,
> ja lobet dich diu menege

---

[7] Haug, 'Vom Imram zur Aventiure-Fahrt', 268ff., 290ff.; also in Haug, *Strukturen*, pp. 382ff., 401–2.

der engel von himele.
ouch fleget dich hie nidene
diu irdiske diet.
diu nelazet daz niet,
si nebete an dine magencraft,
wan si ist din hantkescaft
die du gescuofe von der erde.
nu ruoche des gewerden
daz du mich erhore:
ich wil eine rede erboren,
diu ist also lobesam,
fon einem heiligem man,
fon dem guoten sancte Vite.
er dienet dir alle zite
in siner chintheite.
er was ie gereite
ze dinem dieneste.
nu ferlich mir der liste
durch die sine minne,
daz ich si fure bringe
al nach din eren,
ze lobe dem heiligen herren. (*Sankt Veit*, 1–24)

[Emperor over and above all kings, the host of angels in heaven praises you, and the people down here on earth worship you. They cannot resist worshipping your might, for they are your creation that you fashioned out of earth. Now grant that I may be heard by you: I will commence a poem of praise about a holy man, about good Saint Vitus. He served you unceasingly in his youth. He was always ready at your service. Now grant me for love of him the skill to compose it in your honour, in praise of that holy lord.]

Christian poetry, seen from the perspective of a world imbued with God's presence, must perforce become a hymn of praise. If God is addressed in all his omnipotence, humankind, as his creation, like the angels cannot but praise him. The prologue to *Sankt Veit* therefore asks for the strength to create a poem worthy of God. Since its subject is a saint whose life was spent in the service of God, the poet, in praising the praiseworthy saint, thus praises the Creator. There is no other Early Middle High German prologue which sets out the Christian concept of poetry as praise in the light of the Resurrection in so consistent and lucid a manner.

II

We will now turn to a consideration of the contrasting type, which is less concerned with demonstrating the presence of the divine in the world than with exposing the discrepancy between God and the human perception of him, between eternal bliss and what those on earth may know and realize of it. Let us first consider an intermediate form which may be seen as a transition between the two types, the prologue to *Die Wahrheit*:

> Nu wil ich bitten den got,
> der von den Juden wart gemarterot,
> daz er mir verlihe den sin,
> daz ich muozze chundin
> den armen unde den richen
> di chunft fraisliche,
> den jungen joh den alten,
> waz uns ist behalten,
> wa wir uns sulen enden.
> wir sin in dem ellende,
> unser heimot ist uns ungewis,
> dar in helfe uns der heilige Christ. (*Die Wahrheit*, 1–12)

[I will now beseech that God who was martyred by the Jews to grant me such understanding that I may announce to rich and poor alike the terrible things to come, proclaim to young and old alike what is in store for us, where we shall find ourselves at the end. We are in a foreign land, uncertain of our return home: may holy Christ help us to get there.]

Although the topical prayer for *sin* ('understanding') to be granted recurs here, it is not in this instance directed towards the interpretation of the world but towards the description of death and the Last Things. It is significant that it is the Christ of the Passion who is addressed; what is at issue is the moment of decision or commitment in the face of death, the anxious hope that we may find the way out of the exile of this world and into our true home in heaven. The theme of the poem itself is likewise human existence in the face of death and judgement. Thus the prologue sets the scene for what the poem *Die Wahrheit* will present.

If one now considers history from this eschatological perspective, the former is necessarily reduced to a sequence of right and wrong

decisions. The prologue of *Die jüngere Judith* may serve to illustrate
how mechanical this concept of history can appear:

> Nû vernemet, ir lîben lûte:
> ich wil û gerne sagen ze dûte
> eine rede vil wunnesame:
> dâ muget ir gerne denchen ane.
> derne solde mich nîht erdrîzen
> mahte ich ir genîzen
> vor den nîdêren
> dî vil ofte phlegent ze beswêren
> des mannes mût.
> der dem lûte îht ze gûte getût
> mit sîner gûten lêre
> des sint sî spottêre.
> daz sî phlegent ze schelten
> daz mugen sî bringen selten
> unde enlâzent iz doch âne nît nîht:
> dar umbe mûzen sî verlîsen daz êwichliche lîht.
> Ich wil û sagen von unserm heilêre,
> wî manige lêre
> er uns vore hât getragen,
> dî uns vil wale mugen behagen,
> an dem êbrêischem dîte:
> dî wîl iz sîn gebot gehîlte
> sône mohte im nîht leides ergân:
> swer sû mit arge wolde bestân
> der mûse des enallen gâhen
> wal grôzen schaden enphâhen,
> alsô an disem lîde ist vil gût schîn,
> wî er sû beschirmôte mit einem blôden wîbelîn
> unde mit welcher schande
> er Nabuchôdônôsors her sande wider ze lande.
> (dazne wirt û nîht verdaget
> izne werde û allez gesaget.)
> swenne aver sî gechêrten
> von dem ir trehten,
> daz sî sînem gebote nîne wâren undertân,
> daz mûse sâ an ir schaden gân,
> sô wurden sî von den heiden
> bedwungen mit manigen leiden,
> unze sî danne getâten widerchêre
> zû ir rehten scheffêre:

sô half er danne drâte
ûz maniger slahte nôte. –
dâ lâze wir dise rede stân
unde grîfe wir daz lît an. (*Judith*, 1–44)

[Now listen, you dear people, I would like to interpret for you a
delightful tale, one that you will be pleased to recall. To do so
would be no hardship if I could be spared the criticism of those
envious people who so often cause a man to be depressed. Whatever good one does for people with one's teaching is mocked by
them. That which they abuse, they themselves are incapable of
producing, and yet they will not desist in their envy of it: for that
they will surely be deprived of the light of eternity. I will tell you
of our Saviour and how many lessons He gave us through the
Hebrew people, from which truly pleasure can be derived. As long
as they kept His command they could not be made to suffer.
Whoever would attack them out of malice was immediately compelled to suffer great harm, as is well demonstrated in this poem
about how He protected them by means of a frail woman and how
He sent Nebuchadnezzar's army back home in such shame. That
will not be withheld from you, you will be told everything. Yet
when they themselves turned against their Lord and ceased to be
subject to His command, that immediately led to their downfall,
and they suffered many hardships at the hands of the heathen until
they turned back to their rightful creator. He then swiftly released
them from perils of all kinds. We shall break off here and embark
on the poem.]

History is here viewed in terms of a kind of divine pedagogy. It
follows a pattern as simple as it is striking: no ill can befall the people
who keep God's commandments. When, however, they turn away
from God, his punishment strikes them. As soon as they come to
their senses and turn to God again, he is there ready to save them. The
poet uses the story of the biblical figure Judith to demonstrate this.

The exemplary nature of history gives poetry a specific function,
namely *lêre* ('teaching'), since it lifts historical events from their actual
linear sequence and sees them simply as a reflection of the changing
relationship between God and his people. In the face of the absolute,
history is reduced to a series of isolated incidents, a mere collection of
exempla.

This is true of the present as well as the past. In the Old High
German period the *Ludwigslied* had considered current events from
precisely this perspective, albeit in a slightly different form. The

55

simple pattern whereby turning away from God implies ruin, and turning towards him means grace, contradicts everday experience in that the good may suffer misfortune, whereas evil-doers live happily. The neat pattern of correspondences thus has to be qualified by an explanation of those examples which apparently disprove it. The solution runs as follows: if a good person suffers misfortune, this must be regarded as a trial. Thus the invasion of the Vikings, in the *Ludwigslied*, may be seen as a test for the king.[8] If, on the other hand, an evil-doer is fortunate, this is because God, in his forbearance, wishes to give him a last chance before plunging him even more deeply into damnation when he fails to seize it. This is the argument used, for example, by Giraldus Cambrensis in *De principis instructione*, when called upon to explain why God is taking so long to punish the wrongdoings of Henry II. In any case, all accounts will be settled at the Last Judgement.[9]

Given this idea of history as a just correspondence between merit and fortune, including an explanation of the exceptions, each individual moment of history can be interpreted directly in the light of God's acts and his judgements: history becomes a storehouse of exempla illustrating the relationship between God and humanity.

The contrast between the people loyal to God, who are thus rewarded, and those who turn away from God and are punished for it, is reflected in the relationship between poet and audience in the prologue to *Die jüngere Judith*, namely the opposition between the good *lêre* and the *nîdære* ('detractors', or 'envious men'). Just as it is possible to decide for or against God, so it is possible to accept or reject the good advice offered by the poet's teaching. The device of reward and punishment outlined above is repeated in the context of poetic representation and reception, so that the poet can ultimately proclaim that anyone who is against his poem will go to Hell. Thus even the reception of the poem takes place with the Last Judgement in mind.

The motif of the evil critics and envious rivals, to return to the *nîdære*, has a long-standing tradition of its own; this has already been mentioned in the context of rhetorical topoi. Jerome forms the primary historical starting point for this literary tradition, having as

---

8 On the view of history in the *Ludwigslied*, see Berg, 'Das Ludwigslied'; Kemper, 'Das Ludwigslied im Kontext' places even more emphasis on the contemporary political situation. See Müller, 'Der historische Hintergrund des Ludwigsliedes' on this point.
9 Altmann, *Strukturuntersuchungen zu Giraldus*, pp. 89ff.

he did constantly to defend himself against malevolent critics.[10] Otfrid was the first to take up the motif in the vernacular, making specific reference to Jerome.[11]

The more directly the poet sees himself as a prophet of divine truth, the more there is a tendency for those who do not wish to listen to be compared to those who scorn God's word itself. Thus in the introduction to the *Deutung der Meßgebräuche*:

> iht mer hilfet, daz man dem brideget,
> der darumbe niene tuot, wan daz er bespottet gotes wort.
> (*Deutung der Meßgebräuche*, 2,4–5)
>
> [It is no good preaching to a man who does nothing but mock the word of God.]

It must be assumed that some listeners will remain obdurate; they are not worth bothering about. This is supported by the biblical quotation that one should not cast pearls before swine (Matthew 7,6).[12] The passage itself is especially concerned with the relationship between word and deed, i.e. the reception process is expected to result in a conscious choice. The authority of poetry is vouchsafed by the appeal to the assistance of the Holy Spirit. The doctrine of inspiration functions here first and foremost as a guarantee of the poetic claim to truth and the obligation that this entails.

Der Wilde Mann, in his poem *Van der girheit*, seeks to demonstrate how the dying can be saved through God's grace (lines 19–20). It opens with the *invocatio* topos; the justification given is that human frailty requires divine assistance in the process of composition:

> Der heilich engil birichti minen sin,
> want ich ein brodich mennischi bin ... (*Van der girheit*, 1–2)
>
> [May the holy angel direct my wit, for I am a frail man ...]

With respect to the attack on avarice, on which he is resolved, Der

---

[10] Schönbach, 'Otfridstudien III', 400ff.; Schwietering, 'Demutsformel', pp. 164ff.; Simon, 'Untersuchungen', I, 87ff.; Beumann, 'Der Schriftsteller und seine Kritiker', 500ff.; Jones, *Prologue and Epilogue*, pp. 53ff.; Unger, 'Vorreden deutscher Sachliteratur des Mittelalters', p. 221; Richert, *Wege und Formen der Passionalüberlieferung*, pp. 320ff. On Early MHG literature, see Wilkerson, 'Form and function of the prologue', pp. 95ff.

[11] V,25 69ff.; cf. Ernst, '*Liber Evangeliorum*', pp. 42ff., who attempts to establish how far Otfrid is merely making use of rhetorical strategies and how far he argues in terms of Christian categories of good and evil.

[12] This is a common prologue topos: Alan of Lille uses it in the prose prologue to *Anti-claudianus* (ed. R. Bossuat, 1955, p. 56). Cf. also Wirnt von Gravenberc's *Wigalois* prologue; see below, chapter 14, p. 277. The topos persists for a long time; cf. Beheim; for references see Schanze, *Meisterliche Liedkunst*, p. 235.

Wilde Mann hopes to soften hard hearts, and once more it is those who mock who are seen as the opponents. Their contempt, he claims, has no substance, and vanishes like hoar-frost before the sun (15ff.).

The Early Middle High German prologues discussed so far do indeed, as has become clear, employ arguments from the Christian poetic tradition. However, it is not essentially a question of the deployment of a stock of conventional strategies designed to influence reception, selecting topoi according to the requirements of the situation; rather, the individual elements cited are used to evoke the basic positions of Christian aesthetics. These are, on the one hand, an understanding of nature and history with regard to their hidden significance in the context of *Heilsgeschichte*, and on the other, an awareness that the absolute realization of the Kingdom of God, to which this significance refers, still remains remote. An awareness of this overall concept can be presupposed for author and audience alike, so that it is sufficient merely to allude to those elements which are to be emphasized. Thus it is not surprising that a reference to this traditional Christian literary theory does not – as might have been expected by analogy with rhetorical prologue theory – represent a preliminary form of establishing contact with the audience without reference to the subject matter. Rather, both principal theoretical positions are specifically related to the corresponding thematic concepts; this determines the perspective from which the subject is to be treated. The ambivalence in the Christian aesthetic tradition permeates the presentation of the subject matter, and although a particular perspective may be inferred from the prologue, such a theoretical introductory passage can only ever achieve limited independence from the poem it precedes. Early Middle High German prologues often lead without a break into the actual narrative, indeed the introduction is often so closely interwoven thematically with the actual subject matter that it is sometimes debatable whether a prologue as such exists at all, or whether in fact the work should be seen as beginning directly with the presentation of the subject matter. This is the case for example with *Memento Mori*, *Vom Rechte* and *Die Hochzeit*.[13] Strictly speaking, it is only justifiable to speak of a prologue when the introductory part takes the form of a general theoretical statement which can be distinguished reasonably clearly from the actual subject matter. This is more readily achieved with a

---

[13] See Gerhaher, *Der Prolog des Annoliedes*, who attempts to establish separate prologues here too.

concrete subject – i.e. where nature and history are dealt with – than where the subject is of a moral or dogmatic nature and is thus itself essentially theoretical.

The prologue to the *St. Trudperter Hohes Lied* (*c.* 1160) illustrates the extent to which a religious prologue may be closely related to the subject of the work and at the same time stand on its own. The starting point is once again the invocation of the Holy Spirit. However, this is not merely an instance of an exordial reflection on the search for truth; rather, the author is attempting in his introduction to evoke the presence of the Holy Spirit by showing how everything is pervaded by it. He depicts its presence and its workings in the world and in history – and this as the introduction to a work that has as its theme the encounter of the human soul with God. Thus from the beginning the listener is drawn into the process which the author goes on to describe as the workings of the Holy Spirit in the work itself.

The structural conception of this prologue has been illuminated by Friedrich Ohly.[14] The main outline runs as follows: the prologue describes how the Holy Spirit has always operated, and continues to operate, by means of its seven gifts. Three stages may be distinguished: first, the Holy Spirit played a part in the creation; secondly, it is the redeeming power in the history of salvation; thirdly, it is the force which has power to transform the inner self. At the time of the creation, the first human beings were given seven parts or members: feet, hands, eyes, and head. These correspond to the seven gifts of the Holy Spirit: thus, *timor* and *pietas* are allocated to the feet, and indicate their negative and positive functions respectively, that is, to go away from evil, and to do good. Similarly, the left hand has a passive, the right an active role – deflecting attack versus readiness to fight in a just cause; *scientia* and *fortitudo* are the corresponding gifts. *Consilium* and *intellectus* are associated with the eyes, while *sapientia* is allocated to the head.

This is then followed by a historical account of how, by means of the Fall, the devil negated the power of the seven parts and their attendant gifts, opposing them with the seven deadly sins. In opposition to this, the working of the Holy Spirit is introduced on a second level, that of salvation history; its influence is shown *ante legem* in the seven patriarchs, *sub lege* from Moses to the Incarnation, and finally

---

[14] Ohly, 'Der Prolog des St. Trudperter Hohenliedes'.

sub gratia in the seven stages of the life of Christ. However, the devil once more opposes this with his seven vices, and then the process begins a third time, completing the three-stage ascent of the inner self towards *unio* with God; this process is itself in turn divided according to the seven gifts.

The prologue to the *St. Trudperter Hohes Lied* may thus be seen as a process of initiation. It leads upwards in three major steps: from the creation, via salvation history, to the redemption of the individual. In this way, the listener is prepared for the mystical interpretation of the Song of Songs, which presents the encounter of bride and bridegroom as the union of the soul with God. The topos of the prayer for inspiration is developed here into a theory of the omnipotence of the Holy Spirit, which in turn prepares the listener for a process of interpretation which is not only pervaded by the Holy Spirit but which also includes the audience in this process. The prologue thus prepares the way for the process of redemption, a process in which the literary work, inspired by the Holy Spirit, itself becomes an instrument of divine grace.

III

Since Sulpicius Severus' *Life of Saint Martin*, the rejection of secular poetry had also been a standard topos in religious prologues. As has been stated, this applied to profane writings of the classical tradition as well as the indigenous oral traditions.[15] In the context of vernacular literature the argument is already set out by Otfrid in the letter to Liutbert, when he says that he hopes to supplant the 'laicorum cantus obscenus' with his own work.[16] It occurs again in the Early Middle High German period, this time, strikingly enough, in prologues to works which themselves engage with the secular sphere in a new way, such as the *Annolied* and the *Kaiserchronik*.[17] Both works make a bold attempt to combine secular history with salvation history. This obviously prompts the authors to draw a sharp distinction in the

---

[15] On the orthodox ecclesiastical rejection of pagan classical literature, especially where this occurs as a motif in the prologue, see Nat, 'Die Praefatio der Evangelistenparaphrase', pp. 251ff.; Moos, 'Poeta und Historicus im Mittelalter', 105, note 22; Fichte, 'Einfluß der Kirche', 5–6. On the rejection of native secular poetry, see above, chapter 2, pp. 25–6.

[16] See above, chapter 2, p. 31.

[17] A further example is provided by the epilogue to an admittedly religious poem, *Das himmlische Jerusalem*: 'der tumbe der haizet ime singen / von werltlichen dingen / unt von der degenhaite, / daz endunchet in arbaite' ('The simple man asks to hear songs about worldly things and the deeds of warriors, he sees no hardship in that.' (449–52)).

respective prologues between their own work and those of purely profane content.

The poet of the *Annolied* (written between 1077 and 1081) does this as follows:

> Wir hôrten ie dikke singen
> von alten dingen:
> wî snelle helide vuhten,
> wî si veste burge brêchen,
> wî sich liebin vuiniscefte schieden,
> wî rîche kunige al zegiengen.
> nû ist cît, daz wir dencken,
> wî wir selve sulin enden.
> Crist, der vnser héro gût,
> wî manige ceichen her vns vure dût,
> alser ûffin Sigeberg havit gedân
> durch den diurlîchen man,
> den heiligen bischof Annen,
> durch den sînin willen.
> dabî wir uns sulin bewarin,
> wante wir noch sulin varin
> von disime ellendin lîbe hin cin êwin,
> dâ wir îmer sulin sîn. (*Annolied*, 1,1–18)

[We have often heard songs about deeds of old: how brave heroes fought, how they destroyed strongholds, how close friendships were severed, how mighty kings were destroyed. Now it is time to think about how we ourselves shall finish up. Christ, our good Lord – how many miracles he performs for us, as he did on the Siegberg through and for the benefit of that worthy man, the holy Bishop Anno. With these in mind we should provide for ourselves, for one day we shall make the journey from this life of exile to eternity, where we shall reside for ever.]

The characterization of profane literature given here – heroic battles, devastation, the breaking of friendships and the downfall of kings – clearly alludes to oral heroic poetry, particularly of the kind characterized by tragic inevitability and hopelessness: the *Nibelungenlied* springs to mind. Heroic action is thus seen in the light of a conclusion which brings destruction and annihilation. But this negative conclusion is now offset by a positive aim in life; the programmatic change of direction occurs in lines 7–8: 'nû ist cît, daz wir dencken, / wî wir selve sulin enden' ('Now it is time to think about

61

how we ourselves shall finish up'). It is crucial that life should not end in a meaningless act of profane heroism, but rather that one should discover the way out of the exile of this world and into eternal life. Moreover, miracles are provided to indicate the way. The life of St Anno, that is to say, the story of what Christ did on his behalf and for his sake, thus comes to be seen as a sign and in this sense can lead to our salvation: 'dabî wir uns sulin bewarin' (15) – 'with these (=miracles) in mind we should provide for ourselves'. This is what justifies poetry of this kind. It represents a new type of literature, one which is not bound up with the past – unlike the heroic lay, which, being thus constrained, can convey no such significance – but which rather looks to the future, inasmuch as it is concerned with our future goal and end. A commitment to the profane tradition means damnation; in the face of the Last Things, if damnation is to be avoided, a commitment to the new literature is required. The function of this new literature is thus nothing less than the establishment of this connection: it must act as a mediator for the salvation of the soul. This appears surprising from a modern point of view, since current notions of literature ascribe to it no such existential effects or implications for immortality. In the *Annolied* this eschatological dimension is achieved by prefacing the *vita* of Anno with a summary both of secular history and of *Heilsgeschichte*, so that Anno appears as the veritable focal point of universal history.

The opening section presents an outline of salvation history in seven strophes. God's programme for salvation, in which the apostles are sent out to all parts of the world, after which the main action moves to Cologne, forms the wider framework within which secular history is then treated. The latter appears initially to pursue an independent path, but upon closer inspection the crowning achievement of secular history, the uniting of all countries in the Roman Empire, is seen to prepare the ground for the proselytizing of the world. The work follows the traditional pattern: Daniel's vision, with the interpretation of the four beasts as the four successive kingdoms, is seen as a revelation of the divine planning of history. Here salvation history and secular history intersect; Hugo Kuhn has referred to this as a 'christened *translatio imperii*'.[18] However, the broad scope given to secular history should not be overlooked; safely embedded in the context of the *Heilsgeschichte*, as it were, it is allowed a certain degree

---

[18] Hugo Kuhn, 'Gestalten und Lebenskräfte', p. 124.

of independent existence. This corresponds to the increased emphasis on the material world which is a characteristic of the late eleventh century. However, this complex religious and secular movement is centred on an actual historical figure, Anno of Cologne. He first makes an appearance in the seventh strophe, at the end of the outline of *Heilsgeschichte*, and he also represents the vanishing point or culmination of secular history in the heavily symbolic strophe 33. Moreover, he appears as the thirty-third bishop of Cologne, and as the seventh of the Cologne bishops to be venerated as a saint. In the figure of Anno, then, the *Heilsgeschichte* and the history of the world converge, and this is of course intentional. At this point the gap between the two alternative histories – secular and salvation history – was necessarily at its most apparent, and it was thus at this point that a solution had to be found. This solution is Anno himself; his own personal biography was intended to effect the reconciliation between the two historical perspectives, and his *vita* to show the way out of the conflict that had arisen from their differing claims.

The second strophe states that God initially divided his creation into two parts: on the one hand the affairs of this world, and on the other the concerns of the spirit. In mankind, however, God combined the two: it was intended that Adam should constitute a third world.[19] However, this was destroyed by the Fall. The process of salvation history has the ultimate effect of restoring this situation, and after the Harrowing of Hell reconciliation once more becomes possible. The aim of the *Heilsgeschichte* is thus the re-creation of that original third world, and when it culminates in the figure of Anno, he is then both *bîspili* ('exemplum') and *spiegel* ('mirror': 34,2–3) of this possibility. When Anno arrives with his entourage in Cologne, his progress is compared to the sun which moves between heaven and earth (34,8ff.): an image of the reconciliation of nature and spirit, and thus of the restoration of the original blueprint for creation.

This does not, however, prevent Anno from having to undergo a further process of purification. He is forced to leave Cologne after becoming involved in political intrigues; the poet interprets this as a divine trial. The final stage is reached when Anno, after a premonition in a dream, forgives the citizens of Cologne for their injustice towards him: only now is he ready to enter Heaven.

Is Anno then nothing but an exemplary moral figure?[20] One

---

[19] See Haas, 'Der Mensch als *dritte werilt*' on this concept.
[20] Eggers, 'Annolied'.

possible answer would be that the separate processes of secular and salvation history converge in each individual as they do in Anno. The conflict between the material world and the spirit is reconciled when man becomes aware of his situation in the face of the absolute. In this way the drama of universal history is re-enacted in each individual.

Yet Anno is more than a mere exemplum, more too than just a guarantor of the possibility of redemption, for as a saint, he is able to intercede on behalf of others. After he has entered Heaven, miracles occur at his tomb. Thus it is related that a certain Volprecht fell into the clutches of the devil, denying God and reviling even the holy bishop, with the result that his eyes fell out of his head. At this, Volprecht confessed his sins and asked Anno for forgiveness, where-upon his eyes were restored. The last strophe of the poem is devoted to the interpretation of this miracle:

> Von altin êwin ist daz kunt,
> wî sich wîlin ûf tedde der merigrunt,
> dů Moyses daz liut Israêl
> mit trukkenim wegge leite ubir sê
> ci demi allir bezzistin lante
> (des die gůtin ouch sulin waltin):
> dâ die becche miliche vluzzin,
> diz sůze honig dar inzuschin;
> diz olei ûz eime steine sprunge,
> sân dir bî der sůze brunne;
> diz brôt vane himele reginete,
> allis gůdis si seide habiten.
> mit wuntirlîchen ceichinin
> êrete got Moysen, den heiligin,
> vnz ein sîn selbis suster
> bigondimi sprecchin laster.
> ô wî starche si dî misilsuht bistûnt,
> vnz iri gewegete der brůder gût!
> alsô gewegete seint Anno disim man,
> daz her sîni gesunt gewan,
> ci diu daz wir virstûntin
> des rîchin godis gůte,
> wî her sô lônit unti ricchit,
> suaz man sînin[21] holtin sprecchit,
> der sô sůze leidit albihanten

---

[21] By contrast to the first edition I no longer follow Rödiger's reading *sinim*, preferring to follow Nellmann (ed.), *Das Annolied*, p. 120.

ci demi scônin paradysi lante. (*Annolied*, 49,1–26)

[It is known from the Old Testament that once upon a time the depths of the sea rose up, when Moses led the people of Israel along a dry path across the sea to that excellent land, where the good folk too shall reign, where streams of milk and sweet honey flow alternately, where oil sprang from a rock, close at hand the sweet spring, where bread rained from the sky, where they had their fill of all good things. God honoured Moses, that holy man, with great miracles until his own sister vilified him. Oh how severely she was smitten with leprosy until her good brother interceded for her. Thus did Anno intercede for this man, so that his health was restored, in order that we might recognize the grace of almighty God and how he rewards and punishes whatever is said about his loyal servants, whom he in his sweet grace leads directly to the beautiful land of paradise.]

In this final strophe, a significant parallel is established between Anno and Moses. Just as Moses showed the way to the Promised Land, so Anno points the way to heaven. The scene where Miriam is afflicted with leprosy corresponds to the Volprecht episode, and no doubt some kind of typological relationship is intended. The question is just how to place it in the interplay between a typological interpretation in the strict sense, and mere literary illustration.

Typological exegesis provides a key to the specific relationship between the Old and New Testaments; the historical events of the Old Testament foreshadow those of the New, or, to put it another way, the New Testament fulfils what is prefigured in the Old.[22] Seen from the viewpoint that history culminates in Christ, life *sub gratia* can only be understood and represented as an imitation of Christ. An example of this is the *humilitas–exaltatio* model used by the German emperors to express their relationship to Christ.[23] On the other hand, history continues to exist after Christ, in that the Kingdom of God has yet to be realized here on earth. In this respect, humanity *sub gratia* – i.e. after Christ's act of redemption – is nevertheless still progressing towards redemption. Seen from a typological viewpoint, this means that what was prefigured in the Old Testament must

---

[22] Only a few standard introductory works can be cited here from the wealth of relevant literature: Goppelt, *Typos*; Auerbach, 'Figura'; Boer, 'Graeco-Roman historiography', 45–6; Daniélou, *Sacramentum futuri*; Lubac, *Exégèse médiévale*; Meier, 'Überlegungen', 34ff.; Wehrli, *Literatur im deutschen Mittelalter*, pp. 246ff.; cf. also Haug (ed.), *Formen und Funktionen der Allegorie*, index, under 'Typus' and 'Typologie'.
[23] Bornscheuer, *Miseriae regum*.

continually be fulfilled anew. Thus if Anno is seen, *sub gratia*, as being in some sense an antitype of Moses, this implies a comparison with Christ, in whom, as the antitype of Moses, the typological progression has already been fulfilled and made possible for others. The typological fulfilment of Old Testament figures after Christ is thus always also an *imitatio Christi*. A kind of triangular relationship is established between the Old Testament type, the New Testament antitype, and the imitative antitype in time present.[24] That this is not – at least in the *Annolied* – merely an abstract game with illustrative analogies, is demonstrated by the unusual scope of the historical introduction which prefaces the life of Anno. *Heilsgeschichte* and the history of the world both culminate in the figure of Anno. This is intended to be understood in an exemplary sense, in that, because of Christ's act of redemption, it is possible for every individual to experience history in this way. The 'typological triangle' provides the frame of reference within which the identity of humanity can be defined *sub gratia*. As such it represents both a reassurance and a challenge; it demands, as the life of Anno demonstrates, a personal commitment, since there can be no escaping a constant awareness of death and judgement. Thus strophe 40 of the *Annolied*, with its images of historical chaos, in particular the apocalyptic image of the battle between kinsmen, evokes an end-of-the-world scenario. Here the interweaving of secular history and salvation history is seen in terms of conflict. From this perspective, the life of Anno becomes a warning to each individual to change his ways. Although the reconciliation of world and spirit may have been realized, for the individual it remains an opportunity each must grasp, a personal commitment to be pledged by each individual: 'nû ist cît, daz wir dencken, / wî wir selve sulin enden' ('Now it is time to think about how we ourselves shall finish up').

IV

The *Kaiserchronik* differs from the *Annolied* in that it presents the history only of the Fourth, or Roman, Empire. Composed about

---

[24] This is how, upon closer consideration, one may regard the issue which has been given the not entirely satisfactory designation of 'postfiguration'. I prefer the term 'typologisches Dreieck' (typological triangle) to both this term and the alternative concept of 'Mehrstufigkeit der Exegese' (multilevel exegesis) used by Haverkamp, *Typik und Politik im Annolied*, especially pp. 35ff., to describe the complex phenomenon of typological relations in the time after the New Testament.

seventy years later than the *Annolied*, it gives an account of this Empire up to around the middle of the twelfth century: to be more precise, it breaks off mid-sentence during the description of the events of 1147. Like the *Annolied*, which it takes as a source, the historiographical conception of the *Kaiserchronik* is committed to the idea of a succession of empires, although this pattern undergoes considerable modification. The four beasts in Daniel's dream now no longer refer to kingdoms but to kings, and they appear in a different order from the usual one. The series begins with the leopard, symbolizing Alexander the Great. Then follows the bear, without any interpretation. The third animal, a wild boar, is identified with Caesar, while the lioness, now placed at the end, signifies the Antichrist. Friedrich Ohly sees this, no doubt correctly, as a conscious and programmatic re-arrangement and thus re-interpretation.[25] What is of interest in the *Kaiserchronik* is less the succession of ages, than the last age itself with its expectation of the Antichrist and the Last Judgement. Here the *Heilsgeschichte* is presented entirely from an eschatological perspective. This means that the fates of individual rulers are seen in isolation even though they form part of a chronological sequence; each individual must either prove himself or fall down before the divine judgement. On their death, the souls of the kings and emperors are gathered up either by angels or by devils, in accordance with this judgement. While it is true that a certain historical development may be perceived, in that a majority of good rulers is found in Christian times, the progression is not so marked that a consistent typological pattern could be established throughout. The chronological framework serves first and foremost to bring historical figures from the time of the last kingdom face to face with the Last Judgement; this is anticipated in the individual judgement on the death of each.

This eschatological perspective is explicitly set out in the prologue to the *Kaiserchronik*. Here too the argument displays both allusions to, and characteristic deviations from, the prologue strophe of the *Annolied*.

> In des almähtigen gotes minnen
> sô wil ich des liedes beginnen.
> daz scult ir gezogenlîche vernemen:
> jâ mac iuh vil wole gezemen
> ze hôren älliu frumichait.

[25] Ohly, *Sage und Legende*, pp. 46ff.

die tumben dunchet iz arebait,
sculn si iemer iht gelernen
od ir wîstuom gemêren.
die sint unnuzze
unt phlegent niht guoter wizze,
daz si ungerne hôrent sagen
dannen si mahten haben
wîstuom unt êre;
unt wære iedoch frum der sêle.
Ein buoch ist ze diute getihtet,
daz uns Rômisces rîches wol berihtet,
gehaizzen ist iz crônicâ.
iz chundet uns dâ
von den bâbesen unt von den chunigen,
baidiu guoten unt ubelen,
die vor uns wâren
unt Rômisces rîches phlâgen
unze an disen hiutegen tac.
sô ich aller beste mac
sô wil ich iz iu vor zellen.
iz verneme swer der welle.
Nu ist leider in disen zîten
ein gewoneheit wîten:
manege erdenchent in lugene
unt vuogent si zesamene
mit scophelîchen worten.
nû vurht ich vil harte
daz diu sêle dar umbe brinne:
iz ist ân gotes minne.
sô lêret man die luge diu chint:
die nâch uns chunftich sint,
die wellent si alsô behaben
und wellent si iemer fur wâr sagen.
lugene unde ubermuot
ist niemen guot.
die wîsen hôrent ungerne der von sagen.
nû grîfe wir daz guote liet an. (*Kaiserchronik*, 1–42)

[In the love of almighty God 1 begin my poem. Listen to it with good manners: it may indeed benefit you to hear about many good deeds. Simple people consider it to be a strain if ever they have to learn something or extend their knowledge. They are good for nothing and witless that they do not want to hear what could be a source of wisdom and honour for them; despite the fact that it would benefit the soul. This book, which provides a good account of the Roman Empire, is presented clearly, it is called a 'chronicle'. It tells of the popes and kings, good and bad alike, who lived in the past and ruled over the Roman Empire right up to the present day. I will recite it to you as well as I can. Anyone who wishes may listen. Now, alas, there is today a widespread custom: many men think up lies and make songs out of them, like scops.[26] It is my great fear that their souls will burn for it, for there is no love of God there. In this way children are taught lies, those who come after us will maintain them and will constantly give them out for true. Lying and swaggering does no one any good. Wise men do not like to hear of it. Now let us begin this good poem.]

The prologue to the *Kaiserchronik* employs a series of arguments from the stock of rhetorical exordial topoi, for example the demand that the work be given due attention, since it has profitable things to offer – only the stupid would miss a chance to acquire wisdom and honour. However, these arguments are presented from a particular angle. When the poet states at the beginning that he intends to commence 'in des almähtigen gotes minnen' ('in the love of almighty God'), this must be an allusion, at least, to the theme of inspiration; God's *minne* ('love') stands for his workings both in the world and in the mind of the poet. The terms *wîstuom* and *êre* (13: 'wisdom and honour') belong in the context of the salvation of the soul. Next the subject of the poem is set out: a tale of popes and emperors set in the Roman Empire, featuring both good and evil characters. Here too there follows a discussion of the rival tradition of secular heroic poetry, but by contrast with the *Annolied*, this tradition is branded from the first as consisting of lies. The prologue to the *Annolied* had taken heroic poetry seriously, albeit in a negative way, interpreting it as an expression of a doomed world; such poetry was seen to condemn itself on account of its tragic outcome. For the author of the *Kaiserchronik*, however, the heroic lay appears as a narrative which is beyond the reach of Christian interpretation; it is 'ân gotes minne' ('without the love of God'), that is, heroic poetry is composed without regard for the workings of God, and as such can only be false.

This does not, however, prevent the poet or poets from repeatedly interpolating legendary material. Indeed, the rendering of the Lucretia story goes one stage further, adapting Ovid's plot in imitation of an

---

26 On the problems of determining the exact meaning of *scoph/scophelîch*, see Wissmann, *Skop*.

indigenous heroic model. Lucretia's husband is transformed into an exiled warrior; the conflict between him and the Roman king Tarquinius begins with a boast about the qualities of their wives, and a wager; the final catastrophe is set in motion by the Roman queen, who imagines herself to have been insulted. All in all, this constellation of figures and motifs is strongly reminiscent of the *Nibelungenlied*.[27] Here, then, heroic poetry is alluded to without being rejected as a lie; instead it is incorporated into the chronicle as a negative example. Significantly enough, Tarquinius is immediately introduced as 'der ubermuotigeste man, / der ie von muoter in dise werlt bekom' (4303–4: 'the most arrogant man ever born of woman'). Moreover, the conclusion – with the suicide of Lucretia, the murder of Tarquinius, the disappearance of the murderer – appears as a fitting judgement on this world of *Frauendienst* ('the service of women') and knightly combat with its attendant social irresponsibility and unpredictable risks.

v

In the Early Middle High German period, the problem of language continues to be a fundamental preoccupation of Christian poets. However, they are no longer concerned with specific linguistic problems: rather, the question is whether they will be able to find a form of language appropriate to their task. As a rule, the appropriateness or otherwise of German in particular is not an issue – as far as our sources reveal, the relationship between Latin and the vernacular is not discussed. The questions of form and style pale into insignificance beside the problem of the essential inadequacy of human speech before God and its dependence on the assistance of the Holy Spirit.

One exception to this is the author of the *Pilatus* fragment from the end of the twelfth century. He protests that German is *unbetwungen* ('unbridled') – a formulation which is surprisingly similar to Otfrid's criticism of the vernacular:

> Man sagit von dûtscher zungen,
> siu sî unbetwungen,
> ze vôgene herte.
> swer si dicke berte,

---

[27] Mohr, 'Lucretia in der Kaiserchronik'.

si wurde wol zêhe,
als dem stâle ir geschêhe
der in mit sîme gezowe
ûf dem anehowe
berte, er wurde gebouge. (*Pilatus*, 1–9)[28]

[It is said of the German language that it is unbridled and inflexible. If it is beaten again and again it becomes quite supple, like steel when it is beaten with the hammer on the anvil and becomes malleable.]

While the poet here appears to characterize German as an inflexible instrument, at the same time he also envisages the possibility of rectifying this, and rendering it supple. He continues by stating that he will do his best to achieve this, even if he feels himself to be too weak for his *rede* ('speech', or 'poem'). However,

mac sih enthalden mîn gedanc,
unz ich sî geenden,
sô weiz ih daz genenden
mê tût dan mâze
an sulhen anlâze. (*Pilatus*, 14–18)

[If I can remain firm in my intention until I have finished it [the poem], then I will realize that daring is more effective than caution in such an undertaking.]

The poet then explains the source from which he derives his courage and strength: once again it is the Holy Spirit who prepares the ground, shows the way, and, as *erster sin* ('the primary sense of the work'), provides support for the human *sin* ('sense' or 'meaning'), however terrifying the gulf between God's spirit and the human spirit is felt to be:

Der êrste sin is sô getân
den ich ze fullemunde hân
under di andren geleit,
is irschricket mîn frevilheit,
swenne ih neigen darane.
er ist allir sinne vane,
ir zil unde ir zeichen.
ihne mac sîn niht gereichen,
swî ih in lege unde
zô dem fullemunde. (*Pilatus*, 31–40)

28 Weinhold, 'Zu dem deutschen Pilatusgedicht', 272–3.

[The 'primary sense', which I have placed beneath the others as a foundation, is such that whenever I turn to it, bold as I am, I take fright. It is the banner of all the senses, their goal and their sign. I cannot attain it, even though I lay it down as a foundation.]

It is God who gives his *sin* ('spirit') to the poet and determines what 'sense' the latter is capable of conveying (44–51). This brings the argument round full circle to the initial idea of rendering the German language pliant and of becoming versed in the art of poetry:

> ih bin gebougit unde gebogen
> baz dan ich wêre.
> ih spien mich ze sêre,
> dô ih dî sinne beschiet.
> noh nentlâzen ih mih niet,
> ih wil an mîner mâze donen
> unz ich gweichen unde gwonen
> in dûtscher zungen vorbaz;
> sî ist mir noh al ze laz. (*Pilatus*, 52–60)

[I am better worked and formed than I was formerly. I overtaxed myself when I made use of my own senses. But I will not let up, I will stretch to the right extent until I become supple and better accustomed to the German language; I still find it too weak.]

The imagery of forging and working metal is here transferred from the language to the poet himself. The distinctions between working with the language and aspiring to articulacy become blurred. Both are however combined with an insight into the role played by the Holy Spirit in this process.[29]

The prologue to *Pilatus* is a unique theoretical document. It differs from Otfrid's work, and from that of the other Early Middle High German writers, in that there is no direct transition here from the inadequacies of language and linguistic competence to the subject matter, invoking the Holy Spirit to convey the truth of the latter; rather, the Holy Spirit is expected to exert a direct influence on the form of the language and the linguistic facility of the poet, so that language may become sufficiently supple to meet the demands of the subject, or so that the poet himself may become supple by adapting the language into an appropriate formal and stylistic vehicle.

This is not a traditional idea, nor does it re-surface at a later stage; indeed, reflection on the formal potential of the vernacular is, as has

---

[29] On the imagery of forging and metalwork, see Kibelka, '*der ware meister*', p. 223.

been suggested earlier, not documented in the eleventh and twelfth centuries other than in *Pilatus*. Even at later stages in the Middle Ages, hardly any parallels are to be found; when occasional remarks as to the inadequacy of the German language do occur, they take a different direction. The author of *Moriz von Craun* – written around 1220–30 – says in the epilogue:

> tiuschiu zunge diu ist arn:
> swer dar inne wil tihten,
> sal die rîme rihten;
> sô muoz er wort spalten
> oder zwei zesamene valten. (*Moriz von Craun*, 1778–82)

[The German language is impoverished. Anyone who wishes to write poetry in it using rhymed verse has to split his words or press pairs of words together.]

This is primarily the voice of the translator struggling faithfully to recreate the French verses in the German language at his disposal: in order to meet the metrical requirements, he is obliged on occasion to replace one word in the original with a compound, or conversely to convey two words by means of one.

In comparison with Latin, too, the German language may be described as *arm* ('poor') on account of its relative imprecision. Thus the following statement is found in a confessional text:

> tiutschiu zunge ist vil armer an dehein ding ze bescheidenne denne latîne.[30]

[The German language is poorer in its capacity to designate something than Latin.]

Such utterances, however, remain rare. This demonstrates the extraordinary degree to which the use of German had become a matter of course from the eleventh century onwards. This new vernacular self-consciousness, which is at the same time filtered through an awareness of the fundamental inadequacy of human language, is a consequence of confronting the sphere of human language directly with the Absolute. Since this is a universal problem, the question of form becomes irrelevant. By comparison with the strict rules of Otfrid's verse, Early Middle High German metre is surprisingly free. Precedence is given to the practical difficulties of striving to render the content; indeed, the wide range of permissible

---

[30] Quoted by Weinhold, 'Zu dem deutschen Pilatusgedicht', 255.

forms is an expression of this intense struggle to formulate the subject matter. The return, ultimately, to a strict metrical form towards the end of the twelfth century may be seen as the result of a development within poetic language towards greater suppleness, technical skill and elegance. This, however, is then accompanied by the establishment of a new secular literature in the vernacular. The autonomy which this implies effectively abolishes any linguistic self-doubts. Only when humanism brings about a renewed comparision with Latin is the old discussion as to the semantic and formal limitations and possibilities of German re-opened.[31]

[31] Cf. Johannes von Tepl, *Der Ackermann aus Böhmen*, ed. W. Krogmann, p. 10: 'Multa quoque alia et tamquam omnia utcumque inculta rethorice accidencia, que possunt fieri in hoc ydeomate indeclinabili, ibi vigent, que intentus inveniet auscultator' ('Also many other, indeed virtually all possible – even unrefined – appurtenances of the art of rhetoric that can be achieved in this uninflected language flourish here and will be observed by the attentive listener').

4

Religious adaptation of secular forms: the *Rolandslied, Brautwerbungsepen* ('bridal quests'), the Alexander romance

I

After the time of the church fathers – to take up a theme from chapter 1 – three possible responses to the cultural challenge to Christianity from pagan classical literature emerged: first, an unconditional denial and an attempt at eradication;[1] secondly, toleration, since it was needed as a source of formal and stylistic models;[2] and finally, a re-interpretation made possible by the positing of a meaning which, it was claimed, had hitherto been hidden, of which indeed the author himself may not have been aware and which was now ripe for revelation: this led to the allegorical and typological interpretation of the classical canon.[3] Initially, the three approaches co-existed in a more or less competitive fashion. On the whole, despite their inherent problems, they remained adequate as long as what was under discussion was secular classical literature. However, these approaches could only be applied in a limited sense to the native oral heroic tradition found in areas where a Germanic dialect was predominant, or those which had at some time been within the Germanic sphere of influence. Although there could be no stylistic reasons for tolerating the indigenous tradition, a rigorous rejection of it was not tenable in the long term in view of the influence still exerted by the native heroic lays. Nor was it really possible to submit the subject matter in question to an allegorical exegesis.[4] Although attempts were made to present the heroic material as a negative example, such reductive

---

[1] See chapter 3 above, p. 60.
[2] See chapter 1 above, pp. 15–16, and chapter 2, pp. 42–3.
[3] Rahner, *Griechische Mythen*; on medieval interpretations of Ovid and Virgil, see Born, 'Ovid and allegory' and Lubac, *Exégèse médiévale*, vol. II, pp. 233–60 respectively; Brinkmann, *Mittelalterliche Hermeneutik*, pp. 292ff.; cf. also Haug (ed.), *Formen und Funktionen der Allegorie*, index, under 'Antikenallegorese'.
[4] On northern European attempts to give Christian allegorical interpretations to pagan myths, see Gschwantler, 'Christus, Thor und die Midgardschlange'.

approaches necessarily failed to do justice to the vitality of the living oral tradition. Thus, for example, Theoderic was branded a child of the devil, riding to hell on a demon horse, but this interpretation failed to supplant the popular Dietrich legend.[5] Moreover, as the *illitterati*, whose tradition it was, achieved increasing cultural and political importance from the eleventh century onwards, so it became increasingly necessary to take this poetry seriously. Thus an alternative solution was brought into play, which, in effectively transposing the indigenous oral subject matter into a written form, devised a way of placing a religious interpretation on it without altering its narrative substance. Such was the method applied to the heroic tale of Roland's defeat at Roncevaux and to the *Brautwerbungsepen* in the manner of *König Rother*: those epic poems, in other words, in which the dominant theme is that of the 'wooing expedition' (the hero's quest to win a bride). Even secular subjects from antiquity – such as the Alexander legend – were retold in this light. This Christian transformation of the profane tradition could only be understood theoretically in terms of the traditional method of interpretation, i.e. as a revelation of hidden truth – even though this meant that the relationship between subject matter and interpretation necessarily became more complex. At any rate, the Christian interpretation was presented according to these conventional models.

Thus Konrad opens his *Rolandslied* – which dates from around 1170 –[6] with a prologue which on the whole follows the traditional pattern:

> Schephære allir dinge,
> cheiser allir chuninge,
> wol du oberister êwart,
> lêre mich selbe diniu wort;
> du sende mir ze munde
> dîn heilege urkunde,
> daz ich die luge virmîde,
> die wârheit scrîbe
> von eineme tûrlichem man,
> wie er daz gotes rîche gewan:
> daz ist Karl der cheiser.
> Vor gote ist er,
> want er mit gote uberwant

---

5 See, most recently, Szklenar, 'Die Jagdszene von Hocheppan', pp. 432ff., with comprehensive bibliography.
6 For the establishment of date and place, see Bumke, *Mäzene im Mittelalter*, pp. 85ff.

vil manige heideniske lant,
dâ er die cristin hât mit gêret
alse uns daz bûch lêret. (*Rolandslied*, 1–16)

[Creator of all things, emperor over all kings, praise to you, highest
of priests, teach me your words, place in my mouth your holy
message, that I may not lie and may write the truth about an
admirable man, how he won the kingdom of God: Emperor
Charles. He is now there in the presence of God, for together with
God he conquered so many heathen lands, thereby bringing honour
to the Christians, as the book tells us.]

Konrad begins with the traditional *invocatio*, appealing to God as
Creator and preserver of order in the world, and asking for his Word
and his truth. After this the poet states his theme, namely how the
Emperor Karl (Charlemagne) earned a place in the Kingdom of
Heaven by his victory over the heathens. It is striking that the appeal
for God's *heilege urkunde* ('holy message') is in no sense invalidated
by the fact that the poet is here drawing on a written source, that is,
one that has already been 'interpreted'. While the original is in a
foreign language, since it is not a sacred text, the appeal for inspiration
can hardly – as is the case in the *Exodus* prologue – be seen as a
request for divine aid in translation. A passage from the epilogue
confirms that the problems did indeed lie on another plane:

Also iz an dem bûche gescribin stât
in franczischer zungen,
sô hân ich iz in die latîne bedwungin,
danne in di tûtiske gekêrct.
Ich nehân der nicht an gemêret,
ich nehân dir nicht uberhaben. (*Rolandslied*, 9080–5)

[Just as it was written in the book in French I cast it into Latin and
then translated it into German. I have not added to it, nor have I
omitted anything.]

Leaving aside the rather dubious reference to the intermediary
Latin stage, Konrad emphasizes that he has produced a translation
which faithfully follows the French source text. How, then, can there
be any question of truth and falsehood in the poetic fashioning of the
work? Either the appeal for inspiration has become merely an empty
topos, or Konrad's concept of faithfulness to the original source
differs from our own.
A comparison with the French shows the latter to be the case.

There can be no doubt that Konrad interfered with his source material, less in terms of the external structure of the plot – this is no doubt what is meant by Konrad's statement that he had added nothing and taken nothing away – than with regard to his interpretation of events.[7] The assistance of the Holy Spirit is thus essential in order that the translator should recognize this true meaning and set it out in perhaps clearer or more emphatic terms than in the original French. Translation thus means the discovery of truth in the original and perhaps beyond or beneath it.[8] This begs the question as to the precise literary-historical relationship between the subject matter, the original French version, and the translation.

The *Rolandslied* is based on historical events of the eighth century. Charlemagne had led an army to Spain at the request of one of the political factions involved, there to intervene in the Moorish power struggles. The venture was not a success; the emperor was forced to retreat, and in the process the rearguard of his army was attacked and defeated.

Legend has fashioned this defeat into an heroic tragedy. The defeat was blamed on the treachery of Ganelon, one of Charlemagne's retinue, a betrayal which is further motivated by the rivalry between Ganelon and Roland, the leader of the Frankish rearguard, as set out below.

The heathens, beleaguered by Charlemagne in Saragossa, make an offer of peace. The Franks remain suspicious, and want to send an envoy into the town to obtain more detailed information. Since Roland is out of the question as an envoy on account of his violent temperament, he suggests Ganelon, the model courtier, who had already put the case for accepting the heathens' offer. Pale with anger, Ganelon accepts the task, knowing that Christian negotiators had once before lost their heads in this way. He is, however, determined to seek revenge if he should return alive. He negotiates a false truce with the heathens, and while Roland is covering Charlemagne's retreat with the rearguard, the Moors attack and defeat them.

---

[7] This may be assumed despite the fact that a comparison with the actual version used by Konrad is not possible, since this has not survived. Cf. Ott-Meimberg, *Kreuzepos oder Staatsroman*, pp. 25ff.

[8] Werner and Zirnbauer (eds.), *Das 'Rolandslied' des Pfaffen Konrad*; Ott-Meimberg, *Kreuzepos oder Staatsroman*, pp. 43ff., with emphasis on the relationship with the *Kaiserchronik*. For an essential introduction to the relationship between truth and historical facts in the religious literature of the Middle Ages, see Schreiner, 'Wahrheitsverständnis'.

The political conflict is thus focussed on the clash of personalities between Roland and Ganelon, and becomes a human drama which culminates in Roland's refusal, in the full flush of his pride, to blow his horn and call on the aid of Charlemagne and the main body of the army when the heathens attack with all their might. Thus he brings about the destruction of his own side.

It is not known in exactly what form the legend was passed down through the centuries.[9] By the time a written version appears in the twelfth century, this heroic and human drama is already interpreted from the perspective of salvation history: Charlemagne's embarrassing military venture appears as a crusade, and Roland and his men become martyrs to the faith; there is an unmistakable echo of Judas Maccabeus in the figure of Roland. Ganelon for his part is allotted the traitor's role of Lucifer-Judas in the universal struggle between God and the devil; his courtly beauty reflects the false brilliance of the fallen angel. Like Christ, Charlemagne knows in advance that he is to be betrayed. Moreover, a new conclusion is added: when the dying Roland finally blows the horn after all, Charlemagne comes down from the heights of the Pyrenees to avenge the treacherous attack. As in the Old Testament, God bids the sun stand still so that the emperor may have enough time to destroy the heathens.[10]

In the French *Chanson de Roland*, the Christian perspective is superimposed on the conflict of the heroic epic. The author of the German version takes this a crucial stage further, reducing the emphasis placed on heroic motivation so as to present a black-and-white drama of martyrdom. It is no longer overweening pride which prevents Roland from blowing his horn and calling on Charlemagne's assistance, but his wish to die as a martyr and enter the Kingdom of

---

[9] Christmann, 'Neuere Arbeiten zum Rolandslied'; Rohr, *Matière, sens, conjointure*, pp. 144ff., with further bibliography.

[10] Geppert, 'Christus und Kaiser Karl'; Rohr, *Matière, sens, conjointure*, pp. 125–6; Ohly, 'Die Legende von Karl und Roland'; Stackmann, 'Karl und Genelûn', 264ff.; Geith, *Carolus Magnus*, pp. 98ff. Heinzle, 'Entdeckung der Fiktionalität', 59, raises the objection that the *Chanson de Roland* is not a religious adaptation of secular subject matter but rather a legend which was conceived from the outset in a Christian context. For this reason, he argues, the 'psychological emphasis' is not a remnant of an earlier stage but one of the 'achievements of the written version' of the *Chanson* and thus belongs to the most recent stage. As far as his first objection is concerned, nothing is known about this stage of composition. Some very unchristian heroic lays date from the Christian era – cf. the Dietrich legend. Even if Heinzle's arguments are correct, though, it may be assumed that traditional heroic forms continued to have an effect and might well have been able to resist a Christian interpretation. As for the 'psychological emphasis', it is conceivable that 'modern' elements have crept in, but these are only of secondary importance, since the underlying pattern of conflict is based on the old heroic tradition.

Heaven. The heathens are transformed into devils, whom Charlemagne opposes on God's behalf. History is thus reduced to a mere variation of the eternal conflict between heaven and hell.

Inasmuch as the *Rolandslied* echoes on the one hand an Old Testament configuration, and on the other allows events to be interpreted in the light of the New Testament, the representation may, by analogy with the *Annolied*, be seen in terms of the 'typological triangle', in that, at Roncevaux, Christ's victory over the devil is re-enacted in the form of religious *imitatio*. It thus transpires that it was for this Christian re-interpretation that Konrad sought divine assistance in the prologue; this is the true meaning which had to be conveyed. It gives Konrad the authority to explain and set out explicitly in his version what had been unobtrusively implicit as a second level of meaning in the French original. What he has lost in characterization and human drama, he has gained in unambiguous interpretation and propagandist religious impact. Moreover, a certain contemporary political relevance cannot be overlooked; Konrad's version should be viewed in the light of the German cult of Charlemagne at this time.[11] In the epilogue, Konrad compares Henry the Lion – who commissioned the work – with David, a prefiguration of Christ. Since Henry, as a crusader, is also implicitly compared with Charlemagne, he too is woven into the typological system on several levels.[12]

II

An alternative means by which the religious tradition was able to assimilate the secular oral tradition in a written form was in the adaptation of the *Brautwerbungsepen*, a genre which in all probability dates back to the middle of the twelfth century. Instead of interpreting the heroic plot in the light of salvation history, thus giving it a new level of meaning, the new interpretation in these epics based on the wooing expedition (or 'bridal quest') is arrived at by means of a duplication of the action, whereby the second cycle repeats the action of the first but places it in a different perspective, thus to some extent qualifying it. Instead of two superimposed levels of meaning, here the two variations on the plot follow one another.

---

[11] Ott-Meimberg, *Kreuzepos oder Staatsroman*, interprets the *Rolandslied* as a political epic.
[12] Bertau, 'Das deutsche Rolandslied'; on the *imitatio* of David by medieval rulers, see Steger, *David Rex et Propheta*, pp. 121ff.; cf. also Nellmann, 'Karl der Große'.

This may be demonstrated most clearly by the example of *König Rother*; however, other epics of this type, especially *Sankt Oswald* and *Orendel*, also employ this contrasting narrative principle to convey their meaning, despite their respective differences imposed by the requirements of the subject matter and the interpretative solutions adopted.[13]

King Rother needs a wife of equal rank; the council is assembled, and someone tells of the beautiful daughter of Constantine of Constantinople. However, to woo her seems hopeless, since all her previous suitors have been put to death. Rother is determined to try nonetheless. He sends messengers to King Constantine, who has them thrown into a dungeon. Concerned about their fate, Rother himself takes to the seas. So as not to endanger his imprisoned messengers, he enters Constantinople in the guise of a fugitive warrior, accompanied by a retinue of violent giants who proceed to terrorize the town. At the same time, Rother puts on a dazzling display of wealth and power. His generosity wins him friends, and he assembles a whole army among the homeless and disenfranchised. Constantine, alarmed and intimidated, does not dare to take action against the foreigners, and Rother finally succeeds in gaining access to the princess. In a daring move, he confides his identity to her and succeeds in winning her for himself. In a war against King Ymelot of Babylon, Rother helps the Byzantines to victory. He is sent as a messenger to bring the glad tidings to the town, but uses this opportunity to elope with the princess, and they and the liberated messengers set sail for Italy.

The basic pattern of the *Brautwerbungsepos* with its characteristic motifs of the 'bridal quest' are unmistakable in this first part of the action of *König Rother*: the king seeking a wife, the council assembly with the report of a remote and inaccessible princess, the sending of messengers, the daring yet surreptitious approach to the bride, her co-operation, military service in the army of the prospective father-in-law, and finally flight.[14] However, these typical elements are viewed from a particular perspective, in that everything is focussed on Rother's display of power. This has, admittedly, a strategic purpose, but it is carried further than the situation demands. Its deeper

---

[13] A basic introduction to type and structure is given in Curschmann, *Der Münchener Oswald*; on *Oswald*, see Haug, 'Das Komische und das Heilige', 23ff.: also in Haug, *Strukturen*, pp. 268ff.; on *Orendel*, see Ebenbauer, '*Orendel*', pp. 54ff.

[14] On the topical nature of these motifs, see Frings and Braun, *Brautwerbung I*; Geissler, *Brautwerbung in der Weltliteratur*; cf. also Curschmann, *Der Münchener Oswald*, pp. 10ff.

significance is only revealed in the contrast to Rother's behaviour in the second part of the action; in other words, the first cycle is planned by the author in anticipation of the second cycle, which repeats the motif of the wooing expedition in contrasting circumstances.

The second cycle opens with a counter-move on Constantine's part. By cunning means he succeeds in abducting his daughter back from Italy. Rother is thus forced to set out again and win his wife a second time. Once again he travels with an army to Constantinople; this time, however, he conceals his forces at a short distance from the town and enters Constantine's palace by stealth, disguised as a pilgrim and accompanied by only two followers. They are discovered, and are sentenced to be hanged. On the way to the gallows, however, Rother manages to blow his horn and call his hidden army to his aid. After they have been liberated, he generously forgives his father-in-law. Rother returns with his wife to Italy, where she gives birth to a son, who is christened Pippin. After twenty-four years he takes over the rule of the country, and Rother and his wife retire to a monastery. Pippin's son, however, will become the Emperor Charlemagne.

There can be little doubt that the second part of *König Rother* did not belong to the legend in its original form.[15] However, it is no longer possible to discover in what the original core of the story consisted, since the later duplication of the action transformed it, fusing it into the larger plan. In the first cycle, Rother sets out confident of wooing and winning his queen. His entry into Constantinople is calculated to display the maximum splendour and power. Since his aim in courting the princess is to found a universal empire uniting East and West, the journey becomes a political operation. The second cycle, however, presents a contrast in every respect. Rother slips into the town disguised as a pilgrim; once discovered, he places himself in the hands of God. The change of costume is symbolic of the difference in attitude: whereas on the first trip, Rother wins his queen as a warrior, by cunning and bravery, on the second he gives himself up in pilgrim's clothes, is led to the gallows and has to rely on help from others. Once he has been saved, he allows generosity to prevail; thus violence and power are replaced by self-denial and grace.[16] At the very end, however, the political perspective is reintroduced with the distant view of the Carolingian

---

[15] Curschmann, '*Spielmannsepik*', pp. 29ff.
[16] W. J. Schröder, '*König Rother*'; Reiffenstein, 'Erzählervorausdeutung', pp. 557ff.; Curschmann, '*Spielmannsepik*', pp. 74ff.

empire: Rother is the grandfather of Charlemagne. This is why, as the poet claims (4785ff., and also in 3483–4), the work cannot be compared with any other, since it is 'von lugenen gedihtet niet' ('not fashioned out of lies') but is a true story. Its claims to truth are thus derived from the historical perspective introduced at the end. Truth is here taken to mean the foundation of the universal empire based on the principles set out in the double wooing expedition: state power and the authority of the ruler are transformed through personal discipline and divine grace.

III

In the twelfth century, individual French *chansons de geste* and native oral poetry were not the only works to be adapted and given new meaning by the clergy within the vernacular written tradition; as has been stated above, a number of the secular works of classical antiquity were also included in this process of re-interpretation. Around 1150, the romance of Alexander was translated into German by a cleric named Lambrecht, from the Moselle-Franconian area. His immediate source was the Provençal version by one Alberic of Pisançon, which was in turn based on the Latin version of Julius Valerius. Whereas 105 original lines of Alberic's version have survived, nothing has been preserved of Lambrecht's work in its original form. However, a Bavarian re-working is preserved in the *Vorau Manuscript*, taking the romance up to the death of Darius, though this has a curiously abrupt ending, with the statement that Alberic's and Lambrecht's work also only reached this point. Regardless of how this sudden conclusion is to be interpreted, however, it is almost certain that Lambrecht did not translate the whole of the Alexander romance, though it was not long before his fragment was continued and concluded by another hand, on the basis of the Latin version of Leo of Naples. Two versions of this sequel have survived: an adaptation dating from *c.* 1170, the *Straßburger Alexander*, and a late re-working from the fifteenth century, the *Basler Alexander*.[17]

It should be pointed out that Alberic's version and its sequels and adaptations represent only one of the many strands by which the story of Alexander passed into the vernacular languages in the Middle Ages. This multiplicity of documents reflects a wide variety of

---

[17] Urbanek, 'Ferdinand'; Stein, 'Ein Weltherrscher als *vanitas*-Exempel', pp. 146ff.

perspectives in the adaptation and interpretation of the classical biography of King Alexander. Two aspects stand out in the Christian Latin reception of the story. On the one hand, Alexander occupies a clear position within the traditional sequence of empires, and thus acquires a specific function in salvation history. He ushers in the third empire, which, embracing Orient and Occident, prepares the way for the last – the Roman – empire and thus for the spread of Christianity. On the other hand, the Alexander tradition furnishes a rich vein of exempla: the figure of the Macedonian king is interpreted from widely contrasting perspectives, for he is seen now as an example of hubris, now of wisdom; now of excess, now of self-discipline; now of unrestrained behaviour, now of moderation, and so on.[18]

Surprisingly enough, the first vernacular Alexander poem is completely at variance with any of the usual interpretations. In his prologue, Alberic justifies his interest in Alexander as a subject thus:

> Dit Salomon, al primier pas,
> Quant de son libre mot lo clas:
> 'Est vanitatum vanitas
> Et universa vanitas.'
> Poyst lou me fay m'enfirmitas,
> Toylle s'en otiositas!
> Solaz nos faz' antiquitas
> Que tot non sie vanitas. (*Alexandre*, 1–8)[19]

> [Solomon says right at the beginning, when he begins to speak of his book: *Vanity of vanities, all is vanity.* Since my infirmity provides the opportunity, let idleness take flight; let the world of the ancients give us the comfort that not everything is vanity.]

Alberic thus begins with a reference to Solomon, citing the *vanitas* passage from Ecclesiastes 1,2 and 1,14, which he uses as an opening *sententia*. It is not entirely clear how the next two lines (5–6) follow on logically. The translation given above deliberately leaves the meaning of *enfirmitas* open.[20] One might suppose that this word is a variation on the concept of *vanitas*;[21] in this case one might rather

---

[18] Cary, *The Medieval Alexander*.
[19] Mölk, *Französische Literarästhetik des 12. und 13. Jahrhunderts*, No. 23, p. 20.
[20] Both Foerster, 'Zu V. 5 des Alexanderfragments', and Szklenar, *Bild des Orients*, p. 33, translate *enfermitas* as 'illness'. Ehlert, *Deutschsprachige Alexanderdichtung*, p. 33, agrees with Szklenar. However, the latter's suggestion (p. 33, note 5) that a translation of *enfirmitas* as 'weakness' or 'inadequacy' would result in an 'inappropriate contrast' to the idea of *vanitas* seems to me unconvincing.
[21] *infirmitas*, 'frailty', appears as a synonym for *vanitas* in Eccl. 5,12 and 15. Laugesen,

expect that the poet – or perhaps Solomon?[22] – would continue along the following lines: 'even though I am fallible, I shall not give way to sloth' – the danger of sloth being likewise a motif from Ecclesiastes: 'multam enim malitiam docuit otiositas' (33,29), and moreover a common prologue topos.[23] Be that as it may, the conclusion to be drawn is as clear as it is unusual: the poet intends to turn to examples from antiquity in order to demonstrate that all is *not* vanity. The life of Alexander the Great is offered as proof of this, implying that a classical pagan figure is being set up against the authority of Solomon: the example of Alexander is intended to refute the pessimism of Solomon's sayings on vanity! This is a preposterous notion; it is unlikely that many parallels could be found from the early twelfth century. It is, then, hardly surprising that Lambrecht fails to follow up this bold claim on the part of the original text. He opens with a preamble of his own devising, during which he introduces himself, his theme, and his source:

> Diz lît, daz wir hî wurchen,
> daz sult ir rehte merchen.
> sîn gevûge ist vil reht.
> Iz tihte der phaffe Lambret.
> Er tâte uns gerne ze mâre,
> wer Alexander wâre.
> Alexander was ein wîse man,
> vil manec rîche er gewan,
> er zestôrte vil manec lant.
> Philippus was sîn vater genant.
> Diz mugit ir wol hôren
> in libro Machabeorum.
> Alberich von Bisinzo
> der brâhte uns diz lît zû.
> er hetez in walhisken getihtet.
> Nû sol ich es euh in dûtisken berihten.

'Commentaire', 287, takes a different view, interpreting *enfirmitas* as a modesty formula: 'puisque mon infirmité m'en "donne lieu" (?) = ne s'y oppose pas = puisque je peux entreprendre une telle œuvre malgré mon peu de talent, eh bien! que l'oisiveté s'éloigne . . .' However, the interpreter is obliged to pursue a tortuous route in order to arrive at this point!

[22] Spitzer, 'Des guillemets', suggests that lines 5ff. also refer to Solomon. Ehlert, *Deutschsprachige Alexanderdichtung*, p. 33, is probably right in preferring to link *nos* (line 7) with the activity of the poet, as did Foerster, 'Zu V. 5 des Alexanderfragments'.

[23] Curtius, *Europäische Literatur und lateinisches Mittelalter*, pp. 98–9; Arbusow, *Colores rhetorici*, pp. 98ff., p. 102; Lausberg, *Handbuch der literarischen Rhetorik*, col. 275α; Gottfried von Strassburg, *Tristan*, ed. Ganz, vol. I, pp. 342f., note to 41–2; Jungbluth, 'Ein Topos in Lamprechts *Alexander*'.

Nîman inschulde sîn mich:
louc er, sô leuge ich. (*Alexander*, 1–18)

[Listen carefully to the poem that we compose. Its form is most appropriate. Lambrecht the priest has written it. He wanted to make known to us who Alexander was. Alexander was a wise man who conquered many kingdoms and destroyed many lands. Philip was his father's name. You can hear this in the Book of Maccabees. Alberic of Pisançon passed this poem on to us. He wrote it in French. I will now tell it to you in German. Let nobody blame me: if he was lying then I am lying.]

The recommendation of one's own work, the demand for a proper degree of attentiveness, the naming of oneself as author, and the indication of contents and source are all common prologue elements. There is nothing unusual about this list, apart from the fact that it merely enumerates topoi without attempting to place especial emphasis on any one thing in particular. It is tempting to suggest that the return to profane material is accompanied by a return to the formal tradition of secular rhetoric. Only the mischievous aside in lines 17 and 18 might appear surprising. However, it too contributes to the impression that a new attitude to literature is emerging here. Lambrecht presents himself as a mediator of Alberic's work, and in so doing – whether seriously or in jest – places the responsiblity for anything suspect which may have crept in firmly on the original.[24] Something of the new spirit one senses in Alberic seems to have been influential here. The way in which Lambrecht proceeds to translate and reinterpret Alberic's prologue, however, shows how soon this spirit comes up against limitations:

Dô Alberich diz lît inslûc,
dô heter ein Salemones pûch,
dâ er ane sach

---

[24] The exculpation of the self by putting the blame on the author of the original also occurs in other works. A comparable formula is found in the epilogue to Veldeke's *Eneide*. He says, with reference to Virgil, 'Louc her nicht, so ist iz war / Das Heynrich machte dar nah' (13514–15, MS. G, ed. T. Frings and G. Schieb, Berlin 1964/65); '... Wan als her do geschreben vant, / Als har hers uns vorgezogen, / Das her anders nicht hat gelogen / Wan als her an dem buche las. / Ob das nicht gelogen was, / So wil her unschuldic sin / Als ist walsch und latin / Ane misse wende' (13520ff.). There is nothing which corresponds to this in the French original. Is Veldeke echoing Lambrecht? He probably knew the Strasbourg version of the *Alexander*, which puts it less strongly: 'alse daz bûch saget, sô sagen ouh ih' (ed. K. Kinzel, 1884, line 18). Cf. also *König Rother*, line 16. Later, Wolfram and Der Stricker make use of the play on lying in order to draw attention to the fictional nature of their work; Der Stricker quotes Lambrecht directly. See below, chapter 9, p. 166 and chapter 14, p. 276 respectively.

vanitatum vanitas:
daz ist allez ein îtelcheit,
daz diu sunne umbe geit.
Daz hete Salemon wol virsûht.
Dar umbe swar in sîn mût.
Er ne wolte niht langer ledec sitzen,
er screip von grôzen witzen
wande des mannes mûzecheit
ze deme lîbe noh ze der sêle niht versteit.
Dar ane gedâhte Alberich.
Denselben gedanc hân ich.
Unt ich ne wil mih niwit langer sparn,
des liedis wil ich volvarn. (*Alexander*, 19–34)

[When Alberic began this poem he had before him a book by
Solomon in which he read: *Vanity of vanities*, everything under the
sun is vanity. Solomon had truly tested that out. For that reason
Alberic's heart was weary. He did not want to stay idle any longer.
In his great wisdom he started writing, for idleness is good neither
for the body nor for the soul. That is what Alberic thought. And
that is what I think; and I will hesitate no longer, I will get on with
the poem.]

Lambrecht thus takes over Alberic's opening *sententia* from Ecclesiastes; lines 23 and 24 refer to the biblical source. He reads in
Alberic's problematic lines 5 and 6 the topos of the dangers of sloth,
which he clearly attributes to Solomon. However, this topos here
provides the exclusive motivation for Alberic's work, and Lambrecht
claims it for his adaptation as well. The provocative idea that the life
of Alexander could refute Solomon's statement about the vanity of
the world has been dropped, and the main thrust of Alberic's
argument is therefore lost. Later Solomon is expressly placed above
Alexander; after Lambrecht, following the original, has singled out
Alexander for his incomparable virtue, he qualifies this by saying
'Salemon der was ûz getân ... (62), man mûste in wol ûzsceiden, /
wande Alexander was ein heiden' (69f.) ('Solomon was an exception
... he had to be considered apart, for Alexander was a heathen').
Similarly, in the rest of the work Lambrecht repeatedly modifies
Alberic's glorification of Alexander with critical interpolations,[25]
giving rise to a curiously contradictory picture: on the one hand,
Lambrecht is unable to escape the fascination which emanates from

---

[25] Cf. Grammel, *Wandel des Alexanderbildes*, pp. 37–8.

Alberic's portrait of the Macedonian king, while on the other he feels it necessary, as a cleric, to express his reservations.

This represents a less than happy compromise. The redactor of the *Vorau Manuscript* restored Lambrecht's fragment to its Christian historical framework and interpreted it accordingly; in his collection of texts he places the *Alexander* between the episodes from the Old and New Testaments, and thus views it from the conservative viewpoint of salvation history.[26]

The Strasbourg version, on the other hand, points forward to the future. It is an expression of that particular stage of development with which we are here concerned: the elaboration of the life of Alexander in all its colourful details is associated with a sensitivity towards the strange and wonderful variety of history and the natural world. However, although narrative is here given a dynamic of its own, signalling a sense of the autonomy of the literary work, nonetheless secular affairs are once again placed into a religious context. From Alexander's conquest of the world through to his experience of the wonders of the Orient, all ultimately culminates in one episode, the 'Iter ad Paradisum', which here occurs for the first time in the context of a romance. Having conquered the world, Alexander tries to conquer paradise too. However, he is rebuffed, and taught by means of a parable that all human ambition must become as naught in the face of death. The traditional means of interpreting individual episodes as exempla is thus used here to provide the crucial turning point in a life which encompassed the world in an unprecedented fashion. The life of Alexander, for all the fascination it exerts at a secular level, is retrospectively put into perspective with the introduction of the religious viewpoint at the end.[27]

Alexander did not fail to draw the appropriate conclusions from this lesson, for in future he lived a life of *mâze* (7263: 'moderation', 'measure'). *Mâze* is in the first instance the opposite of hubris, the term which characterizes the conqueror of the world who also wants to bring paradise within his orbit. Yet *mâze* is not completely synonymous with the moderation and restraint appropriate to the limits of human potential. The idea of a life of *mâze* anticipates the courtly ideal of *mâze*, implying an ideal inner balance of individual

---

[26] Polheim, *Die deutschen Gedichte der Vorauer Handschrift*, especially pp. XIVff.
[27] Haug, 'Struktur und Geschichte', 131ff., 135ff.; also in Haug, *Strukturen*, pp. 238ff., 241ff. Vollmann-Profe, *Wiederbeginn*, pp. 209ff., takes a more positive view: she refers to a process of mediation between 'classical humanity and heroism and the Christian ethos'.

and social forces. In no sense can the *Straßburger Alexander* be read as an epic on the renunciation of worldly affairs.[28]

IV

The *Rolandslied, König Rother* and the *Alexander* represent three ways in which the new open attitude to the material world may engage with history and the natural world, and at the same time translate it onto a higher plane of meaning. The *Rolandslied*, by superimposing the universal drama of salvation onto a heroic plot, is able to interpret the historical action in just such a religious sense; world history is incorporated into the eternal scheme of the *Heilsgeschichte*. The interpretation is based, *sub gratia*, on the pattern of thought expressed in the 'typological triangle'. *König Rother* likewise makes use of a two-level poetic model. In this case, however, the would-be interpreter is dealing with a variant of the plot which uses contrastive analogy to repeat the action on a higher plane, thus giving the purely secular elements a religious dimension. Finally, the *Alexander* gives meaning to earthly matters by reverting to an exemplary interpretation of reality. However, this is no longer achieved by breaking down the life of Alexander into a series of exemplary episodes; rather, the secular side of his biography culminates in a scene in which an exemplary truth is presented in such a way as to pass judgement on what has gone before, determining the form the rest of Alexander's life will take.

These are all epic adaptations and variations of the religious interpretative models that were available to vernacular writers in the Early Middle High German period. What is new is the amount of space devoted to secular matters before they are, ultimately, re-integrated into the religious framework. No new theoretical basis is established here as yet, but the traditional approaches are transformed to such an extent as to anticipate future developments, not least in the unusual way traditional forms are re-established.

Finally, what is remarkable with respect to the development of an autonomous status for literature is the interplay between the breaking of new literary ground and the repeated retreat to the traditional

---

[28] Stein, 'Ein Weltherrscher als *vanitas*-Exempel', pp. 156ff., emphatically refuting W. J. Schröder, *König Rother*. On the central importance of *mâze* in *Alexander*, cf. also Stackmann, 'Die Gymnosophisten-Episode', 339, 350ff. As Jungbluth, 'Ein Topos in Lamprechts *Alexander*', has already pointed out, the *vanitas* topos of the prologue may not be used in the thematic interpretation of the work.

political notions and implications of salvation history. The *Rolands-lied* and *König Rother* both derive their particular contemporary relevance from the veneration of Charlemagne as an ideal ruler, a cult which reaches a new peak in Germany precisely in the twelfth century. The *Alexander* is once more situated in the context of salvation history, towards the end of the twelfth century, in the *Vorau Manuscript*. Other examples might be added, notably the *Eneide*, which was given a renewed political impact by Heinrich von Veldeke, for example through the inclusion of the Hohenstaufen interpolations concerning Barbarossa.[29]

---

[29] Dittrich, *Die 'Eneide' Heinrichs von Veldecke*, pp. 126ff., 433ff.; Wenzelburger, *Motivation und Menschenbild*, pp. 270ff., 321ff. The less one is prepared to follow Dittrich's interpretation, based on typology and salvation history, the more one is obliged to speak in terms of re-politicization; cf. Ruh, *Höfische Epik*, vol. I, pp. 86–7.

5

Chrétien de Troyes' prologue to *Erec et Enide* and the Arthurian structural model

I

Chrétien de Troyes' *Erec et Enide*, the first Arthurian romance, marks the beginning of an important new phase in Western literature. It represents the first vernacular romance of the Middle Ages which may be described as fictional. Moreover, not only is it fictional in its structure, but there is at the same time a high degree of awareness of this fictional status and the problems and attendant literary possibilities this entails. Such a statement, however, will not meet with universal approval: there has been an ongoing controversy as to whether Chrétien and his successors really intended their romances to be viewed as fiction.[1]

The terms 'romance' and 'fiction' require further clarification. The English language allows a distinction between 'epic', 'romance', and the (modern) 'novel'; in German 'romance' and the 'novel' are subsumed in a single word, *Roman*. The 'novel' is considered fictional, whereas this is not necessarily the case with 'epic', which is generally considered to be based, however loosely, on historical events. Whereas in English the term 'courtly romance' has come to be established for such works as *Erec et Enide*, in German the terms *höfisches Epos* ('courtly epic') and *höfischer Roman* ('courtly romance/novel') are used side by side.

According to current definitions, the term 'epic' assumes the hero to be integrated in a structured and coherent existence having a definite order and values, whereas the term 'novel' is used when the hero begins to question this social commitment, breaking away from it in order to discover himself and his true place in society. In the epic, the action unfolds within an ordered and self-contained world,

---

[1] See e.g. Gumbrecht, 'Wie fiktional war der höfische Roman?'

from which it in turn derives its meaning, so that success and failure occur according to fixed and at times harsh rules which are never called into question. In the novel, on the other hand, the meaning of the action remains open, that is to say the work itself becomes instrumental in the process of discovering and establishing meaning.[2]

The Arthurian romance differs from the modern novel in that the protagonists of the former appear more as figures in a preordained pattern of events than as fully rounded and individual characters in their own right. The rules which govern the movements of the Knights of the Round Table within their own world are however so different from the fixed order of the epic universe as to create a sharp distinction between the new literary form of the 'romance' and the traditional epic, thus marking the former as more akin to the novel.

This definition of the Arthurian romance is supported by the fact that it seeks to establish meaning by the use of a particular fictional model, and that the romance, in the course of its development, experiments with and explores its possibilities and limitations until a crisis point is reached and the type disintegrates.

The fictional status of Arthurian romance as a genre can hardly be doubted when viewed from a modern literary-historical perspective, since its world is manifestly a freely invented literary construct. Such sources as there are serve primarily as a repository of motifs.[3] This freedom is essential for the development of the experimental structure by which the meaning is realized and conveyed within the text itself. In concrete terms, this is made possible by turning away from the historically based subject matter of classical antiquity and Frankish heroic poetry, and using instead the *matière de Bretagne*, i.e. by operating with primarily oral and popular subjects of Celtic origin which, having no firm historical basis, may be adapted at will.

It is less easy to determine how far the Arthurian poets were conscious of the scope and implications of this new genre, and to what extent they were in a position to analyse it and establish a

---

[2] On the distinctions between epic and romance, see Jauss, 'Epos und Roman'; 'Theorie der Gattungen', pp. 334ff.; and 'Fiktionalität und Realität', pp. 428–9; also Stierle, 'Die Verwilderung des Romans', pp. 255ff. On Chrétien's terminology, see Ollier, 'The author in the text', pp. 27ff. Gumbrecht, 'Wie fiktional war der höfische Roman?', has expressed reservations about the use of the term 'fictional'. In referring to the courtly romance as 'fictional', the present author does not wish to ignore the differences between medieval fictional literature and the novel: these distinctions, which have been repeatedly stressed – for example by Jauss, *Alterität und Modernität*, p. 15, and Hugo Kuhn, 'Versuch über das 15. Jahrhundert', pp. 149ff. – must not be overlooked. See below, p. 106.

[3] Haug, 'Tristansage', 670ff. esp. 673: also in Haug, *Strukturen*, pp. 484ff., esp. pp. 486–7.

theoretical basis for it. Only by examining the Arthurian structural model in relation to theoretical statements in prologues, epilogues and excursuses, where – for the first time since Otfrid – the aims and function of literature and the position of the poet are explicitly discussed, can one hope to answer this question.

II

Erec, a knight of the Round Table, sets out to avenge an insult to the queen, who had been slighted by a stranger whilst out riding. Erec, who was accompanying her while the other knights were at the hunt, follows the stranger, although he is unarmed. They reach a town where many people are assembled. Erec finds a meagre lodging with a poor knight at the edge of the town, where he is waited on by the latter's daughter Enide, a maiden whose extraordinary beauty shines through her ragged clothes. It transpires that a kind of beauty contest is to be held in the town: it is so devised that the best fighter can win the 'beauty prize' – a sparrowhawk – for his mistress; the victory thus proves that the winner's lady is the fairest, since bravery and beauty belong together. The stranger whom Erec has been pursuing has already won the sparrowhawk twice for his *amie*, and now he wants to attempt to win it a third time. Seeing his chance, Erec obtains weapons from his host, together with the permission to try to win the sparrowhawk for Enide. He manages to defeat the offending knight and thus avenges the queen; at the same time he wins Enide, with whom he returns to Arthur's court, where a wedding feast is prepared for them. Their wedding and the return to Erec's own court bring the first part of the action to a close.

With Erec's journey of *avanture*[4] Chrétien had devised a narrative structure which was to become the basis of the type of the Arthurian romance. It is characterized by three structural elements:

1. Arthur's court as the ideal starting point and goal of the action.

2. The challenge, in which the ideal status of the court is called into question by an outsider, and a knight of the Round Table sets out to take up this challenge on behalf of society.

3. The hero's 'adventures': his setting out and journey lead to a crisis, at the low point or nadir of his fortunes. Here there comes a

---

[4] On the term *avanture/âventiure*, see Eberwein, *Zur Deutung mittelalterlicher Existenz*, pp. 27ff.; Köhler, *Ideal und Wirklichkeit*, pp. 66ff.; Haug, '*Aventiure* in Gottfrieds *Tristan*'; Green, 'The concept *aventiure*'; Zumthor, 'Le Roman courtois', 86.

turning point which is associated with the winning of a bride, with whom the hero returns to the court.

However, the action of the romance is not contained solely within this basic pattern, but is repeated in a typical variation. The first series of *avantures* ends as it were in a precarious state of equilibrium; there then follows a crisis which forces the hero to set out again.

After returning with Enide to his residence, Erec devotes himself entirely to love, neglecting his knightly duties, so that the court begins to complain. Enide comes to learn of this, and on one occasion, believing Erec to be asleep, she begins to lament it aloud. However, he has heard her, and presses her to let him know the cause of her grief; she tells him of the general dissatisfaction at court. Erec's reaction is as abrupt as it is strange. He sets out once more in search of an *avanture*. Enide is obliged to ride on ahead in silence, a decoy for robbers and adventurers. The couple's path takes them through a double series of *avantures*, each with three stages, which mirror each other in a striking fashion. The first triad runs as follows:

1. Erec has to defend himself against two attacks from robbers. In each case, Enide, who is riding ahead, notices the danger first and warns her husband, ignoring the command of silence laid upon her. Erec kills his attackers and reprimands his wife.

2. The couple meet a count, who falls in love with Enide. She manages to stall him, and finally warns her husband. They flee; the count, who follows them, is defeated by Erec after another warning from Enide.

3. The next attacker is an enormously strong though short knight called Guivret. Once more Enide warns her husband. In a hard fight, Guivret is overcome, but Erec is sorely wounded. However, they enter a bond of friendship, and Guivret invites the couple to stay at his castle. The next day they chance upon Arthur and his retinue in the forest. Erec's wounds are tended there, but he cannot be persuaded to stay long. The couple move on again, and after this interim stay with the court the second triad of *avantures* begins.

Once again:

1. violent opponents put in an appearance. This time they are giants, leading off a man they have captured. Erec frees him, out of sympathy with his desperate wife, and slays his ferocious opponents. Afterwards however he faints from exhaustion. Enide assumes her husband is dead and begins to lament aloud. At this, there appears

2. yet another seducer. He drags Enide, and Erec whom he takes

for dead, off to his castle, Limors. A wedding feast is served, but the grieving Enide rejects the suit of the count. Finally he strikes her, and she cries out. At this, Erec regains consciousness; he leaps up and deals the count a fatal blow. Then the couple flee in haste from the castle. In doing so, they no longer ride separately one after the other, but together on one horse – a symbol of reconciliation which shows that the crisis is past. There follows the

3. third *avanture*: Erec encounters Guivret again. In the darkness, they fail to recognize each other. They fight, and Erec, weak and exhausted, is defeated. At the last moment Enide intervenes, tells Guivret the name of his opponent, and thus manages to save her husband's life. Now Guivret too reveals his identity, and, reconciled, the friends spend the night together in the wood. Then Guivret takes the couple to his castle, where they spend a fortnight recovering.

The parallel construction of the two triads is immediately apparent. Position 1 is occupied by the fights with the villains – the robbers and giants. Position 2 contains the scenes where Enide is tempted: the count who attempts to overcome Erec and win Enide, and parallel to this the lord of Limors, who drags Enide off to his castle in the belief that Erec is dead. In third position are the fights with Guivret.

The significant and deliberate contrast between these two *avanture* triads is unmistakable. The fights with the robbers in the first triad are mere displays of strength by means of which Erec once more proves his fitness for knighthood. In the second triad, the fight with the giants is an act of mercy, arising from compassion for the wife of the man they are torturing. The seduction scenes likewise form a contrasting pair. In the first triad, Enide is wooed by a count, whom she is able to fend off by seeming to agree with his demands; the couple flee, and Erec defeats his pursuers. In the second triad, Erec is helpless, and the danger of the situation extreme, yet Enide remains faithful to Erec even though he appears to be dead. Finally, in the fight with Guivret the change of perspective is made especially plain. In the first encounter, the opponents are equally matched. In a long fight, Erec succeeds in overcoming Guivret, who asks for mercy. In the second encounter, Erec is sorely wounded, but he nevertheless defends himself courageously although in a hopeless situation. He owes his life to the intervention of Enide.

This whole double cycle of *avantures* through which Erec has to pass is obviously constructed down to the last detail around such parallels and contrasts. The *avantures* of the first cycle to some extent anticipate those of the second, and the structure of the latter itself consists of a double cycle of two contrasting triads. Clearly, what was easily achieved by good fortune in the first cycle has to be lost again in order that possession of it may be properly secured. The external challenge at the beginning of the first cycle corresponds to and contrasts with the inner crisis which triggers the action of the second cycle. The first triad of the latter also seems set to demonstrate the vigour and valour of the hero: Erec is trying to prove that he is still the victorious hero he was at the beginning. However, this new series of *avantures* leads to a low point or nadir which, as shown in the name of the castle Limors (= La Mort), is intended as a symbolic passage through death. At this turning point, Erec also experiences the saving love of Enide, i.e. he learns that what is truly important cannot be won by fighting: rather, one must accept it as a gift through love.

At this stage it would be possible for Erec and Enide to return to the court. However, Chrétien inserts one final adventure, which stands alone from a structural point of view. This is the controversial episode of the 'Joie de la Cort' (5416ff., ed. M. Roques).

On the journey home, Erec stops in Brandigan where he has heard of an enchanted orchard. A knight, Mabonagrain, is imprisoned in this orchard with his lady. He is praised as a model of knightly valour, she is a lady of great beauty, and the garden is of fabled splendour. However, the couple are compelled by the power of love to remain in the seclusion of the enchanted garden. Only when Mabonagrain has been defeated by another knight can they be set free. Many have taken up the challenge; eighty heads are impaled on stakes in the magic garden, while the eighty widows of those defeated live out their days in mourning in the castle of Brandigan; the court is bereft of joy. Erec survives this last and most perilous exploit: he defeats Mabonagrain and restores the 'Joie de la Cort'.

How then is this episode, lying as it does outside the main scheme of events, to be interpreted? One possible reading is that the couple imprisoned in the garden once again represent the situation of Erec and Enide at the end of the first cycle. By setting free Mabonagrain and his *amie*, Erec is symbolically freeing himself. Thus at the end of the work the theme of the whole is presented once more in a strikingly visual form: the 'Joie de la Cort' episode demonstrates graphically how absolute love is exclusive of society and leads to self-absorbed isolation. At the same time, however, the analogy with

Erec's situation is not complete, since this love-spell leads not to passivity but to murderous action. This may however also be seen as reflecting Erec's situation when he sets out for the second time. Absolute love thus ultimately leads to extremes of behaviour which, whether expressed in terms of action or inaction, are equally detrimental to society. Instead of these extremes, the encounter with the beloved must be integrated into society: the knight returns to the court and to the Arthurian festivities. In order to reach this goal, however, he is first obliged, for the sake of the courtly ideal, to encounter its antithesis, must indeed subject himself to it in order to rediscover, at its furthest extreme, in defeat and on the brink of death, the relationship with his beloved, and be able to celebrate this symbolically in the festival on his return to court.

It is thus possible to see the 'Joie de la Cort' episode as a quasi-allegorical representation of the theme of *Erec*. This is supported by the special position of this last stage within the structure of the work. At the same time, of course, it still forms a part of the linear action of the main narrative. However, even if there is no departure from the actual narrative plane, a symbolic interpretation of the action suggests itself here with more force than usual, disrupting to some extent the linear continuity of the narrative.[5]

This insight into the structure of *Erec et Enide* and its inherent meaning has come to be generally accepted through the work of Wilhelm Kellermann, Reto R. Bezzola and Hugo Kuhn.[6] An important study by Hans Fromm has shown this remarkable structure to be a genuine achievement of Chrétien's, rather than something derived from a number of earlier structural experiments which might be thought to have influenced Chrétien's conception of the double cycle.[7] Without wishing to undermine this position in any way, it still seems permissible to enquire as to the literary origins and antecedents of this two-phase narrative model. This might shed more light on the special meaning inherent in the hero's twofold passage through the world of *avanture*. First of all, however, it should be noted that

---

5   Hugo Kuhn, '*Erec*', in: Hugo Kuhn, *Dichtung und Welt im Mittelalter*, pp. 144–5; Wünsch, 'Allegorie und Sinnstruktur'; a different view is found in Cormeau, '*Joie de la curt*'. A review of the literature, which however omits Germanist interpretations, is given by Sturm-Maddox, '*Hortus non conclusus*'.

6   Kellermann, *Aufbaustil und Weltbild Chrestiens*, p. 6 and passim.; Bezzola, *Le sens de l'aventure*, pp. 82ff.; Hugo Kuhn, '*Erec*'; Köhler, *Ideal und Wirklichkeit*, pp. 236ff.; Ruh, *Höfische Epik*, vol. I, pp. 115ff.

7   Fromm, 'Gottfried von Straßburg und Abaelard'.

repetition of the action is a universal feature of narrative literature – it has already been encountered in the context of *Brautwerbungsepen*, or 'bridal quests'. In the case of Chrétien de Troyes, however, it seems likely that in this respect his structural model is based on dual narrative forms, such as the Breton lays, familiar at the courts of Northern France. These do indeed display the characteristic sequence of motifs: the hero's encounter with the beloved, and her subsequent loss and recovery.[8] The crucial step then lay in transforming this simple form into the graduated double cycle, with its different levels and complex mirroring of related episodes.

Rainer Warning has put forward the theory that the relationship between the two cycles is based on a typological pattern.[9] This would presuppose that in the Middle Ages such a thought pattern existed independently of specifically exegetical and typological interpretations; indeed, the question of the partial – or indeed complete – emancipation of typological interpretation from its original biblical context is highly controversial. The further one moves away from typology in the strict sense, the more one enters the general sphere of varying repetitions of action and contrasting figures, and the outcome of such a discussion depends on whether, and to what extent, this 'typological' scheme can be distinguished from other types of repeated action or mere contrastive effects. This point will be taken up again later.[10]

The question of Chrétien's possible models for the structure of his romances is, however, less important than the establishment of the interdependence between his narrative structure and the subject matter it conveys. Thus, the structural elements established on the basis of the first cycle have to be reviewed and reformulated in the light of the double cycle of two series of *avantures*, and then expanded in accordance with their thematic implications. This can be done as follows:

1. The starting and finishing point of the action is King Arthur's Round Table. Its ideals are manifested in *vröude* ('joy'), the festivities. Arthurian romances typically begin and conclude with just such a celebration.

2. The action consists in the *avantures* encountered by a knight of the Round Table after he sets out from court. This takes him through

[8] Ruh, *Höfische Epik*, vol. I, pp. 102ff., 120–1; Haug, 'Symbolstruktur', pp. 671ff.: also in Haug, *Strukturen*, pp. 485ff.; J. Schulze, '*Guigemar*'.
[9] Warning, 'Heterogenität', 561ff.   [10] See below, chapter 11, pp. 244–5.

an 'anti-world', i.e. a world of anti-Arthurian figures and behaviour. Here the hero encounters human and supernatural enemies – giants, dwarves, villains, monsters – which he overcomes in order to return to the court and take part in – or reinstate – the joy of the festivities.

3. The journey along a path beset with *avantures* is repeated, but the motivation of the two cycles differs sharply. The first cycle is initiated by a challenge to the ideals of the Round Table from outside, jeopardizing the joy of the courtly festivities. The Arthurian knight undertakes to answer the challenge on behalf of the court. However, he returns not without personal gain, having obtained a wife in the process. The second cycle is occasioned by an inner crisis, in which the hero's relationship to both his partner and to society is rendered problematical. This second journey again follows the same path through the non-Arthurian anti-world, but this time is governed by new conditions.

4. Within this framework, a dual theme is developed: first, chivalric action, that is to say the possibility of conquering the world by means of deeds. In this context the Arthurian knight both exercises violence and experiences it at first hand, coming face to face with death. The second theme is love: the hero experiences Eros as desire and as an absolute claim to, or on the part of, the other person.

The Arthurian model thus serves as a vehicle for rehearsing the relationship of action and love, violence and desire, death and Eros. The individual romances are variations on this scheme, with differing emphasis placed on individual elements; however, the point of reference remains the courtly festival, with its balance of these forces, or in more concrete terms, the channelling of violent action within the ritualized scope of the tournament, and of desire in the social integration of love. There is an ideal, even Utopian element to this balance.

The non-Arthurian anti-world which the knights enter when they set out from the court is characterized by forces intrinsically opposed to such a balance, namely love in its most absolute form, and the irreversible finality of death. The path of action therefore symbolically leads the hero through death: Erec lies unconscious in Castle Limors while the lord of the castle seeks to overpower his wife Enide. In this anti-world, Eros takes the form of desire, possession and infatuation. However, in his symbolic passage through death, the hero receives love as a gift; it is his wife who saves him from death. Having passed through this extremity, the couple are able to return to the court. The Utopian ideal of the Arthurian festivities is thus sustained by and can only be experienced through the anti-world which opposes it, i.e. the former is only conceivable in the context of the latter, and can only be realized by traversing the utmost limits of this realm and so experiencing the full force of those powers which challenge and negate the Arthurian ideal. While this process forms the basis of the narrative, if the latter is to convey its message effectively, the audience must also be in a position to grasp the underlying structural principle.

However, before turning to the problem of reception, we should first investigate how far Chrétien de Troyes was himself aware of the limitations and possibilities of his structural concept and to what extent he was able to formulate this in theoretical terms.

III

I intend to begin by analysing Chrétien's first attempt at formulating a narrative theory, the prologue to *Erec et Enide*. In accordance with the tradition of the rhetorical prologue, Chrétien opens the 'dialogue' with his audience with a *sententia*:[11]

> Li vilains dit an son respit
> que tel chose a l'an an despit
> qui molt valt mialz que l'an ne cuide; (*Erec et Enide*, 1–3)
>
> [The common man has a proverb which says that some things are despised that are worth much more than one thinks.]

So the opening *sententia* here takes the form of a well-known proverb. Its function is clear: Chrétien apparently intends to present his audience with something which has long been reviled. In rhetorical terms, the subject of his discourse is not essentially appealing in itself, so prejudices against it must be forestalled or overcome. Chrétien attempts to win over his audience by means of a piece of proverbial wisdom about the hidden worth of something which at first sight appears contemptible.[12] From this the logical conclusion is drawn:

---

[11] Cf. Arbusow, *Colores rhetorici*, pp. 97, 99; Schirmer, *Motivuntersuchungen*, p. 66; Hunt, 'Tradition and originality', 320. For the exordial *sententia* or *proverbium* in French, see Jones, *Prologue and Epilogue*, pp. 31, 35; Niemeyer, *Exordia*, pp. 100ff. See also chapter 1 above, p. 12.

[12] On this motif, see Hilty, 'Zum *Erec*-Prolog', p. 247.

> por ce fet bien qui son estuide
> atorne a bien quel que il l'ait;
> car qui son estuide antrelait,
> tost i puet tel chose teisir
> qui molt vandroit puis a pleisir. (*Erec et Enide*, 4–8)

[Consequently that man does well who directs whatever knowledge he has to a good end; for he who neglects such efforts may thereby easily pass over something which might later give a lot of pleasure.]

Instead of 'a bien', two manuscripts have the wording 'a san', which was adopted by Wendelin Foerster.[13] If – as Gerolt Hilty suggests – one may understand *a san* in a modal sense,[14] there is in fact not too much difference in meaning. Instead of 'directs whatever knowledge he has (*estuide*) to a good end', it would read 'directs whatever knowledge he has in a meaningful way'. The term *estuide* ('knowledge', 'efforts') in any case implies – again following Hilty[15] – a positive attempt at understanding, and it is this which forms the link with the opening *sententia*, since in order that the hidden worth of a hitherto under-rated matter can be recognized, a degree of intellectual effort is required which cannot necessarily be taken for granted. In what follows, this general argument is applied to the subject matter itself:

> Por ce dist Crestïens de Troies
> que reisons est que totevoies
> doit chascuns panser et antandre
> a bien dire et a bien aprandre;
> et tret d'un conte d'avanture
> une molt bele conjointure
> par qu'an puet prover et savoir
> que cil ne fet mie savoir
> qui s'escïence n'abandone
> tant con Dex la grasce l'an done: (*Erec et Enide*, 9–18)

[So Chrétien de Troyes declares that it is right that everyone should always remember to strive to speak well and teach well; and from an adventure story he derives a most fine *conjointure*, whence it can be demonstrated and recognized that he does not act at all wisely who relinquishes what he knows, as long as God in His grace supports him.]

Once the true worth of something has been recognized, the main

---

[13] 3rd edn, 1934, p. 194, note to line 5.   [14] Hilty, 'Zum *Erec*-Prolog', p. 247, note 11.
[15] Ibid.

concern is then to express and transmit this, too, *a bien* – which could be rendered more emphatically as 'in its whole meaning'. What that implies is set out in the controversial lines 13 and 14. First of all, the underrated subject matter is named – the *conte d'avanture*. Anyone who brings all their powers of reasoning and understanding to bear will recognize its real worth, however, and will then succeed in communicating this worth by 'deriving' a particularly fine *conjointure* from the story of *avanture*. However one may decide to translate the term *conjointure*,[16] it refers to the way in which the meaning is realized in literary form. Hilty has rightly stressed that *conjointure* cannot be an established poetic *terminus technicus*.[17] Even if what the learned poet had in mind was the Latin *junctura*,[18] the Old French expression would still have seemed almost as strange to Chrétien's audience as it does today. They may well have seen it in relation to *conjoindre* and have understood something like 'joining together'. However, in view of the preceding argument of the prologue, what is meant in concrete terms must be the organization of the individual elements of the narrative into a meaningful whole, in short the structure by means of which the meaning is transmitted. It is *molt bele* in that it structures the subject matter so as to reveal the meaning; the beauty of the form is an expression of the meaningfulness of the content.[19] This is followed by another familiar prologue topos, the poet's duty to pass on his knowledge (15f.),[20] used here to justify the communication of the meaning thus revealed.

The really provocative aspect of this whole argument lies in the fact that it represents an apology for the hitherto underrated *conte d'avanture*. The aims of such a reassessment, and the extent to which it is necessary, becomes clear in the following lines:

[16] For secondary literature on this subject, see Hilty, 'Zum *Erec*-Prolog', p. 249, note 14; cf. Haug, '*Der aventiure meine*', p. 102: also in Haug, *Strukturen*, p. 455.

[17] Hilty, 'Zum *Erec*-Prolog', p. 249.

[18] Both Nitze: 'Arthurian problems', 76–7, and '*Conjointure in Erec*', and Kelly: 'Source and meaning', 181–2, and 'Topical invention', p. 243, connect this with Horace; Robertson, 'Some medieval literary terminology', 671, believes the term is found in Alan of Lille; cf. Hilty, 'Zum *Erec*-Prolog', pp. 249–50, note 15; Ollier, 'The author in the text', p. 30; Hunt, 'Tradition and originality', 321–2; on the context of the argument in the Alan of Lille passage, see Knapp, 'Historische Wahrheit', 619–20.

[19] Köhler, 'Selbstauffassung', pp. 26ff.; Haug, '*Der aventiure meine*', pp. 100ff.

[20] Brinkmann, *Wesen und Form*, p. 19; Curtius, *Europäische Literatur*, pp. 97–8; Arbusow, *Colores rhetorici*, pp. 99, 102; Lausberg, *Handbuch*, col. 275α; Beumann, 'Schriftsteller', 505; Hunt, 'Tradition and originality', 321; Hilty, 'Zum *Erec*-Prolog', p. 246, note 4; Knapp, 'Historische Wahrheit', 585.

d'Erec, le fil Lac, est li contes,
que devant rois et devant contes
depecier et corronpre suelent
cil qui de conter vivre vuelent.
Des or comancerai l'estoire
qui toz jorz mes iert an mimoire
tant con durra crestïantez;
de ce s'est Crestïens vantez. (*Erec et Enide*, 19–26)

[This tale is about Erec, the son of Lac, a story which those who try to earn their living by storytelling are accustomed to spoil and corrupt when they tell it in the presence of kings and counts. Now I will begin the story which will long be held in memory, for as long as Christianity endures. That is Chrétien's boast.]

This sets out the actual subject matter: the story of Erec, the son of King Lac. It is, apparently, already familiar, although not in the correct form but only in distorted and corrupt versions. There is, however, more than merely the topos of denigration of rivals in play here;[21] it is rather a critique of a whole literary form, namely the short narrative form of oral tradition, which could never have achieved the level of form and meaning of Chrétien's version, since such a sophisticated rendering was only possible in written literature. According to Chrétien, it is the wandering minstrels who have sold short the subjects of the *matière de Bretagne* which he now wishes to take up. The self-confidence of the scholar-poet, with his awareness of the potential of the written word, is demonstrated by the conclusion of his prologue, where Chrétien prophesies that his poem will be remembered until the end of time! This appears all the more bold in that he has just claimed that the material he was presenting would be familiar to many.[22] It is, therefore, crucial that the subject matter be completely transformed by the *conjointure*; only thus can the author hope to offer something outstanding and new to his audience. In terms of the development of poetic theory, then, the transition from an oral to a written tradition opens up important new dimensions for literature; what is more, Chrétien himself must have been highly conscious of the significant threshold in literary history that he was crossing in setting down the Arthurian material in written form.

Significant as this step was, it was obviously difficult to express the

21 On this topos, see Hunt, 'Rhetorical background', p. 3.
22 This is true even if the idea is a variation on a commonplace. Cf. Nitze, 'Arthurian problems', 77.

new position in theoretical terms. When Chrétien suggests that a hitherto hidden meaning must be discovered in the orally transmitted material, he is making use of a metaphor based on the notion of *integumentum*, the poetic and hermeneutic theory that was especially prevalent in the school of Chartres and which starts from the premise that moral or philosophical truths are 'clothed' or veiled in literary forms and can be readily communicated by this means.[23] Yet if Chrétien is identified with the Chartres school too readily, this would tend to lead to an interpretation of *Erec* – and thus of subsequent romance literature in this tradition – in terms of a second level of meaning as suggested by the *integumentum* theory, in other words, reading romance essentially as allegory: the results of such an interpretation cannot, however, be other than misleading.[24] Rather, Chrétien makes use of the exegetical metaphor in order to claim for his work a truth which is not identical with the literal meaning, while at the same time making it clear that it is not in any sense the truth of a second, allegorical plane. In this sense, *conjointure* stands on the one hand in opposition to *conte*, inasmuch as the former has to be discovered in the latter; on the other hand, since the *conte* presents its material in a fragmented and debased manner, *conjointure*, by contrast, represents the meaningful organization of the whole: it is this structured whole which contains and communicates the truth. The meaning is thus not just the hidden significance waiting to be revealed; it is, rather, realized in the act of poetic formulation itself. Unlike the exemplum, or an allegorical construct, it is not hidden beneath a *narratio fabulosa*, but is inherent in the fictional structure itself, and is thus not to be taken as either *sensus moralis* or *sensus allegoricus*. The exegetical idea of a revelation of meaning by interpretation is thus alluded to but then placed in a completely different perspective. This shift of perspective heralds the new literary form of the fictional romance, with its own way of representing and communicating meaning: *conjointure* thus ultimately refers to the Arthurian model and implies an awareness that the meaning lies in the structure itself.

What is lacking, however, is an adequate theoretical discussion or statement corresponding to this new stage of development in narrative literature. To be able to deal explicitly with the fictional character of the new romance genre and the conditions of its production and

---

[23] On this point, see below, chapter 12, pp. 230–2.
[24] Bloomfield, 'Symbolism in medieval literature'; Frappier, 'Le *Conte du Graal*'; Beichner, 'Allegorical interpretation'; Wolf, 'Erzählkunst'; Schnell, 'Grenzen', 253.

reception, a whole new poetological terminology was needed. This theoretical equipment was not available, and instead it was necessary to fall back on the standard repertoire of terms and concepts supplied by tradition. Nor was it possible to step outside the framework of the argument in which questions of poetics were traditionally discussed, namely prologue rhetoric.[25]

This led in practice to the use of traditional theoretical terms and concepts while at the same time showing up their inadequacy. By demonstrating that they were no longer appropriate, the new position was indirectly referred to, but it is not always possible to determine whether this practice is merely an expression of the inadequacy of the terminology available, or whether it is not, rather, a deliberate strategy to ensure that the audience is fully aware of this unsatisfactory state of affairs.

IV

The discovery of the new fictional approach made possible by the *matière de Bretagne* marks a decisive new stage in literary history. Although fiction as a distinct literary category was already recognized and described in Ancient Greece, the classical notion of fiction was seen from a completely different perspective and accordingly received quite different theoretical treatment.

The Greek discovery of fiction resulted from the confrontation between science and poetry. Since science had claimed truth for itself, poetry was automatically defined as untrue. Plato's harsh verdict on poetry, based on this opposition, caused Aristotle to reflect on the specific status of poetry and accord it a truth of its own – the truth of the probable: in his opinion it is superior to historical and factual truth, being 'more philosophical'.[26]

The medieval notion of fiction, as represented in Arthurian romance, is however precisely not based on the idea of the probable; on the contrary, this new category of fiction finds its true identity in free interplay with the *im*probable. Its truth is not that something could really be as the poet invents it; rather, experience of truth is here transposed onto a fictional level and presented as a kind of

---

25 What Gumbrecht, 'Wie fiktional war der höfische Roman?', sees as a loosening of the commitment to a religious and moral claim to represent the truth may thus be seen as an inadequate attempt on the part of theory to justify the actual fictional practice.

26 Fuhrmann, *Einführung in die antike Dichtungstheorie*, pp. 4ff.; Kannicht, 'Der alte Streit'; Rösler, 'Die Entdeckung der Fiktionalität in der Antike', esp. 309–10.

experiment, so that the very improbability of the plot leads the listener to seek the meaning all the more eagerly.[27] Taken to its logical conclusion, the idea that literature is the art of the probable limits poetry to the presentation of exempla. That Aristotle's theory thus lags behind the powers and the function he imputes to poetry is demonstrated by his concept of catharsis, which, as a socio-psychological category, goes beyond what is merely didactic.

The rediscovery and reformulation of Aristotle's *Poetics* in the Renaissance and Enlightenment represents, in its linking of fiction and probability, a regression by comparison with the medieval position. Not until the modern period does literary theory manage to liberate itself from this classical concept by defining the fictional in the light of communication theory.[28] Since, in this context, the probable is only of relevance as a stylistic category, the freedom which had already been a salient feature of the medieval Arthurian romance – despite the fact that, as has been shown, there was at the time no clearly defined concept of fiction – is finally restored.

The question remains, however, as to how far the medieval concept of fiction may be equated with the modern one.[29] A grasp of the Arthurian structural model is an essential prerequisite for an understanding of the romance; nevertheless, the traditional idea of an actual historical Arthurian world co-existed alongside its fictional representations, though the relationship between them was never precisely defined. For this reason, it was always possible to appeal to historical authenticity as a guarantee of truth. While there thus seems little reason to doubt that Chrétien discovered fiction, it should nevertheless be emphasized that the literary context and associations of fiction in the Middle Ages are by no means identical with modern conceptions of the fictional, since in the Middle Ages there is no concept of an autonomous aesthetic sphere comparable to that found in later centuries.

[27] Anderegg, *Fiktion und Kommunikation*, p. 106. One might suggest that it is particularly this possibility of operating with improbable elements which serves to characterize fiction here.
[28] Anderegg, *Fiktion und Kommunikation* and 'Das Fiktionale und das Ästhetische'; Assmann, *Die Legitimität der Fiktion*, pp. 9ff., with further literature.
[29] This is in response to reservations expressed – despite my caveats in note 2 on p. 92 – in the reviews by Huber, 'Literaturtheorie', and Heinzle, 'Entdeckung der Fiktionalität'.

6

Divine inspiration and the changing role of the poet in Chrétien's *Lancelot* and *Cligés*

I

Chrétien de Troyes' reflections on poetics in the prologue to *Erec et Enide* are to some extent continued in the prologues to the *Chevalier de la Charrette* (*Lancelot*) and *Cligés*.

Like the prologue to *Erec*, the *Lancelot* prologue culminates in a pair of contrasting terms: *matiere* and *san*. It is tempting to see this as a variant of the controversial word pair *conte* and *conjointure* in *Erec*, thus, if not directly identifying the two pairs, at least using the concepts of the *Lancelot* prologue as an aid to interpreting the problematic terms of the *Erec* prologue, since the meaning of *matiere* and *san* appears straightforward. Can *conte* and *conjointure* then be reduced to nothing more than the opposition of content and meaning? It should first be observed, however, that the shift from *conte* and *conjointure* to *matiere* and *san* represents a move from the specific to the general. This shift means that there is now no discussion of the relationship between the oral tradition and the complex new structures: a specific discussion of genre is omitted in *Lancelot*, possibly because *Erec* had already established the new type within the literary tradition, so that Chrétien was now able to integrate these specific aspects into general theoretical considerations. This provides another clear illustration of the principle that the subject matter has to be interpreted in order to establish the meaning. The contrasting of *matiere* and *san* instead of *conte* and *conjointure* means that the latter pair has become so abstract as to serve no purpose other than to indicate the broad theoretical tradition in which these terms belong.

However, these preliminary considerations do not dispense with the need to investigate how far the pair of concepts in question is integrated into the argument of the prologue, and how this affects its relationship to the theoretical statements in the introduction to *Erec*. Here the characteristic theoretical components of the relationship between poet and audience are encountered once more, albeit in a striking new configuration.

Chrétien begins by naming his patron, Marie de Champagne:

> Puis que ma dame de Chanpaigne
> vialt que romans a feire anpraigne,
> je l'anprendrai molt volentiers
> come cil qui est suens antiers
> de quan qu'il puet el monde feire
> sanz rien de losange avant treire; (*Lancelot*, 1–6)

> [Since my lady (= Marie) of Champagne wishes that I should undertake to write a romance, I shall do so most willingly, as one who is entirely devoted to her in whatever he does in this world, without wishing to flatter in any way.]

It is striking that the opening maxim used in *Erec* to establish a relationship with the audience is missing here. Its place is taken by the reference to Marie de Champagne's wish that he should compose a romance for her. However, in some sense the patron also assumes the role of audience, so that the homage is at one and the same time addressed to both patron and recipient of the work. Chrétien's charmingly hyperbolic flattery which follows may also be viewed from this dual perspective. Chrétien states – after claiming in line 6 that he has no intention of flattering his patron – that it could be claimed she far excels any other lady living today, just as the warm wind which blows in April or May is superior to any other wind – but he, of course, is not one of those who would wish to flatter his mistress unduly. He could even say that Marie surpasses all queens, but he would say nothing of the kind, even though it were true. He then introduces the linked concepts of *matiere* and *san*:

> Mes tant dirai ge que mialz oevre
> ses comandemanz an ceste oevre
> que sans ne painne que g'i mete.
> Del Chevalier de la charrete
> comance Crestïens son livre;
> matiere et san li done et livre
> la contesse, et il s'antremet
> de panser, que gueres n'i met
> fors sa painne et s'antancïon. (*Lancelot*, 21–9)

[But I will go so far as to say that her commands have done more for this work than either the thought or the trouble that I have put into it. Chrétien commences his book about the knight of the cart; the subject matter and the sense have been provided and given to him by the Countess, and he undertakes to see to it that nothing is supplied other than his trouble and his effort.]

Chrétien's statement that his patron provided not only the subject matter, but also the *san*, the meaning, is unusual. Since Gaston Paris' interpretation this has always been read as an attempt on Chrétien's part to disclaim responsibility for the idea of his romance, since its theme is Lancelot's adulterous love for the queen; it was claimed that the idea of love propounded here was one diametrically opposed to that of *Erec*, and one against which Chrétien took up a definite stance in *Cligés*, his *Tristan* parody.[1]

This hypothesis, that Chrétien's praise of Marie de Champagne expresses his dissatisfaction with the subject matter imposed on him, remained virtually unchallenged until Jean Rychner put forward a counter-argument in 1967. Rychner wished to include lines 21–9 in the homage to Marie. Chrétien's attribution of not only the subject matter, but also the *san*, to her would in his view fit the pattern of excessive flattery which characterizes the prologue thus far; any conclusions as to Chrétien's own attitude to his subject matter drawn from the final part of the prologue would thus be invalidated.[2]

Whether or not one is willing to accept all the details of Rychner's argument, it at least had the merit of highlighting the need to question, or even revise, the prevailing theory of Chrétien's dislike of a theme which was apparently thrust upon him.

However, with regard to the place of the prologue in the context of tradition – even in the light of Rychner's interpretation of the whole prologue in terms of homage – it is necessary to look carefully at the arguments used. First, it should be borne in mind that Marie de Champagne fulfils a function which is normally made manifest in three distinct roles. Not only is Marie the patron and supplier of the subject matter, and then also, as has been noted above, the audience; she is also looked to as the source of inspiration. In *Erec*, Chrétien claimed authority for his poem by referring to the fact that God had

---

[1] Paris, 'Etudes II', 516ff.; cf. Haug, *'Das Land, von welchem niemand wiederkehrt'*, pp. 19–20.
[2] Rychner, 'Le Prologue du *Chevalier de la charrette*', and 'Le Prologue du *Chevalier de la charrette* et l'interprétation du roman'. On the debate arising from Rychner's theories, see Haug, *'Das Land, von welchem niemand wiederkehrt'*, pp. 20ff.

bestowed on him the requisite knowledge and skill, deriving from this an obligation not to let these gifts lie fallow. Here, however, it is his patron who urges the poet to carry out the work, even giving him the *san*, so that, in the terms of the tradition of the inspiration topos, it is she who enables him to discover the meaning in the subject matter.[3]

There can be no doubt that the audience will, on the one hand, have seen the transferral of divine inspiration to the patron as a bold variation on the traditional form of homage. On the other hand, however, such a transferral could not be wholly explained in terms of flattery. It is, rather, indicative of a change in the prevailing theoretical conditions governing literature. The fact that it was possible to dissociate the idea of inspiration from God shows that the process of establishing poetic meaning had moved beyond the traditional scheme: the concept of *conjointure*, seen as a structure through which meaning is conveyed, is not easily connected with the idea of divine inspiration. The *science* which Chrétien received from God thus occupies an indeterminate position between divine revelation of meaning and technical skill.

Whatever one's view of Rychner's theory, a change in the contemporary perception of poetic inspiration is evinced by the fact that Chrétien is able to attribute the *san*, too, to his patron. A hint as to the direction of this change may possibly be contained in line 4, where Chrétien describes his relationship to Marie in the same words with which the relationship between Lancelot and the queen are later characterized (5656). Chrétien styles his poetry a service to his mistress, and the playful extravagance of his praise deliberately approximates the excesses of Lancelot's services in courtly love.[4] The hyperbolic homage thus anticipates the theme of the romance. In this way, poetry may function as a gift both from and to the revered lady, and in this game of give and take one may indeed see the commissioner and dedicatee of the work as its true inspiration. In other words, Chrétien's homage, in alluding to the subject of the romance, ultimately makes the experience of love the source of poetry:

---

[3] Although it strikes an unusual and surprising note in twelfth-century French literature, there are classical antecedents for the transferral of the source of inspiration to the commissioner of the work or the addressee: cf. Janson, *Latin Prose Prefaces*, pp. 121–2; Thraede, *Studien zur Sprache und Stil des Prudentius*, p. 39.

[4] Cf. Haug, '*Das Land, von welchem niemand wiederkehrt*', p. 24. We are dealing with a stock formula which also occurs in *Cligés*, where it is commented on as such: lines 4367, 4388ff. (ed. A. Micha, 1957).

acknowledging the revered lady as the source of inspiration would thus signify nothing other than inspiration by love itself.

The introduction to *Lancelot* thus provides a particularly clear example of the fact that a prologue which appears completely separate from the text and seems only to be concerned with such preliminary matters as befits a prologue, may, on a deeper level, be connected to and interact with the subject of the work. This becomes increasingly applicable the more a prologue, in discussing the conditions of its production and reception, makes reference to the literary-historical circumstances in which a work has arisen, since it is in this context that the choice of *matiere*, and the *san* according to which it is presented, may be understood. If the level of theoretical reflection is sufficiently high, it goes beyond the conventional rhetorical use of prologue topoi, so that the subject brings its own specific problems of communication to bear.

II

With his treatment of adulterous love in *Lancelot*, Chrétien would seem to be turning in the direction of the subject of the *Tristan* legend. This would present an extreme contrast to the concept of love he put forward in *Erec*. If, then, the *Chevalier de la Charrette* is not to be regarded as a commissioned work for which the poet disclaims responsibility, it becomes necessary to establish what position the 'Knight of the Cart' occupies in relation to Chrétien's other Arthurian romances.

As has already been stated, Chrétien varied the model he created in *Erec* on more than one occasion, notably in *Yvain* and in *Perceval*; this can be shown to be true of *Lancelot* also. Such experimentation with the Arthurian scheme suggests that it may well have contained problematic elements which called for new, experimental narrative configurations in which they could be tested. These elements may be sought where the Arthurian scheme makes its most exaggerated claims, namely in the attempt to realize a Utopia which is achieved by quite remarkable means. The ultimate goal of the narrative progression is arrived at by taking a path which leads off in an opposite direction, where counter-positions opposed to the ideal have to be overcome, so that the goal is in the end only realized through the recognition of these extreme positions as 'boundary experiences' at the limits of human capabilities. It is, then, an exceedingly bold

111

attempt, in which the absolute nature of love and the irreversible fact of death are encompassed within a unified fictional process.

This is especially true of *Lancelot*, where Chrétien stretches his model to the utmost. In this work, he attempts to adapt the subject of adulterous love to fit his scheme, limiting its destructive potential by integrating it into the fictional Arthurian model.[5]

In accordance with this model, *Lancelot* too begins at the Arthurian court with a challenge. A stranger has succeeded in abducting Queen Guenievre. Lancelot, who suddenly appears from nowhere at the crucial moment, sets off to win her back – however he is motivated less by the desire to avenge the insult than by his all-consuming passion for the queen. As if in a trance, he follows the quest through perils and combat, finally arriving in a country which bears all the characteristics of the realm of the dead. Here he overcomes Guenievre's captor, which, according to the model, should mean that the queen is rescued and the quest safely fulfilled. However, this victory is ambiguous, since when Lancelot appears triumphantly before Guenievre, she brusquely rejects him. In despair, he tries to take his own life; but at the last minute the complications are resolved, and Lancelot learns why the queen had behaved so harshly. During the quest, after losing his horse he had come across a dwarf with a cart. The dwarf had invited him to get in, this being the only means of proceeding in the search for the queen. Lancelot had hesitated for one brief moment, since the cart was of the kind used to convey criminals to the gallows. Then he had accepted the invitation. He was now to be the butt of everyone's mockery and was henceforth called the Knight of the Cart. Guenievre however, having heard about the incident, rejected her deliverer on account of his hesitation before mounting the cart of shame.

After this crisis, which here too is placed in the appropriate position after the victory, albeit in an unusual form, Lancelot secretly spends a night with the queen. Then he is ambushed and taken prisoner while Guenievre is allowed to return to Arthur's court. Only after he has defeated the queen's captor a second time in a tournament, to which he makes his way incognito from prison, does Lancelot become free again. Now the plot can be brought to its conclusion, but, because of the particular configuration of the characters, there can be no ultimate reunion of the protagonist with his beloved. The conclusion of the

---

[5] What follows is discussed in more detail in Haug, *'Das Land, von welchem niemand wiederkehrt'*, pp. 26ff.

romance – which was not composed by Chrétien – remains somewhat unsatisfactory.

Despite its major deviations from the basic pattern of *Erec* and *Yvain*, the underlying structural model is still clearly discernible in *Lancelot*: the Arthurian court at the start and end of the action, the double cycle, the central crisis with the passage through death and then salvation through love. However, Lancelot's love is of such an absolute nature as to ride roughshod over all social considerations, and would thus theoretically break the mould. Chrétien manages to save his model by limiting the union of the lovers to a single night, and this in a land 'whence', it is said, 'none may return' – a symbolic Otherworld which clearly has no connection with any social reality. Although love is here placed in direct and irreconcilable opposition to society, this does not lead to a conflict, since Lancelot's adultery takes place outside the Arthurian world and thus preserves the absolute nature of love as well as its isolation from the social context. In other words, if love is not to destroy the *avanture* model, the absolute claims of Eros can only be satisfied in secret, in an unreal or supernatural world.

In *Lancelot*, then, Chrétien ventured to treat the *Tristan* theme of absolute love within the Arthurian framework. In so doing, he took seriously the idea in *Tristan* that Eros is an anti-social and destructive force, and at the same time neutralized it by integrating it into his scheme. The love-act in the symbolic realm of the dead becomes a moment in which the absolute may realize its claims, but as such it is also necessarily excluded from social reality. Although Lancelot is able to draw strength from love in order to win Arthurian *avantures* in the traditional manner, the actions which result from this strength repeatedly show signs of the supernatural realm from which it is drawn. The hero becomes a kind of ecstatic introvert who lives half his life in another world. From the point of view of 'normality', the here-and-now of earthly existence, he represents a bizarre and incomprehensible phenomenon.

III

In *Cligés*, Chrétien also takes issue with the *Tristan* material, although here in the form of a parody.[6] Here too, the prologue presents a

---

[6]   Bertau, 'Versuch über den späten Chrestien', pp. 24ff., and *Deutsche Literatur*, pp. 498ff.

theoretical approach which is, albeit indirectly, specifically geared to the subject of the work.

Chrétien opens the *Cligés* prologue with a list of his own works, beginning with *Erec*. There follow translations of Ovid, and he also makes mention of his tale of King Marc and Ysalt, which has not survived, so that there is no way of ascertaining whether it was a Tristan romance or an episodic poem. Since only the king and Ysalt feature in the title, and no mention is made of Tristan himself, the latter would seem more likely. Then Chrétien announces his new work,[7] the story of a young man from Greece who was related to King Arthur (the mother of the eponymous hero Cligés is the sister of Gauvain, and thus the king's niece); first of all, however, he wishes to tell of the hero's father, who came from Greece to England in order to win fame and fortune at Arthur's court.

This is a surprising beginning. In order to establish contact with the audience, it seems that it suffices for the author to remind them of his own work: Chrétien's name will guarantee the interest of the audience, and so the poet is able to proceed directly to his theme, without any long preparation. After introducing his hero, he begins with a reference to his source. He claims to have found the story of Cligés in an old book in the library of Saint-Pierre in Beauvais, adding that this should make the tale all the more credible, and remarking in passing that books enable us to bring the deeds of the ancients to life. In contrast to *Erec*, then, there is a specific reference to a written source, and a consequent emphasis on the authenticity of the tale.

This is all the more striking in that, in *Erec*, Chrétien had himself created a literary type in which the truth was not so much guaranteed by the authenticity of the material as revealed in the structure and its meaning. Is *Cligés* an example of a new genre? Although the hero of the new romance lives in Greece, he is of Arthurian descent. In other words, a story with pretensions to historical credibility is nevertheless located in the fictional Arthurian world. This is disconcerting, and one is tempted to ask whether this is really an introduction to the subject – as it would appear – or whether the question of the hero's origins is not a pretext for opening a discussion of the genre. For the moment the question must remain open; but one may anticipate by

[7] Since *Lancelot* is not mentioned in this list, it is generally assumed that *Cligés* was composed first. I have chosen here to present *Lancelot* first, since it is closer in type to *Erec* than is *Cligés*, and may thus be more readily understood from the perspective of Chrétien's first Arthurian work.

stating that Chrétien's reference to a written source in the prologue of *Cligés* (his *Tristan* parody) may already be an allusion to Thomas, who for his part had also cited a written source and still presented a romance belonging to the new, fictional, type. It is possible that Chrétien is satirizing the *Tristan* prologue from the perspective of his awareness of the different genres. If this is indeed the case, then only on a superficial level is the poet seen to discuss the subject matter directly; in reality the prologue represents a playful distancing from Thomas on Chrétien's part, implying a veiled discussion of the literary form. Be that as it may, Chrétien in the rest of the prologue returns to traditional prologue topoi, without any specific references to the subject of his work.

> Par les livres que nos avons
> Les fez des ancïens savons
> Et del siegle qu fu jadis.
> Ce nos ont nostre livre apris
> Qu'an Grece ot de chevalerie
> Le premier los et de clergie.
> Puis vint chevalerie a Rome
> Et de la clergie la some,
> Qui or est an France venue.
> Dex doint qu'ele i soit maintenue
> Et que li leus li abelisse
> Tant que ja mes de France n'isse
> L'enors qui s'i est arestee.
> Dex l'avoit as altres prestee:
> Car des Grezois ne des Romains
> Ne dit an mes ne plus ne mains,
> D'ax est la parole remese
> Et estainte la vive brese. (*Cligés*, 25–42)

[It is through books that we possess what we know of the deeds of the ancients and bygone times. Our books have taught us that praise of chivalry and learning originated in Greece. Then chivalry came to Rome, together with the highest learning, which has now come to France. God grant that it be cherished here and that this region please it so much that the honour which has taken up its abode here shall never depart from France. God had given it to the others as a loan, for nothing at all is said any more of the Greeks and Romans, talk of them has ceased and the glowing coals are extinguished.]

The theory of the *translatio studii*, the transfer of learning from

Greece via Rome to France, is part of a long tradition with its origins in antiquity. It has been traced by Franz Josef Worstbrock and A. C. Jongkees.[8] Chrétien's scheme is characterized by the dual concept of *chevalerie* and *clergie*. Erich Köhler sees here a vernacular rendering of *fortitudo et sapientia* – the formula for the new ideal of the Christian knight, the *miles christianus*, although he sees the term *clergie* as now completely divorced from its religious context. Köhler translates *clergie* as 'education' or 'culture', i.e. he interprets the dual concept as an expression of the new cultural consciousness of the ideal of chivalry. The inclusion of the chivalric culture of the twelfth century in the *translatio* process was intended to express its superiority over the ancient world.[9]

But how is this cultural superiority to be understood? Curtius saw in the *Cligés* prologue an anti-classical and anti-humanist note, but was immediately contradicted.[10] Ultimately this sense of superiority not only implies a new, modern cultural consciousness, but also comprises a new awareness of the role of literature in the historical process; the deeds of the ancients may have vanished, and their voices be silent, yet we still know of them through their books. The literary work thus outlasts time.[11] The cultural-political aspect of the *translatio* concept cannot be ignored, but equally its position and function within the context of the literary programme outlined here should not be underestimated. The term *clergie* here is meant not only to stand for education and culture in general; Chrétien, as a learned man, a *clerc*, claims this *clergie* for himself too, that is to say his poetic vocation is to establish this connection between *chevalerie* and *clergie*. Chivalry finds an identity in the meaning conferred on it by *clergie*. The terms *chevalerie* and *clergie* thus refer to knighthood from the perspective of its own literary identity. The poet, as the custodian of *clergie*, takes *chevalerie* as his literary subject. The twin concepts of *chevalerie/clergie* may thus ultimately be understood as the reformulation, on a cultural-political level, of the contrasting pairs *conte/conjointure* and *matiere/san*. The poet's relationship to society can be

---

[8] In Middle High German literature, the idea appears in *Moriz von Craun* – cf. Folz, 'L'histoire de la chevalerie' – and is also suggested in Konrad von Würzburg's *Trojanerkrieg*, lines 298ff.

[9] Köhler, *Ideal und Wirklichkeit*, pp. 39ff., 52ff.

[10] On this controversy, see Lyons, 'Interprétations critiques'.

[11] This idea occurs in one of the earliest works of the new literature, in Wace; see Bezzola, *Les Origines*, vol. III, pp. 184ff.

seen as analogous to the relationship between the creation of meaning and the subject matter.

This however is to beg the question as to why such a programme should be found in the prologue to a *Tristan* parody. It should be borne in mind that with this programme Chrétien is setting himself up in opposition to a work which called into question the very basis of courtly society, and thus also challenged the very ideals which Chrétien was promoting in his romance. It is precisely the social interaction of *chevalerie* and *clergie* put forward in *Cligés* which is seen to break down in *Tristan*, since in the character of Tristan, chivalry and culture turn on and reject the society symbolized by Marc's court in the name of absolute love. *Cligés* attacks this by using a parodistic adaptation of the plot of *Tristan*: the tragic love story becomes a grotesque joke. The new fictional type opens the way for an ironic manipulation of the Tristan motifs.[12] The prologue sketches in the literary and cultural outline which forms the basis for this attack.

[12] Cf. Haidu, *Aesthetic Distance in Chrétien de Troyes.*

7

Hartmann von Aue's fictional programme: the prologue to *Iwein*

I

In the last two decades of the twelfth century, Hartmann von Aue's translations of *Erec* and *Yvain* assured Chrétien's Arthurian romances lasting success in the German-speaking world.[1] There can be no doubt that he recognized and understood the structural scheme of Chrétien's romances and its theoretical implications, since on those occasions where Chrétien deviates from the model on points of detail, Hartmann emphasizes the strict formal scheme.[2] If his commentaries in the text fail to live up to the challenge posed by the new literary form, in which meaning is conveyed by means of the fictional process, this is because they must be considered as conscious simplifications, intended as aids for those who could not be expected fully to understand, rather than as a reflection of Hartmann's own level of comprehension.[3]

As far as Hartmann's explicit poetic theory in the *Iwein* prologue is concerned, no direct comparison with *Erec* is possible, since the prologue of that work has been lost, along with the beginning of the work. One can only speculate as to which, if any, of Chrétien's arguments would have been applicable to the German literary situation.[4] The

---

[1]   This was in all probability preceded by an earlier period of reception on the Lower Rhine: see Ruh, *Höfische Epik*, vol. I, pp. 110–11.

[2]   Hugo Kuhn, '*Erec*', in Hugo Kuhn, *Dichtung und Welt im Mittelalter*, pp. 135–6; Ruh, *Höfische Epik*, vol. I, p. 117. In *Erec*, however, Hartmann adds a preview of the further life of Erec and Enide which goes further than the conclusion of Chrétien's second cycle. Hartmann's additions were probably made with the expectations of the audience in mind. While Hartmann did not, however, succumb to this temptation in *Iwein*, a scribe, borrowing from Rudolf von Ems' *Willehalm von Orlens*, was later to do so; see Gerhardt, '*Iwein*-Schlüsse'.

[3]   Ruh, *Höfische Epik*, vol. I, p. 112. Worstbrock, 'Dilatatio materiae', 26–7 uses the description of Enite's horse to demonstrate that the new fictional awareness is also expressed within the narrative proper.

[4]   What follows is discussed in more detail in Haug, '*Der aventiure meine*'.

literary excursus in Gottfried's *Tristan* offers certain clues, since it appears that Gottfried, in his characterization of Hartmann, drew on a series of motifs from the latter's lost prologue to *Erec*. It is thus possible that the contrasting pairs of concepts central to Gottfried's literary criticism, namely *wort/sin* and *rede/meine*, go back to reflections in Hartmann's *Erec* prologue which are in turn derived from Chrétien. On the other hand, it was clearly not possible to apply Chrétien's statements as to the relationship of his romance to the oral – i.e. Breton – tradition to the German situation. It may thus be assumed that Hartmann reformulated the specific opposition of *conte d'avanture* and *conjointure* so as to bring it into line with the general opposition of subject matter/interpretation – *âventiure/meine* – used by Gottfried to characterize Hartmann's art in particular. Such reflections must, however, to a large extent remain speculative.

Hartmann's prologue to *Iwein* demonstrates that he was capable of highly independent theoretical thought. In *Yvain*, Chrétien had dispensed with a prologue as such, beginning directly with the action in the description of the Whitsuntide feast at King Arthur's court. Admittedly, certain reflections occur in this context which do in fact represent prologue elements; at any rate, Hartmann was able to spin them out into an independent prologue in his version of *Iwein*.

Chrétien's work opens thus:

> Artus, li buens rois de Bretaingne,
> La cui proesce nos ansaingne,
> Que nos soiiens preu et cortois,
> Tint cort si riche come rois
> A cele feste, qui tant coste,
> Qu'an doit clamer la pantecoste.
> Li rois fu a Carduel an Gales.
> Aprés mangier parmi cez sales
> Li chevalier s'atropelerent
> La, ou dames les apelerent
> Ou dameiseles ou puceles.
> Li un recontoient noveles,
> Li autre parloient d'amors,
> Des angoisses et des dolors
> Et des granz biens, qu'an ont sovant
> Li deciple de son covant,
> Qui lors estoit riches et buens.
> Mes ore i a mout po des suens;
> Que a bien pres l'ont tuit leissiee,

S'an est amors mout abeissiee;
Car cil, qui soloient amer,
Se feisoient cortois clamer
Et preu et large et enorable.
Ore est amors tornee a fable
Por ce que cil, qui rien n'an santent,
Dïent qu'il aimment, mes il mantent,
Et cil fable et mançonge an font,
Qui s'an vantent et droit n'i ont.
Mes por parler de çaus, qui furent,
Leissons çaus, qui an vie durent!
Qu'ancor vaut miauz, ce m'est avis,
Uns cortois morz qu'uns vilains vis.
Por ce me plest a reconter
Chose, qui face a escouter,
Del roi, qui fu de tel tesmoing,
Qu'an an parole pres et loing;
Si m'acort de tant as Bretons,
Que toz jorz mes vivra ses nons;
Et par lui sont ramanteü
Li buen chevalier esleü,
Qui an enor se traveillierent. (*Yvain*, 1–41)

[Arthur, the good king of Britain, whose prowess teaches us to be brave and courteous, held a court of truly royal splendour on that feast which is so costly that it truly deserves to be called Pentecost. The king was at Carduel (= Carlisle) in Wales. After they had eaten, the knights congregated in the chambers to which they were summoned by the ladies, damsels and maidens. Some of them were telling the latest stories, others were speaking of love, of the adversities and sorrows and the great blessings which are frequently experienced by the disciples of the order of love, which was rich and flourishing in those days. But now it has very few members, for they have nearly all left it, and love has been greatly degraded thereby. For those who practised love earned a reputation for being courtly and brave, generous and honourable. Now love has become an empty word, because those who have no experience of it claim to be in love, but they are liars and they turn it into an empty phrase and an untruth, boasting of it yet having no right to it. But let us speak of those who lived hitherto and leave aside those who are alive now. For in my opinion a courtly man dead is still worth more than a common man alive. Therefore I take pleasure in recounting something worth hearing of that king who was held in such esteem that he is spoken of far and near, and I am in agreement with the

Bretons that his name will live for ever more. And for his sake those goodly chosen knights are remembered who strove for honour.]

Chrétien makes use of this introductory description of Arthur's Whitsuntide festivities to distinguish the debased values of the present from the ideal age of King Arthur. This common prologue topos[5] is here so intertwined with the beginning of the story that one is inclined to view this *laudatio temporis acti* more as a glorification of the past by contrast with the present than as a specific theoretical statement in the context of the contemporary literary situation.

Hartmann, by contrast, focusses on precisely these theoretical elements woven in to the narrative, extrapolating them to form a separate prologue:

> Swer an rehte güete
> wendet sîn gemüete,
> dem volget sælde und êre. (*Iwein*, 1–3)[6]

[That man who strives with all his heart to attain real goodness finds himself the recipient of good fortune and honour.]

This is the characteristic opening maxim, used here to present a strikingly optimistic moral point. Whether it has any validity outside the context of a fictional world, in which merit and reward can coincide, must remain doubtful. At any rate, the evidence which Hartmann goes on to supply serves to identify the work as part of the Arthurian tradition:

> des gît gewisse lêre
> künec Artûs der guote,
> der mit rîters muote
> nâch lobe kunde strîten.
> er hât bî sînen zîten
> gelebet alsô schône
> daz er der êren krône
> dô truoc und noch sîn name treit.
> des habent die wârheit
> sîne lantliute:

---

5 Delbrück, 'Die gute alte Zeit'; on the French sphere in particular, Jones, *Prologue and Epilogue*, pp. 31–2.

6 The interpretation of these lines is controversial; cf. Endres, 'Der Prolog von Hartmanns *Iwein*'; Nagel, 'Hartmann "zitiert" Reinmar'; Endres, 'Die Bedeutung von *güete*'. Kern, 'Der Roman und seine Rezeption', 247, and Mertens, 'Imitatio Arthuri', 352–3, both rightly argue that the range of meaning should be left open, at least initially. The key terms accrue meaning during the course of the romance; cf. pp. 125–6 below.

sî jehent er lebe noch hiute:
er hât den lop erworben,
ist im der lîp erstorben,
sô lebet doch iemer sîn name.
er ist lasterlîcher schame
iemer vil gar erwert,
der noch nâch sînem site vert. (*Iwein*, 4–20)

[A clear example of this is provided by good King Arthur, who succeeded in winning praise by his knightly valour. His fine lifestyle became so famous in his own day that he won the crown of honour at that time and is still accorded it now. His countrymen maintain this: they say that he is still alive today. He won renown, indeed although his body may be dead, his name lives on for ever. The man who follows his example is for ever spared all shame and ill repute.]

Lines 4 to 6 are obviously derived from *Yvain*, 1–3. In the opening *sententia*, Hartmann makes the lesson offered by the shining example of Chrétien's Arthur generally valid: *Artus, li buens rois/künec Artûs der guote* led to the concept of *rehtiu güete* ('true goodness'), and in accordance with the idea of 'fighting for knightly honour' (7) attributed to the king, all those who turn to *güete* and strive towards it will attain both *sælde* ('good fortune') and *êre* ('honour'); recognition, then, in the eyes of both God and the world.

Hartmann derives the reflections in the following lines (8–17) from lines 37ff. of *Yvain*. Chrétien had already modified the popular British belief in the return of King Arthur into the suggestion that his fame made him immortal. Finally, in lines 18–20, Hartmann returns to the initial idea of teaching by the example of excellence.

Then the poet speaks of himself, justifying his undertaking and stating his name:

Ein rîter, der gelêret was
unde ez an den buochen las,
swenner sîne stunde
niht baz bewenden kunde,
daz er ouch tihtennes pflac
(daz man gerne hœren mac,
dâ kêrt er sînen vlîz an:
er was genant Hartman
und was ein Ouwære),
der tihte diz mære. (*Iwein*, 21–30)

Hartmann von Aue: the prologue to Iwein

[A knight who was learned and had read this tale in books – whenever he had no better use for his time and could occupy himself with writing poetry, devoting himself to the composition of what people take pleasure in hearing – he was called Hartmann and he came from Aue, he composed this story.]

Thus lines 1–10 open – in a similar manner to *Erec* and *Lancelot* – with a reference to the genre, incorporating a discussion on how meaning is conveyed. This is then established as part of a poetological concept which in turn bases its authority on learning and the poet's access to the written tradition. Well-known topos strategies are employed here: the opening maxim, teaching by example, evidence of the poet's competence, reference to a written source, poetry as entertainment,[7] the poet's naming of himself. However, these topoi are fused into a completely self-contained argument.

Hartmann does not make reference to the subject matter itself in his prologue, since at line 31 the narrative proper commences straight away with a reference to *Yvain*, 3ff.:

> Ez hete der künec Artûs
> ze Karidôl in sîn hûs
> zeinen pfingesten geleit
> nâch rîcher gewonheit
> ein alsô schœne hôchzît
> daz er vordes noch sît
> deheine schœner nie gewan. (*Iwein*, 31–7)

[One Whitsun King Arthur arranged such a splendid festival in his traditional lavish style in the castle at Karidol that he never held a finer one before or since.]

The fact that the festivities at Arthur's court are used as a starting point for the narrative confirms the expectations of the genre aroused by the mention of the king's name in line 5. The story could in theory proceed straight from there, but Hartmann interrupts the narrative again in order to insert those of Chrétien's exordial reflections which he had not used at the beginning. A connection with the prologue is established by elaborating the motif in which the praise of Arthur in the prologue culminated, namely the endurance of his fame in

---

7 Ruh, *Höfische Epik*, vol. I, p. 107, and Kern, 'Der Roman und seine Rezeption', 248, interpret lines 23–6 in this sense; it is not a question of a lack of commitment to the poetic work, as has been claimed, since in the medieval sense entertainment does not imply distraction, but was rather seen as a meaningful activity in itself: cf. Suchomski, *'Delectatio' und 'Utilitas'*, p. 72.

posterity. The occasion for introducing this is given by the lament, after the depiction of the Arthurian Whitsuntide festivities,

> daz nû bî unseren tagen
> selch vreude niemer werden mac
> der man ze den zîten pflac. (*Iwein*, 50–2)

[that nowadays such celebrations as they had in those days have become impossible.]

This is clearly a brief recapitulation, in general terms, of the complaint of the decline of the art of love which Chrétien put forward in lines 18ff. Hartmann connects it in the following lines with lines 29ff. of *Yvain*, giving them a new slant:

> doch müezen wir ouch nû genesen.
> ichn wolde dô niht sîn gewesen,
> daz ich nû niht enwære,
> dâ uns noch mit ir mære
> sô rehte wol wesen sol:
> dâ tâten in diu werc vil wol. (*Iwein*, 53–8)

[But we too must live our lives. I would not like to have lived in those days, for then I would not be alive now, when we can enjoy such benefits from the tales of the past: whereas they had all the benefits of the events themselves.]

How, then, is one to live in an age in which the Arthurian ideal can no longer be realized? Hartmann gives the surprising answer that it is nevertheless still possible to *genesen*, that is to live in the pursuit of meaning, happiness and salvation. Indeed, the present is even superior to the past: Hartmann, in a startling reversal of the *laudatio temporis acti*, claims that the poetic representation of events is preferable to the events themselves.

Hartmann scholars were until recently able to make little sense of this *volte-face*. Initially, they attempted to explain it as a misunderstanding of the original on Hartmann's part.[8] Chrétien had said, 'But let us speak of those who lived hitherto and leave those who are alive now. For in my opinion a courtly man dead is still worth more than a common man alive.' However, closer examination reveals that Hartmann's version of these lines is in fact not so far from the idea of the

---

[8] Bertau, *Deutsche Literatur*, vol. I, p. 713 and 'Versuch über den späten Chrestien', p. 38, and Mertens, 'Imitatio Arthuri', 353ff., see the issue in its true perspective. Cf. also Hugo Kuhn, 'Soziale Realität und dichterische Fiktion', p. 36.

original after all. When Chrétien says that a dead knight is worth more than a living commoner, this is not intended as a comment on the relative merits of social classes; rather, the emphasis is on the reference to the chivalric past in a present which fails to live up to it. Hartmann merely makes this idea more radical by developing it into an opposition between literature and life in general. Far from being a misunderstanding, then, this is a deliberate programme. The superiority of literature over life is here formulated explicitly for the first time.[9] However, what lies behind it is basically the same opposition which has already been encountered in various guises in Chrétien: *conjointure* versus *conte*, *san* versus *matiere*, *clergie* versus *chevalerie*. What counts is not the plot, nor the subject matter, nor the actual events, but the meaning derived from them by literary interpretation. However, like Chrétien before him, Hartmann lacks the theoretical equipment to analyse the process by which this meaning is realized in, and conveyed by, the literary work. Where Chrétien alludes to the

---

[9] Various objections have been made to this admittedly provocative statement on my part, and to the argument behind it. It has been seen as the culmination of a dangerous tendency to apply modern aesthetic concepts to medieval literature: thus Huber, 'Höfischer Roman als Integumentum?', 86–7, and 'Literaturtheorie', 63ff.; by contrast, Curschmann, 'Literaturtheorie', 349–50, and Heinzle, 'Entdeckung der Fiktionalität', 65–6, at least accept the arguments; while Wolf, 'Der Roman vom Löwenritter', p. 220, agrees with my position. In fact I start from the point of view that the dividing line between literary or historical epochs cannot be fixed once and for all but has to be reassessed in the case of each individual cultural phenomenon. The question of 'literary autonomy' which is at issue here is in no way an appropriate criterion for establishing to which epoch a work may be attributed, since in some sense literature can be said to have existed as an independent phenomenon ever since human beings began to sing or to tell tales. Even works composed to order are able to achieve a measure of freedom in this respect. It should, however, be added that this autonomous element has to be determined anew for each individual work. Thus Arthurian romances based on Chrétien's model seem to display a high degree of literary automony. With Hartmann's romances there is already evidence of concern with the act of narration itself, i.e. with the narrative as a mode of experience, indeed as a forum for experimenting with new imaginative possibilities (see also chapters 9 and 11), and this becomes quite explicit in the case of Wolfram and Gottfried. This is not to deny that simpler, more didactic models of behaviour may sometimes play a part in, influence or indeed obstruct these new narrative possibilities, though I would hesitate to agree with Huber, 'Höfischer Roman als Integumentum?', 87, that the participation of the audience in the narrative process is subsumed in an all-embracing didactic moral perspective. Clearly the path followed by the Arthurian hero may be termed exemplary, in that the audience is invited to identify with it, but it seems to me more fruitful to emphasize the difference rather than to view this as another aspect of the medieval didactic mode. The crucial difference is finally articulated by Wolfram: namely, the opposition between following a definite pattern of behaviour and embarking on an intellectual process in which the individual reader participates in the narrative experiment. Some medievalists may well find this too modern for their liking, but as I have said, the question of where to draw the line between 'medieval' and 'modern' should not be prejudged. From an impartial viewpoint, the theoretical evidence would seem to indicate that the turning point comes somewhere in the twelfth century, even if the boldest advances here are far ahead of their time and are to some extent retracted in later epochs.

integumentum metaphor, Hartmann makes use of the idea of the exemplary function of literature. In line 4 he refers explicitly to the teaching (*lêre*) which we can derive from King Arthur; in line 20 he recommends following his example (*sînem site*). Both instances refer to the exemplary figure of Arthur. Is Hartmann then claiming a *sensus moralis* for his romance? Yet if it were simply a matter of imitating the figure of Arthur, then surely one would have to wish to have participated in the Arthurian *âventiure* themselves! Instead of which, the tales of these *âventiure* are preferred to the deeds themselves, and if there is talk of enjoying the benefit of such tales (*wol wesen mit ir mære*) at the end, this must mean, with due regard to *lêre*, more than just pleasurable entertainment; in other words, it is not just a question here of completing the traditional concept of *prodesse et delectare* by adding the Middle High German equivalent of *delectare* to the didactic element implicit in *lêre*. The phrases *wol wesen* ('to benefit'), *wol tuon* ('to do good'), and the term *genesen* ('to live') in line 53, which also belongs in this semantic context, all refer to a process which affects humanity on a far more fundamental level and which in a certain sense concerns its salvation. That is to say, we are dealing here at the highest level with the communication of truth. This truth is precisely not reducible to a moral formula, nor can it be transformed into a practical catalogue of prescriptive norms; rather it is understood via the fictional narrative as an autonomous form of experience.

This prompts a re-examination of Hartmann's opening maxim: what does he mean by *rehtiu güete*? In view of the emphasis placed on the fictional nature of the romance, the answer can only be that 'true goodness' has to be perceived as the ultimate goal of the Arthurian *âventiure*; these adventures would be neither conceivable nor desirable in any historical 'Arthurian age', but are only meaningful within a literary and intellectual process. Hartmann places the prologue in the service of this new concept of aesthetics, taking as his starting point the traditional function of the prologue, which is to prepare the audience for the work to be presented, and to win them over to his cause. However, in the newly created genre of fictional romance this priming of the audience is effected by a discussion of the genre itself, with the aim of making them aware of the autonomy of the literary medium by referring explicitly to its fictional character. As has been stated, however, Hartmann, like Chrétien before him, had no adequate poetic terminology for this at his disposal, and so was obliged to fall back on traditional concepts. On closer investigation it becomes apparent that these concepts are inadequate, indeed that they are perhaps deliberately allowed to culminate in contradictions which expose their inadequacy.

This idea of the new function of poetry is at the root of Hartmann's understanding of his role and identity as a poet. He refers to himself as a learned knight, a 'rîter, der gelêret was', in other words he is able to read and thus has access to the written tradition. This self-characterization is clearly important to him, since it occurs in almost the same words in the prologue to *Der arme Heinrich* (1ff.).[10]

It is important to bear in mind that this is not merely the utterance of a layman proud of his education; the allusions to chivalry and learning are a reference to the cultural programme formulated by Chrétien de Troyes in the prologue to *Cligés*. Being able to read, being learned, here not only implies that the poet has access to the written tradition, but also that he sees himself as justified in taking up, interpreting, and passing on this same tradition. Education implies that literature can and should provide a model for the actual experience of life. The contrast between Arthurian *âventiure* and *mære* is reflected in the opposition of *chevalerie* and *clergie*, and, by extension, of Hartmann the knight and Hartmann the scholar.

II

A characteristic feature of the opening of *Iwein* is the 'interlacing' of rhetorical topoi and narrative. This may be seen in the way in which the prologue is incorporated into the depiction of the Arthurian festivities, both here (in *Iwein*) and even more markedly in Chrétien's *Yvain*. Another instance of this device of interweaving occurs after the beginning of the narrative proper, in the setting of a scene which leaves room for the inclusion of further exordial motifs, as will be seen from what follows.

Kalogrenant begins to tell a tale to several knights who have assembled for the courtly festivities. Ginover, who had retired to bed with Arthur, learns of this and joins the gathering, at which point the story-teller interrupts his tale in order to greet the queen, as is proper. Keie spitefully mocks such hasty courtesy; this gives rise to a heated dispute. Kalogrenant refuses to continue his tale in Keie's presence; the queen attempts to pacify him by explaining that Keie usually

---

[10] On cross-references and quotations between Hartmann's prologues and epilogues, see Grosse, 'Beginn und Ende'.

denigrates anything good, so that his insults in fact amount to a compliment. Keie tries to smooth things over and attempts to win the queen round, at which Kalogrenant observes that he, Keie, is speaking true to form, since

> ezn sprichet niemannes munt
> wan als in sîn herze lêret:
> swen iuwer zunge unêret,
> dâ ist daz herze schuldec an.
> in der werlte ist manec man
> valsch und wandelbære,
> der gerne biderbe wære,
> wan daz in sîn herze enlât.
> swer iuch mit lêre bestât,
> deist ein verlorniu arbeit. (*Iwein*, 194–203)

[The mouth speaks only as it is instructed by the heart. If you abuse someone with your tongue, then your heart must take responsibility. There are many fickle and deceitful people in society who would like to be worthy, if only their hearts would let them. It is a waste of effort to offer advice to you.]

When, finally, the queen succeeds in persuading Kalogrenant to continue his tale, he begins with an exordium which supplies a whole series of prologue topoi not deployed at the beginning:

> sît ir michs niht welt erlân,
> so vernemet ez mit guotem site,
> unde mietet mich dâ mite:
> ich sag iu deste gerner vil,
> ob manz ze rehte merken wil.
> man verliuset michel sagen,
> man enwellez merken unde dagen.
> maneger biutet diu ôren dar:
> ern nemes ouch mit dem herzen war,
> sone wirt im niht wan der dôz,
> und ist der schade alze grôz:
> wan si verliesent beide ir arbeit,
> der dâ hoeret und der dâ seit.
> ir muget mir deste gerner dagen:
> ichn wil iu keine lüge sagen. (*Iwein*, 244–58)

[Since you refuse to let me off, listen with decorum, let that be my reward. If you will listen properly I will tell my tale all the more willingly. Much of what is said is wasted if people will not listen

128

attentively and quietly. Many people listen with their ears. Unless they also take it in with their hearts, they will get nothing but the sound, and the loss will be most considerable, for both parties will waste their effort, the listeners and the storyteller. You have all the more reason to be quiet and listen to me, for I shall tell you no lies.]

What is belatedly included here, then, is first the exordial topos of the importance of the correct attitude on the part of the audience.[11] Keie here features not only in his usual role of cynic but also in that of the obstinate listener. In terms of the argument, Hartmann is here employing general psychological concepts which in turn have a specific meaning in the context of reception: what is good, both in the word and the work, depends on the inner attitude, or *muot* ('heart'/ 'mind'), of the audience. Those whose thoughts and intentions are evil will remain evil, and cannot be changed by arguments. In other words, only those whose *muot* is prepared for goodness (*güete*), which the work aims to transmit, will be able to understand it fully. At the same time we find here an ironic play on the question of truth and falsehood which draws attention to the fictional nature of the work.[12]

What is here only hinted at with regard to the relationship between the meaning of the narrative and the *muot* of the listener later becomes a definite programme on the part of Wolfram von Eschenbach and Gottfried von Strassburg: they demand of the audience from the very beginning an unconditional acceptance of and commitment to the idea behind the work. In more specific terms, this means that the argument employed as a model for the reception of the new fictional genre is the same as the one which had previously based its authority on, and derived its meaning from, the religious context of the connection between truth and language.[13]

A further point should also be noted: the narrative situation at the Arthurian court is in marked contrast to the narrative situation of the contemporary poet, in that the relationship between word and deed is reversed. While for the contemporary writer, the narration must distance itself from the world of deeds in order to come into its own, Kalogrenant's tale is anything but a glorification of his own deeds,

---

[11] Kern, 'Rezeption und Genese des Artusromans', 250: 'The romance discusses the conditions of its reception'; on Keie as the typical bad listener, ibid., 251. Cf. *Yvain*, 151ff., discussed by Gallais, 'Recherches sur la mentalité des romanciers français du moyen âge', 491. Cf. also Scholz, *Hören und Lesen*, p. 175, note 697.

[12] Cf. Wolf, 'Der Roman vom Löwenritter', pp. 214ff.

[13] Lines 251ff. are probably a deliberate allusion to Matthew 13,15; likewise in *Yvain*, 150ff.

since he has to tell of an *âventiure* in which he failed miserably. This causes Iwein to set out to make good his disgrace. The tale thus initiates the *âventiure*, and in this sense itself functions as the challenge motif.

On the path which Iwein must follow, it is, however, precisely chivalric action which is called into question. Following Kalogrenant's directions, the hero arrives at a place where he sets off a thunderstorm by pouring water onto a stone, and then is obliged to fight the lord of the fountain. However, unlike Kalogrenant he is able to defeat this knight of the fountain, fatally wounding him. He then marries his widow Laudine, but immediately takes his leave again in order to perform knightly deeds. However, he misses the agreed date for his return, and Laudine withdraws her love; this drives him to madness. Miraculously cured, he finally finds his way back to Laudine after a second series of *âventiure*. This second cycle is again characterized by the complex structure already deployed in *Erec*.[14]

Kalogrenant's tale thus leads to a questioning of the concept of knightly *âventiure*. The concept is explicitly discussed in the narrative: on the way to the magic fountain, Kalogrenant comes across a terrifying wild man, to whom he attempts to explain, when the latter asks, what *âventiure* is. The famous definition goes as follows:

> ich heize ein riter und hân den sin
> daz ich suochende rîte
> einen man der mit mir strîte,
> der gewâfent sî als ich.
> daz prîset in, und sleht er mich:
> gesige aber ich im an,
> sô hât man mich vür einen man,
> und wirde werder danne ich sî. (*Iwein*, 530–7)

> [I am called a knight and it is my intention to ride seeking a man armed as I am myself who will fight with me. He will win honour if he defeats me, whereas if I defeat him, then I will be considered a brave man and my reputation will increase.]

This definition of *âventiure*, concise to the point of caricature, holds true to a certain extent for Iwein also. At all events, it is when knightly deeds have become an end in themselves that they result in a personal crisis for the hero. After he has sunk to – or below – the level of the wild man, who knows nothing of *âventiure*, he has to learn, in

---

[14] Ruh, *Höfische Epik*, vol. I, pp. 154ff.

a second cycle, to make proper use of his knighthood in the service of fellow mortals in distress. Following a pattern analogous to the structure of *Erec*, the crucial transformation takes place in the crisis between love and action. In falling prey to madness and living like an animal in the wilderness, the protagonist here too symbolically passes through death; in this the romance hero is once again led to the limits of human experience. This boundary experience is not explicitly formulated, since it can be neither taught nor learned, and its meaning can only be conveyed effectively if the thematic and structural scheme is grasped by the listeners. The exemplary aspect of the Arthurian world cannot for this reason be sufficient unto itself, but must continually re-emerge from the same movement which finds narrative expression in the journeys of *âventiure* undertaken by individual knights. Where the Arthurian ideal 'rests on its laurels', it becomes brittle and vulnerable. This is demonstrated particularly clearly in the quarrel about Keie which opens the action in *Iwein*, in that one of its prime functions is to challenge the complacency of the Utopian state – which would of course, as a contradiction in terms, render it invalid as an ideal. On the other hand, the discussion of *âventiure* in anticipation of the narrative represents an implicit criticism of the idea that the Utopian ideal can be achieved by effort alone: the tale of the encounter between the knight, who regards the path into the Other-world as a mere trial of strength, and the uncourtly wild herdsman, to whom the whole problem is totally foreign, foreshadows the central *âventiure* of Iwein, in the course of which he must himself sink to the level of the wild man – or indeed below it – in order to appreciate the relationship between action and the experience of compassion and grace.

8

Hagiographical legend or romance? – Hartmann's prologue to *Gregorius*

I

With *Gregorius*, Hartmann turns to a new literary form: the hagiographical romance. He prefaces his narrative – based on a French source, the anonymous *Vie du pape Grégoire* – with an extensive prologue which goes far beyond the scope of the original.[1] It is one of the most controversial passages in Middle High German literature,[2] of particular significance for literary theory, and it continues to engage the attention of scholars, in that the problems which it poses still remain, on the whole, unresolved.

It may seem unusual to place a discussion of the *Gregorius* prologue immediately after an analysis of the theoretical passages from Hartmann's Arthurian romances. The different genres each have their own characteristic elements,[3] but the separate development of the different prologue types should not be overemphasized, since there is a certain tendency, especially at a more sophisticated level, for an interchange of exordial topoi between the different genres. It is nevertheless possible to trace a continuous development from the prologues of Early Middle High German religious literature, via for example Heinrich von Veldeke's *Servatius* prologue, down to the time of Hartmann. Such a development would indeed confirm the continuity of tradition in a most gratifying way: Veldeke appeals to the Holy Spirit to lead the 'sense', the *sin*, along the right paths for him, to make its abode in his heart so that God's word and his teachings might lead in turn to good works – a later interpolation

---

[1] 176 lines, as opposed to the 62 of the original: cf. Sol, *La Vie du Pape Saint Grégoire*.

[2] Neubuhr, *Bibliographie zu Hartmann von Aue*, pp. 120ff.

[3] For the religious prologue, see Brinkmann, 'Prolog im Mittelalter', pp. 101ff.; Naumann, 'Vorstudien zu einer Darstellung des Prologs', p. 27; Schulmeister, *Aedificatio und Imitatio*; Wyss, *Theorie der mittelhochdeutschen Legendenepik*, pp. 76ff.; in addition, see the references to critical works in chapter 1, note 10.

goes on to discuss spiritual wakefulness. There follows the introduction of the saint and the plea for assistance in composing the work, accompanied by the usual modesty topoi.[4]

This brief allusion to Veldeke should suffice to call to mind the continuity of the religious prologue tradition, in order that the *Gregorius* prologue may be contrasted with it. It is notably lacking in those characteristic elements of prologues to the lives of saints encountered in the *Servatius* prologue, namely the *invocatio*, the request for assistance with the work, the appeal to the saint and the modesty topoi. The prologue to *Gregorius* develops its theoretical arguments from a single, admittedly traditional, motif, namely the idea of doing penance for one's sins by means of a literary work, and thus at the same time showing audience and readers the way out of their own sinful existence and into a state of grace.[5] These remarks about the aims and intentions of the work then lead, in lines 43–50, straight into the introduction of the subject matter, with the announcement that this very theme is to be illustrated by means of a concrete example, the Life of Gregorius.

Hartmann develops the argument of 'poetry as penance' as follows. First he uses self-reproach: led astray by his youth, he has until now only written for *der werlde lôn* ('worldly gain'). However, it is wrong to assume that old age will be time enough to repent of one's sins, since death may come swiftly. Indeed it is in any case perverse to regard the relationship of sin and repentance as a kind of trade or bargain which can be settled when the time is ripe; rather, the following is the case:

> und wære aber er geborn
> von Adâme mit Abêle
> und solde im sîn sêle
> weren âne sünden slac
> unz an den jungisten tac,
> sô hæte er niht ze vil gegeben
> umbe daz êwige leben
> daz anegenges niht enhât

---

[4] On the authenticity of the prologue and its relationship to the tradition, see Woesler, 'Heinrich von Veldeke'; cf. Wyss, *Theorie der mittelhochdeutschen Legendenepik*, pp. 83ff.

[5] On the theme of poetry as penance, especially for secular youthful works, see Thraede, *Studien zur Sprache und Stil des Prudentius*, pp. 28ff.; Nat, 'Die Praefatio der Evangelien-paraphrase des Iuvencus', p. 254; Suchomski, *'Delectatio' und 'Utilitas'*, p. 69; Jones, *Prologue and Epilogue*, pp. 26ff.; Schwietering, *Demutsformel*, pp. 203ff.; Sayce, 'Prolog, Epilog, und das Problem des Erzählers', p. 68.

und ouch niemer zegât. (*Gregorius*, 26–34)

[If a man had been born as a child of Adam along with Abel and if his soul were then to be spared the devastation of sin until the Day of Judgement, then he would not have given too much to gain eternal life, which has no beginning and will never end.]

This leads Hartmann back to his own work:

Durch daz wære ich gerne bereit
ze sprechenne die wârheit
daz gotes wille wære
und daz diu grôze swaære
der süntlîchen bürde
ein teil ringer würde
die ich durch mîne müezikeit
ûf mich mit worten hân geleit. (*Gregorius*, 35–42)

[Consequently I would like to speak the truth, the will of God, in order that the great weight of the burden of sin, which I have imposed on myself with abandon through my poetry, might be lightened somewhat.]

The introduction to the subject matter now follows on from this without a break. Referring to the subject of the poem, Hartmann voices his hope that his new, religious work might lessen the burden of his sins:

wan dâ enzwîvel ich niht an:
als uns got an einem man
erzeiget und bewæret hât,
sô enwart nie mannes missetât
ze dirre werlde sô grôz,
er enwerde ir ledic unde blôz,
ob si in von herzen riuwet
und si niht wider niuwet. (*Gregorius*, 43–50)

[For I have no doubt, as God has demonstrated and shown to be true through one man,[6] no one on earth has ever committed so great a sin that he cannot be freed of it if he truly repents in his heart and does not do it again.]

After line 51, the subject of the new work is outlined: Hartmann intends to tell the story of a man who heaped the worst kind of guilt

---

[6] Pretzel, 'Zum Prolog von Hartmanns *Gregorius*', reads 'einem man' as referring to Christ, which does not seem convincing in this context.

upon himself but who, since he never doubted in God's grace, was nonetheless ultimately saved.

There have been attempts to place a biographical interpretation on this very public confession of sins, a temptation which was all the more natural in that Hartmann's penitental act of turning away from Arthurian romance to a religious subject matter could be seen as the expression of a personal crisis, of which there seems to be some indication in his lyrical works, where the poet laments the loss of his patron. He also seems to have taken part in a crusade. Could his rejection of the courtly romance perhaps be explained by such a biographical incident? Yet such an interpretation not only involves playing down Hartmann's later return to a secular genre in *Iwein* as something merely coincidental – it is generally agreed that this second Arthurian romance was completed at the end of Hartmann's poetic career – but also means ignoring the fact that the prologue relies heavily on conventional topoi. The confession of one's own sins, the rejection of secular literature, the religious work as an act of penance or as a commendable spiritual act are all motifs which would have been familiar to the audience from the religious prologue tradition. What appears to be personal – however biographically accurate the data may be – would therefore have served in the first instance as an indication of the genre. Hartmann is known as a secular poet; for whatever reasons he changes to the religious type, and in this connection presents a series of topoi in the prologue to make the audience aware of the change of genre.[7]

The confession of sins also has another function in this prologue, which may explain the way it comes to be emphasized: it serves to establish contact with the audience in a very specific way. By presenting himself as a penitent sinner,[8] the poet can demand that his audience likewise reform, and is thus able to present his work as a living proof that this is possible even for the most hardened sinner. Hartmann's 'ich' or poetic persona is, in fact, the true narrator of this hagiographical romance, precisely because of the way in which the relationship with the audience is skilfully interwoven with the subject matter. At the same time, this smooth transition to the second part of the prologue, in which the subject matter is introduced, makes it

---

[7] Sayce, 'Prolog, Epilog, und das Problem des Erzählers', pp. 69–70; Mertens, *Gregorius eremita*, pp. 76ff., 81ff.

[8] Mention of oneself is also a traditional topos directed at the audience: Schirmer, *Stil- und Motivuntersuchungen*, p. 72.

apparent that this thematic perspective is increasingly important in determining the course of the prologue as a whole, and that, indeed, it has been the focus from the outset.

The discussion of the subject matter extends from line 51 to 176, and may be divided into four sections. The first of these ends at line 96. Hartmann announces that he intends to tell a tale which is 'vil starc ze hœrenne' (53), that is, a dreadful tale, full of frightful things. He feels however that he may not withhold it from his audience, since it also contains evidence of great faith in God, demonstrating as it does – and with this he takes up the argument of line 42 – that even the greatest sins may be forgiven if one places one's trust in the grace of God, provided always that one does not fall into despair but shows repentance and does penance in the unshakeable hope of redemption.

It should be borne in mind that when the author here turns to the subject matter, he does not lose sight of the audience altogether, for the work continues to take their response into account, so that the exposition of the subject matter and the relationship with the audience are continually intertwined.

The section ends with the biblical image of the parting of the ways: the broad path which leads to destruction and the narrow gate which promises eternal salvation.[9] This image of the parting of the ways is then linked to the next section, starting at line 97, as follows:

> Den selben wec geriet ein man:
> zer rehten zît er entran
> ûz der mordære gewalt. (*Gregorius*, 97–9)

> [A certain man found himself on that same path (=the straight and narrow path leading to paradise).[10] He escaped from the clutches of murderers in good time.]

Hartmann next introduces another parable, that of the Good Samaritan from Luke, chapter 10. The description and interpretation of this passage comprises the second section of this part of the prologue.

[9] Matthew 7,13f.; on the history of the motif, see Siefken, '*Der sælden strâze*'; Harms, *Homo viator*.

[10] The expression 'that same path' ('den selben wec') can only refer to the path leading to salvation, not, as one might expect and as indeed previously was thought, the broad path. However, this is the view taken by Spitz, 'Zwischen Furcht und Hoffnung', p. 176; for bibliography on this point, see his note 27. The reference to the narrow way in the context of lines 98–9 either anticipates the final outcome, or already at this stage indicates the paradox that it is precisely that individual who believed himself to be following the right path who went astray.

Luke 10,30–4 relates the following:

> Homo quidam descendebat ab Jerusalem in Jericho, et incidit in
> latrones, qui etiam despoliaverunt eum: et plagis impositis abierunt
> semivivo relicto. Accidit autem ut sacerdos quidam descenderet
> eadem via: et viso illo praeterivit. Similiter et Levita, cum esset secus
> locum, et videret eum, pertransiit. Samaritanus autem quidam iter
> faciens, venit secus eum: et videns eum misericordia motus est. Et
> appropians alligavit vulnera ejus, infundens oleum, et vinum: et
> imponens illum in jumentum suum, duxit in stabulum, et curam ejus
> egit.

> [A certain man was going down from Jerusalem to Jericho, and he
> fell among robbers, who stripped him: and having beaten him they
> departed, leaving him half dead. Now it happened that a priest was
> going down that same road: and when he saw him he passed by on
> the other side. So likewise a Levite, when he came to the place and
> saw him, he went on. But a Samaritan, as he journeyed, came to the
> place where he was: and on seeing him he was moved with
> compassion. He went to him and bound his wounds, pouring on oil
> and wine: then he set him on his own beast and brought him to an
> inn, and took care of him.]

The church fathers and, in turn, their medieval commentators
interpreted this parable in terms of salvation history. The man who
comes down from Jerusalem and falls among thieves stands for Adam,
who fell from grace by sinning and thus forfeited paradise. The
robbers signify the devil, who defrauds the human race by robbing
them of the robes of innocence and immortality. The priest and the
Levite stand for the Law and the Prophets, who are incapable of
assistance, while the Good Samaritan is to be understood as a Christ
figure who redeems the human race from sin and restores it to its
heavenly home.[11]

Hartmann's version fuses the *narratio* with its allegorical interpretation in such a way that the biblical parable increasingly resembles a
metaphorical illustration of the Fall and the Redemption:

> er was komen in ir walt,
> dâ hâten si in nider geslagen
> und im vrevellîche entragen

---

[11] Bennholdt-Thomsen, 'Die allegorischen *kleit* im *Gregorius*-Prolog'; Monselewski, *Der
barmherzige Samariter*, esp. pp. 18ff. and 29ff.; Flügel, *Prolog und Epilog*, pp. 159ff.;
Goebel, 'Hartmanns "Gregorius-Allegorie"'; and Spitz, 'Zwischen Furcht und Hoffnung',
pp. 174ff., on the whole spectrum of previous interpretations.

aller sîner sinne kleit
und hâten in an geleit
vil marterlîche wunden.
ez was zuo den stunden
sîner sêle armuot vil grôz.
sus liezen si in ...[12] blôz
unde halp tôt ligen.
do enhâte im got niht verzigen
sîner gewonlîchen erbarmekeit
und sande im disiu zwei kleit,
gedingen unde vorhte,
diu got selbe worhte
daz si im ein schirm wæren
und allen sündæren:
vorhte daz er erstürbe,
gedinge daz er iht verdürbe.
vorhte liez in dâ niht ligen.
doch wære er wider gesigen,
wan daz in der gedinge
machete alsô ringe
daz er doch weibende saz.
dar zuo sô starcte in baz
diu geistlîche triuwe
gemischet mit der riuwe.
si tâten im vil guotes
und ervurpten in des bluotes.
si guzzen im in die wunden sîn
beidiu öl unde wîn.
diu salbe ist linde und tuot doch wê,
daz öl diu gnâde, der wîn diu ê,
die der sündære haben muoz:
sô wirt im siechtuomes buoz.
alsus huop in bî sîner hant

---

[12] The manuscript evidence is inconclusive here ('ungebloss', 'siglos'). Spitz, 'Zwischen Furcht und Hoffnung', p. 177, follows a suggestion of Friedrich Ohly's in amending to 'tugende blôz'. This would mean that the interpretation of the clothes (103) as *tugende* ('virtues') would conflict with the interpretation of them as *sinne* ('senses'). Spitz gets round this by making use of the variant in manuscript J: 'gar alle die sînen kleit' ('all his clothes'). One hesitates to follow this reading not just because it is the *lectio facilior*, but also because in this case the religious interpretation only begins with line 106; nevertheless, the 'sêle armuot' ('destitution of the soul') can scarcely be understood without the previous suggestion that the robbing of the clothes has an allegorical meaning. Moreover, the expressions 'blôz' ('naked') and 'halp tôt' ('half dead') (108–9), introduced by 'sus' ('so'), which seems to indicate a kind of summing up, form a parallel pair in the sentence: Spitz' reading takes this concluding sentence to consist of a literal and an allegorical statement yoked together, with the latter also carrying the whole allegorical meaning of the passage. This solution seems implausible.

diu gotes gnâde als si in vant
ûf ir miltez ahselbein
und truoc in durch beruochen hein.
dâ wurden im verbunden
sîne verchwunden
daz er âne mâsen genas
und sît ein wârer kemphe was,
er eine über al die kristenheit. (*Gregorius*, 100–43)

[He (= the man who had escaped from the murderers) had entered
their forest, where they had knocked him down and violently
stripped him of the clothes of all his senses and inflicted most
painful wounds on him. At that moment his soul suffered great
destitution. And so they left him lying there ... naked and half dead.
But God had not diverted from him His customary mercy and He
sent him two garments, hope and fear, which God fashioned
himself, that they might offer him and all sinners protection: fear
that he might die, hope that he would not perish. Fear would not
allow him to lie there, but he would have sunk down again if hope
had not made him light, so that he could sit up shakily. In addition
he was given further strength by spiritual trust mixed with contri-
tion. These did him much good and cleaned away the blood, poured
oil and wine onto his wounds. This ointment is soothing and yet
causes pain. The oil is grace, the wine is the Law, both of which the
sinner needs to combat the sickness. God's Grace lifted him up by
the hand as she found him, placed him on her gentle shoulder and
carried him home to be cared for. There his mortal wounds were
bandaged so that he was healed and left free of scars. Afterwards he
became a true warrior, singled out from the whole of Christendom.]

The opening of this passage retains the situation of the biblical
parable, with the attack by the robbers. However, the expressions
'sîner sinne kleit' ('the clothes of his senses') and sîner sêle armuot'
('destitution of the soul') already begin to interpret the incident on
an allegorical level, and where, according to the parable, the Samaritan should enter, God himself appears, presenting the victim with
the clothes of fear and hope, while faith and repentance come to his
assistance, cleansing him and anointing his wounds with oil and
wine; the oil is interpreted as grace and the wine as the Law. Finally,
a different image obtrudes from the allegorical level of meaning;
God, carrying the wounded man home, evokes not so much the
image of the Good Shepherd, as has often been suggested, but the
idea of Christ bearing the burden of the world's sins on his

shoulders.[13] Finally, the last two lines adapt the parable to fit the Gregorius legend, since the warrior in the vanguard of Christendom can only mean the protagonist of Hartmann's narrative, who in the end receives the call to the papal throne. Gregorius is thus deliberately identified with the man who fell among thieves and was saved by the Samaritan, that is to say the sinner steeped in sin who is redeemed by Christ despite the grievous nature of his sins.

This parallel is dealt with in the third part of this prologue section, in lines 144–70. Here Hartmann announces his intention to explain what kind of wounds had been inflicted on the man who fell among thieves, and how difficult had been his recovery. Hartmann's intention, clearly, is to illustrate the human situation implicit in the parable of the Good Samaritan by telling the story of one individual. Finally he includes once more the warning to the audience to follow the example of the reformed sinner, and not to doubt in the grace of God.

The six lines following then form a kind of colophon to mark the end of the introduction:

> Der dise rede berihte,
> in tiusche getihte,
> daz was von Ouwe Hartman.
> hie hebent sich von êrste an
> diu seltsænen mære
> von dem guoten sündære. (*Gregorius*, 171–6)

[He who fashioned this story into a German poem was Hartmann von Aue. Here begins the extraordinary tale of the good sinner.]

II

Characteristic of this prologue, as of others discussed in this book, is the fact that Hartmann is not content merely to establish contact with the audience in a general way before introducing the theme: rather, the prologue seems to offer definite guidelines for the understanding of the romance. On the one hand, this applies specifically to the idea, repeated on several occasions, that even the greatest sin may be forgiven, and on the other hand to the biblical parables of the two ways and the Good Samaritan, which seem to refer specifically to the central theme of the work. The theoretical interest must thus focus on the question of how far the specific idea of the work is represented

[13] Goebel, 'Hartmanns "Gregorius-Allegorie"', 216–17.

and discussed in the prologue, or, alternatively, whether and to what extent the considerations of the prologue fail to reflect adequately the complexity of the action itself. This complexity is at least hinted at at the end of the prologue in the reference to the extraordinary (*seltsæne*) tale and the paradox of the 'good sinner', which immediately precedes the beginning of the narrative in line 177. The deliberate emphasis placed on this paradox should not be overlooked.

How far may the tale which Hartmann intends to relate be seen as *seltsæne*?[14] The Gregorius legend is a Christian variation on the Oedipus myth which was current in various forms in the Middle Ages. The legend intensifies the sense of inexorable fate which characterizes the Greek myth by repeating the incest motif: not only does the protagonist marry his mother, but is himself the child of an incestuous union between brother and sister. This child of sin is secretly put out to sea in a casket and abandoned. It is washed ashore in the vicinity of a monastery and discovered by fishermen. The abbot adopts the child, gives him the name Gregorius and has him brought up and educated. When he is older, Gregorius discovers he is a foundling and, obeying an inner longing for a secular life of knightly glory, he decides to leave the monastery. Unable to dissuade him, the abbot finally gives him a stone tablet which had been placed in the casket with him and which, without giving his name or place of origin, explains the circumstances of his birth. Gregorius sets out, armed as a knight, and arrives at a town in which a princess is being besieged by hostile forces. He intervenes, rescues the lady, and marries her. One day the tablet, which Gregorius had kept hidden, is discovered by chance, and it is thus revealed that he has married his own mother. To absolve this sin, Gregorius is prepared to submit to the severest penance, and has himself chained to a rock in the middle of a lake by a fisherman; the key is cast into the water. Nourished miraculously by God, he lives in this way for seventeen years. When the papal throne in Rome falls vacant, a divine voice ordains that the penitent Gregorius on the rock is destined to be the new spiritual leader of Christendom. Messengers are sent out, and eventually they discover the fisherman who guides them to the man on the rock. The key to the chains is discovered in the belly of a fish, and this circumstance convinces the penitent Gregorius that his sins have been forgiven and that he may follow his calling. Thus Gregorius becomes

---

[14] On the use of the term *seltsæne* in the context of prologue topoi, see Schirmer, *Stil- und Motivuntersuchungen*, pp. 67ff.

Pope; rumours of his saintliness spread and his mother comes to beg forgiveness for her sins. When she confesses, they recognize each other, and Gregorius is able to reconcile his wife and mother with God.

The plot of the romance would thus seem to live up to Hartmann's statement that it is a powerful and awful tale, 'vil stark ze hœrenne'. Moreover, it seems to fit readily into the perspective suggested by the prologue maxim about the grace of God which grants absolution from all sin, and the parables of the parting of the ways and the Good Samaritan. However, critics have adopted widely differing positions on the relationship of prologue and narrative. Since the poet applies the situation at the crossroads to the man who fell among thieves, who is in turn identified with the protagonist, it is certainly possible to postulate a clear development from the opening maxim, by way of the parables in the prologue, through to the action of the poem, but on closer examination it proves difficult to reconcile the maxim and parables with Hartmann's narrative in any meaningful way.

Hartmann states that what matters is to turn aside from the broad and easy road which leads to hell and to follow instead the straight and narrow path which leads to eternal happiness. If this is the theme of the work one would expect the protagonist to be faced with this choice, and that despite the overwhelming burden of his sins he would follow the right path and find grace. Gregorius at the crossroads: this situation does indeed form the crux of the action. By marrying his mother, Gregorius has made himself guilty of the ultimate sin. However, he does not give way to despair, but follows the path of penitence. And it seems that along this path the images from the parable of the parting of the ways recur down to the last detail. The description given in the prologue of the narrow path which leads to heaven is reflected in the representation of the path Gregorius must follow through the wilderness to the rock in the lake.[15]

How, then, are the events in *Gregorius* linked to the situation of choice at the parting of the ways? Logically, the hero's departure from the monastery and his journey of *âventiure* would represent the easy road to hell, from which he manages to turn away despite the greatest of sins. However, Hartmann in no sense describes his hero's entry into the world as implying that he has turned to evil. On the

[15] Siefken, '*Der sælden strâze*', pp. 452–3; Picozzi, 'Allegory and symbol', pp. 21ff.

contrary, Gregorius' actions are all good: he succours a beleaguered princess and brings peace to her country. It is clear that any consistent attempt to use the two ways of the biblical parable as a guiding principle of interpretation must, inevitably, result in irreconcilable contradictions, as Gregorius' way into the world is clearly at once both right and wrong. The biblical parable thus proves too schematic to encompass adequately the different levels of the action.

What of the other parable of the Good Samaritan? Hartmann adapted the allegorical interpretation of the parable from Luke 10 in order that it might apply to his protagonist. Just as in the parable the robbers ambush the man, that is tempt him into sin, so Gregorius is tempted by the devil into the trap of incest. The Samaritan, i.e. Christ, saves the man who has fallen; he brings him home, i.e. admits him to heaven; likewise, the grace of God saves the sinner Gregorius, so that finally, without any visible signs of his wounds – that is, his sins – he may become the leader of Christendom.

Hartmann's conclusion to the story of the Good Samaritan falls outside the scheme of the biblical parable, since it only makes sense with respect to the particular fate of Hartmann's protagonist.

Seen in the light of the parable of the Good Samaritan and its allegorical exegesis, *Gregorius* appears as a variation of the myth of the Fall and subsequent salvation – a version which, with its dual incest and seventeen years' penance on the rock, transforms the simple biblical myth into something terrible, indeed grotesque, re-inforced with a moral and didactic purpose, in that it takes the form of an exhortation not to despair of God's saving grace, even under the burden of the greatest of sins.

However, this approach too leads to contradictions, since if Gregorius could be fully identified with the man who fell among thieves, then he would be like Adam, the first man, who sinned against God, was punished, and had to be redeemed. Yet in what does Gregorius' guilt consist? Great efforts have been made to determine the extent to which Gregorius can be held responsible for his sins in terms of medieval moral theology, yet neither his parents' incest, nor his leaving the monastery, nor his marriage to his mother can be levelled against him as a deliberate and knowing transgression.[16] This,

---

[16] Cormeau, *Hartmann von Aue*, pp. 97ff.; Ohly, *Der Verfluchte und der Erwählte*, p. 10; on the history of this controversy in the secondary literature, see Gössmann, 'Typus der Heilsgeschichte'.

then, undermines the neat parallel between the allegorical use of the Good Samaritan parable and Hartmann's *Gregorius*.

III

If all such attempts to establish a precise correspondence between the two parables of the parting of the ways and the Good Samaritan with the events of the poem seem doomed to failure, this would suggest that they are not after all intended – as has often been thought – as models for understanding the work, but have a different function. Bearing in mind the prologue to *Iwein*, it is tempting to conjecture that here, too, what is envisaged is a discussion of the literary form, with the two parables representing the exemplum type. *Gregorius* too is presented as an exemplary, moral, tale, and it is precisely the use of the parables which seems to suggest an interpretation on this basis. However, to assume a simple exemplum-type structure does not provide an adequate basis for interpreting Hartmann's poem. One may therefore surmise that this juxtaposition might be a deliberate strategy on the part of the author, with the express intention of confronting the exemplum type with that of the romance, and so involving a discussion here, too, of the specific mode of reception appropriate to the genre.

The Gregorius story also exists in the form of a simple hagiographical exemplum, taking up only a few pages in the *Gesta Romanorum*. This provides a splendid illustration of the differences between the genres of simple hagiographical legend on the one hand, and romance on the other; there is no need to examine the literary-historical relationship and influences between the two here, as it is not particularly relevant whether an early version of the *Gesta Romanorum* legend formed the basis of Hartmann's source, or whether the more elaborate Gregorius 'romance' was subsequently reduced to a simple hagiographical legend: this does not affect the rules governing the different literary forms, which are equally applicable in either case.

Disregarding the greater scope of Hartmann's work, a number of differences between the legend of Gregorius in the *Gesta Romanorum* and Hartmann's *Gregorius* may be distinguished:[17]

1. In the *Gesta Romanorum*, brother and sister confess their incest

---

[17] Haubrichs, 'Einleitung: Für ein Zwei-Phasen-Modell', pp. 13ff.

and are reconciled with God. This absolution motif is missing in Hartmann's version.

2. When Gregorius learns the truth about his origins in the *Gesta Romanorum*, he seeks to atone for his parents' sin and decides to go to the Holy Land as a crusader. On the way, however, he is diverted to the town where his mother lives. Hartmann's version omits the motif of the penitential journey; instead, Gregorius leaves the monastery in search of knightly *âventiure*.

3. Gregorius fights his mother's enemy. In the *Gesta Romanorum* he defeats him and puts him to death, whereas in Hartmann's version a reconciliation is effected.

4. When the mother–son incest is discovered, in the *Gesta Romanorum* Gregorius immediately takes the blame upon himself and decides to do penance. In Hartmann's version, however, in his indignation Gregorius is tempted for a moment to defy God, but overcomes this impulse and succeeds in accepting his guilt.

5. At the end of the *Gesta Romanorum* version, Gregorius has an abbey built for his mother, who becomes the abbess; soon, however, they both die and achieve eternal salvation. In Hartmann's version, Gregorius continues to lead an active life as Pope for some time.

Regardless of whether these variants are deviations in Hartmann's poem from the original hagiographical legend, or changes in the latter which took place when Hartmann's text came to be reduced to an exemplum, in either case there is a definite pattern to them. When, in the *Gesta Romanorum*, Gregorius sets out to do penance for the sins of his parents, despite having received absolution for the guilt of incest, the coincidence which leads to the second act of incest is all the more cruel, in that the evil trap is set for a man who was prepared to do penance for a sin which had already been forgiven. By contrast, Hartmann's version on the one hand avoids all mention of forgiveness of the first incest, and on the other still has the protagonist take no action over the sin of his parents, other than weeping daily for their sins. Instead, he decides to lead a normal life in keeping with his knightly status. In place of the crusade – which the protagonist of the version in the *Gesta Romanorum* never in fact joins – Hartmann's Gregorius follows an exemplary knightly path into the world, commending himself to God's guidance so that he allows his ship's course to be determined by the wind. This last motif is, in fact, an invention of Hartmann's which is not found in the French source. Gregorius helps a beleaguered princess and achieves peace: instead of killing his opponent in the battle, Hartmann's hero reconciles him with his (i.e. Gregorius') mother.

The crude coincidences of the hagiographical legend must be taken at face value, since this literary form precludes all possibilities of reflection. By elaborating the theme into a romance according to the *âventiure* pattern, Hartmann prepares the ground for the second incest by presenting the protagonist's adventures as a knight, even though this chivalric lifestyle is deliberately shown from a positive viewpoint. Accordingly, and in contrast to the hagiographical legend, the hero's decision to accept his guilt is not presented as unproblematic: Hartmann's Gregorius at first flares up in indignation, only commending himself to God's mercy when he sees the despair of his wife-and-mother.

The *Gesta Romanorum* version thus displays a relentless alternation of guilt and penitence, sin and grace, demonstrating exemplary behaviour with no concessions to psychology. The situations presented are so extreme as to appear almost grotesque if taken at face value rather than seen as paradigms or models. Hartmann, however, goes out of his way to avoid such a mechanistic technique, replacing the sudden *volte-face* with the idea that innocent and guilty are equally at risk when it comes to sin.[18] This change of perspective then corresponds to the altered ending. In the exemplum, the earthly goal was fulfilled with Gregorius' calling to the papal throne and the reconciliation of his mother with God; the protagonists are then allowed to die and go to heaven. Hartmann's Gregorius, however, finds a new mission: as Pope, he is able to realize what he has achieved both in the world and for the sake of the world.

Unlike the hagiographical exemplum, then, Hartmann's *Gregorius* is not concerned to demonstrate a straightforward mechanistic sequence of 'sin–penitence–grace', but rather to show the effect of the experience of guilt along a way which the hero believes to be right and good, and the dangers or temptations into which this belief leads him: the temptation to rebel against a fate which overtakes him in spite of his good intentions.

The straightforward *sententia* of the prologue – that one should not despair of God's grace even when guilty of the greatest sin – cannot adequately express the complexity of this state of affairs. However, it

[18] Hartmann also reflects on the hagiographical type, but using other means, in *Der arme Heinrich*; cf. Haug, 'Poetologische Universalien', pp. 292ff.: also in Haug, *Strukturen*, pp. 16ff.

does overlap neatly with the sense offered by the straightforward hagiographical exemplum. Is the prologue then to be understood as offering a brief preview of the work, a simplified approach analogous to Hartmann's commentary technique, which similarly fails to deal adequately with the problems raised in the *narratio*? The key to this question lies in the position and function of the parables in linking the action of what is essentially a romance with the moralizing maxim which precedes it.

It should be noted that Hartmann makes an unusual connection between the parable of the Good Samaritan and that of the parting of the ways. After describing the narrow path which leads to paradise, he says that the man who fell among thieves in the parable of the Good Samaritan also finally attained this path. Clearly, in an objective and topographical sense there can be no such parting of the ways at the scene of the ambush, that is to say the image of the two ways is only included in the parable of the Good Samaritan in a metaphorical sense. From the turning point in the objective course of salvation history, conjured up by the parable of the Good Samaritan, Hartmann has thus derived a new kind of choice which Gregorius must confront. Gregorius is no longer in the position of Adam, who still had a genuine free choice between the right and the wrong way; after the Fall he is of necessity already following the way of sin. He is an innocent sinner; as a human being he cannot avoid original sin. However, this essentially different situation presents a new possibility, dictating a conscious choice between accepting one's guilt and trusting in grace, or rebellion and despair. In assimilating the motif of the parting of the ways into the Samaritan parable, Hartmann gives expression to the possibility of this new, positive choice: the allegory of salvation history is thus adapted in such a way as to apply to humanity after the Fall and after Christ's act of redemption. As already indicated in the prologue, what matters is not the guilt or innocence of the protagonist, but the consequences arising from the inevitable experience of sin.

This shift in emphasis, away from the usual configuration of salvation history – the traditional sense of the allegorical interpretation of the parable of the Good Samaritan – to the new situation of humanity after Christ, is also responsible for certain details in Hartmann's exegesis of the parable which depart from the traditional interpretation. The man on the road to Jericho is stripped of his clothes by the robbers: this is conventionally interpreted as an allegory of humanity's loss of innocence and immortality at the Fall. In Hartmann's version, however, the man who fell among thieves is robbed of 'the clothes of his senses'. This is usually understood as 'he fainted' or 'he lost consciousness': however, that would mean Hartmann had failed to include this statement in his allegorical interpretation. This reading is all the more unsatisfactory in that, in the traditional allegorical interpretation of the parable – e.g. in Bede – it is asserted that at the Fall humanity did not at all take leave of its senses, or more exactly of the *sensus rationalis*.[19] It is scarcely possible to interpret 'der sinne kleit' without taking this particular traditional view into account. The following interpretation might offer a solution: the loss of the *sinne* ('senses') does not refer to a loss of reason, but to the impossibility of understanding what has taken place. Gregorius believes he has followed the right path, yet he has entered into a state of sin. He is faced with the paradox of innocent guilt, which he is unable to solve by reason alone. In this situation he has to rely on God for assistance; God gives him new clothes. In Hartmann's version, however, these are not the traditional clothes of immortality and innocence, which are restored, according to the allegorical interpretation, to the man who fell among thieves, but rather fear and hope. The lost *sinne* are thus replaced by emotions; the fear of dying of the wounds incurred, in other words of being condemned to hell as a punishment for sin, and the hope of being cured, in other words of achieving forgiveness through God's grace.[20] Traditionally, fear and hope were signified by oil and wine. Hartmann however uses a different interpretation from that of Bede, providing a striking parallel to the tension between fear and hope: for Hartmann, oil and wine represent grace and the Law.[21] It should be noted that he also omits the figures of the priest and the Levite, which the conventional allegorical interpretation had used to establish a connection with the Old Testament Law and Prophets respectively. The reasons for this omission are clear: it was Hartmann's intention to disrupt the linear continuity of the *Heilsgeschichte*, since he was

[19] PL 92, col. 469A, 94, col. 294D. Bennholdt-Thomsen, 'Die allegorischen *kleit*', pp. 206–7, simplifies matters by reading 'der sinne kleit' as an objective genitive: the senses are thus only robbed of their clothing, which could then, in keeping with the tradition, be *immortalitas* and *innocentia*. On this point, see Goebel, 'Hartmanns "*Gregorius*-Allegorie"', 218–19.

[20] The interpretations by Goebel, 'Hartmanns "*Gregorius*-Allegorie"', 221ff., and Mertens, *Gregorius eremita*, pp. 168ff., follow a similar line.

[21] This is not a new interpretation: it occurs in Origen. Cf. Monselewski, *Der barmherzige Samariter*, p. 39. The whole exegetical tradition is documented in Spitz, 'Zwischen Furcht und Hoffnung', pp. 181ff.

concerned not with a universal process following the sequence paradise – Fall – Age of Law – Age of grace, but with the conflict between good intentions and the basic sinfulness of humanity, the very paradox alluded to in the 'title': 'diu mære von dem guoten sündære'. The good sinner stands for the human race, caught betwen hope and fear, between the Law and grace. This contradiction cannot be apprehended by means of reason – that is, by the *sinne*: in order to do so, anyone attempting to weigh up the relative measure of guilt or innocence must pass through indignation and rebellion and run the risk of *desperatio*, the abyss on the brink of which Hartmann's Gregorius also momentarily teeters. The only way out of this paradox lies in absolute faith in God's grace. This is the new choice with which humanity is faced after Christ's act of redemption.

It follows from this that the parables of the Gregorius prologue have the function of challenging the moral thesis which is Hartmann's starting point and which would lead the audience to expect an exemplum, and that they thus serve to reveal the inherently problematic nature of the work. The literary form of the simple hagiographical legend is rejected in favour of a 'romance' whose plot is not wholly contained within the simplistic mechanism of sin–penance–grace. The problem here is the paradox of innocent sin: it is precisely the 'right' path, as far as human powers may judge, which leads to the crisis.

The source for this idea is unmistakable: Gregorius' journey of *âventiure* follows the Arthurian model, with the hero setting out, freeing a beleaguered princess, marrying her, facing a crisis and setting out afresh – but with the second cycle suitably adapted to fit the religious theme.[22] This borrowing or copying of a scheme from Arthurian romance implies a similar level of awareness of, and reflection on, the subject matter when the scheme is applied to the representation and interpretation of religious experience. As in the analogous secular process in the courtly romance, the reconciliation comes about not through good deeds or actions but from the recognition of one's own limitations and of human inadequacy. In religious terms, this means admitting and accepting the human need for redemption. The crux of the work is the moment at which

---

[22] Haug, 'Die Symbolstruktur des höfischen Epos', 675–6: also in Haug, *Strukturen*, pp. 489–90; Hirschberg, 'Zur Struktur von Hartmann's *Gregorius*'; on the relationship of romance heroes to the protagonists of hagiographical literature, see Wehrli, 'Roman und Legende', pp. 164ff.

Gregorius flares up and begins to argue with God.[23] The turning point is Gregorius' sudden realization that this weighing up of relative good and evil can lead nowhere, and that he must instead accept the paradox of innocent sin and see in it a symbol of human frailty *per se*. This frailty is described in a mythological sense as original sin, inherited from one's forebears via the Fall. There is a reminder of this in the allegorical exegesis of the parable of the Good Samaritan, and the incest between brother and sister which precedes the main action echoes this theme of original sin within the framework of the narrative. By accepting one's own guilt and God's grace, it then becomes possible to imitate Christ by helping one's fellow humans: this is the sense in which Gregorius' return to the world is to be understood.

On the other hand, as Friedrich Ohly has rightly pointed out,[24] the full horror of the seventeen years of isolation on the rock in the lake should also be appreciated, and not just taken as a reflection on the symbolic significance of the number 17 – the number which represents the sum of the Old and New Testaments, Law and grace[25] – but as a symbol of the terrible isolation of humanity in a world where there is no perceptible order, in which all connection between things has been severed and all human relations broken off, so that the isolated individual is left facing the inhuman images of the absolute: heaven, hell, nature, the sacred, madness, and death.

Thomas Mann was chiefly interested in the grotesque aspect of Gregorius' terrible fate, and the laughter of hell is a perfectly

---

[23] The motif of rebellion does not occur in the French original. In the version B₁ admittedly there is the statement 'Mult es dolent e irascuz' ('he is extremely sad and enraged': 1517), but the hero's fury here is directed at the devil for deceiving him in this underhand manner. In his review 'Entdeckung der Fiktionalität', pp. 67–8, Heinzle takes issue with my interpretation on the grounds that it is not borne out by line 2608: 'sînen zorn huop er hin ze gote' ('he raised his voice in anger against God'), since, he claims, one is entitled to expect Hartmann to have presented the crisis sufficiently clearly (p. 68). Moreover, according to Wapnewski, *Wolframs Parzival*, p. 18, the line in question could be understood as 'he revealed the torments of his soul to God'. This translation does not seem convincing. The parallel passage cited from *Iwein* (1380) also seems to me to refer to anger rather than anguish or inner torment. As far as the clarity of Hartmann's presentation is concerned, line 2068 does not stand alone: rather it is followed by fourteen lines in which God is reproached for fulfilling Gregorius' prayer to lead him to his mother in a such way that it would have been better left unanswered. In other words, Gregorius is accusing God of having wilfully misled him, indeed of having made a mockery of his prayers. In any case the passage implies a loss of faith in God, exposing the protagonist to precisely those dangers of absolute despair mentioned in the prologue.

[24] Ohly, *Der Verfluchte und der Erwählte*.

[25] Schwab, *Lex et gratia*, pp. 22ff.; Ohly, *Der Verfluchte und der Erwählte*, p. 17, takes a different view.

legitimate standpoint, and is, no doubt, that from which he presented his Gregorius puppet show in *Doktor Faustus*. In *Der Erwählte* ('The Holy Sinner'), the material is given a systematically ironic treatment, whereby surface events are thrown into relief by relating them to those of myth:[26] Gregorius shrinks while on the rock to a small hedgehog-like creature; he returns as it were to the womb of nature in order to be reborn. Thus the position of the individual within the symbolic and mythical whole is re-established. The price paid for this by a modern author is precisely what gave rise to the medieval *Gregorius* romance, namely the insight that humanity is at the mercy of discontinuity and chaos, the collapse of order. Through this 're-mythologizing', the modern version avoids confronting the unendurable dimension of the Christian paradox.

However, the unendurable paradox manifested in Hartmann's *Gregorius* was felt long before the modern age; the earliest available evidence testifies to the difficulties which Hartmann's work presented. Around 1210, that is to say ten or fifteen years after *Gregorius* was written, a certain Arnold, from Lübeck (Mann's birthplace), translated the work into Latin. As an educated cleric he shows little respect for Hartmann's poetic achievement, claiming that he is not used to reading this kind of thing, by which he means such vernacular nonsense. Nor is he aiming at literal accuracy in his translation; rather he is concerned to reproduce the meaning. He does not even mention Hartmann by name.

It is illuminating to note the alterations Arnold von Lübeck made to the original.[27] The combination of parables in the prologue seems to have caused him problems from the outset; at any rate he omits the parable of the parting of the ways. At the same time he returns to traditional exegesis in his interpretation of the Good Samaritan parable: the clothes of which the man is robbed once again represent lost immortality, and the problematic dimension of the concept of guilt, introduced by Hartmann in his adaptation of the parable, and his allegorical interpretation of it are thus deliberately overlooked. It is logical enough, then, that Arnold should also omit Gregorius' initial defiance on discovering his unwitting incest. In true exemplum fashion, in Arnold von Lübeck's version Gregorius unhesitatingly chooses the right path, without so much as a moment's anger or

---

[26] Hugo Kuhn, 'der gute sünder – der erwählte?'; Stackmann, 'Der Erwählte'; Wolf, *Gregorius*; Ohly, *Der Verfluchte und der Erwählte*, pp. 126ff.

[27] Cf. Ganz, 'Dienstmann und Abt'.

despair; he is at once ready to do penance and to surrender himself to the grace of God.

These changes affect the very core of Hartmann's narrative structure, reducing the Gregorius story once again to the level of a hagiographical exemplum. The new degree of complexity and self-consciousness which vernacular literature had achieved is abandoned in favour of the rigid framework of the Latin scholastic tradition.

However, this reductive reception gives a very clear indication of what Hartmann had achieved in his prologue. The latter at first seems to promise a kind of exemplum, but by using exempla in the form of parables in his argument, Hartmann implicitly takes issue with the schematic aspects of this literary form. The transparent didacticism of the exemplum is replaced by the unfathomable depths of Hartmann's narrative, just as clear explanations give way to the unveiling of areas of experience inaccessible to human reason. The work aims to represent an experience which no order can accommodate: linear continuity breaks down in the conflict between Law and grace, fear and hope, and in the gulf between terror and faith. Hartmann intertwines the exemplary images and parables to such an extent that his introduction becomes a veritable Chinese puzzle, the aim of which is to draw attention to the complexity and range of problems which the audience will encounter in *Gregorius*.

9

Wolfram von Eschenbach's literary theory: the prologue to *Parzival*, the metaphor of the bow, and the 'self-defence'

I

Hartmann's Gregorius romance strives to achieve a consistent literary representation of religious experience which at the same time takes advantage of the possibilities afforded by the Arthurian structural model. Unlike the plots of Arthurian romances, the plot of *Gregorius* was already a well-established legend; it was now however re-interpreted in the light of Chrétien's model. Religious guilt could thus be understood in a new dimension by making use of the Arthurian pattern with its 'crisis'. Both Chrétien and Wolfram were essentially attempting something similar in the Grail romance, but instead of basing their romances on a hagiographical legend, they made use of Arthurian material. This means that, rather than the Arthurian scheme being employed for a religious subject, here – in *Perceval/Parzival* – the Arthurian structure instead acquires an additional religious dimension: the hero's personal – though profane – crisis is given religious motivation, so that the second cycle of the plot may be used to represent the protagonist's conflict with God – thus again leading, though by the opposite route, to the position of Hartmann's *Gregorius*. While the basic outline of the Arthurian model is preserved in this adaptation of it, the differences are so profound as to raise the question of whether the whole structure is not distorted beyond all recognition in the process.

The hero of the romance – called Perceval in Chrétien's version, Parzival in Wolfram's – follows the double cycle prescribed in the Arthurian model.[1] Accordingly, he sets out from Arthur's court to do battle with a challenger who has insulted the court. However, Perceval/Parzival is no knight of the Round Table, but an unschooled

[1] Haug, 'Symbolstruktur', 678ff.; also in Haug, *Strukturen*, pp. 490ff.

youth who, although of knightly descent, has grown up in the wilderness remote from contact with the Arthurian world, his mother having withdrawn from society after the death of her husband. Perceval/Parzival appears at Arthur's court and then, with the reluctant approval of the king, goes out to meet the Red Knight, the issuer of the challenge, asks for his armour, is attacked, and kills him.

This represents the opening of the first cycle of the Arthurian model, in the course of which the hero – still conforming to the familiar pattern – wins a wife, after receiving a belated knightly education at the court of Gornemans/Gurnemanz. The cycle ends with Perceval/Parzival's return to Arthur's court, where he is fêted and accepted as a member of the Round Table.

The episodes in Parzival's progress from wilderness to court are reflected in a parallel set of episodes in the sequence of *âventiure* (reminiscent of the corresponding structure in *Erec*) which ultimately leads him back to the Arthurian court. After leaving the woods the artless youth brings ruin upon Jeschute, Cunneware and Antanor respectively (thus their names in Wolfram's version), but Parzival makes amends – in part intentionally and in part by chance – for the havoc he has wrought there on his return from his first journey of *âventiure*. However, whereas in *Erec* the parallel episodes characterized the second cycle, and served to reveal the vulnerable side of an otherwise dynamic hero – showing the victor as vanquished – the corresponding episodes of the Grail romance portray quite another kind of experience. Parzival moves in a world in which wrongs can be put right; the world of chivalry is thus represented as a reality in which mistakes can be rectified. For this reason it is not the negative, anti-court realm in which the factors which give rise to the crisis originate. It is significant that the hero does not bring the wife he has won to Arthur's court, but leaves her behind in her home town, so that here too there is no question of the crisis being triggered by the hero's failure to reconcile the respective claims of his relationship with the beloved and society. In the Grail romance, the roots of the crisis are rather to be found in an incongruous episode which is completely at odds with the sequence of adventures: on the way back to Arthur's court the hero suddenly happens upon the Grail castle; there he sees the ailing king, but fails to ask the question which could have relieved his suffering. This omission cannot, however, be made good in the same way as the other misdeeds of the callow youth Parzival; on the contrary, the hero is unable to deal with it effectively

154

and so carries this burden with him until it eventually becomes the stumbling block which initiates the crisis. This latter also follows the standard Arthurian pattern, at least superficially: in Chrétien's version, Perceval, now a fully fledged knight, again comes across the Arthurian court and is led by Gavain to the king and queen; together they go to Carlion, where the festivities which mark the end of the cycle take place. However, three days later the Grail messenger arrives and curses the hero for his failure to relieve the king of his suffering at the Grail castle. In the hope of expiating his guilt, Perceval sets out once more in search of the Grail castle.

Wolfram's version accentuates the crisis by placing it in a particular context, which gives a new angle to the problems involved.[2] When Parzival, as in Chrétien's version already an accomplished courtier, is received by Arthur and the queen, in contrast to the *Conte du Graal*, grief is mingled with the joy of the Arthurian festival, for Parzival's arrival reminds them of the death of the Red Knight, whose armour he wears. In Chrétien's version, the Red Knight had played the traditional role of the challenger; in killing him, and avenging the insult which the court had received at his hands, the young Perceval was thus conforming to the Arthurian scheme. His deed was one isolated incident, without any further consequences. Wolfram, on the other hand, makes the Red Knight a relative of the king and of Parzival. The killing of the challenger, which hitherto had merely been one incident within the Arthurian framework, becomes problematic the moment it involves the murder of a kinsman, since then the matter cannot be allowed to rest; indeed, Wolfram will ultimately establish an inner connection – puzzling at first – between this deed and Parzival's failure to ask the appropriate question at the Grail castle.

An episode which had derived its significance from its position in the narrative and from its structural function within the Arthurian scheme thus here becomes a motif that has lasting influence on the action, and so Chrétien's strict correspondence between structure and meaning, based on a series of episodes, comes into conflict with a different, more linear narrative principle at a critical juncture. The first cycle of action thus no longer achieves a completely harmonious conclusion on the courtly level; if the praise of Parzival on his acceptance as a member of the Round Table seemed distinctly

---

[2] Ibid., 692ff.; also in Haug, *Strukturen*, pp. 502ff.

exaggerated, this only makes the entrance of the Grail messenger appear all the more striking, as she reveals to this perfect gentle knight his total depravity and calls him a disgrace to the Round Table. Parzival has, it is true, attained the status of an Arthurian knight, the ideal for which he set out and for which he was destined; his exceptional beauty was understood wherever he appeared as a sign of this destiny.[3] Now, however, the Grail messenger is able to say that despite his beauty he is *ungehiurer* ('more monstrous') than she in her own frightful ugliness. He has mistaken the goal for which he was destined, or only half understood it: in *Parzival*, the splendour of the hero's appearance ultimately points to a dimension beyond the Arthurian world of knightly deeds. The crisis does not arise out of the precarious balance of individual and social claims, but from the breakthrough to this new dimension. The ambivalence of beauty and ugliness, taken over from Christian aesthetics, is used to signal this new perspective.[4]

This alters the basis from which the action of the second cycle starts: Parzival leaves Arthur's court in rebellious mood. Unable to acknowledge his culpable omission at the Grail castle as guilt, he perceives himself as betrayed by God and sees himself as justified in renouncing his own obligations, his *triuwe*, in return. In this state he journeys around for years without finding his way back to the Grail castle. For the audience, these aimless wanderings remain for the most part hidden from view. Gawan takes over from Parzival as the main protagonist, and his courtly *âventiure* conceal the exploits of the hero, at any rate until the turning point in the action when, on Good Friday, Parzival happens upon Trevrizent in his hermit's cell. Here the despairing knight of the Round Table learns to appreciate his guilt in the context of *Heilsgeschichte* and original sin. Only after further dangers in combat with his relations Gawan and Feirefiz, however, is he able to realize the extent of his own helplessness which will prepare him to receive God's grace. Now he is able to find his way back to the Grail castle again and ask the redeeming question, in order finally to be summoned as Grail king.[5]

The use of the Arthurian model to represent religious experience, and the restructuring of it which this implies, means that the Grail

---

[3] For collected references, see Johnson, 'Parzival's beauty'; cf. also Hahn, 'Parzivals Schönheit'.

[4] Knapp, 'Gralsbotin'; Haug, 'Transzendenz und Utopie', pp. 14–15; also in Haug, *Strukturen*, p. 522.

[5] See the recent articles by Haug, '*Conte du Graal*' and 'Parzival ohne Illusionen'.

romance faces similar difficulties to those encountered in the Gregorius story: a courtly journey of *âventiure*, in itself positive, involves the hero in innocent guilt. The ensuing crisis leads the hero, who is unable to grasp what has happened, to defy God. In both works the portrayal of the hero's rehabilitation, involving a change in the way in which the world is experienced, presents difficulties: the second cycle, in the Grail romance as in *Gregorius*, contains almost no narrative action. The main difference between the two works, as far as the crisis and turning point are concerned, lies in the fact that Gregorius rebels against God only for a moment, so that the second cycle relates a long period of penitence, while in the Grail romance the crisis initially alienates the hero from God, so that the moment of insight which leads to repentance and atonement only comes about much later, flaring up for a brief instant amid the dark wanderings of the second cycle.

II

Wolfram was aware of the problematic issues raised by his undertaking, and, unless we are much mistaken, of how it differed from *Gregorius*. The theoretical considerations of the *Parzival* prologue are devoted in large measure to defining his own position *vis à vis* his predecessor.[6]

This prologue is a free invention on Wolfram's part. There is scarcely anything in Chrétien's introduction to the *Conte du Graal* which Wolfram might have imitated, since it is almost completely taken up by an encomium of Chrétien's patron, Philip of Flanders, who gave him the *livre* containing the Grail material.

Wolfram begins his prologue in the traditional manner with a *sententia*:

> Ist zwîvel herzen nâchgebûr,
> daz muoz der sêle werden sûr. (*Parzival*, 1,1–2)
>
> [If despair takes up residence in the heart the soul will come to a bitter end.]

The term *zwîvel* conveys a wide range of meanings, from religious *desperatio* to mere uncertainty. The decision to translate *zwîvel* as

---

6 For bibliography, see Pretzel and Bachofer, *Bibliographie zu Wolfram von Eschenbach*, pp. 81ff.; cf. Bumke, *Wolfram-Forschung*, pp. 275ff. Rupp, 'Wolframs *Parzival*-Prolog', and Haug, 'Die Symbolstruktur des höfischen Epos', 699ff. (also in Haug, *Strukturen*, pp. 508ff.), build on the fundamental study by Lachmann, *Über den Eingang des 'Parzivals'*; more recently, see Brall, '*Diz vliegende bispel*'.

'despair' (cf. modern German *Verzweiflung*) here is in accordance with the strategy which may be seen as typical of prologues to the courtly romances: the poet chooses an opening maxim which will be found generally acceptable so as to be able to build up his argument on the basis of this common understanding. If *zwîvel* in line 1,1 has often been accorded a weaker rendering, e.g. 'inconstancy' – as for example in 'That man who lacks constancy endangers his immortal soul', this is in order that these opening lines may be applied to Parzival, since he is characterized precisely as inconstant and in danger of forfeiting his immortal soul, although he is saved in the end. However, to have the first lines of a prologue refer so specifically to the theme of the work would run counter to conventional exordial techniques.[7] It is more likely that the poet is initially concerned with establishing the position of his work within the literary tradition. It seems safe to suggest – as Hermann Schneider argues[8] – that the reference to the dangers of *zwîvel* is a conscious allusion to the corresponding argument in Hartmann's *Gregorius*. The audience would no doubt have understood Wolfram's opening *sententia* as a quotation from Hartmann and thus as Wolfram's re-stating of the position of his predecessor. However, contrary to the usual strategy of presenting a universally acceptable *sententia*, Wolfram immediately counters Hartmann's thesis with criticism:

> gesmæhet unde gezieret
> ist, swâ sich parrieret
> unverzaget mannes muot,
> als agelstern varwe tuot. (*Parzival*, 1,3–6)

[Shame and honour mingle where fearless courage is two-toned like a magpie.]

This is unquestionably an attack on *Gregorius*: Wolfram is saying that there is an argument – put forward, as is well known, by Hartmann – that whoever despairs will go to hell. This, however, has to be set against the fact that the world consists not only of people who are wholly good or wholly bad, but also of those in whom good and evil are combined. Of these piebald people, he says:

---

[7] Adolf, 'Wolframs *zwîvel*'; Brinkmann, 'Prolog im Mittelalter', pp. 80, 90ff; Bumke, *Wolfram-Forschung*, pp. 99ff. The opposite view is put forward by Rupp, 'Wolframs *Parzival*-Prolog', pp. 373–4, 376–7; he would like the range of meanings at least to be left open. The fundamental problem has already been touched on in chapter 1.

[8] Schneider, *'Parzival'-Studien*, pp. 11ff.; this has been forcefully restated by Brall, *'Diz vliegende bispel'*, 5ff.

der mac dennoch wesen geil:
wand an im sint beidiu teil,
des himels und der helle.
der unstæte geselle
hât die swarzen varwe gar,
und wirt och nâch der vinster var:
sô habet sich an die blanken
der mit stæten gedanken. (*Parzival*, 1,7–14)

[Such a man may yet have cause to be glad, for both Heaven and
Hell are represented in him. Inconstancy's companion is all black
and will take on the colour of darkness, whereas the man of steadfast
thoughts keeps to the colour white.]

Wolfram thus accuses Hartmann of only distinguishing between
good and bad people in a simplistic, black and white manner.
However, humanity consists not only of those who are damned on
account of their absolute *zwîvel* and others who will be saved because
of their unerring *stæte* ('constancy'): a third type must be taken into
consideration, namely those in whom good and evil co-exist at one
and the same time. Wolfram is of course saying that it is precisely this
third type which is characteristic of humanity in general. Only in this
oblique manner does he prepare his audience for the fact that the hero
of his romance will not arrive at an unambiguous decision, such as
that to which Gregorius manages to win through, but must instead
follow a path on which he will waver for a long time between good
and evil.

If it is correct to assume that Wolfram's opening maxim alludes to
the thesis from *Gregorius* of the dangers of *zwîvel*, then the traditional establishment of a relationship with the audience is here
effected by means of reference to a predecessor; in other words, by
engaging with the literary tradition. Regardless of whether or not his
criticism does justice to his predecessor, Wolfram may be seen as
stating his own theoretical position by distancing himself from the
Hartmann passage he has cited.[9] His plea for a black *and* white hero
ultimately challenges the traditional form of the crisis and the way it
is portrayed, since it is here that the co-existence of good and evil can
most clearly be demonstrated. According to Wolfram, then, a correct
interpretation of this duality is essential for a proper understanding of

---

[9] Whether – and if so, to what extent – the prologue reflects a discussion with Gottfried von
Strassburg is a matter for debate. Like Rupp, 'Wolframs *Parzival*-Prolog', pp. 370ff., I am
inclined to treat this question with caution; see however note 27 below.

the new type of romance, in order to avoid the reduction of the crisis to a straightforward and unproblematic turning point. However, this is not without its difficulties:

> diz vliegende bîspel
> ist tumben liuten gar ze snel,
> sine mugens niht erdenken:
> wand ez kan vor in wenken
> rehte alsam ein schellec hase.
> zin anderhalb ame glase
> gelîchet,[10] und des blinden troum.
> die gebent antlützes roum,
> doch mac mit stæte niht gesîn
> dirre trüebe lîhte schîn:
> er machet kurze fröude alwâr. (*Parzival*, 1,15–25)

[This winged comparison flies too fast for dullards. They cannot grasp it, for it will dart away from them like a startled hare. Glass backed with tin (= a mirror) pleases, as does the blind man's dream. They both show the surface image of a face, and yet this dull insubstantial semblance cannot last: in truth it grants short-lived pleasure.]

Wolfram's starting point for his argument seems clear enough, but what follows is less obvious and has given rise to a long-standing debate among scholars. Recently Bernd Schirok has suggested an interpretation which seems to offer the clearest explanation yet of Wolfram's argument.[11]

Wolfram suggests initially that his *vliegende bîspel* of the black and white magpie will be incomprehensible for *tumbe liute* ('dullards'). In other words, a hero who is both good and bad at the same time is as hard to follow as the twists and turns of a March hare. His audience is obviously not accustomed to this kind of hero and is no match, it is implied, for the demands such a protagonist makes, since it means admitting that there is no clear distinction between good and evil, that what is perceived as good may unexpectedly turn out to be evil or lead to evil; seen in terms of narrative technique, this means that Wolfram will continually present the action from a surprising new angle.

---

[10] The reading offered in Lachmann's edition, *geleichet* ('deceives'), which I adopted in the first edition of this book, is not attested in any of the manuscripts.

[11] See Schirok, 'Zu Lachmanns Konjektur *geleichet*'.

Instead of setting this out explicitly, in a clear argument, however, Wolfram introduces new images: the reflection in a mirror, and the dream of a blind man; they have in common that they are mere fleeting illusions, quickly dispelled. Should these insubstantial images then be seen as variants on the elusive hare? How one answers this question depends in no small degree on the interpretation of *gelîchet* in line 1,21. If one rejects Lachmann's conjectured reading, *geleichet* ('deceives'), three possible interpretations present themselves: 1. 'to resemble' (modern German *gleichen*); 2. 'to smooth out flat'; 3. 'to please'. Of these, the second reading has met with most approval: 'tin, smoothed onto the back of glass' as a circumlocution for mirror. The variation on this in *Der jüngere Titurel*, a 'glas mit zinn vergozzen' ('glass plated with tin': 51,1) would seem to support this. If *gelîchet* is taken to mean 'resemble' (modern German *gleicht*), *zin* (20) and *troum* (21) would have to be in the dative case, with *diz vliegende bîspel* still the subject: the metaphorical example (*bîspel*) of the hare resembles a mirror, or a blind man's dream, but both are mere images, quickly dispelled. The difficulty with both these solutions is that they fail to explain the precise connection of the hare metaphor with the mirror or dream image. As Schirok has noted, it is not a mere variation on one and the same idea, since failing to keep up with the twists and turns of the fleeing hare is quite a different matter from allowing oneself to be taken in by a false and fleeting image.[12] Schirok therefore suggests that *gelîchet* be interpreted as 'pleases'.[13] In this way, both the following images can be understood as substantiating the hare metaphor: the 'dullards' are unable to follow the twists and turns of the hare – in other words the new kind of hero – because they have previously derived pleasure from insubstantial images, that is to say a kind of literature far removed from reality and thus illusory and misleading. This reading would take up the possible literary allusion in the opening sentence, with its mention of *zwîvel* ('doubt', 'despair': 1,1) – a critical reference to a simple, readily assimilated poetic world in which the distinction between good and evil is clear-cut.

Wolfram is well aware that he will be criticized for such a demanding and sophisticated technique. Indeed, he has often been reproached for his refusal to present his argument unequivocally. In the controversial lines quoted below he seemingly attempts to deflect

---

[12] Ibid., 120–1.   [13] Ibid., 122.

and undermine ironically such criticism arising from a lack of understanding:

> wer roufet mich dâ nie kein hâr
> gewuohs, inne an mîner hant?
> der hât vil nâhe griffe erkant.
> sprich ich gein den vorhten och,
> daz glîchet mîner witze doch. (*Parzival*, 1,26–30)

[Who is that trying to tweak me where no hair ever grows, in the
palm of my hand? If I cry out in fear that only reflects my state of
mind!]

Wolfram is clearly amusing himself at the expense of those who
believe their criticisms will hurt him. Anyone so stupid as to try to
seize him at a point where he cannot be attacked at all is hardly
anyone he need fear! Nor will he expect much of such people:

> wil ich triwe vinden
> aldâ si kan verswinden,
> als viur in dem brunnen
> unt daz tou von der sunnen? (*Parzival*, 2,1–4)

[Am I going to find trustworthiness where it can vanish like fire in
water and dew in the sunshine?]

The whole sequence of argument, with its spate of rapidly changing
metaphors, presents considerable difficulties of interpretation, and the
details of the text may be interpreted in various ways; however, the
intention behind the imagery is unmistakable. Wolfram is deliberately
trying to confuse the audience by playing hide-and-seek with them,
characterizing his art as a changeable thing whose meaning eludes all
those who think they understand it readily. This is precisely why he
insists on *stæte* ('constancy') in his audience. However, he is happy to
dispense with those who cannot follow the thread, and who even
reproach him for not giving them anything to hold on to.

On the other hand – as Wolfram has to admit – it is completely in
order for the audience to ask about the meaning of a work:

> ouch erkante ich nie sô wîsen man,
> ern möhte gerne künde hân,
> welher stiure disiu mære gernt
> und waz si guoter lêre wernt. (*Parzival*, 2,5–8)

[Indeed I have never known a wise man who was not desirous of finding out what course these tales hold to[14] and what good teaching they have to offer.]

However, Wolfram retracts these apparently justified demands, taking up in his reply those same fleeting images which he has already used to cover his tracks:

> dar an si nimmer des verzagent,
> beidiu si vliehent unde jagent,
> si entwîchent unde kêrent,
> si lasternt unde êrent.
> swer mit disen schanzen allen kan,
> an dem hât witze wol getân,
> der sich niht versitzet noch vergêt
> und sich anders wol verstêt. (*Parzival*, 2,9–16)

[In that they are quite steadfast: they give chase and take to flight, they speed away and then turn about, they bestow shame and honour. That man who knows how to take such risks, who neither gets stuck (= sich versitzet) nor goes astray (= sich vergêt) and yet still knows where he stands (= sich verstêt), he is blessed with real wisdom.]

It may thus be seen that the clever, too, make demands on the narrator: they ask about the lesson which the tale promises to reveal. But Wolfram has an answer ready: only those who are able to follow all the twists and turns of the action – the metaphor is taken from the joust – are considered truly clever; they alone will finally discover the meaning. The play on the words *versitzen, vergên* and *verstên* can scarcely be adequately rendered in a modern translation. It has been remarked that, far from being merely a gratuitous play on words, the

---

14 The interpretation of *stiure* is controversial. Kratz, 'Prologue to Wolfram's *Parzival*', and Schweikle, 'Zum *Parzival* Wolframs von Eschenbach', would like to interpret it as the expectations which the work presupposes in its audience. I cannot agree here. Not only is it significant that Albrecht did not interpret the passage in this light in *Der jüngere Titurel*, but furthermore Rudolf von Ems does not use *stiure* in this sense either: see *Alexander*, 12968 and 13055, and chapter 16 below, p. 314; cf. also *Parzival*, 115,29–30; see below, p. 175. Even more convincing is the logic of Wolfram's argument. Wolfram announces at the outset that his work contains surprises, indeed contradictions, and states clearly what he expects from his audience: constancy (*stæte*). Line 2,7 cannot therefore reopen the question of what he expects from the audience. Rather, after having dealt with the *tumbe* ('dullards') he turns to the expectation of the *wise* ('wise'), who in theory have the right attitude: they expect to be enlightened with regard to *stiure* and *lêre*. The *stiure* the tale demands is thus quite literally the steering (modern German *Steuerung*) it requires, in other words the direction in which the understanding of the audience should be steered. If, then, the *wise* ask about the *stiure* and *lêre* ('message' or 'moral') of the tale, they are referring to help in understanding and an indication as to the meaning.

terms *versitzen* and *vergên* allude to key failings on the part of Erec and Iwein respectively.[15] The key to this wordplay lies in equating the listeners who fail to respond appropriately with the crisis situations in the Arthurian romance; it is precisely in such crises that the meaning of these works is revealed. It is also possible that this is intended as a jibe at Hartmann, since in Wolfram's view his romances allow moral conclusions to be drawn all too easily from the crisis of the protagonist. At any rate, Wolfram makes it quite plain to his audience that there is no patent formula for understanding his own works; instead, he expects them to follow the action through all the twists and breaks in the narrative. Meaning, therefore, can only be revealed in retrospect; the progressive enlightenment of the hero is paralleled by the listener's progressive recognition of the meaning.[16] No other aids to understanding are possible.

In conclusion Wolfram returns once more to the *tumbe* to deliver a final warning:

> valsch geselleclîcher muot
> ist zem hellefiure guot,
> und ist hôher werdekeit ein hagel.
> sîn triwe hât sô kurzen zagel,
> daz si den dritten biz niht galt,
> fuor si mit bremen in den walt. (*Parzival*, 2,17–22)

[Comradeship with duplicity[17] is fine for hell-fire, and it hails down on true worthiness. Its trustiness is so short in the tail that it would not be able to avenge one bite in three if it ran into the forest driven by horseflies.]

The image of animals fleeing from horseflies is probably an allusion to a fable which has come down to us through Nigel of Canterbury, about two cows whose tails become frozen to the ground in winter so that they are unable to move away. One of them waits for the thaw; the other, impatient to get free, tears off her own tail. When summer comes around, the impatient one is unable to defend herself against flies and is consequently goaded to death.[18]

---

15 Rupp, 'Wolframs *Parzival*-Prolog', p. 382.
16 On this parallel process, see Green, *The Art of Recognition*, Index, under 'points of view'.
17 On the difficulties of translating line 2,17, see Johnson, '*valsch geselleclîcher muot*'.
18 Martin, *Wolframs von Eschenbach 'Parzival'*, p. 10, on 2,20–2; cf. Knapp, 'Antworte dem Narren', 48f. Heinzle, 'Entdeckung der Fiktionalität', 70–1, is not convinced of this allusion to Nigel's fable. I cannot however share his scepticism, since Wolfram is clearly alluding to a well-known tale, the essential features of which correspond to those in the fable cited by Nigel of Canterbury.

Wolfram uses the image of the cow without a tail to describe those of his audience who are too impatient and who thus forfeit the opportunity to save their souls, since according to the boldest turn of his argument, those who understand his work and keep pace with the hero will, like the latter, find the road to salvation, whereas those who give up will go to hell. As a claim for the work's significance, this can scarcely be bettered. We are dealing here with a consciously fictional work which has no intention of providing the usual instructive examples, but which conceives of itself as a touchstone for eternal salvation or damnation. However, there is a well-established tradition for such a claim in exegetical works, where it derives its legitimation from direct inspiration from the Holy Spirit, who guarantees the truth of the poetic word: cf. the prologue to *Die jüngere Judith*. In the new romance form, however, the meaning is conveyed by the fictional structure itself, although its fictional status necessarily entails forfeiting any claim that the truth it seeks to convey is absolute and guaranteed. When, in the Grail romance, the realm of fiction is extended into the sphere of absolute religious truth, this seems to have been sufficient justification for returning to the traditional claim to truth – in fact this was a necessary step if this truth, too, was not to risk being seen as fiction. Thus old and new concepts are mingled here in the most disconcerting fashion. What originally might have appeared presumptuous, is in fact a reassuring return to the tradition of religious literature – even if this return concerns 'only' the underlying truth and does not substantiate the claims made by the form in which it is represented, in other words the new fictional genre. Or, to put it another way, because of the discrepancy between absolute truth and fiction, the only possible solution was to develop an ambitious theory of literature which in practice could never hope to fulfil its own exaggerated claims.

III

By no means all of Wolfram's contemporaries were prepared to accept his poetic claims and the demands thus made on the audience. He was reproached for his enigmatic mode of thought and presentation,[19] and suspected of being an idle poetic trickster. This accusation

---

[19] Cf. *Willehalm*, 4,19ff. and 237,11.

is made in a malicious caricature by Gottfried von Strassburg in the literary excursus in *Tristan*.[20]

Wolfram of course was not slow to defend himself against such criticism. The metaphor of the bowstring in book 5 of *Parzival*, incorporated into the scene in the Grail castle, in which he refers again to his poetic craft, should probably be seen in this context. Once more, then, the argument proceeds by means of images.[21]

As the meal in the Grail castle is being cleared away, Parzival catches sight of a handsome, grey-haired man through the door that leads to an ante-chamber. However, the narrator has no intention of revealing the identity of this figure at this point in the story. He justifies this as follows:

> Wer der selbe wære,
> des freischet her nâch mære.
> dar zuo der wirt, sîn burc, sîn lant,
> diu werdent iu von mir genant,
> her nâch sô des wirdet zît,
> bescheidenlîchen, âne strît
> unde ân allez für zogen. (*Parzival*, 241,1–7)

> [Who this was you are to hear later. In addition the host, his castle and his land will be made known to you, but later on, when the time is right, I will name them properly and without reluctance or hesitation.]

Wolfram thus deliberately leaves his audience in the dark about certain things. The explanation of events has to take place at the most appropriate moment in the story from a narrative point of view. The listener – in accordance with what was demanded in the prologue – is supposed to accompany the hero on his quest; the meaning of the puzzling situations in which he finds himself is not to be revealed prematurely. With regard to the mysterious events in the Grail castle, the listener remains as much in the dark as Parzival himself. This is a deliberate strategy on Wolfram's part, and an important part of his narrative technique.

Wolfram now goes on to justify this, using the image of the bow and bowstring:

---

[20] See below, chapter 11, pp. 219–20.
[21] Hirschberg, *Untersuchungen zur Erzählstruktur*, pp. 308ff.; Green, *The Art of Recognition*, pp. 31ff.

> ich sage die senewen âne bogen.
> diu senewe ist ein bîspel.
> nu dunket iuch der boge snel:
> doch ist sneller daz diu senewe jaget. (*Parzival*, 241,8–11)

[My story is the bowstring without the bow. The bowstring is a comparison. Now you may think the bow is powerful, but what is propelled by the string is even more powerful.]

This *bîspel* ('comparison') is thus concerned with the relationship of the bowstring to the bow. Wolfram states that his narrative is to be compared to the bowstring, not the bow, since ultimately it is the former which is important, as it is responsible for shooting the arrow. The point of such niceties is made plain in what follows:

> ob ich iu rehte hân gesaget,
> diu senewe gelîchet mæren sleht:
> diu dunkent ouch die liute reht.
> swer iu saget von der krümbe,
> der wil iuch leiten ümbe.
> swer den bogen gespannen siht,
> der senewen er der slehte giht,
> man welle si zer biuge erdenen
> sô si den schuz muoz menen. (*Parzival*, 241,12–20)

[If what I have told you was right, the bowstring may be compared to straightforward (= *sleht*) tales such as people approve of. Whoever tells you they are curved is trying to lead you astray. Anyone who sees a strung bow must admit that the string is straight (= *sleht*), except when it is drawn at an angle to fire a shot.]

Wolfram is thus declaring his support – in principle at least – for a narrative form which is straightforward and linear. The image for this is the taut bowstring. The audience, he hastens to add, is right to prefer such a narrative technique. It is nevertheless true that to shoot the arrow it is necessary that the string be bent or plucked back – *zer biuge erdenen* ('to draw at an angle'). This cunning justification, by means of imagery, of the 'straight' and yet 'convoluted' (*krümbe*) style, contains a key point with regard to the reception of the work: Wolfram claims that the action is of itself straightforward, but that it is necessary to depart from this straightforward narrative in order to get through to the audience – for only when the bowstring is bent can the arrow be loosed, that is to say only then can the target – the audience – be reached by the story. The issue is thus, once again, by what means the effect of a narrative on the audience may be directed or 'steered' by its author. By keeping the audience in suspense, continually leaving them in the dark as to the significance of individual elements within the work as a whole, Wolfram is able to capture their attention, causing them to identify with the progress of the hero and exacting from them that degree of perseverance which he had described in the prologue as a necessary prerequisite to the understanding of the work. Wolfram is nevertheless forced to admit here too that this technique does not always achieve the desired effect. The following lines allude rather cynically to this resigned but realistic attitude:

> swer aber dem sîn mære schiuzet,
> des in durch nôt verdriuzet:
> wan daz hât dâ ninder stat,
> und vil gerûmeclîchen pfat,
> zeinem ôren în, zem andern für.
> mîn arbeit ich gar verlür,
> op den mîn mære drunge:
> ich sagte oder sunge,
> daz ez noch paz vernæme ein boc
> odr ein ulmiger stoc. (*Parzival*, 241,21–30)

[Yet if I were to shoot my story at someone who can only find fault with it – as it would not stick there and would follow a wide path in at one ear and out at the other – it would be a total waste of effort if my story were to pay court to him, so that, whether I were to recite or to sing, a billy-goat or a rotten tree stump would listen better.]

This is Wolfram's version of the topos of the obstinate listener.[22] The reproach that he is being deliberately obscure misses the point, Wolfram says: his mode of narration is quite clear and straightforward, in so far as it follows the path of its protagonist.[23] Of course, this necessarily also means that its scope is limited to the latter's own horizons. However, those who are not prepared to accept this narrative technique, calling instead for an omniscient narrator, are a lost cause: it is futile to hope that they will summon up sufficient interest to follow Parzival.

Wolfram was by no means the first to use the bow metaphor to refer to a work of poetry; as Hans-Jörg Spitz and Arthur B. Groos

---

[22] See chapter 3 above, pp. 56–8, and chapter 7, p. 129.
[23] Curschmann, 'Das Abenteuer des Erzählens', 640.

have pointed out, the topos has its origins in the tradition of biblical exegesis.[24] Traditionally, the image of the bow bent by the bowstring is interpreted as the rigid Law of the Old Testament whose intransigence is 'bent' by the New Testament. This also means that the literal sense of the Old Testament is given a secondary, spiritual level of meaning in the New Testament. The arrows which are shot from the bowstring stand for the apostles or the divine message. This exegetical use of the bow metaphor, which may be traced back to Augustine and Gregory the Great, may be found in over a hundred works before Wolfram's time, and it is quite probable that he was familiar with the use of the bow metaphor in biblical commentaries. For this reason, Spitz interprets the image in *Parzival* in accordance with the exegetical tradition, identifying the bowstring as the meaning which Wolfram will release at the appointed time. However, this interpretation is too narrow to do justice to this complex nexus of images. Groos sees Wolfram's bow metaphor as a justification of the *ordo artificialis* by comparison with the *ordo naturalis*. This too misses the crucial point, namely the relationship with the audience, since Wolfram's primary concern in his argument is the choice of the most effective narrative strategy with which to reach the audience. Seen in this light, there can be no question of an alternative between the two *ordines*, since the straightforward mode of narration, following as it does the quest and point of view of the hero, is at the same time the tortuous one; this however is permissible, since only in this way can an optimal effect be achieved.

Nevertheless, the exegetical use of the metaphor is of great interest for Wolfram's re-interpretation of it. If it may be assumed that Wolfram and his audience were familiar with the traditional interpretation, his citation of it must initially have been seen as an indication that his version too was concerned with the discrepancy between appearances and the hidden meaning. Depending upon how far the listeners were prepared to engage with Wolfram's use of the metaphor, they would become aware that this traditional image is here seen from a new theoretical perspective. Whereas traditionally, the bow metaphor presents the discovery of meaning by means of allegorical exegesis – whereby the meaning of the Old Testament is revealed through its typological relationship to the New – Wolfram, by reformulating this metaphor, demonstrates that his romance

24 Spitz, 'Wolframs Bogengleichnis'; Groos, 'Wolfram von Eschenbach's "bow metaphor"'.

conveys its meaning in an essentially different manner, not by presenting an allegorical interpretation, but through the listeners' own experience of the meaning in following the deeds of the hero. Thus the meaning is transmitted by means of the literary structure itself. The bowstring, at once taut and bent, stands for a dialectic process which can only lead by stages to its goal, calling into question each new position as it is attained: 'That man who knows how to take such risks is blessed with real wisdom' (2,12–13).

Michael Curschmann has shown how far Wolfram's particular narrative technique is geared to this specific purpose:[25] the disconcerting manipulation of the role of the narrator finally culminates in the point at which the poet comes to a tacit agreement with the audience as to the truth of fictional material.[26] This represents a wilful distortion of the 'mendacity formula' which Lamprecht in his day used to evade authorial responsibility:

> man sagte mir, diz sag ouch ich
> ûf iwer ieslîches eit,
> daz vorem grâle wære bereit
> (sol ich des iemen triegen,
> sô müezt ir mit mir liegen)
> swâ nâch jener bôt die hant... (*Parzival*, 238,8–13)

[It has been said to me, and I say it myself on the oath of each one of you – if I am deceiving anybody in saying this then you are liars too – that before the Grail there lay spread out whatever anyone might desire ...]

This adaptation of the mendacity formula, extended to include the audience, makes the listener, too, an accomplice of the poet in the creation of meaning in the fictional structure. This is ultimately the key to the understanding which Wolfram demands for his work, which may be 'straightforward', but nevertheless appears 'bent' or refracted in this fictional representation of truth.

In terms of techniques of argument, any observations on Wolfram's treatment of the bow metaphor should be taken in conjunction with what has already been noted in the context of Chrétien's and Hartmann's reflections on literary theory. All three poets make use of elements from the traditional forms of discovering and establishing

---

[25] Curschmann, 'Das Abenteuer des Erzählens'. For a general discussion of the relationship between conscious fictionality and irony in MHG literature, see Pörksen, *Der Erzähler im mittelhochdeutschen Epos*, pp. 184ff.

[26] Curschmann, 'Das Abenteuer des Erzählens', 638.

meaning. The role of the *integumentum* metaphor for Chrétien de Troyes and the importance of the exemplum for Hartmann finds a parallel in Wolfram's use of the exegetical metaphor of bow and bowstring. Here, too, traditional methods are alluded to by way of introduction. This is intended as an indication of the general sense in which the remarks which follow are to be understood, namely with regard to the possibility and manner of conveying meaning. At the same time, however, the traditional techniques are abandoned, since they cannot do justice to the new type of fictional literature. As exegetical concepts or images are superseded, a new theoretical position is reached, even if Wolfram, like Chrétien and Hartmann before him, has great difficulty in defining and formulating this position in explicitly theoretical terms. This does not, however, mean that the full implications and problems of the new type have not been recognized. Wolfram's work in particular demonstrates the difficulties an attempt to justify literature from the new position may entail. Fictional literature now claims for itself the same authority and status as truth as does religious literature, and the onus is now more than ever on the poet to do all in his power in order to win over the audience. The very elements which might be expected to deter an audience in fact open up new possibilities: concealment provokes and fascinates, defamiliarization and the excitement of anticipation can begin to play their familiar role in audience response. However, any appeal to the audience no longer carries the full weight of authority that it had in religious literature: with those not prepared to listen, the tale will go in one ear and out the other: one might as well talk to a billy-goat or a tree-trunk! However, Wolfram does not turn this to positive account by acknowledging a legitimate free response of the listener to fictional material. Once again he employs metaphors from the religious tradition: whoever will not listen is lost. This represents a further connection with the prologue, here with regard to the absolute claims made for poetry.

Wolfram is well aware of the problems of reception facing fictional literature. With the bow metaphor, he is defending his narrative technique and compelling the listener to go along with him. Inasmuch as this is a deliberate strategy, there is clearly an element of manipulation about it, so that the accusation of poetic counterfeiting which Gottfried levels at him is to some extent understandable. However, the strategy is justified by the claim of the new literary form, the romance, to represent a genuine experience of truth through the medium of fiction. Despite suggestions to the contrary, Wolfram is not ultimately concerned to seduce his audience with narrative tricks, but rather to commit them from the very outset to a complex and difficult process, perseverance in which is of itself proof of commitment to the truth which it conveys.

IV

Having set out in the prologue to *Parzival* what he expects of his audience, as well as the meaning and implications of true understanding, Wolfram devotes a short passage to the women in his audience. He starts from the premise that what he has presented as *unterbint* (2,23), that is 'distinctions', oppositions and limitations, applies not only to men but also to women. Here again the central opposition is between *stæte* and *valschheit*. However, it is now seen from a completely different perspective, and is noticeably abridged: a woman must take care to whom she offers her respect, love and honour, so as not to regret it afterwards. Wolfram implores God to grant her *rehte mâze*, which may here be understood as equanimity and restraint combined with considered and discerning judgement. In this, Wolfram continues, lies woman's whole salvation, for:

> diu valsche erwirbet valschen prîs.
> wie stæte ist ein dünnez îs,
> daz ougestheize sunnen hât?
> ir lop vil balde alsus zergât.
> manec wîbes schœne an lobe ist breit:
> ist dâ daz herze conterfeit,
> die lob ich als ich solde
> daz safer ime golde.
> ich enhân daz niht für lîhtiu dinc,
> swer in den kranken messinc
> verwurket edeln rubîn
> und al die âventiure sîn
> (dem glîche ich rehten wîbes muot).
> diu ir wîpheit rehte tuot,
> dane sol ich varwe prüeven niht,
> noch ir herzen dach, daz man siht.
> ist si inrehalp der brust bewart,
> so ist werder prîs dâ niht verschart. (*Parzival*, 3,7–24)

[The false woman earns praise without substance. How lasting is thin ice under the hot August sun? Her reputation is just as quickly gone. Many women's beauty is praised far and wide. If their hearts are counterfeit I can praise them only as I would zaffre (= blue glass) set in gold. I do not consider it a worthless thing when a noble ruby with all its wonderful powers is set in common brass. That I liken to the heart of someone who is truly a woman. I will not examine the facial appearance of one who is true to her womanhood, nor what can be seen shielding her heart. If she is well defended within her breast, her good name remains unblemished.]

As in the first part of the prologue, the juxtaposition here of true and false, constant and inconstant, refers to the differences between essence and appearance, between inner truth and deceptive outer surface. However, applied to women these opposites appear in concrete terms as the contrast between *herze* ('heart') and *schœne* ('beauty'), *muot* ('inner disposition') and *varwe* ('complexion'). Just as woman may be deceived with respect to the man to whom she accords her *prîs* ('good name'/'reputation'), so too she may deceive the world so that the *prîs* she attracts is also false; neither has any lasting substance. The image of ice in the August sun is reminiscent of the inconstancy metaphors in the first part of the prologue.[27]

All this, however, is extraneous to the theoretical issues expressed, in this first part of the prologue, in the relationship between fleeting image and actual truth. Clearly at this point Wolfram is already referring to the actual subject matter of his narrative, since the following lines (4,9ff.) mark the beginning of the introduction to the subject and material: he intends to relate a new tale of joy and pain, *von grôzen triuwen* ('of great constancy'), of *wîplichez wîbes reht* ('rights and obligations of women') and *mannes manheit* ('manly courage'). He goes on to characterize his hero as brave, famous and victorious, women's joy and torment, but at the same time as *træcliche wîs*, that is to say as one who only gradually (*træcliche*: 'belatedly') achieves the wisdom associated with maturity.

What Wolfram has to say about women in the prologue is however not exhausted at this point; later it is supplemented by certain aspects which are omitted here. This occurs in the so-called 'self-defence' passage which forms the transition between the second and third books.[28] This interpolation occurs after the description of

---

[27] Lines 3,7ff., especially 13f., should probably be read as a reference to Gottfried's Isolt; cf. Bumke, *Wolfram von Eschenbach-Forschung*, pp. 82–3, 288–9. More recently, see Brall, '*Diz vliegende bispel*', 26ff., for a closer study of the feud between Wolfram and Gottfried.

[28] Bumke, *Wolfram von Eschenbach-Forschung*, pp. 72ff., 288ff., 326ff.; more recently:

Herzeloyde's collapse on receiving the news of the death of Gahmuret, and after the birth of their child, Parzival. Wolfram depicts a
woman experiencing the greatest joy and the deepest sorrow at one
and the same time. This deeply moving description ends with the line
'ir schimph ertranc in riwen furt': 'her joy was drowned in the flood
of her sorrow'.

At this point Wolfram inserts reflections on the way in which he
sees women in his poetry. He recalls first the general situation of
poets who sing the praises of women, and then defines his own role in
this chorus. Others might sing of *minne* better than he, he says, yet he
can only agree that it is right to write poetry for the pleasure of ladies.
There is one woman, however, to whom he will not gladly grant this
pleasure, and there follows an invective against an unnamed woman
who was unfaithful to him and is therefore the object of his anger,
even though he too lost his sense of proportion. Nevertheless this will
not prevent him from judging women fairly, singing their praises and
sharing in their suffering. On the other hand, no poet should carry his
Frauenlob ('praise of women') to excess; dismissing all women for the
sake of a single one means the poet's praise '(lop) hinket ame spat' –
limps like a lame horse.

Wolfram here evokes the characteristic features of the *Minnesang*
tradition, such as the literary figure of the lady who abruptly
dismisses the poet, or the exaggerated veneration of the poet's own
lady at the expense of all others, which is brought in by citing
Reinmar's famous *mat-sprechen* ('checkmate').[29] Wolfram now counters the praise of women in *Minnesang* with his own position,
declaring 'schildes ambet ist mîn art' ('I am born to the profession of
arms'). Hugo Kuhn has definitively disproved the suggestion that
with this statement, Wolfram wished to boast of himself to the ladies
as a participant in tournaments;[30] he argues that Wolfram's statement
that he wanted to win love 'mit schilde und ouch mit sper' ('with
shield and lance') can in this context only be intended in a metaphorical sense. Wolfram, he suggests, is contrasting the praise of women
in the courtly romance with the *Frauenlob* of the *Minnesänger*. 'And
then, *art* ("schildes ambet ist mîn art"), far removed from any
biographical speculations (= about Wolfram) – is almost like *ars*,

---

Curschmann, 'Das Abenteuer des Erzählens', 648ff. and 'Hören – Lesen – Sehen', 233ff., and
Kuhn, 'Wolframs Frauenlob'.
[29] Further possible echoes are given in Curschmann, 'Das Abenteuer des Erzählens', 651.
[30] Hugo Kuhn, 'Wolframs Frauenlob', p. 47.

literary art.'[31] Thus, Kuhn continues, when Wolfram then returns to his narrative, there is a logical transition:

> hetens wîp niht für ein smeichen,
> ich solt iu fürbaz reichen
> an disem mære unkundiu wort,
> ich spræche iu d'âventiure vort. (*Parzival*, 115,21–4)

> [But that women might take it for flattery I would continue to offer you things as yet unheard of in this tale, I would go on telling the story.]

The stages of this argument must be kept in mind if the controversial theoretical remarks which follow are to be interpreted correctly and not wrenched out of context, as has often happened. Rather, they should be seen, in accordance with Kuhn's view, as part of the *Frauenlob*:

> swer des von mir geruoche,
> dern zels ze keinem buoche.
> ine kan decheinen buochstap.
> dâ nement genuoge ir urhap:
> disiu âventiure
> vert âne der buoche stiure.
> ê man si hete für ein buoch,
> ich wære ê nacket âne tuoch,
> sô ich in dem bade sæze,
> ob ichs questen niht vergæze. (*Parzival*, 115,25–116,4)

> [Anyone who wants me to do that (= to go on telling the story) should not think of my story as a book. I am not literate. There are storytellers enough who make that their starting point. This tale sails without the steerage of books. I would rather sit naked in the bath without a towel than have it thought of as a book – as long as I hadn't forgotten my birch sprigs.]

The debate as to whether Wolfram is trying to say in this passage that he is unable to read or write requires no further comment here.[32] Wolfram's dictum 'ine kan decheinen buochstap' ('I know no letters') is to be taken in the context of his discussion of the other poets who have sung the praises of women, each in their own way. After

---

[31] Ibid.
[32] Cf. Hugo Kuhn, 'Wolframs Frauenlob', p. 48, with reference to Grundmann, 'Dichtete Wolfram von Eschenbach am Schreibtisch?'; cf. also Bumke, *Wolfram von Eschenbach-Forschung*, pp. 74–5, 326–7.; Knapp, 'Der Lautstand der Eigennamen im *Willehalm*'.

Wolfram has distanced himself – as an epic poet – from the *Minne-sänger*, he goes on to criticize the book-learning of poets like Hartmann. He does not want to don borrowed robes of learning, he says, and were anyone to accuse him of it, he would rather sit naked in the bathtub. He then gives a humorous twist to the situation by saying that of course he would not – here, in the context of his speech to the ladies – forget the birch sprigs!

It seems entirely possible that the statement 'ine kan decheinen buochstap' alludes to the traditional exegetical opposition between the letter which kills and the spirit which gives life; the specific formulation, as Friedrich Ohly and Hans Eggers have shown, goes back to the Vulgate reading, *non cognovi litteraturam*, in Psalm 70,15.[33] However, the point is not the opposition between *litteratus* and *illitteratus*, but between those whose knowledge comes only from books and those who are divinely inspired. If it may be assumed that the passage from the Psalms and its attendant tradition inform line 116,7 of *Parzival*, it is tempting to connect this in turn to the prologue to *Willehalm*, in which Wolfram, indirectly at least, claims divine inspiration for his poetic craft. This connection has, on occasion, been made all too readily, without regard for the different contexts.[34] By contrast, it should be noted that in so far as the passage from Psalms and its exegetical tradition do find resonance here, it is at the very least given a quite specific angle in the context of the distinctive argument of the prologue. Wolfram presents his Parzival romance as written in praise of women. What he has in mind is the idea of woman outlined in the prologue and amplified in the second book in the figure of Herzeloyde. Of such a woman he now says:

> der lobes kemphe wil ich sîn:
> mir ist von herzen leit ir pîn. (*Parzival*, 115,3–4)

> [I shall be the champion of her honour, I shall grieve with all my heart at her sorrow.]

Wolfram claims this ability to praise and still to sympathize as a specific qualification which also provides justification for what may be termed his *Frauenlob* in romance form. However, the combination of praise and compassion ultimately means love; and indeed it is Wolfram's declared aim to *verdienen*, with his poem, *der minne solt* ('to earn love's reward'). If 'ine kan decheinen buochstap' implies

---

[33] Ohly, 'Wolframs Gebet'; Eggers, '*Non cognovi litteraturam*'.
[34] Nellmann, 'Wolframs *Willehalm*-Prolog', 407; cf. chapter 10, pp. 188–90 below.

living experience rather than knowledge derived from books, then such experience is embodied here in the image of woman found in Herzeloyde, in Sigune and Condwiramurs. However, this is nothing more than the theoretical counterpart of the passage devoted to women in the prologue. Just as Wolfram demands of his audience an empathetic following of the action which goes far beyond any ready-made formulae for grasping the meaning, so now he bases poetic art itself on an empathy for and involvement in the literary destiny he has devised for his characters, sharing their joys and sorrows. The particular role of women in this derives from the fact that the *âventiure* of the men is reflected as personal experience in the women.[35] The women's personal involvement with the fate of the men thus commends to poet and audience alike intense participation in their praise – and in their suffering.

[35] W. J. Schröder, 'Der Prolog von Wolframs *Parzival*', p. 188.

10

Wolfram's *Willehalm*: a return to historical romance?

I

The epoch-making rise of the courtly romance in the twelfth century came about as a result of the emancipation of narrative literature from its earlier commitment to history as *fact*, and the discovery of fiction as an autonomous medium for the expression of human experience. In *Erec*, Chrétien de Troyes had devised a structural model which enabled him to treat one specific topic on a purely fictional level, namely the possibility of an ideal society, or, to be more precise, to set out the limitations of a non-transcendental Utopia given the restrictions imposed by the human condition. The solution which Chrétien's model presented in the romance was the recognition that the Utopian ideal can only be perceived by contrast with that which negates it; in other words it can only be realized by the hero's progress through an anti-Utopian counter-world.

This model, then, as shown in the preceding chapter, underwent modification as it developed through various stages. Its limitations became apparent with the attempt, in the Grail romance, to employ it to represent the experience of religious guilt. In accordance with the Arthurian structural model, the relationship between human guilt and divine grace was developed in a double cycle of action, and the crisis given a religious interpretation. However, this meant that the goal could no longer be represented as any Utopia conceivable by the human imagination. It was, nevertheless, construed as analogous to the Arthurian Utopia, and thus the 'Grail community' came into being, a scintillating, imaginary world which represented a fantastic and often uneasy mixture between a religious order of knights and a supra-temporal or eschatological *civitas Dei*.

After *Parzival*, Wolfram worked on a further Arthurian romance, *Titurel*, which was intended to fill in the action preceding those scenes in the Grail romance where Parzival meets his cousin Sigune, who is mourning her dead lover Schionatulander. Only two fragments of this romance have survived, and it seems likely that these were the only parts of this project that Wolfram was able to execute. The strikingly new feature about this outline is that Wolfram does not merely have his hero pass symbolically through death, which would correspond to Chrétien's model – but actually has him die in the course of his *âventiure*. This however strikes a blow at the very heart of Chrétien's scheme. It is difficult to imagine how a full-scale Arthurian romance could have been composed on this basis without calling the whole genre radically into question.[1] Later attempts to take up this challenge in spite of the obvious problems will be discussed in the context of Albrecht's *Der jüngere Titurel.*

Apart from the *Titurel* fragments, Wolfram left another, much more substantial unfinished work, namely *Willehalm.* This too breaks with the traditions of the courtly romance, but the change takes a different direction; instead of dissolving the *âventiure* model from within, it abandons the fictional plane and returns to the realm of facts, i.e. historical material. *Willehalm* is a historical romance with hagiographical features; it thus represents a return to a genre which predates the courtly romance. However, unlike Hartmann in *Gregorius*, Wolfram does not project the hagiographical material onto the Arthurian model; rather, he deliberately refuses any attempt to convey the meaning through the structural principle of the work. The meaning of the work must therefore be sought in the truth of the historical narrative itself, regardless of the form this truth may take. Yet Wolfram does not fall back on the usual interpretative techniques of the traditional historical epic, in which the facts are presented as typological figures or exempla, so that history is represented not as a continuum but as a series of individual moments which are judged by reference to a higher truth. Instead, Wolfram here unreservedly embraces the concept of history as a linear development. However, he is here again concerned with precisely those issues which had motivated his fictional works and led him to challenge the premisses on which Chrétien's model was based – the question of human guilt and the problem of how to come to terms with the gulf between human guilt and divine grace. How was it possible to resolve these on a factual or historical level, that is to say without recourse to a fictional scheme?

---

[1] See chapter 20, pp. 366–7 below.

Willehalm draws for its subject matter on the French heroic epic, the *chanson de geste*,[2] which has its origins in the eighth-century battles with the Moors in the South of France and Northern Spain. Besides the cycle centred on the figure of Charlemagne, a second cycle develops around the figure of William, count of Toulouse. He became known as the true liberator of the South of France; after leading a life filled with heroic deeds he retired to a monastery; at his death there in 812 he was known as a holy man.

The *Chanson de Guillaume* centres on the crucial battle at Aliscans. From this starting point the story is extended in both directions: an elaborate *Vorgeschichte* is developed, relating the events leading up to the main action, and William's life as a monk is added at the end. The most varied material was used for these accretions: historical material was interspersed with a whole variety of stock epic motifs, so that in the end the whole narrative cycle came to consist of around twenty branches. When Wolfram set about transposing the material into German, he found himself faced with the task of isolating the core of the work – the battle of Aliscans – from the cycle in order that it could be understood as a story in its own right. To this end he drastically curtailed the *Vorgeschichte*, introducing details from it in flashbacks in the course of the action. How he envisaged the conclusion is unclear, since the work remains incomplete.

The *Vorgeschichte* runs as follows: Willehalm, imprisoned by the Saracens, falls in love with the daughter of the heathen King Terramer, Arabel, the wife of Tybalt. The lovers succeed in fleeing to France, where Arabel is baptized and marries Willehalm; she is given the Christian name Gyburc. However, the Saracens soon land in France with a mighty army. Willehalm and his people resist them, but the small Christian army is defeated in this first battle of Alischanz by the superior strength of the heathen forces. Willehalm just manages to escape to his own town of Oransche. The main emphasis of this introductory section, in Wolfram's version as well as in the original *geste*, is placed on the heroic struggle and death of Willehalm's nephew, Vivianz. Wounded by a lance, Vivianz pulls out the shaft, binds his entrails back into his body with his banner, and returns to the battlefield. When his strength finally forsakes him, he lies for a while among the dead, but comes round again and manages to reach a

[2] On the relationship of *Willehalm* to history and the *chanson de geste*, see Kienast, 'Zur Tektonik von Wolframs *Willehalm*'; Wiesmann-Wiedemann, *Le Roman du 'Willehalm'*.

river valley, where he lies down to die. An angel appears to him and promises to grant his request to see his uncle, Willehalm, once more before he dies. Wolfram describes with vivid intensity how Willehalm slips away from the battle, how he rubs down his froth-covered horse and allows it to recover; how he then rides through the undergrowth to the bed of the stream, comes upon Vivianz' shield and finally discovers where he is lying. He takes the head of the dying youth on his lap and speaks a moving lament. Willehalm's experience here haunts him constantly, driving him to seek revenge for Vivianz' death.

This, then, may be seen as the key to the action: suffering will beget suffering, history appears as a series of violent acts. The question of whether this sequence is inexorable, or whether the chain of murder and revenge can be broken, forms the true theme of the work.

The account of the first battle of Alischanz is followed by a substantial central section, relating how Willehalm goes to seek help from the French king; Gyburc meanwhile is to attempt to hold the town, which has been left almost defenceless. At the court in Munleun Willehalm finds himself shunned, since it is feared that his arrival can bring no good, that he will come asking for help and expecting sacrifices. At the grand reception given by the king and queen he is deliberately ignored, until he vents his anger in a fit of rage. The situation threatens to get out of control, but in the end a reconciliation is effected. A large army is assembled, and sets off for Oransche with Willehalm at its head. The distant glow of fire in the sky leads them to fear the worst; part of the town has already fallen to the heathens. Willehalm and the Christian army arrive just in time to save Gyburc.

This leads in to the final section of the romance, the second battle of Alischanz. The romance breaks off after Wolfram's description of the Christian victory; how and whether he intended to redeem the action, breaking out of the inexorable sequence of murder and revenge, remains open. Nevertheless, the text ends with a gesture of generosity when Willehalm frees Matribleiz, the leader of the Saracen army, without asking anything in return, and honours the enemy's dead. Nor does this deed stand out as an isolated gesture; the way is carefully prepared for it in the contrasting scene at the beginning of the narrative, where Willehalm, wishing to avenge the death of Vivianz, brutally slaughters the vanquished and helpless Arofel despite his pleas for mercy. The attitude expressed in this gesture then further characterizes Willehalm's journey from Oransche to Munleun. His violent temper is directed against anyone who stands in his way. Thus he strikes down the chief collector of tolls at Orlens and almost kills his own brother. Since he is shunned at the castle, he spends the night at a merchant's house, but cannot sleep for anger, and goes to the court with the intention of splitting the king's head open. Eventually his rage is pacified and the king promises him every assistance; however, when the queen, his sister, raises an objection, Willehalm pulls off her crown, seizes her by the hair, and would have struck off her head if their mother had not thrown herself between them. The queen flees, but Willehalm continues to strike wildly about him. However, at the very moment when catastrophe seems inevitable, Wolfram inserts a symbolic contrasting scene with the entry of Alyze, the king's daughter and Willehalm's niece. Richly attired, and enchanting in her youthful beauty, she approaches the raving Willehalm and kneels before him. Willehalm is stunned: his anger vanishes and he declares himself ready to do her every bidding.

Not only did Wolfram make no attempt to diminish the violent element in these scenes by comparison with his source; he even went to some lengths to intensify their dramatic contrast. In the French *Chanson*, the king appears as a weak and rather pathetic figure, so that Willehalm in his anger has all the sympathy on his side. Wolfram makes the king a more positive figure and gives Willehalm his fair share of the blame. The extremity of Willehalm's situation compels him to ruthless actions. Thus, he refuses his relatives the traditional kiss of greeting; there can be no rest and no reconciliation as long as Gyburc is still in peril – and yet Alyze's curtsey is enough to banish his anger. Admittedly, it flares up once more when the king appears reluctant to overlook Willehalm's insulting behaviour towards his wife, but after this no further mention is made of it. On the contrary, Willehalm shows unusual patience and forbearance towards another angry young man, Rennewart, whom he has taken into his service and who, when insulted, reveals his mighty strength in more or less comic, not to say grotesque, outbursts of rage.[3]

Alyze's decisive intervention at the court in Munleun may be seen as anticipating the second appearance of a woman at a critical juncture, when the whole issue of the justification of rage and the violence it implies is of paramount importance, challenging the

---

[3]   Haug, 'Parzivals *zwîvel*'.

inevitability of fighting and killing, and the necessity for violent action in a conflict of interests where both parties have right and wrong on their side. I refer to the so-called tolerance speech delivered by Gyburc in Oransche before the Christian army sets out for the second battle of Alischanz. Like Alyze's intervention, Gyburc's speech raises the crucial question of whether the sequence of violent deeds, the chain of suffering and revenge can be broken.

It may well have been the problems he experienced in attempting to integrate negative forces within a fictional and symbolical construct in *Parzival* and *Titurel* that led Wolfram to turn, in *Willehalm*, to a historical subject. Historical reality, with its incontrovertible facts, did not permit pain, injustice and death to be merely cancelled out in a fictional scheme, unless the facts were contextualized, as in the *Rolandslied*, within a metaphysical frame of reference. Wolfram deliberately chose a subject where such a schematic treatment was out of the question. The struggle between Christians and heathens takes the form of a battle between kinsmen, and Gyburc's personal relationships place her between the two sides: both parties, heathen and Christian, are equal when it comes to chivalry and courtly behaviour. The paradox presented by the reality of history appears insoluble. How is it possible for the literary form to establish meaning where it is permissible neither to construct meaning through fiction, nor to fall back on a metaphysical scheme based upon *Heilsgeschichte*? Or, to couch the question in more general terms, what can be the function of literature, set against the hopelessly paradoxical nature of historical reality? Wolfram did not complete his work: was it this question that was responsible for his failure? To answer this, we should examine how he dealt with the altered literary parameters in theoretical terms. An examination of the prologue should be able to shed light on this, or at the very least on Wolfram's intentions.

II

The prologue to *Willehalm* follows the model of religious narrative, beginning with the traditional *invocatio*: the three-personed God is addressed and his powers described according to each of the three persons of the Trinity respectively. This results in a tripartite structure, though the triadic principle is not rigidly adhered to. There is likewise a fluid transition from this first part of the prologue to the second part, the introduction of the subject matter, which begins with line 2,23, or to be more precise, mid-sentence in line 2,26, ending at line 4,16. The hero of the story, the holy man Willehalm, is introduced in line 2,27. Wolfram then comments on the transmission of the source material and talks about himself.

The traditional division of the prologue into two main parts is thus more or less clear; as Friedrich Ohly and Ingrid Ochs have pointed out, Wolfram also deploys the traditional range of topoi found in religious prologues.[4] Nevertheless, this prologue is highly original on account of the particular combination and arrangement of the motifs employed. Its internal structure is so complex as to make it one of the most disputed passages of Middle High German literature.[5]

First, the *invocatio*: 1,1–2, 23 (25).

> Âne valsch dû reiner,
> dû drî unt doch einer,
> schepfære über alle geschaft,
> âne urhap dîn stætiu kraft
> ân ende ouch belîbet. (*Willehalm*, 1,1–5)

> [You who are pure and undefiled by falsehood, you who are three and yet one, creator over all creation, your abiding power has no beginning and endures without end.]

First, Wolfram addresses the Trinity: the three-personed God is immaculate and perfect (*rein*), and undefiled (*âne valsch*), or in positive terms, he is fidelity and trust (*triuwe*) itself. Line 1,3 marks the start of the consideration of God according to the three attributes of his three persons. The term *schepfære* ('creator') refers to the first person of the Trinity, while *kraft* ('power') presumably takes up the first attribute of the trinitarian formula *potentia–sapientia–bonitas*. This is confirmed when, later, the attributes of the second and third persons, *wîsheit* ('wisdom') and *güete* ('goodness') are taken up. The so-called 'doctrine of appropriation' which is thereby invoked is not however strictly adhered to throughout.[6]

---

4   Ohly, 'Wolframs Gebet'; Ochs, *Wolframs 'Willehalm'-Eingang*; on the apostrophizing of the Creator and the praise of creation, see especially Jaeger, 'Der Schöpfer der Welt'.

5   For further details, in addition to the works cited in note 4 above, see Meissburger, 'Zum Prolog von Wolframs *Willehalm*'; Nellmann, 'Wolframs *Willehalm*-Prolog'; Flügel, *Prolog und Epilog*, pp. 119ff.; Kartschoke, '*Willehalm*', pp. 266ff.; Bumke, *Wolfram von Eschenbach-Forschung*, pp. 326ff.; Lutz, *Rhetorica divina*, pp. 311ff.; Heinzle (ed.), *Wolfram von Eschenbach. Willehalm*, pp. 813–14 (with most recent bibliography). The translation and interpretation which follows is based on these studies; see also Haug, 'Wolframs *Willehalm*-Prolog'.

6   Ruh, 'Drei Voten zu Wolframs *Willehalm*', pp. 283ff.

ob diu von mir vertrîbet
gedanke die gar vlüstic sint,
sô bistû vater unt bin ich kint,
hôch edel ob aller edelkeit.
lâ dîner tugende wesen leit,
dâ kêre dîne erbarme zuo,
swâ ich, hêrre, an dir missetuo!
lâz, hêrre, mich niht übersehen,
swaz mir sælden ist geschehen,
und endelôser wünne!
dîn kint und dîn künne
bin ich bescheidenlîche,
ich arm und dû vil rîche: (*Willehalm*, 1,6–18)

[When that power drives away those thoughts of mine that lead to perdition, then you are my father and I am your child. You have supreme nobility over and above all nobility.[7] Lord, may your loving kindness have pity on me, have mercy on me whenever I do you wrong. Lord, do not allow me to forget the blessings and that joy from eternity that have been granted to me. I am most definitely your child and your kinsman: I am poor and wretched, you are rich and mighty.]

The concept of God the Creator thus leads in to that of God the Father, who adopted humanity as if it were his own offspring. This is expressed, Wolfram suggests, by preserving his children from thoughts that would cause them to forfeit eternal life. This is followed by the plea that he should take pity on the sinful state of mankind and cause it to be grateful for the *sælde* ('blessings') and *endelôse wünne* ('endless joy' – i.e. a foretaste of eternal bliss) already granted. At the end of the passage, the tension between the intimate relationship of God and humanity on the one hand and the unfathomable chasm between the sinful creature and the all-powerful Creator on the other is emphatically re-stated: 'ich arm und dû vil rîche'. This paradox, as will be shown, emerges as the true theme of this praise of the Trinity. In what follows, Wolfram elaborates on the parent–child relationship by connecting it with the second person of the Trinity, Christ, who first established the relationship between God and humankind:

dîn mennischeit mir sippe gît
dîner gotheit mich âne strît
der pâter noster nennet

---

[7] On the punctuation here, see Heinzle (ed.), *Wolfram von Eschenbach. Willehalm*, p. 815.

z'einem kinde erkennet.
sô gît der touf mir einen trôst,
der mich zwîvels hât erlôst,
ich hân gelouphaften sin [8]
daz ich dîn genanne bin,
wîsheit ob allen listen:
dû bist Krist, sô bin ich kristen. (*Willehalm*, 1,19–28)

[Your humanity makes me kinsman of your divinity. The *Pater noster* indubitably recognizes and designates me as a child in relation to your divinity.[9] Baptism has granted me consolation and freed me from despair. I believe in my heart that I am named after you. O Wisdom over and above all knowledge, you are Christ, then I am a Christian.]

It is the incarnation of God in the person of Christ which *mir sippe gît*, i.e. 'which establishes his relationship to me'; this provides an occasion, via the interpretation of the Lord's Prayer, to discuss the act of baptism, in which the name of the Son of God is conferred on Christians. Thus the Incarnation serves to bridge the unfathomable distance between God and humankind. In baptism, each individual receives the *trôst* ('reassurance') of their own personal salvation, and this certainty is based on the belief in the relationship to Christ, as expressed and guaranteed by the act of baptism or 'christening'.

Wolfram thus develops his praise of the Trinity from the idea of the *stæte kraft* ('abiding power'), the *potentia* of God which permeates all creation. The idea of the parent–child relationship of God to humanity then leads to the discussion of the Incarnation, that is to say the second person of the Trinity, who created this special relationship and set the seal on it in the ritual of baptism. Ingrid Ochs is probably right in seeing the idea of supernatural adoption as proceeding not from the beginning of the argument, from creation, but from its end, in other words from the Incarnation.[10] Although the idea of the parent–child relationship is initiated from the perspective of God the Creator, it is comprehended through the experience of divine mercy. In placing the sinfulness of man on the one side and divine mercy on

---

[8] Heinzle (ed.), *Wolfram von Eschenbach. Willehalm*, p. 10 places this line in brackets, seeing it as an explanation and reinforcement of line 24. His argument for setting this line off from what follows is that the bearing of a Christian name can scarcely be a matter of belief or the lack of it. However, this argument is only convincing if *genanne* is defined very narrowly; if the bearing of a Christian name is taken to include all that has already been said about the relationship between God and humanity, these reservations are superfluous.

[9] Ibid., p. 816, on the punctuation.

[10] Ochs, *Wolframs 'Willehalm'-Eingang*, pp. 36–7.

the other, the endless distance between God and mankind is emphasized, while at the same time it is qualified by the suggestion that, through the Redemption, God was and is prepared to abolish this distance.

In line 1,29 Wolfram begins a praise of creation striking for its great poetic power and intensity:

> dîner hœhe und dîner breite,
> dîner tiefe[11] antreite
> wart nie gezilt anz ende.
> ouch loufet in dîner hende
> der siben sterne gâhen,
> daz si den himel wider vâhen. (*Willehalm*, 1,29–2,4)

[The disposition of your height and breadth, and of your depth has never been completely followed through to the end. And the race of the seven planets, supporting the heavens by their contrary motion, runs through your hands.]

Thus the movement of the heavens is located within the image of the incommensurable cosmos. Line 2,4 depends on the medieval idea that the sun, the moon and the planets all run counter to the movement of the firmament with its fixed stars, so that the whole cosmos is held together in a sublime equilibrium of forces and movement.[12]

> luft, wazzer, fiur und erde
> wont in dînem werde.
> ze dînem gebot ez allez stêt,
> dâ wilt unt zam mit umbe gêt.
> ouch hât dîn götlîchiu maht
> den liehten tac, die trüeben naht
> gezilt und underscheiden
> mit den sternenlouften beiden. (*Willehalm*, 2,5–12)

[Air, water, fire and earth dwell in your glory. It all stands at your command, everything that all creatures need, wild or tame. Your divine power established the bright day and the dark night and distinguished them from one another by the course of the two stars.[13]]

---

[11] The reading *tiefe* seems to me preferable to *tiefen*: cf. Heinzle (ed.), *Wolfram von Eschenbach. Willehalm*, p. 818.
[12] Cf. ibid., p. 818.
[13] This probably refers to the sun and moon: ibid., pp. 819–20.

After the description of the cosmos, the elements and time, Wolfram turns to the inner forces of nature:

> niemer wirt, nie wart dîn ebenmâz.
> al der steine kraft, der würze wâz
> hâstû bekant unz an den ort. (*Willehalm*, 2,13–15)

[There will never be, nor has ever been your equal. You know the powers of every stone and the fragrance of every plant down to the last jot.]

God thus not only holds the universe in the palm of his hand, he can also see into the innermost heart of nature, commanding the forces which lie hidden in plants and stones. This links up with the *stætiu kraft* with which God is characterized in line 1,4; it is God's powers which are at work in even the smallest detail of nature. There then follow the lines, as famous as they are controversial, in which the workings of God in the human individual are set out in analogous terms:

> der rehten schrift dôn unde wort
> dîn geist hât gesterket.
> mîn sin dich kreftec merket.
> swaz an den buochen stât geschriben,
> des bin ich künstelôs beliben.
> niht anders ich gelêret bin:
> wan hân ich kunst, die gît mir sin. (*Willehalm*, 2,16–22)

[The song of praise that rises from words written down as truth is reinforced by the power of your Holy Spirit. I have a strong sense of your power working within me: I am not bound by book-learning. My learning is of only one kind: What artistic skill I have is granted by that 'sense'.]

The interpretation of line 2,16 presents particular difficulties. Does *rehtiu schrift* (literally 'true writing') mean the Bible – a use of the expression not attested elsewhere – or does it refer to any work which is *reht*, in the sense of 'true', since what it represents is informed by the Holy Spirit? The expression *dôn unde wort* (literally 'melody and words') is also problematic. Ingrid Ochs, having considered the various interpretations, suggests that it is based on such set phrases as 'singing and saying' (*cantare et dicere*), or 'singing and reading' (*cantare et legere*), meaning liturgical recital and praise.[14] The more

---

[14] Ochs, *Wolframs 'Willehalm'-Eingang*, pp. 62ff. Cf. also Heinzle (ed.), *Wolfram von Eschenbach. Willehalm*, pp. 820–1 (with further references).

convincing these religious connotations, the more likely it appears that the Bible is what is meant by *rehtiu schrift*. The possibility cannot be ruled out, however, that Wolfram deliberately selected an unusual expression in order not to restrict what he wanted to say about divinely inspired truth to a specific text. The translation given above deliberately attempts to take this into account.

As to the meaning of *sin* in line 2,22, it is almost certainly to be understood as that artistic ability which is based on the *kraft* ('power') which is at work in nature and also informs the *dôn* and *wort* of the *rehtiu schrift*. Ohly goes so far as to interpret *sin* as 'the organ by which the Holy Spirit is perceived'.[15] Werner Schröder has taken issue with this,[16] asserting that *sin* here means human powers of reasoning. This criticism is only justified at a superficial level, for what Wolfram is trying to say is that natural human faculties, like the whole of nature, are permeated by the spirit of God, and that for this reason all book-learning can be dispensed with.

This bold renunciation of scholarly knowledge in favour of poetic wisdom that is a natural gift of the Creator was not without consequences. Until then, vernacular literature had been eager to legitimate itself by recourse to scholarship. As a writer, Chrétien distanced himself from the 'singers' of the oral tradition; Hartmann too prided himself on his learning. Gottfried also refers to a written source to guarantee the correctness of his own version, and, more importantly, uses his 'catalogue of poets' to place himself within the written literary tradition.[17] Wolfram, on the other hand, categorically rejects all book-learning. The scholar whose knowledge is derived from books is replaced by the lay poet, whose art springs not from knowledge but from that poetic force which is at work in each individual, and which may ultimately be identified with the divine force or *potentia* which permeates all of creation.[18]

Clearly though the issues are presented here, it is still difficult to connect these reflections with Wolfram's claim to illiteracy, 'ine kan decheinen buochstap', at the end of the second book of *Parzival*. The reasons for such caution have been given above, in the discussion of

[15] Ohly, 'Wolframs Gebet', p. 482.
[16] W. Schröder, '*kunst* und *sin* bei Wolfram von Eschenbach'.
[17] See below, chapter 11, p. 221.
[18] This development enabled Wolfram's followers to take on a new poetic 'role' or persona, that of the inspired lay poet: see Ragotzky, *Studien zur Wolfram-Rezeption*; Wachinger, *Sängerkrieg*, pp. 88–9.

Wolfram's 'self-defence'.[19] Common to both passages, however, is the fact that Wolfram is distancing himself from any kind of pre-conceived interpretation laid down in the written tradition. In *Parzival*, Wolfram presents the declaration that he 'knows no letters' 'rather mischievously', as Hugo Kuhn put it,[20] with the express intention of setting himself apart, as a lay poet, from his learned colleagues and rivals. His main concern here is with his praise of women. In concrete terms, what he is saying is that his representation and understanding of women is not studied or learned artificially – as is the case with other poets – but acquired from experience and personal encounters. Not until *Willehalm* – that is to say, in a quite different context – does he give the explicit religious motivation underlying his personal declaration of 'ignorance'; here, the relationship between letter and spirit is reformulated as a contrast between acquired knowledge and the direct discovery of meaning through the power of the divine spirit. Though Wolfram later comes to be seen as the epitome of the inspired lay poet, it should not be forgotten that in *Willehalm* he speaks as a hagiographical writer, and thus, with his opening prayer to the Holy Spirit, is part of a much older literary tradition. In other words, Wolfram's poetic self-consciousness is directly rooted in the traditional trinitarian praise of creation found in the earlier religious prologues. In retrospect it may be shown that this theoretical perspective is present from the very beginning in the references and appeals to the Holy Spirit. By contrast with God the Father, the Holy Spirit guarantees humankind's child–parent relationship with God by means of baptism; it is operative as a creative force in nature, and at the same time it is the most intimate force at work in humanity, making possible the expression of truth through poetry. Of course, taken separately none of these prologue elements is new; what is striking is the bold way they are combined so that the poetic *sin* of humanity is given a special and distinct place within the universal trinitarian process, since the Holy Spirit is immanent in both the poetic word and the word of God, and this in a quite natural way, on a plane beyond any book-learning or scholarship. In the same way as God is at work in the cosmos, he is also at work as a creative force in the human spirit when it comes to the poetic word. Never before had this been stated in this way in the Middle Ages.

---

[19] See chapter 9 above, pp. 175–6.
[20] Hugo Kuhn, 'Wolframs Frauenlob', p. 48.

In line 2,23 Wolfram appeals directly to God for assistance in his poem:

> diu helfe dîner güete
> sende in mîn gemüete
> unlôsen sin sô wîse,
> der in dînem namen geprîse
> einen rîter, der dîn nie vergaz.
> swenn er gediende dînen haz
> mit sündehaften dingen,
> dîn erbarme kunde in bringen
> an diu werc, daz sîn manheit
> dînen hulden wandels was bereit.
> dîn helfe in dicke brâhte ûz nôt.
> er liez en wâge iewedern tôt,
> der sêle und des lîbes,[21]
> durh minne eines wîbes
> er dicke herzenôt gewan. (*Willehalm*, 2,23–3,7)

[May your grace assist me and send into my heart such profound sense and wisdom as will pay tribute, in your name, to a knight who never lost sight of you. Whenever he incurred your anger by his sinful deeds your mercy had the power to allow him to turn around and direct his heroic courage to such deeds as would regain for him your favour. Often he escaped danger through your help. He risked both death of the soul and death of the body for love of a woman, for love of her he often suffered great sorrow.]

In accordance with the tradition of the hagiographical legend, *Willehalm* takes the form of poetry as praise. This act of praise draws on the spirit of God and represents the human response to his all-pervasive grace. The subject of the tale is in keeping with this: a knight to whom God gave the chance of preparing for grace by means of his actions. The reference to *diu werc* ('such deeds') however also implies the dangers and sorrow which Willehalm took upon himself out of love for Gyburc. This love is thus sanctified in advance, regardless of how much it is later justified on a Christian political level, on the one hand, and how much bloodshed it will cause on the other.

In the final part of his prologue, Wolfram mentions his patron, Hermann von Thüringen, who in all probability provided him with the French manuscript. Then he introduces the hero, Willehalm, and

---

[21] Heinzle (ed.), *Wolfram von Eschenbach. Willehalm*, places this line in brackets.

at the same time appeals to him directly, as a holy man, to intercede on his behalf. He concludes by naming himself as the poet of *Parzival*, a work which received a mixed reception; now, however, he wishes to offer a tale without equal in the German tongue. Finally he declares his faithfulness to the source:

> underswanc noch underreit
> valschete dise rede nie:
> des jehent si dort – nû hœrt se ouch hie! (*Willehalm*, 5,12–14)

[Nowhere is this tale falsified by cuts or intrusions. They tell it over there (= in France), now you can hear it here as well.]

As is usual in such cases, here too fidelity to the source refers of course not to the actual material, but to its truth.

III

It is no easy matter to reconcile the light in which Wolfram presents his *Willehalm* in the introduction with the impression formed on reading the work. One might therefore be tempted to see the prologue as consisting of those topoi usually employed as introduction in the hagiographical tradition, so creating a strict division between the prologue and the actual subject matter. That such an approach would be misguided is demonstrated by the remarkably intimate connection between the prologue and the core of the romance, Gyburc's speech on the subject of tolerance (306,12ff.).

Before the Christians engage in the second battle of Alischanz, Willehalm calls a council in order to discover the attitude of his followers and reassure himself of their loyalty. Gyburc attends this meeting, and after the princes have had their say and decided to do battle, she unexpectedly speaks out. First she tells of her suffering, the burden of which has increased to the point where she feels she is about to collapse under it. She describes her personal situation: her relatives and friends are fighting on opposite sides, so that the outcome, no matter what it is, can only mean new torment for her. Even if there is no one who can help her, she can at least appeal for consideration of the difficult situation she is in. On her account countless heathens and Christians were slain in the first battle of Alischanz, earning her the hatred of both sides; however, all she can do is to accept this and leave the judgement as to how far she is to blame to God. Then she goes on to make her position as a Christian quite clear, demanding that the princes should avenge the death of the young Vivianz on her relatives and their army. However, revenge is not her last word, for she continues: 'When you have defeated the heathens, then act in a manner that shows clearly that you, as Christians, stand in God's grace. Spare your enemies while remembering that they too were created by God' (306,25ff.).

This plea that mercy be shown to her relatives springs from a recognition of the fact that all, friend and foe alike, are God's creatures. Indeed, Gyburc demands such mercy, since God not only was and is ready to forgive sinners, but also sacrificed himself to redeem the sins of the world. God's love also extends to the heathen peoples. After this approach from the perspective of Christ's redemption has been widened to include all humanity as God's creatures, as in the prologue, the whole of creation is now considered in this light. The universe itself is borne by God's love, says Gyburc, and so her speech becomes a celebration of nature: God causes the planets to orbit that they may in turn give warmth and coldness to the earth, now turning water to ice, now causing sap to rise in the trees. And this Creator God also led her away from Mohammed to be baptized. For this reason, she says, her relatives hate her, whereas the Christians hate her because they believe she has caused a war for no better reason than an earthly love. This however was not the case, since she had already known love in the heathen country, and had left behind riches and children and a husband with whom she could not find fault. She ends her speech with the words: 'Believe me, all of you, that the death of your relatives fills me with deep sorrow, all my joy has died with them' (310,27ff.). And with this she bursts into tears.

Thus at the very stage of the action which marks the start of new bloodshed, Wolfram repeats the celebration of creation from the prologue, and this through the mouth of the very character who is the most deeply caught up in the pain and guilt of the action. In the order of creation the workings of the Holy Spirit are made manifest; the beauty of the universe bears witness to the fact that creation is sanctified by God. This guarantees that there is a purpose to the world, and this hidden meaning may be recognized to the extent that the spirit of God also pervades the human spirit. For this reason, traditional hagiographical prologues usually combine the celebration of creation with the plea for assistance in the poetic representation and interpretation of the world – as, for example, in the Early Middle

193

High German texts considered earlier. Wolfram follows this pattern in his prologue to *Willehalm*. However, contrary to the practice of the Early Middle High German poets, the interpretation of the world along allegorical lines or in terms of exempla is here replaced by the question as to its meaning. This is not yet explicitly formulated in the prologue, where the subject of the poem is given as the celebration of the saint's life. When this celebration of creation is repeated within the narrative itself, it is juxtaposed with an almost insoluble problem of interpretation which questions whether it is possible to discover meaning in the world at all. Even if the prologue is seen as containing a guarantee that divine grace will in the end cancel out guilt and suffering, in order to reach this point it is necessary to pass through a world in which humanity finds itself precariously and helplessly poised between the divine assurance of salvation on the one hand and inexorable killing and revenge on the other. Gyburc's praising of God in the beauty of creation at the moment of her greatest inner conflict would appear absurd but for the fact that it re-iterates the poet's position in the prologue, in which the hope that there is a meaning in the order of the world proceeds from just such an act of praise. Gyburc places her trust in the existence of precisely such a connection between beauty and hope. This gives her courage to act, even though it means that she incurs more guilt because of it; indeed, it is ultimately the awareness of guilt and sin which offers the possibility of acknowledging, through God, the other as Other.[22] And it is hope which ultimately assures a continuous development from the prologue, through Gyburc's 'tolerance speech', to the final scene with Matribleiz, where Wolfram provides a symbolic echo of the celebration motif in the context of Willehalm's generous gesture after the second battle.[23]

If one looks back from the end of the work to the poetics of the prologue, the theoretical scheme of the latter is revealed in a new and problematic light. In this work too, Wolfram's narrator accompanies his characters through the romance. Representation here is not the revelation of a given meaning through traditional poetic techniques under the auspices of the Holy Spirit, but rather a search for meaning. Even though this meaning is not the unstated aim of an open process

---

[22] Thus Karl Bertau's interpretation: Bertau, 'Das Recht des Andern', p. 258.
[23] Weber, *Wolframs von Eschenbach Antwort auf Gotfrids 'Tristan'*, pp. 225–6. The most recent work on the problem of the ending of *Willehalm* is Knapp, 'Heilsgewissheit oder Resignation?'

but something pre-ordained, at work both in nature and in human-kind by virtue of God's resplendent power, its realization in art, as in everyday life, involves the hazarding of both body and soul, 'der sêle und des lîbes' (3,5); this cannot be achieved by human strength alone. This lends the conventional invocation of the Holy Spirit a new significance in the context of a new, problematic poetic self-con-sciousness. What now matters is no longer insight into the meaning of earthly phenomena and the ensuing choice – conversion to God – but the experience of hopelessness, and the possibility, by the grace of God, of success. Nothing could demonstrate this more clearly than the impossibility of imagining what form the missing conclusion of *Willehalm* might have taken.

11

Ethics and aesthetics: Gottfried von Strassburg's literary theory

I

Tristan presents a challenge to the Arthurian romance model in that it represents a type of romance arising from a fundamentally different literary-historical tradition. Instead of being based on a freely invented structural model, *Tristan* evolved gradually, in several stages, and it is possible, to some extent at least, to trace and/or reconstruct this process. The core material in all probability derives from a Celtic Irish legend about the love of a queen for her husband's nephew; the adulterous couple flee from the court into the wilderness and finally die while being pursued by the deceived husband. This so-called *aithed* ('tale of elopement') is then combined with a courtship epic in such a way that, in the first instance, the nephew wins a bride for his uncle, and indeed brings her to him, although he himself then falls in love with her: this fateful situation is brought about by the device of a magic potion.[1] This is the point at which the directly accessible history of the Tristan legend begins. Two major stages of development may be distinguished, marked by an early French version, fragments of which are known under the name of Béroul, and by the courtly adaptation of the Anglo-Norman poet Thomas. Eilhart von Oberg's Middle High German translation corresponds to the stage of Béroul, while Gottfried von Strassburg's *Tristan* is based on Thomas.[2]

By re-casting the archetypal constellation of the 'eternal triangle' as a courtly romance, Thomas focussed the narrative interest on the one hand on the relationship between King Mark of Cornwall and his nephew, Tristan, before the beginning of the love story proper; and

---

[1] For an outline of the history of the legend, and a bibliography, see Loomis, *Tristan and Isolde* and Haug, 'Die Tristansage', 408ff.; also in Haug, *Strukturen*, pp. 586ff.
[2] Ruh, *Höfische Epik*, vol. I, pp. 46ff., and vol. II, pp. 208ff.

on the other hand on the situation which arises at Mark's court as a result of the adulterous liaison between Tristan and Queen Isolt. Thomas' elaboration of the events which precede the love story, and of Tristan's early years, clearly appeared all the more fascinating the more the material was contrasted with Arthurian romance – even coming to be seen as a challenge to the Arthurian model[3] – in that Tristan's relationship to Mark's court could be seen in terms of a contrastive analogy to the relationship of the Arthurian protagonist to the Round Table. In the terms of the Arthurian romance, then, Tristan plays the role of the knight who takes on the challenger to the court – represented here by the Irish tribute-collector Morolt – and defeats him. In keeping with the Arthurian scheme, there follows an *âventiure* journey – the first sea-voyage to Ireland, on which Tristan encounters a woman to whom he then pays suit on a second voyage, although not on his own account, but on behalf of his uncle, Mark, only to win her in the end – almost in spite of himself – as his own beloved.

However, because of the ambiguous triangular configuration which results from the 'courtship voyage', not only is Tristan not a typical Arthurian knight in search of *âventiure*: his relationship with the court is also different from the outset, since the Cornish court with its intrigues lacks the Utopian dimension of the Arthurian Round Table. The passivity of the king, a fixed element of the Arthurian romance which is often used to lend a playful touch to the narrative structure, appears, in Mark, as a sign of weakness. When Tristan sets out on his 'quest', therefore, it is not in order to re-establish the challenged ideal by passing through an anti-courtly world; rather, Tristan does battle with Morolt because no one else among the cowardly courtiers has the courage to fight. The voyages to Ireland, too, arise primarily from personal causes: Tristan has to be cured in the enemy land of Ireland of the poisoned wound he has received from Morolt's sword, and the voyage of courtship is instigated by a malicious plan of the courtiers, who wish to ruin him. The tension between the hero and the court is intensified after the marriage of Mark and Isolt, resulting in an ever more complex web of concealment and intrigue which moves inex-orably towards the critical *dénouement*. By contrast to the Arthurian romance, the threat posed by Eros to the perfect balance of the courtly ideal is not neutralized through its integration into a narrative

---

[3] See Haug, 'Der *Tristan* – eine interarthurische Lektüre', for a more detailed analysis of what follows.

structure. The marriage between Mark and Isolt initially masks the problem of absolute love as far as the outside world is concerned, yet slowly but surely it begins to destroy the world of the court. This love ultimately finds fulfilment with the flight of the couple into the wilderness, which is transformed by Thomas/Gottfried from an anxious exile full of hardships into a sojourn in a lovers' paradise. Life in the lovers' cave is an image for surrender to the absolute claims of Eros, whose place can only ever be outside society; any attempt to integrate it leads to an undermining of the very foundations of society, culminating in destruction of the world and of love itself. What in the Arthurian romance appears as a boundary experience, only approached at the furthest limit of the hero's path away from the Utopian ideal, in *Tristan* represents the essential, incontrovertible fragmentation of earthly existence, which can only be transcended in the perfect and timeless moment of love.[4]

The structure of *Tristan*, in Gottfried's version at least, is derived from the specific configuration of characters in the plot.[5] As an orphan, Tristan has no secure social position. Left to his own devices, he faces a world in which the laws of cause and effect are, at best, obscure. He develops strategies to deal with this, countering the unpredictability of the world with rational calculation. The structural principle of the *Tristan* plot consists in the ever-changing variations of this interaction between the hero and the world. Initially, this takes the form of conflict with external foes such as Morolt, Morgan or the dragon; these are superseded by a long series of variations on Tristan's deceiving of the courtly society in which he is obliged to live. The spiral of repetition and variation of the action becomes ever more intense, until the moment is reached when the tension becomes too great and the whole precarious construct collapses. The lovers' parting scene leaves Isolt with the possibility of seeking solace within the self, whereas in Tristan's case his virtuoso performance, alone against the world, rebounds on him and eventually results in his own self-deception.[6]

It is not clear how Gottfried would have treated the new series of adulterous episodes following the lovers' separation which his source provided for the second part of the work. The conclusion at any rate is determined by the love-potion scene: Brangaene's words 'the

---

[4] See Haug, 'Gottfrieds *Tristan*. Sexueller Sündenfall' for a more detailed interpretation.
[5] Haug, '*Aventiure* in Gottfrieds *Tristan*' and 'Die Tristansage'.
[6] Wapnewski, 'Tristans Abschied'.

potion will be the death of both of you' (12488f.[7]) hang over the whole plot. Whereas in the Arthurian romance the symbolic passage through death is intrinsically bound up with the transformation of desire into a more self-denying, charitable form of love, here absolute love can only culminate in death. At the end, the metaphor with which Tristan reacted to Brangaene's words becomes reality: 'solte diu wunneclîche Isôt / iemer alsus sîn mîn tôt / sô wolte ich gerne werben / umb ein êweclîchez sterben' ('If the delightful Isolt meant death to me for all time, I should strive to die eternally'; 12499ff.). Love and death can no longer be integrated into life as ultimate possibilities of experience representing the furthest limits of its horizon, but rather point, the more closely these absolutes are approached, beyond the reality of life: thus existence in the Lovers' Cave, seen as a flight into the hyperreality of Eros, corresponds to the failure to come to terms with the demands of the world expressed in the final *Liebestod*.

II

Gottfried sets out the theoretical basis for his concept of romance in the prologue to *Tristan* and in the literary excursus. The interpretation of these two passages is complicated, however, by the extensive use of rhetorical devices. Ever since the pioneering work of Stanisław Sawicki, these passages had served as excellent examples from which to demonstrate the extent to which the tradition of Latin poetics had influenced vernacular literature.[8] Valuable as this may be, however, the fact remains that there is little to be gained by reducing Gottfried's line of argument and mode of representation to mere lists of topoi and rhetorical techniques. In addition to demonstrating the individual emphasis placed on traditional elements, by assessing the role of set phrases within the structure as a whole, it is important to show to what extent the poet was aware of the innovative nature of his work within the literary tradition, and how far he was able to give a

---

[7] Line numbering follows the edition of F. Ranke, 1959.

[8] Sawicki, *Gottfried von Straßburg und die Poetik des Mittelalters*, pp. 56ff., 155ff.; Wilke, 'Zur Literaturschau in Gottfrieds *Tristan und Isolde*'; Jaeger, 'The "strophic" prologue to Gottfried's *Tristan*'; Eifler, 'Publikumsbeeinflussung'; Peschel, *Prolog-Programm*; Haupt, 'Zum Prolog des *Tristan*'; Dilg, 'Der Literaturexkurs des *Tristan*'; Jaffe, 'Gottfried von Straßburg and the rhetoric of history'; Glendinning, 'Gottfried von Strassburg and the school-tradition'. Interest has increasingly shifted from a mere identification of topoi to an analysis of the strategies of reception.

theoretical account of this within the framework of the exordial argument.

Gottfried's prologue consists of 244 lines, and is divided into three sections, marked by the use of distinct rhyme schemes. The first section consists of ten monorhymed quatrains. In addition it is characterized by the acrostic GDIETERICH, formed from the initial letter of the first line of each quatrain. The ten quatrains may be sub-divided into two groups of five, and these two groups are distinguished by the use of alternating and embracing patterns of rhyme words respectively. An eleventh quatrain (lines 41–4), again using alternating rhyme, marks the transition to the stichic prologue. A new acrostic begins with the initials of lines 41 and 45: T–I. These are repeated in inverse order in the first line of the second inserted monorhyme quatrain – 131–4 – and the first line of the following section: I–T. These are of course the first letters of the names Tristan and Isolt, and this acrostic is continued in a series of monorhyme quatrains inserted at various points into the narrative.[9] The inserted quatrain, 131–4, marks the end of the second part of the prologue which began at line 45. The third section culminates in the two famous quatrains, 233–40, which repeat the *tôt/brôt* rhyme four times – always provided that there were originally two quatrains, and not just one stanza; the manuscript evidence we have leaves room for doubt on this.[10] These two quatrains may be seen as forming the conclusion of the prologue, while the four lines which follow, 241–4, may be seen as leading into the narrative proper.

The formal division of the prologue into a strophic and a stichic part is particularly striking; it goes without saying that this reflects the structure of the argument. Nor is the division made by the quatrain comprising lines 131–4 without significance, occurring as it does after the first naming of the lovers Tristan and Isolt. Hennig Brinkmann sees in this the transition to the *prologus ante rem*:[11] however, the transition is a fluid one, beginning as early as line 123.

This artfully constructed formal organization suggests a carefully devised prologue argument. This may be set out as follows:

---

[9] Ruh, *Höfische Epik*, vol. II, gives a summary of the results of the various interpretations and attempts at de-coding. Cf. also Stein, 'Formaler Schmuck und Aussage im "strophischen" Prolog', and most recently Schirok, 'Zu den Akrosticha in Gottfrieds *Tristan*'.

[10] Cf. Gottfried von Strassburg, *Tristan*, ed Ganz, vol. I, pp. 343–4, on 235–8 and 235a/236a respectively.

[11] Brinkmann, 'Der Prolog im Mittelalter', p. 94.

First section: strophic prologue, 1–40

(1)

Gedæhte man ir ze guote niht,
von den der werlde guot geschiht,[12]
sô wærez allez alse niht,
swaz guotes in der werlde geschiht. (*Tristan*, 1–4)

[If one failed to hold those people in good memory through whom good was given to society, then whatever good is done in society would be entirely worthless.]

In more concrete terms, what this means is that *daz guote*, goodness, would be as good as non-existent if it were not recognized and actively borne in mind. The opening thus provides yet another example of the traditional exordial *sententia* – and here too it does not fail to strike a certain provocative note. Is something intrinsically good really called into question if it goes unacknowledged? This idea poses ethical problems, and is later contradicted, indeed inverted, by Rudolf von Ems. The question remains as to whether Gottfried's maxim really is intended to be understood in a universal, moral sense, or whether *daz guote* refers from the outset to the good work of art. In either case, the listener is entitled to expect further explanation. This, however, is not supplied by the second quatrain, which seems rather to restate the same issues in a negative light:

(2)

Der guote man swaz der in guot
und niwan der werlt ze guote tuot,
swer daz iht anders wan in guot
vernemen wil, der missetuot. (*Tristan*, 5–8)

[Whatever the good man does with good purpose and selflessly, only for the benefit of society – whoever is determined to take that other than in good part does wrong.]

Thus it is stated once again that *daz guote* must be respected as such; moreover, it is evil not to recognize what is good. This attack on those who disparage goodness introduces the topos of the

---

12 Here I disagree with Ranke's reading and follow the manuscripts; cf. Gottfried von Strassburg, ed. Ganz, *Tristan*, vol. I, p. 342 on this passage.

grudging listener.[13] The most obvious parallel is to be found in Eilhart's prologue to *Tristrant*, a work with which Gottfried may well have been familiar. Eilhart mentions the ill-will of those who do not want to hear his *Tristrant*, and continues:

> her ist klûkir sinne ein kint,
> swer sulche rede vorstôret
> die man gerne hôret
> und die nutze ist vornomen
> und gûten lûten wol mag vromen. (*Tristrant*, 26–30)

[That man has the intelligence of a child who disparages poetry that gives pleasure and profit and has the capacity to benefit good people.]

The topos of the obstinate or unwilling listener has already been encountered frequently, notably in the works of Hartmann and Wolfram. If Gottfried's argument is to be understood in this sense, then the general statement that *daz guote* needs to be recognized could be taken to refer to poetry from the outset. The prologue tradition and the fact that the prologue occurs in the context of a poetic work both support such a specific interpretation. However, the fact that Gottfried expresses himself in such general terms must of itself be of some significance.

The tension between the general formulation and the apparently specific meaning has spawned a controversy among scholars as to whether the opening strophes of the prologue refer to good poetry, or to goodness as such. Helmut de Boor opts for a general interpretation, and the wording of the text would indeed seem to support this.[14] However, the listener would have been aware of the possibility of a reference to poetry, even if only in the form of the question which gave rise to the controversy in the first place. Thus here again, it is fruitless to try to adhere to a rigid scheme of interpretation for the prologue: Gottfried deliberately leaves the argument open.

This presents difficulties for the interpretation of the third quatrain, all the more so since the wording itself is not entirely clear:

(3)

> Ich hœre es velschen harte vil,
> daz man doch gerne haben wil:

[13] Boesch, *Die Kunstanschauung in der mittelhochdeutschen Dichtung*, p. 105; Kobbe, 'Funktion und Gestalt des Prologs', 444; see also the references in chapter 3, note 10 above.
[14] Boor, 'Der strophische Prolog zum *Tristan*', especially p. 51. Schöne, 'Zu Gottfrieds *Tristan*-Prolog', had in essence already come to the same conclusion: see pp. 154ff.

dâ ist des lützelen ze vil,
dâ wil man, des man niene wil. (*Tristan*, 9–12)

[Very often I hear people deprecating that which in truth they
desire. And yet there is too much that is worthless, where people
want what they don't want at all.]

Most interpreters assume that the phrase 'des lützelen ze vil' refers
to the way in which a good thing can be denigrated: an emphasis on
pettiness would thus contain the implicit reproach that a poem pays
too much attention to detail, and the last line would then in some way
have to be read in opposition to this, and mean something like 'on the
other hand, people demand that which they had professed not to
want, that is to say the opposite: more details'.[15] However, this is to
read more into the text than the actual wording contains, while at the
same time pinning it down as explicitly referring to the work of art.
De Boor, who here too maintains that it is goodness in general which
is being discussed, interprets the lines as meaning that anyone who
denigrates *daz guote* would find even a small *guot* 'too much of a
good thing'. The last line would then have to be read as an antithesis:
'More is called for, they are demanding something more on top of all
this goodness, but they don't seriously want it.'[16] Josef Quint has,
understandably enough, called this interpretation awkward and
obscure.[17] However, he also rejects all earlier interpretations, suggesting instead that line 11 should not be seen as qualifying 'velschen'
('to falsify'), but as a direct expression of Gottfried's displeasure with
the critics. Faced with malevolent critics – Quint's reading – the little
which one gives them is in itself too much, in other words a waste of
effort, pearls before swine. Line 12 would accordingly read, 'There
(i.e. with such an attitude) they are asking for something they don't
want in the first place (i.e. which they reject or belittle).' Quint
himself recognized that this interpretation involves textual difficulties
of its own, since the genitive 'des lützelen' would then have to be
translated as 'of a little' or 'with a little'. Unable to find evidence for
this, he then surmised that the text might originally have read 'dâ ist
daz lützele ze vil' ('there a little is too much').[18] However, this leaves

---

[15] Spiewok, 'Zur Interpretation des strophischen Prologs'; Gottfried von Strassburg, ed. Ganz, *Tristan*, vol. I, p. 4, on line 12.
[16] Boor, 'Der strophische Prolog zum *Tristan*', pp. 50–1.
[17] Quint, 'Ein Beitrag zur Textinterpretation', especially p. 78.   [18] Ibid., pp. 80–1.

his interpretation no less encumbered with conjectures than those of other critics.[19]

Here too it is appropriate to start from the premise that we are dealing with a general statement on *daz guote* – or rather the distortion of it – and one which accordingly embraces the work of art and its critics only by implication, if at all. Seen in general terms, lines 9 and 10 state that good things are often disparaged, even though *daz guote* is often what is really wanted. On the other hand – as expressed in line 12 – people often ask for what in fact they do not want. By contrast to lines 9 and 10, this would have to mean that something of little value is being promoted, although it is precisely what is not wanted. If this interpretation is correct, then 'des lützelen ze vil' could stand for the bad qualities which are being played off against the good. The two lines in question could then be understood as follows: 'on the other hand, there is more than enough which is of little value, and there (= with regard to this, i.e. if this is what is wanted) something is sought which is not wanted'.

This interpretation would correspond exactly to what is said in quatrain 8, i.e. the third strophe of the second group of five quatrains, about the denigration by the critics of what is good and the elevation of what is bad. If one bears this parallel in mind, Gottfried's imprecision in the third strophe may perhaps seem less disconcerting. What is described in concrete terms as *übel* ('bad' or 'evil') with regard to the work of art in the eighth quatrain, appears here in very general terms as *lützel* in the sense of 'insignificant' or 'inferior'. The issue here is the mode of reception as a whole: what is good must be recognized as such – and indeed all pretend to want what is good – yet it still happens that the latter is denigrated while things of little value, of which there are more than enough, are encouraged.

It should however be remembered that there is as yet no explicit reference to art and criticism here; rather, the wording suggests a concern with ethical considerations regarding the relationship of what is good to the various forms or ways in which it is received or recognized.

The next quatrain reflects this:

[19] On the discussion of line 11, see also Winkelman, 'Zur Erkenntnisproblematik', who would prefer to apply 'des lützelen ze vil' to the malevolent attitude of Gottfried's critics.

(4)

Ez zimet dem man ze lobene wol,
des er iedoch bedürfen sol,
und lâze ez ime gevallen wol,
die wîle ez ime gevallen sol. (*Tristan*, 13–16)

[It becomes a man to praise well that which above all he needs, and may it please him well as long as it is his to have.]

With the word *loben* ('to praise'), a key term is introduced in the first part of the prologue which will run through the whole of the second part. This is the passage in which the ethical perspective most closely approaches the aesthetic one. However, the fifth strophe emphatically rejects such a connection:

(5)

Tiur unde wert ist mir der man,
der guot und übel betrahten kan,
der mich und iegelîchen man
nâch sînem werde erkennen kan. (*Tristan*, 17–20)

[I hold that man in esteem who knows how to assess good and evil and who can judge me and every man according to his worth.]

The formulation 'mich und iegelîchen man' leads the listener quite deliberately away from the idea that Gottfried was primarily thinking of himself, as the artist: it refers to a general ability to pass judgement on one's fellow humans and to distinguish between good and evil.

Only in the second group of five quatrains does the thematic perspective alter, in keeping with the form. Here the ideas of the first five strophes are recapitulated and applied to art:

(6)

Êre unde lop diu schepfent list,
dâ list ze lobe geschaffen ist:
swâ er mit lobe geblüemet ist,
dâ blüejet aller slahte list. (*Tristan*, 21–4)

[Recognition and praise create art, where art is so made as to be worthy of praise. When it is decked out with praise, art of every kind will blossom.]

The use of *loben* (what causes art to flourish) in this quatrain corresponds to *gedenken* ('to remember') in strophe 1, i.e. the consideration which makes *daz guote* effective. The first line presents a striking variation of a well-known Cicero quotation: *honos alit artes* ('public esteem is the nurse of the arts').[20] In stating that recognition and praise *schepfent* ('create') works of art which are fashioned in order to be recognized as such, Gottfried uses an apparently circular argument to justify the existence of the work of art by emphasizing its communicative function.

In strophe 7, parallel to the second quatrain, this same argument is restated from a negative point of view:

(7)

Reht als daz dinc zunruoche gât,
daz lobes noch êre niene hât,
als liebet daz, daz êre hât
und sînes lobes niht irre gât. (*Tristan*, 25–9)

[Just as whatever receives neither recognition nor praise will meet with indifference, so that which is accorded recognition and which is not deprived of praise will find favour.]

The eighth strophe, as has already been suggested, addresses itself to those who invert values. The key word of the first five quatrains, *guot*, occurs again here, re-establishing the connection between the aesthetic argument and the ethical one:

(8)

Ir ist sô vil, die des nu pflegent,
daz si daz guote zübele wegent,
daz übel wider ze guote wegent:
die pflegent niht, si widerpflegent. (*Tristan*, 29–32)

[There are so many people today who are in the habit of judging good to be evil and evil to be good. That is not proper conduct, it is misconduct.]

This is followed by the *Kritikerstrophe*, which all too often has provided the basis for a one-sided interpretation of the strophic prologue as a whole:

---

[20] *Tusculanae disputationes* I,ii. On *ars* and art, see Ehrismann, *Studien über Rudolf von Ems*, pp. 3ff.

(9)

> Cunst unde nâhe sehender sin
> swie wol diu schînen under in,
> geherberget nît zuo zin,
> er leschet kunst unde sin. (*Tristan*, 33–6)

[However well artistry and precise understanding may illuminate one another, if they are joined by spite, it will extinguish both art and understanding.]

This refers to the interaction of art and the appreciation of it: such collaboration can only be of benefit to both when it takes place without resentment or ill-will. The word *nît* ('spite') however calls to mind the ethical perspective of the first five strophes. The final strophe then reiterates this standpoint with surprising vehemence:

(10)

> Hei tugent, wie smal sint dîne stege,
> wie kumberlîch sint dîne wege!
> die dîne stege, die dîne wege,
> wol ime, der si wege unde stege! (*Tristan*, 37–40)

[O perfection, how narrow are your tracks, how arduous your pathways! Fortunate is he who treads (= judges) and walks your tracks and pathways!]

The concept of *tugent*, the epitome of excellence, acquires a decidedly ethical, even religious sense from the subsequent biblical image of the narrow path which leads to eternal happiness. The play on the verb *wegen*, which as well as meaning to tread or prepare a path or way, can also mean 'to weigh up', serves to bring in the motif of fair judgement.

To summarize: the argument of the strophic prologue opens with general reflections on *daz guote*. This ethical perspective prevails for the first five strophes, although the aesthetic aspect is implicit throughout and almost becomes explicit in strophe 4. From the sixth strophe onwards there is a marked change of perspective: the arguments used in the first five quatrains are now explictly applied to works of art. However, the eighth strophe already begins to re-introduce the ethical perspective, and the whole argument returns to its starting point in the tenth quatrain, in that the judgement of a work of art becomes part of a wider ethical dimension and is as it were elevated onto a religious plane.

What critics have always found disconcerting about this prologue – the blurring and overlapping of the ethical and aesthetic dimensions – clearly constitutes a deliberate and well thought-out stratagem on Gottfried's part. The technique of argument and representation employed here is that of contrastive repetition, and is thus reminiscent of the scheme of the double cycle. Here, of course, it does not serve critically to subsume one plane or perspective into another; rather, the point of the repeated pattern of argument is to allow the interplay of two dimensions: the ethical perspective leads into the aesthetic one, which in turn is set in a wider ethical context. In its underlying principle, the challenge implicit in the conclusion to the strophic prologue is surprisingly close to that of the prologue to *Parzival*: anyone capable of appreciating what is good, and thus able to appreciate the true value of the good work of art and its relevance, has automatically chosen the narrow path which leads to salvation. The true appreciation of the work of art, therefore, leads to the salvation of the soul.

Second section: stichic prologue, part 1, 41–130

The quatrain which forms the link between the strophic and the stichic prologue (41–4) is distinguished on a formal level from the second group of five quatrains by its use of alternating rhyme words. It also introduces a new theme: Gottfried now speaks of himself and his art. This is continued without a break in the couplets of the stichic prologue, introduced by the quatrain:

> Trîbe ich die zît vergebene hin,
> sô zîtic ich ze lebene bin,
> son var ich in der werlt sus hin
> niht sô gewerldet, alse ich bin. (*Tristan*, 41–4)

> [If I were to pass my time idly when I am ripe for living, then my path through the world would be out of keeping with my true alignment in the courtly world.]

Even here, where Gottfried is introducing himself, he thinks in terms of a wider context. In coining the term *gewerldet*, he defines his identity with regard to his place in society (*werlt*). The following lines then apply this specifically to poetic practice:

> Ich hân mir eine unmüezekeit
> der werlt ze liebe vür geleit
> und edelen herzen zeiner hage,
> den herzen, den ich herze trage,
> der werlde, in die mîn herze siht. (*Tristan*, 45–9)

[I have put myself to some effort to bring joy to society and consolation to noble hearts, to those hearts to whom I feel heartfelt attachment, to that society onto which my heart looks out.]

Gottfried wishes to serve and delight society, and his relationship to it is accordingly described in the most intimate terms, as from *herze* to *herze*, heart to heart. This in turn presupposes a particularly select audience – the key new term here is *edele herzen*. What is meant by this is defined more precisely in what follows:

> ine meine ir aller werlde niht
> als die, von der ich hœre sagen,
> diu keine swære enmüge getragen
> und niwan in vröuden welle sweben:
> die lâze ouch got mit vröuden leben!
> Der werlde und diseme lebene
> enkumt mîn rede niht ebene:
> ir leben und mînez zweient sich.
> ein ander werlt die meine ich,
> diu samet in eime herzen treit
> ir süeze sûr, ir liebez leit,
> ir herzeliep, ir senede nôt,
> ir liebez leben, ir leiden tôt,
> ir lieben tôt, ir leidez leben.
> dem lebene sî mîn leben ergeben,
> der werlt wil ich gewerldet wesen,
> mit ir verderben oder genesen. (*Tristan*, 50–66)

[I do not mean everybody's world, that society of which I hear tell that it can tolerate no hardship and wishes only to float along in joy. They are welcome to their life of happiness. My story does not fit that world and that way of life. Their life and mine part company. It is another world that I have in mind, one where in a single heart there are combined sweet bitterness and delightful grief, heartfelt love and yearning sorrow, pleasant life and grievous death, pleasant death and grievous life. May my life be dedicated to this life, incorporated into this world, and with it live or die.]

It is a traditional feature of the prologue that the poet should define his ideal audience by appealing on the one hand to the indulgence and attentiveness of the clever and the good, while on the other rejecting those who neither will nor can understand. Gottfried draws on this convention to establish the ideal characteristics of his desired audience.[21] An intimate understanding between the poet and his audience is of crucial importance, based on a shared outlook on life, and in particular on love. Gottfried describes this attitude as a characteristic of what he terms *edelez herze*, 'noble heart'. It is of no great relevance whether this term is derived from the classical idea of *nobilitas cordis*, the Old French *gentil cuer*, or the 'noble soul' of the mystics,[22] since Gottfried furnishes it with a specific content of his own: a *herze* is *edel* when it is prepared to accept and affirm in equal measure both desire and torment, pain and happiness, bitterness and sweetness.[23] By identifying with this paradoxical combination, Gottfried implicitly demands the same of his audience, since it forms an essential prerequisite to an understanding of his work. In other words, the call for an audience consisting of *edele herzen* implies they should identify in advance with the idea of love expressed in the work. The 'good person' appealed to in the strophic prologue, who is able to appreciate a good work of art, has become the *edelez herze*, the 'noble heart' who is in harmony with a work which deals with *edele herzen*.

Why does Gottfried lay down these specific conditions for audience response? Why, indeed, this demand for identification with the idea of love before the narrative has even begun? In what follows, Gottfried attempts to justify this: with his tale, he says, he intends to assuage the sorrow of the 'noble hearts', 'to halve their suffering' (75: 'ze halber senfte bringen'), since leisure only exacerbates the pain of love. This combines the topoi of, first, the *senften* ('assuaging') of *swære* ('suffering') through poetry – the most likely source for this is Hartmann von Aue, who uses an almost identical formulation[24] – and, secondly, the topos of poetry as an opportunity for escape from such oppressive leisure, reminiscent of the prologue to the *Alex-*

---

[21] In principle this corresponds to Wolfram's practice; in the prologue to *Parzival* he too demands quite specific qualifications on the part of his listeners; see above, chapter 9, pp. 159–60.

[22] Speckenbach, *Studium zum Begriff 'edelez herze'*; Kunisch, *'edelez herze – edeliu sêle'*; Ganz, 'Tristan, Isolde und Ovid', p. 411.

[23] On the tradition of this stylistic device, see Ganz, 'Tristan, Isolde und Ovid', pp. 406–7, and Gottfried von Strassburg, ed. Ganz, *Tristan*, vol. I, p. 343 – on lines 60ff.

[24] *Der arme Heinrich*, 10f. The connotations of this topos too may vary according to genre – cf. Schulmeister, *Aedificatio und Imitatio*, pp. 156ff. – but cross-referencing between genres also occurs.

ander.[25] However – Gottfried continues – as distraction from the pains of love an occupation should be sought which is not unworthy of love. Love stories are particularly to be recommended:

> ein senelîchez mære
> daz trîbe ein senedære
> mit herzen und mit munde
> und senfte sô die stunde. (*Tristan*, 97–100)

[A passionate lover should occupy himself, heart and lips, with passionate love stories and thus while away the hours of pain.]

However, there is one objection to this *remedium amoris* which Gottfried is unable – or unwilling – to ignore:

> Nun ist aber einer jehe ze vil,
> der ich vil nâch gevolgen wil:
> der senede muot sô der ie mê
> mit seneden mæren umbe gê,
> sô sîner swære ie mêre sî. (*Tristan*, 101–5)

[Now there is something that is said all too often, that I almost go along with: The more the yearning heart occupies itself with stories of amorous passion, the greater will be its own suffering.]

Gottfried's argument thus ultimately contradicts itself. However, this is none other than the inherent contradiction which characterizes the very essence of the *edelez herze,* and so Gottfried draws the inevitable – paradoxical – conclusion (108ff.) that even though love may make one suffer, one nevertheless holds on to it; the greater the love, the more painful the emotion. Nevertheless the 'noble heart' loves this pain, and therefore also stories about love: 'der edele senedære / der minnet senediu mære' (121–2: 'the noble and passionate lover loves tales of passionate love').[26]

Thus the way is prepared for the introduction of the subject matter, for Gottfried now promises to relate a love story which will illustrate and illuminate all of this: the story of Tristan and Isolt.

A love story, then, for lovers. The 'noble hearts' are the lovers who

---

[25] See above, chapter 4, p. 85, and the works cited there under note 23. Gottfried's source may well have been Ovid: cf. Gottfried von Strassburg, ed. Ganz, *Tristan*, vol. I, p. 343, on lines 81f.; also the references to French sources in Niemeyer, 'A rhetorical study of the exordia of romans courtois', pp. 74–5.

[26] One may agree with Fromm, 'Gottfried von Straßburg und Abaelard', p. 196, in seeing a dialectical argument here, although the *solutio* is replaced by acceptance of the paradox. To accuse the author of illogicality – as does Fourquet, 'Prologue du *Tristan* de Gottfried', 253 – is to miss the point.

are prepared to accept both the joys and pain of love and therefore listen to stories about lovers so as simultaneously to intensify and to assuage their pain. Poetry thus comes to represent an encounter with the self in which these inherent contradictions – an essential feature on the part of both work and audience – so far from being resolved, are justified, deepened and intensified.

Third section: stichic prologue, part 2, 131–240/244

Gottfried now comes to speak of the subject matter directly, but this does not take the form of a self-contained *prologus ante rem*. The considerations of source and subject matter are integrated into the ethical and aesthetic perspectives of the first and the second sections of the prologue respectively:

> Ich weiz wol, ir ist vil gewesen,
> die von Tristande hânt gelesen;
> und ist ir doch niht vil gewesen,
> die von im rehte haben gelesen. (*Tristan*, 131–4)

[I well know that there have been many who have told the tale of Tristan, and yet not many of them have told it the right way.]

Gottfried is thus concerned with the authentic version, as distinct from other versions by those who did not have the skill or opportunity to reproduce the tale *rehte* ('aright'). This is reminiscent of the corresponding argument in Chrétien's prologue to *Erec*. By contrast to Chrétien, however, the judgement Gottfried pronounces on his rivals is very mild:

> Tuon aber ich diu gelîche nuo
> und schepfe mîniu wort dar zuo,
> daz mir ir iegelîches sage
> von disem mære missehage,
> so wirbe ich anders, danne ich sol.
> ine tuon es niht: sî sprâchen wol
> und niwan ûz edelem muote
> mir unde der werlt ze guote.
> binamen si tâten ez in guot:
> und swaz der man in guot getuot,
> daz ist ouch guot und wol getân. (*Tristan*, 135–45)

[If, however, I were now so to act and speak as if nothing that any one of them had ever said with regard to this tale had found favour with me, then I would not be acting as I should. I shall not do that. They spoke well and without exception from a noble heart, for my benefit and that of society. They did so with truly good intentions. Whatever a man does with good purpose is in itself good and such conduct is good.]

Unlike Chrétien, then, Gottfried comes to the defence of those who have previously dealt with the same material, imputing to them good intentions which, as enlarged upon in the strophic prologue, at least deserve recognition. This may be explained both by the different literary-historical circumstances, and the particular requirements dictated by the Tristan material. Unlike Chrétien in *Erec*, Gottfried is not dealing with an oral tradition on which, after first transposing it into a written form, he has to impose a structural pattern of meaning. Instead, he is able to situate himself within an established literary tradition, which he also uses to justify his own position – as will be shown in the discussion of the literary excursus. This perspective adds a further angle to the discussion of *daz guote* in the strophic prologue. Gottfried, then, excuses his predecessors on account of their honest efforts. He restricts his criticism to noting that they did not have access to the right source. In referring to the authentic version – the one offered by *der âventiure meister* (151), the Anglo-Norman poet Thomas of Britain, Gottfried places himself in the tradition of *poetae docti* who base – or claim to base – their versions on a written source. This statement is all the harder to verify in that Gottfried claims to have gone back even to Thomas' original source, of which nothing is known; in the process, he adapts formulae used by Thomas himself when referring to his own source.[27] Whatever one's final verdict on these references, fictitious or otherwise, the fact remains that Gottfried uses them to give himself leeway to create his own version. This enables him to postpone the discussion of the relationship between the subject matter and his interpretation of it: he will return to this issue later in another context.

The problem of how meaning is to be conveyed is, however, another matter. Here Gottfried is able to take up the points made on the function of *senemære* ('tales of passion') in the second section of

---

[27] Thomas, *Fragm. Douce*, 841ff.; cf. W. Schröder, '*Die von Tristande hant gelesen*', 313ff. As has been frequently shown above, it is necessary to examine the function of references to the original afresh each time. Further material (though frequently presented all too schematically) is given in: Blumenröder, 'Quellenberufungen'; Ertzdorff, 'Die Wahrheit der höfischen Romane'; Falk, 'Wolframs Kyot'; Pörksen, *Der Erzähler im mittelhochdeutschen Epos*, pp. 61ff.; Lofmark, *The Authority of the Source*.

the prologue: he wishes to present the story of Tristan to the 'noble hearts', 'daz sî dâ mite unmüezic wesen' (171: 'to engage them'). Once again, the effect of such stories on the listener is described, although now in such a way as to leave behind the ambiguities of the possible *remedium amoris* in favour of a wider perspective. Of Tristan and Isolt's *senemære*, it is said:

> ez liebet liebe und edelt muot,
> ez stætet triuwe und tugendet leben,
> ez kan wol lebene tugende geben;
> wan swâ man hœret oder list,
> daz von sô reinen triuwen ist,
> dâ liebent dem getriuwen man
> triuwe und ander tugende van. (*Tristan*, 174–80)

[It enhances happiness and ennobles the heart, it makes fidelity enduring and grants life its perfection. Truly it has the capacity to bestow the highest qualities on life, for whenever one hears or reads about such pure fidelity, fidelity and other fine qualities come to please a man of true fidelity all the more.]

This is then brought, in the four lines below, to the decisive conclusion:

> liebe ist ein alsô sælic dinc,
> ein alsô sæleclîch gerinc,
> daz nieman âne ir lêre
> noch tugende hât noch êre. (*Tristan*, 187–90)

[Love is such a blessed thing, such a blissful endeavour, that no one can attain perfection and honour without its teaching.]

The theme of love is thus seen in the light of the considerations with which the strophic prologue concludes: the key concepts *êre* and *tugent* also appear here, albeit this time in relation to that process which is set in motion in the lover as he or she listens to love-stories.

In characteristic fashion, Gottfried proceeds to formulate the same thing once again from a negative perspective. By excluding those who are not prepared to open their hearts to both the pain and the joy of love, he once more arrives at the inherent contradiction in which the second section of the prologue culminated, and which he now incorporates into the narrative itself:

> liep unde leit diu wâren ie
> an minnen ungescheiden.

> man muoz mit disen beiden
> êre unde lop erwerben
> oder âne sî verderben.
> von den diz senemære seit,
> und hæten die durch liebe leit,
> durch herzewunne senedez clagen
> in einem herzen niht getragen,
> son wære ir name und ir geschiht
> sô manegem edelen herzen niht
> ze sælden noch ze liebe komen. (*Tristan*, 206–17)

[Joy and sorrow have always been united in love. One must earn recognition and praise by means of them both – or perish without them. If those lovers of whose grievous passion this story tells had not borne sorrow for love's sake, if they had not endured together the heartache of sorrowful love for the sake of heartfelt delight, then their names and their fate would not have brought bliss and happiness to so many noble hearts.]

Furthermore, by incorporating the story of Tristan and Isolt into his concept of 'noble hearts', Gottfried is able to develop, by way of conclusion, his most important theoretical argument. Today, he says, we still listen to the tale of the former joy and enduring sorrow of the long-dead lovers:

> al eine und sîn si lange tôt,
> ir süezer name der lebet iedoch
> und sol ir tôt der werlde noch
> ze guote lange und iemer leben ... (*Tristan*, 222–5)

[Even though they have long been dead, nonetheless their sweet names live on, and their deaths shall live on for all time to the benefit of society.]

These ideas are developed further, to the point where finally they culminate in the great crescendo of the final two monorhymed quatrains of the introduction, which then lead into the narrative proper:

> wan swâ man noch hœret lesen
> ir triuwe, ir triuwen reinekeit,
> ir herzeliep, ir herzeleit,
> **D**eist aller edelen herzen brôt.
> hie mite sô lebet ir beider tôt.
> wir lesen ir leben, wir lesen ir tôt

215

und ist uns daz süeze alse brôt.
Ir leben, ir tôt sint unser brôt.
sus lebet ir leben, sus lebet ir tôt.
sus lebent si noch und sint doch tôt
und ist ir tôt der lebenden brôt. (*Tristan*, 230–40)

[For whenever the tale can still be heard being recounted of their fidelity and its purity, of their heartfelt joy and their heartfelt sorrow, that is bread to all noble hearts. Thereby the death of the two lovers lives on. We read their life, we read their death, and we find it as sweet as bread. Their life and their death are our bread. Thus their life lives on and their death lives on. Thus they still live and yet are dead, and their death is the bread of the living.]

With these reflections Gottfried is unmistakably alluding to certain formulations used by Hartmann. Lines 222–3, 'al eine und sîn si lange tôt, / ir süezer name der lebet iedoch' ('even though they have long been dead, nonetheless their sweet names live on'), are a variation on what is said about King Arthur in the prologue to *Iwein*: 'Ist im der lîp erstorben, / so lebet doch iemer sîn name' ('Even though he is now dead, nonetheless his name will live on forever'). Here too the name represents the essence of poetic immortality, and where Hartmann spoke of 'wol wesen ... mit ir mære' ('finding contentment in their story'), and of 'genesen' ('to live, to get along'), Gottfried employs a striking new image by describing the *senemære* ('tale of passion') as bread for the living. The echoes of the Eucharist here are unmistakable. The representation and realization of the life and death of Tristan and Isolt in the act of narration is compared implicitly with the participation, in the sacrament, in Christ's triumph over death: death for love's sake becomes bread, nourishment for those who come later, and this in both cases is seen as the way to eternal salvation.[28] Helmut de Boor even describes Tristan and Isolt in terms of *Minneheilige*, saints or martyrs of love.[29] However, it would be inappropriate to see in Gottfried's romance an elevation of the profane erotic sphere to a kind of sacred cult of love which claims to be on a par with, or even to replace, the Christian act of redemption. In alluding to ideas drawn from the context of the Eucharist, Gottfried is in one sense availing himself of established images; however, his use of them is based on an aesthetic awareness of

---

[28] Schöne, 'Zu Gottfrieds *Tristan*-Prolog', pp. 175ff.; Wolf, 'Zu Gottfrieds literarischer Technik', pp. 387ff.; Stein, 'Formaler Schmuck und Aussage im "strophischen" Prolog', pp. 384ff.
[29] Boor, 'Die Grundauffassung von Gottfrieds *Tristan*', p. 40.

such high seriousness that it does not so much present a challenge to the religious sphere – by offering love as an alternative religion – as lift the action onto a higher, religious plane. In terms of reception, by employing the image of the Eucharist Gottfried is attempting to evoke processes for which, like Hartmann and Wolfram before him, he lacks an adequate terminology. Here too the issue is how far it is possible for a genuine experience of meaning to be conveyed through the medium of literary fiction. The precedence accorded by Hartmann to narrative, as opposed to historical facts, is emphatically re-iterated here; the story of Tristan and Isolt, that is to say the subject matter or plot, provides the basis for a narrative which, in conveying a higher meaning, is intended to lead the audience towards the perfection of *tugent*, to true virtue. This is the sense in which the lovers' *name* lives on and their death is the bread of the living. This use of narrative to convey a higher level of meaning affects the listeners' whole being to such an extent that the work becomes instrumental in their personal salvation. The distinction between the *tumbe* and the *wise* in Wolfram's prologue to *Parzival* corresponds to the exclusion from this process of those hearts which are not 'noble'. The listeners are required to pledge themselves in advance to a positive commitment to salvation, since in order to appreciate the work they must be willing to accept the argument put forward in the work, even before hearing the story.

This again illustrates the problems which the emergence of the romance as a *fictional* construct presented for reception, namely the vicious circle arising from the fact that the 'lack of authenticity' of fictional works can only be remedied by a commitment from the outset to the meaning which the fictional work conveys. Admittedly Gottfried also employs the word *lêre* (189), but it is not meant in the narrow sense, as a moral lesson. Rather, love's *lêre* represents an initiation of the listener into, and an affirmation of, the continually renewed interplay of joy and sorrow, achieved by the identification of the audience with the fictional representation of the doctrine of love, as enshrined in the narrative process.

The arguments of the prologue may be summarized as follows:

1. The opening consists of a *sententia*-like statement: *daz guote* can only be effective if it is recognized and acknowledged as such. The poetic work is then incorporated into this general ethical perspective in such a way that the appropriate aesthetic attitude acquires ethical significance.

2. On the aesthetic level, what characterizes *daz guote* is then defined with reference to the subject matter, namely love as the inextricable interweaving of delight and torment. Gottfried expresses this succinctly in the concept of the *edele herzen* or 'noble hearts'.

3. Adequate response on the part of the good listener presupposes that the latter possesses appropriate qualifications. A *mære* about *edele herzen* will only make sense to, and be understood by, 'noble hearts'.

4. The narrative function of the love-story is fulfilled in the intensification of the conflicting emotions of joy and sorrow in love which is professed by the *edele herzen*. Since *daz guote* is realized in this way in the 'noble hearts', identifying with the narrative must necessarily lead the listeners to ethical perfection.

5. In an aesthetic context, this interdependence of ethics and aesthetics means that the reception process is described by means of religious analogies. These consist on the one hand of metaphors which, in the absence of an adequate theoretical terminology, are pressed into service to describe the way meaning is conveyed in literature, while on the other hand the religious imagery serves to emphasize the existential significance of the experience of meaning in the new fictional medium.

6. Since the romance, as a fictional construct, lacks 'authenticity' – the authority of truth – the poet demands of his listeners, by analogy with religious experience, a personal commitment from the outset to the work and its specific subject matter.

III

One problem which was of central importance to Chrétien, namely the way in which meaning may be established by and within the fictional medium, plays little or no part in Gottfried's prologue. The subject matter appears to contain the meaning in itself, that is to say the problem of meaning is referred back to the authentic source and its correct transmission through *rehtez lesen* ('reading correctly'). This would leave scope for meaning to be determined by interpretation, for where the authenticity of the source was guaranteed, there could be no question of meaning being established via the structure of the work itself.

However, Gottfried too addressed this problem – from his own characteristic perspective – in his literary excursus, in the question of the relationship of words and meaning, *wort* and *sin*. This takes the form of a critical catalogue of poets which is inserted into the description of Tristan's investiture. Gottfried develops it out of the 'protestation of incapacity' or 'inadequacy topos', interrupting his description of the investiture with the excuse that others had described such ceremonies with such excellence in the past that he does not dare to compete with them (4597ff.). This provides him with an occasion to discuss the Middle High German epic and lyric poets to whom he feels himself indebted. Hartmann von Aue takes pride of place: he is accorded the laurel wreath;[30] then come Bligger von Steinach, and Heinrich von Veldeke, who 'inpfete daz êrste rîs in tiutscher zungen' (4738ff.), i.e. was the first to graft a German branch onto the tree of poetry.[31] Then he recalls Reinmar von Hagenau and Walther von der Vogelweide. These poets are discussed in the light of the very problem omitted from the prologue: the relationship of *wort* and *sin*. The aesthetic ideal expressed here is that of 'transparency', the degree to which the word reveals the meaning behind it, as illustrated by the recurring stylistic metaphors of clarity and translucence: *lûter, rein, cristallîn, geliutert*. The antithesis of this ideal of lucidity is embodied by an unnamed poet who is accused of being obscure, and of using lies and deception to trick the listeners into believing that he is offering them something substantial, whereas in fact it is mere empty rhetoric; in short, Gottfried says, he is trying to provide shade with the trunk of the tree instead of with the leafy crown.[32] This rival poet is traditionally identified with Wolfram, and this – even after the many possible reservations have been taken into account – seems highly probable.[33]

[30] On the history of this motif, see Schulze, 'Literarkritische Äußerungen im *Tristan*', pp. 491ff.

[31] Ibid., pp. 506ff., and Winkelman, 'Die Baummetapher im literarischen Exkurs', on the tree of poetry and Veldeke as an author with whom a new literary era begins.

[32] As Brinkmann, *Mittelalterliche Hermeneutik*, pp. 80–1, has shown, this is a traditional image for an unsubstantiated claim.

[33] I am guided in this perennial controversy by the considered position of Norman, 'Meinung und Gegenmeinung'. For an extremely sceptical view, see Geil, *Gottfried und Wolfram als literarische Antipoden*. There is evidence for the view that Wolfram replied to Gottfried's attack in an interpolation of thirty lines that now forms the prologue to the Gawan books (338). In this passage, Wolfram states that there are some poets who show their heroes in such an ideal light that they are unable to live up to these demands and instead end up as shady characters. Unfortunately, he continues, these perpetrators of falsehood are popular with the audience, whereas he, committed to truth (*wârheit*) as he is, does not receive the acclaim he deserves. If my interpretation is correct, this means that Wolfram does indeed here engage with Gottfried's discussion on the connection between art and success, though this question had not previously engaged his attention – rather, his earlier theoretical comments state that he is completely indifferent to the *tumbe* ('dullards'). This would imply

Gottfried does not, in any case, approach the relationship of *wort* and *sin* with the aim of discovering and conveying a meaning hidden behind the words. Rather, the *wort–sin* relationship is presented as a stylistic problem: in theoretical terms, Gottfried appears to be taking up the rhetorical ideal of *perspicuitas* – as indeed he employs a specific rhetorical terminology for his criticism of the various poets.[34] According to this ideal, then, *wort* and *sin* are identical: the *wort* should be of such crystalline clarity that the *sin* is perfectly manifest. Despite the critical exaggeration with which it is presented, it is clear what Gottfried is rejecting by elaborating on this counter-ideal: he is attacking a metaphorical and allegorical means of establishing meaning, for example when he says of the 'tricksters' accused above, 'sî müezen tiutære / mit ir mæren lâzen gân' (4684f.: 'they have to send interpreters to accompany their stories'), or when he remarks that he has no time to look for 'die glôse in den swarzen buochen' (4689f.: 'the gloss in works of black magic'), that is to say that he is not prepared to consult a secret commentary in order to find out what the story means. Gottfried's stylistic ideal of the 'transparency' of the word thus implies that there is no longer any tension between the phenomenon and its significance, and that there is therefore no hidden meaning behind the object; instead, word and meaning are identical. This is an emphatically anti-allegorical principle.[35]

However, to restrict oneself to a purely stylistic interpretation would be to undervalue the significance of Gottfried's aesthetic concept; here, too, Gottfried goes beyond the scope of mere rhetoric, since as far as the conveying and experiencing of meaning is concerned, his ideas here once again follow his distinctive principle of the correlation between *wort* and *sin*. Thus *sin*, on the one hand, indicates the subjective act of establishing meaning on the part of the poet, while on the other, it denotes the concrete product of this act, both in

that Wolfram, annoyed by the charge of falsehood, had become sensitive to the poet's dependence on the audience, and felt forced to respond to the challenge and claim the rights to truthfulness for himself. This is not, however, the same truth as that referred to by Gottfried, which is justified by the goal towards which the narrative process is directed. For Wolfram, a work is 'false' if, like *Tristan*, the narrative remains to some extent independent of any such goal, thus calling into question the idea of an absolute truth, or at best leaving it unanswered. For a more detailed analysis, see Haug, 'Ein Dichter wehrt sich'.

34   The most recent work on this is Huber, 'Wort-Ding-Entsprechungen', pp. 283ff.
35   W. J. Schröder, 'Bemerkungen zur Sprache Gottfrieds', pp. 388–9; Marchand, 'Tristan's Schwertleite', p. 190. However, this need not imply that Wolfram deliberately constructed *Parzival* as an allegory! Gottfried's prologue follows the Latin tradition of the rejection of deliberate obscurity – cf. Moos, 'Literaturkritik im Mittelalter', especially p. 932 – though this would not provide an adequate basis for interpretation.

terms of 'transparency' with regard to the meaning of the individual word, and as the meaning of the work as a whole. The third aspect of *sin* refers to the listener; in other words, *sin* is also used to refer to the act of reception and those abilities which enable the listener to respond to the *sin* of the work and thus 'bring it to life'. However, it is vital to note that it is actually not legitimate to subdivide the term *sin* semantically in this way, since what is important for Gottfried is the dynamic relationship between the establishing of meaning and the experiencing of it; in other words, *sin* is a function of the processes of both production and reception.[36]

Yet by what means or by what authority may this *sin*, perceived as a communicative act, be vouchsafed? Perhaps surprisingly, at the end of his excursus Gottfried turns to the nine Muses on the throne of Mount Helicon, requesting that they distil and purify his words to make them clear and transparent as gems. This appeal to the Muses, the first in the new vernacular tradition, presents a curious fusion of a classical topos with the medieval prayer for inspiration to the Holy Spirit. The nine Muses are seen in conjunction with the nine choirs of angels, raising the question as to the underlying intention behind this Christian transfiguration of the classical mythical tradition, or, one should perhaps say, this mythological appropriation of Christian tradition. What is important is the way Gottfried freely adapts these inspiration topoi for the purposes of his own aesthetic programme, using them metaphorically to justify the new concept of fiction as a free literary invention; the traditional references are merely deployed as a device to lend credibility to his undertaking. Gottfried is thus using the catalogue of poets to reflect and substantiate his own aesthetic programme of the correlation of *wort* and *sin*: this seems to the present writer to be the true purpose of the literary excursus.

If the unity of *wort* and *sin* is seen as an autonomous poetic principle, it is in theory conceivable, in an ideal sense, that language itself can become wholly transparent with regard to meaning, and thus self-sufficient. At the same time, however, this means that there is no longer any external authority capable of guaranteeing the truth of the *wort*; nor do the traditions evoked do more than lend support to this aesthetic principle. Significantly enough, even the appeal to the

---

[36] Hahn, 'Zu Gottfrieds Literaturschau', pp. 424ff.; Winkelman, 'Die Baummetapher im literarischen Exkurs', 93ff., and *'ze guote und ouch ze rehte'*, 86–7; Ruh, *Höfische Epik*, vol. II, p. 261; Huber, 'Wort-Ding-Entsprechungen', p. 293.

Muses is concerned not so much with the truth of the *sin*, as with the perfection of language as a means of communication. Since the truth of poetry is no longer guaranteed by any external authority, language becomes divorced from external reality, and words become susceptible to manipulation. The way out of this dilemma is, however, anticipated in the prologue in the advance commitment of the audience, which is intended to compensate, at the level of reception, for the impossibility of guaranteeing truth within the new autonomy of the fictional construct, which in turn derives from the ideal of the unity of *wort* and *sin*.

However, the intricacies of the truth–language problem go far beyond the question of the establishing of meaning in, and the conveying of it through, the work, since ultimately it touches on the heart of the subject matter itself.[37] In addition to his courtly accomplishments, Tristan is gifted with an uncommon degree of skill with words. Thus it is his skill in the art of concealment, combined with his familiarity with fashionable hunting jargon, which make him a success with Mark's huntsmen and thence at the Cornish royal court. Similarly, it is his artistic, musical and poetic gifts which gain him admission to the Irish court and the post of tutor to the young Isolt. He uses a play on words – reversing the syllables of his name to give Tantris instead of Tristan – to conceal his identity in Ireland. Isolt, too, a good pupil, uses a pun to disclose her love for him, speaking of *lameir*, which can mean 'the sea' or 'bitter', but can also mean 'love'. The ambiguity of the word permits Tristan and Isolt to tell the truth and yet at the same time to be false. A striking example of this is found in the orchard scene, where the lovers meet in secret and discover just in time that they are being observed by Mark. Isolt is able to say, 'I swear I love no man other than him to whom I gave my virginity.' Mark has to believe that this refers to himself, whereas in fact Tristan was Isolt's first lover. The boldest example of this manipulation of the truth is found in the ordeal episode, where Isolt swears that she has lain with no man save her husband, with the exception of the pilgrim who shortly before had carried her from the ship and stumbled as he did so, so that briefly she lay under him. The scene however was stage-managed: the pilgrim was Tristan in

---

[37] On what follows, see Wolf, 'Zu Gottfrieds literarischer Technik', pp. 397ff., 405ff.; Fromm, 'Tristans Schwertleite' and 'Gottfried von Straßburg und Abaelard', pp. 204ff.; Haug, '*Aventiure* in Gottfrieds *Tristan*', p. 124; also in Haug, *Strukturen*, pp. 581–2; Stein, 'Tristans Schwertleite', 347; Wehrli, *Geschichte der deutschen Literatur*, pp. 268ff.; for an alternative, linguistic, account, see Huber, 'Wort-Ding-Entsprechungen', pp. 298ff.

disguise. Finally, however, the possibility of deception through language rebounds on the lovers themselves. Tristan falls under the spell of another woman merely because she too is called Isolt, and this second Isolt believes that Tristan really loves her, because he sings of Isolt, whereas in fact he means another, the Cornish queen. Once words no longer refer to an established range of meaning but are used to create a fictional reality, the way is open for lies and deception to flourish; language which is 'transparent' in itself is particularly liable to ambiguity. It becomes a ready tool which Tristan and Isolt place at the disposal of their love; on the one hand, love, as an absolute ideal, justifies such manipulation; on the other hand, however, it is precisely this manipulation of the power of language which, in dissolving the order of the external world, drives the lovers to their fate: their death too will ultimately be brought about by a lie. The problematic nature of autonomous fiction, which the poet seeks to by-pass in the reception process by demanding the prior commitment of the audience to the concept of love propounded in the romance, thus reappears all the more forcefully within the story itself.

IV

Although the structural concept of *Tristan* differs greatly from that of the Arthurian romance, one of the principal techniques used to establish meaning is nevertheless common to both types of romance. This is the technique of 'variierende Überhöhung', or 'intensified repetition' – the rendering of meaning by superimposing one layer or set of events on another: in more concrete terms, the contrasting repetition of a given pattern of events on a higher level. It is a principle which characterizes both the relationship of the second cycle of action to the first in the Arthurian romance, and that between the love of Tristan and Isolt as compared to the love of Riwalin and Blanscheflur in *Tristan*. This pattern may also be applied to the analogies Gottfried establishes between various classical elements: thus, for example, Isolt is seen as a new Helen, the prayer for inspiration in the literary excursus is analogous to the classical appeal to the Muses, love in the *Minnegrotte* or lovers' cave is set alongside the love stories from Ovid which Tristan and Isolt tell each other, and so on. In *Erec*, the relationship of the new concept of love to that in the older stories represented on Enite's saddle might be cited as a similar example.[38] The variety of material which may be cited in illustration of this technique of 'intensified repetition' – the repetition of a pattern of events on a higher level – has been the subject of numerous studies. Since Julius Schwietering's article of 1925,[39] the technique has been described as a form of typology, or at least as a pattern of thought based on typology. There seems little point in continuing the debate about the appropriateness of extending the exegetical concept of typology to include the techniques outlined above. Nonetheless, there could be no objection if agreement were to be reached on a definition of typology, or of the different forms of the principle of variation and repetition derived from it.[40] The implications for literary theory of such an application of exegetical technique are, moreover, of the greatest importance. The unthinking wholesale adoption of the term typology, by including everything in the idea of a general medieval typological pattern of thought, risks obscuring important historical developments. Rather than merely applying techniques taken from exegetical typology to the courtly romance, it would be more fruitful to investigate the differences between these exegetical techniques, on the one hand, and the patterns of repetition and variation outlined above, on the other.

The semiotic potential of typological, or, in more general terms, figural, exegesis depends on the possibility that things or events can be signifiers of something else while at the same time existing as independent historical facts. For example, the Israelites' crossing the Red Sea and thus being saved from the Egyptians has the status of historical fact; in this capacity however it also anticipates the New Testament rite of baptism, through which the Christian is saved, i.e. is preserved from the devil. History in the Old Testament is devised by God with a view to the New Testament, and in such a way as to prefigure the latter.

The almost inestimable significance, in terms of intellectual history, of typological or figural exegesis lies in the fact that the latter made it possible to derive meaning from history and nature without belittling or even denying their factual existence. This development was,

---

[38] Haug, 'Gebet und Hieroglyphe', 168ff.; also in Haug, *Strukturen*, pp. 114ff.
[39] Schwietering, 'Typologisches in mittelalterlicher Dichtung'. Cf. also the works cited in note 44 below; also chapter 3 above, p. 98. Keuchen, *Typologische Strukturen im Tristan*, may be cited as an example of a consistently typological interpretation of *Tristan*.
[40] Hoefer, *Typologie im Mittelalter*; Jentzmik, *Zu Möglichkeiten und Grenzen typologischer Exegese*; W. Schröder, *Zum Typologie-Begriff*, take a decidedly critical view of this. See also Ohly, 'Typologische Figuren', p. 144, note 1.

however, by no means a foregone conclusion. Only when Alexandrine allegorical exegesis was finally superseded by Antiochene figural interpretation did it become certain that historical reality would not prove evanescent in Christian thought, but would be retained on account of its literal meaning. In spite of considerable resistance, this meant that a positive attitude to the world was possible.[41]

With the aid of this exegetical concept, it also became possible to interpret and justify human artefacts: thus for example a church both *is* the house of God and at the same time signifies this in the eschatological sense of the eternal Heavenly Jerusalem, or of the culmination of *Heilsgeschichte* in the *civitas Dei*.[42] As far as literature is concerned, inasmuch as it refers to facts it will serve as a means of representing the figural tension between the immanence of the divine in earthly phenomena and at the same time its transcendence of the latter.

The semiotic structure of this exegetical scheme disintegrates when it is applied to the fictional realm of courtly literature, since in the fictional pattern of repetition and variation, events cannot simultaneously *mean* and *be*. The story of the love between Riwalin and Blanscheflur does indeed anticipate the love of Tristan and Isolt in a simpler and less problematic or less extreme form, but it cannot be said to 'mean' or stand for this love. The pattern of repetition and variation is thus essentially dependent on the similarity of the subject matter in the two instances; this is, however, not essential in typological exegesis, inasmuch as the latter can also take its cue from incidental features, seeing them in isolation to such an extent that one and the same object may be made the basis of quite different interpretations. The application of typology, as a form of thought and representation, to the new, fictional, literature could only take place at the expense of the underlying semiotic principle. In more positive terms, the adoption of this scheme liberated interpretation from the narrow confines of *Heilsgeschichte*. The technique of repetition and variation, therefore, no longer meant the narrative had to illustrate the fulfilling of a predetermined meaning, and thus the way was opened for innovation. The adaptation of the typological scheme thus permits precisely what its original principle would have prevented, namely the

---

[41] Auerbach, 'Figura'; Bloomfield, 'Symbolism in medieval literature'.
[42] Bandmann, *Mittelalterliche Architektur*; Ohly, 'Die Kathedrale als Zeitenraum'; Brinkmann, *Mittelalterliche Hermeneutik*, pp. 123ff.

idea of progression: repetition as development, or, in more cautious terms, as a first experimental step towards the idea of a development, using a pattern of intensification, variation and repetition to approach the possibility of a meaning which is not laid down in advance but which is left open.

The objection may be raised that even in the realm of fiction it is possible for something to mean and be at the same time, pointing to the 'Joie de la Cort' episode in *Erec*, or the *Minnegrotte* in *Tristan*. However, such fictional constructs which imply a given meaning cannot be of a truly typological nature, but are, rather, allegorical, that is to say they are constructed with a view to a secondary level of meaning which takes precedence over their position in the narrative sequence of action.[43]

It is a well-known fact, however, that even in the early Christian period the range of typological exegesis extended beyond historical facts to the fiction of classical mythology and poetry. Since the appearance of Hugo Rahner's work, *Griechische Mythen in christlicher Deutung* ('Christian Interpretation of Greek Myths', 1944), a great deal of evidence has been accumulated, especially by Friedrich Ohly:[44] Christ is thus seen not only as the true David, the true Gideon, the true Solomon, but also as the true Orpheus and the most high Jupiter. The techniques of typological interpretation seem to have been applied indiscriminately to both historical and poetic or mythological figures and events, so that it is tempting to agree with Herbert Kolb that *der wâre Êlicôn* in Gottfried's literary excursus (4897) refers to nothing other than the Christian source of poetic inspiration, that is to say the Trinity or the Holy Spirit, and that this represents a typological transfiguration of the corresponding classical notions.[45] Ohly by contrast saw in the passage a 'most sublime parody of the openings of religious poems', and Max Wehrli too senses a 'deliberate ambiguity' in this fusion of classical and Christian

---

[43] On the allegorical character of the 'Joie de la Cort' episode, see above, pp. 96–7; on the allegory of the *Minnegrotte*, the most recent comprehensive work is Ernst, 'Gottfried von Straßburg in komparatistischer Sicht', 18ff.

[44] Rahner, *Griechische Mythen*, and *Symbole der Kirche*; Ohly, 'Halbbiblische und außerbiblische Typologie', 'Außerbiblisch Typologisches', 'Typologische Figuren', and 'Skizzen zur Typologie'; cf. also Wehrli, 'Mehrfacher Schriftsinn', 'Antike Mythologie', and *Literatur im deutschen Mittelalter*, pp. 255ff.

[45] Kolb, '*Der ware Elicon*'; on the pre-Christian invocation of the Muses, cf. also Flügel, *Prolog und Epilog*, p. 187, and for the post-medieval tradition Klotz, 'Muse und Helios', pp. 16–17; see also the references in conjunction with the discussion of the *invocatio*, chapter 2 above, p. 40.

ideas.[46] The instincts of these two writers with their subtle feeling for nuances would seem to be justified. The differences between the exegetical and fictional positions should not be overlooked; Christian exegesis, in imposing a figural interpretation on classical poetry and mythology, assumes these works to have contained Christian truths in an encoded form, whether unconsciously or as a deliberate ploy on the part of their poets. The truth to be found in the fictional romance of the twelfth and thirteenth centuries, on the other hand, is that of literary experimentation. Anything which appears typological in this context can only be a kind of game reflecting the new poetic consciousness.[47] Gottfried's Muses are located somewhere between the seductive magic of the sirens and the absolute Truth of God, in a realm of their own whose autonomy is still becoming established; in the juxtaposition of classical and Christian *invocatio*, poetic reflection set its sights on something new, namely the refinement of the poet's word in the 'tegel ... der camênischen sinne' ('crucible of Camenian inspiration'; 4890f.), that is to say, Gottfried is concerned to refine poetic language, making it lucid and effective, so that it is capable, both in and by means of itself, of representing a truth to which, in this very process of refinement, it may be seen to aspire.

---

46 Ohly, 'Wolframs Gebet', 494; Wehrli, 'Antike Mythologie', 31, and *Literatur im deutschen Mittelalter*, pp. 264ff.
47 Hahn, 'Zu Gottfrieds Literaturschau', p. 432 and especially p. 441; Schulze, 'Literarkritische Äußerungen im *Tristan*', pp. 512ff.

The truth of fiction: Thomasin von Zerklære
and *integumentum* theory

I

This chapter is especially indebted to Peter von Moos and Fritz Peter Knapp for their sensitive and critical investigations of the subtle relationship between historical and poetic truth in the Latin tradition of antiquity and the Middle Ages.[1] The fundamental insights achieved by these studies may on the one hand be viewed in connection with the theoretical positions described above in chapters 1–4 (to some extent this has been done already), while on the other they may be contrasted with the new aesthetics of fiction which I have attempted to set out in the analyses given in chapters 5–11.

In what follows, I intend to take up Knapp's argument at the point at which he breaks off, that is to say with the question of the literary-historical significance of the confrontation between Latin-Christian literary theory and the aesthetics of the new romance. Knapp sees the development of the courtly romance as a series of attempts to break free from and/or adapt to its own ends a poetics whose norms are determined by theological criteria, and he describes the 'splendour and misery' of these attempts.[2] What is most striking is the failure of the Latin-Christian tradition to understand the new phenomenon of the fictional romance. If vernacular literature and its explicit and implicit poetics are taken as a starting point, it becomes much more apparent to what extent this literature was capable of achieving autonomy and also of reflecting on and representing its own position. The 'splendour and misery' of the development of the medieval romance owe less to its struggle to come to terms with an inap-

---

[1] Moos, 'Poeta und historicus'; Knapp, 'Historische Wahrheit'; on the changing usage of the term *historia/historie*, see Knape, *'Historie' im Mittelalter.*
[2] Knapp, 'Historische Wahrheit', 582.

propriate poetic theory than to its own internal tensions. However, the confrontation between the Latin and vernacular traditions should not be dismissed lightly, since in some respects it is anything but insignificant from a literary-historical point of view. Before the independent development of the genre is examined further in the chapters which follow, therefore, the perspective should be opened out to include not only an examination of the position of vernacular literature in the High Middle Ages with regard to Latin and theologically based poetics, but also the concrete influence of the latter on the former. It will be remembered from chapter 1 that the question of the relationship between early Christianity and Latin literature was initially governed by a general problem of cultural history, in that it was not possible to ignore the secular tradition and culture completely. The basic solution – albeit one continually called into question – was to incorporate secular subjects into the basic curriculum of liberal arts, thereby effectively reducing them to the status of tools or teaching aids – *instrumenta*, as Notker says – and in this way to some extent neutralizing them and undermining their effect. This did not, however, as we have seen, resolve the basic stylistic conflict, which – rooted as it is in fundamental theological oppositions – continues to recur in varying forms throughout the centuries to come.

However, the existence of poetry as a sphere *sui generis* could not be eliminated by confining it within even the limited scope granted, however reluctantly, to the Liberal Arts. Although the orthodox religious position which equated poetry with vain invention, condemning it out of hand as a lie, was to re-assert itself time and time again, it was, for a variety of reasons, never quite able to win through. The question of the relationship between truth and art, history and poetry, remained open,[3] and the search for literary forms which could serve to convey truth and meaning continued. Even genuine Christian writing made use of figurative or non-literal, that is to say rhetorical or poetical, speech – a prime example being the biblical parables. This ambivalence, indeed polyvalence, of language became increasingly significant as exegetical techniques became diversified in accordance with the possibility of a multiple interpretation of Scripture. However, since the possibility of figurative speech plays such a key role in the Christian understanding of the Word, it was a natural step to usurp classical literature for Christian ends by re-interpreting it in

---

[3] See Moos, 'Poeta und historicus', especially 107ff.

the light of a higher meaning. Furthermore, the creation of new works of fiction for Christian purposes could scarcely be prevented. This led to the adoption of classical theoretical categories, with Macrobius playing a key literary-historical role.[4]

In his commentary on Cicero's *Somnium Scipionis*, Macrobius devised a theory of *fabula* which was to be of central importance for medieval poetics.[5] Macrobius distinguishes three types of *fabula*: first, invented tales told merely for pleasure, such as the Hellenistic romance; secondly, invented tales which exhort us to be good, fulfilling a moral purpose, for example Aesop's *Fables*; and thirdly, the *narratio fabulosa*, in which truth is presented with the help of fictitious material: the example given by Macrobius is the myth of Orpheus, which he sees as a symbolic illustration of a higher truth. Isidore of Seville then takes up this scheme on a much smaller scale, contrasting Aesop's moral fables with a *narratio fabulosa*, which he understands as the fictional representation of natural and historical facts, as when Vulcan becomes a symbol of fire. In the twelfth century, however, the *narratio fabulosa*, as defined by Macrobius, is developed further into the doctrine of *integumentum*. Bernardus Silvestris defines *integumentum* as 'sub fabulosa narratione verum claudens intellectum', 'a true meaning enclosed in an invented tale'.[6] However, Bernardus' use of the term not only covers such cases as the Orpheus myth, but also an epic work such as the *Aeneid*, which he interprets as the journey of the human spirit through the world. In the prologue to his commentary on the *Aeneid* Bernardus returns to this scheme, differentiating between the *delectatio* offered by the tale, particularly its rhetorical and poetic ornamentation; the moral of the story; and finally the deeper meaning, the *integumentum* in the narrow sense. Thus Macrobius' juxtaposition of three forms of fable is elaborated, in Bernardus' poetics, into a tripartite scheme. This is quite simply an ambitious attempt to justify the use of poetic and fictional means to convey meaning on different levels, in analogy to and by contrast with the traditional model of biblical exegesis, which is based on the multiple levels of meaning derived from Scripture. The

---

[4] Brinkmann, 'Die Zeichenhaftigkeit der Sprache', 8ff., and *Mittelalterliche Hermeneutik*, pp. 169ff.; Dronke, 'Eine Theorie über *fabula* und *imago*', pp. 162ff.; Moos, 'Poeta und historicus', 122–3; Meier, 'Überlegungen', 9ff.; Knapp, 'Historische Wahrheit', 61ff. Cf. also Dronke, *Fabula*, pp. 14ff.

[5] On the reception history of this work, see Hüttig, *Macrobius im Mittelalter*. For the continued influence of Macrobius' *fabula* theory, see Minnis and Scott, *Medieval Literary Theory and Criticism*, pp. 118ff.

[6] Quoted in Brinkmann, 'Die Zeichenhaftigkeit der Sprache', 8.

concept of fiction is crucial for this contrast, since within Bernardus' model the factual, literal meaning – corresponding to the first level of truth in biblical exegesis – is replaced by pleasure in the form alone: in other words, fiction, which necessarily lacks this factual level, can possess truth only in its meaning.

Bernardus' scheme was not without influence, even if it never became elevated to the status of a general principle.[7] Alongside it there exists a bewildering variety of attempts to distinguish between the exegetical, philosophical and literary modes of establishing meaning, resulting not only in terminological confusion, but also in a tendency towards over-simplification. However, the lowest common denominator, the basic – over-simplified – position to which all ultimately return, is interpretation according to the *sensus moralis*, which can be applied to everything in a straightforward fashion, whether invented or factual, biblical or secular, Nature or history.

It has on occasion been asked whether the concept of *integumentum* could provide a framework for a theoretical understanding of the fictional romance. This has been answered above, at least in part, in the discussion of Chrétien de Troyes' *Erec* prologue: Chrétien's poetic theory could not be entirely explained in terms of *integumentum*, in that the courtly romance is not simply a vehicle for a philosophical truth clothed in a fictional plot.[8] The kind of poetic composition for which the concept of *integumentum* is an appropriate model is illustrated by the allegorical – to be more precise one should say 'integumental' – poems of Alan of Lille.[9]

Whether the *integumentum* theory was used in the Middle Ages in an attempt to justify the new romance form – against which, on account of its marked fictional content, the charge of falsehood was frequently levelled[10] – is another matter altogether. Hennig Brinkmann claims that Thomasin von Zerklære attempted this;[11] Knapp

---

[7] Knapp, 'Historische Wahrheit', 617–18.

[8] See above, chapter 5, p. 104. Nor does the *integumentum* theory offer the key to *Tristan*, despite Jaeger, *Medieval Humanism*, pp. 153ff. The only contemporary theoretical statement which has been ascribed to an allegorical conception of fictional courtly literature, a remark in Marie de France's prologue to her *Lais* – cf. Spitzer, 'The Prologue to the Lais of Marie de France'; Robertson, 'Marie de France' – has been wrongly interpreted; see Donovan, 'Priscian and the obscurity of the ancients'.

[9] Cf. Wetherbee, *Platonism and Poetry* – who does not however always take into account the difference between the genres.

[10] Cf. chapter 13 below, p. 252 and note 26.

[11] Brinkmann, 'Verhüllung als literarische Darstellungsform', p. 322, and *Mittelalterliche Hermeneutik*, pp. 179–80.

disagrees.[12] In either case, Thomasin's attempt at a theoretical justification of the new romance – and the fact that Thomasin's own *Wälscher Gast* dates from 1215–16 – is of considerable interest with regard to the possibilities of reception in Wolfram and Gottfried's time.

II

After an entirely conventional preface which – naturally enough, given that it is a textbook of moral instruction – emphasizes the didactic aspect of the work,[13] Thomasin draws up a kind of educational programme.

First he addresses the young, beginning with the young ladies:

> nu wil ich sagen waz diu kint
> suln vernemen unde lesen
> und waz in mac nütze wesen.
> juncvrouwen suln gern vernemen
> Andromaches, dâ von si nemen
> mügen bilde und guote lêre,
> des habent si beidiu vrum und êre. (*Wälscher Gast*, 1026–32)

> [Now I shall tell you what young people should listen to and read, and what can be of profit to them. Young maidens should take pleasure in hearing of Andromache, from whom they can take example and derive good instruction. From that they will benefit and earn recognition.]

Thomasin thus first presents the young ladies with a figure from the story of Troy as an example to follow, namely the wife of Hector. He then moves on to characters from courtly romance, but almost immediately intersperses these with legendary historical figures:

> si suln hœren von Ênît,
> daz si die volgen âne nît.
> si suln ouch Pênelopê
> der vrouwen volgn und Oenonê,
> Galjênâ und Blanscheflôr,
> ... unde Sôrdâmôr.
> sint si niht alle küneginne,
> si mügen ez sîn an schœnem sinne. (*Wälscher Gast*, 1033–40)

---

[12] Knapp, 'Historische Wahrheit', 623.
[13] Rocher, *'Der Wälsche Gast'*, pp. 269ff.; Ruff, *Der 'Wälsche Gast' Thomasins'*, pp. 20ff.

232

[They should hear about Enit and emulate her without protest. They should also emulate Penelope and Oenone, Galiena and Blanscheflor ... and Sordamor. Even if these are not all actually queens, they are such in beauty of spirit.]

On the one hand, these are names from the story of Troy and the Charlemagne legend:[14] Galiena is the legendary wife of Charlemagne, while Oenone is Paris' beloved – and on the other hand characters from the new courtly romance: Enite from *Erec*, Sordamor from *Cligés*, while Blanscheflur may refer to either Perceval's *amie* or the heroine of the Floris romance; the name which preceded Sordamor in the original has been corrupted and can no longer be identified.

Two things are striking about this sequence. First, Thomasin does not recommend authors, or even works, but rather individual figures as models; chosen for their exemplary behaviour, they offer valuable instruction, *guote lêre* (1031). What matters is not their rank, but their *schœner sin* ('beauty of spirit'; 1040); this describes an inner attitude which is revealed in the form of calm and beautiful dignity. Secondly, it is striking that the series of examples cuts across all genres; examples are taken from the *matière de Rome* as well as the *matière de Bretagne* and the *matière de France*. The literary type is thus largely irrelevant:[15] theme and subject matter seem of little or no importance, since all that counts is the exemplary character of the individual figures.

When Thomasin then turns to the young men in his audience (1041ff.), he follows the same pattern. The sequence runs as follows: Gawein, Cligés, Erec, Iwein, Charlemagne, Alexander, Tristan, Sagremors, Kalogrenant. It can hardly be a coincidence that Gawein is placed first; he is the epitome of the courtly knight, perfectly formed and almost entirely unproblematic. In later romances he is promoted to a major figure, while in the 'classical' period he plays at best a supporting role as a kind of personification of the Arthurian ideal. Either way, he makes a particularly apt exemplary figure. Here too the distinctions between genres are disregarded: characters from courtly romance rub shoulders with historical figures. The three figures at the end – Tristan, Sagremors and Kalogrenant – provide a clear illustration of how far Thomasin is able to play down or set aside the problematic aspects of courtly romance, since all three characters

---

[14] See Düwel, 'Lesestoff für junge Adlige', on the forms of the names, possible identities and probable sources.

[15] It is significant that the native heroic epic is omitted, as Fechter has noted: see *Das Publikum der mittelhochdeutschen Dichtung*, p. 71.

can only be seen as exemplary in a very limited sense. Admittedly, Tristan may be considered exemplary, at least with regard to *gevuoc*, in other words the command of courtly etiquette; but Sagremors' reckless behaviour in the Grail romance meets deserved punishment at the hands of Parzival, and Kalogrenant's defeat at the fountain in *Iwein* can scarcely be said to recommend him.

Thomasin goes on to present negative examples by way of warning:

> kint, lât iuch niht an trâkeit
> und volget vrumer liute lêre,
> des komt ir ze grôzer êre.
> irn sult hern Key volgen niht
> von dem mir vil unwirde geschiht:
> der tuot mir allenthalben nôt.
> jâ ist her Key noch niht tôt
> und hât dar zuo erben vil;
> ichn weiz war ich mich kêren wil.
> sîniu kint heizent alsam er:
> ê was ein Key, nu ist ir mêr. (*Wälscher Gast*, 1056–66)

[Young people, keep clear of sloth. Heed the instruction of good people, and that will lead to great honour. Do not emulate Sir Key, through whom I have suffered great dishonour. He is always tormenting me. Sir Key is certainly not dead yet, and furthermore he has many heirs. I do not know which way to turn. His children all take on his name. There used to be one Key, now there are more.]

Key is not dead; this statement gives a curious new twist to the idea of the immortality of the name of courtly heroes first formulated by Hartmann. However, in this instance the motif is not used to justify poetry as fiction; rather, a figure from romance is used metaphorically in connection with actual reality. Key, that is to say the wicked type of person whom he embodies, is actually still with us today, and not merely in one single example but in such numbers that there is no avoiding him. In the case of Parzival, unfortunately, the situation is quite different:

> ez schînt daz Parzivâl nien lebet,
> wan der her Key nâch êren strebet
> mit lüge und mit unstætekeit,
> mit spotte und mit schalkeit.
> gelouben sult ir mir ein mære,
> ob ichz Parzivâl wære,

daz ich etlîchen Key stæche,
daz ich im ein rippe noch zebræche.
ouwê, wâ bistu Parzivâl?
wan wær noch inder dehein grâl
und stüende er umb einn phenninc phant,
in erlôst niht Keyes hant. (*Wälscher Gast*, 1067–78)

[It seems that Parzival is no longer alive, but Sir Key pursues honour with lies and duplicity, mockery and knavery. Believe me, if I were Parzival I would unhorse any number of Keys and break their ribs. Alas, where are you, Parzival? If there was still a grail somewhere that could be redeemed for as little as a penny, Key would not do so.]

Key's broken rib represents a somewhat imprecise allusion to the scene with the drops of blood in Wolfram's Grail romance, where Parzival punishes Keie for his impudence by unseating him from his horse with his lance. This episode here becomes an image of the victory of courtly behaviour over its uncouth opposite, of good over evil. However, this battle is long since past; the only one of the former heroes still living is Key.

Thomasin is thus judging the present by the standards of the idealized Arthurian past, and this provides the new, moral sense of the romance. Reception here is not understood as a narrative process with which the listener must engage; instead, the literary figures and scenes illustrate universal patterns of behaviour. The aesthetic counter-position to the process of audience identification is instruction by exemplum.[16] The exemplum, then, merely demands *imitatio*, presenting itself as an example to be followed; the identification of the audience with the narrative, however, is intended to represent and resolve, on a fictional level, the fundamental questions of human experience.

Ir habt nu vernomen wol
waz ein kint hœrn und lesen sol.
ave die ze sinne komen sint
die suln anders dann ein kint
gemeistert werden, daz ist wâr.
wan si suln verlâzen gar
diu spel diu niht wâr sint:
dâ mit sîn gemüet diu kint.
ich enschilte deheinen man

---

[16] Jauss, *Ästhetische Erfahrung und literarische Hermeneutik*, pp. 156–7.

der âventiure tihten kan:
die âventiure die sint guot,
wan si bereitent kindes muot.
swer niht vürbaz kan vernemen,
der sol dâ bî ouch bilde nemen.
swer schrîben kan, der sol schrîben;
swer mâlen kan, der sol belîben
ouch dâ mit; ein ieglîcher sol
tuon daz er kan tuon wol.
von dem gemâlten bilde sint
der gebûre und daz kint
gevreuwet oft: swer niht enkan
verstên swaz ein biderb man
an der schrift verstên sol,
dem sî mit den bilden wol. (*Wälscher Gast*, 1079–1102)

[You have now heard what young people should listen to and read. But, in truth, those who have reached maturity should be instructed differently from children. For they should completely abandon such mendacious stories, those are used for taxing children. I am not criticizing anybody who writes poems of 'adventure'. Such poems are of benefit in that they have an improving effect on the young person. Anyone whose understanding goes no further than that should find models for himself there. He who can write should write. He who can paint should stick to that. Everybody should do what they can do well. The man of no education and the child often take pleasure in a painted picture. He who fails to grasp from a written text what a man of experience would get from it should content himself with pictures.]

Here the traditional cultural and historical opposition between the educated and uneducated, *litteratus* and *illitteratus* re-emerges, but in a very different situation and with correspondingly different emphasis.[17] Vernacular writing had been campaigning against this dualism for more than a century, until finally a lay consciousness of education developed which found particular expression in courtly literature. This emancipation of the vernacular ultimately reached the point where Wolfram was able to bid farewell to any dependence on book-learning. Thomasin is here taking one step forwards and one step back at the same time. On the one hand, his didactic moral poem

---

[17] The relationship between the new position and the traditional opposition is not entirely consistent, as shown by Curschmann, 'Hören – Lesen – Sehen', pp. 238ff.

opens up a new sphere of knowledge to the vernacular which had formerly been a prerogative of the Latin tradition; but at the same time he falls back on a position which undermines the status which the courtly romance had achieved meanwhile in terms of secular educational awareness. The courtly romance, says Thomasin, although not true, has some benefit, though it is only of use to the uneducated, i.e. young people and *gebûre* ('rustics'). Just as those who are unable to read may and should stick to pictures, so too it is permissible for those whose powers of reason are not yet ready for higher knowledge to listen to or read *âventiure* romances. There is no reason they should not enjoy them; 'wol dermite wesen' (1110), and they may also derive moral benefit from such tales: 'daz bezzert (ir) sinne' (1112).[18]

The idea of *wol wesen* (literally 'to make content'), corresponding to the traditional *delectare*, was in Hartmann's works given a deeper meaning within the context of the living reality of the fictional world. In connection with 'ouch nû genesen' ('to live nowadays'), he applied it to a new, autonomous form of literary experience. In Thomasin, on the other hand, the meaning is once more reduced to the simple pleasure in the story which is to be recommended and justified on account of the improvement or *bezzerunge* it may confer. However, anyone not obliged to rely on such indirect understanding through images is exhorted not to waste time on *âventiure*, but rather to seek a direct approach to the truth. Thomasin then returns to an explicit discussion of the relationship between truth and falsehood in the romance:

> die âventiure sint gekleit
> dicke mit lüge harte schône:
> diu lüge ist ir gezierde krône.
> ich schilt die âventiure niht,
> swie uns ze liegen geschiht
> von der âventiure rât,
> wan si bezeichenunge hât
> der zuht unde der wârheit:
> daz wâr man mit lüge kleit. (*Wälscher Gast*, 1118–26)

[The stories of 'adventure' are often decked out with the most

---

[18] On the Latin tradition that saw poetry as a form of instruction in 'nurseries', see Dronke, *Fabula*, pp. 17–18, and 'Eine Theorie über *fabula* und *imago*', p. 164. On the *bezzerunge* argument, see Boesch, *Die Kunstanschauung in der mittelhochdeutschen Dichtung*, pp. 30ff.; Schulmeister, *Aedificatio und Imitatio*, pp. 127ff., 168.

elaborate lies. The lie is the very crown of their embellishment. I am
not criticizing the 'adventure' stories, even though they induce us to
lie, for such tales may signify good behaviour and truth: Truth is
clothed in untruth.]

Thomasin's attitude towards courtly literature seems ambivalent.
On the one hand, he does not wish to reproach the poets of *âventiure*,
indeed he even expressly thanks them that they have 'put many
stories of *âventiure* into German' (1136f.: 'der âventiure vil / in
tiusche zungen hânt verkêrt'), since these *âventiure* are excellent
examples of *vrümkeit* ('worthiness'; 1134), which is all the uneducated
have to rely on. However, these works are still tainted with falsehood,
that is to say they are fictitious, and it is preferable to seek a direct
way to the truth.

The idea of truth clothed in falsehood is reminiscent of the concept
of *integumentum*, and there can be no doubt that Thomasin's
justification of the romance is based on those Latin discussions
regarding the 'legitimacy' of fiction which ultimately led to the
doctrine of *integumentum*. At the same time it must be borne in mind
that such an interpretation would go beyond the scope of Thomasin's
own theoretical scheme, since the courtly romance has no allegorical
or philosophical pretensions. Thomasin sees in it nothing more than a
vehicle for exemplary individual figures illustrating models of behaviour; he regards moral philosophy, as presented in his *Wälscher
Gast*, as more advanced by comparison. In the romance, according to
Thomasin, philosophy does not borrow the robes of fiction which
would fit her; rather, fiction is seen as merely the ante-chamber to
truth itself and should be traversed as quickly as possible. Thomasin
is thus no advocate of a theory of the courtly romance derived from
the doctrine of *integumentum*,[19] but instead takes up the general
interpretation of fiction according to its *sensus moralis*, or moral
sense, thus occupying – as, *inter alia*, his use of courtly characters as
exemplary figures shows – a theoretical position less advanced than
those of Chrétien, Hartmann and Wolfram, who progressed beyond
the doctrine of *integumentum* to a poetics which attempted to
account for the autonomous truth of fiction. It is thus not surprising
to find Thomasin launching an attack on Hartmann's introduction to

---

[19] Huber, 'Höfischer Roman als Integumentum?', has recently attempted once more to
interpret Thomasin's literary theory from the point of view of *integumentum* theory.
His arguments have been opposed by Knapp, 'Integumentum und Âventiure', Nellmann,
'Wolfram und Kyot', 42, note 65, and Heinzle, 'Entdeckung der Fiktionalität', 75–6.

Iwein. The critical issue here is the survival of the *name* (3520ff.). Thomasin condemns as futile all striving for worldly fame – in the end we must all leave this world, he says, and the *name* is then irrelevant:

> seht, Artûs was wol erkant
> und ist ouch hiute genuoc genant:
> nu sage mir, waz hilft in daz?
> im tæte ein pâter noster baz.
> ob Artûs gots hulde haben sol,
> er enbirt unsers lobes wol:
> ist aver er in der helle grunde,
> unser lop mêrt sîne sunde,
> wan er uns materge gît
> grôzer lüge zaller zît. (*Wälscher Gast*, 3535–44)

> [Look, Arthur was well known, and even today many people talk of him. Now tell me, what good is that to him? He would benefit more from a *Pater noster*. If Arthur has found favour with God, he doesn't need praise from us. And yet if he is down in hell, our praise will increase his sin, for his doings are a constant source of material for huge lies.]

This shows clearly enough that Thomasin did not perceive the survival of the *name* to be the epitome of the new, autonomous fiction: he thus, by extension, either failed to understand Hartmann's literary theory, or, at least, was unable to accept it. In his view, the *Iwein* prologue did no more than to promote vainglory, the desire for fame, and when he finally takes up the idea that the fame of a king can furnish material for tales, these 'lies' are here referred back to the historical figure of Arthur; they would represent a burden in the hereafter, Thomasin claims, especially should he be condemned to hell. This seems far more radical than the declaration of pedagogic intentions at the beginning of the work.

Thomasin thus reduces the new theory of fiction – in so far as he is prepared to allow the *âventiure* any significance at all – to the traditional moral formula. Not all modern critics of courtly romances have been able to resist the temptation to follow this easy path.[20]

However, the importance of this reductive, moralistic mode of reception in the Middle Ages should not be underestimated: Thomasin testifies to its significance for the contemporaries of the

---

[20] For example Dittmann, '*Dune hâst nicht wâr, Hartman!*'; Carls, 'Die Auffassung der Wahrheit im *Tristan*'.

'classical' romance writers. It represents the fall-back position for all those not prepared to risk committing themselves to the fictional process, or who lack the necessary insight and understanding to do so: another prime example of the critical significance of Wolfram's brusque rebuttal of all those who expect to find a clear moral lesson in his work.

At the same time, however, in view of the later development of the courtly romance it is important to note that there had always been a tendency for the audience to demand a return to the didactic mode. The chapters which follow aim to investigate how the pressure of these demands was met, and the problems of representation and theory that this involved. These problems came to be a crucial factor in the later Arthurian romance, and are also central to the theoretical reflections of Rudolf von Ems and Konrad von Würzburg.

However, it should be pointed out that this process cannot readily be distinguished from the effects produced by the increasing distance in time from the poets of the 'classical' courtly era, their works and the specific socio-cultural conditions of the age. The poets of the *Blütezeit*, the creators of the new courtly literature, later acquire the status of classics. Lists of them are drawn up, in imitation of Gottfried von Strassburg's literary excursus, but with an increasing disregard for individual traits, so that all that counts is a general awareness of the quality of formal achievement. This corresponds to an increasing uniformity of content, in which the problematic aspects and open questions in the subject matter are reduced to a representation of unambiguous norms of behaviour. All that remains of Gottfried's 'correlation', or unity of form and meaning, is the idea of stylistic excellence and moral excellence respectively. This leads on the one hand to giddy heights of exaggerated artistry, particularly in the case of the lyric; and on the other, in the late courtly romance, to a new type of hero who incontestably fulfils the requisite norms of behaviour. The problem which faced these 'post-classical' authors, however, as will be seen, was how to bridge the gap which had reopened between form and meaning, with regard to poetic self-consciousness and to reception, both of which had become problematical as formal artistry ceased to be identified with the concept of moral excellence.

13

The *Lucidarius* A-prologue in the context of contemporary literary theory, and the origins of the prose romance

I

The composition of the *Lucidarius*, the first German *summa*, marks an important stage in the ongoing appropriation of Latin literary forms by means of vernacular translations and adaptations. Written in the form of a dialogue between master and pupil, it presents an encyclopaedic outline of contemporary knowledge of the universe and the world, the doctrine of salvation, the institutions of the church, and the Last Things. The main source is Honorius Augustodunensis, but a number of other authors are also cited.[1] The history of the manuscript transmission remains in many respects complex and obscure. Georg Steer has been endeavouring to throw light on these questions.[2]

The *Lucidarius* is written in prose. Only the prologue, which is extant in two versions (A and B) is in verse. The two versions differ considerably. Prologue B has a carefully planned trinitarian structure, corresponding to the tripartite structure of the work itself. Steer has produced a convincing account of this, absolving the author from the popular charge of incompetence.[3] The author of prologue A is concerned with quite different matters, including the relation of the circumstances under which the work was composed. He also discusses the literary form:

> Diz buch heizet elucidarius
> vnde ist durch recht geheisen sus,
> wan ez ist ein erluchtere.
> Swer gerne vremde mere

---

[1] Steer, '*Lucidarius*', col. 940f.; Sturlese, 'Filosofia e scienza', 165ff.
[2] This is in the context of his work on a new edition of the text: see Steer, 'Der deutsche *Lucidarius* – ein Auftragswerk?', 3.
[3] Ibid., 4ff.

von der schrift vernemen wil,
der mac hie horen wunders vil
in disme cleinen buche.
man soldes verre suche,
e man ez vunde entsam geschriben.
Got selbe hat den sin gegebin
deme herzogen, der ez schriben liez.
Sine capellane er hiez
die rede suchen an den schriften
vnd bat, daz sie ez tihten
an rimen wolden,
wan sie ensolden
nicht schriben wan die warheit,
als ez zv latine steit.
Daz taten sie willecliche
dem herzogen heinriche,
der es in gebot vnd bat.
Zv brunswic in der stat
wart ez getihtet vnde geschriben.
Ez enwere an dem meister niht bliben,
er hette ez gerimet, ab er solde.
Der herzoge wolde,
daz man ez hieze da
Aurea gemma.
Do duchte ez den meister bezzer sus,
daz ez hieze lucidarius,
wan ez ein irluchter ist.
Der heilige geist gab im die list.
Er was der lerer
vnde ouch der vrager,
der daz buch tichte. (*Lucidarius*, 102*1–104*12 [1–35])

[This book is called the 'Elucidarius' and is rightly so called, for it is
a lantern. Whoever desires to hear strange things taken from books
can learn many marvellous things here in this little book. You
would have to look far before you would find it all set out in one
place. God himself gave the idea to the duke who commissioned it.
He instructed his chaplains to seek out this matter from books and
requested that they should not set it down in rhymed verse, for they
were to write down nothing but the truth, as it is in the Latin. They
did this willingly for Duke Henry, who put the request to them and
issued this command. It was composed and written down in the city
of Braunschweig. The master would not have failed to do it: he
would have written it in rhymed verse if that had been what he had

to do. The duke wanted it to be called the 'Aurea gemma', but the master thought it better that it should be called the 'Lucidarius', for it gives illumination. The Holy Ghost gave him the skill, He who composed the work was both the master and the disciple who put the questions.]

The *herzoge Heinrich* (20) named here has in the past been identified as Henry the Lion, Duke of Saxony, and he has traditionally been held responsible for commissioning the first large-scale German work in prose – a major innovation, the cultural significance of which critics have not been slow to recognize.[4] Recently, however, Steer has cast doubt on this.[5] On the basis of his examination of the manuscript transmission, he has established that the A-prologue, hitherto considered to be earlier than the B-prologue (and thus the authentic, original version), only appears in a relatively small and quite evidently secondary branch of the stemma.[6] The question remains as to whether the author of prologue A had access to real facts about the origins of the work, or whether he simply invented this information, making use of current prologue topoi, for the greater glory of Henry the Lion. Steer, who takes the latter view, furthermore doubts whether the *Lucidarius* even originated in Braunschweig. He maintains that the work was originally written not in Low German – as one would have to expect in Braunschweig – but in Upper German, and the pattern of transmission is from the South to the North, and not the other way around.[7] A decision about these matters is complicated by the fact that, if Henry the Lion cannot be assumed to have commissioned the work, it is not possible to establish a precise date for it with any degree of certainty. The oldest manuscript for prologue A dates from the last third of the thirteenth century,[8] and it is an open question as to how far back this branch of the textual tradition may actually be traced.[9] However, there are no

4   Stackmann, '*Lucidarius*', col. 624.
5   Steer, 'Der deutsche *Lucidarius* – ein Auftragswerk?'.
6   See the manuscript stemma in ibid., 7. Prologue A is attested only in the y branch, where in y4 the work is reduced to the first two books only: it is not found until MS y15. The revision of the prologue would thus seem to be associated with the fact that the trinitarian references had no relevance in the shorter B version.
7   Ibid., 1ff., 24–5.
8   Ibid., 25, note 53.
9   Steer, ibid., 25, dates the composition of prologue A to the mid-thirteenth century, but there is insufficient evidence for this. The supposed borrowings from the *Sidrach*, the *Älterer deutscher Macer*, the *Sachsenspiegel* and Wernher von Elmendorf could also, as was previously assumed, be derived from the *Lucidarius* prologue. Cf. the relevant passages in ibid., 19–22.

good reasons for placing it significantly later than 1195, the year of Henry's death; otherwise it would be necessary to conjecture that the wish expressed at the end of the prologue – that God should receive Henry's soul into his care (44: '[got] neme des herren sele an sin geleite') – was only added to disguise the fact that the prologue was composed much later – a degree of sophistication with which one would scarcely credit the author of prologue A. Nor is the language argument tenable, since the *meister* entrusted with the undertaking may himself have been from southern Germany. Moreover, the origins and direction of the manuscript distribution are far from clear. Convincing as Steer's arguments for the precedence of prologue B are, I am reluctant to accept that the statements in prologue A on the origins of the work are a later invention. Just as the Vorau version of the *Ezzolied*, though later than the Strasbourg version, nevertheless presents authentic information about the origins of the poem,[10] so too the *Lucidarius* A-prologue could well have preserved information about the actual circumstances which gave rise to the work. Be that as it may, there can be no doubt that what lies behind this prologue is the debate about the relationship between truth and the use of verse, which starts around 1200. The statement that Henry insisted on prose because only this form allows a true, i.e. faithful, rendering of the Latin original cannot be explained away, as Steer attempts to do, as a standard element of the German vernacular prologue tradition.[11] Rather, the remark of the *meister* that he could just as well have produced a rhymed version emphasizes just how unusual the duke's demand for a prose version was. Probably in order to demonstrate this competence, the author composes the prologue, at least, in verse – as the author of the B-prologue had done without any explanation.

The fact that the author of prologue A registers the prose form as being unusual reflects the general attitude in Germany at the time:

---

[10] See *Frühe deutsche Literatur*, ed. Haug and Vollmann, pp. 570–1, and commentary, pp. 1411–12 and 1415–16.

[11] Steer in 'Der deutsche *Lucidarius* – ein Auftragswerk?', 19, bases his argument on a somewhat forced reading of lines 16–18. He reads 'wan sie ensolden / nicht schriben wan die warheit, / als ez zv latine steit' as follows: 'rather they should write the truth (of the book) in the form that is used (= *ez*, not *si* = *die warheit*) in the Latin sources (i.e. in prose).' The pronoun *ez* however refers, as parallel uses show, not to the form but to the subject matter; cf. for example Konrad's *Rolandslied*, 9080ff.: 'Also iz an dem buche gescribin stât / in franczischer zungen, / sô hân ich iz in die latîne bedwungin, / dann in die tûtiske gekêret' ('Just as it is written in the book in French, so I have adapted and translated it into Latin, and then put it into German'). Konrad certainly does not mean by this that he has produced a version of the *Chanson de Roland* in Latin verse.

around 1200 and after, the use of verse is still obligatory in all vernacular literary genres – apart from functional texts such as sermons, prayers, medicinal recipes, and so on. The general shift from verse to prose originated in French-speaking areas; the earliest documents available date from the early thirteenth century. There can therefore be little doubt that the thesis in prologue A, that prose is a more truthful form than verse, is indebted to these developments in France and England. It was probably through his family connections with the English royal household, and in particular his exile during Barbarossa's crusade, that Henry the Lion became directly acquainted with contemporary literary trends in the French-speaking world, though one would have to assume that this first occurred about a decade before the oldest surviving French documents of this discussion, which is entirely possible. Anyone who objects to this assumption could argue that this supports a later dating of prologue A; the fact remains that around 1200 the respective merits of the use of verse or prose were, for a while at least, a matter of lively discussion in German-speaking areas.[12]

As far as the subsequent history of German literary works in prose is concerned, it is striking that despite the widespread distribution which *Lucidarius* achieved, this breakthrough in the use of prose did not lead to a general shift to prose comparable to that taking place at the time in France. In Germany, prose continued to be treated warily for at least another fifty years, even longer in the case of the romance. There was an isolated attempt to naturalize the French 'Prose Lancelot', but the German version does not seem to have been a great success, at least not in the first instance;[13] what is more, it failed to initiate a native tradition of prose romance in the thirteenth century. Thus where theoretical discussion is concerned the *Lucidarius* likewise remains an isolated example;[14] the debate about verse *versus*

---

[12] Cf. the examples in note 9 above.

[13] Steinhoff, 'Zur Entstehungsgeschichte des deutschen Prosa-Lancelot'. I have reservations about Heinzle's 'Zur Stellung des Prosa-Lancelot', which attempts to understand the translation of the *Lancelot en prose* in the context of the literary situation in the mid-thirteenth century, pointing out that this romance displays the characteristic features, i.e. the return to a religious dimension and the use of historical material. However, it seems likely that at this time only the *Lancelot propre* had been translated (and this too remained a fragment: cf. Steinhoff, 'Zur Entstehungsgeschichte des deutschen Prosa-Lancelot', pp. 88ff.) – thus the explicitly religious aspects were not even available for discussion at the time.

[14] Such examples as may be found are cited in note 9. The German *Buch Sidrach*, where the verse *versus* prose discussion is presented in a rhymed prologue, is based on a Middle Dutch version of a thirteenth-century French text. Cf. Unger, 'Vorreden deutscher Sachliteratur', p. 225; Beckers, '*Buch Sidrach*'; Steer, 'Der deutsche *Lucidarius* – ein Auftragswerk?', 19–20.

prose in Germany does not begin in earnest until the fifteenth century, and even then occurs only sporadically.[15]

The situation in France is completely different. Until 1200, French literature too almost exclusively employs verse. Then, almost at a stroke, prose takes over; this is true in all genres, albeit to varying degrees.[16] As far as religious literature is concerned, Bible translation continues to use verse into the fourteenth century, apart from a few early attempts in prose, but hagiography goes over to prose around 1200. Moral and didactic genres, including bestiaries, make use of the new form to some extent, although verse remains prevalent until well into the sixteenth century. In historiography, prose chronicles become established on a large scale around 1200 with the works of Pseudo-Turpin, Geoffroi de Villehardouin, Robert de Clari and Henri de Valenciennes. In the romance, prose begins to replace verse around 1200, the first prose romance being Robert de Boron's *Joseph d'Arimathie*. The first romance to be conceived in prose from the outset is *Perlesvaus*, and within a few years it is followed by the extensive romance compilations of the *Lancelot en prose* and the *Tristan en prose*.

The breakthrough of prose is thus particularly marked in historical writing and in the romance; other genres are slower to follow suit. There is nothing comparable to this decisive literary-historical shift in any other Romance literature, and certainly not in German. Nor, indeed, is it shared by medieval Latin literature, since the relationship between verse and prose there had always been of a fundamentally different nature:[17] on the one hand, the use of prose or verse in different genres was fixed by tradition, and on the other hand, verse was viewed as a purely ornamental form, so that alternating use of verse and prose was quite unproblematic. The transposition of a text from one form to the other was a common medieval school exercise, and prose was required to be no less artistic than verse. This does not of course imply that the relationship between verse and prose was not discussed, since it was necessarily drawn into the debate about the *sermo humilis*.[18]

---

[15] Meissner, ' "Dein clage ist one reimen" '; Besch, 'Vers oder Prosa?'; Herkommer, *Überlieferungsgeschichte der 'Sächsichen Weltchronik'*, pp. 216ff.

[16] Ferkinghoff, 'Vers und Prosa'; Stempel, 'Die Anfänge der romanischen Prosa im XIII. Jahrhundert'.

[17] Klopsch, 'Prosa und Vers in der mittellateinischen Literatur'.

[18] Klopsch, 'Prosa und Vers in der mittellateinischen Literatur', 15ff.; Finster, 'Zur Theorie und Technik mittelalterlicher Prologe', pp. 62ff.

II

Not until relatively recently did critics begin to investigate and elucidate the literary-historical significance of the transition from verse to prose in France, especially with regard to the romance form. Leaving aside a few more or less incidental earlier comments, Rudolf Brummer was the first, in 1948, to attempt such a historical interpretation. He explains the sudden emergence of prose by a shift in values from the chivalric and courtly sphere to a more religious and ascetic ideal. This meant that the romance acquired hagiographical traits and started to use prose in imitation of the medieval Latin lives of saints. However, Brummer's theory has been almost universally rejected: it has been pointed out that examples of religious and ascetic idealism occur frequently in verse romances, whereas there are many prose romances which are profane in the extreme. Hermann Tiemann countered such a simplistic explanation with a variety of factors which could have contributed to the increase in the use of prose. The first of these, he suggests, was a change in the nature of the audience, which now comprised, in addition to the nobility, an increasing number of bourgeois listeners or readers. Secondly, the form of reception itself was changing, as reading increasingly took the place of listening. A third factor was the probable imitation of prose historiography, since the use of prose there immediately precedes its use in the romance. Finally, Tiemann posits the possibility of an independent literary development from verse to prose, such as had already occurred in late antiquity with Dictys' and Dares' prose versions of the Trojan material.

Later research took up these points – apart from the fourth – and made them the basis of further discussion. Erich Köhler based his interpretation on Tiemann's third point, the imitation of prose historiography.[19] His argument runs as follows: the classical Arthurian romance derived its contemporary impact from a literary idealization of courtly existence, by means of which the anti-centralist feudal nobility was able to articulate its political and cultural identity. However, the limitations of this concept soon became apparent, and the Arthurian ideal became increasingly stylized and codified into a kind of chivalric guarantee of salvation, a tendency which increased in proportion to the decreasing political importance of the feudal

---

[19] Köhler, 'Zur Entstehung des altfranzösischen Prosaromans'.

nobility. The Arthurian ideal therefore fell into disrepute, accused of being nothing more than an attractive illusion, something made particularly apparent in the skilfully crafted metre of the verse. The criticism of the use of verse was thus aimed at the empty shell of an illusory world. The courtly poets were obliged to counter this charge by re-establishing their legitimacy in a new form. They thus adopted prose, as used in the chronicles, at the same time availing themselves of the claim to historical truth it implied. While verse romances continued to be written, they were, Köhler argues, solely of entertainment value.

Klaus Ferkinghoff, by contrast, took Tiemann's second argument as his starting point, seeing the increasing importance of secular literacy as the decisive factor in the ascendancy of prose. The use of verse, he argues, made sense in the context of a tradition of oral recitation, but was rendered superfluous when reading replaced listening as the chief mode of reception. Since, as a rule, the vernacular audience was unable to read, Latin prose literature in translation was also transposed into verse for oral recitation. However, by 1200 reading had become so widespread that prose was able to establish itself in the vernacular also. According to Ferkinghoff, an additional impulse was provided by the diminishing cost of writing materials brought about by the growth of the paper industry, and by the establishment of municipal schools offering instruction in reading and writing in the vernacular: thus for example by the second half of the twelfth century, Paris had become the largest book market in Europe.

In 1960, finally, Peter M. Schon took up Tiemann's first argument, explaining the change of form in terms of socio-economic developments, which in turn were marked by the use of prose for historiography. Schon argues that the bougeoisie gained importance as a result of the crusades and the ensuing trade with the Orient. The French king, Schon suggests, played off the cities against the landed aristocracy, encouraging the development of the former into economic and cultural centres which, committed as they were to pragmatic styles of thinking, would be likely to reject the fictional world of the verse romances. However, the verse form, Schon suggests, was rejected not only because it represented an illusory and mendacious world; prose also offered the advantage of a clearer, more concise and comprehensible form. The practical needs of the essentially new, bourgeois audience thus gave rise to a new stylistic ideal. Nor is it coincidental that the first French prose chronicle should deal with the fourth crusade, notable for its extremely secular and political character.

In 1966, Hans Günter Jantzen presented a new survey of the various arguments, making some attempt to incorporate Brummer's theory also, by highlighting the suspicion with which strict religious thinking regarded secular courtly verse romances.

Illuminating as all these arguments for the conditions in which the change from verse to prose came about in France around 1200 are, they by no means account for the real cause of this development and the course it took; all the arguments could apply equally to Germany, and yet no such change took place there in the thirteenth century. In Germany the cities likewise achieved increasing cultural and economic importance after 1200, even if political developments in the relationship between the nobility, the cities and central authority took a different course from those in France. In any case, the tastes of a growing literary audience in the cities increasingly had to be taken into account. Manfred G. Scholz has pointed out the extent to which here too a gradual development from listening to reading took place. Although no tradition of prose chronicles existed in the Germany of the early thirteenth century which could have served as a formal model for the romance, around the middle of the thirteenth century the *Lucidarius* and the German version of the *Lancelot en prose* were available as examples.

If all the socio-cultural arguments, important as their role in the development from verse to prose may be, thus prove to be less than watertight when it comes to a convincing historical explanation, there is little option but to seek an explanation in the specific literary-historical situation itself. It is therefore appropriate to examine here some works from the early stages of the new prose literature in which the issue of form is discussed. The following works document the French verse–prose controversy up to the mid-thirteenth century.

1. Pierre: Histoire de Charlemagne et de Roland *(c. 1202)*

> Maintes genz si en ont oi chanter e conter, mes n'est si mançongie non ço qu'il en dient e en chantent, cil jogleor ni cil conteor; nus contes rimés oest verais, car tot est mançongie ço qu'il en dient, car il n'en sievent rienz fors quant per oir dire.[20]

---

[20] Mandach (ed.), *Chronique dite Saintongeaise*, p. 256, lines 5–8.

[Many people have heard tales sung and told about them (= Charlemagne and Roland), but everything these minstrels and players say and sing about them is just lies. No tale in rhymed verse is true, whatever they say is all lies, for they know nothing about it other than from hearsay.]

Pierre, then, justifies the use of prose in his version of the events of Roncevaux, claiming that the oral version is based on hearsay and is therefore untrue; moreover, it uses the verse form. This leads to the conclusion that works in verse must necessarily be false. Therefore, he remarks later, when commissioning the work his patron requested him to translate the book 'de latin en romans sans rime' ('from Latin into Romance without the use of rhyme'; 34f.).

Pierre is, with dubious logic, combining two arguments here; first, there are the traditional criticisms levelled by historiography at the oral transmission of history – despite the fact that written vernacular representations of history, too, had long used the verse form, for example Wace, or the *Kaiserchronik*. Secondly, the use of verse is equated with falsehood: Pierre does not attempt to justify this, but merely appends it to the traditional topos. A second translation of Pseudo-Turpin also states bluntly, 'E pur ceo que estoire rimee semble mensunge, est ceste mis en prose': 'And because a story in rhyme is thought of as a lie, this has been put into prose.'[21] This means that Pierre's argument is based on the equation: verse = lies, which must therefore already have been current shortly after 1200.

2. *Johannes: translation of the chronicle of Pseudo-Turpin commissioned by Renau de Boulogne (1206)*

Et por que rime se velt afeitier de moz conqueilliz hors de l'estoire, voust li cuens que cist livres fust sanz rime selonc le latin de l'estoire que Turpins, le arcevesques de Reins traita et escrit si com il le vit et oï.[22]

[Because rhymed verse has to be made up of words drawn from outside the story, the Count (= Renau de Boulogne) wanted this book to be composed without rhyme from the Latin version of the story which Archbishop Turpin of Reims noted down and wrote as he had heard and witnessed it.]

---

[21] Cited in Schon, *Studien zum Stil der frühen französischen Prosa*, p. 28.
[22] Walpole (ed.), *The Old French Johannes translation of the Pseudo-Turpin Chronicle*, p. 130, lines 10–14.

Here a plausible reason is given for the essential untruthfulness of verse forms, namely that in them words have to be added for metrical reasons which were not in the original source: these are invented, and therefore 'false'. The argument underlying the statements in the Turpin translator's prologue thus becomes clear: only written accounts based on eye-witness reports can guarantee the truth of historical facts. As far as the mode of representation is concerned, prose is preferable, since the use of verse necessitates the addition of words which do not occur in the original, thus distorting the meaning of the latter.

This argument was subsequently applied to other genres, resulting in an exclusive concentration on the relationship between translation and original, as in:

3. Pierre de Beauvais: Bestiaire *(before 1217)*

En cest livre translater de latin en romanz mist lonc travail Pierres qui volontiers le fist et pour ce que rime se vieut afaitier de moz concueilliz hors de verité, mit il sanz rime cest livre selonc le latin dou livre que Phisiologes, uns boens clers d'Athenes, traita ... [23]

[Pierre, who made this book willingly, put a lot of work into translating it from Latin into Romance, and since rhymed verse has to be made up of words taken from beyond the sphere of truth, he translated it without rhyme according to the Latin of the book composed by Physiologus, a good clerk of Athens.]

Pierre clearly derived his argument from Pseudo-Turpin, merely substituting *verité* or *livre* for *estoire* as appropriate.[24]

4. Vies des Peres, *written for Blanche de Navarre (d. 1229)*

Les autres dames de cest mont
Qui plus pensent a val qu'a mont
Si font les mençonges rimer
Et les paroles alimer
Pour les cuers miauz enroïllier

---

[23] Mermier (ed.), *Le Bestiaire de Pierre de Beauvais*, p. 59; cf. also the variants on p. 95 from manuscripts Ma and S, which name Count Robert (Robert II of Dreux, d. 1218) and Bishop Phelippe (Philip of Dreux, Bishop of Beauvais, 1175–1215) respectively as the persons responsible for commissioning the work and demanding that it be executed in prose.

[24] Further evidence for this argument is the rhymed preface to the *Buch Sidrach*. Cf. Unger, 'Vorreden deutscher Sachliteratur', p. 225.

Et pour honesté avillier.
Dame, de ce n'avez vos cure!
De mençonge qui cuers oscure
Et corrompent la clarte d'ame
N'en aiez cure, douce dame,
Laissiez Cliges et Perceval,
Qui les cuers perce et trait a val
Et les romanz de vanite. (*Vies des Peres*, 23–35)[25]

[The other ladies, who are concerned with the world and whose thoughts are directed downwards rather than upwards, have lies put into rhymed verse and the diction filed smooth the better to corrupt hearts and demean integrity. My lady, do not concern yourself with such matters! Do not concern yourself with lies that sully the heart and defile the purity of the soul, sweet lady. Forget about Cliges and Perceval, who pierce the heart and drag it down, and those worthless romances.]

Here too the equation of rhymed verse with lies is taken as read, although it is no longer argued that the verse form is responsible for the invention of words and thus for lies, but rather that these lies call for expression in verse, which lends language a smoothness (*alimer*) whose pleasing accessibility may readily seduce the hearts. The courtly romance, represented here by Cligés and Perceval, is thus dismissed out of hand, and the opportunity is seized for a none-too-subtle pun on the name Perceval. However, the prose translator does not let this stop him from composing a prologue in verse! This may be seen as symptomatic of a rigorist religious attitude which dismisses Arthurian literature as secular lies.[26]

5. Anonymous biography of King Philip Augustus (shortly after 1226)

Issi vos an feré le conte
Non pas rimé, qui an droit conte,
Si con li livres Lancelot
Ou il n'a de rime un seul mot,
Pour mielz dire la verité

---

[25] Cited in Schon, *Studien zum Stil der frühen französischen Prosa*, p. 28.
[26] Jones, *Prologue and Epilogue*, pp. 44ff.; Hirdt, *Studien zum epischen Prolog*, pp. 41ff.; Jauss, 'Zur historischen Genese der Scheidung zwischen Fiktionalität und Realität', pp. 427–8; Boesch, *Die Kunstanschauung in der mittelhochdeutschen Literatur*, pp. 90–1; Unger, 'Vorreden deutscher Sachliteratur', p. 227; Gerhardt, '*Iwein*-Schlüsse', 31, note 38. It should be noted that although evidence of such disapproval of verse is widespread, on the whole an attitude of silent toleration is more usual.

Et por tretier sans fauseté;
Quar anviz puet estre rimee
Estoire ou n'ait ajostee
Mançonge por fere la rime. (99–107)[27]

[Here I have made a story for you which is not rhymed, which is narrated in a straightforward manner like the romance of Lancelot, where not a single word is rhymed, in order better to tell and give account of the truth without any falsehood. For there can hardly be a story composed in rhyme where not a single lie has been added for the sake of the rhyme.]

This prologue would seem to confirm that the change from verse to prose as a medium for the romance was understood as a response to a desire for a greater degree of truth. By the second quarter of the thirteenth century, this argument – that prose is more 'truthful' than verse – had become so prevalent that the prose romance may in turn be taken as evidence for the truthfulness of prose! Nevertheless, this prologue too employs verse to advance its plea for the use of prose.

6. *Translation of the* Prophetia Merlini *of Geoffrey of Monmouth*

Ne le ay pas, sachez, rimé,
Mes eyns si fut tut avant alé
Tut eynsi come il le fist,
Saun ryme, tuit ensy l'ay dist;
Kar cil ky voudra rimer
Ne pot mie tut dis le dreyt aler;
Hors de estorie ly covent trere
Sovent e menter por rime fere.[28]

[Take note, I have not written it in rhymed verse but rather in a straightforward manner, just as he (i.e. Geoffrey) did, without rhyme, so too I have composed it. For whoever wishes to use rhyme cannot express everything in a straightforward manner, he often has to draw on matter outside the story and to lie for the sake of the rhyme.]

This series of documents on the verse–prose discussion makes clear how far the argument that verse is untrue because the metre necessitates the addition of words not included in the original had become standard. In terms of the development of poetic theory, it coincides

---

[27] Mölk, *Französische Literarästhetik*, No. 80, p. 103.
[28] Cited in Schon, *Studien zum Stil der frühen französischen Prosa*, p. 29.

with the rejection of the profane oral tradition on the one hand, and warnings about the seductive beauty of form on the other. Here the idea of the greater truth of plain style recurs; this will come to be explicitly formulated in later prose prologues, merging with a new ideal from an old tradition which aims for clarity, brevity and succinctness of expression.[29] The passages chosen furthermore give some idea of the probable origin of the argument, inasmuch as they are all, with the exception of the life of King Philip Augustus, taken from prologues to translations from the Latin. The discussion was clearly sparked off by the translation into the vernacular of Latin historical texts, and it is here that the oldest concrete evidence of a conscious and programmatic transition from verse to prose is to be found. In England, indirect evidence exists which suggests this may go back to the time of the third crusade.[30] It may be assumed that the question of form was also discussed explicitly at an early stage. The *Lucidarius* A-prologue remains a key piece of evidence for this – even if it should prove to be not quite contemporary – since, as explained above, it is only understandable in the context of the Anglo-Norman literary background. The interest in a vernacular prose form thus originated in the desire for an objective and accurate reproduction of historical facts, as offered by Latin prose historiography. In view of the vital importance of accurate information in connection with contemporary events such as the crusades, this is quite understandable.

The change of emphasis in vernacular historiography went hand in hand with a change in the concept of truth as such. Up to that point, the truth of history had been found in the meaning conveyed in the representation of the facts. The use of rhyme in this process served as a sign that the linguistic form not only reproduced the facts, but also represented a translation in another sense, into a higher dimension of meaning. Now, however, what mattered was the presentation of the facts, and the plainer the form in which this objectivity could be presented, the more justice would be done to the facts; it thus became possible to be completely open to the complex nexus of relationships between earthly phenomena in their own right.[31] The discussion of

---

[29] Schon, *Studien zum Stil der frühen französischen Prosa*, pp. 27ff.
[30] Stempel, 'Die Anfänge der romanischen Prosa im XIII. Jahrhundert', 592–3. On the significance of the relationship between Latin and the vernacular in the change-over to prose, cf. also Schnell, *Prosaauflösung und Geschichtsschreibung*.
[31] This accordingly also applies to the new formal possibilities of the prose romance: see Poirion, 'Romans en vers et romans en prose', 78ff.; Haug, '*Das Land, von welchem niemand wiederkehrt*', pp. 77ff.

form probably first erupted in the vernacular because of the fact that the existing tradition consisted almost exclusively of verse. Be that as it may, it was Latin prose historiography which provided a model for the new form of representing truth.

Other genres then adopted the new concept of truth, along with the prose form, with varying degrees of consistency and justification, until finally the romance took it over and made it its own. The significance of this becomes apparent if one considers that the first narrative work to be re-cast in prose was Robert de Boron's *Joseph d'Arimathie* ('L'Estoire dou Graal').

III

Robert de Boron's romance takes the form of a programmatic reintegration of the Grail story into salvation history. The Grail is identified with the chalice from the Last Supper; it comes into the possession of Joseph of Arimathea, who uses it to catch Christ's blood on the Cross. When Joseph is imprisoned, the risen Christ appears to him, bringing him the dish of blood and prophesying that after him two others will be appointed as its keepers. When Vespasian enters Jerusalem, Joseph is freed; he sets out and together with his companions, among them Bron, his sister's husband, sets up the table and the service of the Grail; a fish caught by Bron is placed beside the sacred vessel, for which reason he becomes known as the 'Rich Fisherman'. Twelve sons are born to Bron, and the youngest, Alain, goes to the West. Meanwhile, Bron also takes the Grail to the West, where he waits for Alain's son, who according to the prophecy will be the *tierz hon*, the third and final keeper of the Grail.[32]

We do not know exactly how far Robert got with his work.[33] The beginning of a Merlin narrative has survived, and this is clearly intended, with the foundation of the Round Table, to form the historical link between Joseph's table commemorating the Last Supper and the 'Grail community' of Alain's son – who can of course be none other than Perceval. Furthermore, much of the underlying narrative structure remains unclear, revealing fundamental contradictions. However, it is unmistakably based on a tripartite scheme,

[32] Struss, 'Le Roman de L'Histoire du Graal (Robert de Boron)'.
[33] Nitze, 'What did Robert de Boron write?' and 'Messire Robert de Boron. Enquiry and summary'.

and so Kurt Ruh ventured the thesis[34] that it was inspired by Joachim of Fiore's trinitarian interpretation of history as an ascent through three successive ages. It seems that Robert's Joachite model was recognized and became influential, since the five-part compilation of the *Prose Lancelot* is also informed by the idea of a three-phase, trinitarian scheme. The first stage is the history of the first generation, corresponding to the Age of the Father, the history of which is related in the *Estoire del Saint Graal* and precedes the actual Lancelot cycle. The second Age, that of the Son, is represented in the chivalric world of King Arthur and Lancelot, while the Age of the Holy Spirit is represented by Galahad. Naturally not all of the vast corpus of material available could be incorporated in this scheme, and there is room for debate about the position and significance of individual figures within this trinitarian structure; nevertheless, the presence of a three-phase historical and metaphysical structure underlying the scheme is difficult to disregard entirely.[35]

Robert originally composed the work in verse. However, he had barely completed it when it became caught up in the wake of the new idea that historical truth could be more appropriately conveyed in prose, and so a prose trilogy was produced, consisting of *Joseph*, *Merlin*, and the so-called *Didot-Perceval*.[36] The probable dates are c. 1200 for the verse romance, and 1202 for the prose version.[37]

The development then proceeds at an alarming pace. At around the same time, the first romance to be written in prose is produced, namely *Perlesvaus*. Already, it demonstrates a perfect command of the new medium.[38] Thematically, this romance too is a Grail narrative which has been completely transposed into the religious dimension, even if it does not – unlike Robert's work – expand to include a universal *Heilsgeschichte*. Instead it may be read 'allegorically' with reference to contemporary political events, so that it is tempting to

---

[34] Ruh, 'Joachitische Spiritualität im Werke Roberts von Boron', and 'Der Gralsheld in der *Queste del Saint Graal*', 260ff.; cf. also Bertau, *Deutsche Literatur im europäischen Mittelalter*, pp. 640ff.

[35] Cf. Fromm, 'Zur Karrenritter-Episode im Prosa-Lancelot', pp. 89ff., and his critique of Ruh's categories. These are emphatically rejected by Speckenbach, 'Endzeiterwartung im *Lancelot-Gral-Zyklus*'. Convincing though his argument for the surviving version of the *Lancelot en prose* is, it has little relevance for Robert's own version. A familiarity with Joachim's work in Northern Europe at this time cannot definitively be ruled out – see Speckenbach, 'Endzeiterwartung im *Lancelot-Gral-Zyklus*', p. 214 – as research on the survival and transmission of the manuscripts is still in its early stages.

[36] Bogdanow, 'La trilogie de Robert de Boron'.

[37] Le Gentil, 'The work of Robert de Boron'.   [38] Nitze, '*Perlesvaus*'.

interpret it as a historical *roman à clef*.[39] However, by far the greatest achievement in the new form, the *Lancelot-Grail* cycle, does not emerge until between 1215 and 1230.

Both the first and the most important representatives of the new prose romance, then, revert to the pattern of universal history. The Arthurian world, hitherto a purely fictional construct, is integrated into a Christian plan of salvation, and thus acquires historical status; the use of the prose medium corresponds to the new form of historical truth. Or – to take up the reference to Chrétien's Arthurian model – Robert, far from allowing the classical Arthurian concept to disintegrate into a fictional spinning out of the various strands of the narrative as did the many continuators of *Perceval*, jettisoned this tradition completely, replacing the fictional structure with the trinitarian scheme of universal history. Even if this does not spell the end of the verse romance in France, the line which future developments are to take is nonetheless determined by the new form. The discovery of the literary and artistic possibilities inherent in prose opens up a perspective which soon becomes detached from its initial connection with history, as well as from the serious purpose of its claim to truth, becoming diffused in fictional works in precisely the same way as does the verse romance after Chrétien.

In Germany, literary history unfolds along completely different lines. Seen against the background of the French tradition, as outlined above, the reasons for this can be clearly perceived. It is significant that neither the continuations of Chrétien's romances nor Robert's romance found an echo in Germany. In other words, no attempts were made to continue the Grail cycle, nor to integrate the Arthurian world into the scheme of salvation history. Instead, the challenge of Chrétien's model was addressed in new romances, discussed exhaustively from different perspectives, and finally used as a starting point against which alternative models were defined. This process of experimental adaptation and challenging of Chrétien's structural concept, which continued throughout the thirteenth century in Germany, presupposed a continued adherence to the medium characteristic of fictional literature, namely rhyming verse.

In contrast to earlier theories on the question of verse as opposed to prose, then, it may be noted that it was neither the new realism of an urban culture, nor the exaggerated stylization of the Arthurian

---

[39] Adolf, 'Studies in the *Perlesvaus*'.

ideal in the fictional romance form, which demanded the use of prose; rather, the change came about through the medium of vernacular historiography. Starting from a new historical concept of truth, this took as its model Latin prose, or at any rate sought to render the Latin originals as faithfully as possible in the vernacular. However, the romance arrived at the medium of prose – established meanwhile as the appropriate vehicle for historical representation – by way of a re-integration of the fictional Arthurian world into the *Heilsgeschichte*. Only thus can the different course taken by the development from verse to prose in Germany be explained – through the lack of a crucial link in the chain, namely a type of Arthurian romance which laid claim to metaphysical, and thus historical, truth. The debate on the truth of fictional works in Germany took place on the basis of Chrétien's original model and in the form most appropriate to this, i.e. in verse.

14

Magic, morals and manipulation: the emergence of the post-classical Arthurian romance

I

Chrétien's model for romance composition was based on premisses as bold as they were problematic. He sought to present the Utopian ideal as the ultimate goal of a movement that constantly advanced towards the very positions which undermined and threatened it, namely the absolute positions of love and death. Such boundary experiences – encounters with ultimate reality – form an integral part of the process represented in the action. Just as these experiences can only be integrated momentarily into this process, the Utopian position with which they are contrasted can also only appear as an exceptional situation, in the form of the Arthurian festivities. The disturbing elements to which this literary model gives rise are at the same time an integral part of the concept. This led Chrétien to test his model repeatedly in new romances, gradually taking the action closer and closer to the extreme positions which called it into question. His continual re-adaptation of the model had the effect of emphasizing its limitations and relentlessly revealing its unresolved tensions.

In *Yvain*, by contrast with *Erec*, the hero does not symbolically pass through death by losing consciousness; instead, he goes mad and sinks to sub-human, bestial depths, whence only a miracle can restore him to humanity. In *Le Chevalier de la Charrette*, the claims of Eros are pressed to the utmost; only by placing the moment of absolute Eros in a symbolic otherworld can it be incorporated into the model without destroying it. In *Perceval*, Chrétien attempts to depict a sin which cannot be absolved in this world by extending his model to include the religious dimension. Wolfram's version of this story intensifies these tensions by assimilating the absolute position which had previously been situated beyond the limits of the model – namely death – into the action of the romance itself. In *Titurel*, however, he planned a work in which the hero would not merely die symbolically but would actually lose his life, which necessarily distorted the model beyond recognition; he finally abandoned the fictional type altogether in *Willehalm*.

Inevitably, then, the destabilizing element which was a characteristic feature of Chrétien's model ultimately led ever more inexorably towards the critical limit which challenged and thus defined it, until the point was reached at which not only did the model break down, but the fictional type itself came to be seen as inappropriate and was abandoned.

Apart from these experiments at and beyond the limits of the fictional, however, another possibility presented itself: that of resolving the almost unbearable tensions of the model as it were from within, by modifying it in such a way as to neutralize these destabilizing elements or make them disappear altogether. This was achieved by omitting the crisis of the hero, thereby reducing the model to a mere external framework; the twofold action loses its symbolic function, and the characteristic pattern of movement from a Utopian starting point through a counter-world and back is abandoned. Arthur's court thus loses its ideal function and becomes a purely topographical point of reference; as such, it can now figure actively in the plot, becoming a factor in the action which the protagonist must take into account; that is to say it has become one element within a homogeneous realm rather than a Utopian ideal which appears only at certain clearly defined points in the narrative. The court can then also be given negative characteristics, so providing an occasion for social criticism. This in turn means that the hero becomes the sole repository of the Arthurian ideal; he is transformed into an unproblematic personification of exemplary behaviour. However, this transformation means that the Arthurian romance has renounced all claims to precisely that principle which gave rise to it in the first place. It is no longer conceived of as a fictional process which opens up a unique possibility of genuine human experience; instead, it becomes a mere illustration of norms of behaviour, a moral lesson with a practicable application to life. This, then, is precisely the position emphatically rejected by the 'classical' Arthurian romance; but at the same time it is the basis for the reductive, moralistic mode of reception exemplified by Thomasin, which must always be reckoned with from the outset.

The new type reveals its potential and its limitations most strikingly in Wirnt von Gravenberc's *Wigalois*, and in *Diu Crône* by Heinrich von dem Türlin; it is given a new angle in Der Stricker's *Daniel von dem Blüenden Tal* and in Der Pleier's *Garel*.[1]

II

Wigalois opens with the story of the hero's parents. It begins with the conventional challenge motif: Joram, a stranger, challenges the knights of the Round Table to a fight. They are defeated, and even Gawein is forced to give in in the end. For him however it is an honourable defeat, since the strange knight was only able to win with the help of a magic girdle. Joram then befriends Gawein, taking him to his distant kingdom and giving him his niece's hand in marriage. When Gawein leaves this foreign land after some time in order to return to Arthur's court, he is unable to find the way back.

Meanwhile, Gawein's wife bears a child: Wigalois, the hero of the story. When he has grown up he comes to Arthur's court in search of his father. To everyone's amazement, he is able to sit on a particular perilous stone, something only possible for one who is entirely without guile. He is accepted at court and invested as a knight. There then follows his *âventiure*. It begins as usual with the challenge motif. A young woman appears, seeking assistance from Arthur's court for the queen of Korntin, whose kingdom is being threatened by an adversary. Against the wishes of the messenger – who had hoped for an experienced knight – Wigalois sets out with her. On the way he gives several demonstrations of his extraordinary bravery, so that he is finally accepted as a worthy helper. Eventually he is told what is in store for him: Roaz of Glois, who has made a pact with the devil, has robbed the queen of Korntin of her land and killed her husband. With her daughter, Larie, she has taken refuge in the castle of Roimunt and is there awaiting a knight who will do battle with Roaz and win back her lands. The reward will be the hand of her daughter and the rule over the country of Korntin. On reaching Roimunt, Wigalois meets Larie for the first time, and her extraordinary beauty makes the *âventiure* seem all the more worthwhile. The goal of the first sequence of *âventiure* is thus arrived at, and the second cycle begins.

Equipped with a magic loaf of bread and a consecrated sword, the

---

[1] Ruh, 'Epische Literatur des deutschen Spätmittelalters', pp. 191ff.; Haug, 'Paradigmatische Poesie'. For equivalents in French and English literature, cf. Schmolke-Hasselmann, 'Der französische höfische Roman' and 'Der französische Artusroman', and Fichte, 'Middle English Arthurian verse romance' respectively.

hero sets out from Korntin to challenge Roaz. First, however, he must successfully accomplish a number of additional tasks or adventures. A leopard-like beast gives Wigalois directions; this turns out to be the king of Korntin whom Roaz had killed, and whose spirit, like those knights of his who have suffered a similar fate, must roam at large without finding peace until he has been avenged. The leopard-man gives Wigalois a flowering branch to protect him against the pestilential breath of a dragon he will encounter along the way, and helps him to obtain a magic lance with which to despatch it. After a fierce battle, Wigalois manages to slay the monster, but he himself is left lying unconscious. He is robbed while in this helpless state, and is finally rescued by women who nurse and re-equip him. The next dangerous character he meets is the wild woman Ruel, who overcomes him and ties him up. In this extremity he is aided by his horse, which sets up a loud neighing: at this, Ruel believes the dragon to be approaching, and flees. Wigalois prays, and his bonds are loosed. Finally he reaches Roaz' fortress, Glois. It is surrounded by a swamp which is obscured by a thick black fog; the way is blocked by a dwarf. Wigalois wounds him mortally, and he vanishes into the mist with a scream; the fog is suddenly sucked into the swamp and reveals a path along which Wigalois is able to ride to the castle. Once there, however, he comes upon a revolving wheel armed with swords and clubs barring the way. Meanwhile, the black fog has closed in behind him, cutting off his retreat. Once more Wigalois asks God for help: the wheel stops. After he has passed it he has to contend with a fire-throwing centaur, then with two guards; after this he is finally able to enter Roaz' domain. There is thunder and lightning; total darkness envelops him. Twelve maidens with candles come up to him and disappear again. Then Roaz rushes out, preceded by a magic cloud containing the devil. Protected by his consecrated sword, Wigalois finally manages to vanquish the demon knight. At the end of the story, as is to be expected, there is the wedding with Larie and the coronation feast. Before he finally takes over the governing of Korntin, another campaign, against a certain Lion, is inserted, in the course of which Wigalois returns to Arthur's court once more.

This sequence of *âventiure* appears to follow the Arthurian pattern closely,[2] revealing several characteristic elements: Arthur's court as

---

[2] Heinzle, *Stellenkommentar zu Wolframs Titurel*; Cormeau, '*Wigalois' und 'Diu Crône'*. On Wirnt's reception and use of the Arthurian tradition, see most recently Kern, 'Auseinandersetzung mit der Gattungstradition'.

the starting point and point of reference, the series of *âventiure* leading through a counter-world, the dual structure of the action associated with winning the hand of a woman, and culminating in the festivities at court. However, one fundamental element of the 'classical' Arthurian romance is missing: the crisis of the hero. There is nothing in *Wigalois* to compare with the disturbing vehemence of Erec's second departure or with Iwein's madness or the cursing of Parzival by the Grail messenger. The division of the action into two parts remains superficial, since when Wigalois leaves Korntin it is not as the result of a crisis, but in order to fulfil his original task; thus the hero's unconsciousness after the fight with the dragon, like his immobilization at the hands of Ruel, has no symbolic significance. At most, the episodes amount to an increasingly dramatic linear sequence building up to a single climax: the confrontation with Roaz. There is thus no complex structure of parallel and contrasting episodes, in the sense of Chrétien's model, to illuminate the meaning of the action. The omission of the crisis implies that the hero is not being subjected to any kind of test or trial; he already *is* the perfect embodiment of Arthurian knighthood, so that the unfolding of the action can only serve to reveal ever more of his virtues.[3]

By contrast with the immaculate perfection of the protagonist, the world of *âventiure* appears transformed: it now attracts all the negative elements which previously were situated not only within the counter-world but also within the complex figure of the hero. The counter-figures, along with their setting, become demoniac and indeed evil, making use of magic and the black arts; the main antagonist, Roaz, is in league with the devil himself.

However, the negative supernatural features in turn conjure up positive supernatural elements: thus the hero too is equipped with magic objects which enable him to overcome his devilish adversaries. The bonds placed on the hero by Ruel are loosed by divine intervention, and the hellish machinery barring the entrance to Glois can likewise be overcome only with God's help. The degree to which the hero is dependent on supernatural aid is in direct proportion to the extent to which the devil is involved in the counter-world; he, the hero, needs a particular kind of luck which interacts with divine providence. Wigalois bears this new quality as a device in his coat of arms: a golden wheel. This is explained as follows: when Gawein

---

[3]   Gottzmann, 'Wirnts von Gravenberc *Wigalois*'.

arrives at Joram's royal castle, he finds there a wheel made of gold with human figures on it which rise and fall with its movement. It is the wheel of fortune, but it does not, as is usually the case, signify the inevitable changes of fortune, but is instead a symbol of its constancy. Gawein adopts this wheel of fortune as a device for his shield, and when his son comes to Arthur's court he passes it on to him. The devil's wheel in Glois, with its swords and clubs, later comes to a standstill when confronted with the knight who bears the golden wheel of fortune on his coat of arms.

However, the supernatural transformation of the world of *âventiure* is, though predominantly daemonic, not wholly evil; it is also curiously ambivalent. Thus, although Roaz is in league with the devil, and although his castle is situated in a perilous and fog-ridden swamp, this same castle nevertheless shines like crystal in the moonlight. Before the final battle, the women of Glois approach the hero in a kind of candle-lit procession. Roaz himself is radiant with gold and precious stones, and after his defeat his wife dies of a broken heart, and an expensive monument is built to her. The opposites of good and evil, light and darkness here take on a strangely ambiguous quality, so that there seems to be something positive in the negative aspects, a glimmering of light even in the dark and dangerous realm of the demoniac forces of evil.

This has, moreover, a certain structural logic in the context of the rejection of the classical Arthurian romance type; if meaning is no longer conveyed by the positioning of the episodes within the structure as a whole, the individual scenes can become ambivalent, reflecting at the same time despair and hope, danger and fortune, evil and redemption. The particularly atmospheric quality of *Wigalois* has always been admired;[4] the work's subtle indication of shades and mood suggests a new element in the world of *âventiure*, expressing its Janus-like quality and introducing an interplay of heavenly and hellish aspects which, far from being unfolded by degrees and resolved in the crisis, continually confounds the protagonist with its lack of any clear message. In ever more fantastical surroundings, things lose their contours and begin to metamorphose according to irrational and obscure principles. A shifting reality is created, in which the only constant element is the fairy-tale good fortune of the hero.

[4]   Wehrli, '*Wigalois*', pp. 227, 235–6.

III

This development is taken further in Heinrich von dem Türlin's great Gawein romance, *Diu Crône*, which dates from around 1230. It is a multi-stranded *âventiure* complex of some 30,000 lines, arranged to form a series of *âventiure* sequences punctuated by scenes at Arthur's court.[5] In accordance with the new concept, Gawein too turns out to be a model hero. However, to an even greater extent than in *Wigalois*, the world portrayed in the narrative becomes increasingly opaque; whole episodes at times resemble nothing more than a surreal kind of waxworks or dumbshow. One example may serve to illustrate this: Gawein comes upon a band of knights being fought by a sword and lance wielded by invisible hands above a pair of horses. The knights are killed and the two horses move on with their invisible riders and their weapons. Gawein follows them. Looking back, he sees the dead knights consumed by flames. He rides through fire-ravaged country and reaches a range of mountains. There he encounters a naked girl hitting out with a club at birds who are tearing the flesh from a giant in chains. Gawein is unable to save him; he rides on and meets a hideous beast, as green as grass, with three horns on its head. An old woman in costly attire is seated on a blood-red saddle; her ashen hair falls to below her waist, and she wears a golden wreath upon her head. Her face is a deathly yellow and her eyes glow like fire. She leads a terrible naked Moor on a hemp rope, lashing him with a scourge so that he runs alongside screaming. Gawein moves on and meets a black knight carrying a woman's head by its braids; he is being pursued in turn by a red knight. Gawein cannot await the outcome of the fight; he has to keep moving. He comes to a great forest; under one of the trees is a shield, a half-drawn sword and a pair of blood-stained greaves. A saddled horse is tied to the trunk of the tree and a helmet hangs from the saddle. Beside it is a standard, with the head of a knight impaled upon its point and a wounded dog lying at its foot. Gawein hears the sound of women weeping, but can see no one. He rides on, and on the other side of a range of hills he comes upon a magnificent castle keep in the middle of a meadow, surrounded by a wall of crystal, where he hears the sound of maidens singing. Then a terrifying naked giant appears, at least six fathoms tall

---

5   On the work's construction and its relationship to the classical Arthurian romance, see Cormeau, *'Wigalois' und 'Diu Crône'*, pp. 155ff.; Ebenbauer, 'Fortuna und Artushof'; Reinitzer, 'Zur Erzählfunktion der *Crône*'.

and black as a raven. He begins to batter the crystal wall with a heavy club of steel. The wall collapses and bursts into flames along with the keep, and the black giant then thrusts the singing maidens into the fire with his club. Gawein is unable to help; he rides through the night once more, and in the morning reaches a beautiful heath covered in roses whose wonderful scent gives him renewed strength. He comes across a handsome young man in expensive attire; an arrow has been shot through his eyes, and he is bound to a bed by iron chains. He holds a fan in his hand, and when he moves it a fiery wind blows up and causes the roses to wither. On a red coverlet on the bed lies the ermine-white body of a maiden. A dwarf rests in her right arm, wearing a crown of rubies which outshines the roses on the heath. Beside him lies a knight, black as a Moor, wounded to the heart with the broken end of a lance still protruding from his breast. And so on (ed. G. H. F. Scholl, 1852; 14024ff.).

There are other surreal sequences of this kind to be found in *Diu Crône*;[6] it is not always easy to guess their meaning. Taken individually, these tableaux are reminiscent of conventional Arthurian scenes: dangerous characters and evil powers are engaged in actions which should really demand the intervention of the hero, but here everything remains spectacle, and the hero moves on to the next scene. The daemonic world of *Wigalois* has here become a bizarre phantasmagoria in which beauty is mingled with horror, brilliance with the grotesque, the fascinating with the repulsive. The ambivalent nature of reality has become transfixed in its most extreme manifestations, and appears as a series of isolated *tableaux vivants* which appear to be devoid of any specific function and significance, i.e. they have come to signify only the contrast which they portray, manifestations of a hypothetical world able to juxtapose its most extreme features in a bizarre and apparently random montage. This represents the furthest limit of the development of German romance, first suggested in *Wigalois*, towards an opaque and ambivalent reality.

Obviously not all the scenes in *Diu Crône* are of this type; the majority are *âventiure* sequences in the conventional sense, with the usual Arthurian themes of helping those in distress, love entanglements, tests of valour, and so on. However, *Diu Crône* does illustrate a marked tendency to favour such series of grotesque tableaux, and in

---

6 Lines 15998ff., 28608ff. Cf. also Wyss, 'Die Wunderketten in der *Crône*'.

this sense may be said to verge on the world of pure fantastic spectacle.

It will come as no surprise that Gawein should require, in addition to his already perfect qualities, a still higher guarantee of fortune in order to pass unharmed through such a world; he accordingly encounters *Sælde* (Fortuna) in person. Shining with the light of its precious stones, her marvellous palace stands on the other side of a stretch of water which Gawein crosses with the help of a magic thread. The vaulted roof, the battlements and the hundred windows are all described; it is reported that these last are superfluous, since the gems of which the palace is built shine brighter than daylight. Gawein arrives at the portal, made from a single diamond; the door-frame is fashioned from gold and rubies; and so on. He enters the hall and sees *Vrou Sælde* ('Dame Fortune') on top of a wheel, holding a child, Salvation, in her arms. A wind causes the wheel to revolve while she herself remains immobile. Men and women are suspended from the wheel; its movement plunges some of them into misfortune as it raises others. Sælde and her child are of great beauty and dressed in costly apparel on their right side, while on the left they are old and wan, their clothes threadbare and ragged. Likewise, the whole room is magnificent on one side while the other is in ruins. However, when Gawein enters the wheel stops and Sælde, the child and the whole palace appear in complete and undivided splendour. Sælde welcomes Gawein and prophesies that victory and good fortune will be his. This is the counterpart to the wheel of fortune in *Wigalois*, but with the dramatic difference that Gawein's entrance causes the wheel to stop, thus negating the dual aspect of Fortuna.[7] However, as if this were not enough, Gawein soon arrives in a blessed land of women, where he may choose between love and power on the one hand and eternal youth on the other. Gawein opts for the latter, and is thus finally established as the hero who has attained absolute perfection and eternal happiness in a world beyond time.

IV

The perfect gentle knight who brings the wheel of fortune to a standstill: this new type of hero is characteristic of the later Arthurian

---

[7] On the 'Sælde' episode, see Boor, 'Fortuna in mittelhochdeutscher Dichtung', pp. 320ff.; Schouwink, *Fortuna im Alexanderroman Rudolfs von Ems*, p. 104; Ebenbauer, 'Fortuna und Artushof', pp. 38–9; Knapp, 'Virtus und Fortuna in der *Krone*'.

romance. However, the restructuring of the classical *âventiure* model takes various forms. Besides *Wigalois* and *Diu Crône* there is a second type, which, although comparable in many ways, stresses very different elements. A prime example is Der Stricker's romance *Daniel von dem Blüenden Tal* (between 1220 and 1250).

The action opens according to the familiar scheme: King Arthur refuses to break his fast until an *âventiure* has taken place. As usual he does not have to go hungry for long, since a hideous giant promptly appears and demands that he submit to his lord, King Matur of Cluse. Cluse is a wondrous land which lies beyond a range of mountains and can only be reached through a tunnel. It is the site of an *âventiure* in which no one has yet succeeded: a beast cast in gold is to be found there with a standard in its mouth; when the standard is pulled out it sets up such a monstrous roaring that anyone hearing it falls from his horse, whereupon the lord of the land appears and despatches the intruder.

While the giant is detained at Arthur's court, Daniel sets out of his own accord to seek the adventure. He arrives at the tunnel, but finds the giant's brother seated in front of it, and he – like the messenger giant – has skin which no normal sword can pierce. However, before he can challenge this giant, Daniel becomes involved in another *âventiure*: a maiden asks for his help in dealing with a threatening and insistent dwarf who is trying to force his attentions on her; this dwarf has a sword which can cut through anything – exactly what Daniel needs. The dwarf is outwitted by means of a trick: at Daniel's instigation the maiden agrees to marriage, on the condition that the dwarf prove himself worthy of her by defeating an opponent with an ordinary sword. Blinded by love, he agrees, and Daniel kills him. There follows another exploit on behalf of a woman in distress. This time the opponent is a devil-like creature consisting only of head, arms and legs, which is terrorizing the land with a kind of Medusa's head. Daniel outwits this trunkless monster and its accompanying army with the aid of a mirror.

Back at the tunnel, Daniel takes on the giant, although he barely reaches to his knee. However, he hacks the giant to pieces with the dwarf's magic sword. Meanwhile, King Arthur appears with the army, on their way to Cluse. They ride through the tunnel and encounter the golden beast. After the standard has been pulled from its mouth it begins to roar, and the knights all fall off their horses. Now Matur appears, to do battle with them. Arthur kills him himself, and a general free-for-all ensues between Arthur's knights and the army of King Matur. During this fight the dwarf's sword also proves its worth against the giant who had brought the original challenge.

After this first day's fighting, Daniel is involved in another private *âventiure*, again a mission of mercy. This time he has to deal with a fiend who robs anyone he speaks to of their senses, and then draws blood from his victims in order to bathe in it. Daniel creeps unnoticed among the victims, pretending that he too has been deprived of his senses. Thus he is able to slay the fiend unawares as he is draining the blood of the first victim into his tub.

During the days that follow, further bloody battles take place against new armies, until it occurs to Daniel to turn the roaring beast against Matur's own troops. Arthur's forces stop up their ears, and the enemy forces drop like flies at the sound of the beast's roar. Finally there are the victory celebrations, which leave nothing to be desired: Daniel receives from Arthur the hand of the vanquished ruler's widow, and the rest of the Knights of the Round Table are married to the widows of Matur's vassals in a mass wedding.

However, in the midst of all the celebrating the father of the two dead giants, an old magician, suddenly appears. He seizes the king, clambers with him up the sheer mountain wall and leaves him perched on an outcrop of rock; he does the same with Parzival. They are left there helpless, and the old man declares that the same will happen to the other knights in turn. Daniel of course sees a way out of the situation; he procures a magic net and uses it to capture the old magician. After the latter has been thus tamed, they are able to explain at leisure that they are innocent of the death of his sons – the giants – since they only acted in self-defence. The old man accepts this argument and is satisfied with the gift of the magic net – which delights his magician's heart – as a gesture of reconciliation.

Der Stricker, who in all probability freely invented this Daniel romance, is fully familiar with the Middle High German 'classics' and is clearly able to count on such familiarity on the part of his audience, since his method of working involves lifting central themes from earlier Arthurian literature and reformulating them in accordance with a scheme of his own which is as bold as it is comic.[8] Not only is the fountain episode from *Iwein* developed to the point of absurdity, and Iwein's already somewhat dubious marriage to his opponent's

[8] Rosenhagen, *Untersuchungen über Daniel*; Boor, 'Der *Daniel* des Strickers'; Kern, 'Der Roman und seine Rezeption'; Schmidt, *Aufbauformen und Erzählstil im 'Daniel'*, pp. 200–1.

widow turned into a grotesque mass nuptials; the traditional abduction of Guinevere is replaced by the kidnapping of King Arthur himself, who is spirited away not to a fortress in the otherworld but onto a mountain peak. Here he could starve in all seriousness: an amusing twist to the favourite motif of refusing food often used by the king to instigate an *âventiure* at the start of a given romance.

Yet this game of literary adaptations has far-reaching consequences, since in effect it distorts the classical Arthurian model almost beyond recognition: Arthur's court as a fixed and ideal point of reference is abandoned, and the whole court goes out on an *âventiure* and gets involved in a battle. There is, admittedly, a second cycle of action and even a kind of crisis – the appearance of the magician – but this is nothing more than a comic – though perilous – interlude which does not affect the hero himself, but merely gives him yet another opportunity to intervene as a rescuer. Finally, the winning of the hand of a woman by means of the *âventiure* here becomes such a superficial mechanism, and is made to appear so ludicrous in the episode of the mass nuptials, that it can only be seen as a parody.

In undermining the classical Arthurian model in this way, Der Stricker adheres all the more closely to the new conception of the hero: in Daniel we once more encounter, albeit in a slightly different form, the unproblematic, idealized Arthurian knight. In Der Stricker's romance, the world of *âventiure* takes a different form from that found in *Wigalois* and *Diu Crône*. Since the court itself sets out in pursuit of *âventiure*, the conventional encounters and trials of strength undertaken by individual knights are in large measure transferred to the whole entourage, taking on the qualities of exaggerated ritual slaughter. On the other hand, the supernatural elements of the *âventiure* world are as it were extrapolated and developed into a particular sphere reserved for Daniel. Only superficially connected with the main action, and thus free from any meaning conveyed by the traditional Arthurian model, this realm is given over to unrestrained fantasy. A grotesque imagination comes into its own here; the world which it creates is, although dangerous in a magical kind of way, more primitively wicked than truly sinister. There is a preponderance of magical devices, and this prevents the development of the more sinister kind of obscure and evil fantastic elements, such as are encountered in *Wigalois* or *Diu Crône*. Thus the sinister supernatural elements are here not counteracted by other, positive ones – that is to say, it is not good fortune which distinguishes the knight who pursues *âventiure*; instead, the magical and irrational dimension is opposed by reason, the hero's most notable characteristic. Daniel uses his own cleverness to oppose the forces of the supernatural, and the grotesque adversaries he encounters, despite their magical powers, are ultimately revealed as essentially rather stupid. Thus Daniel outwits the dwarf by exploiting his infatuation; he outmanoeuvres the trunkless monster by using the mirror trick, and he pretends to be one of the crowd of madmen in order to dispatch the bloodthirsty fiend. This last episode is especially telling: madness, which in the classical Arthurian romance is a sign of crisis, representing the hero's alienation from himself, is here reduced to a mere artifice. Nothing could indicate more clearly Der Stricker's distance from the classical model of Chrétien and Hartmann. Bravery, in conjunction with skill and cunning, combine to make Daniel von dem Blüenden Tal into a superhero in a fantastic game in which, in the twinkling of an eye, all the devices which the tradition provides can be brought into play.

There is a whole series of romances that more or less follow this type, although most fail to live up to the playful mood and light touch which characterize *Daniel*. As the new monsters of the world of *âventiure* become increasingly prone to mindless violence, so too the heroes appear as brainless muscle-men, and there is nothing to prevent a total trivialization of the genre.

Of particular interest for the assessment of literary self-consciousness in the mid-thirteenth century is the variation on *Daniel* attempted by Der Pleier in *Garel von dem Blüenden Tal*. This represents a clear attempt to adapt Der Stricker's romance to fit the original Arthurian model.[9] Der Pleier accordingly not only abandons the parodistic aspect, by omitting all the ironical motifs such as the roaring beast, the marriage to the widows and the abduction of the king; he also censors everything which in his opinion is not compatible with the classical Arthurian romance. Arthur's court thus becomes once more the traditional static point of reference, and the whole series of *âventiure* becomes once again the sole prerogative of the protagonist. Moreover, as Peter Kern has shown,[10] Der Pleier's characters are knowledgeably and skilfully situated in the lineage of the 'classical' Arthurian knights. Nothing could show more clearly the programmatic nature of Der Pleier's attempt to establish for

9   Boor, 'Der *Daniel* des Strickers', 74ff.
10 Kern, *Die Artusromane des Pleier*.

Garel, as well as for his later works, a place in the classical tradition of courtly literature.

As in *Daniel*, the action in *Garel* begins with a challenge from a messenger giant, but here this is more in the nature of a formal declaration of war, which is further justified by an account of previous events. At this, Garel, like Daniel, sets out on an investigative expedition and is faced with a series of five increasingly dangerous individual encounters. The first of these are *âventiure* to help and liberate others from human oppressors. There follows the battle with the giant, Purdan, and his wife – a fierce exchange of blows in a forest, in which Garel repeatedly dodges attacks by hiding behind trees until he finally succeeds in killing the two giants. The series culminates in the encounter with the centaur Vulganus, who – in a clear reference to *Daniel* – carries a Medusa-like head in his hand. In the course of this fight Garel also rescues Laudamie, with whom he has fallen in love, from the monster: the fight with Vulganus is thus at the same time *Minnedienst*, a labour of love. In keeping with the genre, the marriage takes place at the end of the first cycle. In accordance with the scheme of *Daniel*, the second cycle then depicts the pitched battle against the enemies of Arthur's court, which Der Pleier was clearly unwilling to forgo altogether. However, the battle is not fought by the Arthurian army but by auxiliary troops whose assistance the hero has secured in the *âventiure* of the first cycle. Only after all this has been brought to a successful conclusion do Arthur and the Knights of the Round Table appear on the scene.

In *Garel*, then, Der Pleier restores the Arthurian model as he understands it – that is, differently from Der Stricker; he carries through the division of the action into two parts, placing the hero's marriage to the partner he has won during the first cycle between the two parts. In accordance with the model, Arthur's court again has the function of starting point and ultimate goal. What Der Pleier however fails to restore is the crisis: the protagonist's leaving Laudamie to embark on the second cycle has no significance for the relationship between the lovers; it is merely that Garel still has to accomplish the task for which he originally set out. For the rest, Der Pleier's recasting also means the loss of that parodistic delight in invention which makes *Daniel* such enjoyable reading. Der Pleier's restoration of the Arthurian ideal without the problematic aspects of either the hero or the world of *âventiure* means that the action lacks depth, and the courtly ideal becomes a mere formality. Of all the new possibilities opened up by Der Stricker, the only ones retained are the grotesque exaggeration of the adversaries met with in the *âventiure*, and the numerical hyperbole of the battle scenes. Yet without Der Stricker's wit, and without the depths of evil plumbed in *Wigalois* or *Diu Crône*, this is hardly sufficient to captivate the reader's attention. Although Der Pleier's protagonist retains much of the superior cleverness and the irrepressible courage of Daniel, the author is more interested in demonstrating elegant modes of behaviour: in particular, a great deal of attention is lavished on the representation of court ceremonies.[11] The world of the romance is thus sharply divided into a human and courtly sphere – which also includes knightly adversaries – on the one hand, and a brutal world of monsters on the other, creating a dichotomy which is completely at odds with the traditional tension between the idealized world of Arthur's court and the counter-world experienced in the series of *âventiure*. The return to the classical model thus remains a superficial one: the specific problems of Chrétien's Arthurian model are subordinated to the representation of courtly form.

Wigalois and *Diu Crône*, *Daniel* and *Garel* all undermine the Arthurian model in different ways and develop it in different directions, so that the romances appear divergent in the extreme: nevertheless, they are bound by a common aesthetic principle which allows them to be seen, in conjunction with other late Arthurian romances, as a distinct literary type. Here, by contrast with the classical Arthurian romance, we are not dealing with a process which, following a fixed course through the negation or opposite of the ideal world of the court, continually keeps the Utopian moment in view as a goal; rather, the dynamic alternation of ideal and negation, of light and dark, is now reduced to and resolved into an unproblematic sphere of light personified by the hero, and a dark counter-world which sometimes appears cruel and daemonic, sometimes comic and grotesque.

These two worlds are interdependent, each defining the limits of the other, since if all the positive elements are concentrated in the hero, the negative side is as it were liberated for the free play of the poetic imagination. This insight into the wilder depths of human fantasy is what poetry gains in exchange for the loss of Chrétien's Arthurian model. Or, to put it differently, in the works of Chrétien

---

[11] Haug, 'Das Bildprogramm im Sommerhaus von Runkelstein', p. 52; also in Haug, *Strukturen*, p. 704.

and Hartmann fantasy elements were firmly embedded in the *âventiure* scheme, and the narrative dimension was not allowed to become too prominent, since the structure had to be clearly visible beneath it. Once this model was abandoned, the fictional imagination was free to develop its own potential, and was associated with the forces of darkness or the subconscious to the extent to which the latter had become detached from the now faultless hero. The fictional imagination was now set on a course which, in its fascination with evil, offered a distant prospect of the more recent concept of the creative literary potential of the daemonic.

These late Arthurian poets cannot and should not be expected to be capable of formulating such a 'poetics of evil' explicitly, or indeed to have wished to do so. Clearly they take the positive aspect as the starting point for their arguments, thus following the line laid down by the idea of the didactic function of poetry. What is of interest, then, is the establishment of this didactic function in opposition to the classical model, which had rejected a specifically didactic intention for courtly romance as being too narrowly reductive.

v

Wirnt, Heinrich von dem Türlin and Der Stricker accompanied their romances with prologues which contain theoretical reflections; *Garel*, on the other hand, lacks such an introduction. Der Pleier's other works, *Meleranz* and *Tandareis*, which both have prologues, are 'love romances', and thus represent a different type of romance: the prologue to *Tandareis*, with its praise of women, is consequently indebted to the conventions of this second type, whereas the introduction to *Meleranz* makes use of more general arguments, and may be included here instead of the non-existent prologue to *Garel*.

Let us consider first the prologue to *Wigalois*:

> Wer hât mich guoter ûf getân?
> sî ez iemen der mich kan
> beidiu lesen und verstên,
> der sol genâde an mir begên,
> ob iht wandels an mir sî,
> daz er mich doch lâze vrî
> valscher rede: daz êret in.
> ich weiz wol daz ich niene bin
> geliutert und gerihtet

noch sô wol getihtet
michn velsche lîhte ein valscher man,
wan sich niemen vor in kan
behüeten wol, swie rehte er tuot.
dehein rede ist sô guot
sine velschen si, daz weiz ich wol.
swaz ich valsches von in dol,
owê, wem sol ich daz klagen?
ich wilz et harte ringe tragen,
mac ich der besten lop bejagen. (*Wigalois*, 1–19)

[What good person has opened me? If it is someone who can both read and understand me, he should have pity on me if he find any imperfections, and spare me any accusations of incorrectness. That will be to his own honour. I know full well that I have not been so refined and emended, nor indeed so well written, as to escape the easy criticisms of a dishonest man. For no one can protect himself against such people, no matter how correctly he behaves. No poem is so good as to be spared their reproaches. I know that full well. Alas, to whom should I address my complaints at the unfair criticism I suffer from them? I will put up with it lightly if I can earn the praise of truly good people.]

Wirnt begins by speaking in the persona of his book, which appeals to the 'good reader' and asks for forbearance for any shortcomings. The traditional modesty formula here becomes a device for stylistic self-criticism. However – the 'book' continues – it is precisely incomplete or imperfect works which suffer at the hands of those critics who denigrate everything as a matter of principle. No amount of complaining will alter this, so one can only hope for *der besten lop* ('praise from truly good people').

The background for this argument is unmistakably Gottfried's *Tristan* prologue. There are clear verbal echoes: the appeal to the 'good reader', the *velschen* ('deprecation') perpetrated by the *valschen* ('the untrustworthy'), the stylistic terms *geliutert* ('purified') and *gerihtet* ('set right'); later these are supplemented by *zunge* ('tongue') and *sin* ('sense'; 37), and the expression 'swâ von dem guoten guot geschiht' (94: 'by whatever means the good man is treated well'), to mention only the most striking examples.

However, nothing remains of Gottfried's theoretical framework. Wirnt merely draws on *Tristan* to enrich his *captatio benevolentiae* and to forestall malevolent critics. He returns later to the theme of his own inadequacy and his hope that with God's aid he will yet be able to achieve something good (33ff.). Before this, he introduces arguments inspired by Hartmann's *Iwein*. Now the poet speaks directly, rather than in the persona of the book:[12]

> Swer nâch êren sinne,
> triuwe und êre minne,
> der volge guoter lêre –
> daz vürdert in vil sêre –
> unde vlîze sich dar zuo
> wie er nâch den getuo
> den diu werlt des besten giht,
> und die man doch dar under siht
> nâch gotes lône dienen hie;
> den volge wir, wan daz sint die
> den got hie sælde hât gegeben
> und dort ein êwiclîchez leben;
> dar nâch wir alle sulen streben. (*Wigalois*, 20–32)

[Whosoever strives for recognition and loves honesty and honour should heed good instruction – that will benefit him greatly – and endeavour to emulate those people, who are held in highest repute by society, and yet can also be seen striving to earn God's reward at the same time. Let us follow them, for those are the people to whom God has granted good fortune in this world and eternal life in the next. That is what we should all strive to attain.]

The beginning of this passage is clearly a reworking of the prologue to *Iwein*, while the end presents motifs which are particularly reminiscent of the epilogue to *Erec*. Yet although moral teaching and the setting of examples are discussed here, the argument remains – in contrast to Hartmann – on a general level: one should strive to imitate the good, regardless. No reference is made to King Arthur, at least not initially, for Wirnt returns to elaborate on his initial theme, the discussion of his own inadequacy. When reference is finally made to Arthur in lines 145ff., Hartmann's *Iwein* prologue is used again, but robbed of its main point, namely the idea of the supremacy of literature over bare facts:

> Ez was hie bevor, sô man seit,
> ein künic, der ie nâch êren streit,
> des nam wîten ist erkant;

---

[12] On this 'change of speaker' and how it relates to an audience of listeners or readers respectively, see Curschmann, 'Hören – Lesen – Sehen', 225ff.

Britanjâ hiez sîn lant,
selbe hiez er Artûs;
zu Karidôl hêt er hûs.
mit solhen vreuden stuont ez dô
daz uns daz nu machet vrô
sô man der herren vrümicheit
uns niwan mit worten seit
die dô des hoves pflâgen;
die muosen dicke wâgen
durch lop den lîp: daz was ir sit. (*Wigalois*, 145–57)

[Once upon a time there was a king, so it is said, who constantly
fought to win honour. His name is known far and wide. His country
was called Britannia, he himself was called Arthur. He had his seat at
Karidôl. Those were times of such happiness that it makes us happy
today simply to hear stories told about the courage of those noble
lords who were there at the court. Many a time were they obliged to
risk their lives to win renown, such was their custom.]

The tale is thus only a mere echo of the joys (*vreuden*) which once
reigned at Karidol; it is in no way superior to them as Hartmann's
theory had suggested. The discussion of the literary type and its
fictional status is therefore lacking in Wirnt; this is however precisely
what, in Hartmann's prologue, had defined his theoretical position.
Instead, Wirnt reduces the meaning of the tale to the moral lesson it
will provide.

As far as the relationship between poet and audience is concerned,
the initial topos of the critics is followed by further traditional
arguments, and/or proverbs; one should not hide one's light under a
bushel, nor on the other hand should one cast pearls before swine.
Furthermore, he notes, even something which is not made with
complete mastery can be useful; but such an argument will not sway
the obstinate listener. Then Wirnt brings a characterization of those
people who will not listen, with reminiscences of formulations used
by Hartmann and Wolfram: 'si / (= die bœsen) bietent lîhte d'ôren
dar: / ir muot stêt aber anders war' ('they (= the knaves) lend their
ears willingly, but their minds are elsewhere', 98f.) may be compared
to *Iwein* 250f., and 'er (= der valsche) / lât ez durch diu ôren gar, /
zem einen în, zem andern ûz' ('he (= the dishonest man) allows it
[what Wirnt tells him] to enter his ears, in at one and out at the other',
112f.) corresponds to *Parzival* 241,21f. And finally there is a reminis-
cence from Hartmann's *Der arme Heinrich*: 'ob ich mit mînem

277

munde / möhte swære stunde / den liuten senfte machen' ('whether with my words I might enable people to pass wearisome hours more pleasantly', 126ff.): cf. *Der arme Heinrich*, 10–11.

It may thus be seen that the prologue to *Wigalois* does not present a consistent theoretical argument. Wirnt has selected individual elements from the prologues of Gottfried, Hartmann and Wolfram, reduced them to conventional formulae and pieced them together, more or less skilfully, to make a prologue of his own. All that remains of the fundamental theoretical elements of the prologue is the traditional pairing of *prodesse* and *delectare*. Both of these are presented from the perspective of a traditional gesture of modesty which is in part affectation, and in part the product of a genuine lack of experience, since Wirnt says of himself that he has had no previous practice: *Wigalois* is his first work. None of the forward-looking narrative possibilities opened up by the romance itself are mentioned in the prologue, unless the didactic intention is to be seen in conjunction with the new model figure of the hero.

VI

By contrast with Wirnt's more or less eclectic collection of exordial topoi, Heinrich's prologue to *Diu Crône* is at least of some artistic merit. A quotation from Cicero serves as the opening *sententia*: 'Eloquence without wisdom is meaningless; wisdom without rhetoric is useless.'[13] This is elaborated on, using the contrast between *sin* ('sense') and *rede* ('speech'),[14] and then illustrated metaphorically: he who draws his sword and runs away without having struck a blow with it is unlikely to win; anyone who acts in this way is like someone who washes an unfired tile and keeps finding more dirt, or someone who grinds a jewel into the mud. One has to know whether one is in a position to fight or whether it would be better to take flight; in other words, what matters is to be able to judge one's own abilities accurately. This leads Heinrich – like Wirnt – to speak of his own poetic abilities:

> Ich vüer ouch wol, ob ich möht,
> von den tôren ein teil

[13] *De inventione*, 1,1; this quotation was used by Augustine, who helped to familiarize it: CCSL, *De doctrina christiana* IV, v 10/11; cf. also Suchomski, *'Delectatio' und 'Utilitas'*, p. 215.
[14] Cf. Mentzel-Reuters, *Vröude, Artusbild, Fortuna*, p. 84.

und spræch gern âne meil,
liez mich mîn unheil. (*Crône*, 36–9)[15]

[Indeed I would set myself apart from the fools, if I could, and did
misfortune not prevent me I would gladly speak unblemished verse.]

Heinrich proceeds to counter this conventional topos of self-
criticism with the reminder that nobody is perfect; a worthless crystal
may still shine beside an emerald, the Imperial crown is not set with
the one outstanding jewel known as 'der Waise' alone, and precious
and less precious metals are fused into one. Thus he, Heinrich, is not
afraid of being set alongside more brilliant jewels. However, after
elaborating the theme of such companionship (*genôzschaft*) further,
he returns once more to the theme of his own lack of ability:

Der sin, der diu wort zieret
und die rede florieret,
der ist mir leider tiur. (*Crône*, 89–91)

[I lack that intelligence which embellishes words and creates florid
language.]

Heinrich compares himself to a fire which only smoulders but does
not truly glow, and to a piece of glass which, unlike a diamond, does
not shine with its own fire. Nevertheless he wishes to remain true to
what is true and perfect (*stæte unde ganz*), not that which is faithless
and worthless (*valsch unde swach*):

Ich bit an disem buoche,
swer ez lesen geruoche,
ob wandel eteswâ sî
und ob anderhalp dâ bî
iht von künste schîn,
daz diu arbeit mîn
iht gar werde verlorn
und ân schulde verkorn
umb einen ungefüegen spruch.
An einem purper ein bruch
sol in niht gar verswachen. (*Crône*, 140–50)

[I ask all those who deign to read this book, if on the one hand there
are faults, on the other some element of lustre and artistry, that my
efforts should not be entirely wasted and unjustly rejected because

---

[15] I have followed the text established by Mentzel-Reuters, ibid., pp. 292ff., but without
necessarily adopting his punctuation.

of some inappropriate turn of phrase. One tear in a costly piece of silk cannot make it completely contemptible.]

This imagery of precious stones, metals and brilliance finds an echo in the epilogue, where Heinrich refers to his poem as a crown which is set with fine precious stones ('<mit> guoten steinen … über al beleit'; 29966ff.), so that it would be quite fitting for the good to wear. Here all the conventional exordial modesty is forgotten; the poet declares confidently that if the jewels in his 'crown' are taken to be glass, this reflects not on the goldsmith but on the beholder. Even if the splendid imagery of the prologue had not already revealed Heinrich's self-deprecation as the rhetorical device it is, the conclusion would make perfectly clear how confident he is of his own ability and with what degree of calculation he employs these strategic devices.

In lines 161ff. he too refers to King Arthur, and once again this is an echo of the prologue to *Iwein*.

> Uns ist oft geseit
> von maneger hant vrümekeit,
> die Artûs der künec begienc. (*Crône*, 161–3)

> [We have often heard tell of all kinds of brave deeds performed by King Arthur.]

He, Heinrich, now wishes to give an account of the king's early years:

> und wâ sich anevienge
> sîner tugend loblîcher strît,
> den im noch diu werlt gît.
> Mit sîner reinen tugende sage
> sich mêret sîn lop alle tage,
> die wîl werlt vröuden phligt.
> Er hât mit êren sô gesigt,
> daz er nie vant sînen gnôz. (*Crône*, 172–9)

> [and how that fine contest of virtues first began that the world still attributes to him. Such are the reports of his excellent qualities that his reputation is enhanced daily for as long as courtly life endures. His honour has won such a round of victories that he has never ever encountered his equal.]

This theme of supreme fame is continued in several variations, repeatedly echoing expressions of Hartmann's, for example:

Leider ob der lîp erstarp,
Im lebt doch sîn reiner nam; (*Crône*, 199–200)

[Even if he were, alas, to die his untarnished name would live on.]

Hartmann's complaint at the world of his own time is also taken up, but Heinrich has his own answer to it:

In möhte wol diu werlt clagen
Cumberlîchen in disen tagen,
Het sich nû lîp unde guot
Gewendet an sô reinen muot.
Ez zimt den besten wol
Tuon wol, swaz man sol.
Iemer sunder widerwanc
Haben die bœsen undanc,
Triuwen die vrumen hân vruom; (*Crône*, 206–14)

[Society today would not lament his passing with such sorrow, if it were committed, at risk of life and possessions, to the attainment of such inner excellence now. It well becomes the best of men to do well what one has to do. May the evil men always get their deserts, and the honest men the benefit of their honesty too.]

The poet thus intends, as a source of betterment ('ze bezzerunge') and pleasure ('ze kurzwîle'), and in honour of women, to translate from French into German the Arthurian story he has announced, 'wan er sô gelêret was, / Daz er die sprâche kunde' ('for his learning was such that he knew that language'; 224f.):

Ez ist von dem Turlîn
Heinrîch, des zung nie
wîbes ganzen lop verlie,
der vant ditz mære,
wannen geborn wære
künec Artûs der guote,
der ie in rîters muote
bî sînen zîten hât gelebt.
Wie er nâch êren ie strebt,
daz muget ir wol hœren nuo. (*Crône*, 246–55)

[Heinrich von dem Türlin, who has never been lacking in his praise of women, composed this story about the origins of good King Arthur, who in his day lived a life of knightly valour. Now you may hear the story of how he strove to win renown.]

The Hartmann quotations and echoes here follow so closely upon one another that it would be possible to reconstitute almost the whole of the *Iwein* prologue from them. However, this only serves to illustrate all the more clearly how and where Heinrich deviates from *Iwein*: the deploring of the present by comparison with the past does not lead here to the bold claim that the tale (*mære*) more than compensates for the lost world of Arthur's court; instead, Heinrich calls for precisely what Hartmann did not intend, namely good deeds in imitation of those of King Arthur. This moral *bezzerunge* ('improvement') is his prime motive for telling the story.

It must be assumed that Heinrich von dem Türlin, unlike Wirnt, was at least aware of the key theoretical point of Hartmann's *Iwein* prologue. Not only did he omit the latter's theory of the supremacy of literature over life, he deliberately opposed it: for him, the Arthurian world acts as an inspiration for 'die besten', a spur to 'tuon wol, swaz man sol' ('to do their duty as well as possible'). This implies, at least theoretically, the abandoning of the autonomous status of fiction as a literary medium and as a genuine form of experience. In reality, however, *Diu Crône* is anything but an idealized moral tale of *âventiure* with exemplary figures which gradually reveals a definite moral lesson. In fact, the work breaks new poetic ground in a positively pioneering spirit, discovering new areas whose sinister or chimerical aspects are represented in an extremely bold and vivid way, without any attempt to integrate them in a coherent literary world. The theoretical justification of literature provided in the prologue is – if it is to be seen as more than a precautionary strategy – most readily to be understood as a kind of poetic self-reassurance, a declaration of the poet's intention to retain, at the very least, a clear distinction between good and evil in the face of a world of *âventiure* in which the supernatural elements are beginning to run riot, and are threatening to take an uncontrollable hold on the imagination.

VII

The particular significance which Hartmann's *Iwein* prologue held for the post-classical romance poets is illustrated – possibly even earlier than in Wirnt and Heinrich von dem Türlin – by Der Stricker, whose *Daniel* prologue presents a clearly focussed consideration of the issues raised by Hartmann.[16] The delicate balance, in Hartmann's text, between literary representation and facts or subject matter is transformed, in the version by Der Stricker, into a triangular relationship between the act of listening, the attitude of the listener, and action:

> Swer gerne allez daz vernimt
> daz guoten liuten wol gezimt,
> der wirt es selten âne muot,
> unz er der werc ein teil getuot. (*Daniel*, 1–4)

[That man who likes to hear everything that it is appropriate for good people to hear never ceases to dwell on it until he has performed some of those deeds himself.]

Der Stricker thus postulates as a starting point a correlation between *wort* ('word') and *werc* ('deed') which is established by means of the heart (*muot*); an ethical concept with unmistakable biblical connotations.[17] It is Der Stricker's declared intention to integrate literature directly into life, and in such a specific way that a fourth dimension, the material or practical aspect, is taken into consideration: the *guot* is seen in terms of material possessions, a necessary prerequisite for right action:

> Swer lop und êre wil bejagen,
> der sol dar umbe niht verzagen,
> irret in etswâ daz guot.
> sô man den willigen muot
> an ime erkennet unde siht,
> man giht im, des man dem giht
> der den willen und diu werc tuot.
> gar âne willigen muot
> wirt selten ieman wol gelobet,
> swaz er mit gebene getobet. (*Daniel*, 23–32)

[He who desires to win praise and recognition should not be put off if he is at all lacking in wealth. As soon as his willing disposition is recognized he will be spoken of in the same terms as the man who both has the will and puts it into action. A man who lacks a willing disposition never earns praise, no matter what show he makes with his bounty.]

---

[16] Kern, 'Rezeption und Genese des Artusromans', 19ff; Ragotzky, *Gattungserneuerung*, pp. 45ff. Both offer apt comments, although the deviation from Hartmann could be stressed more strongly.

[17] Ragotzky, *Gattungserneuerung*, p. 48.

Once one has realized that this passage is based on the beginning of the *Iwein* prologue, the extent to which the basis of the argument has shifted becomes obvious. Hartmann's prologue stated that whoever devoted his meditations and endeavours to *rehtiu güete* ('true goodness') would also be granted *sælde* and *êre* ('fortune' and 'honour'). This is the key concept of the Arthurian ideal, which is based on the correlation between inner and outer reality, merit and reward: all the action takes place according to this principle. Der Stricker however abandons this equivalence, restricting himself essentially to the intention to do good deeds. This alone is important, he suggests, and can indeed take the place of action if the material conditions for the latter are lacking. It is significant that the material aspect is mentioned here; in the classical Arthurian romance it was of no relevance, since there the correlation between inner and outer spheres, including the material aspect, could be achieved without difficulty in the medium of fiction. At the moment when the concept of an autonomous fictional medium is abandoned, however, so that direct transformation of *wort* into *werc* is called for, difficulties necessarily arise, since the application of Arthurian ways of living and modes of behaviour to actual reality places too great a strain on the material resources of most people. The logical conclusion of the discrepancy revealed here between the Arthurian ideal and its chances of practical realization can only be a retreat into an ideal inner world, since the only recourse left is to good intentions. This solution then becomes programmatic, particularly in Rudolf von Ems' *Der guote Gêrhart*.

The adaptation of the opening to *Iwein*, transforming it into a discourse on the primacy of good intentions, is followed in Der Stricker's poem – as one might expect – by praise of King Arthur. However, Hartmann's 'des gît gewisse lêre / künec Artûs der guote' ('noble King Arthur provides definite teaching on this') becomes 'des giht der künic Artûs' ('King Arthur declares this to be so'). In other words, Der Stricker makes Arthur the guarantor of the new idea. Praise of Arthur then leads to the usual catalogue of virtues, again with echoes of Hartmann, e.g. 'ern begie nie lasterlîche schame. / dâvon sîn lop und sîn name / reine lebt unde wert' ('He never did anything shameful. Hence his praise and his good name have endured and remained untarnished'; 39ff.), yet without the idea of the survival of the name leading, as it does elsewhere, to an autonomous concept of fiction. If there is anything

284

which goes beyond the level of stereotype, it is the slightly mischievous tone which comes through at certain times during the praise of Arthur:

> Der künic Artûs was vollekomen.
> swaz wir von künigen hân vernomen,
> daz was ein wint wider im. (*Daniel*, 47–9)

> [King Arthur attained perfection. No other king that we have ever heard of can stand comparison with him.]

Der Stricker continues by stating that he cannot possibly set down all the things that Arthur accomplished in his youth, for fear of being thought a liar or a madman. However, he intends, he says, to reveal a small part, at least, to his audience, saying of Arthur:

> er was sô rehte wârhaft
> daz er sprach dehein wort,
> ezn wære stæter denne der hort
> der iemer und iemer weren mac. (*Daniel*, 60–3)

> [He was so true to his word that he never spoke a single sentence that did not surpass in its immutability the treasure that lasts for ever.]

Such empty hyperbole anticipates the playful manipulation of the Arthurian tradition which characterizes the narrative proper. However, the more obvious it becomes that Der Stricker does not take the world of *âventiure* which he presents in *Daniel* entirely seriously, the more the apparent demands of the prologue for a direct application of the ideals of Arthurian romance to everyday reality are lost to view. The distancing of the *werc* from the intentions behind it seems, by contrast, to some extent to restore a certain degree of freedom to the *wort* also: here too, what matters is *muot*, the underlying feeling; there is no reason why the world in which its potential is realized should not be a fictional one. What is important for Der Stricker is not the make-believe world of the *âventiure*, but the demonstration of clever reasoning on the part of his hero Daniel.[18] The whole Arthurian setting is in essence nothing more than an amusing and decorative backdrop, designed to display the new type of hero and his own particular brand of *muot* to advantage. Since this last quality is ultimately the only thing that matters, the background

---

[18] Wuttke, 'Didaktische Dichtung', pp. 614–15, has drawn attention to the extent to which Der Stricker's idea corresponds to the didactic theory put forward by Thomasin.

against which it is represented can be given over to the free play of the imagination.

Der Stricker's casual attitude to the subject matter of his romance may also be considered responsible for the following unexpected reference to a source, which takes the form of a bold plagiarism of Lambrecht's prologue to the *Alexander*:

> Von Bisenze meister Albrich,
> der brâhte ein rede an mich
> ûz wälscher zungen.
> die hân ich des betwungen,
> daz man sie in tiutschen vernimet,
> swenne kurzwîle gezimet.
> nieman der enschelte mich:
> louc er mir, sô liuge ouch ich. (*Daniel*, 7–14)

[Master Alberic of Pisançon passed on to me a tale that was written in French. I have so reworked it that it can now be heard in German whenever there is a need for entertainment. Let no one criticize me. If he was lying to me, then I am lying too.]

With this obviously fictitious source, introduced at the very beginning of the 'word–work–will' discussion, Der Stricker makes clear, in a deliberately programmatic way, the status he wishes to be accorded to his poetic world. He thus first removes the *wort* from the correlation already established between *wort* and *werc*, going on to remove *werc* too by falling back on good intentions: the subject matter itself is thus neutral and of little relevance. In the end, then, the very elements which had initially been seen and presented in a new constellation – namely imagination, morals, and the deeds of the world of action – ultimately appear to have no common unifying factor after all.

VIII

As in Der Stricker's poem, so too in Der Pleier's prologue to *Meleranz* the problem of the material basis of the Arthurian festivities (*vröude*) is of central importance, though it is seen here from a different perspective and has correspondingly different connotations. The interrelationship of goodness (*daz guote*) and joy (*vröude*) is discussed in the context of a *laudatio temporis acti*. In former times, *gefuoge*, *zuht* and *hübescheit* ('decorous behaviour', 'good manners', 'courtesy'; 8) were the rule, and men and women could be observed striving to attain honour (*nâch êren strîten*; 15). Since then, times have changed for the worse:

> ez nimt abe an guoten dingen.
> die uns fröude solten bringen,
> ich mein die edelen rîchen,
> die lebent unfrôlichen.
> die wîben solten lachen
> und fröude solten machen,
> ich mein die edelen jungen,
> die lebent unbetwungen
> an tugenthaftem muote.
> manec bî grôzem guote
> lebt unfrôlîchen. (*Meleranz*, 27–37)

[Good living is in decline. Those who ought to maintain courtly festivities, namely the rich and the noble, live paltry lives. Those who ought to bring laughter and joy to the ladies, namely the young and noble, are not guided by a virtuous inner disposition. Many a man has great wealth and yet lives a life of no cheer.]

Der Pleier then demands that anyone who owns property should use it in order to achieve fame; this will bring him respect in this world and eternal happiness in the hereafter.

Der Pleier's poetic work has the stated aim of realizing the courtly ideal; his *Garel* is a veritable textbook on Arthurian ceremony. For this reason, his theoretical reflections have a primarily practical intention, since he is concerned with the possibility of enacting the Arthurian ideal in the real world. However, in the conflict which necessarily arises between this bold claim and the possibilities of its practical implementation, Der Pleier does not – unlike Der Stricker – fall back on good intentions, but rather insists on the actual realization of the Arthurian ideal. He attempts to solve the practical problems this presents by appealing to the rich and powerful to employ their wealth and power to make the Arthurian ideal a reality.

Only after these general statements does Der Pleier mention Arthur himself in the introduction to *Meleranz*, following the prologue to *Iwein* closely to provide a concrete example of the lost ideal state. King Arthur thus becomes a prime example of an ideal attitude to be realized in the here and now.

In retrospect, then, it is clear that Hartmann's prologue to *Iwein* provided the theoretical starting point for all the 'post-classical' prologues which have been discussed here. The discussion takes shape around the didactic concept of *lêre*, which is now taken to mean that the Arthurian world represents a direct and positive example for the present. The programmatic step taken by Hartmann, away from the historical reality of the Arthurian past in favour of the fictional reality of the narrative, is ignored, and this idealized past instead gives rise, among post-classical authors, to the *laudatio temporis acti* with regard to what – by comparison with this lost age – is an inferior present time. However, attempts to recreate the Arthurian world in real terms were inevitably forced to confront the discrepancy between such an ideal on the one hand, and the actual *guot*, in the sense of the material possibilities available, on the other. The respective solutions posited by Der Stricker and Der Pleier are diametrically opposed: whereas Der Stricker takes the course of internalization, Der Pleier opts for externalization. In other words, Der Stricker's retreat to the ideal world of good intentions makes *daz guote* – what is good – independent of any worldly goods, while Der Pleier's incursions into the outside world have as their goal an application of the Arthurian ideal to actual social forms – an experiment often repeated in the long series of Arthurian festivals and Round Table societies in the Late Middle Ages. While the theoretical discussion centred on the feasibility of applying the lessons of the Arthurian world to contemporary reality, in the poetic works themselves the very area neglected by the theory, namely the fictional world of *âventiure*, shows a dynamic development which, uninhibited by theoretical considerations, is left to its own devices, in other words given over to the free play of the imagination.

15

Rudolf von Ems' *Der guote Gêrhart*: a programmatic rejection of the correlation between merit and reward

I

The work of the two most important romance authors of the second half of the thirteenth century, Rudolf von Ems and Konrad von Würzburg, covers a relatively broad range of genres: hagiographical romances, historical romances, love-romances – but this range no longer includes the Arthurian romance. In contrast to the post-classical Arthurian romances, then, their theoretical reflections are unlikely to be derived from Hartmann's *Iwein* prologue. Konrad, by and large, pursues an independent course, while Rudolf takes up the *Tristan* prologue and Wolfram's introduction to *Willehalm*. However, this does not mean that the scheme of the Arthurian romance was no longer influential. On the contrary, Rudolf programmatically takes issue with it in *Der guote Gêrhart*, and Konrad's *Partonopier und Meliur* relies for its effect on an appreciation of how it deviates from the classical *âventiure* pattern. To put it another way, the open questions which the post-classical era inherited from the great romances of Wolfram and Gottfried are taken up by both Rudolf and Konrad in a completely new way, that is to say outside the Arthurian framework. This leads to new, fruitful solutions, opening up new paths which in turn give rise to further open-ended problems.

I shall begin with a consideration of Rudolf's first work, *Der guote Gêrhart*. In terms of its relationship to the 'classical' Arthurian romance, it can be seen as a programmatic work, testifying to the new moral tendency in the romance tradition already anticipated by Der Stricker in the prologue to *Daniel*.

Rudolf introduces his romance with a prologue which takes up Gottfried's theme of the relationship between good deeds and society's recognition of them. The first four lines may be read as a paraphrase of the introductory quatrain of *Tristan*:

> Swaz ein man durch guoten muot
> ze guote in guotem muote tuot,
> des sol man im ze guote jehen,
> wan ez in guote muoz geschehen. (*Der guote Gêrhart*, 1–4)

> [Whatever a man does out of the goodness of his heart, with good intentions, that is for the good, should be accredited to him as a good deed, for it should have its good effect.]

This allusion to Gottfried clearly functions as an exordial *sententia*, and Rudolf may thus be seen to follow Wolfram's example in transforming the general prologue *sententia* into a specific literary reference. It is tempting at first to read these four opening lines as an affirmation of Gottfried's statement that it is right and necessary to recognize *daz guote* as such. It is striking, however, that the crux of Gottfried's argument is omitted, since no mention is made of his point that the good is lost if it does not meet with recognition. Moreover, the phrase 'durch guoten muot' seems to strike a new note, and may at least be seen as an indication that *daz guote* here is not as closely associated with the reception of the work as it was for Gottfried. The lines which follow make it abundantly clear that Rudolf only takes up the argument from the *Tristan* prologue in order to distance himself from it all the more emphatically:

> swen sîn gemüete lêret
> daz er ze gote kêret
> herze, sinne unde muot,
> daz er daz beste gerne tuot,
> der hüete an dem guote sich,
> sô ist ez guot und lobelich. (*Der guote Gêrhart*, 5–10)

> [Whoever is inwardly disposed to turn his heart, mind and senses to God and to do gladly what is best, should be on his guard with respect to his goodness, to do that is good and praiseworthy.]

Despite the echoes of Hartmann and Wirnt in this passage, the combination of *guot* and *muot* points in a quite a new direction: the key phrase is *sich hüeten* ('to be on one's guard'). What is meant by it is explained in the following lines:

> swer durch guot iht guotes tuot,
> durch guotes herzen guoten muot,

wil er sich selben rüemen vil,
sô jagt er ûf des ruomes zil
den ruom hinz an ein ende
mit solher missewende
daz mit des ruomes missetât
des guoten ruom an im zergât. (*Der guote Gêrhart*, 11–18)

[If a man who does a good deed out of goodness and with the good
intentions of a good heart indulges in self-praise, then by aiming for
approbation he will pursue fame to the point where because of his
boastfulness his good deed will no longer be praised.]

Whereas Gottfried had been concerned to demonstrate the interdependence of *daz guote* and the recognition of it – the concept of
'correlation' – and had translated this correlation into the aesthetic
sphere with his theory of the identification between audience and
work, Rudolf deliberately disrupts this relationship and warns against
seeking praise for a good deed ('des guoten ruom'), since pursuit of
such recognition necessarily entails the loss of *daz guote*. From this
he draws the following conclusion, emphatically stating the new
position:

von swem guotes iht geschiht,
des ruom ist gên der welt ein niht; (*Der guote Gêrhart*, 19–20)

[The worldly fame of a man who does a good deed is in itself
meaningless]

And one might, Rudolf continues, quite well leave the business of
praise to the *guote* and *wîse*, since they are well able to recognize
and appreciate what is truly good. This leads to the logical conclusion that

er sol daz rüemen lâzen sîn;
wan den guoten wirt wol schîn
ob er durch guotes herzen rât
guotes iht geprüevet hât. (*Der guote Gêrhart*, 33–6)

[A man should never boast, for to good people it will be apparent if
he has done good out of the goodness of his heart.]

This, then, is the moral indicated by the various reflections: one
should not boast of one's own good deeds – a fairly banal conclusion
to an argument which had promised to take issue with Gottfried's
literary theory! Is the allusion to the *Tristan* prologue therefore

intended as nothing more than a tag on which to hang a moral, which the following story is then designed to illustrate? The end of the prologue would seem to suggest this, in that Rudolf, after further remarking that his moral lesson is directed at wise and foolish people alike (41; 'gegen wîser und an tumber diet'), i.e. 'to all', concludes with the following statement:

> dise lêre mir beschiet
> ein mære, daz mit wârheit
> nâch rehter ebenmâze seit,
> wie sêre ein man missevert
> des ruom sîn lob sô gar verzert
> daz man in fürbaz prîset niht
> wan als er im selben giht. (*Der guote Gêrhart*, 42–8)

> [I learned this lesson from a story which gives a true and balanced account of how badly that man goes wrong whose good reputation is so consumed by boastfulness that he no longer enjoys any praise save that which he speaks himself.]

The impression one gains from this is that the prologue has shrivelled to nothing more than an explanation of a moral precept; the tale related is apparently intended to be no more than an exemplary illustration, with no function beyond the moral it is intended to convey. Should one, then, expect nothing more than an exemplum blown up to the scale of romance?

At first glance, the structure of the work would seem to confirm this. *Der guote Gêrhart* consists of a story within a story, taking the form of an exemplum within a framework, as set out below.

The subject of the frame narrative is Emperor Otto, who has led an exemplary life and who therefore believes he may reasonably expect God to reward him for his good deeds with eternal life. On asking God to confirm him in this hope, he is informed by an angel that he has forfeited his heavenly reward because he sought earthly praise when performing his good deeds. He would have done better to act in the spirit of a certain merchant from Cologne whose good deeds were performed quietly, without boasting, and whose name is therefore inscribed in the Book of Life. After the emperor has made enquiries about the life of this man – known as 'der guote Gêrhart', or Gerhart the Good – he seeks him out and eventually, despite his reluctance, persuades him to tell his story. This runs as follows:

Gerhart has travelled to the Orient to make his fortune on a commercial voyage. During the homeward journey, a storm forces him to take refuge in an unfamiliar heathen city in Morocco, where some Christians are being held prisoner. Gerhart is given the opportunity of purchasing the liberty of the twenty-four men and fifteen women in exchange for his valuable cargo. Among the women is a Norwegian princess who had been on her way to marry the English prince William when her ship was driven off course. Her bridegroom's ship was sunk in the storm. Although Gerhart may expect that the prisoners will repay him handsomely after their return home, he still hesitates to take the risk, until warned by an angel to overcome his scruples, since a good deed is never done in vain: 'If you do it for gain, the prisoners will reward you; if you do it for fame, you will be praised; if you do it because God commands it, he will reward you for it' (1860ff.). Gerhart therefore buys the prisoners' freedom and allows them to return to their own country. However, he takes the Norwegian princess with him to Cologne while waiting to see whether the lost English prince will turn up. When no news comes within a year, Gerhart suggests that she marry his son, and after waiting for another year she agrees to this. A Whitsun wedding is arranged, a magnificent courtly festival with jousts and tournaments in which the whole city takes part, burghers, clergy and nobility alike. Then Gerhart notices a lone sad face among the joyful crowd. It belongs, of course, to the long-lost prince, whose years of wandering in search of his bride have finally brought him to his goal in the nick of time. Gerhart urges his son to renounce his claim. There follows a moving reunion scene, and Gerhart adds that when he saw this he would gladly have given a dozen times as much gold and silver in order to be able to bestow such happiness.

After this, William seeks Gerhart's advice as to how he might regain his land and his throne. England is in uproar, since the pretender to the throne is believed to be dead and no one can agree on a new king. Gerhart sets out to discover more, and comes across a council assembly which is at that very moment attempting to elect a new king. Among those present are the twenty-four prisoners whom Gerhart had freed. When they recognize him they are convinced that they have found in him their new king, and before he can protest the crown is placed on his head. Then however he tells them that their prince, whom all had believed lost, has returned with his wife. The couple are given a rapturous reception, and a magnificent feast is prepared, the like of which, it is said, has not been seen since the days of King Arthur. William wishes to enfeoff Gerhart with the dukedom of Kent or the county of London, and, when Gerhart refuses this, to shower him with gold and silver. But Gerhart accepts only a brooch and a ring for his wife and returns to Cologne, happy that he has been able to do so much good with his wealth. Thereafter he is referred to as *der guote*. However, concluding his tale, Gerhart emphasizes once again that he does not deserve this title, stating that if he has done any good, then it is for God to weigh it in the balance against the sin of pride he has committed in telling of his deeds.

The emperor acknowledges the moral superiority of the modest merchant from Cologne, who did not forfeit the heavenly reward for his good deeds by singing his own praises.

Der guote Gêrhart is thus clearly a romance designed to illustrate a moral principle. It could be termed a moral tale which has been expanded into a romance; the inner narrative is indeed derived from the tradition of the exemplum.[1]

What, then, is the significance of this elaboration of a simple exemplary tale into a romance? What does it have to offer beyond the simple exemplum apart from the breadth of illustration, which is included only at the expense of sacrificing some of the story's impact? The answer lies in the fact that the re-casting of the tale on a large scale was undertaken in imitation of courtly romance, thus implicitly engaging in the theoretical discussion of the genre which the prologue fails to supply. This illustration, within the narrative proper, of the thesis put forward in the prologue of the correlation between merit and reward, here becomes a programmatic critique of the underlying premisses of the Arthurian model. The inner narrative, based on a double cycle, thus – as Thomas Perry Thornton and Christoph Cormeau[2] have pointed out – only makes use of the scheme of the Arthurian *âventiure* in order to distance itself from it, as is explained in what follows.

Gerhart sets out on a commercial voyage, which however leads to the freeing of prisoners, although not, as in a romance of *âventiure*, in knightly combat but by Gerhart's buying their liberty. He brings a king's daughter home with him from this voyage, and at the end of the first 'cycle' there is the traditional wedding celebration. Admittedly Gerhart does not marry the princess himself, but he wishes to wed her to his son. However, this is prevented, since at the crucial

<hr/>

[1] Ertzdorff, *Rudolf von Ems*, pp. 160ff.
[2] Cormeau, 'Rudolf von Ems: *Der guote Gerhart*'.

moment her rightful suitor appears, and Gerhart persuades his son to renounce her; thus after the end of the first cycle a kind of crisis occurs, although in completely different circumstances from the usual Arthurian pattern. There then follows, in accordance with the model of the double cycle, a new expedition designed to consolidate the first: Gerhart is crowned king in England, prematurely, as it turns out, and steps down in favour of the rightful ruler, subsequently refusing both fief and personal riches.

The classical Arthurian model is thus cited quite explicitly in the structuring of the narrative: the hero's setting out and encountering danger, the turning point and the winning of a wife, the return home and the Whitsuntide wedding feast, a second expedition, renewed danger and the concluding celebrations. Moreover, on two occasions the action actually seems to enter the world of courtly romance, namely in the festivities in Cologne and London: the key concept of *vröude* is introduced, and the London celebration is explicitly compared with the Arthurian feast (*hôchgezît*). However, precisely at those moments when a parallel with Arthurian romance is most apparent, the action abruptly changes course: thus the merchant's son does not win the hand of the princess after all, and when Gerhart is proclaimed king and crowned, and could become ruler over all England – or at least over Kent and London – here too the action is deliberately prevented from becoming a traditional courtly romance; this is clearly the point of the narrative as a whole. The key positions at which, in courtly romance, the series of *âventiure* find temporary or absolute fulfilment, i.e. at the end of the first and second cycles respectively, are occupied in *Der guote Gêrhart* by acts of renunciation. Such renunciation is the manifestation of a principle diametrically opposed, on both ethical and aesthetic grounds, to the Arthurian principle of correlation between merit and reward, inner and outer realms.[3]

The angel who encourages Gerhart to purchase the prisoners' release describes to him what he stands to gain from this action: material reward, or social respect, or eternal life. Initially Gerhart is interested in the business aspect of the bargain, yet when he returns home he makes no attempt to recover his money, being now more interested in social advancement and arranging for the marriage of his son to the Norwegian princess. However, when the original bride-

---

[3] Haug, 'Struktur und Geschichte', pp. 149ff.: also in Haug, *Strukturen*, pp. 253ff.; Walliczek, *Rudolf von Ems: 'Der guote Gêrhart'*, pp. 95ff.

groom turns up, he renounces this plan too, and in addition refuses all social advancements subsequently offered to him. His actions are henceforth directed towards the third possibility, seeking the good deed for its own sake, a deed which will be rewarded by God.

Such clear-cut alternatives are foreign to the Arthurian romance. In the latter, a correspondence exists between the spiritual and material worlds, and the inner position is represented by the outer dimension. The hero's achievements find recognition in the eyes of God and the world, and personal virtue is rewarded by worldly success. This is the sense of the conclusion of Hartmann's *Erec*, where it is stated that God granted the happy couple eternal life 'nâch der werlde krône' ('after having achieved their crown in the world'; 10127ff.). By contrast, Gerhart achieves eternal life precisely because he has renounced 'der werlde krône'.

The journey of the new hero is no longer intended to represent his *social* progress in addition to his spiritual development. While the knight of the Round Table always has the distant goal of the Utopian moment of celebration in the *werlt* – as represented by the Arthurian festivities – in view during his journey through the anti-courtly world of *âventiure*, Gerhart's merchant expedition is a purely private venture. Nor does Gerhart set out from a court; if the course of his journey at times resembles that of the Arthurian romance, this is only so that he may distance himself all the more clearly from the courtly world. This is the reason for making a merchant the hero of a romance; not because a new class, the bourgeoisie, is here deemed worthy of literary treatment, but because the use of a merchant figure makes possible a starting point that is situated outside courtly society – which is not to say that this movement away from the courtly sphere does not open up new, sociological, dimensions for literature.[4] Be that as it may, the tension between courtly society and the individual *âventiure* which characterized the Arthurian romance is no longer a factor. The existential crisis of the protagonist, which in the Arthurian romance had opened the way for a vision of a social utopia, is replaced by an isolated moral act, carried out for its own sake and leading to a form of personal salvation which is not only independent of all social relationships, but for which such independence is indeed an essential prerequisite.

This is not without consequences in determining the nature of

---

[4] On the sociological aspect, see Peters, *Literatur in der Stadt*, pp. 36ff.

literary fiction. Just as the *âventiure* sequence, with its Utopian goal, and the symbolic counter-world of *âventiure* complement each other in the Arthurian romance, so in *Der guote Gêrhart* the quasi-realistic settings for the action go hand in hand with the structuring of the narrative with the goal of the isolated moral act in view. It is a realm with fixed historical and geographical reference points, stretching from Northern and Western Europe to the Near East and North Africa, ranging over Norway, England, Cologne, Damascus, Morocco and so on. The events take place during the reign of Otto the Great, and historical details are mentioned, such as his founding of Magdeburg. The unfolding of the action also seems more 'realistic', with the everyday life of the merchant providing concrete details. This all becomes possible, indeed necessary, because meaning is no longer conveyed through a symbolic fictional construct but instead is made apparent in the good deeds of the hero. No longer bound by the symbolic structure of the Arthurian model, fiction can aim at a certain degree of verisimilitude, since good deeds become more convincing the more they are perceived as taking place within a clearly imaginable, 'real' world. The fact that the plot is, by comparison, revealed as a clearly artificial construct does not necessarily detract from the impact of the narrative, since this depends for its effect on the individual deed within a specific situation, rather than on the fictional coincidences and twists of fate, however adventurous or improbable these may be.

The action of the 'frame narrative' reflects on the subject of the romance, while at the same time demonstrating the new mode of reception and function of narrative through the use of exemplary figures. Emperor Otto represents the traditional Arthurian position of the identification of honour (*êre*) and fortune (*sælde*), in the sense of a correlation between earthly success and divine grace; however, from a religious viewpoint his expectation of divine recognition of his earthly deeds must, strictly speaking, appear as *superbia*.[5] Through Gerhart's tale, the emperor learns that the expectation of divine recognition and heavenly rewards cancels out all his good deeds; ultimately, then, the *êre* of the world and the *sælde* of God are irreconcilable. The relationship between society and individual action is redefined in the course of the narrative, so that Otto's act of reception itself automatically implies a discussion of the genre. Those

---

[5] Walliczek, *Rudolf von Ems: 'Der guote Gêrhart'*, esp. pp. 71ff.

who, sharing Otto's traditional position, expect something Arthurian, will find what they are looking for in those elements of the narrative which echo the structure of the Arthurian romance. The new position, meanwhile, is achieved through the dismantling of the Arthurian model exemplified in the narrative.

If one looks back at the prologue, then, it may be said on the one hand that the tale fulfils the promise set out at the beginning in giving an example of how goodness is its own reward; while on the other hand it is undeniable that there is more to the tale than a demonstration of this moral principle would strictly demand. The prologue thesis does no more than focus on the moral aspect of a discussion which has far wider implications, namely the fundamental relationship between inner and outer worlds, or, in a literary context, the possibility of experiencing meaning in and through the world. The problem is presented as a debate with the 'classical' Arthurian model, which is based on the correlation between inner and outer realms, and its corresponding social ideal. It is evident that an ideal correlation of this kind could only be realized in terms of a fictional construct: goodness and the recognition of it, merit and reward, diverge sharply in the real world. The rejection of this fictional correlation on the one hand opens the way for a more 'realistic' representation; on the other hand the meaning can then only be redeemed as a purely internal value. The path Gerhart pursues follows an ascending scale of values until at the highest point he discovers that goodness contains its own meaning and is its own reward: the greatest satisfaction is to be found in the contemplation of the happiness one is able to bring about. The problem is no longer an inner conflict, nor the question of guilt versus innocence; instead, the principal theme is now the discrepancy between inner and outer realities, between moral values and social success. The characteristic crisis of the Arthurian hero is represented by means of the narrative structure, which in turn supplies its meaning: the conflict between merit and reward calls for a new type of hero who becomes perfect by degrees. The path through the crisis taken by the Arthurian knight can only be followed through and identified with in the imagination. By contrast, the hero who gradually develops towards moral perfection represents an example of model behaviour based on an absolute system of values, which remains valid regardless of whether it is adopted by society or its proponents granted recognition; indeed, its autonomy is demonstrated precisely by the fact that it is able to dispense with any correlation with external events. This is the meaning which ultimately underlies the demand in the prologue that one should not boast about one's own good deeds.

All this cannot, of course, be adequately expressed in this one maxim; it may nevertheless serve to give a moral slant to the introduction. This suggests a new function for the prologue, which is thus reduced to little more than a peg on which to hang a subject which gives rise to questions of a far more fundamental nature. In other words, an aphorism is employed to capture the attention of the listeners, in the hope that once captivated, they will also be receptive to the more complex problems underlying this moral precept. In terms of the sociology of reception, this means that the possibility of committing a narrowly defined group of listeners to a particular idea from the outset no longer exists. Rudolf's romance is aimed at *wîse* and *tumbe* alike; in other words, the advance commitment imposed on the audience by Gottfried and Wolfram is replaced by an appeal to the moral sense of the individual. The new strategic device, which the exordial *sententia* here becomes, is in some sense – albeit indirectly – indicative of the fundamental changes in the literary-historical situation. Seen from this wider perspective, Rudolf's citation of the *Tristan* prologue and subsequent distancing from it seems less irrelevant than might at first be supposed – Gottfried's poetics were based just as much on the 'concept of correlation' as those of the Arthurian poets. The interweaving of ethical and aesthetic perspectives in the opening passages of *Tristan* implies an awareness of the autonomy of the fictional sphere, as the only level on which this correlation can be successfully realized; at the same time a corresponding mode of reception is envisaged, in which the audience engages with and enters upon the fictional process under certain specified thematic conditions. When Rudolf, at the beginning of his romance, calls this concept to mind by quoting Gottfried, in order then to contradict it by stating that his aim can in no way be the correspondence of inner and outer realms, he is indicating to his audience that they are dealing here with a new literary type, and will accordingly have to be prepared to adjust to a new mode of reception. Of course, the listener or reader only becomes aware in the course of the narrative that this is not the straightforward mode of reception appropriate to the exemplum. It goes without saying that it is this gradual process of recognition which is all-important in *Der guote Gêrhart*; indeed, it is the main factor motivating Rudolf's retelling of an exemplum in romance form.

16

Chance, fortune and virtue: Rudolf von Ems' *Alexander*

I

In *Der guote Gerhart*, Rudolf held up a mirror to the highest representative of secular power, the emperor himself. However, the choice of this figure was motivated not by political concerns but by both literary and theoretical considerations. A retreat to the self-satisfaction engendered by good deeds is hardly an adequate framework for the concrete demands of an ethics of government. When Rudolf embarked on the Hohenstaufen court's commission for a *Fürstenspiegel*,[1] he found himself obliged to reassess the relationship between merit and fortune, morals and success, and to discover a solution that was both positive and politically practicable. This he undertook in his treatment of the Alexander story, like Wolfram before him abandoning fiction in favour of historical events. However, since Wolfram's day the basic literary premises had altered. In *Willehalm*, Wolfram was concerned to present his hero – and his audience – with the insoluble conflict between moral obligation and guilt. While this could also be played out on a fictional level, the full impact of the irrevocable and fatal consequences of violent deeds could only be realized by referring to the realm of historical fact. Rudolf, then, turned his attention to the more factual realm of history in order to find a way of resolving that other earthly contradiction, namely the discrepancy between *êre* and *sælde*, between virtue – *virtus* – and (good) fortune, or *fortuna*. Within the realm of fiction this did not present a problem, since the opposing elements could always be reconciled artificially. In the real world of facts,

---

[1] It is the idea of a *Fürstenspiegel* (a treatise on statecraft in literary form, literally a 'mirror for princes'), which gives the work its distinctive character, even if in all probability Rudolf's connection with the Hohenstaufen court only dates from the second half of the work. See Brackert, *Rudolf von Ems*, pp. 29ff.

however, there tends to be a wide gulf between merit and reward. If the conditions for bridging this gulf were ever to be created, examples from history would have to be presented as evidence.

It was a bold move to attempt this with the Alexander *vita*, since the figure of Alexander the Great had often been the subject of controversial judgement in literary history.[2] As Rudolf did not complete his poem, it is hard to say whether he could have successfully maintained this scheme throughout the work and applied it to the conclusion. The fragment which has come down to us however gives an unmistakable indication of the line he was attempting to follow. One of the high points of the romance – especially with regard to the question of merit and reward – is Alexander's encounter with King Darius. The victory over the Persians has crowned Alexander's success, since it brings with it the rule of the world. At this point, Rudolf confronts the victor with the dying Darius. The Persian king exhorts Alexander to change his ways in a speech which achieves its purpose, to the extent that Alexander adopts it as a guiding principle for the rest of his life. Darius says – to quote the most important passages:

> sich der welte lôn an mir
> und welhen lôn ir endes zît
> nâch dienste den liuten gît!
> swaz gelückes dir geschehe,
> swie grôzer hêrschaft man dir jehe,
> swie grôz heil sich dir vüege,
> sô sich daz dich genüege
> diu Mâze gar! ... (*Alexander*, 14942–9)

[Look how the world has rewarded me and how it repays people for their services at the end! Whatever good fortune is yours, however great the power granted to you, however great the blessings you enjoy, see to it that you are fully satisfied by a life of moderation and restraint! ...]

> swie grôz êre dû bejagst,
> in swelhen sælden dû betagst,
> sô gedenke ie der geschiht
> wie man die welt uns lônen siht,
> daz dir iht alsam geschehe
> sô man dîn leben enden sehe!

---

[2] See chapter 4 above, pp. 83–4.

diu Mâze sol dich lêren
nâch weltlîchen êren
werben wol mit sinnen,
sô mahtû sî gewinnen. (*Alexander*, 14953–62)

[However great the honour you attain, whatever good fortune
accompanies you all your life, always remember what has happened
here and how the world is seen to reward us, so that the same may
not happen to you, when your life is drawing to a close! Let
moderation teach you to strive to attain worldly honours with
discretion, so that you may indeed win them.]

swer wil êre koufen,
der mac ir niht erloufen,
er muoz lîp sêl unde guot
nâch ir arbeiten und den muot
und muoz zallen zîten
mit kumber nâch ir strîten.
als er sî danne ergriffen hât,
sô muoz er haben wîsen rât
mit kündeclîchem sinne
dazs im iht entrinne. (*Alexander*, 14969–78)

[He who desires to buy honour will never catch up with it, he must
set his body, soul, heart and all his resources to work for it and
must ever struggle laboriously to attain it. And when he has seized
it, he will need shrewd advice and discernment, so that it does not
escape from him.]

ir gunst ist wankel gemuot
wan swer ir reht mit rehte tuot:
unmâze und überêre
schadent dicke sêre.
bî der êre ist mâze guot,
unmâze unde übermuot
wanket vil oft underz rat
von der hœhesten stat.
swer êre hât mit witzen,
des heil siht man gesitzen,
sô überêre wanken muoz … (*Alexander*, 14985–95)[3]

[(Honour's) good favour cannot be relied on, if one fails to treat her

---

[3]   I have corrected Junk's text to follow C. von Kraus, *Text und Entstehung von Rudolfs
'Alexander'*.

rightly. Exorbitance and excessive concern with honour often do great harm. Honour is best accompanied by restraint, exorbitance and arrogance very often throw you down from the highest position to under the wheel. The good fortune of the man who combines honour with intelligence is often seen to remain seated, when excessive honour loses its hold.]

The concept of *mâze* ('moderation') had already played a key role in the *Straßburger Alexander*. There, it had the function of qualifying Alexander's lust for power, as exemplified in his attempt to conquer paradise. In Rudolf's version, *mâze* belongs to a different set of values. It is offered as a solution to the nexus of problems characterized by the tension between merit and reward. Seen as the opposite of hubris, *mâze* serves here to connect fame with fortune. Only with the help of *mâze* is it possible to stay at the top of the wheel of fortune instead of plummeting to the depths.

Alexander takes the lesson of his dying adversary to heart. At the end of the fifth book, Rudolf is able to state:

> Sus vuocte sich nâch saelden ie
> swaz Alexander ane gie
> daz er dâ von mit sælden schiet.
> sîn witze alsô ze sælden riet
> daz er nie nihtes began,
> im gelunge wol dar an:
> sîn hôher prîs, sîn sælde was
> staet als ein herter adamas.
> diu glesîn sælde in ie vlôch,
> diu staete sælde in nâch ir zôch
> eht ûf und ûf hin ûf daz rat
> unz er sô hôhe wart gesat
> und alsô verre ûz genomn
> daz niemen zuo zim mohte komn.
> diz werte gar unz an den tac
> daz sînes lîbes zil gelac,
> daz im niht arges nie gewar,
> er überwunde ez ie vil gar
> mit sælden sæleclîche. (*Alexander*, 20545–63)

[Thus everything turned out for the best that Alexander ever turned his hand to, he always benefited from good fortune. His wise judgement advised him in his dealings with good fortune so that nothing he ever began failed to bring him success. His luck and his illustriousness were as enduring as an unbreakable diamond. Brittle

Fortune always fled from him, whereas lasting Good Fortune pulled him after her further and further up the wheel, until he was placed so high, in such a unique position, that no one was able to approach him. This lasted right up to the day his life ended, for never did an evil befall him, but he had the gratification of vanquishing it totally by the power of good fortune.]

Alexander thus achieves what was not granted to Darius; in other words, Rudolf presents Alexander's life in such a way that it provides an exemplary illustration of the overcoming, by *mâze*, of the inconstancy of fortune. However, there is no guarantee of the correlation between merit and fortune, and Rudolf is at pains to point out that the hand of fortune cannot be forced; if one nevertheless strives for it with all one's energies, though, there is a good chance that one will indeed be favoured by fortune. Once this occurs, one is then in a position to halt the wheel of fortune, as it were, stepping outside the cycle of fortune and misfortune to secure *sælde* for oneself. Rudolf repeatedly reflects on the subject of *sælde* (good fortune), considering how far it is possible to seize or to hold on to it.[4] However, he is unable to dispel one final element of uncertainty: the fact that everyday experience would seem to disprove his theory. He does, however, manage to play down this factor to such an extent that in this Hohenstaufen *Fürstenspiegel* – which is what his *Alexander* is intended to be – a didactic optimism nevertheless retains the upper hand.

II

The concept of *sælde* is also the theme of the introduction with which Rudolf prefaces the first book of his romance. Here too he cites Gottfried, even imitating his division of the prologue into a strophic and a stichic part. The seven quatrains of the strophic part are further linked by an acrostic which spells out the name of the principal characters and which is continued in the narrative proper. What is more, the themes treated in the prologue, as well as the technique of developing varying patterns of thought, are indebted to Gottfried's example, even if they are now seen from a completely different perspective. Rudolf's opening, like Gottfried's, is of a general nature:

> Rîchiu sælde, hôher sin
> daz ist von Gote ein grôz gewin

---

4   See Wisbey, *Das Alexanderbild Rudolfs von Ems*, pp. 48ff., for references.

den Got alsô besinnet
daz er sælde gewinnet. (*Alexander*, 1–4)

[Mighty fortune, noble sense (= *sin*), these are great gifts of God,
when God grants a man that 'sense' that will win good fortune.]

The subject matter of his work, then, is *sælde* ('(good) fortune') and
sin in general. Both of these qualities are gifts of God, and lines 3 and
4 present the situation in such a way that God is the provider of the
sin which makes it possible to achieve *sælde*. Since the term *sin* in itself
has a wide range of possible meanings, as well as having been
endowed by the theoretical tradition with meanings which are
divergent in the extreme, an exact definition scarcely seems possible.
It may be assumed that this was already a problem for Rudolf's
contemporary audience, and that the meaning of the term was
deliberately left open. However, looking back at Gottfried's prologue
there is a case for starting from a general definition of *sin* as 'understanding' or 'wisdom', while bearing in mind the specific *sin* of artistic
ability. At any rate, the issues introduced in the second strophe are
clearly concerned with poetic theory:

Ûf hôhe kunst ist ahte niht,
ist si sunder sælden phliht,
sô wirt si gar vernihtet,
ob sælde ir niht zuo phlihtet. (*Alexander*, 5–8)

[Great art is held in no esteem if it is not linked to good fortune, it is
destroyed if good fortune is not associated with it.]

That Rudolf has adopted Gottfried's ideas is unmistakable here,
just as the way in which he adapts them demonstrates his different
perspective. As in Gottfried's prologue, here too it is stated that art
can only achieve its true effect if it meets with recognition. However,
the recognition envisaged here does not depend on finding a good
and knowledgeable listener, but on good fortune. In concrete terms,
this presumably refers to whether conditions for reception are favourable or otherwise. What for Gottfried was a question of ethics, is here
dependent on *sælde*.

Orthabunge rehter kunst
ist sælden heil, gelückes gunst,
der sî nâch sælden werben kan
daz im Got gelückes gan. (*Alexander*, 9–12)

[The origin of true art lies in the blessing of good fortune, the gift of luck, in that God bestows good fortune on that man who can lead art to good fortune.]

Where the second quatrain dealt with the aspect of luck involved in success, the third is concerned with the beneficial gift of artistic ability: God bestows *sælde* not only in the form of worldly success, but also as *orthabunge*, the basis and foundation of artistic expression.[5]

> Der kunst geleite sælde treit.
> swer iht tihtet oder seit,
> der muoz kunst bî sælden tragn
> odr sîn kunst der sælde entsagn. (*Alexander*, 13–16)

[Good fortune is art's escort. Whoever composes or performs poetry must have both artistry and good fortune, otherwise his art must renounce good fortune.]

The play on the two meanings of *sælde*, on the one hand as a condition for artistic creation and on the other as a condition for its success, is not always easy to unravel. The presentation of a negative example in the next strophe, however, makes the situation sufficiently clear:

> Ofte ergât ouch diu geschiht
> daz man den künste rîchen siht
> dem selten ist daz heil geschehn
> daz sîn kunst sælec sî gesehn. (*Alexander*, 17–20)

[Now it often happens that one encounters an artistic man who has not experienced the good fortune that his art be successful.]

There are thus talented artists who are not successful in worldly terms. This is Rudolf's variation on Gottfried's maxim that goodness, or rather a good work of art, is worthless if it is not recognized as such. However, the obstinate listeners or detractors are here replaced, in accordance with the altered perspective, by the lack of *sælde*.

> Lobelich guot getihte
> daz vindet ie die rihte,
> als ez diu sælde tihtet
> und ez gelücke rihtet. (*Alexander*, 21–4)

---

[5] Kolb, '*Orthabunge rehter kunst*', p. 95, refers to 'objective' and 'subjective' *sælde*; I prefer to refer to the two aspects in more concrete terms, namely *sælde* as artistic gift and *sælde* as success.

[An admirable and well-written poem will always be successful in
so far as it is composed by good fortune and formed by luck.]

Florieret sælde künste kraft,
sô edelt sich diu meisterschaft
und wirt diu kunst gekreftet,
der sin gemeisterscheftet. (*Alexander*, 25–8)

[If good fortune decks out the power of art with its flowers,[6] the
artistry will take on true nobility, the art will be invigorated, the
poetic talents (= *sin*) will turn into mastery.]

In the strophic prologue to the first book, then, Rudolf discusses
the relationship between art and success. In this way the theme
running through the work as a whole, the correlation between merit
and fortune, acquires a poetological interpretation. The argument is
based on two traditional prologue motifs; on the one hand the idea of
inspiration, and on the other the dependency on the goodwill of the
audience. In both cases, *sælde* is seen as a gift of God. It is thus not the
divine force itself which is at work through the artist: what the latter
receives from God, i.e. the gift of fortune, is, rather, a latent artistic
talent which must be developed. This process, however, is in turn also
dependent on *sælde*, since only success can cause art to flourish. This
means that *sælde* replaces that authority which traditionally inter-
vened directly to guarantee the truth of the work of art (that is to say,
divine inspiration), and also takes the place of the specific demands
which the poet was wont to make on the audience in order to
guarantee a favourable reception. The conventional prologue motif of
divine inspiration is thus reduced to the 'good fortune' of artistic
talent, and the relationship with the audience is reduced to the 'luck'
of success. God is still mentioned by name, it is true, but has to a large
extent become interchangeable with *sælde*; it is significant that his
assistance is no longer called upon. An intangible, indeed irrational,
element has been interposed between the traditional components of
the poetological communication model.

In the stichic prologue, Rudolf firstly introduces himself, before
going on to discuss his subject directly:

Nû was ich, als ich eht noch bin,
als gemuot daz ich den sin

---

[6] The term *florieren* is used in a technical sense here: *sælde* gives art poetic ornamentation. Cf.
Finster, *Zur Theorie und Technik mittelalterlicher Prologe*, pp. 137–8.

ie dar ûf arbeite
daz Got zuo geleite
geruochte vüegen mîner kunst
sælde und edeler herzen gunst. (*Alexander*, 29–34)

[Now it was always my desire, as indeed it still is, so to exercise my
inner powers (= *sin*) that God might consent to grant my art good
fortune and the favour of noble hearts as an escort.]

Rudolf thus places himself within the tradition outlined in the
strophic prologue. The key terms *sin*, *sælde* and *kunst* ('sense', 'good
fortune' and 'art') reappear here; Rudolf intends to exercise his
powers to such an extent that God cannot fail to grant his work
success. Thus the gulf between artistic endeavour and God's gift of
fortune reveals once again the element of uncertainty which characterizes the relationship between virtue and fortune. It is surprising to
encounter the concept of 'noble hearts' in this connection. However,
the context in which Gottfried placed the expression, and thus its
meaning, is lacking here; if the *edele herzen* are not to be dismissed as
an empty reference, the phrase might be rendered, rather flatly, as
something like 'an audience able to appreciate the challenge of the
poem'. Nor is the term further defined in what follows; instead, *sælde*
continues to function as a kind of *leitmotif*:

sol des gelücke walten
und mir den prîs behalten
ûf den ich sus garbeitet hân,
sô wil ich ûf den süezen wân
und ûf des lônes gewin
arbeiten aber mînen sin
und wil iu bescheiden hie
an dirre âventiure wie
ein der tugentrîchste man
der ritters namen ie gewan
dirre welte prîs erwarp,
wie er warp, wie er verdarp,
wier zer welte wart geborn,
wie im besunder wart erkorn
der welte hœhstiu werdekeit,
wie er die werdekeit erstreit
daz sîn lop, sîn name, sîn lebn
an lobe ze mâze ist gegebn
den tumben und den wîsen: ... (*Alexander*, 35–53)

[If luck is with me and endows me with the prize for which I have so exerted myself, then once again, in the sweet hope that I may be so rewarded, I will exert my poetic powers and will recount to you in this story how the most excellent man who ever earned the title of knight won worldly fame, how he persevered, how he died, how he was born into the world, how he was singled out to win the highest honour in the world, how he became so celebrated that his renown, his name and his life are all presented as a model of excellence to wise men and fools alike ...]

Rudolf thus wishes to depict the life of a man who achieved the highest possible fame. Birth, rise to fame and death: this is the standard formula for a biographical work, while *werdekeit, lop* and *name* are all concepts which recall the patterns of argument in classical prologues, where the survival of the name is used as a metaphor for the autonomy of literary fiction. The phrase 'ze mâze geben' (52) expresses the idea of the subject as a model of excellence, in other words, the justification of literature by its exemplary function. However, this topos is not merely used here as a kind of provisional shorthand, a convenient term which is then superseded, as in Hartmann: rather, in the case of a historical, i.e. non-fictional, subject, it is completely in accordance with the mode of reception. The reference to the survival of the *name* in posterity refers to nothing more than its continued function as an exemplum. Since the audience is only envisaged extremely vaguely, there is no question – despite the mention of Gottfried's *edele herzen* – of a particular group of listeners being addressed to whom the phrase might refer. As far as 'exemplary' morals are concerned, Rudolf refers in the most general way to *werdekeit*, and this is in accordance with the fact that this work too is addressed to everyone, both *tumbe* and *wîse*. The fact that no specific audience is designated means that the audience response cannot be anticipated, and is thus quite unpredictable. Thus the idea of success as *sælde* has its basis in the new conditions of audience reception.

III

Rudolf supplied prologues, or prologue-type introductions, not only for the first but also for the subsequent books into which he divided his romance. I propose to deal with the prologue to the fifth book first, since it takes up the theme of *sælde* again. By and large, the argument coincides with that of the prologue to the first book. Again, *sælde* is presented as having a dual function, for on it depends both art (*kunst*) and its success. And once again *sælde* and God are almost synonymous:

> An sælden stât
> diu beste kunst,
> swaz iemen kan,
> von sælden gât
> der welte gunst,
> dem Got des gan
> daz er sî hât ... (*Alexander*, 20573–9)

> [The best art is dependent upon good fortune – whatever anyone can achieve; the world's favour is dependent upon good fortune, if God consents that a man should have it ...]

Rudolf then applies to the specific context of the realm of art what the plot of the romance demonstrates in general terms, namely that if one has come into good fortune, what then matters is finding a way of keeping it. Thus the poet who has been granted *sælde* in the form of talent and success should endeavour 'daz er ir rât / mit der vernunst / dâ wendet an, / wie er bejage / der welte prîs' ('to apply its teachings with reason in order to obtain worldly fame'; 20582ff.). The term *vernunst* corresponds in principle to *witze* in 20548. One has to prove oneself worthy of the *gunst* of *sælde*, in order that one might earn the laurels of good fortune ('daz rîs / daz sælde gît, / ze rehte trage'; 20589ff.). Then the irrational and unpredictable aspect of the gift of fortune is discussed again, and here too the echoes of Gottfried are unmistakable: as in Gottfried's poem, *daz guote* needs to be recognized in order that it may achieve its effect, but here this depends not on the ethical criteria of the listeners, but on *sælde*:

> swem sælde ist bî,
> den hilfet iht
> sîn reiner muot.
> ist er ir vrî,
> sô'st gar ein wiht
> swaz er durch guot
> Je getet ze guote
> mit lîbe und ouch mit guote.
> Sælde und êre
> wilde sint ... (*Alexander*, 20600–9)

> [Whoever enjoys good fortune will derive some benefit from his

purity of heart. If he lacks it, then whatever he ever did out of his own goodness that was for the best, either in person or at his own expense, is just worthless. Fortune and honour are wild creatures.]

The argument of this prologue runs counter to that of the prologue to book 1. This is analogous to the two groups of 5 quatrains in Gottfried's introduction to *Tristan*; whereas in the first prologue general comments on the theme of *sælde* led into a discussion of the specific *sælde* of the poet, here the movement is from the specific *sælde* of *kunst* ('art') back to the relationship between merit and success. As evidence for the *wilde* nature of *sælde*, the poet recalls a *Spruch* attributed to Gottfried, in which luck or fortune is described as being as fragile as glass; it is easier to win *gelücke* than to keep it (20621f.). As far as the winning of *sælde* is concerned, he cites a saying of Freidank's: while it is impossible to acquire good fortune by force, if one makes every effort to secure it, it generally happens that it comes one's way after all (20632f.). It is in the hope that this may happen – and here he picks up the poetological argument again – that Rudolf presents his poem to the audience (20641ff.). Since he realizes that it will not be to the liking of everyone, he asks those who would rather hear something else not to spoil his *Alexander* for those others who take pleasure in it. This allows him to review the current literary genres: Dietrich epic, Arthurian romance, love poetry, religious literature etc. The traditional division between good and bad, clever and dull listeners has been transformed into a wide variety of literary interests. On the one hand, this means that the question of reception becomes less problematic, while on the other hand, it results in the fragmentation of the audience into an indefinite number of individuals whose only link is their taste in literature. Once again this clearly demonstrates the extent to which reception has become an unpredictable factor, in which audience success can no longer be guaranteed.

IV

The prologue to the second book is of particular interest in terms of Rudolf's literary theory, since here he contrasts his own art with that of the *meister*, and by stressing the unattainable superiority of the latter, creates an opportunity for the first catalogue of 'classic' romance authors. Clearly the impulse for this came from Gottfried's own survey of contemporary literature in the literary excursus in *Tristan.*[7]

Rudolf begins his catalogue with Heinrich von Veldeke, of whom he – like Gottfried – says that he founded the art of German poetry; like his predecessor, Rudolf also uses the image of grafting new growth onto the tree of poetry. Three branches, he claims, blossomed from this: Hartmann, Wolfram and Gottfried. Rudolf gives an impression of the style of the three poets, capturing – albeit very subtly – something of their individual character. Hartmann's art is described as *sleht*, *süeze* and *guot*, i.e. full of straightforward elegance, charm and excellent skill; Wolfram's as *starc, in mange wîs gebogn, wilde, guot, spæhe* and *wæhe*, that is to say 'forceful', 'artfully wrought', 'striking', 'excellent', 'artistic' and 'richly ornamented'. Gottfried, however, to some extent combines the qualities of the other two: his art is described as *spæhe* ('artistic'), *guot* ('excellent'), *wilde* ('striking'), *reht* ('true'), *sîn süeziu bluot ebensleht* ('charming elegance'), *wæhe* ('ornamental'), *reine* ('pure') and *vollekomn* ('perfect'). Hartmann and Wolfram thus represent here different aspects of the same stylistic ideal, which is then realized by Gottfried in a kind of synthesis of the two. What in Gottfried's own catalogue still represented an extreme contrast – *sleht* and *süeze* as opposed to *gebogn* and *wilde* – is here reconciled; Hartmann's lucidity and Wolfram's more oblique style have become mere shades in a broad spectrum of styles, whose common factor is represented by the highest possible level of stylistic awareness. When Rudolf then repeats this catalogue in a slightly different form in his romance *Willehalm von Orlens*, even this small amount of individual characterization is abandoned, leaving only a list of names and works.

This demonstrates the general theoretical trend: the general artistic excellence of the poets is emphasized at the expense of their individual personalities.[8] The practical consequence of this is precisely that synthesis which Rudolf – with somewhat dubious justification – claims for Gottfried, namely a synthesis between the formal and

[7] Rudolf's survey is preceded by that of Heinrich von dem Türlin in *Diu Crône*, 2348ff., which however takes up a different aspect of Gottfried's excursus, namely the survey of poets as a lament for the dead. On the different functions of post-classical catalogues of poets, see Vollmann-Profe, 'Der Prolog zum *Heiligen Georg*', pp. 323–4; a collection of texts is given by Schweikle in *Dichter über Dichter*. On earlier examples, see Walde, 'Untersuchungen zur Literaturkritik', pp. 67ff.; Reinitzer, 'Geschichte der deutschen Literaturkritik', pp. 36ff.; Finster, *Zur Theorie und Technik mittelalterlicher Prologe*, pp. 177–8; Brinkmann, *Mittelalterliche Hermeneutik*, p. 11.
[8] Ragotzky, *Studien zur Wolfram-Rezeption*, pp. 35–6.

stylistic skill represented by Gottfried, and Wolfram's visual imagination: this is achieved in the second half of the century by Konrad von Würzburg.

Characteristic of the new position is an awareness of the distance separating the new generation of poets from their 'classical' predecessors and models. The earlier poets of the *Blütezeit* are now seen as the unattainable *meister* against whom Rudolf measures his art and to whose judgement – in a rhetorical apostrophe – he submits his work:

> Aller mîner meister kür
> wil ich diz mære legen vür
> unde wil sie vlêhen und bitn
> daz sie nâch meisterlîchen sitn
> ir hôhe kunst mir zeigen ... (*Alexander*, 3063–7)

> [I wish to submit this tale to be examined by all my masters, and I beg and beseech them to grant me the benefit of their great artistry, in accordance with their position as masters of the art ...]

> dâ von ich lêre suochen wil,
> wan ich mich niht gelîchen
> mac den künsterîchen. (*Alexander*, 3082–4)

> [So I go in search of instruction, for I cannot compare myself to the great artists.]

Conventional though it is, Rudolf's emphasis on his own lack of ability is given a new angle here; this is no longer the playful reference to tradition established by Gottfried in order to claim an assured place within it for himself and his art. The continuity of the poetic tradition can no longer be taken for granted; rather, classical predecessors have become models from whom the later poet must strive to learn, so that the relationship acquires a certain technical, stylistic dimension. However, it is important to note that the rhetorical gesture of seeking assistance from the *meister* already contains the same irrational or unpredictable element as was expressed above in the term *sælde*. The request for *lêre* by no means implies that art is now a skill that can be learned, although this is the view held by those who believe poetry is merely about writing verse. In this way, praise of the unattainable classical masters is combined with lament for the debased art of the poet's contemporaries (3090ff.). Their art has become *gemeine* ('commonplace'; 3094, 3102), in other words 'available to all'.[9] An awareness of a difference in standard between contemporary works and those of the *meister* becomes an indication of the correct appreciation of art – an art which cannot be achieved by craftsmanship alone. This kind of two-edged argument will become characteristic of theoretical discussion from now on.

v

The prologues to the other books of Rudolf's romance supply information which one would have expected at the start of the work, namely details about the source and tradition of the material. In the prologue to the fourth book, Rudolf names his sources: Leo of Naples, Q. Curtius Rufus, Josephus, Methodius. In his introduction to the fifth book, he also refers to German versions of the Alexander story, going back to Lambrecht. The description and comparison of the different versions goes far beyond the traditional topos of reference to sources.

Whereas Gottfried was probably only pretending to have looked for the authentic version of the *Tristan* legend on which Thomas drew, Rudolf did indeed research his source material;[10] he makes explicit reference to this when imitating the appropriate passage in *Tristan* (155ff.). This of course is not to be understood as a critical evaluation of the sources in the modern sense; rather, Rudolf's interest in earlier versions of the subject matter was in keeping with his search for the version which best fitted his idea of Alexander as a historically credible, yet still ideal, ruler-figure. Rudolf calls this a search for the 'stiure, / die sie der âventiure / gegeben hânt mit wârheit' ('the guidance which they (i.e. the chroniclers of Alexander) gave to the narrative by their employment of the truth'; 13055ff.). This he found primarily in the work of Curtius Rufus, which also provided material for the prologue to his fourth book.[11] However, even Curtius was not able to satisfy Rudolf's requirements completely; in particular, his version did not connect merit and fortune in the way that Rudolf's theory demanded. Instead, the classical historian juxtaposed ethics and fortune as co-existent but unrelated entities; thus he showed how fortune long remained loyal to Alexander, even as he became increas-

---

[9] On the motif of the decline of art, see Walde, 'Untersuchungen zur Literaturkritik', pp. 236ff.; Kobbe, 'Funktion und Gestalt des Prologs', 449; Finster, *Zur Theorie und Technik mittelalterlicher Prologe*, p. 174.
[10] Brackert, *Rudolf von Ems*, pp. 153–4.   [11] Bulst, 'Zum *prologus* der *Natiuitas*', 255ff.

ingly cruel, tyrannical and licentious. In order to retain his theory of *sælde* based on *mâze*, therefore, Rudolf was obliged to amend his source accordingly. This he did without any qualms, as Karl Stackmann has shown; in other words, Rudolf had to treat the historical facts as fiction in order to make them fit in with his concept.[12]

As has been shown, the correlation of merit and fortune can only be completely realized on the level of fiction, and even here it loses credibility when it is presented as an unproblematic 'happy ending'. However, in so far as fiction displays a tendency to reflect upon itself and the problems presented by its fictional status, the relationship between merit and fortune is inevitably drawn into the discussion: as in the Arthurian romance, meaning can be transmitted through the tension between the projected ideal and the movements which oppose it. In seeking a positive solution to the problem on a historical level, Rudolf had no option but to seek to adapt the historical data to fit the fictional concept: an attempt which was ultimately doomed to failure. This is already indicated in the theoretical concession he makes with regard to the expectation that goodness will lead to success. He is obliged to qualify this with the statement that one can only aspire to good fortune; it cannot be guaranteed as a natural and inevitable consequence of merit. Furthermore, historical evidence contradicts the theory that fortune inevitably abandons those who do not observe moderation. Here all Rudolf can do is to retouch the historical facts, and in so doing he of necessity reverts to fiction.

In Rudolf's work, then, the technique of interpretation traditionally employed to derive an exemplary meaning from history comes into conflict with the other form of constituting meaning that had come to be established in the courtly romance. In order to illustrate the theory that *mâze* is able to establish a causal connection between merit and fortune, the historical romance – in its function as exemplary biography – of necessity developed into a semi-fictional construct, in that Rudolf found himself obliged to sacrifice historical accuracy for the sake of his scheme. At the same time, however, he had to respect historical events, since these alone could furnish evidence of the truth which he sought to demonstrate. From a didactic point of view, there admittedly remained the weakness that this evidence could not be definitively proven historically, on account of the inevitable element of uncertainty regarding the winning of *sælde*; at the same time,

---

[12] Stackmann, *'Der Alten Werdekeit'*; Fechter, *Lateinische Dichtkunst und deutsches Mittelalter*, pp. 140ff.; Brackert, *Rudolf von Ems*, pp. 155ff.

however, the admission of this uncertainty lent support to the work's claim to historical truth.

There is of course a point to Rudolf's introduction of this element of uncertainty into his poetic theory, since it enables him to give *sælde* a decisive role here too. Nor is this merely an idle association of ideas: there is an inner connection which goes deeper than the rhetorical rule that the exordial *sententia*, if it refer to the subject of the work at all, must do so indirectly, since the inner connection here derives from the status and function of the work of art. Uncertainty as to the ultimate success of the work is an integral part of the mode of reception of exemplary literature, since this type of literature, conscious of its role as a vehicle for demonstrating a model of behaviour, has a clear didactic function from the outset. It thus presupposes a distance between poet and audience which has to be overcome by means of persuasion. This is a completely different relationship between work and audience from that pertaining in the Arthurian romance, which had demanded from its 'congregation' of listeners a prior commitment to following the course of the action. The success of a given work was irrelevant, since anyone refusing to accept the work was automatically damned. By contrast, with a work which is to be understood as a moral lesson there is necessarily the implication that it must first win over its audience, and the unpredictable quality of *sælde* therefore replaces the ethical and aesthetic commitment. This element of uncertainty also affects the poet's own understanding of his role: to the extent to which he becomes conscious of his own artistic techniques, he also experiences their limitations. The writer's existence thus begins to be problematic in a new sense.

VI

After Rudolf von Ems, the Alexander story occurs in several other German versions. None of these however displays an approach which deals with the problems of the subject as boldly and in as much depth as Rudolf's work.[13] Ulrich von Etzenbach's *Alexander* was composed before the end of the thirteenth century. It is largely based on Walter of Châtillon, with individual additions from other sources, especially

[13] Surveys are given in Hübner, 'Alexander der Große in der deutschen Dichtung'; Buntz, *Die deutsche Alexanderdichtung des Mittelalters*; Ruh, 'Epische Literatur des deutschen Spätmittelalters', pp. 148ff.

the *Historia de Preliis*.[14] Ulrich's perspective is in part determined by his choice of source: he presents a courtly, stylized picture of Alexander, marked by a strong tendency towards sentimentality. As with Der Pleier, this idealization goes hand in hand with a marked fondness for form and ceremony. For the rest, Ulrich uses the theory of the sequence of empires as a guiding principle, citing Daniel's dream in the prologue to his first book. The work was probably intended as a *Fürstenspiegel* for Ottokar II of Bohemia, and, after his death, for King Wenceslas II.[15] The prologues unashamedly exploit Wolfram's introduction to *Willehalm*, either directly or *via* Ulrich von dem Türlin, who had already made use of this prologue for his own version of *Willehalm*. The imitation of Wolfram goes so far as to take over individual expressions verbatim.[16] No particular slant to his account can be discerned, apart from a reverence for the *meister*, Wolfram, who is praised in the famous words of Wirnt von Gravenberc: 'leien munt gesprach nie baz' (127: 'never did a layman speak so well'; ed. W. Toischer, 1888).

[14] Paul, *Ulrich von Eschenbach*, pp. 12ff.; Behr, *Literatur als Machtlegitimation*, pp. 143ff.
[15] On the problem of dedication, see Kleinschmidt, 'Literarische Rezeption und Geschichte', 622.
[16] Paul, *Ulrich von Eschenbach*, pp. 21ff.

17

Wolfram's prologue to *Willehalm*: a model for later hagiographical romances

I

No other 'classical' romance prologue had such a lasting influence as Wolfram's introduction to *Willehalm*,[1] which was copied out and adapted time and time again. Rudolf von Ems drew on it three times, in *Der guote Gêrhart*, in *Barlaam*, and in his *Weltchronik*. Reinbot von Durne used it in *Georg*.[2] Ulrich von Türheim and Ulrich von dem Türlin paraphrased it in *Rennewart* and *Willehalm* respectively.[3] Ulrich von Etzenbach also adapted it in his own *Willehalm*, and finally Albrecht, in *Der jüngere Titurel*, fused it with elements of Wolfram's prologue to *Parzival*. It may be asked whether the introduction to *Willehalm* might not itself be considered as simply a model hagiographical prologue, always available for imitation where the literary type demanded it, or whether this 'reception by imitation' was in fact a means of engaging with and discussing Wolfram's theoretical concept. There is no straightforward answer to this question, especially since the process of reception is often an indirect one. Moreover, there exists an independent tradition of prologues to saints' lives which must also be taken into account, as illustrated for example in Lamprecht von Regensburg's *Tochter von Syon*.[4] Here I shall investigate, by way of example, the author who was the first to imitate and thus comment on Wolfram's prologue, and who may be expected, from his general high standard, to have taken some pains over his adaptation of the original, namely Rudolf von Ems. Ulrich

---

[1] Kleinschmidt, 'Literarische Rezeption und Geschichte'.
[2] Wyss, 'Rudolf von Ems *Barlaam und Josaphat*', pp. 131ff.; a critique of this is given in Vollmann-Profe, 'Prolog zum *Heiligen Georg*'. See also Kleinschmidt, 'Literarische Rezeption und Geschichte', 607ff.
[3] Cf. Flügel, *Prolog und Epilog*, pp. 147ff. and 143ff. respectively.
[4] Ibid., pp. 111ff.

von Etzenbach's and Albrecht's reception of Wolfram will be dealt with in chapters 18 and 20 respectively.

The three works in which Rudolf draws on Wolfram's prayer to the Trinity each adapt it from a different perspective.[5] The first instance, in *Der guote Gêrhart*, is not concerned with theoretical reflection, since the prayer is not used here as a prologue, but is placed in the mouth of the emperor (lines 300–446): Otto turns to God to discover what rewards await him for his good deeds in the life to come, and he introduces his prayer with a hymn to God which is a free adaptation of and elaboration on the introduction to *Willehalm*. It is noticeable that the trinitarian scheme is brought out much more strongly by comparison with Wolfram. Otto refers to the three powers (*krefte*) of God and characterizes them as *gewalt* (*potestas*), *wîsheit* (*sapientia*) and *güete* (*bonitas*), corresponding to Father, Son and Holy Spirit respectively. Apart from the substitution of *gewalt* for *kraft* as an equivalent for *potestas*, the terminology agrees with Wolfram's usage. However, whereas in *Willehalm* the attribution of these characteristics to the three persons of the Trinity respectively is not clearly defined, Rudolf adopts a more schematic approach. In connection with the Father he describes the movements of the cosmos, and then the heavenly spheres which sing the praises of their Creator. The elements are allocated to the Son, as the Word of the Creator, while the Holy Spirit is understood as the life-giving force. Three forms of life are distinguished: first the vegetable world, which, although endowed with life, lacks consciousness; then the world of animals, which, although capable of perception, is incapable both of expressing itself and of representing itself symbolically; and finally humanity, which receives from the Holy Spirit the gifts of *wizze*, *sinne*, *rât* and *vernunst*, corresponding roughly to the Latin terms *mens*, *ingenium*, *consilium* and *ratio* respectively – an ontological scheme which dates back to Aristotle's distinction between *anima vegetativa*, *sensitiva* and *rationalis*. Otto goes on to refer to the Fall and to Redemption, in other words he gives a brief outline of salvation history, including Christ's virgin birth, his death, resurrection and the harrowing of hell.

Clearly, there could be no place, within the narrative context of Otto's prayer, for the theoretical dimension which Wolfram gives the

---

[5] Detailed analyses may be found in Lutz, *Rhetorica divina*, pp. 193ff.; 243ff.; 289ff.

Willehalm prologue. It is, however, remarkable that another peculiarly characteristic element is also missing in Rudolf's version, namely the tension inherent in the distance which determines the relationship between the worshipper and God. Wolfram's prologue is based on an awareness that, despite the infinite distance between God and creation, since Christ provided a bridge between God and humanity, the latter is entitled to place hope and trust in him. In omitting this Christian paradox, Rudolf simplifies the prologue; by thus removing all sources of tension, he reduces the prologue to the simple form of a prayer. Given Rudolf's familiarity with Wolfram's work, one may assume that this was deliberate. Seen against the background of the *Willehalm* prologue, the prayer is used to characterize and criticize the emperor's ambivalent relationship to God; as a hymn of praise it lacks the crucial 'inner' dimension, since it does not spring from genuine personal emotion, but is merely a devotional exercise.[6] This crucial dimension is then supplied by Gerhart's journey. His tale concludes with a confession of his own unworthiness and sinful state, and at this the emperor, his sense of self-righteousness shaken, decides to do penance.

The themes and problems which form the basis of Wolfram's work only emerge gradually in the course of *Der guote Gêrhart*. The function of the romance is to make this a conscious process. The emperor has Gerhart's story set down in writing, and when Rudolf comes to compose a German version of it, he is able to take credit for these good intentions in his prologue (6861ff.). However, he does not take such acknowledgement for granted, since at the same time he says he is prepared to accept criticism and if possible to do better next time. Although this may sound like a conventional modesty topos,[7] the context of caution regarding any benefit which might be derived from good deeds does lend it a certain individuality.

II

The prologue to *Barlaam* is also characterized by imitation of the introduction to *Willehalm*, and here too Rudolf brings out the

---

[6]   Cf. the controversy between Brackert, *Rudolf von Ems*, and Walliczek as to the function of Otto's prayer, in Walliczek, *Rudolf von Ems: 'Der guote Gêrhart'*, pp. 77ff.

[7]   On the use of the request for correction, see Schwietering, 'Die Demutsformel mittelalterlicher Dichtung', pp. 182–3; Beumann, 'Der Schriftsteller und seine Kritiker', 511; Simon, 'Untersuchungen', II, 125ff.; cf. also Vollmann-Profe, *Kommentar zu Otfrids Evangelienbuch*, p. 71.

trinitarian scheme more strongly than does Wolfram.[8] He begins with an apostrophe to God: 'Alphâ et Ô, künec Sâbâôt, / got, des gewaltes kraft gebôt / leben ân urhap ... ' ('Alpha and omega, King Sabaoth, God, your power and might called into being life without beginning'), followed in lines 7ff. by an extended *amplificatio* devoted to the first person of the Trinity as *principium – non de principio*.[9] Only after this does Rudolf include the Trinity, which Wolfram had invoked at the beginning of his work. Rudolf then immediately connects the Trinity with the idea of eternity:

> dîn gewalt, dîn geist, dîn wort,
> got vater mensche unde kint,
> gewaltes ungescheiden sint,
> als ie ân anegenge was
> dîn einic drîvalt unitas. (*Barlaam*, 20–4)

> [Your power, your spirit, your word – God-father, man and child – are inseparable in their power, just as your single threefold unity was without beginning.]

Here the three persons of the Trinity are seen as one, and, since Rudolf also attributes *potentia* to the second and third persons, the traditional participation of all three persons in all the attributes is fulfilled.

It will be recalled that Wolfram connects the concept of *stæte kraft* in line 4 of *Willehalm* with the idea of supernatural adoption (*Gotteskindschaft*); it is the *kraft* of the Father which frees humanity from evil thoughts, and these reflections culminate in the tension between the intimate bonds between parent and child on the one hand, and the infinite distance separating humankind from God on the other:

> dîn kint und dîn künne
> bin ich bescheidenlîche,
> ich arm und du vil rîche. (*Willehalm*, 1,16–18)

> [I am most definitely your child and your kin: I am poor and wretched, you are rich and mighty.]

The following lines then discuss both how this relationship between God and humanity was established and the seal set on it by Christ.

---

8   Haug, 'Wolframs *Willehalm*-Prolog'; on the current state of research, cf. ibid., 302, note 9; also in Haug, *Strukturen*, pp. 617–18, note 9.
9   On the theological speculation underlying Rudolf's concept, see Ehrismann, *Studien über Rudolf von Ems*, pp. 49ff.; Flügel, *Prolog und Epilog*, pp. 130–1.

Whereas Wolfram starts from the omnipotent and supreme *potentia* of God and moves on to relate this to the father–child relationship between the all-powerful divinity and a weak and sinful humanity, Rudolf, after a speculative passage on God's eternity, introduces the following argument:

> dir sich biegent älliu knie
> ze himel und ûf der erde hie
> biz durch der helle künde.
> vor dir daz abgründe
> bibent unde in vorhten swebet. (*Barlaam*, 25–9)

[Every knee is bent before you in heaven and here on earth and throughout hell (there too you are known). The abyss quakes before you and shakes in fear.]

Rudolf logically follows his principal concern, the representation of the timeless nature of God's supremacy, by showing, not so much humanity as children of God, but rather the whole of creation – even down to hell – respectfully worshipping the *künec Sâbâôt*. At an infinite distance, creation echoes the idea of the supreme Creator with fear and trembling. The Christian paradox of an intimate relationship combined with infinite distance, with which Wolfram is primarily concerned, gives way to an increasing sense of the distance separating the human and divine spheres.

Finally Rudolf comments briefly on the workings of the Holy Sprit:

> von dînem süezen geiste lebet
> swaz lebelîche sich verstât
> unde lebende sinne hât. (*Barlaam*, 30–2)

[Everything living that possesses understanding and sense takes its life from your sweet spirit.]

This appears to be an abridged version of the three orders of life discussed in the prayer to the Trinity in *Der guote Gêrhart*. Be that as it may, here too the workings of the third person of the Trinity – a theme which in Wolfram's work does not emerge clearly until the end of the first part of the prologue – is brought forward to round off the trinitarian concept. In this position in Rudolf's work it loses most of its impact, since the workings of the Holy Ghost are put into perspective by the concept of the supreme God outlined here. Anything possessed of life and spirit is seen as directly dependent on the divine spirit.

Both poets then continue with a section comprising a hymn of praise to creation. However, Rudolf's version of this is almost twice as long as Wolfram's. The main motifs employed by Wolfram are: 1. the movement of the heavens; 2. the elements; 3. living organisms; 4. day and night; 5. God's all-pervasive knowledge of creation. All these recur in Rudolf's version, albeit in a different order; he also extends Wolfram's four elements by adding *kelte, regen, hitze, tuft* ('cold', 'rain', 'heat', 'dew' or 'vapour') and, finally, thunder and lightning to the list; living organisms, which are not specified further, are represented as dependent on the movement of the heavens. By contrast, only praise of the sun is retained from Wolfram's description of the alternation between day and night. The final motif, however, which deals with God's relationship to the innermost forces of nature, shows a significant variation:

> dir ist niht verborgen vor,
> dû sihst durch aller herzen tor
> in menschlîcher sinne grunt ... (*Barlaam*, 59–61)

> [Nothing is concealed from you, you see through the gateway of every heart into the depths of the human spirit ...]

Wolfram's idea that God is also aware of the innermost workings of nature is here replaced by the idea that even the most intimate secrets of the human heart cannot be hidden from God. Only after Rudolf has run through all aspects of the Trinity does he introduce the central christological concept, which in Wolfram's version had preceded the section praising creation:

> Got vater nâch der gotheit,
> dînes sunes name treit
> die menscheit, in der er leit
> den tôt durch unser brœdekeit,
> der megede schepfer unde ir kint ... (*Barlaam*, 63–7)

> [God, father in your divinity, in the person of the Son you have taken on humanity – as a man he suffered death on account of our weakness, he who was the virgin's creator and her child.]

This passage is shorter than the corresponding passage in Wolfram (1,19–28). Rudolf omits the interpretation of the Lord's Prayer, thereby radically altering the emphasis. Wolfram was concerned to establish the parent–child relationship of God and humanity; this is sealed by baptism in the name of Christ. When Rudolf comes to speak of the second person of the Trinity, he introduces a central christological concept omitted by Wolfram, namely Christ's Passion. By inserting the christological argument at this point, Rudolf brings his eulogy of creation, and with it the section on the second person of the Trinity, to a definite conclusion, thus creating a clear caesura. By contrast, Wolfram's praise of creation led straight into the representation of the workings of the Holy Ghost in the human spirit: 'der rehten schrift dôn unde wort / dîn geist hât gesterket / mîn sin dich kreftec merket' ('The song of praise that rises from words written down as truth is reinforced by the power of your Holy Spirit'). Rudolf, too, follows this with a discussion of the workings of the Holy Spirit, but this not only begins in quite a different way from Wolfram's, it is also much more general and more extensive. Whereas Wolfram was concerned solely with the workings of the Holy Spirit in the *sin* of the poet, here the Holy Spirit is considered in all its manifestations: Rudolf presents a catalogue of the debt human abilities and characteristics owe to God's spirit and grace: *wîsheit, kunst, list, bescheidenheit, tugende, gesunder lîp, vrœlîcher muot* ('wisdom', 'knowledge', 'skill', 'knowledge' or 'discernment', 'virtue', 'health', 'joy'). He follows this with thanks that God has granted him a share of these, if only to a modest degree; especially however he gives thanks to God for granting him grace in the form of faith and redemption. Only now does Rudolf return to Wolfram's model, asking God for help in his poetic work.

> durch die gnâde bite ich dich,
> daz dû geruochest hœren mich
> und mir in mîne sinne
> des heilegen geistes minne
> ze lêre geruochest senden,
> daz ich wol müge verenden,
> des ich mit kranken sinnen
> alhie wil beginnen
> ze sprechenne von einem man,
> wie des lêre dir gewan
> vil der heidenischen diet,
> wie er von ungelouben schiet
> mit dîner lêre liute, lant
> und den glouben tet erkant
> in dînem namen, süezer Krist. (*Barlaam*, 103–17)

[By your grace I beg you that you should consent to hear me and

that you should consent to send the love of the Holy Spirit into my
heart (= *sinne*) and so teach me how to accomplish what I will now
begin to tell here through my own feeble powers about a certain
man, how through his teaching many heathen people were won
over to you, how by instructing them about you he converted lands
and peoples from their false belief and made the faith known to
them in your name, sweet Christ.]

Wolfram had asked the Holy Spirit to help him in the praise of a
knight who never forgot ('nie vergaz': 2,27) God and who, although
he did not escape sin – having indeed risked both body and soul for
the sake of his love – was allowed to redeem himself by the grace of
God. In Rudolf's case, however, the Holy Spirit is to teach the poet
how to give an account of a man whose teachings spread the Christian
faith. At this point it becomes abundantly clear how far Wolfram's
and Rudolf's lines of argument have diverged.

To sum up: a comparison of the two prologues shows that while
Rudolf is greatly influenced by Wolfram's introduction to *Willehalm*,
retaining the most important ideas in the trinitarian concept, he
nevertheless introduces substantial re-arrangements and variations.
Only a few things are dropped, for example the interpretation of the
Lord's Prayer, while others are expanded or elaborated. These alterations suggest a deliberate tendency on Rudolf's part to represent the
trinitarian idea in a clear-cut tripartite scheme, viz. 1. God and
eternity (1–32); 2. the creation (33–67); 3. humankind (68–88). At the
same time, the whole trinitarian scheme is rehearsed – seen under a
different aspect each time – in connection with each person of the
Trinity. Thus, in the first complex, seen under the aspect of divine
potentia, the perspective of the second Person is already taken into
consideration, and the whole trinitarian picture is rounded off with
additional lines on the Holy Spirit at the end. The second complex, in
praise of creation, is likewise constructed from the perspective of the
interaction of divine power and divine wisdom, and at the end – in a
striking variation of Wolfram's lines 2,14ff. – inasmuch as humankind
is considered as endowed with spirit, the third person of the Trinity is
at least implicitly included here. Finally, the section on humanity,
which is placed more clearly than the others under the influence of
one person of the Trinity, namely the Holy Spirit, at least begins most
emphatically with the Trinity. By comparison with Rudolf's new
version of the prologue, which combines a clear division into three
parts with an integrated description of the workings of the individual

persons of God in the general framework of the Trinity in each of these parts, Wolfram's prologue, although unmistakably based on a trinitarian structure, to some extent appears to blur the distinctions between the three thematic complexes. Thus for example Wolfram showed God as the Creator, but at the same time presented him under the aspect of *paternitas*, that is to say as the father of Christ, thus establishing a connection with the second person of the Trinity, in whom the parent–child relationship of God and humanity is realized. He then directed his praise of creation at the workings of *sapientia* in nature, yet this passage too led directly into the relationship of the Holy Ghost to the human spirit.

In eschewing such fluid transitions in favour of a more marked trinitarian structure, Rudolf also dispensed with certain connections which had been central to the sequence of Wolfram's argument. The three connections omitted in this way are as follows:

1. A central idea of the *Willehalm* prologue was unquestionably the parent–child relationship between God and humanity, mediated by the second person of the Trinity, Christ. Rudolf cut out this central section, re-locating the christological argument after the praise of creation. It may be claimed that in so doing he was following the logical sequence of the *Heilsgeschichte*: the second person is primarily manifest in creation, and the incarnation follows as an act of redemption for post-lapsarian humanity. Wolfram, on the other hand, was concerned to stress the special position of humanity in the context of creation at the beginning of his work: humankind is seen primarily in terms of its parent–child relationship with God, and the historical act of Christ's redemption is as it were incorporated, in lines 1,10ff., into the awareness of sin and the hope of forgiveness.

2. The guiding thread of Wolfram's praise of creation was the relationship between the Creator and nature, seen as parallel to the intimate but fraught relationship between God and humanity. Creation only exists through God, but its scope and measure are defined by the second person of the Trinity. Despite its absolute dependence on God the Creator – the first person of the Trinity – the order of creation is at the same time dependent on the continuous presence of *sapientia*, in other words the second person. Absolute distance is thus mitigated by the workings of God's law in nature. In lines 2,14f., finally, Wolfram presented the subject matter in such a way as to establish a connection between God and the innate forces in plants and stones; thus it is not only the far-reaching movements of the

cosmos which are occasioned and controlled by God, but rather he *bekennt* ('has knowledge of') the innermost forces at work in nature. If this *bekennen* can be seen as God's representation of himself in creation, this implies that the force which is at work in nature is ultimately God's own power. Rudolf on the other hand has his praise of creation culminate, in lines 59ff., in humanity itself. What Wolfram claimed for the innermost forces of nature is applied by Rudolf to the depths of the human heart. Unlike Wolfram, Rudolf is clearly trying to avoid moving directly from a discussion of the workings of God in nature to the effects of the Holy Spirit in the human individual, and so, logically, he also omits the second key element of Wolfram's scheme, namely the connection of Creator and creation through the innermost forces of nature.

3. Whereas Wolfram had no clear division between his description of the relationship of God and creation and the passage about the working of the divine spirit in the mind of the poet, Rudolf makes a new start with his discussion of the third person of the Trinity. He shows the Holy Spirit in relationship to what comprises human spirituality, namely the *sinne*, placing wisdom and knowledge in first position. Poetic abilities are not explicitly discussed here. There can be little doubt that this is intended as a deliberate attack on Wolfram, since it is precisely those aspects of the human mind or spirit denigrated by Wolfram which Rudolf connects with the workings of the Holy Ghost: 'swaz an den buochen stêt geschriben'; in other words, scholarship based on the general intellectual capacities of humanity, which appear in Rudolf's work as gifts of the Holy Spirit.

It may thus be seen that Rudolf, in his reworking of Wolfram's prologue to *Willehalm*, deliberately chooses to omit those three elements which form the basis of Wolfram's scheme: first, the parent–child relationship between God and humanity; secondly, the workings of God in the innermost depths of nature; and thirdly, the relationship of the spirit of the poet to the creative spirit of God. In abandoning these three elements, Rudolf effectively demolishes the argument of Wolfram's prologue. This accordingly affects the transition from the *prologus praeter rem* to the request for divine assistance: whereas Wolfram's request arose directly from an awareness of the origins of poetic ability in the Holy Spirit, Rudolf inserts a general prayer of thanks between his request and his representation of the third person of the Trinity. The request thus returns to its traditional function as a transition to the subject matter.

At the end of the prologue, Wolfram announces the story of a knight who finds himself in dire straits (*nôt*), that is to say who becomes caught between the conflicting claims of militant defence of Christianity on the one hand, and respect for God's creation, which also includes the heathen peoples, on the other. This conflict finds particular expression in Gyburc's speech before the second battle. The route followed by the hero, as by the narrator, thus takes the form of a search for meaning, an attempt to resolve the dilemma which the conflict of interests presents.

Rudolf's version of the Barlaam and Josaphat legend likewise represents a conflict between Christians and heathens; however, Josaphat is no knight at arms, but a wise man who is able to convince and convert the heathens by his teachings. It is conceivable that Rudolf deliberately intended to present this conversion through teaching as a contrast to Willehalm's battle with the heathens. In Wolfram's work, too, a disputation takes place – between Gyburc and her father – but it is fruitless, and the issue has to be decided by the use of force. Rudolf, on the other hand, presents a subject which centres not on a battle but on a successful religious disputation. The inner connection between aesthetic approach and poetic subject matter becomes evident in *Barlaam* also: Rudolf is asking the Holy Spirit to teach him how best to execute his poem. This is no daring leap of faith, as we have seen elsewhere in the context of the search for meaning through the poetic act, but rather a question of divine support and assistance in the traditional form of religious mediation of truth. Accordingly, the work itself is seen as having a didactic function, and this in turn finds a parallel in the subject matter, since *Barlaam* is concerned with the idea that belief can be taught, and it is therefore important to show how the Christian faith can be demonstrated by the persuasive powers of its own conviction. In this, the prologues to *Willehalm* and *Barlaam* reflect the differences in aesthetic approach and subject matter between the respective works. Rudolf presents the trinitarian action in his work as an independent and universal process, an essential feature of which is that it initially appears to take place at a great distance from humanity; in other words, the latter is only involved in this universal process at one particular point in connection with the gift of spirit (literally inspiration). The central motifs here are neither supernatural adoption nor the intimate connection between the divine and the human spirit, but rather the respect of creation for its supreme Creator, and the dependence of humanity on divine gifts. As the recipient of knowledge, the poet's function is to impart it to others: this is the sense in which he is assigned responsibility for the realm of art.

Rudolf's adaptation of the *Willehalm* prologue reveals an astonishingly perceptive awareness of the critical points of Wolfram's aesthetic programme. Whether this may be attributed to intuition or to conscious programmatic intent, Rudolf unerringly homes in on the fundamental elements of Wolfram's prologue structure, and, by omitting these, radically alters its theoretical conception. Inherent in his representation of the Trinity in the prologue to *Barlaam* is an intrinsically different theory, compelling in its concision. Rudolf's adaptation of Wolfram's prologue is thus revealed as a fundamental critical preoccupation with, and discussion of, his work and the literary self-consciousness which produced it, and this is achieved by referring back to the traditional format of the prologues to saints' lives. It can come as no surprise, then, that the epilogue supplies further traditional topoi, for example: faithfulness to the source while digressing for the sake of truth; the idea that those who refuse to listen are sinners; *Barlaam* as a work of expiation for the youthful sin of composing *Der guote Gêrhart*. The use of such topoi confirms that Rudolf was also influenced by conventional notions of what was appropriate to the genre.

III

Finally, in his *Weltchronik* Rudolf presents yet another variation on the introduction in the form of a prayer. Here the Trinity is played down in favour of the Creator, whose omnipotence is impressively presented. God is the *richter* ('judge'), the *herre* ('lord'), the *vogt* ('master') of the heavenly host who sing his praises; his Word is the origin, driving force and goal of all action. God, himself without beginning and end, determines both beginning and end, creating time in the alternation of day and night; the whole universe is permeated with the divine force, from the choirs of angels in the highest reaches of heaven down to the very depths of the abyss; all living things are comprehended by him. Rudolf follows this praise of creation directly with a plea for inspiration:

> Got herre, sit daz nu din chunst
> bi dir ie was ane begunst
> und anegenge nie gewan,

und doh wol mag und machin kan
anegenge und endis zil,
alse din gebot gebietin wil:
so wil ich bittin dich dastu
begiezest mine sinne nu
mit dem brunnin dinir wisheit,
der ursprinc allir witze treit;
und schoffe ein anegenge mir,
wan ih beginnen wil mit dir
ze sprechinne und ze tihtinne,
ze bescheidenne und ze berihtinne
wie du von erst mit dinir kraft
himil und erde und alle geschaft
von anegenge irdahtest,
in sibin tagin vollebrahtest
gar allir geschepfide undirscheit ... (*Weltchronik*, 61–79)

[Lord God, since your wisdom was always with you, without beginning, since it never began and yet is well able to make a beginning and an end according to your command, therefore I entreat you to drench my senses now with the fountain of your wisdom, which contains the origin of all knowledge; allow me to begin, for I desire to begin along with you to speak and to set out in poetry, to recount and to describe how first of all you conceived through your power, from the very beginning, heaven and earth and all creation, and in seven days brought to fulfilment the whole range of created things ...]

From this starting point Rudolf proceeds to unfurl the history of the world; the plea for inspiration thus leads directly into the representation of the subject matter. In asking God to 'allow him to begin' (71), Rudolf is including his own art within God's process of creation. He wishes to unfold the history of the world speaking and composing together with God, and in this undertaking, surprisingly enough, Rudolf regains something of the poetic consciousness which marked Wolfram's prologue to *Willehalm*. The spirit of God and the mind of the poet work together in harmony. Admittedly there is a fundamental difference, in that Rudolf, unlike Wolfram, is not concerned to find a meaning in a secular history which has become problematical; in his *Weltchronik*, Rudolf is, rather, following the pre-ordained meaning of universal history, and is able to demonstrate the truth of God's plan of salvation by means of the traditional doctrine of the Ages of the World.

18

The new genre of love-romance: suffering as a way to fulfilment. From Rudolf von Ems' *Willehalm von Orlens* to Ulrich von Etzenbach's *Willehalm von Wenden*

I

By omitting the crisis of the hero, the post-classical Arthurian romance may be said to deconstruct Chrétien's model from within; in the process, the erotic element implicit in the crisis is lost. Wigalois and Daniel, Garel and the Gawein of *Diu Crône* all still win their *amours*, it is true, and the *âventiure* is still arranged so as to culminate in a wedding feast, but love – *minne* – itself is no longer a problematic area. Parallel to this development, however, there emerges in the post-classical period a new type of 'love-romance'. It might reasonably be expected that this new type would take its lead from *Tristan* and confront the theme of absolute love. Although this expectation is on the whole vindicated, critical discussion of the earlier romance makes its appearance in Germany comparatively late. *Lancelot*, Chrétien's early response to *Tristan*, was not translated into German; Ulrich von Zatzikhoven's *Lanzelet* came into being under different literary-historical circumstances and did not give rise to a tradition of its own.[1] The French *Lancelot en prose*, in which the erotic element occupies a central position, remained initially without impact in German-speaking countries, although it was translated relatively early. For the rest, various continuations of Gottfried's *Tristan* appear, but neither Ulrich von Türheim nor Heinrich von Freiberg prove truly equal to the task.[2] By reverting to the pre-courtly version, Ulrich reduces the whole issue almost to the point of incomprehensibility; in the process, while the love between Tristan and Isolt von Irlanden ('Ysolt the Fair') is condemned and the marriage with Isolt as blanschemains ('Ysolt of the White Hands') emphasized, the *triuwe* of the adulterous couple is

---

[1] Haug, '*Das Land, von welchem niemand wiederkehrt*', pp. 52ff., 62ff.
[2] Wachinger, 'Zur Rezeption Gottfrieds von Straßburg', pp. 59ff.; Ruh, 'Epische Literatur des deutschen Spätmittelalters', pp. 119ff.

nevertheless praised to the skies. The resulting work is uneven in the extreme. It lacks any kind of theoretical reflection, and the prologue is restricted to an *in memoriam* for Gottfried and a passage addressed to Ulrich's patron, Ulrich von Winterstetten. Heinrich von Freiberg's version is scarcely more satisfactory.

Rudolf von Ems' *Willehalm von Orlens* may be seen as the first work of any significance to take up the issues raised by Gottfried's *Tristan*. Rudolf makes the reference to Gottfried clear at the very beginning by citing Gottfried's concept of the *edele herzen*:

> Rainer tugende wiser rat
> Von edeles herzen lere gat.
> Ob alles lobes werdekait
> Den pris dú zuht allaine trait. (*Willehalm von Orlens*, 1–4)

[The teaching of a noble heart wisely proclaims the virtue of pure excellence. Discipline combined with gracious behaviour takes the first prize among all virtues that are worthy of praise.]

However, this opening establishes a connection with Gottfried in which Rudolf is at the same time distancing himself from the latter's example. In this connection, Burghart Wachinger has noted that by placing the term *edelez herze* at the beginning as a kind of gnomic statement, Rudolf is taking as read something which in Gottfried's romance was the result of a much longer process of argument.[3] Gottfried set apart the noble hearts from *alle werlde* ('society at large'), identifying them by their willingness to affirm the joys and sorrows of love in equal measure. Only those committed in advance to the inherently inseparable mixture of bliss and torment – thus Gottfried – will really be able to understand a work which has *edele herzen* as its subject. This argument, demanding the identification of the audience with the subject matter, is omitted by Rudolf altogether. The concept of *edelez herze* is taken as a fixed value, and as such carries a message, urging the audience to observe *tugent* ('virtue'), which attains its highest expression in *zuht* ('good conduct'). Other features of this ideal of virtue are then listed: *wîsheit, triuwe, êre* and *bescheidenheit* ('knowledge', 'fidelity', 'honour', 'discernment'). Whoever follows this advice of an *edelez herze* will also be honoured by society, the recipient of *der werlte prîs* (9). No explicit mention is made of love in this first section of the prologue, which comprises sixteen lines and, following Gottfried's example in *Tristan*, is linked

---

3 Wachinger, 'Zur Rezeption Gottfrieds von Straßburg', p. 67.

by an acrostic. Yet is love not an essential prerequisite for the concept of *edelez herze*? Caution is necessary here, since by contrast to Gottfried's work the *edelez herze* in Rudolf is not characterized by ideal love, which contains all the virtues (*tugende*) within itself. Here it rather 'advises' the exercise of the virtues, the first of which is given as *zuht* – a term which does not occur in Gottfried's prologue. The audience's expectations associated with Gottfried's central concept are thus quite deliberately thwarted. Only now, in line 17, does Rudolf address his audience directly, asking whether there is anyone present who has 'spotliche sitten' (19: 'is inclined to mock'); if so, he is asked to leave – a more polite formulation of the familiar *nîdære* or 'detractor' topos. However, anyone who 'gûti mêr erkennen kan' (34: 'can appreciate a good tale') and whose disposition is such that 'sûze rede im sanfte tût' (36: 'sweet words appeal to him') is welcome. The key expressions *sûze* and *sanfte tûn*, echoing expressions of Gottfried's, prepare the way for the introduction to the subject of the work, which is presented in the following lines using direct quotations from Gottfried's concept of love:

> Ich wil si gerne wissen lan
> Baide liep unde lait
> Von rittherlicher werdekait,
> Von wiplichen trúwen,
> Von sender herzen rúwen,
> Von lieplicher geselleschaft
> Und wie die minne mit ir kraft
> Sûsis sur und liebes lait,
> Laides lieb mit arebait
> Zwai gelieben lerte
> Und unverhǒwen serte
> Ir minne gerenden herzen
> Mit so nach gǎndem smerzen,
> Der vil nach gegen dem ende wac. (*Willehalm von Orlens*, 40–53)

[I will gladly tell them (i.e. the audience) of both joy and sorrow, of knightly prowess, of womanly fidelity, of heartfelt passion, of happy companionship, and of how love through its power taught two lovers to know sweet bitterness and delightful grief as well as the delight of suffering combined with distress, and how unhindered it wounded their yearning hearts with such intense pain that it almost led to their deaths.]

Rudolf's characterization of love, indebted as it is to Gottfried, is

333

nevertheless not formulated as a challenge to the audience, but instead refers exclusively to the subject matter, namely the joy and sorrow of the hero and heroine of the romance; thus the introduction leads without a break into a summary of the plot (69ff.). Towards the end of the prologue, however, Rudolf again addresses the audience directly, setting out in detail what his tale has to offer:

> Die minnere vindent minne dran,
> Die getriuwen stâte trúwe,
> Die seneden senede rúwe,
> Die erbarmherzigen claigendes lait,
> Die manlichen vil manhait,
> Die gûten rehte gûte,
> Die werden hohgemûte: ... (*Willehalm von Orlens*, 112–18)

[Lovers will find love here, the faithful enduring fidelity, the passionate passionate sorrow, the merciful lamentable grief, the courageous great courage, good people true goodness, the distinguished social *élan* ...]

Rudolf ends with the comment that he, 'ûf der sâlden bejag' – in striving for success – that is, in order to win the favour of *werde lúte* ('good people'), will now turn to his task.

The passage beginning with line 112 is clearly an allusion to Gottfried, lines 174ff., where he speaks of the manner in which love may be said to incorporate the other virtues: *tugent, triuwe, êre* are all closely bound up with it. In Rudolf's prologue, this complex is refracted into a spectrum of virtues which can be individually combined, as it were, according to the specific wishes of the listener. This is in accordance with the line taken in the prologue, since if the *edelez herze* first and foremost teaches *zuht*, this will provide a kind of ethical or moral framework to the story; although love is the subject of the romance, it is no longer perceived as its absolute guiding principle. This is why Rudolf abandons Gottfried's complex interweaving of ethics and aesthetics, instead taking as his starting point a general concept of virtue, which is intended to be mirrored in the audience by a general willingness to understand. Those who will not or cannot understand are accordingly shown the door without further ado.

This direct addressing of the audience, then, deliberately avoids any commitment to a particular subject matter. What Gottfried saw as a necessary prerequisite for an appropriate audience response, namely an acceptance on the part of the audience of the indissoluble link between the joys and sorrows of love, is here treated purely as material for the romance, in other words Rudolf's concept of love corresponds to and is designed around the particular fate of the lovers who are his subject. Accordingly, the anticipated effect of this on the listeners is also situated in a more general context; the romance is intended not only for lovers but also for those possessed of mercy and courage, indeed for anyone who is *guot* and *werde*.

This brief introduction should serve to demonstrate just how systematic Rudolf was in his dismantling of Gottfried's theoretical scheme and approach, starting with its most basic premises. What is announced in the theoretical implications of Rudolf's prologue is fulfilled in the most consistent manner imaginable by the romance itself.

II

As in Gottfried's *Tristan*, the tale begins with the story of the hero's parents.[4] Willehalm, the father, is engaged in a feud with Jofrit von Brabant. An over-bold advance sees him captured, and Jofrit is unable to prevent his death. The news that Willehalm has been killed reaches his wife on the very day that she has given birth to a son; she dies beside her husband's bier. Jofrit then adopts the child, gives him his father's name and brings him up as his own. Once the young Willehalm has grown up and his foster-father has had the emperor confer his own fief on him, he goes to the court of the king of England, where he becomes the centre of courtly *vröude*.

This story of the parents clearly alludes to and contrasts with Gottfried's *Tristan* from the outset. In both cases the father is killed and the mother dies during or after childbirth. However, whereas the infant Tristan has to be hidden from his father's enemy, and receives a courtly upbringing despite his lack of inheritance, Jofrit not only takes the son of his slain opponent into his care, but also arranges for his own fief to be conferred on him. Like Tristan, Willehalm then travels to England, but while the former arrives by chance at his uncle's court, knowing nothing of his relationship to Mark, Willehalm plans to finish his education at a court with which he has no ties

---

[4] The comparison which follows is explored in greater detail in Haug, 'Rudolfs *Willehalm* und Gottfrieds *Tristan*'.

whatsoever. This constellation automatically precludes certain points of conflict which were crucial in *Tristan*.

At the English court, Willehalm spends a great deal of time with Amelie, the king's daughter, and their childhood affection gradually develops into a passionate love, at least on the part of the precocious thirteen-year-old Willehalm. Amelie, however, a mere nine, rejects his passionate advances, with the result that Willehalm rejects all food and comes close to death. At this point Amelie acknowledges the strength of his devotion and is prepared to return his love, but first he must prove himself as a knight. Willehalm accepts this condition and goes to Brabant, where he is invested as a knight, enters on his inheritance, and proceeds to prove his skill at tournaments.

Meanwhile, the king of England decides to marry his daughter to King Avenis of Spain. Hearing this news, Willehalm returns to England in some haste, arriving on the day appointed for the wedding. The lovers flee; however, they are captured, and Willehalm is brought before the king severely wounded. He is obliged to submit to a strange penance: he must leave England and agree never to return unless the king himself should invite him. What is more, the point of the spear which is still embedded in his wound may only be removed by a royal lady. Finally he is forbidden to speak until Amelie gives him permission to do so in person. Willehalm thus goes silently into exile. He reaches the Norwegian court, where the king's daughter Duzabel removes the spear point from his wound.

As in *Tristan*, then, the hero's love brings him into conflict with his lord and master. However, in *Willehalm* this love is directed not at the latter's wife, but at his daughter; the adulterous passion of Tristan and Isolt is thus replaced by the apparently unproblematic relationship between Willehalm and Amelie. This love develops naturally out of childhood affection, with no obstacles requiring a magic potion to overcome them. The problems which arise are the result of natural circumstances – namely the difference in age between the two partners. In Rudolf's romance, this difficulty is ultimately bridged by the absolute nature of Willehalm's love. This does not, however, lead to mutual surrender to passion; instead, the girl demands that he should first prove himself as a knight. In spite of the fact that unrequited love has already just brought him close to death, Willehalm accepts this condition. If a conflict with his lord is still to be brought about despite the – by comparison with *Tristan* – completely non-critical situation, then it must be imposed from outside: the father plans to marry his daughter to another. As in *Tristan*, the lovers leave the court, but not in order to live together in the paradise of a lovers' cave; instead, their flight misfires and leads directly to their separation.

After Willehalm's banishment, the king of England attempts to bring about the marriage of his daughter to Avenis. However, in the face of the girl's refusal the Spaniard is generous enough to renounce his claim.

Like *Tristan*, then, *Willehalm* contains a rival figure who, superficially at least, would seem to have a more rightful claim on the woman who is the object of the dispute. However, whereas in the earlier tale the protagonist's beloved is forced to marry the husband chosen for her, giving rise to the fateful adulterous relationship, in *Willehalm*, Avenis retracts his claim of his own accord. His role is thus restricted to initiating the confrontation with the heroine's father, thereby bringing about the separation of the two lovers.

Meanwhile, the silent Willehalm performs acts of heroism in the service of the Norwegian king. On one occasion he participates in a campaign to relieve the besieged abbey on the island of Desilvois, whose abbess, Savine, happens to be the sister of the king of England. When she hears of her lovesick niece pining away in England, and the circumstances which have brought about this situation, she begins to suspect the true identity of the silent knight in the Norwegian army, and sets to work to bring about a reunion of the lovers. She has Amelie come to the abbey and then sends her to Norway, where she is able to release Willehalm from his enforced vow of silence. There remains, however, one more obstacle to be overcome; Duzabel claims the hero for her own in return for saving his life. This conflict is resolved when it is established that Willehalm's mother was the aunt of the king of Norway, so that a marriage is out of the question.

In *Willehalm*, as in *Tristan*, the period of separation is a time of anguished anticipation. Whereas Tristan is determined to continue meeting his beloved in secret at any price, however, Willehalm obeys the conditions imposed upon him, which restrict him to an entirely passive role; outside help is needed to re-unite the lovers. Rudolf introduces a new character to bring about this reunion.

Finally, Rudolf too uses the motif of the other woman, but whereas Gottfried has Tristan hope for a relief of his emotional torment from Ysolt of the White Hands, Duzabel heals Willehalm's physical wounds – a motif used in *Tristan* in connection with the first Ysolt.

Whereas Tristan marries Isolt as blanschemains, however, thereby involving himself in a whole web of deceit and self-deception, in Rudolf's tale the problem of the other woman is resolved of its own accord.

Finally Amelie – like Ysolt – crosses the sea in order to rejoin her lover and relieve his suffering. However, here too the circumstances have changed and the situation is reversed: Ysolt should have healed Tristan of his poisoned – physical – wound, but arrives too late. Amelie, on the other hand, is able to heal Willehalm psychologically, as it were, by restoring his power of speech.

In *Tristan*, the lovers' ruin is brought about by a lie on the part of the other woman. In *Willehalm*, the final 'healing' results from the intervention of a third, disinterested party; this passivity on the part of the lovers is balanced by a certain amount of stage-managing of the plot, in order that the complications may be resolved, and a general reconciliation at the end made possible, by outside intervention.

Rudolf, then, relates a love-story in which the listener or reader is continually referred back to the configuration of *Tristan*, but where, at the same time, the circumstances and solutions presented diverge from this model at every important juncture. There can be no doubt that the work is intended to be seen against the background of *Tristan*, indeed understood as a critical reworking of the latter. In order for Rudolf to be able to present the action from a contrasting viewpoint, however, a number of contradictions and inconsistencies inevitably arise. Thus in the background story, Jofrit – whose hostility towards the protagonist's father is in no way less motivated than that of Gottfried's Morgan – quite unexpectedly turns into the caring guardian of the young Willehalm. The violence of Willehalm's passion, which brings him close to death, is in marked contrast to the fact that the merest promise of marriage is sufficient to restore him to life, and even to cause him to accept a voluntary separation. The king's sudden disregard for his daughter's feelings when arranging a marriage for her – which moreover accords ill with the idealized portrayal of the English court – is no more accounted for than the sudden reversal at the end, where the king begs his daughter's forgiveness. Amelie, on the other hand, does not initially appear able to oppose her father's plans for her marriage, yet after the failed elopement she unexpectedly succeeds in resisting his wishes. Since Avenis proceeds to renounce Amelie with good grace, the conflict is essentially resolved, and Willehalm could in fact have been recalled;

yet the narrative pattern introduced with the lovers' separation is set to run its course regardless of the change in circumstances. Finally, the conflict regarding the other woman is introduced as arbitrarily as it is resolved.

All these discrepancies and inconsistencies were a consequence of Rudolf's attempt to structure the action of *Willehalm* by analogy with and in contrast to *Tristan*, and indeed may serve to show the extent of his programmatic deviation from Gottfried's model. They draw the attention of the listener or reader to the fact that the action must run its course despite any improbable or inconsistent elements, in order that *Willehalm von Orlens* can become an 'anti-*Tristan*'. For these purposes it is irrelevant how far Rudolf's source – which has not survived – had already gone in this direction. What is important – as the direct references to Gottfried in the prologue show – is that Rudolf's *Willehalm* is intended as a critical reworking and adaptation of Gottfried's *Tristan*.

III

It is clear that the love-story of Willehalm and Amelie, conceived as it was in opposition to the idea and story of *Tristan*, at the same time necessarily called into question Gottfried's aesthetic concept, since this latter was intimately bound up with his specific concept of love. In *Willehalm*, Rudolf is thus implicitly taking issue with Gottfried's literary theory. Rudolf's poetic identity and literary standpoint emerge as a contrast to Gottfried's position; the meaning of the work is to a large extent revealed and fulfilled within this critical literary relationship.

Tristan demanded of its audience from the outset an identification with that paradox which characterizes the highest form of love, as exemplified by Tristan and Ysolt. In Rudolf's scheme, these paradoxes, or rather the conflicts in which they become apparent, are easily capable of resolution, and the scenes are re-arranged in such a way that the contradictions may be overcome; where this is not possible, a solution is simply imposed from outside, regardless of its probability or the logic of the situation. Joy and sorrow, then, are no longer inextricably interwoven; love is no longer intensified by its inherent and characteristic paradoxes, but instead joy and sorrow follow abruptly on one another, positive and negative aspects alternate and the passage through suffering leads ultimately to a joyful conclusion. The tightly interlocking pattern of contradictions is replaced by the successive alternation of opposites. This means that this new type of love-story no longer demands of its audience an identification with, and empathetic appreciation of, the paradoxes of love, but rather presupposes a sympathetic following of the action and an identification with patterns of behaviour which demonstrate the exemplary resolution of conflicts. Rudolf therefore no longer has need of a 'congregation' which is required to profess its faith in the subject matter in advance; rather, the doctrine conveyed by *Willehalm* is intended for, and accessible to, all. This demonstrates once again the new relationship of literature and society by contrast with the 'classical' aesthetic concept – a new postion already illustrated in Rudolf's *Der guote Gêrhart* and *Barlaam*.

Rudolf's critical reworking of the themes of *Tristan* also represents an implicit reformulation of the function of poetry. Gottfried had postulated the extreme intensity of the contradiction between joy and sorrow in love as the highest possible form of human existence. As such it is to be understood in an ethical sense, i.e. in the context of society, even if the relationship with society itself becomes one aspect of this conflict. If Rudolf sets against this paradoxical situation a conflict which is essentially resolvable, this does not necessarily mean that he is seeking to disregard the negative aspects of love; however, sorrow is no longer seen as an inevitable concomitant of love, but rather on the one hand has to be lived through as a subjective experience, and on the other is an objective state which has to be overcome in a practical way. The social conflicts arising from love are resolved in *Willehalm* by political settlements, which ultimately go so far as to marry Willehalm and Amelie's son to the daughter of Avenis! At the same time, the subjective aspect of the conflict is isolated from the social context, so that personal suffering is entirely contained within an 'inner', subjective sphere, creating new scope for individual emotional experience. However, in the first instance this experience takes the form of a test of endurance; it signifies a process of growth and maturing in patient trust and fidelity (*triuwe*). This new scope, or inner space, finds its own particular expression in a specific literary device, that of the interpolated letters, which is more or less irrelevant to the action but serves to represent the dimension of inner experience. Thus the letter which Amelie writes to Willehalm when she is about to be married to the Spaniard is not a cry for help – as one might be justified in expecting – but an outpouring of grief.

The second part of the action, in particular, may be seen to be based on the principle of the protagonist having to prove himself; the scheme of *Robert le Diable* clearly provided the model for this part.[5] The vow of silence which Willehalm accepts effectively isolates his suffering from any social context; his knightly deeds must, perforce, remain anonymous. This anonymity is quite different from Tristan's incognito, which, a direct result of the conflict with society, is a deliberate strategy. Equally, it is to be distinguished from the anonymity of the Arthurian knight, since by contrast to the latter, acts of chivalry do not for Willehalm represent a means of regaining his lost identity; rather, Rudolf deliberately abandons the character-istic Arthurian interweaving of and interplay between subjective suffering (*nôt*) and the conflict with society. The realm of political and social conflict and the realm of subjectivity co-exist alongside each other, but there is no connection between them; the one has, it is true, an effect on the other, but practical political action and emotional experience go their own separate ways. Moreover, just as personal suffering is brought about by external causes, it is likewise resolved through external agents. Yet precisely because subjectivity and indivi-dual experience no longer present a problem within society, Rudolf's new love-romance can be avowedly social in a new sense, with, on the one hand, its theory of the possibility of practical solutions to external conflicts, and on the other, its idea that sorrow can and must be overcome within the enclosed inner world of the heart. Both strands converge at the end in the happy reunion of the lovers. The conclu-sion then portrays an exemplary prince's life, opening out the action of the romance to illustrate exemplary ethical and religious stan-dards.[6]

IV

Only someone as self-sufficient as the protagonist of *Der guote Gêrhart*, who acts solely on his own behalf and expects no other

---

[5] Haug, 'Rudolfs *Willehalm* und Gottfrieds *Tristan*', p. 90; also in Haug, *Strukturen*, p. 643.

[6] The divergent approaches and interpretations of Brackert, *Rudolf von Ems*, p. 222, and Schnell, *Rudolf von Ems*, p. 56 – interpreting the romance as *Fürstenspiegel* and in terms of the religious dimension respectively – are by no means incompatible. Besides *Willehalm von Orlens*, there are other variations on the theme of absolute love adumbrated in *Tristan*. Some of these return to the Arthurian model in an attempt to come to terms with Eros by integrating it firmly within the romance structure; cf. Cormeau, '*Tandareis und Floribel* von dem Pleier'; Haug, 'Von *aventiure* und *minne* zu Intrige und Treue' and 'Der *Tristan* – eine interarthurische Lektüre', pp. 348ff.

reward than his own sense of virtue, is able to retreat with impunity into the moral certainty of a good deed; yet even in that work Rudolf was obliged to gloss over certain aspects in order not to make this moral appear problematic; thus for example no mention is made of the feelings of the son who is obliged to sacrifice his love. If, however, it is the fate, not of one individual, but of two people which is being enacted in a world in which personal experience has become divorced from society and benefits the latter at best indirectly – in this case, a world in which love is not incorporated into any large-scale social process but rather, as a private affair, runs counter to any social concerns – then the only consolation, if one does not want to challenge the *werlt* as Tristan does, is a retreat into the moral virtue of individual suffering. Suffering then appears as a value in its own right, and is prized so highly that it finally carries the day against all outward circumstances; *triuwe* in suffering has the power to prevail in a world subject to the whims of chance. In *Willehalm von Orlens*, which is superficially structured according to the 'double cycle' model, the crisis forms the starting point for a second cycle, depicting the hero's endurance and patience in suffering. Since this is the actual point of the story – leaving aside the meaning derived from the contrast with *Tristan* – what precedes it becomes nothing more than a prelude, and the crisis is reduced to a device to bring about the separation of the lovers. This approximates to a romance type in which the first part is dropped altogether, so that the action begins more or less directly with the first union of the lovers; this is then followed by the depiction of the separation and the long 'path of suffering' until they are reunited. This is the literary type to which the Placidas/Eustachius legend belongs, which, although Indian in origin, combines with certain motifs of the Hellenistic romance and is introduced in different versions into the vernacular literature of the High Middle Ages.[7] Indeed Rudolf himself wrote a *Eustachius*, although this has not survived.

The oldest German version of this story – dating from around 1230 – is the short romance known as *Die gute Frau*, which is based on French models. The works it most closely resembles are *Guillaume d'Angleterre* – dating from Chrétien's time, although probably not composed by him – and *Escoufle*. The most important German

---

[7] Aarne and Thompson, *Types of the Folktale*, No. 938.

version is Ulrich von Etzenbach's *Willehalm von Wenden*, written around 1290 for King Wenceslas II of Bohemia and his wife Guta.[8]

The subject of Ulrich's romance is the journey to Jerusalem of the eponymous hero, a heathen prince of the Wends. Driven by an inner longing for Christ, Willehalm secretly leaves his own country, accompanied by his pregnant wife Bene. On the way she gives birth to twins, whom Willehalm sells, leaving Bene behind in good hands. He reaches Jerusalem, and fights on the side of the Christians against the infidels; meanwhile, Bene is chosen as a ruler in the town in which she has been nursed back to health. The two children have also grown up, isolated from one another; they go out into the world, meet by chance, and set out in search of their parents, are led astray and end up as leaders of a gang of robbers in their mother's country. On his way back from Jerusalem, Willehalm by chance comes to his wife's court; they fail to recognize each other. Willehalm sets out on Bene's behalf to deal with his bandit sons, and while negotiating with them discovers their identity. They follow him back to the town, and Willehalm succeeds in obtaining forgiveness for them; when he relates his and their stories, he and his wife recognize each other also. Bene and her followers then convert to the Christian faith.

By contrast with the Eustachius legend, where the protagonist loses wife and children in a series of appalling coincidences and then wanders around aimlessly until – also by chance – they are all reunited, in *Willehalm von Wenden* it is the protagonist himself who is responsible for the loss of his family. He sacrifices them to his desire to become a Christian. Thus an active hero once more replaces the passive suffering hero tried by God; the plot combines intention and coincidence. In *Willehalm von Wenden* the literary type is thus accommodated to the tradition represented by Wolfram's *Willehalm* and Rudolf's *Barlaam*; indeed it may be said that Ulrich was deliberately attempting to combine the themes of these two romances – fighting the infidel, and conversion by instruction – within the general framework of the Eustachius legend.

Ulrich also establishes his position within this tradition in his prologue; in imitating Wolfram's introduction to *Willehalm*, he places

---

8 Masser, 'Zum *Willehalm von Wenden* Ulrichs von Etzenbach'; Kohlmayer, *Ulrich von Etzenbachs 'Willehalm von Wenden'*; Behr, *Literatur als Machtlegitimation*, pp. 175ff.

himself clearly in the hagiographical tradition.[9] At the beginning, the *invocatio Dei* – combined with a reference to the work's patrons – is followed by the usual prayer to the Trinity and then the praising of creation. This is followed by a short version of the christological section, which, following Wolfram's example, ends by pointing out that it is by being baptized in Christ's name that we may be called Christians. However, at this point Ulrich unexpectedly inserts a lament for his sins: the charms of the world seduced him, he says, and led him to break God's commandments; however, he hopes God will show mercy. Ulrich asks Christ for absolution from his sins and for guidance so that he may not again fall into temptation. He then, without a break, adds the request that Christ give him *wort* and *sin*, so that he may represent the success of his – i.e. Christ's – conversions among the heathens. The confession of one's own sins is a common hagiographical prologue topos; Hartmann used it in his introduction to *Gregorius*, and Rudolf too used it in *Barlaam*, albeit in the epilogue. Ulrich, however, does not explicitly present the poetic work as a penitential exercise; instead, there follows the traditional plea for inspiration, which here takes a dual form, as follows: he first asks for help in representing the works of Christ, and then repeats the request in order to sing the praises of Willehalm:

> Von Parrit sante Willehalm
> der junge was ûf der erde
> ein vürste in hôhem werde.
> got gebe mir sin sô wîse
> dêr in sîm namen prîse
> des vürsten leben unde tât ... (*Willehalm von Wenden*, 74–9)

> [St Willehalm of Parrit, who while still in his youth was held to be a prince of high renown – God grant me the wisdom that I may praise in his name the life and deeds of that prince ...]

The echoes of Wolfram's introduction to *Willehalm* are quite unmistakable in this passage. The plea to the saint for intercession which now follows is also taken from Wolfram, in part word for word.

Ulrich intends his romance as straightforward praise of Christ and of the saint, Willehalm of Wenden. At the same time, he brings the action up to date by using contemporary figures and events to lend

---

[9] Flügel, *Prolog und Epilog*, pp. 137ff.; Kleinschmidt, 'Literarische Rezeption und Geschichte', pp. 618–19.

colour and form to the events and characters of the romance. The most striking example of this is the allusion to Guta, King Wenceslas' wife, in the name Bene. Ulrich's work is at one and the same time praise of a model prince and a lesson for other princes to follow. This is why the Bohemian king and queen are included in the *invocatio Dei* at the very beginning of the prologue. By highlighting the renewed active role of the hero at the expense of the theme of passive suffering characteristic of the Eustachius story, Ulrich is to some extent able to restore a social dimension to the hagiographical 'love-romance', although this social aspect has a concrete political dimension. This however need not imply that those problems which characterized Wolfram's *Willehalm* will be found here, since the author remains insensitive even to certain awkward questions which the protagonist's behaviour may well suggest – such as when, without any scruples, he sells his children and abandons his wife. The idealization of the protagonists, which is intended to mirror the Bohemian rulers, brooks no criticism.

After Ulrich, the new love-romance continues to function as a vehicle for the praise of princes, as well as in subtle adaptations of the Eustachius legend with emphasis on the new 'path of suffering'. This second variation also generates an alternative version with a female protagonist, in the type of the persecuted woman;[10] in the second half of the thirteenth century the diverse history of this type acquires a German offshoot in the romance *Mai und Beaflor*.

[10] Aarne and Thompson, *Types of the Folktale*, No. 712.

19

Konrad von Würzburg: spellbinding artistry and individual moral action

I

As has been shown above, the critical process of coming to terms with the Arthurian model and with the themes and problems associated with it took three forms. Since the 'classical' model for Arthurian romance aimed to subsume (and thus to some extent neutralize) the absolute positions of love and death into a fictional scheme by construing them as 'boundary experiences' at the furthest limits of the hero's journey of *âventiure*, one way of developing an alternative model was to confront the classical scheme with the reality of absolute love and the incontrovertible fact of death. Outstanding examples of this are Wolfram's *Titurel* and *Willehalm*. However, it was also possible to dissolve the classical model from within, as it were, by omitting the crisis of the hero and making him instead into a kind of ideal knight, thereby robbing the classical model of its problematic aspects and thus also of its critical tension. In such a work, interest necessarily shifts to a world of *âventiure* which opens up, in its grotesque and daemonic dimensions, whole new worlds of sinister fantasy. This was the course taken by the 'post-classical' Arthurian romance. The third possibility of subverting Chrétien's 'classical' model consisted of abandoning the underlying principle of correlation between the hero and the world in which he moves, internalizing the values in question to such an extent that they became independent of any relation to the real world, indeed of any external expression at all. This is what occurs, programmatically, in *Der guote Gêrhart*, and this development leads ultimately to the 'suffering hero'; thus the romance gradually takes on the characteristics of hagiography.

As might be expected, Konrad von Würzburg's narrative works are based on and develop these 'classical' types, and to this extent all these various possibilities were available to him. However, the social and literary circumstances in which he wrote had changed dramatically since the time of the 'classical' romance authors. By the second half of the thirteenth century, Konrad's audience was a heterogeneous urban one.[1] The position of the poet was different from that of the mid-century, and artistic self-consciousness altered accordingly.

Konrad's love-romance *Partonopier und Meliur* provides a particularly instructive example of the shift towards different models favoured by these new conditions. In this work, Konrad follows a French original;[2] his version however clearly shows the particular angle from which he approaches the subject matter.

Partonopier is a re-working in romance form of the folk-tale of Cupid and Psyche or the 'Monstrous Bridegroom', with the gender roles reversed,[3] so that – unlike the version of Apuleius and its variants – it is the male who takes the part of the human partner. He falls in love with a supernatural being; the relationship is thus subject to certain restraints from the start. Disobeying, he breaks the taboo, loses his beloved and can only win her back at the end after many difficult trials.

To shape this material into a romance in the thirteenth century almost inevitably meant following the 'double cycle' scheme of the Arthurian model.[4] Little alteration was needed to present the wooing and regaining of the beloved as the two cycles of *âventiure*, playing down the folk-tale elements so that the supernatural beloved became a courtly lady, and interpreting the breaking of the taboo in terms of the Arthurian crisis. This is clearly reminiscent of the world of, say, *Yvain*; indeed in his own time Chrétien drew on the Breton minstrels' tales of the love of fairies which were related to the same folk-tale genre. However, for the breaking of the taboo to become an Arthurian crisis, it had to be isolated from the strict logic of the folk-tale and related to the themes and problems of the Arthurian 'double cycle'. Chrétien consistently put this transformation into practice in *Yvain*, integrating the violation of the taboo into his own model. In *Partonopier*, on the other hand, Konrad only alludes to the Arthurian

---

[1] Jackson, 'Konrad von Würzburg's legends'; Bumke, *Mäzene im Mittelalter*, pp. 287ff.

[2] Moret, *L'originalité de Conrad de Wurzbourg*; Werner, *Studien zu Konrads 'Partonopier'*, pp. 1ff.

[3] Aarne and Thompson, *Types of the Folktale*, Nos. 400, 425; Uri, 'Some remarks on *Partonopeus de Blois*'; Werner, *Studien zu Konrads 'Partonopier'*, pp. 45ff.

[4] Garstka, *Untersuchungen zu Konrads 'Partonopier'*, offers an analysis of the correspondences to and deviations from the Arthurian scheme.

model in order ultimately to distance himself all the more strongly from it.

The action unfolds as follows: Partonopier, a young knight, the nephew of the king of France, loses his way while out hunting. Night falls; afraid of wild animals, both real and imaginary, he rides on. Finally he reaches the shore of a lake, where he finds an expensively equipped ship. When he embarks, it sets sail, steered by unseen hands, for a distant city, which turns out to be deserted. He climbs up to the castle, where he is served by invisible hands and is led into a bedchamber, where a mysterious woman – Meliur – lies down beside him. Appearing to resist, she allows herself to be seduced, and then confesses that she used her magical powers to bring him to her, and has chosen him as her husband. For the time being, however, he is not allowed to see her: she will only come to him at night. Despite the happiness of his situation, after a while Partonopier begins to long to visit his home again. There he is made suspicious of his invisible beloved, and so, after visiting his home a second time, he breaks the taboo in order to see whether it is really the devil he has been dealing with, as he has been told. He glimpses a woman of wondrous beauty; at the same time he has lost her, for with this act of disobedience her magical powers are forfeit; their love can no longer remain a secret, and although the court is inclined to forgive Partonopier, and Irekel, Meliur's sister, also puts in a plea for him, Meliur angrily orders him to leave the country. On his return to France his first reaction is to shut himself away. Then he flees in desperation into the wilderness, in the hope of dying there. It is Irekel who soon discovers that deep down Meliur still loves Partonopier, and who stakes everything on bringing the two of them together again to effect a reconciliation. After many a long detour and false trail this is finally accomplished.

In *Partonopier* the breaking of the taboo is no longer brought about by means of the standard devices of the folk-tale. Nor, however, is it an example of wrong behaviour, as in the case of the Arthurian crisis; in other words, it does not represent a pre-ordained position within an established scheme, namely the conflict between the idealized Arthurian world and its counter-world, in which the latter is overcome and integrated within this fictional process. Rather, the crisis – i.e. the breaking of the taboo – is here largely internalized; the cause of the lovers' separation – Meliur's anger, and set against it Partonopier's hopeless despair – takes place on a purely psychological level. This concentration on the psychology of the individual is characteristic of the romance as a whole.[5] The path followed by the lovers is a private one from the first. The process which the hero has to undergo is not anchored by the court as an ideal starting point; on the contrary, his own native land is the location from which the intrigue which destroys the lovers' happiness proceeds. Even in Meliur's domain, the love of the eponymous couple is excluded from any social context, remaining a secret until the moment when Partonopier is banished. Love thus does not here occupy a fixed place within the structural concept of the romance. While the absolute rules which govern love here are reminiscent of *Tristan*, the problems to which love gives rise in *Partonopier* are different, and find a correspondingly different solution: both problem and solution may well have been formulated in conscious opposition to Gottfried's idea of Eros, as I hope to show below.

Partonopier fails to live up to the demands of trust and fidelity (*triuwe*) imposed on him by a love which has manifested itself with all the signs of the supernatural and miraculous. After his breaking of the taboo has destroyed the relationship, Partonopier flees into the wilderness. This flight marks a departure from the model of the folk-tale, bearing instead the hallmarks of the Arthurian scheme, according to which it would correspond with the 'classical' Arthurian motif of symbolic death. However, this process, following the course of the traditional double cycle, remains, as stated above, devoid of any social context: the crisis is a purely personal one, and the conflict takes place between two individuals: the outside world serves only to set the wheels of the action in motion. Partonopier's own country and the miraculous foreign land to which he is so mysteriously led are both equally ambiguous and opaque for the hero; he is unable to move with assurance in either. Intrigue brings about his downfall; intervention by Irekel on his behalf is needed in order finally to deliver him from his despair.

Yet this action, indebted as it is to the folk-tale, is adapted to a certain extent to fit the Arthurian scheme; increasingly subject to a psychological approach, it in turn brings with it a range of problems for which Konrad was unable to find convincing solutions. For example, it proved difficult to adhere to the Arthurian model and simultaneously to establish a psychological motivation for the reac-

---

[5] Werner, *Studien zu Konrads 'Partonopier'*, pp. 73ff. However, it is not permissible to interpret *Partonopier* on these grounds as an *Entwicklungsroman*.

tions of the protagonists; in other words, Konrad continually presents spontaneous or instantaneous reactions which arise from a given set of circumstances but do not readily fit individual characterizations. When Partonopier, lying alone in the dark bedchamber, hears someone come creeping in, his first reaction is fear. This emotion is depicted vividly, but when he then realizes that an attractive young woman is lying in his bed, he seduces her without further ado. Or, in another example, after Partonopier has broken the taboo, Meliur gives voice to heart-rending laments that she will now lose her beloved, and yet when a chance is offered of resolving the conflict by marrying him, it is she, and not, as she claims, the court, who prevents this. Thus one is continually faced with a disconcerting spontaneity in the reactions of the individual characters which renders the action completely unpredictable. That is to say, even coincidence, which plays a specific, though different, role in both the Arthurian romance and *Tristan*, here acquires psychological significance. This makes for an atmosphere of uncertainty and instability, not only as far as external events are concerned, but also with regard to the inner action. Despite all the new developments, then, it is ultimately still the set pattern of the folk-tale, rather than any psychological consistency within the action, which brings about, *ex machina*, the happy ending.

II

Even if, in *Partonopier*, love is removed from the social context into a purely private sphere, social considerations nevertheless have an important part to play. Partonopier's knightly deeds in and for society, however, represent a separate realm which, despite being repeatedly introduced into the main – love – action, is in fact only connected with it on a superficial level. This world of the court and society is in fact curiously unstructured as a whole; modelled now on one, now on another scheme, it too is at the mercy of chance and coincidence. This means that certain isolated episodes, which are clearly intended programmatically, to counteract this unpredictable quality, appear all the more striking by contrast. Two examples follow:

On his first visit to France, Partonopier intervenes in the French king's conflict with the Saracens. Before the crucial battle is due to take place, Sornagiur, the heathen king, sends a messenger to his opponent suggesting that, in order to avoid further bloodshed, the

350

outcome of the war should be decided by single combat. He, Sornagiur, is prepared to fight with one of the French king's knights; the kingdom of the loser shall be subject to the rule of his victorious opponent. The French king takes up this offer, and Partonopier volunteers to fight for him. In a clear space between the two armies, who have sworn on oath not to intervene, he joins battle with Sornagiur. For a long time it is impossible to predict the outcome of the fight, since both antagonists are equally matched in their outstanding bravery. The two armies follow the progress of the duel with bated breath. Among the Saracens is one Count Mareis, who had already incurred the king's displeasure with a cowardly suggestion. He now feels the moment has come to restore himself in the king's favour, and has his followers secretly conceal weapons beneath their clothes. When Sornagiur's position eventually becomes critical, Mareis leaps into the battleground with all his followers. Sornagiur calls to him not to break the sworn agreement, but in vain. Partonopier is taken prisoner and led away. Weeping with anger, Sornagiur watches helplessly as the slaughter begins. Finally night puts an end to the fighting. Lamenting the loss of Partonopier, not knowing whether he is alive or dead, the French retreat to their own city. Meanwhile, under cover of darkness Sornagiur mingles unrecognized among the retreating Christians. In this way he is able to reach the French court, where the king and his followers are cursing the treachery of their opponent and grieving for Partonopier. At this, Sornagiur steps forward, offers the king his sword and explains that he is not responsible for this breach of the agreement. If Partonopier has been killed, he says, they should take their revenge on his own person; if on the other hand he is still alive, they can effect his release in exchange for himself, i.e. Sornagiur. By means of this selfless moral act, he succeeds in making amends for Mareis' misdeeds and thus in breaking the desperate chain of murder and revenge (4715ff.).

A second, analogous episode is found at the end of the romance in another lengthy battle between Christians and heathens. The sultan, a rejected suitor of Meliur's, has raised an army and invaded her country. Meliur finds a pretext for calling a truce in order to summon troops to her assistance. Nevertheless, isolated battles continue to take place, in particular between the heathen camp and the castle of one Arnold. On one occasion the latter's son Walter follows a group of heathen soldiers, passing so close to the sultan's camp that he is noticed; a thousand horsemen are sent out against this one man, with

Appatris at their head. Walter flees at their approach. Appatris sets off in pursuit, soon leaving his troops far behind. When within earshot of Walter, he challenges him to stand and fight. Walter replies that not being a king he is not of equal rank; Appatris answers that anyone of free birth who aspires to glory is entitled to fight with kings and emperors; it is the honour of a knight's name which counts. At this, Walter turns and gallops to the attack; a fierce battle ensues. Meanwhile, however, the thousand heathens have ridden up. Recognizing the hopelessness of his situation, Walter throws himself at Appatris' feet, whereupon the latter gives him his own horse and allows him to escape (19709ff.).

The battle with the Saracens in the first part of the romance culminates in the moral act of generosity on the part of the heathen king, with which he makes good the perjury of one of his vassals. In the battle with the heathens at the end, Appatris' act of generosity occupies the same striking position. This kind of chivalrous behaviour, which transcends all the differences between opponents, is on both occasions exercised by heathens, and this is clearly of great significance on a thematic level. The battles of the knights, falling as they do outside any structural plan, remain obscure and unpredictable as they rage back and forth; peace negotiations and truces cannot be relied upon. In this situation there remains only one solution: an act of moral generosity on the part of an individual is the only way of resolving the web of intrigue and deception.

This model solution is not only important in *Partonopier*. When Konrad later – like Wolfram or Rudolf von Ems – comes to abandon the form of the love-romance in favour of historical fact when writing *Der Trojanerkrieg*, he nevertheless retains this fictional model. This, incidentally, provides a clear illustration of the critical point at which the development of the romance had arrived; in his version of the Trojan war, instead of a folk-tale structure guaranteeing a happy ending, we have the relentless tragedy of a battle between two peoples. However, just as Konrad, in bringing the love-romance into line with the Arthurian romance model, opened the way for individual psychological reactions, so in the historical romance the inclusion of courtly patterns of behaviour offers greater scope for spontaneous individual action, as Christoph Cormeau has so convincingly demonstrated.[6] Yet whereas, in *Partonopier*, the individual

---

[6] Cormeau, 'Quellenkompendium oder Erzählkonzept?'

moral act appears in the context of a folk-tale ending as a sign of optimism, in *Der Trojanerkrieg* the individual is seen to fail even within the small scope available for personal action, making the tragic confines of the situation all the more desperate. This is in spite of the fact that, here too, isolated acts of generosity nevertheless make momentary and tantalizing appearances, transcending the lines of battle, and seemingly promising to break the tragic chain of violence and destruction. Thus Paris spares the wounded Panfilot, after the latter has previously come to his aid; Hector rescues Theseus, who had once advised him well in a difficult situation.[7] However, acts of moral generosity are here able to achieve no more than a brief respite; they cannot alter the tragic course of history.

III

To what extent did Konrad make the specific position of his romance within the development of the genre the subject of conscious reflection? Do his theoretical utterances address or offer solutions to the problems raised in his work? And in what, within the given parameters, does he perceive his task as a poet to consist? These are the questions to which a detailed analysis, in particular of the introduction to *Partonopier*, must address itself.[8]

The prologue to *Partonopier* comprises 230 lines and is divided, according to the traditional arrangement, into two sections, with general theoretical statements at the beginning which, after line 160, merge smoothly into an exposition of the personal situation of the poet, concluding with remarks on the genesis of the work.

The opening is surprising, for Konrad immediately asks about the purpose and useful function of poetry. This takes up the well-established theoretical tradition outlined above in the context of Thomasin's poetics. The characteristic combination of general and specific aesthetic viewpoints found in the prologues to Wolfram's and Gottfried's works is thus missing here. Nevertheless, a series of theoretical arguments is rehearsed – arguments which had, in the works referred to above, derived their specific meaning from the interlocking pattern of general and specific viewpoints. However,

---

[7] Ibid., p. 317.
[8] Konrad's prologues to saints' lives may be largely disregarded here, since they are almost exclusively conventional: cf. Jackson, 'Konrad von Würzburg's legends', pp. 204ff., esp. p. 210.

353

since they appear here in a quite different context, their purpose and meaning change accordingly.[9]

> Ez ist ein gar vil nütze dinc,
> daz ein bescheiden jungelinc
> getihte gerne hœre
> und er niemen stœre,
> der singen unde reden kan.
> dâ lît vil hôhes nutzes an
> und ist ouch guot für ürdrutz. (*Partonopier*, 1–7)

> [It is beneficial for an intelligent young man to enjoy listening to poetry and not to obstruct those who are skilled in singing and storytelling. There is enormous benefit in this, and it is also an antidote to despondency.]

There is an unmistakable didactic note to these comments on the use of poetry, addressed as they are to the *bescheiden jungelinc* in particular. The idea that poetry can serve as a remedy for *ürdrutz*, that is, boredom and *ennui*, takes up the traditional topos of pernicious leisure. This is then defined in detail:

> ich zel iu drîer hande nutz,
> die rede bringet unde sanc.
> daz eine ist, daz ir süezer klanc
> daz ôre fröuwet mit genuht;
> daz ander ist, daz hovezuht
> ir lêre deme herzen birt;
> daz dritte ist, daz diu zunge wirt
> gespræche sêre von in zwein. (*Partonopier*, 8–15)

> [I will tell you three kinds of benefit that are brought by storytelling and song. One is that its sweet sound fills the ear with delight. The second is that courtly refinement conveys its teaching to the heart. The third is that the tongue becomes most eloquent as the result of the first two benefits.]

Literature is thus useful on three counts:

1. It gives rise to aesthetic pleasure, particularly through its musical possibilities. In terms of the theoretical tradition, this corresponds to Horace's *delectare*; what is striking however is that the emphasis is not on the general aspect of entertainment but specifically on the formal, musical side.

---

[9] Ehlert, 'Zu Konrads Auffassung vom Wert der Kunst', 81ff., interprets this from the conventional perspective of traditional topoi.

2. It will come as no surprise to find this followed by *docere*. What is taught is however not wisdom in general but courtly manners (*hovezuht*). This is one more example, with regard to Konrad's potential audience, of a familiar phenomenon, confirming that the new urban élite emerging in the thirteenth century was concerned to preserve the chivalric way of life of the High Middle Ages.[10]

3. Finally, the third aspect, the eloquence which can be achieved through a literary education, refers to the rhetorical component of the poetic tradition. However, it is mentioned here more or less in passing, since the following lines are primarily concerned with the first two aspects, pleasure and instruction, or aesthetic enjoyment and the courtly way of life.[11]

> ich bin des komen über ein,
> daz beide fröude und êre
> sanc unde rede sêre
> den liuten bringent unde gebent,
> die nâch ir zweier râte lebent
> unde in beiden volgent mite.
> si lêrent hovelîche site
> und alle tugentlîche tât. (*Partonopier*, 16–23)

> [I have come to be of the opinion that song and storytelling give those people who are guided by them and are receptive to their teaching a good deal of both joy and honour. They teach courtly behaviour and excellent conduct of every kind.]

In the classical Arthurian sense, *fröude* and *êre* refer to the festive mood of celebration and to social standing respectively, particularly in the tradition of Chrétien's Arthurian model, where they represent the ideal goal of the narrative process. In Konrad's prologue, the first association is with *fröuwen* and *hovezuht* in the preceding lines 11 and 12, thus establishing a link between them and the concept of the benefits of poetry with which Konrad justified his work. In this sense, then, *fröude* would refer to an enjoyment of poetry, and *êre* would have to be understood as a product of courtly manners which literature is in a position to impart. However, too sharp a distinction between aesthetics and ethics, between artistic enjoyment and moral instruction is problematic, since when Konrad says that poetry teaches 'hovelîche site / und alle tugentliche tât' (22f.), this contains

---

[10] On the subject of courtly literature in the cities, see Peters, *Literatur in der Stadt*.

[11] The combining of pleasure, instruction and avoidance of pernicious leisure as a poetological concept also occurs elsewhere in Konrad; cf. the prologue to *Silvester* (ed. P. Gereke, 1925).

the idea of a correlation between courtly attitudes and behaviour and corresponding deeds: ultimately, then, the goal is again a synthesis of chivalric forms and personal ethics. What is new, however, is the fact that this correlation is no longer taken for granted, as in the Arthurian romance; indeed, from the perspective of reception form and content seem to diverge, so that the question arises whether it is not precisely this striven-for synthesis which is at the root of the problem.

The following lines refer specifically to the exemplary nature of what the poet intends to portray, as well as to the appropriate attitude for the audience to adopt:

> wie sol der iemer wîsen rât
> in sînen muot gesliezen,
> der sich des læt verdriezen,
> daz man singet oder seit
> von aller der bescheidenheit,
> der wîlent pflâgen alle die,
> der lîp nâch hôhen êren hie
> mit flîze kunde werben?
> sîn wirde muoz verderben,
> der guot getihte smæhen wil. (*Partonopier*, 24–33)

[How will that man ever allow wise teaching to penetrate his heart, who takes offence at songs and stories about good deeds performed long ago by people who strove with all their might to attain great honour? Whoever reviles a fine poem does so at the cost of his honour.]

Familiar topoi are introduced here: the exemplary quality of predecessors, which – handed down through poetry to the present day – demands an appropriate contemporary response. Interwoven with this is the argument that an exemplary work of literature must be good in itself, and that anyone who sees fit to deprecate it will lose the very qualities of worthiness and honour (*wirde* and *êre*) it presents. These reflections are then developed along familiar lines; what is striking is how readily the connection is made between the exemplary function of the subject of the poem on the one hand, and on the other the poet's conception of his task and the ideal response to it.

> man überhüebe tugende vil,
> die niht ze liehte würden brâht,
> ob sanges unde rede gedâht
> nie wære in tiutscher zungen. (*Partonopier*, 34–7)

[One would pass over many good matters, which would otherwise not be brought to light, if song and poetry had never been cultivated in German.]

This is a variation of the *memoria* topos, used here not to justify literature from the point of view of the deserving object but with regard to the German literary tradition, which, as Konrad states, had always justified itself in this way. This provides an occasion for the poet to refer to his debt to his predecessors:

> gesprochen und gesungen
> die meister hânt sô rehte wol,
> daz man guot bilde nemen sol
> an ir getihte schœne. (*Partonopier*, 38–41)

[The masters have produced such fine works of poetry and song that one should take example from their fine literary productions.]

The exemplary function of these predecessors thus also sets a standard for the poet to follow, and so the *meister*, the Middle High German 'classics', are invoked as models or examples to follow. The poet thus derives the justification for his work from his indebtedness to his literary models. In this way it may be seen that Gottfried's turning away from extra-poetic inspiration in favour of a justification of poetry by and through itself was just as clearly worked through by Konrad in his poetics as by Rudolf von Ems: literary traditions create their own norms, and the high style of the courtly era here too becomes a measure of poetic truth. What is considered 'masterly' now appears so self-evident that a catalogue of poets whose works set this standard is no longer felt to be necessary.

How, then, does Konrad perceive meaning to be conveyed in his 'classical' models, and thus by extension in his own works? Since he has already committed himself to demonstrating the usefulness of poetry for entertainment and instruction, it is hardly to be expected that he will give Wolfram and Gottfried credit for a theory of reception which had dispensed with precisely this overt didactic moment. Rather he says of the works of the *meister*:

> ir rede und ir gedœne
> ist nützebære und frühtic:
> reht als ein boum genühtic
> durch sîner tugende güete
> gît obez nâch der blüete,

sus birt getihte mit genuht
nâch schœner blüete guote fruht.
Hie merket wie ichz meine.
diu bluot schœn unde reine,
die von êrst getihte birt
und diu dar nâch ze frühte wirt,
daz ist diu kurzewîle guot,
diu sich alsam des meien bluot
in daz gemüete ströuwet
und im sîn ougen fröuwet
der guot getihte hœret,
wan ez im trûren stœret
und alle sorge mit genuht.
waz meine ich danne mit der fruht,
diu nâch getihtes blüete gât?
daz ist der nütze wîse rât
und ûz erweltiu bîschaft,
diu beide mit ir lêre kraft
ze bezzerunge bringent die,
die willeclichen merkent hie
swaz man in singet oder seit. (*Partonopier*, 42–67)

[Their words and their melodies are edifying and fruitful. Just as a flourishing tree bears fruit after the flowers according to its particular properties, similarly a poem produces fine fruit in profusion after the lovely flowers. Note what I mean here. The lovely pure blossom, which a poem bears first of all and which afterwards turns into the fruit, signifies the pleasant entertainment which is strewn into the mind like blossoms in May and causes the eyes of those listening to such fine poems to light up, for it completely banishes all sorrow and care. What do I mean then by the fruit, which follows on after the poem has blossomed? That is the profitable edification and the exemplification of good behaviour, which are both, by the power of their teaching, of benefit to those who are willing to heed what is said in verse or song.]

Konrad thus uses a simile to explain how the effects of literature are produced by the interaction of aesthetic pleasure and instruction. He explains it thus: a tree which has produced beautiful blossom will also bear plentiful fruit, in other words delight in its beauty leads to an appreciation of its fruitfulness and its usefulness.[12] Underlying this is the traditional concept of clothing instruction in beautiful form in

---

[12] Cf. the prologue to *Silvester*, 8f.

order to make it more palatable.[13] However, to see this simile as nothing more than a superficial and conventional device is to do Konrad a disservice; a closer examination shows that the imagery contains a specific, and in some respects quite new, aesthetic programme. It is most readily to be grasped from the semantic context of the word 'blossom' (*blüete* or *bluome*) in Konrad's work. These terms appear in conjunction with *spaehe*, *vremde* and particularly with *wilde*. Konrad uses *wilde* (literally: 'wildness'; 'untamed complexity') in this context to denote a sophisticated and ornate narrative style, based on an artistic principle which is highly conscious of the artistic means at its disposal and is able to deploy them with subtle virtuosity.[14] This 'wild' style attempts to captivate by its use of the unusual, or the esoteric, to seduce by means of the obscure and puzzling, to appeal as much by being grotesque and repellent as by being sublime and mysterious. It is distinguished as much by elegance as by fantasy, as much by mannered artificiality as by baroque excess. In short, it is a style which aims to fascinate and entrance, and this is where Konrad's concept of aesthetics comes in: he aims to compose in such a way that the audience will be captivated by the allure of his exposition, and when once they are caught, so to speak, they are delivered up to what lies behind this dazzling display, namely its didactic or moral point. The fruit thus naturally and inevitably develops from the flower. On the one hand, then, ethics and aesthetics diverge; on the other hand a new connection is established between them. The divergence leads to a stronger emphasis on poetic autonomy; literature has become aware of the variety of means at its disposal to a hitherto unprecedented degree, and these are ruthlessly deployed. The listeners are intended to fall under the spell of the stylish artistic presentation to such an extent that they are ultimately unable to escape the lesson contained within it.

After setting out his concept of poetics, Konrad turns to a discussion of the current state of literature. He says that poetry is in itself extremely useful, yet too many people believe that they are capable of composing it: 'ir ist worden ze vil, / die tihten wænent künnen' (70f.). Composing poetry, he says, has become 'sô gemeine' (75), 'so commonplace', that its effect is lost. Moreover, most of these would-

---

13 On the history of the theoretical use of the terms *delectatio* and *utilitas*, see Olson, *The Medieval Theory of Literature for Refreshment*; Suchomski, '*Delectatio*' und '*Utilitas*', esp. pp. 30ff., 67ff., 70ff.; on the beauty of the form as a bait or lure, Suchomski, p. 276, note 207.
14 Monecke, *Studien zur epischen Technik Konrads*.

be poets are not remotely competent, and this has stifling consequences for the truly talented artist:

> Swie gerne ein künste rîcher man
> wil tihten swaz er guotes kan,
> sô ist der tumben alsô vil,
> der iegelicher tihten wil,
> daz der geswîgen muoz vor in,
> dem edeliu kunst und edeler sin
> wont in sînem herzen bî. (*Partonopier*, 97–103)

[However willing a man skilled in the art may be to compose
whatever good poetry he can, there are so many fools who all want
to be poets, that they bring that man to silence in whose heart true
artistry and poetic talent have made their home.]

This argument had already been put forward by Rudolf von Ems,
but it is expressed more pointedly by Konrad: those without talent
are crowding out the true artists. This is the logical conclusion of
literature's increasing awareness of its own technical possibilities: the
more it is emphasized as a *craft*, a skill which can be acquired, the
more art appears to become generally available, instead of the
prerogative of a chosen few. In *Der Trojanerkrieg*, where Konrad
presents a similar argument, he returns to the idea of art as a gift of
God, in order to dissociate himself from the conception of poetry as a
skill which can be learned.[15] The less the audience is in a position to
distinguish clearly between the *meister* and the mere rhymster, the
more the true artist is forced into a special, isolated position. Konrad
notes this, not without a tinge of regret:

> swaz aber nu der tumben sî,
> die getihten wellen noch,
> ein meister sol nicht lâzen doch
> dar umbe sprechen unde sanc.
> swie lützel man im wizze danc
> sîner meisterlichen kunst,
> sô kêre doch herz und vernunst
> ûf edele dœne und edeliu wort. (*Partonopier*, 104–11)

[However many fools there may be nowadays who try to write
poetry, that is no reason for a true master to give up the art of

---

[15] Lines 72ff. Cf. also Konrad's *Klage der Kunst*. The contradiction between art as a craft and art as a gift of God henceforth becomes a traditional feature of literary discussion: see Burger, *Die Kunstauffassung der frühen Meistersinger*, pp. 32ff.

poetry and song. No matter how little thanks he gets for his masterly art, he should still devote his heart and mind to the composition of fine melodies and fine words.]

After elaborating this further, Konrad illustrates it, by way of justification, with the following parable:

in holze und in geriuten
diu nahtigale singet,
ir sanc vil ofte erklinget,
dâ niemen hœret sînen klanc;
si lât dar umbe niht ir sanc
daz man sîn dâ sô lützel gert:
si hât in selber alsô wert
und alsô liep tag unde naht
daz si durch wünneclichen braht
ir lîbe grôzen schaden tuot:
wan der dunket si sô guot
und alsô rehte minneclich
daz si ze tôde singet sich. (*Partonopier*, 122–34)

[The nightingale sings in woods and clearings, often its song resounds where there is no one to listen. But it does not give up singing because there is so little demand for it. It so values its song and so loves it, night and day, that it does itself great harm in order to sustain the delightful sound. Indeed it finds such beauty and loveliness in its song that it sings itself to death.]

The image of the nightingale which sings itself to death[16] expresses exactly the new experience of the spellbinding power of art. The poet himself becomes spellbound by the beauty of the poetic form; indeed, this is sufficient unto itself, as the following lines make clear:

Hie mag ein künste rîcher man
bild unde bîschaft nemen an,
sô daz er künste niht enber
durch daz man ir sô lützel ger
und alsô kleine ruoche.
der sîne kunst niht suoche
dur tugende rîches herzen site,
sô mache im selben doch dâ mite
fröud unde kurzewîle guot,

---

[16] On this motif, see McCulloch, *Medieval Latin and French Bestiaries*, p. 144; Schmidtke, *Geistliche Tierinterpretation*, p. 353; Ehlert, 'Zu Konrads Auffassung vom Wert der Kunst', 86–7.

361

durch sînen frîen hübeschen muot
sing unde spreche zaller zît. (*Partonopier*, 135–45)

[A man who is skilled in art should take example from this and not
forgo his art because it is in such small demand and valued so little.
If people are not led to seek out his art in pursuit of the qualities of
a heart rich in virtue, he should use it to provide himself with joy
and good entertainment. May he sing and compose poems continu-
ously in pursuit of courtly independence.]

Konrad claims to be one such poet when he says, in lines 150ff.,
that – regardless of how limited his abilities may be (and here the
conventional modesty topos recurs) – he must nevertheless seek a
means of passing the time with his art, inwardly in his mind and
outwardly in words: 'lange stunde / mit herzen und mit munde ...
selben kürzen müeze' (153ff.); and that he furthermore wishes to
'hübeschen trûren stœren' (157), that is to say, he would like to dispel
the sadness of the courtly people.

Hennig Brinkmann, Bruno Boesch and others have rightly insisted
that this reference to the self-sufficiency of poetry, 'art for art's sake',
should not be understood in too modern and individualistic a sense.[17]
Nor, however, would it be sufficient to see it merely as an expression
of defiance; the reference to self-sufficiency is indicative of a change in
the reception process which is confirmed by the poetic programme of
virtuosity and instruction, on the one hand, and, corresponding to
this, an awareness of the widening gulf between poet and audience on
the other.

Finally, Konrad describes his own specific situation:

swie man ungerne hœre
sanc unde süeze rede, doch
sô vindet man die liute noch,
die durch ir tugende rîchen sin
niht werfent guot getihte hin,
swâ man ez singet oder seit;
ez hât noch maneger edelkeit
und alsô reines herzen gir
daz er sîn ôre neiget mir,
swenn ich entsliuze mînen list. (*Partonopier*, 158–67)

[However little interest there may be in listening to song and the

---

[17] Brinkmann, *Zu Wesen und Form mittelalterlicher Dichtung*, pp. 25–6; Boesch, *Die Kunstanschauung in der mittelhochdeutschen Dichtung*, pp. 151ff.; cf. also Ehlert, 'Zu Konrads
Auffassung vom Wert der Kunst', 79f.

delights of poetry, you can still find people who out of their concern to perfect their inner qualities do not reject a fine poem when they hear it spoken or sung. There are still many people of such noble character and purity of heart that they listen to me attentively when I display my artistic skills.]

With this, the ground is prepared for Konrad to praise his patron, Peter Schaler, who supplied Konrad with the French source and commissioned him to produce a German version (183). Schaler is praised as an outstanding connoisseur of literature, so that the patron is here stylized into the ideal listener – a new twist to a very old device.[18] Then the poet gives his own name:

> Von Wirzeburc ich Kuonrât
> erfülle gerne sînen muot. (*Partonopier*, 192–3)

[I, Konrad von Würzburg, do his bidding gladly.]

This takes the introduction to the point where the poet speaks of the work itself: Konrad then goes on to refer to those who have helped him with the translation into German. The prologue ends with a request for the audience's attention, for Konrad is about to tell of a knight whose name was never tarnished with shame.

To sing even when no one is listening: this principle is diametrically opposed to Gottfried's concept of poetics, according to which art has no meaning if it is not heard and appreciated. For this reason Gottfried had postulated his ideal 'congregation' of *edele herzen*, committed from the outset and without reservation to the idea behind the work.

In his first romance, *Engelhard*, Konrad however still seems to wish to remain loyal to Gottfried's concept. After the encomium of *Triuwe* in the prologue, he turns to his theme; he wants to renew a true tale of great trust and fidelity ('von hôhen triuwen / ein wârez mære erniuwen': 153f.), and this with a particular aim in mind:

> ob ieman noch getriuwer lebe,
> daz er sich dâ von sterke,
> ein valschgemuoter merke
> und kenne sîne unstæten art,
> sô daz er ûf die rehten vart
> der ganzen triuwen kêre sich.
> wan ez ist wâr und endelich

---

[18] On this topos, cf. Janson, *Latin Prose Prefaces*, p. 148.

daz der triuwebære
von triuwe rîchem mære
an sînen triuwen stæte wirt,
und daz der valschgemuote enbirt
untriuwen lîhte gar dâ bî ... (*Engelhard*, 160–71)

[that if there are still any true lovers alive today they should draw strength from this story, and that the unfaithful man should take note and recognize his capricious nature and thus be converted to the rightful path of total fidelity. For it is true and certain that the faithful man is fortified in his faithfulness by hearing a story of great fidelity, and that the unfaithful man may perhaps be led to abandon his faithlessness entirely through such a story ...]

Yet Konrad is not really convinced of the powers of persuasion of his work, since – he continues – his efforts are wasted on anyone who has made a habit of inconstancy, to whom *valscheit ist gewon* (173): an unfaithful man will not bother to listen to stories of true love and constancy. He goes on to retract the cautiously expressed hope that his *mære* might be able to convert an unfaithful man:

dâ von sô muoz ich unde wil
komen ûz der zuoversiht
daz ein triuwelôser wiht
von disem mære ûf triuwe kome.
ich wil daz den getriuwen frome
dis âventiure aleine,
sô daz ir triuwe reine
dâ von gesterket werden. (*Engelhard*, 186–93)

[For this reason I am obliged to abandon the conviction that a faithless man may be led by this story to become faithful. I want this story to be of benefit to the faithful alone, so that their pure fidelity will be fortified by it.]

It might be thought that Konrad, after giving up the rash hope of improving the unfaithful, is here returning to Gottfried and his notion that a work of literature can only be understood by those who have already taken its message to heart beforehand. However, despite appearances, this is not the case: what in Gottfried had been a conscious and deliberate programme now becomes the basic position to which Konrad retreats. Gottfried was still able to demand of his audience an unquestioning commitment to the theme of the work, whereas Konrad's starting point is the experience that the effects of art are limited: he realizes that, far from converting his audience to constancy, he will only find an audience for his theme of *Triuwe* among the *getriuwen*. Here the other, problematic side of the autonomy of fiction begins to became apparent. The image of the nightingale which sings for itself alone, in the prologues to *Partonopier* and *Der Trojanerkrieg*, testifies to this, as does Konrad's new concept of aesthetics which, with its conscious emphasis on reception, seeks to bridge the widening gap between poet and audience with the help of artistic virtuosity and the enchantment of form. Gottfried's position was only tenable under the condition of writing for a small social élite. Like Rudolf von Ems before him, however, Konrad no longer has a ready-made and socially cohesive audience for his works – nor even the ideal of such an audience. His work is addressed quite simply to everyone, in other words to any individual, any connoisseur who is able to appreciate his work and is prepared to be captivated by it. This corresponds to the new urban situation with its variety of social groupings. What is more, Konrad stands before this heterogeneous audience as a professional poet who receives commissions from a number of different quarters. If there is any quality which all nobles have in common, it can now only be expressed as a catalogue of relatively abstract ethical values, which are therefore no longer the prerogative of one narrowly defined group. However, the only means the poet has of transmitting these values is through the individual's reception of his work, over which, as it takes place at a distance, he can have no control; the effect of the work on society remains problematic. The equivalent, within the plot of the romance, of this essentially individual act of reception is represented by the isolated moral act of generosity, which, limited in effect as it necessarily is, ultimately remains its own reward.[19]

---

[19] A further consequence of this change, as Karl Bertau, 'Beobachtungen zum Ich in der *Goldenen Schmiede*', pp. 191–2, has pointed out, is a new sense of worth for the poet, based on the awareness of his own autonomy.

20

Albrecht's *Der jüngere Titurel*: magic and moral code in the inscription on the hound's leash

As mentioned above, either during or after the composition of *Willehalm* Wolfram was also working on a tragic love-romance. In it he intended to relate the story of Schionatulander and Sigune, which he had already outlined in *Parzival* by means of flashbacks, starting at the end: Parzival meets Sigune as she is mourning her beloved Schionatulander, lately slain by Orilus. The two sections of this new romance which Wolfram managed to complete depict first, after a review of the family connections, the love of the couple as children, and Schionatulander's departure for the journey to the Orient in which Parzival's father is killed; and secondly, after Schionatulander's return, the episode of the hound's leash with the wondrous inscription. Schionatulander and Sigune are resting in a clearing in the woods when a hound appears, in pursuit of game, dragging behind it a leash encrusted with precious jewels and bearing an inscription. Schionatulander manages to catch the hound and brings it to Sigune, who begins to read the inscription on its leash. However, the hound breaks free before she has had time to finish reading it. She now wants to get the leash back more than anything else in the world, and so sends Schionatulander out on a quest which will lead to his death.

Even considered in conjunction with the Sigune scenes in *Parzival*, the two fragments leave many questions unanswered. However, it is clear that Wolfram intended the work as an anti-Arthurian romance, in that the hero dies in the course of the quest on which the beloved has sent him. In other words, Chrétien's model, in which the counter-world could be integrated within the Arthurian scheme by means of a symbolic passage through death, has now been definitively abandoned: the action does not end in the traditional Arthurian festivities, but in the lonely cell to which Sigune retreats with the body of her beloved. What, though, is the significance of the task Signe sets Schionatulander? Is it intended to demonstrate the futility of *Minne-dienst*, the excessive demonstration of courage and devotion for the beloved? Or does the search for the hound's leash on the contrary stand for the quest for love, so that Signe only experiences the full force of the latter in the death of her beloved, or to be more precise, as a form of *triuwe* ('fidelity') which persists beyond death? Given the fragmentary nature of the romance, it is difficult for a present-day critic to be confident of interpreting it within the correct framework.[1]

However, the seventh and eighth decades of the thirteenth century were already witnesses to an attempt, on the part of one Albrecht, to answer precisely these questions by completing the tale of Signe and Schionatulander in Wolfram's name.[2] In so doing, he constructed around Wolfram's two fragments a universal romance of over 6,000 strophes.[3] First he supplies the story prior to the beginning of the action. Using material from Wolfram's work, he traces the history of the Grail dynasty back to Troy and Rome – the son of the founding father, Senabor of Cappadocia, marries the daughter of the Roman emperor, and they have a son, Titurel, who is given France as his fief; a kind of *translatio* from Troy via Rome to the West. Titurel's education covers chivalry as well as grammar; however, his mother wants to prevent him from hearing anything about love (*minne*), since an angel has ordained that he must live a chaste life. The idea of love he then forms, based on a reading of Ovid, is a very strange one, and so his tutor takes it upon himself to explain to him the differences between true and false love: one should feel love for everything, but especially for God. The two central concepts of the Grail ethos are thus laid down: *kiusche* ('purity') and the love of God.

When Titurel reaches the age of fifty, God sends him the Grail by means of an angel, and he is shown the way to Munt Salvasch, where the Grail temple is to be built. The description of the latter forms one

---

[1] For attempts at an interpretation, see Wehrli, *Wolframs 'Titurel'*; Haug, 'Erzählen vom Tod her'; Ortmann, '*Titurel* im *Parzival*-Kontext'.

[2] This was almost certainly intended as literary play, even if later it was no longer perceived as such. See Ragotzky, *Studien zur Wolfram-Rezeption*, pp. 103, 137, 147; Kleinschmidt, 'Literarische Rezeption und Geschichte', 625–6; Ruh, 'Drei Voten zu Wolframs *Willehalm*', pp. 126ff.; Nyholm, 'Pragmatische Isotypien im *Jüngeren Titurel*', 123. W. Schröder, *Demontage und Montage*, on the other hand, attributes 'arrogance' and 'intention to deceive' to the author, thus effectively blocking in advance any understanding of the work in the context of the literary tradition. Cf. also Fromm, 'Der *Jüngere Titurel*', 14ff.

[3] On the structure of the work, see Huschenbett, *Albrechts 'Jüngerer Titurel*'; on the technique, see Huschenbett, 'Der *Jüngere Titurel* als literaturgeschichtliches Problem'.

of the most fascinating parts of the romance.[4] When he is 400 years of age, Titurel finally marries Richaude of Spain; they have a son, Frimutel, who marries Klarisse; she bears him five children. On her death, Titurel retires from the world. This is the point at which Albrecht introduces the first of Wolfram's fragments. Inserted among Wolfram's original strophes – which are also greatly extended – is a doctrinal section, a kind of moralizing aside suggesting the possibility of an allegorical reading of the description of the Grail temple: thus a human being may represent a temple of God; the candelabra could stand for the Ten Commandments, the three doors for *miltekeit*, *kiusche* and *wâre minne* ('generosity', 'purity', 'true love'); the powers of Aaron's twelve precious stones are explained, and so on. This section ends with the passing of the Grail to Frimutel.

This is followed by the portrayal of the childhood love of Tschinotulander (Albrecht's version of the name) and Sigune, taken from Wolfram, and then by the journey to the Orient and the death of Gahmuret. With his dying breath, Gahmuret begs Tschinotulander to look after Herzeloyde, to care for their child Parzival, and to marry Sigune. After Tschinotulander's return, the central theme – the quest for the leash – takes pride of place, based on Wolfram's second fragment. Tschinotulander and Sigune are on their way home from Soltane, where they have paid a visit to Herzeloyde and the young Parzival. For the sake of the plot, a connection has to be established between the search for the hound's leash and the figure of Orilus, who has already made an enemy of Tschinotulander by invading, together with his brother Lähelin, the lands which constitute Parzival's birthright – for which, until Parzival comes of age, Tschinotulander feels himself responsible. This connection is brought about in the following manner: after the hound escapes from Sigune, it falls into the hands of Orilus, who gives its leash to Jeschute. However, Ekunat, the hound's true owner, disputes his possession of the leash. King Arthur tries to settle the quarrel, but without success. In this context the author takes the opportunity of describing the magical properties of the inscription on the hound's leash (*brackenseil*). Anyone hearing it finds relief from sorrow, pain and sickness. Jeschute is asked to read out the inscription, and this is to be repeated on the occasion of a great feast at Floritschanze, to which Sigune has also been invited. The leash is handed to her, she herself reads the

---

[4] Haug, 'Gebet und Hieroglyphe', 176–7: also in Haug, *Strukturen*, p. 120; Huschenbett, *Albrechts 'Jüngerer Titurel'*, pp. 41ff.

inscription aloud to the eighty maidens at the Arthurian court and forgets her grief. After the audience has been prepared at length in this way, the feast in question takes place, and in this context the full text of the wondrous inscription is finally given.

Sigune's discovery of what is written on the leash makes the task which she has set Tschinotulander superfluous; and she is consequently prepared to grant him her love without further proof. However, he wishes to prove his worthiness by even greater acts of chivalry. So Tschinotulander now goes to the Orient to avenge the death of Gahmuret, and after his return he sets about restoring to Parzival the lands which are his by right. This conflict ends with the duel with Orilus, in which Tschinotulander is defeated and killed, although not because his opponent was in any way superior but because the latter (Orilus) was protected by a talisman which had in fact been intended for Tschinotulander. This brings the action up to the scene where Parzival, coming from Jeschute, encounters Sigune and her dead lover. This provides the occasion for a brief résumé of *Parzival*, in which Albrecht deals in greater detail with those elements omitted by Wolfram, that is to say Sigune's life in the wilderness, her connections with the Grail castle and Parzival's five years of wandering. The history of the Grail sword is also given in some detail. At length it comes into Ekunat's hands; he uses it on Orilus to avenge the death of Tschinotulander, killing him with its blows. Ekunat wears on his helm the hound's leash, which has meanwhile been returned to him: during the fight with Orilus it is completely destroyed. There then follows the Lohengrin story and the transfer of the Grail to India – the sinfulness of the Western world having caused the knights of the Grail to remove it to the Orient; there follows a description of the ideal world of Prester John, a kind of Utopian alternative to contemporary affairs.[5] God finally removes the Grail temple itself to India as well, and in conclusion the romance fills in the origins of the Grail – the story of how Joseph of Arimathea saved the vessel used at the Last Supper, and how it then, with the help of an angel, came to be handed down to Titurel.

The leash and its inscription play a singular role in Albrecht's universal Grail history. In Wolfram's second fragment, Sigune had begun to read an *âventiure* inscribed on the leash, a story telling of Claudite and Ehkunat: Claudite had sent the leash to Ehkunat as a

---

5   Zatloukal, 'India – ein idealer Staat'.

kind of love letter. In Wolfram's *Titurel*, Ehkunat is called *de Salvâsch flôrîen* (151,1), which he translates as *von Bluome diu wilde* (152,4).[6] Albrecht's Clauditte adapts the name as *von den blûmen ... der wilde* ('the wild man of the flowers': 1879,1), and interprets this in such a way that all crimes or outrages are *wilde*, 'foreign', to him, while the *bluomen* rcfer to his virtues (strophes 1881f.) Then the hound is named: *Gardivias, hûte der verte* ('guard the path': 1882,4; 1883,2); Albrecht then makes this a *leitmotif* of the code of ethics which then follows. It is divided into four sections: 1. a code of duties; 2. a code of morals; 3. a code of love; 4. a code of virtue.[7]

1. The 'code of duties' comprises ten strophes. The first three run as follows:

> Des ersten hût der verte   vil wol an gotes minne,
> sit ie vil gerne werte   der tiuvel swer zu got hat edel sinne,
> daz lutzel ieman got zu rehte minnet.
> nu hûte wol der verte!   der sin ob allen sinnen stet besinnet.
>
> Swer sine vart in hûte   hat an allen dingen,
> zeselden und zu gûte   iz im vrumt, so daz im mûz gelingen
> hie und dort, in ewiclichem heile.
> nu hûte wol der verte,   daz dir des himels krone werd zu teile!
>
> Des libes girde hûte   vor schemelicher verte.
> gedultikeit, diemûte   und kiusche nim dir zeiner zuhte gerte
> und minn die waren minn fur werltlich sûze.
> nu hûte wol der verte,   daz sich din vart mit selden enden mûze!
> (*Jüngerer Titurel*, 1884–6)

[First of all guard the path well with respect to the love of God; for the devil has always tried to hinder the man whose noble inclinations are turned towards God, so that very few people love God truly. Guard the path well! That sense is endowed with sense that surpasses all sense.

Whoever guards his path in every respect will find that that is for the best and that it brings good fortune, with the result that he has success in this world and in the next, in eternal bliss. Now guard the path well, that you may be granted the crown of heaven!

---

[6] There is some debate as to whether this means 'of the wild flower' or whether it should be read as *von bluomediu wilde* – 'of the flowering wilderness'. Cf. Heinzle, *Stellenkommentar zu Wolframs Titurel*, p. 202, on this passage.

[7] On this subdivision, see Huschenbett, *Albrechts 'Jüngerer Titurel'*, pp. 224ff.; cf. Hermann, 'Die Inschrift des Brackenseils', p. 41; Nyholm, *Studien zum sogenannten geblümten Stil*, pp. 56ff.; Hahn, 'Kosmologie und Zahl', pp. 241ff.

Guard the desires of the body, keep them from the path of shame. Chastize yourself with the rod of patience, humility and chastity and love true love over and above the sweet pleasures of the world. Now guard the path well, that your journey may come to a happy end.]

In the strophes which follow, everything which might be expected in a true courtesy book is brought in: e.g. the clergy should be greeted with respect and their teachings listened to; one should believe in the faith of the Church, show compassion to widows and orphans, pronounce a fair sentence at trials, fulfil chivalric obligations. This catalogue is thus concerned with duties in connection with God and the Church, ruling and knighthood.

2. The 'moral code' comprises seven strophes. These are devised in such a way that particular attributes of animals are used as graphic metaphors for parts of the human body: e.g. your eyes should be like those of the ostrich, your ears like those of the lynx, your neck as long as that of the crane – since words should not be allowed out of the throat until they have been well considered. The strength of the lion should be in one's heart, the feet should be as steady as those of the bear, and so on.[8]

3. The 'code of love' comprises ten strophes. It begins with courtly love: *minne* must be guarded – it needs *huote*; through this *vröude* is achieved; where the former is lacking, the latter is lost. One should choose a beloved, one's *minnetrût*, who is *von edeler wurze smac* ('has the fragrance of fine herbs'), which is to be taken to mean equipped with virtues. Any kind of *unadel* ('ignoble behaviour') is a threat to *tugent* ('virtue'). The ambiguity of *minne* is then discussed, the relationship between *triuwe* and *minne*, married and unmarried love; and the honour of women, which must not be compromised. The final strophes run as follows:

> Pfaffen unde vrowen   an eren nieman krenke.
> sin wirde wirt verhowen,   ich wen, er hoher eren anker senke
> in schanden grunt, da er immer lit versunken.
> nu hûte wol der verte,   du mûst mich anders ungevaren bedunken!
>
> Die vrowen sint uns bernde   zer werlt, zu got die pfaffen.
> wer ist uns hoher wernde   deheiner seld ane got, der da geschaffen

---

8   On these comparisons with animals, see Hermann, 'Die Inschrift des Brackenseils', pp. 19ff.; Parshall, *The Art of Narration*, p. 149 and note 49 on p. 255. Gerhardt, 'Reinmars von Zweter *Idealer Mann*', 56f. and note 12, and Curschmann, *Facies peccatorum – Vir bonus*, p. 175, argue that Albrecht is indebted to Reinmar von Zweter's *Der ideale Mann*.

si hat uns und uns in zallem heile?
nu hůte wol der verte, so bistu hie und dort der selden geile!
(*Jüngerer Titurel*, 1909–10)

[May no one affront the clergy or women. That man's reputation
takes a battering, I think, who sinks the anchor of great honour into
the abyss of shame, where it will lie sunk for ever. Now guard the
path well, otherwise I believe you will make no progress at all!

It is women who give birth to us when we come into the world, the
clergy when we come to God. Who can better grant us blessedness
than God, who created them as a blessing for us and us as a blessing
for them? Now guard the path well, then you will be blessed with
rewards both in this world and the next!]

4. The 'code of virtue' is presented in seventeen strophes as a
garland of twelve flowers. These are: *belde* ('bravery'), *kiusche*
('purity'), *milte* ('generosity'), *triuwe* ('fidelity'), *mâze* ('moderation'),
sorge ('concern'), *schame* ('shame'), *bescheidenheit* ('knowledge', 'discernment'), *stæte* ('constancy'), *diemüete* ('humility'), *gedult* ('patience'), and the twelfth virtue is referred to as 'minne ûzerhalp der
valschen sinne' ('that love that lies beyond the falseness of the
senses'). The central position is occupied by *mâze*, to which five
whole strophes are dedicated.

The inscription on the hound's leash is structured according to a
clear scheme. This love letter from Clauditte to Ekunat contains a
comprehensive chivalric code of conduct with a quite specific intention. The catalogue of duties, representing an external or objective
order, begins with the love of God and then moves on to worldly
obligations. The 'subjective order', the catalogue of the duties contained in the next section, seeks to establish control over the senses
and parts of the body, a theme which echoes elements of the
preceding catalogue of duties. The code of love that follows begins
with courtly love and goes on to intertwine secular and religious
perspectives: honour is due to women and clerics alike. However, the
perspective is opened out at the end to include God, without which
dimension *sælde* cannot be attained, either here or in the hereafter.
The last section, the code of virtues, places *mâze* in the centre with
five strophes to itself; *mâze* is here seen less in terms of the balance of
social and individual aspects which characterized the 'classical'
Arthurian romance than as 'moderation' or 'self-restraint'. Love,
however, appears again as the final flower of virtue, as the love of

God: 'minne ûzerhalp der valschen sinne'. Thematically, then, the inscription has come full circle; earthly virtue and earthly love are seen from the perspective of the love of God, and this scheme is reflected in the use of symbolic numbers in its construction: ten strophes for the various duties, seven for moral conduct, ten for love and seventeen for virtue; ten is the number of the Ten Commandments, seven the number of the Holy Spirit: furthermore, 10 + 7 refers to the Old and New Testaments; in other words, seventeen is the ideal number, embracing both Law and grace. The inscription is thus a synoptic presentation of the Law of the Old and the Love of the New Testament.[9]

II

What is it that moves Sigune to send Schionatulander out to risk life and limb in the quest for the hound's leash? The point of this craving was left open in Wolfram's version of the story; in *Der jüngere Titurel*, Albrecht offers a solution by giving the text of the inscription on the hound's leash. In other words, the inscription is his answer to the problems raised by Wolfram's *Titurel* fragments; it contains in a nutshell his understanding of Wolfram. The quest for the leash, and thus the thematic core of the romance, represents a search for a system of values which combines and interweaves secular and religious concerns from a spiritual perspective. At the nub of the web of *âventiure* is the revelation of the doctrine inscribed on the leash at the feast at Floritschanze. This revelation of the meaning of the romance in an ethical code is able to subsume the tragic aspect inherent in Wolfram's fragments, since the emphasis shifts from the individual fates of Sigune and Schionatulander to the history of the Grail, and the world of the Grail is imbued with that very system of values which is inscribed on the leash. Each individual must justify his or her life in terms of this system – or find justification in it; earthly ambitions and their consequences – victory or death – become largely irrelevant. Thus even in defeat Tschinotulander can continue to represent the ideal faultless hero. The scheme of *Der jüngere Titurel*, then, no longer relies on the absolute success of the hero; it is enough

---

[9] Cf. chapter 8, p. 150 above. More generally on numbers in the composition of *Der jüngere Titurel*, see Huschenbett, *Albrechts 'Jüngerer Titurel'*, passim.; Hahn, 'Kosmologie und Zahl', pp. 240ff.

for him to prove himself by the standards of this moral code, even, indeed especially, if this means forfeiting his life.[10]

The poetic world in which the figures move is defined here too by the tasks with which this new type of hero is faced. The world of *âventiure* contained in *Der jüngere Titurel* aspires to a quasi-historical reality;[11] the action unfolds within a more or less geographically exact space comprising Spain, France, the Near East and India. Whereas in *Wigalois* or *Daniel* the world of the hero is presented as fantastically grotesque and he himself is favoured by either fortune or skill, the principle of moral rectitude confronts the knights in *Titurel* with conflicts on a strictly human scale. For this reason, the fantastical and magical dimension is almost entirely absent. When it does appear, it either takes the form of a divine miracle in connection with the Grail – which arrives on earth in a supernatural manner, just as the ground-plan of the Grail temple appears miraculously at the place where it is to be built, and so on – or else in the guise of magic to explain the defeat of even the best knights, for example the death of Tschinotulander. As there is no longer any need for a particular structure to the *âventiure* sequences, the classical Arthurian scheme can now be abandoned entirely, since on the one hand every action is directly answerable to the moral code, and on the other individual desires and ambitions have little effect on the history of the Grail.[12]

Thus in Germany too – although in a form quite different from Robert de Boron's work – the Arthurian romance is re-integrated into the *Heilsgeschichte*.[13] It is significant that the impetus for this change should have come from Wolfram's radical exposure of the problems of the literary type. This also implies that any subsequent adaptation and elaboration of the model, in order to transcend this critical moment in the development, inevitably has to alter its basic underlying premisses. Thus in Albrecht's romance the narrative is no longer related, as it was in Wolfram's fragments, from the perspective of the characters' experience of death, but instead sets its sights on the moral code of the inscription on the leash. Albrecht avoids the problems inherent in chivalric action by embedding the latter in a fictional world in which *Heilsgeschichte* supplies a framework of a

[10] Ragotzky, *Studien zur Wolfram-Rezeption*, p. 116.

[11] See Ebenbauer, 'Tschionatulander und Artus', 397ff., for an account of the process of 'historicization' in connection with the disintegration of the Arthurian structure.

[12] Ragotzky, *Studien zur Wolfram-Rezeption*, pp. 113ff.; Ebenbauer, 'Tschionatulander und Artus', 385ff.

[13] A. G. Thornton, *Weltgeschichte und Heilsgeschichte*.

greater dimension than the fates of individual characters. Whereas in Wolfram's *Titurel*, the festive *vröude* of the Arthurian romance is replaced by Sigune's mourning in the lonely cell, Albrecht restores the *vröude*. However, the Arthurian feast which is thus revived is no longer the Utopia it represented in Chrétien's model, but instead finds its culmination in the revelation of the code of ethics inscribed on the leash, in other words the representation of an external code of values, which is already anticipated in the concept of the Grail Kingdom: this corresponds on the level of the plot to the universal history of the Grail. In this way the leash with its inscription also ultimately becomes redundant after Parzival has become the Grail king, and can be destroyed in the fight in which Orilus meets his death. The inscription and its code are ultimately realized in the eternal realm of the Grail kingdom – albeit at the same time removed to an ideal, if unattainable, distance.[14]

Thus it will be seen that Albrecht's answer to the questions left open in Wolfram's *Titurel* fragments is diametrically opposed to Wolfram's own scheme, regardless of how the latter is interpreted. What is more, this re-interpretation was a deliberate and programmatic move on Albrecht's part. This could not be shown more plainly than in the eighty-five strophes of the prologue, which paraphrases and interprets the introduction to *Parzival*, with some echoes of the prologue to *Willehalm*.[15] Some of Wolfram's ideas or motifs give rise to elaborate excursuses, for example Wolfram's comment about the people who are said to be both black and white. Albrecht adds a didactic comment of his own on the colour *blank* ('white'), referring to baptism and the cleansing powers of water, which he places in the context of a theory of the elements.[16] Most illuminating, however, is Albrecht's comment on Wolfram's question about the *stiure*, or direction, of the *mære* ('tale'). Wolfram had insisted that the story could only be understood if the hero's progress were followed by the audience. Albrecht turns this into its exact opposite, claiming that the *stiure* of the *mære* is the *sinneriche lere* (59,4), the moral lesson: 'Dirre aventûre kere, si si krump oder slihte, / daz ist nicht wan ein lere'

---

[14] On the complex function of the hound's leash, see Parshall, *The Art of Narration*, pp. 136ff.

[15] Ragotzky, *Studien zur Wolfram-Rezeption*, pp. 102ff.; Kleinschmidt, 'Literarische Rezeption und Geschichte', 624ff.; Huschenbett, *Albrechts 'Jüngerer Titurel'*, pp. 166ff.; W. Schröder, *Demontage und Montage*. Alongside this Albrecht also makes use of quite different sources, such as the sermons of Berthold von Regensburg: see Röll, 'Berthold von Regensburg und der *Jüngere Titurel*', 82ff.

[16] Kern, 'Der Kommentar zu *Parzival*'.

('Whether the direction of this tale be straight or crooked, it continues to be a tale with a lesson'; 65,1f.). Wolfram's theoretical position is thus reversed: the didactic purpose, which Wolfram perceived as emphatically not part of the task of the poet, becomes the guiding principle of Albrecht's work, and so it is only logical that the central symbol of the *Titurel* story, the hound's leash, should become the vehicle for a moral code.[17]

For Albrecht, as for Konrad von Würzburg, using poetry as a medium for imparting a didactic message proves problematic; however, the moral import of the romance means more than simply setting up exemplary models of behaviour embodied in the characters of the romance, as with Thomasin, even though Albrecht readily quotes such figures as examples.[18] Like Konrad, Albrecht reflects on this in comments on the potential effects and reception of his work. These do not, however, take the form of explicit theoretical statements, but rather they are linked to the vehicle for his ethical code, namely the hound's leash. In other words, Albrecht's theory of reception is contained, to all intents and purposes, in what he has to say about the properties and effects of the famous inscription.

The inscription on the hound's leash, it is said, exerts an irresistible, magical attraction, so that any one who begins to read it has to read to the end, and anyone who has once read it is compelled to read it over and over again. Reading the inscription brings release from all cares, heals all ills, and brings happiness. This amazing effect is due, so Albrecht assures us, to the fact that when the inscription was being fashioned something of both the wisdom of Solomon and the song of the Sirens crept in; in other words, wisdom is here combined with magic. The magical effect is said to be derived in particular from the power of the precious stones out of which the inscription is fashioned, although admittedly another passage also states that it is the Code of Virtue on the leash which, when heard, is responsible for the destruction of all evils. Underlying this singular description of the effects of the text, if it is to be taken seriously, is nothing other than the idea of a certain magical element in the poetic transmission of the ethical code. Thus the magic of the poetic form is able to succeed where a merely didactic concept of poetry, seeking to provide exemplary models to illustrate its doctrine, would lack conviction.

[17] Hahn, 'Kosmologie und Zahl', points out that this doctrine is contained within a hymn of praise to creation in the traditional manner.
[18] Cf. Fromm, 'Der *Jüngere Titurel*', 19ff.

That this interpretation is legitimate is confirmed by Albrecht's highly developed stylistic awareness.[19] As will be recalled, the message on the leash is sent by Clauditte to Ekunat, who is given the name 'von den blŭmen ... der wilde'. Albrecht takes up the play on the term *wilde* begun by Wolfram and elaborates on it, and thus the introduction to the inscription culminates in the following strophe:

> Du eren pflicht geselle,   du wilde blŭme riche,
> in wildez walt gevelle   send ich dir wilden boten wildicliche
> und wilden prief mit wilder boteschefte.
> der bot genant Gardivias.   der nam hat richeit vil und tugend krefte.
> (*Jüngerer Titurel*, 1882)

[You who have obliged yourself to win fame, you flower wonderful and wild, I send to you in my wildness into the wild clefted forest a wild messenger and a wild letter with a wild message. The messenger is called Gardivias. That name is full of might and excellent powers.]

Albrecht seems deliberately to have set out to run through all possible shades of meaning of the word *wilde*. Ekunat is *wilde* because all wrong deeds are 'foreign' to him; the woodland ravine is *wilde*, i.e. deeply fissured and impenetrable; the *wilde* messenger refers to the hound, a strange kind of postman; *wildicliche* characterizes the surprising and perhaps secretive behaviour on Clauditte's part in sending her love letter in this form; with reference to the letter, *wilde* can be taken to refer to the astonishing and precious form of the inscription; while finally, with regard to the message, *wilde* can be taken to include all the strange and wonderful things which are related about the inscription. At the same time, this strophe is itself a paradigm of the *wildekeit* of Albrecht's style, which, in his over-sophisticated *Titurel*-strophe, abounds in amazingly convoluted and bizarre figures of speech. *Der wilde von den bluomen* certainly seems a fitting addressee for a message which is itself *wilde* in the sense of 'figurative', 'flowery' or 'mannered'. Finally, this could be seen as a hint that this message should also be taken as a self-portrait of Albrecht's own idiosyncratic style. The precious stones with their magic powers, of which the inscription on the leash is fashioned, stand for the artistry of the form, the magic of which draws the audience into the spell of the moral code propounded on the leash. The modern critic, who has difficulty enough in reading the work, will scarcely be convinced by this claim. However, from the point of

---

[19] Cf. also Ragotzky, *Studien zur Wolfram-Rezeption*, pp. 127ff.

view of the great success of the work in its own time, Albrecht's strategy of reception and his principle of *wildekeit* have been shown to be vindicated.[20]

[20] On the later reception of the work, see Fechter, *Das Publikum der mittelhochdeutschen Dichtung*, pp. 40ff.

Concluding remarks

Albrecht's *Der jüngere Titurel* represents in some respects the culmination of the literary and theoretical development which began in the twelfth century with the arrival of the fictional romance in Germany. If it can be said that the *Lancelot en prose* represents the final response in French to the problems which the emergence of this new type brought with it, then *Der jüngere Titurel* may stand beside it as the equivalent German response, although the solutions it presents are quite different. Both works sought to re-integrate the Arthurian world of *âventiure* into a concept based loosely on the pattern of *Heilsgeschichte*. In France, however, this coincided with the new form of the prose romance, which created scope for a freer, more differentiated treatment of the Arthurian tradition; the new form made possible a complex interweaving of the strands of the plot with a view ultimately to incorporating all the multifarious traditions of romance material. This led to bold combinations and shifts of perspective; the meaning, or the search for it, was intended to emerge from such *entrelacement* of the action – or, alternatively, was to be realized in the awareness of the possibility – or indeed impossibility – of ever escaping from the web of interlocking plots and sub-plots. Thus the *Queste* and the *Mort Artu* represent two opposite extremes of the diversification of the Lancelot material: on the one hand the search for the Grail, and on the other the breakdown of the Arthurian world.

In Germany, a different situation prevailed; there, the verse form was retained with a determination which seems nothing less than programmatic. This means that the development of the Arthurian romance always took the form of critical and experimental variations on Chrétien's model, occasionally leading to the creation of counter-models. Even where it was programatically rejected or subverted, the 'classical' Arthurian tradition was always present as a background, and was never jettisoned completely as in the French prose romance. Ultimately, however, in Germany too the Arthurian material was re-integrated into the framework of the fictitious history of the Grail; that is to say, here too the traditional Arthurian scheme was abandoned or, to be more precise, superseded. It is significant that this development should occur in a work which made use of a metrical form which was itself deliberately mannered: the compli-cated, over-wrought *Titurel*-strophe may serve as a fitting symbol for the extreme formal stylization through which the German tradition ultimately attempts to guarantee the truth of its message. At the same time, there was an acute awareness of the problems associated with this extreme position, inasmuch as the critical adaptation of the Arthurian model had begun, by the end of the thirteenth century, to raise the increasingly urgent question of the relationship between artistry and morals: Konrad von Würzburg explicitly addressed this very question. Albrecht carried the divergence of ethics and aesthetics to its logical extreme, endowing artistic form with magical properties and linking it to a system of values which he is then able to substantiate – at least in part – by reference to the Grail story. Robert de Boron's version of the latter may thus be seen to have had a profound – albeit belated – effect on the Arthurian tradition in Germany also, although this took a form radically different from its earlier impact in France.

After Albrecht, the tradition in Germany had little to offer in the way of new possibilities. The production of new Arthurian ro-mances petered out in the fourteenth century, although the process of reception of course continued. This may be seen as a justification for curtailing our survey of the history of poetic theories and concepts in Germany at this point. Of course, the positions reached at the end of the thirteenth century continue to hold sway for a long time, and it is tempting to trace these poetological developments further, demonstrating at the same time how even elements which remain constant appear in a new light when set against the back-ground of changing historical circumstances. On the other hand, from the fourteenth century onwards a far-reaching process of change may be observed in almost all areas of culture and society, so that it would be impossible to begin to do justice to the new situation without starting afresh and looking forward far into the following centuries.[1] Such an investigation, however, must remain outside the scope of the present study.

---

[1] In the meantime, see Haug, 'Das Bildprogramm im Sommerhaus von Runkelstein'; also the relevant articles in Haug et al., *Zur deutschen Literatur und Sprache des 14. Jahrhunderts*; in Grenzmann and Stackmann, *Literatur und Laienbildung*; and particularly in the series 'Fortuna vitrea', founded and edited by Burghart Wachinger and myself (Tübingen 1991–), which is devoted to research on the transition from the late Middle Ages to the early modern period.

Bibliography

I. PRIMARY WORKS: EDITIONS AND TRANSLATIONS

Alberic of Pisançon, *Alexandre. The Medieval French 'Roman d'Alexandre'*, vol. III, ed. Alfred Foulet (Elliott Monographs in the Romance Languages and Literatures 38), Princeton 1949, pp. 37–41; repr. in Rodney Sampson (ed.), *Early Romance Texts*, Cambridge 1980, pp. 97–100.

Albrecht [von Scharfenberg], *Jüngerer Titurel*, ed. Werner Wolf and Kurt Nyholm, 4 vols. (Deutsche Texte des Mittelalters 45; 56 and 61; 73/1–2; 79), Berlin 1955–96.

Das Alexanderlied [Straßburger Alexander], in *Lamprechts Alexander, nach den 3 Texten mit dem Fragment des Alberic von Besançon und den lateinischen Quellen*, ed. Karl Kinzel, Halle 1884; repr. in Irene Ruttmann, *Das Alexanderlied des Pfaffen Lamprecht (Straßburger Alexander). Text, Nacherzählung, Worterklärungen*, Darmstadt 1974; Engl. trans. by J. W. Thomas, *The Strassburg Alexander and the Munich Oswald*, Columbia 1989.

Das Annolied, ed. and German trans. by Eberhard Nellmann (Reclams Universal-Bibliothek 1416); 3rd edn, Stuttgart 1986.

Augustine, *De doctrina christiana*, ed. Joseph Martin (Corpus Christianorum series latina 32), Turnhout 1962, pp. 1–167; Engl. trans. by D. W. Robertson, Jr., *On Christian Doctrine*, Indianapolis 1958.

Chrétien de Troyes, *Les Romans*, vol. I: *Erec et Enide*, ed. Mario Roques, Paris 1955; Engl. trans. in William W. Kibler, *Arthurian Romances*, Penguin Classics, Harmondsworth 1991, pp. 37–122 (*Erec and Enide* trans. by Carleton W. Carroll).

Les Romans, vol. III: *Le Chevalier de la Charrette*, ed. Mario Roques, Paris 1958; Engl. trans. in Kibler, *Arthurian Romances*, pp. 207–94.

Cligés, ed. Alexandre Micha, Paris 1957; Engl. trans. in Kibler, *Arthurian Romances*, pp. 123–205.

Yvain, Der Löwenritter. Textausgabe mit Variantenauswahl, Einleitung, erklärenden Anmerkungen und vollständigem Glossar, ed. Wendelin Foerster; 4th edn, Halle 1912; Engl. trans. in Kibler, *Arthurian Romances*, pp. 295–380.

Deutung der Meßgebräuche, in Maurer, *Die religiösen Dichtungen*, vol. II, pp. 290–315.

Eilhart von Oberge, *Tristrant*, ed. Franz Lichtenstein, Strassburg 1877; repr. Hildesheim/New York 1973; Engl. trans. by J. W. Thomas, Lincoln, Nebraska 1978.

382

Bibliography: primary works

Exodus. Die altdeutsche Exodus, ed. Edgar Papp (Medium Aevum 16), Munich 1968.

Frühe deutsche Literatur und lateinische Literatur in Deutschland 800–1150, ed. Walter Haug and Benedikt Konrad Vollmann (Bibliothek des Mittelalters 1 = Bibliothek deutscher Klassiker 62), Frankfurt am Main 1991.

Gottfried von Strassburg, *Tristan. Nach der Ausgabe von Reinhold Bechstein*, ed. Peter Ganz, 2 vols. (Deutsche Klassiker des Mittelalters n.s. 4), Wiesbaden 1978.

Tristan, ed. Friedrich Ranke; 4th edn, Dublin and Zurich 1959; Engl. trans. by Arthur T. Hatto, Penguin Classics, Harmondsworth 1960.

Hartmann von Aue, *Iwein*, ed. Georg F. Benecke, Karl Lachmann and Ludwig Wolff; 7th edn, Berlin 1968; Engl. trans. by Rodney W. Fisher, *The Narrative Works of Hartmann von Aue* (Göppinger Arbeiten zur Germanistik 370), Göppingen 1983, pp. 177–270.

Der arme Heinrich, ed. Hermann Paul, Ludwig Wolff and Gesa Bonath (Altdeutsche Textbibliothek 3); 15th edn, Tübingen 1984; Engl. trans. by Fisher, *The Narrative Works*, pp. 157–75.

Gregorius, ed. Hermann Paul and Burghart Wachinger (Altdeutsche Textbibliothek 2); 14th edn, Tübingen 1992; Engl. trans. by Fisher, *The Narrative Works*, pp. 111–55.

Heinrich von dem Türlîn, *Diu Crône*, ed. Gottlob Heinrich Friedrich Scholl (Bibliothek des Stuttgarter Literarischen Vereins 27), Stuttgart 1852; repr. Amsterdam 1966; the passages cited re-edited in Arno Mentzel-Reuters, *Vröude. Artusbild, Fortuna- und Gralskonzeption in der 'Crône' des Heinrich von dem Türlin als Verteidigung des höfischen Lebensideals* (Europäische Hochschulschriften 1,1134), Frankfurt am Main 1989; Engl. trans. by J. W. Thomas, Lincoln, Nebraska 1989.

Heinrich von Melk, ed. Richard Heinzel, Berlin 1867.

Heinrich von Veldeke/Henric van Veldeken, *Eneide*, ed. Gabriele Schieb and Theodor Frings (Deutsche Texte des Mittelalters 58), Berlin 1964; Engl. trans. by J. W. Thomas (Garland Library of Medieval Literature B38), New York 1985.

Das himmlische Jerusalem, in Waag and Schröder (eds.), *Kleinere deutsche Gedichte*, pp. 92–111.

Johannes, *The Old French Johannes Translation of the Pseudo-Turpin Chronicle*, ed. Ronald N. Walpole, Berkeley 1976.

Johannes von Tepl, *Der ackerman*, ed. Willy Krogmann (Deutsche Klassiker des Mittelalters n.s. 1); 4th edn, Wiesbaden 1978; Engl. trans. by K. W. Maurer, London 1947.

Judith. Die jüngere Judith aus der Vorauer Handschrift, ed. Hiltgunt Monecke (Altdeutsche Textbibliothek 61), Tübingen 1964.

Die Kaiserchronik, ed. Edward Schröder (Monumenta Germaniae Historica: Deutsche Chroniken 1,1), Hanover 1892; repr. Berlin 1964.

König Rother, ed. Theodor Frings and Joachim Kuhnt; 2nd edn, Halle 1961; Engl. trans. by Robert Lichtenstein, Chapel Hill 1962.

Konrad von Würzburg, *Engelhard*, ed. Paul Gereke and Ingo Reiffenstein (Altdeutsche Textbibliothek 17); 3rd edn, Tübingen 1982.

Die Klage der Kunst, in *Kleinere Dichtungen Konrads von Würzburg* III, ed. Edward Schröder and Ludwig Wolff; 4th edn, Berlin 1970.

Bibliography: primary works

Partonopier und Meliur. Turnei von Nantheiz. Sant Nicolaus. Lieder und Sprüche, ed. Karl Bartsch, Vienna 1871; repr. Berlin, 3rd edn 1969.

Sylvester. Die Legenden I. Sylvester, ed. Paul Gereke (Altdeutsche Textbibliothek 19), Halle 1925.

Der Troianische Krieg von Konrad von Würzburg, ed. Adelbert von Keller (Bibliothek des Stuttgarter Literarischen Vereins 44), Stuttgart 1858; repr. Amsterdam 1965.

Konrad (Pfaffe), Rolandslied, in Das Alexanderlied des Pfaffen Lamprecht. Das Rolandslied des Pfaffen Konrad, ed. Friedrich Maurer (Deutsche Literatur in Entwicklungsreihen, Geistliche Dichtung des Mittelalters 5), Leipzig 1940; repr. Darmstadt 1964, pp. 47–313; Engl. trans. by J. W. Thomas, Columbia 1994.

Lambrecht, Alexander, in Maurer, Das Alexanderlied des Pfaffen Lamprecht, pp. 21–46.

Das Lob Salomons, in Maurer, Die religiösen Dichtungen, vol. I, pp. 317–26; in Waag and Schröder (eds.), Kleinere deutsche Gedichte, vol. I, pp. 43–55.

Der deutsche 'Lucidarius'. Vol. I: Kritischer Text nach den Handschriften, ed. Dagmar Gottschall and Georg Steer (Texte und Textgeschichte 35), Tübingen 1994.

Maurer, Friedrich (ed.), Die religiösen Dichtungen des 11. und 12. Jahrhunderts, 3 vols., Tübingen 1964, 1965, 1970.

Moriz von Craûn, ed. Ulrich Pretzel (Altdeutsche Textbibliothek 45); 4th edn, Tübingen 1973; Engl. trans. by Stephanie Cain Van D'Elden (Garland Library of Medieval Literature A69), New York 1990.

Otfrid [von Weißenburg], Evangelienbuch, ed. Oskar Erdmann and Ludwig Wolff (Altdeutsche Textbibliothek 49); 6th edn, Tübingen 1973.

Pierre de Beauvais, Le Bestiaire de Pierre de Beauvais (Version courte). Edition critique avec notes et glossaire, ed. Guy R. Mermier, Paris 1977.

Der Pleier, Meleranz, ed. Karl Bartsch (Bibliothek des Stuttgarter Literarischen Vereins 60), Stuttgart 1861; repr. with an afterword by Alexander Hildebrand, Hildesheim/New York 1974; Engl. trans by J. W. Thomas, The Pleier's Arthurian Romances. Garel of the Blooming Valley, Tandareis and Flordibel, Meleranz (Garland Library of Medieval Literature B91), New York and London 1992.

Pseudo-Turpin Chronicle, see under Johannes.

Robert de Boron, Le Roman de l'estoire dou Graal, ed. William Nitze, Paris 1927; Engl. trans. by Jean Rogers, London 1990.

Rudolf von Ems, Alexander. Ein höfischer Versroman des 13. Jahrhunderts, ed. Victor Junk (Bibliothek des Stuttgarter Literarischen Vereins 272, 274), Leipzig 1928–9; repr. Darmstadt 1970.

Barlaam und Josaphat, ed. Franz Pfeiffer (Dichtungen des deutschen Mittelalters 3), Leipzig 1843; repr. Berlin 1965.

Der guote Gêrhart, ed. John A. Asher (Altdeutsche Textbibliothek 56); 3rd edn, Tübingen 1989.

Weltchronik, ed. Gustav Ehrismann (Deutsche Texte des Mittelalters 20), Berlin 1915; repr. Zurich 1967.

Willehalm von Orlens, ed. Victor Junk (Deutsche Texte des Mittelalters 2), Berlin 1905; repr. Zurich 1967.

Bibliography: secondary literature

Sanct Brandan. Ein lateinischer und drei deutsche Texte, ed. Carl Schröder, Erlangen 1871.

St. Veit, in Maurer, *Die religiösen Dichtungen*, vol. III, pp. 615–19.

Der Stricker, *Daniel von dem Blühenden Tal*, ed. Michael Resler (Altdeutsche Textbibliothek 92), Tübingen 1983; Engl. trans. by Michael Resler (Garland Library of Medieval Literature B58), New York 1990.

Thomas, *Le Roman de Tristan* ed. Félix Lecoy, Paris 1991; Engl. trans. in Gottfried von Strassburg, *Tristan*, trans. Arthur T. Hatto, Penguin Classics, Harmondsworth 1960, pp. 299–353.

Thomasin von Zirclaria, *Der wälsche Gast*, ed. Heinrich Rückert (Bibliothek der gesammten deutschen National-Literatur 30), Quedlinburg and Leipzig 1852; repr. with an introduction and index by Friedrich Neumann, Berlin 1965.

Ulrich von Eschenbach, *Alexander*, ed. Wendelin Toischer (Bibliothek des Stuttgarter Literarischen Vereins 183), Stuttgart and Tübingen 1888; repr. Hildesheim/New York 1974.

Ulrich von Etzenbach, *Wilhelm von Wenden*, ed. Hans-Friedrich Rosenfeld (Deutsche Texte des Mittelalters 49), Berlin 1957.

Waag, Albert, and Werner Schröder (eds.), *Kleinere deutsche Gedichte des 11. und 12. Jahrhunderts*, 2 vols. (Altdeutsche Textbibliothek 71–2); 2nd edn, Tübingen 1972.

Die Wahrheit, in Waag and Schröder (eds.), *Kleinere deutsche Gedichte*, vol. II, pp. 184–92.

Wiener Genesis. Die frühmittelhochdeutsche Wiener Genesis, ed. Kathryn Smits (Philologische Studien und Quellen 59), Berlin 1972.

Der Wilde Mann, *Van der girheit*, in *Die Gedichte des Wilden Mannes*, ed. Bernard Standring (Altdeutsche Textbibliothek 59), Tübingen 1963, pp. 31–43.

Wirnt von Gravenberc, *Wigalois der Ritter mit dem Rade*, ed. J. M. N. Kapteyn, Bonn 1926; Engl. trans. by J. W. Thomas, Lincoln, Nebraska and London 1977.

Wolfram von Eschenbach, *Parzival*, in *Wolfram von Eschenbach*, ed. Karl Lachmann; 6th edn, Berlin and Leipzig 1926, pp. 11–388; Engl. trans. by Arthur T. Hatto, Penguin Classics, Harmondsworth 1980.

Titurel, in *Wolfram von Eschenbach*, ed. Lachmann, pp. 389–420; Engl. trans. by Marion E. Gibbs and Sidney M. Johnson (Garland Library of Medieval Literature A57), New York 1988.

Willehalm, in *Wolfram von Eschenbach*, ed. Lachmann, pp. 421–640; Engl. trans. by Marion E. Gibbs and Sidney M. Johnson, Penguin Classics, Harmondsworth 1984.

2. SECONDARY LITERATURE

Aarne, Antti, and Stith Thompson, *The Types of the Folktale. A Classification and Bibliography* (FF Communications 184), Helsinki 1961.

Adolf, Helen, 'Studies in the "Perlesvaus". The historical background', *Studies in Philology* 43 (1945), pp. 723–40.

'The theological and feudal background of Wolfram's *zwivel*', *The Journal of English and Germanic Philology* 49 (1950), pp. 285–303.

Bibliography: secondary literature

Altmann, Michael, *Strukturuntersuchungen zu Giraldus Cambrensis' 'De Principis Instructione'*, diss. Regensburg 1974.

Anderegg, Johannes, *Fiktion und Kommunikation. Ein Beitrag zur Theorie der Prosa*, Göttingen 1973.

'Das Fiktionale und das Ästhetische', in Henrich and Iser (eds.), *Funktionen des Fiktiven*, pp. 153–72.

Arbusow, Leonid, *Colores rhetorici. Eine Auswahl rhetorischer Figuren und Gemeinplätze als Hilfsmittel für akademische Übungen an mittelalterlichen Texten*, Göttingen 1948; 2nd edn, 1963.

Assmann, Aleida, *Die Legitimität der Fiktion. Ein Beitrag zur Geschichte der literarischen Kommunikation* (Theorie und Geschichte der Literatur und der schönen Künste 55), Munich 1980.

Auerbach, Erich, 'Figura', *Archivum Romanicum* 22 (1938), pp. 436–89; repr. in Auerbach, *Neue Dantestudien*, pp. 11–71, and in Erich Auerbach, *Gesammelte Aufsätze zur romanischen Philologie*, Berne and Munich 1967, pp. 55–92; Engl. trans. in Erich Auerbach, *Scenes from the Drama of European Literature*, New York 1959.

'Sacrae Scripturae sermo humilis', *Neuphilologische Mitteilungen* 42 (1941), pp. 57–67; repr. in Auerbach, *Neue Dantestudien*, pp. 1–10.

Neue Dantestudien (Istanbuler Schriften 5), Istanbul 1944.

'Sermo humilis', *Romanische Forschungen* 64 (1952), pp. 304–64; repr. in Auerbach, *Literatursprache und Publikum*, pp. 25–53.

'Lateinische Prosa des frühen Mittelalters', *Romanische Forschungen* 66 (1955), pp. 1–64; repr. in Auerbach, *Literatursprache und Publikum*, pp. 65–133.

Literatursprache und Publikum in der lateinischen Spätantike und im Mittelalter, Berne 1958; Engl. trans. by Ralph Manheim, *Literary Language and its Public in Late Latin Antiquity and in the Middle Ages*, London 1965; repr. with a new foreword by Jan Ziolkowski, Princeton 1993 (Bollinger Series 74).

Baesecke, Georg, 'Die Karlische Renaissance und das deutsche Schrifttum', *Deutsche Vierteljahrsschrift* 23 (1949), pp. 143–216.

Baeumer, Max L. (ed.), *Toposforschung* (Wege der Forschung 395), Darmstadt 1973 (with bibliography).

Bäuml, Franz H., 'Varieties and consequences of medieval literacy and illiteracy', *Speculum* 55 (1980), pp. 237–65.

Baldwin, Charles Sears, *Medieval Rhetoric and Poetic (to 1400), interpreted from Representative Works*, New York 1928; repr. Gloucester, Mass. 1959.

Balthasar, Hans Urs von, *Herrlichkeit. Eine theologische Ästhetik*, 3 vols., Einsiedeln 1961–9; Engl. trans. by Erasmo Leiva-Merikakis et al., *Glory of the Lord. A Theological Aesthetics*, 7 vols., Edinburgh 1982–91.

Bandmann, Günter, *Mittelalterliche Architektur als Bedeutungsträger*, Berlin 1951; repr. Darmstadt 1969; 5th edn, 1978.

Barmeyer, Eike, *Die Musen. Ein Beitrag zur Inspirationstheorie* (Humanistische Bibliothek, I, 2), Munich 1968.

Beckers, Hartmut, 'Buch Sidrach', in Ruh et al. (eds.), *Verfasserlexikon*, vol. I, cols. 1097–9.

Beckmann, Jan P., et al. (eds.), *Sprache und Erkenntnis im Mittelalter* (Miscellanea Mediaevalia 13/1), Berlin and New York 1981.

Bibliography: secondary literature

Behr, Hans-Joachim, *Literatur als Machtlegitimation. Studien zur Funktion der deutschsprachigen Dichtung am böhmischen Königshof im 13. Jahrhundert* (Forschungen zur Geschichte der älteren deutschen Literatur 9), Munich 1989.

Beichner, Paul E., 'The allegorical interpretation of medieval literature', *Publications of the Modern Language Association of America* 82 (1967), pp. 33–8.

Bennholdt-Thomsen, Anke, 'Die allegorischen *kleit* im *Gregorius*-Prolog', *Euphorion* 56 (1962), pp. 174–84; repr. in Kuhn and Cormeau (eds.), *Hartmann von Aue*, pp. 195–216.

Berg, Elisabeth, 'Das Ludwigslied und die Schlacht bei Saucourt', *Rheinische Vierteljahrsblätter* 29 (1964), pp. 175–99.

Bertau, Karl, 'Das deutsche Rolandslied und die Repräsentationskunst Heinrichs des Löwen, *Der Deutschunterricht* 20/2 (1968), pp. 4–30.

Deutsche Literatur im europäischen Mittelalter, 2 vols., Munich 1972–3.

'Versuch über den späten Chrestien und die Anfänge Wolframs von Eschenbach', in Ganz and Schröder (eds.), *Probleme mittelalterlicher Erzählformen*, pp. 73–106; revised version in Bertau, *Wolfram von Eschenbach*, pp. 24–59.

'Das Recht des Andern. Über den Ursprung der Vorstellung von einer Schonung der Irrgläubigen bei Wolfram von Eschenbach', in Alfred Wendehorst and Jürgen Schneider (eds.), *Schriften des Zentralinstituts für Fränkische Landeskunde und Allgemeine Regionalforschung der Universität Erlangen-Nürnberg* 22, Neustadt an der Aisch 1982, pp. 127–43; repr. in Bertau, *Wolfram von Eschenbach*, pp. 241–58.

Wolfram von Eschenbach. Neun Versuche über Subjektivität und Ursprünglichkeit in der Geschichte, Munich 1983.

'Beobachtungen zum Ich in der "Goldenen Schmiede"', in Grenzmann et al. (eds.), *Philologie als Kulturwissenschaft* (Festschrift Karl Stackmann), pp. 179–92.

Besch, Werner, 'Vers oder Prosa? Zur Kritik am Reimvers im Spätmittelalter', *Beiträge zur Geschichte der deutschen Sprache und Literatur* (Tüb.) 94, Sonderheft, Festschrift Hans Eggers (1972), pp. 745–66.

Beumann, Helmut, 'Topos und Gedankengefüge bei Einhard', *Archiv für Kulturgeschichte* 33 (1951), pp. 337–50; repr. in Helmut Beumann, *Ideengeschichtliche Studien zu Einhard und anderen Geschichtsschreibern des früheren Mittelalters*, Darmstadt 1962, pp. 1–14, and in Jehn (ed.), *Toposforschung*, pp. 191–208.

'Der Schriftsteller und seine Kritiker im frühen Mittelalter', *Studium Generale* 12 (1959), pp. 497–511.

'Gregor von Tours und der *Sermo Rusticus*', in Konrad Repgen and Stephan Skalweit (eds.), *Spiegel der Geschichte. Festgabe für Max Braubach zum 10. April 1964*, Münster 1964, pp. 69–98.

Beumann, Helmut, and Werner Schröder (eds.), *Aspekte der Nationenbildung im Mittelalter* (Nationes 1), Sigmaringen 1978.

Bezzola, Reto R., *Le Sens de l'aventure et de l'amour*, Paris 1947; abridged German trans., *Liebe und Abenteuer im höfischen Roman* (rde 117–18), Reinbek 1961.

Les Origines et la formation de la littérature courtoise en occident (500–1200). Troisième partie: la societé courtoise: littérature de cour et littérature courtoise, Paris 1963.

Bibliography: secondary literature

Bischoff, Bernhard (ed.), *Karl der Große. Lebenswerk und Nachleben*. Vol. II: *Das geistige Leben*, Düsseldorf 1965.

Bloomfield, Morton W., 'Symbolism in medieval literature', *Modern Philology* 56 (1958), pp. 73–81; repr. in Morton W. Bloomfield, *Essays and Explorations. Studies in Ideas, Language, and Literature*, Cambridge, Mass. 1970, pp. 82–95.

Blumenröder, Albert, 'Die Quellenberufungen in der mittelhochdeutschen Dichtung', dissertation, University of Marburg 1922.

Boer, Willem den, 'Graeco-Roman historiography in its relation to biblical and modern thinking', *History and Theory* 7 (1968), pp. 60–75.

Boesch, Bruno, *Die Kunstanschauung in der mittelhochdeutschen Dichtung von der Blütezeit bis zum Meistergesang*, Berne and Leipzig 1936.

Bogdanow, Fanni, 'La Trilogie de Robert de Boron: "le Perceval en prose"', in Frappier and Grimm (eds.), *Le Roman*, vol. I, pp. 513–35; vol. II, ed. Grimm, pp. 173–7.

Boor, Helmut de, 'Die Grundauffassung von Gottfrieds Tristan', *Deutsche Vierteljahrsschrift* 18 (1940), pp. 262–306; repr. in Boor, *Kleine Schriften*, vol. I, pp. 136–72, and in Wolf (ed.), *Gottfried von Straßburg*, pp. 25–73.

'Der Daniel des Strickers und der Garel des Pleier', *Beiträge zur Geschichte der deutschen Sprache und Literatur* (Tüb.) 79 (1957), pp. 79–84; repr. in Boor, *Kleine Schriften*, vol. I, pp. 184–97.

'Der strophische Prolog zum Tristan Gottfrieds von Straßburg, *Beiträge zur Geschichte der deutschen Sprache und Literatur* (Tüb.) 81 (1959), pp. 47–60; repr. in Boor, *Kleine Schriften*, vol. I, pp. 173–83.

Kleine Schriften, vol. I, Berlin 1964.

'Fortuna in mittelhochdeutscher Dichtung, insbesondere in der "Crône" des Heinrich von dem Türlin', in Fromm et al. (eds.), *Verbum et Signum* (Festschrift Friedrich Ohly), vol. II, pp. 311–28.

Born, Lester K., 'Ovid and allegory', *Speculum* 9 (1934), 362–79.

Bornscheuer, Lothar, *Miseriae regum. Untersuchungen zum Krisen- und Todesgedanken in den herrschaftstheologischen Vorstellungen der ottonisch-salischen Zeit* (Arbeiten zur Frühmittelalterforschung 4), Berlin 1968.

'Bemerkungen zur Toposforschung', *Mittellateinisches Jahrbuch* 11 (1976), 312–20.

Topik. Zur Struktur der gesellschaftlichen Einbildungskraft, Frankfurt am Main 1976.

Brackert, Helmut, *Rudolf von Ems. Dichtung und Geschichte*, Heidelberg 1968.

Brall, Helmut, 'Diz vliegende bîspel. Zu Programmatik und kommunikativer Funktion des *Parzival*prologes', *Euphorion* 77 (1983), pp. 1–39.

Breuer, Dieter, and Helmut Schanze, *Topik. Beiträge zur interdisziplinären Diskussion* (Kritische Information 99), Munich 1981.

Brinkmann, Hennig, *Zu Wesen und Form mittelalterlicher Dichtung*, Halle 1928; 2nd edn, Tübingen 1979.

'Der Prolog im Mittelalter als literarische Erscheinung. Bau und Aussage', *Wirkendes Wort* 14 (1964), pp. 1–21; repr. in Hennig Brinkmann, *Studien zur Geschichte de deutschen Sprache und Literatur*, vol. II, Düsseldorf 1966, pp. 79–105.

'Verhüllung ("Integumentum") als literarische Darstellungsform im Mittelalter', in Albert Zimmermann (ed.), *Der Begriff der* Repraesentatio *im Mittelalter. Stellvertretung, Symbol, Zeichen, Bild* (Miscellanea Mediaevalia 8), Berlin and New York 1971, pp. 314–39.

'Die Zeichenhaftigkeit der Sprache, des Schrifttums und der Welt im Mittelalter', *Zeitschrift für deutsche Philologie* 93 (1974), pp. 1–11.

'Die Sprache als Zeichen im Mittelalter', in Hartmut Beckers and Hans Schwarz (eds.), *Gedenkschrift Jost Trier*, Cologne and Vienna 1975, pp. 23–44.

Mittelalterliche Hermeneutik, Tübingen 1980.

Brummer, Rudolf, *Die erzählende Prosadichtung in den romanischen Literaturen des XIII. Jahrhunderts*, vol. I, Berlin 1948.

Bruyne, Edgar de, *Etudes d'esthétique médiévale*, 3 vols., Bruges 1946; repr. Geneva 1975.

Bulst, Walther, 'Zum *prologus* der "Natiuitas et uictoria Alexandri magni regis". II. Die Paraphrase im "Alexander" Rudolfs von Ems', *Historische Vierteljahrschrift* 29 (1935), pp. 253–67.

Bumke, Joachim, *Die Wolfram von Eschenbach-Forschung seit 1945*, Munich 1970.

Mäzene im Mittelalter. Die Gönner und Auftraggeber der höfischen Literatur in Deutschland 1150–1300, Munich 1979.

Buntz, Herwig, *Die deutsche Alexanderdichtung des Mittelalters* (Sammlung Metzler M123), Stuttgart 1973.

Burger, Heinz Otto, *Die Kunstauffassung der frühen Meistersinger. Eine Untersuchung über die Kolmarer Handschrift* (Neue deutsche Forschungen: Abteilung Deutsche Philologie 2), Berlin 1936.

Carls, Ottmar, 'Die Auffassung der Wahrheit im "Tristan" Gottfrieds von Straßburg', *Zeitschrift für deutsche Philologie* 93 (1974), pp. 11–34.

Cary, George, *The Medieval Alexander*, Cambridge 1956.

Charland, Thomas Marie, *Artes praedicandi. Contribution à l'histoire de la rhétorique au Moyen Age* (Publications de l'Institut d'études médiévales d'Ottawa 7), Paris and Ottawa 1936.

Christmann, Hans Helmut, 'Neuere Arbeiten zum Rolandslied', *Romanistisches Jahrbuch* 16 (1965), pp. 49–60.

Cieslik, Karen, review of Walter Haug, *Literaturtheorie im deutschen Mittelalter*, *Referatdienst zur Literaturwissenschaft* 19 (1987), pp. 179–80.

Cormeau, Christoph, *Hartmanns von Aue 'Armer Heinrich' und 'Gregorius'. Studien zur Interpretation mit dem Blick auf die Theologie zur Zeit Hartmanns* (Münchener Texte und Untersuchngen 15), Munich 1966.

'Rudolf von Ems: "Der guote Gerhart". Die Veränderung eines Bauelements in einer gewandelten literarischen Situation', in Glier et al. (eds.), *Werk – Typ – Situation*, pp. 80–98.

'*Wigalois' und 'Diu Crône'. Zwei Kapitel zur Gattungsgeschichte des nachklassischen Aventiureromans* (Münchener Texte und Untersuchungen 57), Munich 1977.

'*Joie de la curt*. Bedeutungssetzung und ethische Erkenntnis', in Haug (ed.), *Formen und Funktionen der Allegorie*, pp. 194–205.

'Quellencompendium oder Erzählkonzept? Eine Skizze zu Konrads von

Würzburg "Trojanerkrieg"', in Grubmüller et al. (eds.), *Befund und Deutung*, pp. 303–19.

'"Tandareis und Flordibel" von dem Pleier. Eine poetologische Reflexion über Liebe im Artusroman', in Haug and Wachinger (eds.), *Positionen des Romans*, pp. 39–53.

Coseriu, Eugenio, *Die Geschichte der Sprachphilosophie von der Antike bis zur Gegenwart. Eine Übersicht*. Vol. I: *Von der Antike bis Leibniz* (Tübinger Beiträge zur Linguistik 11), Tübingen 1970; 2nd edn, 1975.

Curschmann, Michael, *Der Münchener Oswald und die deutsche spielmännische Epik* (Münchener Texte und Untersuchungen 6), Munich 1964.

'Spielmannsepik'. Wege und Ergebnisse der Forschung von 1907–1965, Stuttgart 1968.

'Das Abenteuer des Erzählens. Über den Erzähler in Wolframs "Parzival"', *Deutsche Vierteljahrsschrift* 45 (1971), pp. 627–67.

'Hören – Lesen – Sehen. Buch und Schriftlichkeit im Selbstverständnis der volkssprachlichen literarischen Kultur Deutschlands um 1200', *Beiträge zur Geschichte der deutschen Sprache und Literatur* (Tüb.) 106 (1984), pp. 218–57.

review of Walter Haug, *Literaturtheorie im deutschen Mittelalter*, *Germanisch-romanische Monatsschrift* 69 (1988), pp. 348–50.

'Facies peccatorum – Vir bonus: Bild–Text–Formel zwischen Hochmittelalter und früher Neuzeit', in Stephan Füssel and Joachim Knape (eds.), *Poesis und Pictura: Studien zum Verhältnis von Text und Bild in Handschriften und Drucken. Festschrift für Dieter Wuttke zum 60. Geburtstag* (Saecula Spiritalia Sonderband), Baden-Baden 1989, pp. 157–89.

Curtius, Ernst Robert, *Europäische Literatur und lateinisches Mittelalter*, Berne 1948; 9th edn, 1978; Engl. trans. by Willard R. Trask, *European Literature and the Latin Middle Ages*, London and Henley 1953, 7th edn, with an introduction by Peter Godman, Princeton 1990.

Daniélou, Jean, *Sacramentum futuri. Etudes sur les origines de la typologie biblique* (Etudes de théologie historique 19), Paris 1950.

Debus, Friedhelm, and Joachim Hartig (eds.), *Festschrift für Gerhard Cordes zum 65. Geburtstag*, Neumünster 1973.

Delbouille, Maurice, and Hans Ulrich Gumbrecht (eds.), *Généralités* (Grundriß der romanischen Literaturen des Mittelalters 1), Heidelberg 1972.

Delbrück, Hans, 'Die gute alte Zeit', in Hans Delbrück, *Erinnerungen, Aufsätze und Reden*, Berlin 1902, pp. 179–212.

Dick, Ernst S., review of Walter Haug, *Literaturtheorie im deutschen Mittelalter*, *Speculum* 63 (1988), pp. 679–81.

Dilg, Wolfgang, 'Der Literaturexkurs des "Tristan" als Zugang zu Gottfrieds Dichtung', in Krohn et al. (eds.), *Stauferzeit*, pp. 270–8.

Dittmann, Wolfgang, '"Dune hâst niht wâr, Hartman!" Zum Begriff der *wârheit* in Hartmanns "Iwein"', in Simon et al. (eds.), *Festgabe für Ulrich Pretzel*, pp. 150–61.

Dittrich, Marie-Luise, *Die 'Eneide' Heinrichs von Veldeke, I: Quellenkritischer Vergleich mit dem 'Roman d'Eneas' und Vergils 'Aeneis'*, Wiesbaden 1966.

Donovan, Mortimer J., 'Priscian and the obscurity of the ancients,' *Speculum* 36 (1961), pp. 75–80.

Bibliography: secondary literature

Dronke, Peter, *Fabula. Explorations into the Uses of Myth in Medieval Platonism* (Mittellateinische Studien und Texte 9), Leiden and Cologne 1974.

'Eine Theorie über *fabula* und *imago* im zwölften Jahrhundert,' in Fromm et al. (eds.), *Verbum et Signum* (Festschrift Friedrich Ohly), vol. II, pp. 161–76.

Düwel, Klaus, 'Lesestoff für junge Adlige. Lektüreempfehlung in einer Tugendlehre des 13. Jahrhunderts', *Fabula* 32 (1991), pp. 67–93.

Ebenbauer, Alfred, ' "Orendel" – Anspruch und Verwirklichung', in Ebenbauer et al. (eds.), *Strukturen und Interpretationen* (Festschrift Blanka Horacek), pp. 25–63.

'Fortuna und Artushof. Bemerkungen zum "Sinn" der "Krone" Heinrichs von dem Türlin', in Ebenbauer et al. (eds.), *Österreichische Literatur zur Zeit der Babenberger*, pp. 25–49.

'Tschionatulander und Artus. Zur Gattungsstruktur und zur Interpretation des Tschionatulanderlebens im "Jüngeren Titurel" ', *Zeitschrift für deutsches Altertum* 108 (1979), pp. 374–407.

Ebenbauer, Alfred, et al. (eds.), *Strukturen und Interpretationen. Studien zur deutschen Philologie gewidmet Blanka Horacek zum 60. Geburtstag* (Philologia Germanica 1), Vienna and Stuttgart 1974.

Österreichische Literatur zur Zeit der Babenberger (Wiener Arbeiten zur germanischen Altertumskunde und Philologie 10), Vienna 1977.

Eberwein, Elena, *Zur Deutung mittelalterlicher Existenz* (Kölner Romanistische Arbeiten 7), Bonn and Cologne 1933.

Egert, Eugene, *The Holy Spirit in German Literature until the End of the Twelfth Century*, The Hague and Paris 1973.

Eggers, Hans, 'Das Annolied – Eine Exempeldichtung?', in Schröder (ed.), *Festschrift für Ludwig Wolff*, pp. 161–72.

Deutsche Sprachgeschichte. Vol. I: *Das Althochdeutsche* (rde 185–6), Reinbek 1963.

'*Non cognovi litteraturam* (zu "Parzival" 115,27)', in Simon et al. (eds.), *Festgabe für Ulrich Pretzel*, pp. 162–72; repr. in Rupp (ed.), *Wolfram von Eschenbach*, pp. 533–48.

Ehlert, Trude, 'Zu Konrads von Würzburg Auffassung vom Wert der Kunst und von der Rolle des Künstlers', *Jahrbuch der Oswald von Wolkenstein Gesellschaft* 5 (1988/9), pp. 79–94.

Deutschsprachige Alexanderdichtung des Mittelalters (Europäische Hochschulschriften 1,1174), Frankfurt am Main etc. 1989.

Ehrismann, Gustav, *Studien über Rudolf von Ems. Beiträge zur Geschichte der Rhetorik und Ethik im Mittelalter* (Sitzungsberichte der Heidelberger Akademie, philos.-hist. Klasse 1919, Abh. 8), Heidelberg 1919.

Eifler, Günter, 'Publikumsbeeinflussung im strophischen Prolog zum "Tristan" Gottfrieds von Straßburg', in Günter Bellmann et al. (eds.), *Festschrift für Karl Bischoff zum 70. Geburtstag*, Cologne and Vienna 1975, pp. 357–89.

Eisenhut, Werner, *Einführung in die antike Rhetorik und ihre Geschichte*, Darmstadt 1974; 2nd edn 1982.

Eiswirth, Rudolf, *Hieronymus' Stellung zur Literatur und Kunst* (Klassisch-philologische Studien 16), Wiesbaden 1955.

Ellspermann, Gerard L., *The Attitude of the Early Christian Latin Writers toward Pagan Literature and Learning* (The Catholic University of America: Patristic studies 82), Washington D.C. 1949.

Bibliography: secondary literature

Endres, Rolf, 'Der Prolog von Hartmanns "Iwein"', *Deutsche Vierteljahrsschrift* 40 (1966), pp. 509–37.

'Die Bedeutung von *güete* und die Diesseitigkeit der Artusromane Hartmanns', *Deutsche Vierteljahrsschrift* 44 (1970), pp. 595–612.

Erdmann, Carl, 'Fabulae curiales. Neues zum Spielmannsgesang und zum Ezzo-Liede', *Zeitschrift für deutsches Altertum* 73 (1936), pp. 87–98.

'Gunther von Bamberg als Heldendichter', *Zeitschrift für deutsches Altertum* 74 (1937), p. 116.

Ernst, Ulrich, 'Die Magiergeschichte in Otfrids *Liber Evangeliorum*', *Annali dell' Istituto Orientale di Napoli: Sezione germanica* 15/2 (1972), pp. 81–138.

Der '*Liber Evangeliorum*' *Otfrids von Weißenburg. Literarästhetik und Verstechnik im Lichte der Tradition* (Kölner Germanistische Studien 11), Cologne and Vienna 1975.

'Gottfried von Straßburg in komparatistischer Sicht. Form und Funktion der Allegorese im Tristanepos', *Euphorion* 70 (1976), pp. 1–72.

Ertzdorff, Xenja von, 'Die Hochzeit zu Kana. Zur Bibelauslegung Otfrids von Weißenburg', *Beiträge zur Geschichte der deutschen Sprache und Literatur* (Tüb.) 86 (1964), pp. 62–82; repr. in Kleiber (ed.), *Otfrid von Weißenburg*, pp. 251–74.

Rudolf von Ems. Untersuchungen zum höfischen Roman im 13. Jahrhundert, Munich 1967.

'Die Wahrheit der höfischen Romane des Mittelalters', *Zeitschrift für deutsche Philologie* 86 (1967), pp. 375–89.

Falk, Walter, 'Wolframs Kyot und die Bedeutung der "Quelle" im Mittelalter', *Literaturwissenschaftliches Jahrbuch* n.s. 9 (1968), pp. 1–63.

Faral, Edmond, *Les Arts poétiques du XIIe et du XIIIe siècle. Recherches et documents sur la technique littéraire du Moyen Age*, Paris 1924; repr. Geneva 1982.

Fechter, Werner, *Das Publikum der mittelhochdeutschen Dichtung*, Frankfurt am Main 1935; 2nd edn, Darmstadt 1966.

Lateinische Dichtkunst und deutsches Mittelalter. Forschungen über Ausdrucksmittel, poetische Technik und Stil mittelhochdeutscher Dichtungen (Philologische Studien und Quellen 23), Berlin 1964.

Ferkinghoff, Klaus, 'Vers und Prosa. Die Bedeutung der beginnenden Laienschriftlichkeit für die Entstehung der altfranzösischen Prosaliteratur', dissertation, University of Heidelberg 1959.

Fichte, Joerg O., 'Der Einfluß der Kirche auf die mittelalterliche Literarästhetik', *Studia Neophilologica* 48 (1976), pp. 3–20.

'The Middle English Arthurian verse romance. Suggestions for the development of a literary typology', *Deutsche Vierteljahrsschrift* 55 (1981), pp. 567–90.

Finster, Franz, *Zur Theorie und Technik mittelalterlicher Prologe. Eine Untersuchung zu den Alexander- und Willehalmprologen Rudolfs von Ems*, diss. Bochum 1971.

Flügel, Christoph, *Prolog und Epilog in den deutschen Dramen und Legenden des Mittelalters*, diss. Basel 1969.

Foerster, Wendelin, 'Zu V. 5 des Alexanderfragments der Laurentiana', *Zeitschrift für romanische Philologie* 6 (1882), p. 422.

Bibliography: secondary literature

Folz, Robert, 'L'Histoire de la chevalerie d'après "Moriz von Craun"', *Etudes Germaniques* 32 (1977), pp. 119–28.

Fourquet, Jean, 'Prologue du "Tristan" de Gottfried. Fragment pour une initiation à l'étude de la langue et de la littérature allemande du moyen âge', *Bulletin de la faculté des lettres de Strasbourg* 31 (1952–3), pp. 251–9.

Frappier, Jean, 'Le *Conte du Graal* est-il une allégorie judéo-chrétienne?', *Romance Philology* 16 (1962–3), pp. 179–213; 20 (1966), pp. 1–31.

Frappier, Jean, and Reinhold R. Grimm (eds.), *Le Roman jusqu'à la fin du XIIIe siècle* (Grundriß der romanischen Literaturen des Mittelalters 4/1), vol. I, Heidelberg 1978.

Freytag, Hartmut, *Die Theorie der allegorischen Schriftdeutung und die Allegorie in deutschen Texten besonders des 11. und 12. Jahrhunderts* (Bibliotheca Germanica 24), Berne and Munich 1982.

Freytag, Wiebke, 'Otfrieds Briefvorrede "Ad Liutbertum" und die Accessus ad auctores', *Zeitschrift für deutsches Altertum* 111 (1982), pp. 168–93.

review of Walter Haug, *Literaturtheorie im deutschen Mittelalter*, *Germanistik* 27 (1986), pp. 73–4.

Frings, Theodor, and Max Braun, *Brautwerbung I* (Berichte über die Verhandlungen der Sächsischen Akademie der Wissenschaften, Philol.-hist. Klasse 96/2, 1944–8), Leipzig 1947.

Fromm, Hans, 'Tristans Schwertleite', *Deutsche Vierteljahrsschrift* 41 (1967), pp. 333–50; repr. in Fromm, *Arbeiten*, pp. 155–72.

'Doppelweg', in Glier et al. (eds.), *Werk – Typ – Situation*, pp. 64–79; repr. in Fromm, *Arbeiten*, pp. 122–35.

'Gottfried von Straßburg und Abaelard', *Beiträge zur Geschichte der deutschen Sprache und Literatur* (Tüb.) 95, Sonderheft, Festschrift Ingeborg Schröbler (1973), pp. 196–216; repr. in Fromm, *Arbeiten*, pp. 173–90.

'Zur Karrenritter-Episode im "Prosa-Lancelot". Struktur und Geschichte', in Huschenbett et al. (eds.), *Medium Aevum deutsch* (Festschrift Kurt Ruh), pp. 69–97; repr. in Fromm, *Arbeiten*, pp. 191–218.

'Der "Jüngere Titurel". Das Werk und sein Dichter', *Wolfram-Studien* 8 (1984), pp. 11–33; repr. in Fromm, *Arbeiten*, pp. 235–57.

Arbeiten zur deutschen Literatur des Mittelalters, Tübingen 1989.

Fromm, Hans et al. (eds.), *Verbum et Signum* (Festschrift Friedrich Ohly), Munich 1975.

Fuhrmann, Manfred, *Einführung in die antike Dichtungstheorie*, Darmstadt 1973.

Gallais, Pierre, 'Recherches sur la mentalité des romanciers français du moyen âge', *Cahiers de civilisation médiévale* 7 (1964), pp. 479–93.

Ganz, Peter F., 'Tristan, Isolde und Ovid. Zu Gottfrieds "Tristan" Z. 17182ff', in Hennig and Kolb (eds.), *Mediaevalia litteraria* (Festschrift Helmut de Boor) pp. 397–412.

'Dienstmann und Abt. "Gregorius Peccator" bei Hartmann von Aue und Arnold von Lübeck', in Schmidt (ed.), *Kritische Bewahrung* (Festschrift Werner Schröder), pp. 250–75.

Ganz, Peter F., and Werner Schröder (eds.), *Probleme mittelhochdeutscher Erzählformen. Marburger Colloquium 1969*, Berlin 1972.

Garstka, Ruth, *Untersuchungen zu Konrads von Würzburg Versroman 'Partonopier und Meliur'. Funktionsänderung epischer Komposition im nachhöfischen Epigonenroman im Vergleich zu Beispielen aus den 'Klassischen' Artusromanen Hartmanns*, diss. Tübingen 1979.

Geil, Gerhild, *Gottfried von Straßburg und Wolfram von Eschenbach als literarische Antipoden. Zur Genese eines literaturgeschichtlichen Topos*, Cologne and Vienna 1973.

Geissler, Friedmar, *Brautwerbung in der Weltliteratur*, Halle 1955.

Geith, Karl-Ernst, *Carolus Magnus. Studien zur Darstellung Karls des Großen in der deutschen Literatur des 12. und 13. Jahrhunderts* (Bibliotheca Germanica 19), Berne and Munich 1977.

Geppert, Waltraut-Ingeborg, 'Christus und Kaiser Karl im deutschen Rolandslied', *Beiträge zur Geschichte der deutschen Sprache und Literatur* (Tüb.) 78 (1956), pp. 349–73.

Gerhaher, Susanne, *Der Prolog des Annolieds als Typus in der frühmittelhochdeutschen Literatur*, diss. Munich, Straubing 1965.

Gerhardt, Christoph, ' "Iwein"-Schlüsse', *Literaturwissenschaftliches Jahrbuch* n.s. 13 (1972), pp. 13–29.

'Reinmars von Zweter "Idealer Mann" (Roethe Nr. 99/100)', *Beiträge zur Geschichte der deutschen Sprache und Literatur* 109 (1987), pp. 51–84, 222–51.

Gier, Albert, review of Walter Haug, *Literaturtheorie im deutschen Mittelalter*, *Zeitschrift für romanische Philologie* 102 (1986), pp. 632–4.

Glendinning, Robert, 'Gottfried von Straßburg and the school-tradition', *Deutsche Vierteljahrsschrift* 61 (1987), pp. 617–38.

Glier, Ingeborg, et al. (eds.), *Werk – Typ – Situation. Studien zu poetologischen Bedingungen in der älteren deutschen Literatur*, Stuttgart 1969.

Goebel, Klaus Dieter, 'Hartmanns "Gregorius-Allegorie" ', *Zeitschrift für deutsches Altertum* 100 (1971), pp. 213–26.

Gössmann, Elisabeth, 'Typus der Heilsgeschichte oder Opfer morbider Gesellschaftsordnung? Ein Forschungsbericht zum Schuldproblem in Hartmanns *Gregorius* (1950–1971)', *Euphorion* 68 (1974), pp. 42–80.

Goppelt, Leonhard, *Typos. Die typologische Deutung des Alten Testaments im Neuen* (Beiträge zur Förderung christlicher Theologie, series 2, vol. 43), Gütersloh 1939; repr. Darmstadt 1969.

Gottzmann, Carola L., 'Wirnts von Gravenberc "Wigalois". Zur Klassifizierung sogenannter epigonaler Artusdichtung', *Amsterdamer Beiträge zur älteren Germanistik* 14 (1979), pp. 87–136.

Grammel, Elisabeth, *Studien über den Wandel des Alexanderbildes in der deutschen Dichtung des 12. und 13. Jahrhunderts*, diss. Frankfurt am Main, Limburg an der Lahn 1931.

Green, Dennis Howard, *The Art of Recognition in Wolfram's 'Parzival'*, Cambridge 1982.

'The concept *aventiure* in *Parzival*', in Green and Johnson (eds.), *Approaches to Wolfram von Eschenbach*, pp. 83–161.

Green, Dennis Howard, and Leslie Peter Johnson, *Approaches to Wolfram von Eschenbach. Five Essays* (Mikrokosmos 5), Berne etc. 1978.

Grenzmann, Ludger, and Karl Stackmann (eds.), *Literatur und Laienbildung im*

Spätmittelalter und in der Reformationszeit. Symposion Wolfenbüttel 1981 (Germanistische Symposien: Berichtsbände 5), Stuttgart 1984.

Grenzmann, Ludger, et al. (eds.), *Philologie als Kulturwissenschaft. Studien zur Literatur und Geschichte des Mittelalters. Festschrift für Karl Stackmann zum 65. Geburtstag*, Göttingen 1987.

Groos, Arthur B., Jr., 'Wolfram von Eschenbach's "Bow Metaphor" and the narrative technique of *Parzival*', *Modern Language Notes* 87 (1972), pp. 391–408.

Grosse, Siegfried, 'Beginn und Ende der erzählenden Dichtungen Hartmanns von Aue', *Beiträge zur Geschichte der deutschen Sprache und Literatur* (Tüb.) 83 (1961–2), pp. 137–56; repr. in Kuhn and Cormeau (eds.), *Hartmann von Aue*, pp. 172–94.

Grubmüller, Klaus, 'Der Artusroman und sein König. Beobachtungen zur Artusfigur am Beispiel von Ginovers Entführung', in Haug and Wachinger (eds.), *Positionen des Romans*, pp. 1–20.

Grubmüller, Klaus, et al. (eds.), *Befund und Deutung. Zum Verhältnis von Empirie und Interpretation in Sprach- und Literaturwissenschaft*, Tübingen 1979.

Geistliche Denkformen in der Literatur des Mittelalters (Münstersche Mittelalter-Schriften 51), Munich 1984.

Grundmann, Herbert, 'Dichtete Wolfram von Eschenbach am Schreibtisch?', *Archiv für Kulturgeschichte* 49 (1967), pp. 391–405.

Gschwantler, Otto, 'Christus, Thor und die Midgardschlange', in Helmut Birkhan et al. (eds.), *Festschrift für Otto Höfler zum 65. Geburtstag*, Vienna 1968, pp. 145–68.

Gsteiger, Manfred, 'Note sur les préambules des chansons de geste', *Cahiers de civilisation médiévale* 2 (1959), pp. 213–20.

Guillén, Claudio, *Literature as System. Essays toward the Theory of Literary History*, Princeton 1971.

Gumbrecht, Hans Ulrich (ed.), *Literatur in der Gesellschaft des Spätmittelalters* (Grundriß der romanischen Literaturen des Mittelalters: Begleitreihe 1), Heidelberg 1980.

'Wie fiktional war der höfische Roman?', in Henrich and Iser (eds.), *Funktionen des Fiktiven*, pp. 433–40.

Haas, Alois, 'Der Mensch als *dritte werlt* im Annolied', *Zeitschrift für deutsches Altertum* 95 (1966), pp. 271–81.

Hagendahl, Harald, *Latin Fathers and the Classics. A Study on the Apologists, Jerome and Other Christian Writers* (Acta Universitatis Gothoburgensis: Göteborgs Universitets Årsskrift 64,1), Gothenburg 1958.

Hahn, Ingrid, 'Zu Gottfrieds von Straßburg Literaturschau', *Zeitschrift für deutsches Altertum* 96 (1967), pp. 218–36; repr. in Wolf (ed.), *Gottfried von Straßburg*, pp. 424–52.

'Parzivals Schönheit. Zum Problem des Erkennens und Verkennens im "Parzival"', in Fromm et al. (eds.), *Verbum et Signum* (Festschrift Friedrich Ohly), vol. II, pp. 203–32.

'Kosmologie und Zahl. Zum Prolog des "Jüngeren Titurel"', in Grubmüller et al. (eds.), *Geistliche Denkformen*, pp. 226–44.

Haidu, Peter, *Aesthetic Distance in Chrétien de Troyes. Irony and Comedy in Cligès and Perceval*, Geneva 1968.

Halpersohn, Rubin, *Über die Einleitungen im altfranzösischen Kunstepos*, Berlin 1911.

Harms, Wolfgang, *Homo viator in bivio. Studien zur Bildlichkeit des Weges* (Medium Aevum 21), Munich 1970.

Harms, Wolfgang, and Leslie Peter Johnson (eds.), *Deutsche Literatur des späten Mittelalters. Hamburger Colloquium 1973*, Berlin 1975.

Hartmann, Reinhildis, 'Die sprachliche Form der Allegorese in Otfrids von Weißenburg "Evangelienbuch"', in Fromm et al. (eds.), *Verbum et Signum* (Festschrift Friedrich Ohly), vol. I, pp. 103–41.

Haubrichs, Wolfgang, 'Die Praefatio des "Heliand". Ein Zeugnis der Religions- und Bildungspolitik Ludwigs des Deutschen', *Jahrbuch des Vereins für niederdeutsche Sprachforschung* 89 (1966), pp. 7–32; repr. in Jürgen Eichhoff and Irmengard Rauch, (eds.), *Der Heliand*, Darmstadt 1973 (Wege der Forschung 321), pp. 400–35.

'Einleitung: Für ein Zwei-Phasen-Modell der Erzählanalyse. Ausdrucksform und Inhaltsform in mittelalterlichen und modernen Bearbeitungen der Gregoriuslegende', in Wolfgang Haubrichs (ed.), *Erzählforschung 1: Theorien, Modelle und Methoden der Narrativik (LiLi*: Beiheft 4), Göttingen 1976, pp. 7–28.

'Eine prosopographische Skizze zu Otfrid von Weißenburg', in Kleiber (ed.), *Otfrid von Weißenburg*, pp. 397–413.

'Althochdeutsch in Fulda und Weißenburg – Hrabanus Maurus und Otfrid von Weißenburg', in Raymund Kottje and Harald Zimmermann (eds.), *Hrabanus Maurus. Lehrer, Abt und Bischof* (Akademie der Wissenschaften und der Literatur: Mainzer Abhandlungen der geistes- und sozialwissenschaftlichen Klasse, Einzelveröffentlichung 4), Wiesbaden 1982, pp. 182–93.

Die Anfänge: Versuche volkssprachiger Schriftlichkeit im frühen Mittelalter (ca. 700–1050/60) (Geschichte der deutschen Literatur von den Anfängen bis zum Beginn der Neuzeit, ed. Joachim Heinzle, I/1), Frankfurt am Main 1988; 2nd edn, Tübingen 1995.

Haug, Walter, 'Vom Imram zur Aventiure-Fahrt. Zur Frage nach der Vorgeschichte der hochhöfischen Epenstruktur', *Wolfram-Studien* [1] (1970), pp. 264–98; repr. in Haug, *Strukturen*, pp. 379–408.

'Die Symbolstruktur des höfischen Epos und ihre Auflösung bei Wolfram von Eschenbach', *Deutsche Vierteljahrsschrift* 45 (1971), pp. 668–705; repr. in Haug, *Strukturen*, pp. 483–512.

'*Aventiure* in Gottfrieds von Straßburg "Tristan"', *Beiträge zur Geschichte der deutschen Sprache und Literatur* (Tüb.) 94, Sonderheft, Festschrift Hans Eggers (1972), pp. 89–125; repr. in Haug, *Strukturen*, pp. 557–82.

'Rudolfs "Willehalm" und Gottfrieds "Tristan". Kontrafaktur als Kritik', in Harms and Johnson (eds.), *Deutsche Literatur des späten Mittelalters*, pp. 83–98; repr. in Haug, *Strukturen*, pp. 637–50.

'Struktur und Geschichte. Ein literaturtheoretisches Experiment an mittelalterlichen Texten', *Germanisch-romanische Monatsschrift* 54 (1973), pp. 130–52; repr. in Haug, *Strukturen*, pp. 236–56.

'Die Tristansage und das persische Epos *Wis und Râmîn*', *Germanisch-romanische Monatsschrift* 54 (1973), pp. 404–23; repr. in Haug, *Strukturen*, pp. 583–99.

'Wolframs "Willehalm"-Prolog im Lichte seiner Bearbeitung durch Rudolf von

Ems', in Schmidt (ed.), *Kritische Bewahrung* (Festschrift Werner Schröder), pp. 298–327; repr. in Haug, *Strukturen*, pp. 615–36.

'Der aventiure meine', in Peter Kesting (ed.), *Würzburger Prosastudien 2. Untersuchungen zur Literatur und Sprache des Mittelalters. Kurt Ruh zum 60. Geburtstag* (Medium Aevum 31), Munich 1975, pp. 93–111; repr. in Haug, *Strukturen*, pp. 447–63.

'Parzivals *zwîvel* und Willehalms *zorn*. Zu Wolframs Wende vom höfischen Roman zur Chanson de Geste', *Wolfram-Studien* 3 (1975), pp. 217–31; repr. in Haug, *Strukturen*, pp. 529–40.

'Gebet und Hieroglyphe. Zur Bild- und Architekturbeschreibung in der mittelalterlichen Dichtung', *Zeitschrift für deutsches Altertum* 106 (1977), pp. 163–83; repr. in Haug, *Strukturen*, pp. 110–25.

'Poetologische Universalien und Literaturgeschichte', in Wolfgang Haubrichs (ed.), *Erzählforschung 2: Theorien, Modelle und Methoden der Narrativik* (LiLi: Beiheft 6), Göttingen 1977, pp. 277–96; repr. in Haug, *Strukturen*, pp. 3–20.

'Das Land, von welchem niemand wiederkehrt'. Mythos, Fiktion und Wahrheit in Chrétiens 'Chevalier de la Charrete', im 'Lanzelet' Ulrichs von Zatzikhoven und im 'Lancelot'-Prosaroman* (Untersuchungen zur deutschen Literaturgeschichte 21), Tübingen 1978.

'Erzählen vom Tod her. Sprachkrise, gebrochene Handlung und zerfallende Welt in Wolframs "Titurel"', *Wolfram-Studien* 6 (1980), pp. 8–24; repr. in Haug, *Strukturen*, pp. 541–53.

'Paradigmatische Poesie. Der spätere deutsche Artusroman auf dem Weg zu einer "nachklassischen" Ästhetik', *Deutsche Vierteljahrsschrift* 54 (1980), pp. 204–31; repr. in Haug, *Strukturen*, pp. 651–71.

'Transzendenz und Utopie. Vorüberlegungen zu einer Literaturästhetik des Mittelalters', in Jürgen Brummack et al. (eds.), *Literaturwissenschaft und Geistesgeschichte. Festschrift Richard Brinkmann*, Tübingen 1981, pp. 1–22; repr. in Haug, *Strukturen*, pp. 513–38.

'Das Bildprogramm im Sommerhaus von Runkelstein', in Walter Haug et al. (eds.), *Runkelstein. Die Wandmalereien des Sommerhauses*, Wiesbaden 1982, pp. 25–62; repr. in Haug, *Strukturen*, pp. 687–708.

'Das Komische und das Heilige. Zur Komik in der religiösen Literatur des Mittelalters', *Wolfram-Studien* 7 (1982), pp. 8–31; repr. in Haug, *Strukturen*, pp. 257–74.

'Gottfrieds von Straßburg "Tristan". Sexueller Sündenfall oder erotische Utopie', in *Akten des VII. Internationalen Germanisten-Kongresses*, Tübingen 1986, vol. I, pp. 41–52; repr. in Haug, *Strukturen*, pp. 600–11.

Strukturen als Schlüssel zur Welt. Kleine Schriften zur Erzählliteratur des Mittelalters, Tübingen 1989; paperback edn, 1990.

'Parzival ohne Illusionen', *Deutsche Vierteljahrsschrift* 64 (1990), pp. 199–217; repr. in Haug, *Brechungen*, pp. 125–39.

'Der "Tristan" – eine interarthurische Lektüre', in Wolfzettel (ed.), *Artusroman und Intertextualität*, pp. 57–72; repr. in Haug, *Brechungen*, pp. 184–96.

'Von *aventiure* und *minne* zu Intrige und Treue: Die Subjektivierung des hochhöfischen Aventürenromans im "Reinfried von Braunschweig"', in Paola Schulze-Belli and Michael Dallapiazza (cds.), *Liebe und Aventiure im Artus-*

roman des Mittelalters (Göppinger Arbeiten zur Germanistik 532), Göppingen 1990, pp. 7–22; repr. in Haug, *Brechungen*, pp. 301–11.

'Hat Wolfram von Eschenbach Chrétiens *Conte du Graal* kongenial ergänzt?', in Willy Van Hoecke et al. (eds.), *Arturus Rex. Volumen II. Acta Conventus Lovaniensis 1987* (Mediaevalia Lovaniensia Ser. I, Studia 17), Louvain 1991, pp. 236–58; repr. in Haug, *Brechungen*, pp. 109–24.

'Über die Schwierigkeiten des Erzählens in nachklassischer Zeit', in Haug and Wachinger (eds.), *Positionen des Romans*, pp. 338–65; repr. in Haug, *Brechungen*, pp. 265–87.

'Ein Dichter wehrt sich. Wolframs Prolog zu den Gawan-Büchern', *Wolfram-Studien* 12 (1992), pp. 214–29; repr. in Haug, *Brechungen*, pp. 140–52.

Brechungen auf dem Weg zur Individualität. Kleine Schriften zur Literatur des Mittelalters, Tübingen 1995.

Haug, Walter (ed.), *Formen und Funktionen der Allegorie. Symposion Wolfenbüttel 1978* (Germanistische Symposien: Berichtsbände 3), Stuttgart 1979.

Haug, Walter, and Burghart Wachinger (eds.), *Positionen des Romans im späten Mittelalter* (Fortuna vitrea 1), Tübingen 1991.

Haug, Walter, et al. (eds.), *Zur deutschen Literatur und Sprache des 14. Jahrhunderts. Dubliner Colloquium 1981*, Heidelberg 1983.

Haupt, Barbara, 'Zum Prolog des "Tristan" Gottfrieds von Straßburg. Prolegomenon zu einer wirkungs- und rezeptionsorientierten Untersuchung mittelalterlicher volkssprachlicher Prologe', in Gert Kaiser (ed.), *Literatur – Publikum – historischer Kontext* (Beiträge zur Älteren Deutschen Literaturgeschichte 1), Berne etc. 1977, pp. 109–36.

Haverkamp, Anselm, *Typik und Politik im Annolied. Zum 'Konflikt der Interpretationen' im Mittelalter*, Stuttgart 1979.

Heinzle, Joachim, *Stellenkommentar zu Wolframs Titurel* (Hermaea 30), Tübingen 1972.

'Über den Aufbau des *Wigalois*', *Euphorion* 67 (1973), pp. 261–71.

'Zur Stellung des Prosa-Lancelot in der deutschen Literatur des 13. Jahrhunderts', in Friedrich Wolfzettel (ed.), *Artusrittertum im späten Mittelalter. Ethos und Ideologie* (Beiträge zur deutschen Philologie 57), Giessen 1984, pp. 104–13.

'Die Entdeckung der Fiktionalität. Zu Walter Haugs "Literaturtheorie im deutschen Mittelalter"', *Beiträge zur Geschichte der deutschen Sprache und Literatur* 112 (1990), pp. 55–80.

Heinzle, Joachim (ed.), *Wolfram von Eschenbach: Willehalm. Nach der Handschrift der Stiftsbibliothek St. Gallen. Mittelhochdeutscher Text, Übersetzung, Kommentar* (Bibliothek des Mittelalters 9), Frankfurt am Main 1991.

Hellgardt, Ernst, 'Notkers des Deutschen Brief an Bischof Hugo von Sitten', in Grubmüller et al. (eds.), *Befund und Deutung*, pp. 169–92.

Hempel, Heinrich, 'Der *zwîvel* bei Wolfram und anderweit', in *Erbe der Vergangenheit. Germanistische Beiträge. Festgabe für Karl Helm zum 80. Geburtstage 19. Mai 1951*, Tübingen 1951, pp. 157–87; repr. in Heinrich Hempel, *Kleine Schriften*, Heidelberg 1966, pp. 277–98.

Hennig, Ursula, and Herbert Kolb (eds.), *Mediaevalia litteraria. Festschrift für Helmut de Boor zum 80. Geburtstag*, Munich 1971.

Henrich, Dieter, and Wolfgang Iser (eds.), *Funktionen des Fiktiven* (Poetik und Hermeneutik 10), Munich 1983.

Herbst, Hermann, 'Neue Wolfenbüttler Fragmente aus dem Codex discissus von Otfrids Buch der Evangelien', *Zeitschrift für Geistesgeschichte* 2 (1936), pp. 131–40; repr. in Kleiber (ed.), *Otfrid von Weißenburg*, pp. 52–73.

Herkommer, Hubert, *Überlieferungsgeschichte der 'Sächsischen Weltchronik'. Ein Beitrag zur deutschen Geschichtsschreibung des Mittelalters*, Munich 1972.

Hermann, Ernst, *Die Inschrift des Brackenseils. Wandlungen der höfischen Weltanschauung im 'Jüngeren Titurel'*, diss. Marburg 1939.

Herzog, Reinhart, *Die Bibelepik der lateinischen Spätantike. Formengeschichte einer erbaulichen Gattung* (Theorie und Geschichte der Literatur und der schönen Künste 37), vol. I, Munich 1975.

'Exegese – Erbauung – Delectatio. Beiträge zu einer christlichen Poetik der Spätantike', in Haug (ed.), *Formen und Funktionen der Allegorie*, pp. 52–69.

Hilty, Gerold, 'Zum "Erec"-Prolog von Chrétien de Troyes', in Manfred Bambeck et al. (eds.), *Philologica Romanica Erhard Lommatzsch gewidmet*, Munich 1975, pp. 245–56.

Hirdt, Willi, 'Untersuchungen zum Eingang in der erzählenden Dichtung des Mittelalters und der Renaissance', *Arcadia* 7 (1972), pp. 47–64.

Studien zum epischen Prolog. Der Eingang in der erzählenden Versdichtung Italiens (Humanistische Bibliothek, I, 23), Munich 1975.

Hirschberg, Dagmar, *Untersuchungen zur Erzählstruktur von Wolframs 'Parzival'. Die Funktion von erzählter Szene und Station für den doppelten Kursus* (Göppinger Arbeiten zur Germanistik 139), Göppingen 1976.

'Zur Struktur von Hartmanns "Gregorius"', in Grubmüller et al. (eds.), *Befund und Deutung*, pp. 240–67.

Hoefer, Hartmut, *Typologie im Mittelalter. Zur Übertragbarkeit typologischer Interpretation auf weltliche Dichtung* (Göppinger Arbeiten zur Germanistik 54), Göppingen 1971.

Hövelmann, Werner, *Die Eingangsformel in germanischer Dichtung*, diss. Bonn 1936.

Holub, Robert C., *Reception Theory. A Critical Introduction*, London and New York 1984.

Huber, Christoph, *'Wort sint der dinge zeichen'. Untersuchungen zum Sprachdenken der mittelhochdeutschen Spruchdichtung bis Frauenlob* (Münchener Texte und Untersuchungen 64), Munich 1977.

'Wort-Ding-Entsprechungen. Zur Sprache- und Stiltheorie Gottfrieds von Straßburg', in Grubmüller et al. (eds.), *Befund und Deutung*, pp. 268–302.

'Höfischer Roman als Integumentum? Das Votum Thomasins von Zerklaere', *Zeitschrift für deutsches Altertum* 115 (1986), pp. 79–100.

review of Walter Haug, *Literaturtheorie im deutschen Mittelalter*, *Anzeiger für deutsches Altertum* 99 (1988), pp. 60–8.

Hübner, Arthur, 'Alexander der Große in der deutschen Dichtung des Mittelalters', *Die Antike* 9 (1933), pp. 32–48; repr. in Arthur Hübner, *Kleine Schriften zur deutschen Philologie*, Berlin 1940, pp. 187–97.

Hüttig, Albrecht, *Macrobius im Mittelalter. Ein Beitrag zur Rezeptionsgeschichte der*

Commentarii in Somnium Scipionis (Freiburger Beiträge zur mittelalterlichen Geschichte 2), Frankfurt am Main etc. 1990.

Hunt, Tony, 'The rhetorical background to the Arthurian prologue', *Forum for Modern Language Studies* 6 (1970) (= *Arthurian Romance. Seven Essays*, ed. D. D. R. Owen, Edinburgh and London 1970), pp. 1–23.

'Tradition and originality in the prologues of Chrestien de Troyes', *Forum for Modern Languages Studies* 8 (1972), pp. 320–44.

Huschenbett, Dietrich, *Albrechts 'Jüngerer Titurel'. Zu Stil und Komposition* (Medium Aevum 35), Munich 1979.

'Der "Jüngere Titurel" als literaturgeschichtliches Problem', *Wolfram-Studien* 8 (1984), pp. 153–68.

Huschenbett, Dietrich, et al. (eds.), *Medium Aevum deutsch. Beiträge zur deutschen Literatur des hohen und späten Mittelalters. Festschrift für Kurt Ruh zum 65. Geburtstag*, Tübingen 1979.

Iwand, Käthe, *Die Schlüsse der mittelhochdeutschen Epen* (Germanische Studien 16), Berlin 1922.

Jackson, Timothy R., 'Konrad von Würzburg's legends. Their historical context and the poet's approach to his material', in Ganz and Schröder (eds.), *Probleme mittelhochdeutscher Erzählformen*, pp. 197–213.

Jaeger, Charles Stephen, 'The "strophic" prologue to Gottfried's *Tristan*', *Germanic Review* 47 (1972), pp. 5–19.

Medieval Humanism in Gottfried von Straßburg's 'Tristan und Isolde' (Germanische Bibliothek, series 3: Untersuchungen und Einzeldarstellungen), Heidelberg 1977.

The Prologue Tradition in Middle High German Romance, Ann Arbor 1978.

'Der Schöpfer der Welt und das Schöpfungswerk als Prologmotiv in der mittelhochdeutschen Dichtung', *Zeitschrift für deutsches Altertum* 107 (1978), pp. 1–18.

Jaffe, Samuel, 'Gottfried von Straßburg and the rhetoric of history', in Murphy (ed.), *Medieval Eloquence*, pp. 288–318.

Jamison, Robert, and Joachim Dyck, *Rhetorik – Topik – Argumentation: Bibliographie zur Redelehre und Rhetorikforschung im deutschsprachigen Raum 1945–1979/80*, Stuttgart and Bad Cannstatt 1983.

Janson, Tore, *Latin Prose Prefaces. Studies in Literary Conventions* (Acta Universitatis Stockholmiensis: Studia Latina Stockholmiensia 13), Stockholm etc. 1964.

Jantsch, Heinz G., *Studien zum Symbolischen in frühmittelhochdeutscher Literatur*, Tübingen 1959.

Jantzen, Hans Günther, *Untersuchungen zur Entstehung des altfranzösischen Prosaromans*, diss. Heidelberg 1966.

Jauss, Hans Robert, 'Epos und Roman. Eine vergleichende Betrachtung an Texten des XII. Jahrhunderts', *Nachrichten der Gießener Hochschulgesellschaft* 31 (1962), pp. 76–92; repr. in Jauss, *Alterität und Modernität*, pp. 385–410.

'Die klassische und die christliche Rechtfertigung des Häßlichen in mittelalterlicher Literatur', in Jauss (ed.), *Die nicht mehr schönen Künste*, pp. 143–68; repr. in Jauss, *Alterität und Modernität*, pp. 385–410.

'Theorie der Gattungen und Literatur des Mittelalters', in Delbouille and

Bibliography: secondary literature

Gumbrecht (eds.), *Généralités* pp. 107–38; repr. in Jauss, *Alterität und Modernität*, pp. 327–58.
Alterität und Modernität der mittelalterlichen Literatur, Munich 1977.
Ästhetische Erfahrung und literarische Hermeneutik, vol. I: *Versuche im Feld der ästhetischen Erfahrung*, Munich 1977; Engl. trans. by Michael Shaw, with an introduction by Wlad Godzich, *Aesthetic Experience and Literary Hermeneutics* (Theory and History of Literature 3), Minneapolis 1982.
'Zur historischen Genese der Scheidung von Fiktionalität und Realität', in Henrich and Iser (eds.), *Funktionen des Fiktiven*, pp. 423–31.
Jauss, Hans Robert (ed.), *La Littérature didactique, allégorique et satirique* (Grundriß der romanischen Literaturen des Mittelalters 6/1), Heidelberg 1968.
Die nicht mehr schönen Künste. Grenzphänomene des Ästhetischen (Poetik und Hermeneutik 3), Munich 1968.
Jehn, Peter (ed.), *Toposforschung. Eine Dokumentation* (Respublica Literaria 10), Frankfurt am Main 1972.
Jentzmik, Peter, *Zu Möglichkeiten und Grenzen typologischer Exegese in mittelalterlicher Predigt und Dichtung* (Göppinger Arbeiten zur Germanistik 112), Göppingen 1973.
Johnson, Leslie Peter, *'valsch geselleclîcher muot (Parzival 2.17)'*, *Modern Language Review* 62 (1967), pp. 70–85.
'Parzival's beauty', in Green and Johnson (eds.), *Approaches to Wolfram von Eschenbach*, pp. 273–91.
Johnson, Leslie Peter, et al. (eds.), *Studien zur frühmittelhochdeutschen Literatur. Cambridger Colloquium 1971*, Berlin 1974.
Jolivet, Jean, 'Eléments pour une étude des rapports entre la grammaire et l'ontologie au Moyen Age', in Beckmann et al. (eds.), *Sprache und Erkenntnis*, pp. 135–64.
Jones, Paul John, *Prologue and Epilogue in Old French Lives of Saints before 1400*, Philadelphia 1933.
Jongkees, A. G., '*Translatio Studii*: Les avatars d'un thème médiéval', in *Miscellanea Mediaevalia in memoriam Jan Frederik Niermeyer*, Groningen 1967, pp. 41–51.
Jungbluth, Günther, 'Ein Topos in Lamprechts Alexander?', *Germanisch-romanische Monatsschrift* 37 (1956), pp. 289–90.
Kannicht, Richard, 'Der alte Streit zwischen Philosophie und Dichtung', *Der altsprachliche Unterricht* 23/6 (1980), pp. 6–36.
Kartschoke, Dieter, *Wolfram von Eschenbach: Willehalm*, Berlin 1968.
Bibeldichtung. Studien zur Geschichte der epischen Bibelparaphrase von Juvencus bis Otfrid von Weißenburg, Munich 1975.
Kellermann, Wilhelm, *Aufbaustil und Weltbild Chrestiens von Troyes im Perceval-roman* (Zeitschrift für romanische Philologie: Beiheft 88), Halle 1936.
Kelly, Douglas, 'Theory of composition in medieval narrative poetry and Geoffrey of Vinsauf's "Poetria Nova"', *Mediaeval Studies* 31 (1969), pp. 117–48.
'The source and meaning of conjointure in Chrétien's "Erec"', *Viator* 1 (1970), pp. 179–200.
'Topical invention in medieval French literature', in Murphy (ed.), *Medieval Eloquence*, pp. 131–51.
Kemper, Raimund, 'Das *Ludwigslied* im Kontext zeitgenössischer Rechtsvorgänge', *Deutsche Vierteljahrsschrift* 56 (1982), pp. 161–73.

401

Bibliography: secondary literature

Kennedy, George A., *Classical Rhetoric and its Christian and Secular Tradition from Ancient to Modern Times*, London 1980.

Kern, Peter, 'Der Roman und seine Rezeption als Gegenstand des Romans. Beobachtungen zum Eingangsteil von Hartmanns *Iwein*', *Wirkendes Wort* 23 (1973), pp. 246–52.

'Der Kommentar zu *Parzival* 1,13f. im Prolog des *Jüngeren Titurel*', in Werner Besch et al. (eds.), *Studien zur deutschen Literatur und Sprache des Mittelalters. Festschrift für Hugo Moser zum 65. Geburtstag*, Berlin 1974, pp. 185–99.

'Rezeption und Genese des Artusromans. Überlegungen zu Strickers "Daniel vom blühenden Tal"', *Zeitschrift für deutsche Philologie* 93, Sonderheft (1974), pp. 18–42.

Die Artusromane des Pleier. Untersuchungen über den Zusammenhang von Dichtung und literarischer Situation (Philologische Studien und Quellen 100), Berlin 1981.

'Die Auseinandersetzung mit der Gattungstradition im *Wigalois* Wirnts von Grafenberg', in Wolfzettel (ed.), *Artusroman und Intertextualität*, pp. 73–83.

Keuchen, Rolf, *Typologische Strukturen im 'Tristan'. Ein Beitrag zur Erzähltechnik Gottfrieds von Straßburg*, diss. Cologne 1975.

Kibelka, Johannes, *'der ware meister'. Denkstile und Bauformen in der Dichtung Heinrichs von Mügeln* (Philologische Studien und Quellen 13), Berlin 1963.

Kienast, Richard, 'Zur Tektonik von Wolframs "Willehalm"', in Richard Kienast (ed.), *Studien zur deutschen Philologie des Mittelalters. Friedrich Panzer zum 80. Geburtstag am 4. September 1950 dargebracht*, Heidelberg 1950, pp. 96–115; repr. in Rupp (ed.), *Wolfram von Eschenbach*, pp. 427–54.

Kleiber, Wolfgang, *Otfrid von Weißenburg, Untersuchungen zur handschriftlichen Überlieferung und Studien zum Aufbau des Evangelienbuches* (Bibliotheca Germanica 14), Berne and Munich 1971.

Otfrid von Weißenburg (Wege der Forschung 419), Darmstadt 1978.

Kleinschmidt, Erich, 'Literarische Rezeption und Geschichte. Zur Wirkungsgeschichte von Wolframs *Willehalm* im Spätmittelalter', *Deutsche Vierteljahrsschrift* 48 (1974), pp. 585–649.

Klopsch, Paul, 'Prosa und Vers in der mittellateinischen Literatur', *Mittellateinisches Jahrbuch* 3 (1966), pp. 9–24.

Einführung in die Dichtungslehren des lateinischen Mittelalters, Darmstadt 1980.

Klotz, Volker, 'Muse und Helios. Über epische Anfangsnöte und -weisen', in Norbert Miller (ed.), *Romananfänge. Versuch zu einer Poetik des Romans*, Berlin 1965, pp. 11–36.

Knape, Joachim, *'Historie' in Mittelalter und früher Neuzeit. Begriffs- und gattungsgeschichtliche Untersuchungen im interdisziplinären Kontext* (Saecula spiritalia 10), Baden-Baden 1984.

Knapp, Fritz Peter, 'Die häßliche Gralsbotin und die viktorinische Ästhetik', *Sprachkunst* 3 (1972), pp. 1–10.

'Der Lautstand der Eigennamen im "Willchalm" und das Problem von Wolframs "Schriftlosigkeit"', *Wolfram-Studien* 3 (1974), pp. 193–218.

'Virtus und Fortuna in der "Krone". Zur Herkunft der ethischen Grundthese Heinrichs von dem Türlin', *Zeitschrift für deutsches Altertum* 106 (1977), pp. 253–63.

Bibliography: secondary literature

'Historische Wahrheit und poetische Lüge. Die Gattungen weltlicher Epik und ihre theoretische Rechtfertigung im Hochmittelalter', *Deutsche Vierteljahrsschrift* 54 (1980), pp. 581–635.

'Heilsgewißheit oder Resignation? Rennewarts Schicksal und der Schluß des *Willehalm*', *Deutsche Vierteljahrsschrift* 57 (1983), pp. 593–612.

'Integumentum und Âventiure. Nochmals zur Literaturtheorie bei Bernardus (Silvestris?) und Thomasin von Zerklaere', *Literaturwissenschaftliches Jahrbuch* n.s. 28 (1987), pp. 299–307.

'"Antworte dem Narren nach seiner Wahrheit!" Das Speculum stultorum des Nigellus von Canterbury', *Reinhardus* 3 (1990), pp. 45–68.

Kobbe, Peter, 'Funktion und Gestalt des Prologs in der mittelhochdeutschen nachklassischen Epik des 13. Jahrhunderts', *Deutsche Vierteljahrsschrift* 43 (1969), pp. 405–57.

Köhler, Erich, 'Zur Entstehung des altfranzösischen Prosaromans', *Wissenschaftliche Zeitschrift der Friedrich-Schiller-Universität Jena, gesellschafts- und sprachwissenschaftliche Reihe* 5 (1955–6), pp. 287–92; repr. in Köhler, *Trobadorlyrik*, pp. 213–23, 294–6.

'Zur Selbstauffassung des höfischen Dichters', in Rudolf Grossmann et al. (eds.), *Der Vergleich. Literatur- und sprachwissenschaftliche Interpretationen. Festgabe für Hellmuth Petriconi zum 1. April 1955*, Hamburg 1955, pp. 65–79; repr. in Köhler, *Trobadorlyrik*, pp. 228–34, and in Erich Köhler (ed.), *Der altfranzösische höfische Roman*, Darmstadt 1978 (Wege der Forschung 425), pp. 17–38.

Ideal und Wirklichkeit in der höfischen Epik. Studien zur Form der frühen Artus- und Graldichtung (Zeitschrift für romanische Philologie: Beiheft 97), Tübingen 1956; 2nd edn, 1970.

Trobadorlyrik und höfischer Roman. Aufsätze zur französischen und provenzalischen Literatur des Mittelalters (Neue Beiträge zur Literaturwissenschaft 15), Berlin 1962.

Kohlmayer, Rainer, *Ulrichs von Etzenbach 'Willehalm von Wenden'. Studien zur Tektonik und Thematik einer politischen Legende aus der nachklassischen Zeit des Mittelalters* (Deutsche Studien 25), Meisenheim am Glan 1974.

Kolb, Herbert, '*Orthabunge rehter kunst*. Zu den *saelde*-Prologen in Rudolfs von Ems "Alexander"', in *Festschrift Helmut de Boor zum 75. Geburtstag am 24. März 1966*, Tübingen 1966, pp. 92–110.

'*Der ware Elicon*. Zu Gottfrieds Tristan vv. 4862–4907', *Deutsche Vierteljahrsschrift* 41 (1967), pp. 1–26; repr. in Wolf (ed.), *Gottfried von Straßburg*, pp. 453–88.

Kratz, Henry, 'The prologue to Wolfram's "Parzival"', *The Journal of English and Germanic Philology* 65 (1966), pp. 75–98.

Kraus, Carl von, *Text und Entstehung von Rudolfs 'Alexander'* (Sitzungsberichte der Bayerischen Akademie der Wissenschaften, philol.-hist. Abteilung, Jahrgang 1940/8), Munich 1940.

Krohn, Rüdiger, et al. (eds.), *Stauferzeit. Geschichte, Literatur, Kunst* (Karlsruher Kulturwissenschaftliche Arbeiten 1), Stuttgart 1979.

Krywalski, Diether, review of Walter Haug, *Literaturtheorie im deutschen Mittelalter*, *Blätter für den Deutschlehrer* (1986), pp. 123–5.

Kuhn, Helmut, 'Literaturgeschichte als Geschichtsphilosophie', *Philosophische*

Rundschau 11 (1964), pp. 222–48; repr. in Helmut Kuhn, *Schriften zur Ästhetik*, Munich 1966, pp. 159–94.

Kuhn, Hugo, ' "Erec" ', in *Festschrift Paul Kluckhohn und Hermann Schneider*, Tübingen 1948, pp. 122–47; repr. in Kuhn, *Dichtung und Welt*, pp. 133–50, and in Kuhn and Cormeau (eds.), *Hartmann von Aue*, pp. 17–48.

'Zum neuen Bild vom Mittelalter', *Deutsche Vierteljahrsschrift* 24 (1950), pp. 530–44.

'Soziale Realität und dichterische Fiktion am Beispiel der höfischen Ritterdichtung Deutschlands', in Carl Brinkmann (ed.), *Soziologie und Leben*, Tübingen 1952, pp. 195–219; repr. in Kuhn, *Dichtung und Welt*, pp. 22–40.

'Gestalten und Lebenskräfte der frühmittelhochdeutschen Dichtung. Ezzos Lied, Genesis, Annolied, Memento mori', *Deutsche Vierteljahrsschrift* 27 (1953), pp. 1–30; repr. in Kuhn, *Dichtung und Welt*, pp. 112–32.

'der gute sünder – der erwählte?' in *Hartmann von Aue: Gregorius, der gute sünder*. Mittelhochdeutscher Text nach der Ausgabe von F. Neumann. Übersetzung von B. Kippenberg, Ebenhausen 1959, pp. 255–71.

Dichtung und Welt im Mittelalter, Stuttgart 1959; 2nd edn, 1969.

'Wolframs Frauenlob', *Zeitschrift für deutsches Altertum* 106 (1977), pp. 200–10; repr. in Kuhn, *Liebe und Gesellschaft*, pp. 45–51.

Liebe und Gesellschaft (Kleine Schriften 3), Stuttgart 1980.

'Versuch über das 15. Jahrhundert in der deutschen Literatur', in Hugo Kuhn (ed.), *Entwürfe zu einer Literatursystematik des Spätmittelalters*, Tübingen 1980, pp. 77–81; repr. in Gumbrecht (ed.), *Literatur in der Gesellschaft*, pp. 19–38, and in Kuhn, *Liebe und Gesellschaft*, pp. 135–55.

Kuhn, Hugo, and Christoph Cormeau (eds.), *Hartmann von Aue* (Wege der Forschung 359), Darmstadt 1973.

Kunisch, Hermann, '*edelez herze – edeliu sêle*. Vom Verhältnis höfischer Dichtung zur Mystik', in Hennig and Kolb (eds.), *Mediaevalia litteraria* (Festschrift Helmut de Boor), pp. 413–50.

Lachmann, Karl, 'Über den Eingang des "Parzivals" ', *Abhandlungen der Königlichen Akademie der Wissenschaften zu Berlin, philos.- hist. Klasse* Jahrgang 1835 (1837), pp. 227–66; repr. in Karl Lachmann, *Kleinere Schriften*, ed. Karl Müllenhoff, vol. I, Berlin 1876, pp. 480–518.

Lange, Ernst, *Die Eingänge des altfranzösischen Karlsepen*, Greifswald 1904.

Laugesen, Anker Teilgård, 'Commentaire à la première laisse du Fragment d' "Alexandre" ', *Studia Neophilologica* 35 (1963), pp. 275–89.

Lausberg, Heinrich, *Handbuch der literarischen Rhetorik*, 2 vols., Munich 1960.

Le Gentil, Pierre, 'The work of Robert de Boron and the *Didot Perceval*', in Loomis (ed.), *Arthurian Literature*, pp. 251–62.

Lofmark, Carl, *The Authority of the Source in Middle High German Narrative Poetry* (Bithell Series of Dissertations 5), London 1981.

review of Walter Haug, *Literaturtheorie im deutschen Mittelalter*, *Cahiers de civilisation médiévale* 32 (1989), pp. 160–2.

Loomis, Gertrude Schoepperle, *Tristan und Isolt: A Study of the Sources of the Romance*, 2nd edn, with a bibliography and critical essay in *Tristan* scholarship since 1912 by Roger Sherman Loomis, 2 vols., New York 1960.

Bibliography: secondary literature

Loomis, Roger Sherman (ed.), *Arthurian Literature in the Middle Ages. A Collaborative History*, Oxford 1959; 2nd edn, 1961.

Lubac, Henri de, *Exégèse médiévale. Les quatre sens de l'Ecriture*, 4 vols., Paris 1959–64.

Lutz, Eckart Conrad, *Rhetorica divina. Mittelhochdeutsche Prologgebete und die rhetorische Kultur des Mittelalters* (Quellen und Forschungen zur Sprach- und Kulturgeschichte der germanischen Völker 206, n.s. 82), Berlin and New York 1984.

Lyons, Faith, 'Interprétations critiques au XXe siècle du prologue de *Cligès*: La *translatio studii* selon les historiens, les philosophes et les philologues', *Oeuvres et Critiques* 5 (1980–1), part 2, pp. 39–44.

Maierù, Alfonso, ' "Signum" dans la culture médiévale', in Beckmann et al. (eds.), *Sprache und Erkenntnis*, pp. 51–72.

Mandach, André de (ed.), *Chronique dite Saintongeaise. Texte franco-occitan inédit 'Lee'. A la découverte d'une chronique gasconne du XIIIème siècle et de ses poitevinisations* (Zeitschrift für romanische Philologie: Beiheft 126), Tübingen 1979.

Marchand, James W., 'Tristan's Schwertleite. Gottfried's aesthetics and literary criticism', in Luanne T. Frank and Emery E. George (eds.), *Husbanding the Golden Grain. Studies in Honor of Henry W. Nordmeyer*, Ann Arbor 1973, pp. 187–204.

Marigold, W. C., review of Walter Haug, *Literaturtheorie im deutschen Mittelalter*, *Germanic Notes* 18 (1987), pp. 22–3.

Martin, Ernst, *Wolframs von Eschenbach Parzival und Titurel*. Part II: *Kommentar* (Germanistische Handbibliothek 2), Halle 1903; repr. Darmstadt 1976.

Masser, Achim, 'Zum "Wilhelm von Wenden" Ulrichs von Etzenbach', *Zeitschrift für deutsche Philologie* 93, Sonderheft (1974), pp. 141–55.

Matzel, Klaus, *Untersuchungen zur Verfasserschaft, Sprache und Herkunft der althochdeutschen Übersetzungen der Isidor-Sippe* (Rheinisches Archiv 75), Bonn 1970.

McCulloch, Florence, *Mediaeval Latin and French Bestiaries*, 2nd edn (University of North Carolina Studies in the Romance Languages and Literatures 33), Chapel Hill 1962.

McKeon, Richard, 'Rhetoric in the Middle Ages', *Speculum* 17 (1942), pp. 1–32.

Meier, Christel, 'Überlegungen zum gegenwärtigen Stand der Allegorie-Forschung. Mit besonderer Berücksichtigung der Mischformen', *Frühmittelalterliche Studien* 10 (1976), pp. 1–69.

Meissburger, Gerhard, 'Zum sogenannten Heldenliederbuch Karls des Großen', *Germanisch-romanische Monatsschrift* 44 (1963), pp. 105–19.

'Zum Prolog von Wolframs Willehalm', *Germanisch-romanische Monatsschrift* 46 (1965), pp. 119–38.

Meissner, Rudolf, '*Dein clage ist one reimen*', in Julius Wahle and Victor Klemperer (eds.), *Vom Geiste neuer Literaturforschung. Festschrift für Oskar Walzel*, Wildpark-Potsdam 1924, pp. 21–38.

Mentzel-Reuters, Arno, *Vröude. Artusbild, Fortuna- und Gralskonzeption in der 'Crône' des Heinrich von dem Türlin als Verteidigung des höfischen Lebensideals* (Europäische Hochschulschriften, 1,1134), Frankfurt am Main etc. 1989.

Bibliography: secondary literature

Mermier, Guy R. (ed.), *Le Bestiaire de Pierre de Beauvais. Version courte*, Paris 1977.

Mertens, Volker, 'Imitatio Arthuri. Zum Prolog von Hartmanns "Iwein"', *Zeitschrift für deutsches Altertum* 106 (1977), pp. 350–8.

Gregorius eremita. Eine Lebensform des Adels bei Hartmann von Aue in ihrer Problematik und ihrer Wandlung in der Rezeption (Münchener Texte und Untersuchungen 67), Munich 1978.

Minnis, Alastair, and A. Brian Scott (eds.), *Medieval Literary Theory and Criticism c.1100–c.1375. The Commentary Tradition*, Oxford 1988.

Mölk, Ulrich (ed.), *Französische Literarästhetik des 12. und 13. Jahrhunderts. Prologe – Exkurse – Epiloge* (Sammlung romanischer Übungstexte 54), Tübingen 1969.

Mohr, Wolfgang, 'Lucretia in der *Kaiserchronik*', *Deutsche Vierteljahrsschrift* 26 (1952), pp. 433–46.

Monecke, Wolfgang, *Studien zur epischen Technik Konrads von Würzburg. Das Erzählprinzip der* wildekeit, Stuttgart 1968.

Monselewski, Werner, *Der barmherzige Samariter. Eine auslegungsgeschichtliche Untersuchung zu Lukas 10, 25–37* (Beiträge zur Geschichte der Bibelexegese 5), Tübingen 1967.

Moos, Peter von, 'Literaturkritik im Mittelalter. Arnulf von Lisieux über Ennodius', in *Mélanges offerts à René Crozet à l'occasion de son soixante-dixième anniversaire*, Poitiers 1966, pp. 929–35.

'*Poeta* und *historicus* im Mittelalter. Zum Mimesis-Problem am Beispiel einiger Urteile über Lucan', *Beiträge zur Geschichte der deutschen Sprache und Literatur* (Tüb.) 98 (1976), pp. 93–130.

Moret, André, *L'Originalité de Conrad de Wurzbourg dans son poème: 'Partonopier et Meliur'*, Lille 1933.

Müller, Robert, 'Der historische Hintergrund des althochdeutschen *Ludwigsliedes*', *Deutsche Vierteljahrsschrift* 62 (1988), pp. 221–6.

Murphy, James J., *Medieval Rhetoric. A Select Bibliography*, Toronto and Buffalo 1971; 2nd edn, 1989.

Rhetoric in the Middle Ages. A History of Rhetorical Theory from Saint Augustine to the Renaissance, Berkeley etc. 1974.

Murphy, James J. (ed.), *Medieval Eloquence. Studies in the Theory and Practice of Medieval Rhetoric*, Berkeley etc. 1978.

Nagel, Bert, 'Hartmann "zitiert" Reinmar. Iwein 1–30 und MF 150/10–18', *Euphorion* 63 (1969), pp. 6–39.

Nat, P. G. van der, 'Die Praefatio der Evangelienparaphrase', in *Romanitas et Christianitas. Studia Iano Henrico Waszink*, Amsterdam and London 1973, pp. 249–57.

Naumann, Bernd, 'Vorstudien zu einer Darstellung des Prologs in der deutschen Dichtung des 12. und 13. Jahrhunderts', in Otmar Werner and Bernd Naumann (eds.), *Formen mittelalterlicher Literatur. Siegfried Beyschlag zu seinem 65. Geburtstag* (Göppinger Arbeiten zur Germanistik 25), Göppingen 1970, pp. 23–37.

'Ein- und Ausgänge frühmittelhochdeutscher Gedichte und die Predigt des 12. Jahrhunderts', in Johnson et al. (eds.), *Studien zur frühmittelhochdeutschen Literatur*, pp. 37–57.

Bibliography: secondary literature

Nellmann, Eberhard, 'Karl der Große und König David im Epilog des deutschen Rolandsliedes', *Zeitschrift für deutsches Altertum* 94 (1965), pp. 268–79.

'Wolframs Willehalm-Prolog. Ein kritischer Bericht über das Buch von Ingrid Ochs', *Zeitschrift für deutsche Philologie* 88 (1969), pp. 401–9.

'Wolfram und Kyot als *vindære wilder mære*. Überlegungen zu "Tristan" 4619–4688 und "Parzival" 453,1–17', *Zeitschrift für deutsches Altertum* 117 (1988), pp. 31–67.

Neubuhr, Elfriede, *Bibliographie zu Hartmann von Aue* (Bibliographien zur deutschen Literatur des Mittelalters 6), Berlin 1977.

Niemeyer, Karina Hagmann, *A Rhetorical Study of the Exordia of the Romans Courtois*, Ann Arbor 1964.

Nitze, William A., 'What did Robert de Boron write?', *Modern Philology* 41 (1943–4), pp. 1–5.

'Arthurian problems', *Bulletin Bibliographique de la Société Arthurienne / Bibliographical Bulletin of the International Arthurian Society* 5 (1953), pp. 76–8.

'Messire Robert de Boron. Enquiry and summary', *Speculum* 28 (1953), pp. 279–96.

'Conjointure in *Erec* vs. 14', *Modern Language Notes* 69 (1954), pp. 180–1.

'*Perlesvaus*', in Loomis (ed.), *Arthurian Literature*, pp. 262–73.

Norden, Eduard, *Die antike Kunstprosa vom VI. Jahrhundert v. Chr. bis in die Zeit der Renaissance*, Leipzig 1898; repr. Darmstadt 1958.

Norman, Frederick, 'Meinung und Gegenmeinung: Die literarische Fehde zwischen Gottfried von Straßburg und Wolfram von Eschenbach', in *Miscellanea di studi in onore di Bonaventura Tecchi*, vol. I, Rome 1969, pp. 67–86.

Nyholm, Kurt, *Studien zum sogenannten geblümten Stil* (Acta Academiae Aboensis, Ser. A: Humaniora 39/4), Turku 1971.

'Pragmatische Isotypien im "Jüngeren Titurel". Überlegungen zur Autor-Hörer/Leser-Situation', *Wolfram-Studien* 8 (1984), pp. 120–37.

Ochs, Ingrid, *Wolframs 'Willehalm'-Eingang im Lichte der frühmittelhochdeutschen geistlichen Dichtung* (Medium Aevum 14), Munich 1968.

Ohly, Friedrich, *Sage und Legende in der Kaiserchronik. Untersuchungen über Quellen und Aufbau der Dichtung* (Forschungen zur deutschen Sprache und Dichtung 10), Munich 1940; repr. Darmstadt 1968.

'Der Prolog des St. Trudperter Hohenliedes', *Zeitschrift für deutsches Altertum* 84 (1952–3), pp. 198–232.

'Vom geistigen Sinn des Wortes im Mittelalter', *Zeitschrift für deutsches Altertum* 89 (1958), pp. 1–23; repr. in Ohly, *Schriften zur mittelalterlichen Bedeutungsforschung*, pp. 1–31.

'Wolframs Gebet an den Heiligen Geist im Eingang des Willehalm', *Zeitschrift für deutsches Altertum* 91 (1961–2), pp. 1–37; repr. in Rupp (ed.), *Wolfram von Eschenbach*, pp. 455–509, with addenda pp. 510–18.

'Die Kathedrale als Zeitenraum. Zum Dom von Siena', *Frühmittelalterliche Studien* 6 (1972), pp. 94–158; repr. in Ohly, *Schriften zur mittelalterlichen Bedeutungsforschung*, pp. 171–273.

'Die Legende von Karl und Roland', in Johnson et al. (eds.), *Studien zur frühmittelhochdeutschen Literatur*, pp. 292–343; repr. in Ohly, *Ausgewählte und neue Schriften*, pp. 35–76.

Bibliography: secondary literature

'Halbbiblische und außerbiblische Typologie', in *Simboli e simbologia nell'alto medioevo*, Spoleto 1975, pp. 429–72 (discussion pp. 473–9; repr. in Ohly, *Schriften zur mittelalterlichen Bedeutungsforschung*, pp. 361–400.

'Außerbiblisch Typologisches zwischen Cicero, Ambrosius und Aelred von Rievaulx', in Helmut Rücker and Kurt Otto Seidel (eds.), *'Sagen mit sinne'. Festschrift für Marie-Luise Dittrich zum 65. Geburtstag* (Göppinger Arbeiten zur Germanistik 180), Göppingen 1976, pp. 19–37; repr. in Ohly, *Schriften zur mittelalterlichen Bedeutungsforschung'*, pp. 338–60.

Der Verfluchte und der Erwählte. Vom Leben mit der Schuld (Rheinisch-Westfälische Akademie der Wissenschaften: Vorträge G 207), Opladen 1976; Engl. trans. by Linda Archibald, with an introduction by George Steiner, *The Damned and the Elect. Guilt in Western Culture*, Cambridge 1976.

Schriften zur mittelalterlichen Bedeutungsforschung, Darmstadt 1977; 2nd edn, 1983.

'Skizzen zur Typologie im späteren Mittelalter', in Huschenbett et al. (eds.), *Medium Aevum deutsch* (Festschrift Kurt Ruh), pp. 251–310; repr. in Ohly, *Ausgewählte und neue Schriften*, pp. 509–54.

'Typologische Figuren aus Natur und Mythos', in Haug (ed.), *Formen und Funktionen der Allegorie*, pp. 126–66; repr. in Ohly, *Ausgewählte und neue Schriften*, pp. 445–72.

Ollier, Marie-Louise, 'The author in the text. The prologues of Chrétien de Troyes', in Peter Haidu (ed.), *Approaches to Medieval Romance* (Yale French Studies 51), New York 1974, pp. 26–41.

Olson, Glending, 'The medieval theory of literature for refreshment and its use in the fabliau tradition', *Studies in Philology* 71 (1974), pp. 291–313.

Oostrom, Frits P. van, *Lantsloot vander Haghedochte. Onderzoekingen over een Middelnederlandse bewerking van de Lancelot en prose*, Amsterdam etc. 1981.

Ortmann, Christa, '"Titurel" im "Parzival"-Kontext. Zur Frage nach einer möglichen Strukturdeutung der Fragmente', *Wolfram-Studien* 6 (1980), pp. 25–47.

Ostberg, Kurt, 'The "Prologi" of Notker's "Boethius" reconsidered', *German Life and Letters* 16 (1962–3), pp. 256–65.

Ott-Meimberg, Marianne, *Kreuzzugsepos oder Staatsroman? Strukturen adeliger Heilsversicherung im deutschen 'Rolandslied'* (Münchener Texte und Untersuchungen 70), Munich 1980.

Paris, Gaston, 'Etudes sur les romans de la Table Ronde II. Le *Conte de la Charrette*', *Romania* 12 (1883), pp. 459–534.

Parshall, Linda B., *The Art of Narration in Wolfram's 'Parzival' and Albrecht's 'Jüngerer Titurel'* (Anglica Germanica Series 2), Cambridge 1981.

Paul, Hans, *Ulrich von Eschenbach und seine 'Alexandreis'*, Berlin 1914.

Peschel, Gerd-Dietmar, *Prolog-Programm und Fragment-Schluß in Gotfrits Tristanroman* (Erlanger Studien 9), Erlangen 1976.

Peters, Ursula, *Literatur in der Stadt. Studien zu den sozialen Voraussetzungen und kulturellen Organisationsformen städtischer Literatur im 13. und 14. Jahrhundert* (Studien und Texte zur Sozialgeschichte der Literatur 7), Tübingen 1983.

Picozzi, Rosemary, 'Allegory and symbol in Hartmann's Gregorius', in Michael S. Batts and Margareta Goetz Stankiewicz (eds.), *Essays in German Literature in Honour of G. Joyce Hallamore*, Toronto 1968, pp. 19–33.

Bibliography: secondary literature

Pöggeler, Otto, 'Dichtungstheorie und Toposforschung', *Jahrbuch für Ästhetik und allgemeine Kunstwissenschaft* 5 (1960), pp. 89–201; extracts repr. in Jehn (ed.), *Toposforschung*, pp. 69–73; and in Baeumer (ed.), *Toposforschung*, pp. 25–135.

Pörksen, Uwe, *Der Erzähler im mittelhochdeutschen Epos. Formen seines Hervortretens bei Lamprecht, Konrad, Hartmann, in Wolframs Willehalm und in den 'Spielmannsepen'* (Philologische Studien und Quellen 58), Berlin 1971.

Poirion, Daniel, 'Romans en vers et romans en prose', in Jauss (ed.), *La Littérature didactique*, pp. 74–81.

Polenz, Peter von, 'Otfrids Wortspiel mit Versbegriffen als literarisches Bekenntnis', in Schröder (ed.), *Festschrift für Ludwig Wolff*, pp. 121–34; repr. in Ulrich Ernst and Peter-Erich Neuser (eds.), *Die Genese der europäischen Endreimdichtung* (Wege der Forschung 444), Darmstadt 1977, pp. 196–212.

Polheim, Karl Konrad, *Die deutschen Gedichte der Vorauer Handschrift. Codex 276* (Facsimile edition), part 2, Graz 1958.

Pretzel, Ulrich, 'Zum Prolog von Hartmanns Gregorius mit einem Exkurs über einen Sondergebrauch von mhd. *ein*', in Debus and Hartig (eds.), *Festschrift für Gerhard Cordes*, vol. I, pp. 117–25.

Pretzel, Ulrich, and Wolfgang Bachofer, *Bibliographie zu Wolfram von Eschenbach*, 2nd edn (Bibliographien zur deutschen Literatur des Mittelalters 2), Berlin 1968.

Quadlbauer, Franz, *Die antike Theorie der genera dicendi im lateinischen Mittelalter* (Sitzungsberichte der Österreichischen Akademie der Wissenschaften, philos.-hist. Klasse 241/2), Vienna 1962.

Quint, Josef, 'Ein Beitrag zur Textinterpretation von Gottfrieds Tristan und Wolframs Parzival', in *Festschrift Helmut de Boor zum 75. Geburtstag am 24. März 1966*, Tübingen 1966, pp. 71–91.

Ragotzky, Hedda, *Studien zur Wolfram-Rezeption. Die Entstehung und Verwandlung der Wolfram-Rolle in der deutschen Literatur des 13. Jahrhunderts* (Studien zur Poetik und Geschichte der Literatur 20), Stuttgart 1971.

Gattungserneuerung und Laienunterweisung in Texten des Strickers (Studien und Texte zur Sozialgeschichte der Literatur 1), Tübingen 1981.

Rahner, Hugo, *Griechische Mythen in christlicher Deutung*, Zurich 1944; 3rd edn, 1966.

Symbole der Kirche. Die Ekklesiologie der Väter, Salzburg 1964.

Reiffenstein, Ingo, 'Die Erzählervorausdeutung in der frühmittelhochdeutschen Dichtung. Zur Geschichte und Funktion einer poetischen Formel', *Beiträge zur Geschichte der Sprache und Literatur* (Tüb.) 94, Sonderheft, Festschrift Hans Eggers (1972), pp. 551–76.

Reinitzer, Heimo, 'Geschichte der deutschen Literaturkritik im Mittelalter', dissertation, University of Graz 1966.

'Zur Erzählfunktion der "Crône" Heinrichs von dem Türlin', in Ebenbauer et al. (eds.), *Österreichische Literatur zur Zeit der Babenberger*, pp. 177–96.

Rexroth, Karl-Heinrich, 'Volkssprache und werdendes Volksbewußtsein im ostfränkischen Reich', in Beumann and Schröder (eds.), *Aspekte der Nationenbildung*, pp. 275–315.

Richert, Hans-Georg, *Wege und Formen der Passionalüberlieferung* (Hermaea n.s. 40), Tübingen 1978.

Bibliography: secondary literature

Ritter, Richard, *Die Einleitungen der altdeutschen Epen*, diss. Bonn 1908.

Robertson, Douglas W., Jr., 'Marie de France, *Lais*, prologue, 13–16', *Modern Language Notes* 64 (1949), pp. 336–8.

'Some medieval literary terminology, with special reference to Chrétien de Troyes', *Studies in Philology* 48 (1951), pp. 669–92.

A Preface to Chaucer. Studies in Medieval Perspectives, Princeton 1962; 5th edn, 1969.

Rocher, Daniel, *Thomasin von Zerklaere, 'Der Wälsche Gast' (1215–1216)*, 2 vols., Lille and Paris 1977.

Röll, Walter, 'Berthold von Regensburg und der "Jüngere Titurel"', *Wolfram-Studien* 8 (1984), pp. 67–93.

Rösler, Wolfgang, 'Die Entdeckung der Fiktionalität in der Antike', *Poetica* 12 (1980), pp. 283–319.

Rohr, Rupprecht, *Matière, sens, conjointure. Methodologische Einführung in die französische und provenzalische Literatur des Mittelalters*, Darmstadt 1978.

Rosenhagen, Gustav, *Untersuchungen über Daniel vom Blühenden Tal vom Stricker*, diss. Kiel 1890.

Ruff, Ernst Johann Friedrich, *'Der Wälsche Gast' des Thomasin von Zerklaere. Untersuchungen zu Gehalt und Bedeutung einer mittelhochdeutschen Morallehre* (Erlanger Studien 35), Erlangen 1982.

Ruh, Kurt, *Höfische Epik des deutschen Mittelalters. Vol. I: Von den Anfängen bis zu Hartmann von Aue* (Grundlagen der Germanistik 7), Berlin 1967; 2nd edn, 1977.

'Joachitische Spiritualität im Werke Roberts von Boron', in Stefan Sonderegger et al. (eds.), *Typologia Litterarum. Festschrift für Max Wehrli*, Zurich 1969, pp. 167–96.

'Der Gralsheld in der "Queste del Saint Graal"', *Wolfram-Studien*, [1] (1970), pp. 240–63.

'Drei Voten zu Wolframs Willehalm', in Schmidt (ed.), *Kritische Bewahrung* (Festschrift Werner Schröder), pp. 283–97.

'Epische Literatur des deutschen Spätmittelalters', in Willi Erzgräber (ed.), *Europäisches Spätmittelalter* (Neues Handbuch der Literaturwissenschaft 8), Wiesbaden 1978, pp. 117–88.

Höfische Epik des deutschen Mittelalters. Vol. II: Reinhart Fuchs, Lanzelet, Wolfram von Eschenbach, Gottfried von Straßburg (Grundlagen der Germanistik 25), Berlin 1980.

Ruh, Kurt, et al. (eds.), *Die deutsche Literatur des Mittelalters. Verfasserlexikon*, 2nd, completely revised edn, Berlin 1978–.

Rupp, Heinz, 'Otfrid von Weißenburg und die spätantike Bibeldichtung', *Wirkendes Wort* 7 (1956–7), pp. 334–43.

'Wolframs Parzival-Prolog', *Beiträge zur Geschichte der deutschen Sprache und Literatur* (Halle) 82, Sonderband, Festschrift Elisabeth Karg-Gasterstädt (1961), pp. 29–45; repr. in Rupp (ed.), *Wolfram von Eschenbach*, pp. 369–87.

Rupp, Heinz (ed.), *Wolfram von Eschenbach* (Wege der Forschung 57), Darmstadt 1966.

Rychner, Jean, 'Le Prologue du "Chevalier de la charrette"', *Vox Romanica* 26 (1966), pp. 1–23.

Bibliography: secondary literature

'Le Prologue du *Chevalier de la charrette* et l'interprétation du roman', in *Mélanges offerts à Rita Lejeune*, Gembloux 1969, pp. 1121–35.

Salmon, Paul, 'Über den Beitrag des grammatischen Unterrichts zur Poetik des Mittelalters', *Archiv für das Studium der neueren Sprachen und Literaturen* 199 (1963), pp. 65–84.

Sawicki, Stanisław, *Gottfried von Straßburg und die Poetik des Mittelalters* (Germanische Studien 124), Berlin 1932.

Sayce, Olive, 'Prolog, Epilog und das Problem des Erzählers', in Ganz and Schröder (eds.), *Probleme mittelhochdeutscher Erzählformen*, pp. 63–72.

Schanze, Frieder, *Meisterliche Liedkunst zwischen Heinrich von Mügeln und Hans Sachs* (Münchener Texte und Untersuchungen 82), 2 vols., Munich 1983.

Schirmer, Karl-Heinz, *Stil- und Motivuntersuchungen zur mittelhochdeutschen Versnovelle* (Hermaea n.s. 26), Tübingen 1969.

'Antike Traditionen in der *versus*-Vorrede zum Heliand', in Debus and Hartig (eds.), *Festschrift für Gerhard Cordes*, pp. 136–59.

Schirok, Bernd, 'Zu den Akrosticha in Gottfrieds "Tristan"', *Zeitschrift für deutsches Altertum* 113 (1984), pp. 188–213.

'*Zin anderhalp an dem glase gelîchet*. Zu Lachmanns Konjektur *geleichet* und zum Verständnis von "Parzival" 1,20f.', *Zeitschrift für deutsches Altertum* 115 (1986), pp. 117–24.

Schlosser, Horst Dieter, 'Frühe deutsche Texte im Literaturunterricht, 3. Literaturtheorie bei Otfried von Weißenburg', *Literatur in Wissenschaft und Unterricht* 6 (1973), pp. 264–72; repr. in Kleiber (ed.), *Otfrid von Weißenburg*, pp. 387–96.

Schmidt, Ernst-Joachim (ed.), *Kritische Bewährung. Beiträge zur älteren deutschen Philologie. Festschrift für Werner Schröder zum 60. Geburtstag*, Berlin 1974.

Schmidt, Wolfgang, *Untersuchungen zu Aufbauformen und Erzählstil im 'Daniel von dem blühenden Tal' des Stricker* (Göppinger Arbeiten zur Germanistik 266), Göppingen 1979.

Schmidtke, Dietrich, *Geistliche Tierinterpretation in der deutschsprachigen Literatur des Mittelalters (1100–1500)*, diss. FU Berlin 1968.

Schmolke-Hasselmann, Beate, 'Der französische höfische Roman', in Henning Krauss (ed.), *Europäisches Hochmittelalter* (Neues Handbuch der Literaturwissenschaft 7), Wiesbaden 1981, pp. 283–322.

'Untersuchungen zur Typik des arthurischen Romananfangs', *Germanisch-romanische Monatsschrift* 62 (1981), pp. 1–13.

'Der französische Artusroman in Versen nach Chrétien de Troyes', *Deutsche Vierteljahrsschrift* 57 (1983), pp. 415–30.

Schneider, Hermann, *Parzival-Studien* (Sitzungsberichte der Bayerischen Akademie der Wissenschaften, philos.-hist. Klasse 1944–1946/4), Munich 1947.

Schnell, Rüdiger, *Rudolf von Ems. Studien zur inneren Einheit seines Gesamtwerkes* (Basler Studien zur deutschen Sprache und Literatur 41), Berne 1969.

'Grenzen literarischer Freiheit im Mittelalter', *Archiv für das Studium der neueren Sprachen und Literaturen* 218 (133) (1981), pp. 241–70.

'Prosaauflösung und Geschichtsschreibung im deutschen Spätmittelalter. Zum Entstehen des frühneuhochdeutschen Prosaromans', in Grenzmann and Stackmann (eds.), *Literatur und Laienbildung*, pp. 214–48.

Schönbach, Anton E., 'Otfridstudien III', *Zeitschrift für deutsches Altertum* 39 (1895), pp. 369–423.

Schöne, Albrecht, 'Zu Gottfrieds "Tristan"-Prolog', *Deutsche Vierteljahrsschrift* 29 (1955), 447–74; repr. in Wolf (ed.), *Gottfried von Straßburg*, pp. 147–81.

Scholz, Manfred Günter, *Hören und Lesen. Studien zur primären Rezeption der Literatur im 12. und 13. Jahrhundert*, Wiesbaden 1980.

Schon, Peter M., *Studien zum Stil der frühen französischen Prosa (Robert de Clari, Geoffroy de Villehardouin, Henri de Valenciennes)* (Analecta Romanica 8), Frankfurt am Main 1960.

Schouwink, Wilfried, *Fortuna im Alexanderroman Rudolfs von Ems. Studien zum Verhältnis von Fortuna und Virtus bei einem Autor der späten Stauferzeit* (Göppinger Arbeiten zur Germanistik 212), Göppingen 1977.

Schreiber, Hans, *Studien zum Prolog in mittelalterlicher Dichtung*, Würzburg 1935.

Schreiner, Klaus, 'Zum Wahrheitsverständnis im Heiligen- und Reliquienwesen des Mittelalters', *Saeculum* 17 (1966), pp. 131–69.

Schröder, Edward, 'Die Reimvorreden des deutschen Lucidarius' *Nachrichten von der Königl. Gesellschaft der Wissenschaften zu Göttingen philol.-hist. Klasse* 1917 (Berlin 1918), pp. 153–72.

Schröder, Walter Johannes, 'Der Prolog von Wolframs Parzival', *Zeitschrift für deutsches Altertum* 83 (1951–2), pp. 130–143; repr. in W. J. Schröder, *Aufsätze und Vorträge*, pp. 176–89.

'König Rother. Gehalt und Struktur', *Deutsche Vierteljahrsschrift* 29 (1955), pp. 301–22; repr. in W. J. Schröder, *Aufsätze und Vorträge*, pp. 1–22.

'Bemerkungen zur Sprache Gottfrieds von Straßburg', in Karl Bischoff and Lutz Röhrich (eds.), *Volk, Sprache, Dichtung. Festgabe für Kurt Wagner* (Beiträge zur deutschen Philologie 28), Giessen 1960, pp. 49–60; repr. in W. J. Schröder, *Aufsätze und Vorträge*, pp. 385–95.

'rede' und 'meine'. Aufsätze und Vorträge zur deutschen Literatur des Mittelalters, Cologne and Vienna 1978.

Schröder, Werner, *Grenzen und Möglichkeiten einer althochdeutschen Literaturgeschichte* (Berichte über die Verhandlungen der Sächsischen Akademie der Wissenschaften zu Leipzig, philol.-hist. Klasse 105/2), Berlin 1959.

'Zum Vanitas-Gedanken im deutschen Alexanderlied', *Zeitschrift für deutsches Altertum* 91 (1961–2), pp. 38–55; repr. in W. Schröder, *Kleinere Schriften*, vol. IV, pp. 302–19.

'kunst und *sin* bei Wolfram von Eschenbach', *Euphorion* 67 (1973), pp. 219–43; repr. in W. Schröder, *Kleinere Schriften*, vol. I, pp. 74–98.

'Die von Tristande hant gelesen. Quellenhinweise und Quellenkritik im "Tristan" Gottfrieds von Straßburg', *Zeitschrift für deutsches Altertum* 104 (1975), pp. 307–38.

'Zum Typologie-Begriff und Typologie-Verständnis in der mediävistischen Literaturwissenschaft', in Harald Scholler (ed.), *The Epic in Medieval Society: Aesthetic and Moral Values*, Tübingen 1977, pp. 64–85; repr. in W. Schröder, *Kleinere Schriften*, vol. IV, pp. 264–84.

'Zum Verhältnis von Lateinisch und Deutsch um das Jahr 1000', in Beumann and Schröder (eds.), *Aspekte der Nationenbildung*, pp. 425–38.

Bibliography: secondary literature

Demontage und Montage von Wolframs Prologen im Prolog zum 'Jüngeren Titurel' (Abhandlungen der Marburger Gelehrten Gesellschaft 19) Munich 1983.

Kleinere Schriften. Vol. I: *Wolfram von Eschenbach: Spuren, Werke, Wirkungen*, Stuttgart 1989; vol. IV: *Zur frühmittelhochdeutschen Literatur*, Leipzig 1993.

Schröder, Werner (ed.), *Festschrift für Ludwig Wolff zum 70. Geburtstag*, Neumünster 1962.

Schulmeister, Rolf, *Aedificatio und imitatio. Studien zur intentionalen Poetik der Legende und Kunstlegende* (Geistes- und sozialwissenschaftliche Dissertationen 16), Hamburg 1971.

Schultz, James A., 'Classical rhetoric, medieval poetics, and the medieval vernacular prologue', *Speculum* 59 (1984), pp. 1–15.

Schulze, Joachim, 'Guigemar, der höfische Roman und die allegorische Psychologie des Mittelalters', *Archiv für das Studium der neueren Sprachen und Literaturen* 217 (132) (1980), pp. 312–26.

Schulze, Ursula, 'Literarkritische Äußerungen im Tristan Gottfrieds von Straßburg', *Beiträge zur Geschichte der deutschen Sprache und Literatur* (Tüb.) 88 (1967), pp. 285–310; repr. in Wolf (ed.) *Gottfried von Straßburg*, pp. 489–517.

Schwab, Ute, *Lex et gratia. Der literarische Exkurs Gottfrieds von Straßburg und Hartmanns 'Gregorius'* (Università degli studi di Messina: Pubblicazioni dell' Istituto di lingue e letterature straniere 1), Messina 1967.

Schweikle, Günther, *Dichter über Dichter in mittelhochdeutscher Literatur* (Deutsche Texte 12), Tübingen 1970.

'*stiure* und *lêre*. Zum "Parzival" Wolframs von Eschenbach', *Zeitschrift für deutsches Altertum* 106 (1977), pp. 183–99.

Schwietering, Julius, *Die Demutsformel mittelhochdeutscher Dichter* (Abhandlungen der Königl. Gesellschaft der Wissenschaften zu Göttingen, philol.-hist. Klasse n.s. 17/3), Berlin 1921; repr. in Schwietering, *Philologische Schriften*, pp. 140–215.

'Typologisches in mittelalterlicher Dichtung', in *Vom Werden des deutschen Geistes. Festgabe Gustav Ehrismann*, Berlin and Leipzig 1925, pp. 40–55; repr. in Schwietering, *Philologische Schriften*, pp. 269–81.

Philologische Schriften, Munich 1969.

Siefken, Hinrich, '*Der sælden strâze*. Zum Motiv der Zwei Wege bei Hartmann von Aue', *Euphorion* 61 (1967), pp. 1–21; repr. in Kuhn and Cormeau (eds.), *Hartmann von Aue*, pp. 450–77.

Simon, Gertrud, 'Untersuchungen zur Topik der Widmungsbriefe mittelalterlicher Geschichtsschreiber bis zum Ende des 12. Jahrhunderts I–II', *Archiv für Diplomatik* 4 (1958), pp. 52–119; 5/6 (1959–60), pp. 73–153.

Simon, Werner, et al. (eds.), *Festgabe für Ulrich Pretzel zum 65. Geburtstag*, Berlin 1963.

Singer, Johannes, 'Der Eingang von Strickers "Karl dem Großen"', *Zeitschrift für deutsche Philologie* 93, Sonderheft (1974), pp. 80–107.

Sol, Hendrik Bastiaan (ed.), *La Vie du Pape Saint Grégoire. Huit versions françaises médiévales de la légende du bon pêcheur*, Amsterdam 1977.

Sonderegger, Stefan, 'Tendenzen zu einem überregional geschriebenen Althochdeutsch', in Beumann and Schröder (eds.), *Aspekte der Nationenbildung*, pp. 229–73.

Speckenbach, Klaus, *Studium zum Begriff 'edelez herze' im 'Tristan' Gottfrieds von Straßburg* (Medium Aevum 6), Munich 1965.

'Endzeiterwartung im 'Lancelot-Gral-Zyklus'. Zur Problematik des Joachitischen Einflusses auf den Prosaroman', in Grubmüller et al. (eds.), *Geistliche Denkformen*, pp. 210–25.

Spiewok, Wolfgang, 'Zur Interpretation des strophischen Prologs zum "Tristan" Gottfrieds von Straßburg', *Wissenschaftliche Zeitschrift der Ernst-Moritz-Arndt-Universität Greifswald: Gesellschafts- und sprachwissenschaftliche Reihe* Nr. 1/2, Jahrgang 13 (1964), pp. 115–18; repr. in Wolfgang Spiewok, *Mittelalter-Studien*, Göppingen 1984 (Göppinger Arbeiten zur Germanistik 400), pp. 237–47.

Spitz, Hans-Jörg, *Die Metaphorik des geistigen Schriftsinns. Ein Beitrag zur allegorischen Bibelauslegung des ersten christlichen Jahrtausends* (Münstersche Mittelalter-Schriften 12), Munich 1972.

'Wolframs Bogengleichnis: ein typologisches Signal', in Fromm et al. (eds.), *Verbum et Signum* (Festschrift Friedrich Ohly), vol. II, pp. 247–76.

'Zwischen Furcht und Hoffnung. Zum Samaritergleichnis in Hartmanns von Aue "Gregorius"-Prolog', in Grubmüller et al. (eds.), *Geistliche Denkformen*, pp. 171–97.

review of Walter Haug, *Literaturtheorie im deutschen Mittelalter*, *Arbitrium* 6 (1988), pp. 20–2.

Spitzer, Leo, 'The prologue to the *Lais* of Marie de France and medieval poetics', *Modern Philology* 41 (1943–4), pp. 96–102; repr. in Leo Spitzer, *Romanische Literaturstudien*, Tübingen 1959, pp. 3–14.

'Des guillemets qui changent le climat poétique', *Publications of the Modern Language Association of America* 59 (1959), pp. 335–48; repr. in Leo Spitzer, *Romanische Literaturstudien*, Tübingen 1959, pp. 34–48.

Stackmann, Karl, 'Lucidarius', in Ruh et al. (eds.), *Verfasserlexikon*, vol. V, cols. 621–9.

'Der Erwählte. Thomas Manns Mittelalter-Parodie', *Euphorion* 53 (1959), pp. 61–74.

'Der Alten Werdekeit. Rudolfs "Alexander" und der Roman des Q. Curtius Rufus', in Hugo Moser et al. (eds.), *Festschrift Joseph Quint anläßlich seines 65. Geburtstages überreicht*, Bonn 1964, pp. 215–30.

'Karl und Genelûn. Das Thema des Verrats im *Rolandslied des Pfaffen Konrad* und seinen Bearbeitungen', *Poetica* 8 (1976), pp. 258–80.

'Die Gymnosophisten-Episode in deutschen Alexander-Erzählungen des Mittelalters', *Beiträge zur Geschichte der deutschen Sprache und Literatur* (Tüb.) 105 (1983), pp. 331–54.

Steer, Georg, 'Lucidarius', in Ruh et al. (eds.), *Verfasserlexikon*, vol. V, cols. 939–47.

'Der deutsche *Lucidarius* – ein Auftragswerk Heinrichs des Löwen?', *Deutsche Vierteljahrsschrift* 64 (1990), pp. 1–25.

Steger, Hugo, *David Rex et Propheta. König David als vorbildliche Verkörperung des Herrschers und Dichters im Mittelalter, nach Bilddarstellungen des achten bis zwölften Jahrhunderts* (Erlanger Beiträge zur Sprach- und Kunstwissenschaft 6), Nuremberg 1961.

414

Bibliography: secondary literature

Stein, Peter K., 'Formaler Schmuck und Aussage im "strophischen" Prolog zu Gottfrieds von Straßburg *Tristan*', *Euphorion* 69 (1975), pp. 371–87.

'Tristans Schwertleite. Zur Einschätzung ritterlich-höfischer Dichtung durch Gottfried von Straßburg', *Deutsche Vierteljahrsschrift* 51 (1977), pp. 300–50.

'Ein Weltherrscher als *vanitas*-Exempel in imperial-ideologisch orientierter Zeit? Fragen und Beobachtungen zum "Straßburger Alexander"', in Krohn et al. (eds.), *Stauferzeit*, pp. 144–80.

Steinhoff, Hans-Hugo, 'Zur Entstehungsgeschichte des deutschen Prosa-Lancelot', in Peter F. Ganz and Werner Schröder (eds.), *Probleme mittelalterlicher Überlieferung und Textkritik. Oxforder Colloquium 1966*, Berlin 1968, pp. 81–95; repr. in Frits P. van Oostrom (ed.), *Arturistiek in artikelen*, Utrecht 1978, pp. 149–63.

Stempel, Wolf-Dieter, 'Die Anfänge der romanischen Prosa im XIII. Jahrhundert', in Delbouille and Gumbrecht (eds.), *Généralités*, Heidelberg 1972, pp. 585–601.

Stierle, Karlheinz, 'Die Verwilderung des Romans als Ursprung seiner Möglichkeit', in Gumbrecht (ed.), *Literatur in der Gesellschaft*, pp. 253–313.

Strunk, Gerhard, *Kunst und Glaube in der lateinischen Heiligenlegende. Zu ihrem Selbstverständnis in den Prologen* (Medium Aevum 12), Munich 1970.

Struss, Lothar, 'Le Roman de L'Histoire du Graal (Robert de Boron)', in Frappier and Grimm (eds.), *Le Roman*, vol. I, pp. 361–75; vol. II, ed. Grimm, pp. 199f.

Sturlese, Loris, 'Filosofia e scienza della natura nel "Lucidarius" medioaltotedesco. A proposito della diffusione dei testi e delle idee di Guglielmo di Conches nella Germania medievale', *Giornale critico della filosofia italiana* 68 (1989), pp. 161–3.

Sturm-Maddox, Sara, 'Hortus non conclusus: Critics and the *Joie de la Cort*', *Oeuvres et Critiques* 5 (1980–1), part 2, pp. 61–71.

Suchomski, Joachim, *'Delectatio' und 'Utilitas'. Ein Beitrag zum Verständnis mittelalterlicher komischer Literatur* (Bibliotheca Germanica 18), Berne and Munich 1975.

Szklenar, Hans, *Studien zum Bild des Orients in vorhöfischen deutschen Epen* (Palaestra 243), Göttingen 1966.

'Die Jagdszene von Hocheppan – ein Zeugnis der Dietrichsage?', in Egon Kühebacher and Karl H. Vigl (eds.), *Deutsche Heldenepik in Tirol. König Laurin und Dietrich von Bern in der Dichtung des Mittelalters. Beiträge der Neustifter Tagung 1977 des Südtiroler Kulturinstitutes* (Schriftenreihe des Südtiroler Kulturinstitutes 7), Bolzano 1979, pp. 407–65.

Magister Nicolaus de Dybin. Vorstudien zu einer Edition seiner Schriften. Ein Beitrag zur Geschichte der literarischen Rhetorik im späteren Mittelalter (Münchener Texte und Untersuchungen 65), Munich 1981.

Taeger, Burkhard, 'Heliand', in Ruh et al. (eds.), *Verfasserlexikon*, vol. III, cols. 958–71.

Thornton, Alison G., *Weltgeschichte und Heilsgeschichte in Albrechts von Scharfenberg Jüngerem Titurel* (Göppinger Arbeiten zur Germanistik 211), Göppingen 1977.

Thornton, Thomas Perry, 'Unity and meaning in *Der Gute Gerhard*', *Annuale Mediaevale* 3 (1962), pp. 69–79.

Thraede, Klaus, 'Untersuchungen zum Ursprung und zur Geschichte der christlichen

Poesie', I–III, *Jahrbuch für Antike und Christentum* 4 (1961), pp. 108–27; 5 (1962), pp. 125–57; 6 (1963), pp. 101–11.

Studien zur Sprache und Stil des Prudentius (Hypomnemata 13), Göttingen 1965.

Tiemann, Hermann, 'Zur Geschichte des altfranzösischen Prosaromans', *Romanische Forschungen* 63 (1951), pp. 306–28.

Tschirch, Fritz, 'Das Selbstverständnis des mittelaltlerlichen deutschen Dichters', in Paul Wilpert (ed.), *Beiträge zum Berufsbewußtsein des mittelalterlichen Menschen* (Miscellanea Mediaevalia 3), Berlin 1964, pp. 239–85; repr. in Fritz Tschirch, *Spiegelungen. Untersuchungen vom Grenzrain zwischen Germanistik und Theologie*, Berlin 1966, pp. 123–66.

Unger, Helga, 'Vorreden deutscher Sachliteratur des Mittelalters als Ausdruck lyrischen Bewußtseins', in Glier et al. (eds.), *Werk – Typ – Situation*, pp. 217–51.

Urbanek, Ferdinand, 'Umfang und Intention von Lamprechts Alexanderlied', *Zeitschrift für deutsches Altertum* 99 (1970), pp. 96–120.

Uri, S. P., 'Some remarks on Partonopeus de Blois', *Neophilologus* 37 (1953), pp. 83–98.

Veit, Walter, 'Toposforschung. Ein Forschungsbericht', *Deutsche Vierteljahrsschrift* 37 (1963), pp. 120–63; repr. in Baeumer (ed.), *Toposforschung*, pp. 136–209, and, in part, in Jehn (ed.), *Toposforschung*, pp. 74–89.

Viëtor, Karl, 'Die Kunstanschauung der höfischen Epigonen', *Beiträge zur Geschichte der deutschen Sprache und Literatur* 46 (1922), pp. 85–124.

Vollmann, Benedikt K., 'Gregor IV (Gregor von Tours)', in *Reallexikon für Antike und Christentum*, vol. XII, cols. 895–930.

Vollmann-Profe, Gisela, *Kommentar zu Otfrids Evangelienbuch*, vol. I, Bonn 1976.

'Der Prolog zum "Heiligen Georg" des Reinbot von Durne', in Grubmüller et al. (eds.), *Befund und Deutung*, pp. 320–41.

Wiederbeginn volkssprachlicher Schriftlichkeit im hohen Mitteialter (1050/60–1160/70) (Geschichte der deutschen Literatur von den Anfängen bis zum Beginn der Neuzeit 1/2, ed. Joachim Heinzle), Königstein 1986; 2nd edn, Tübingen 1994.

Voorwinden, Norbert, review of Walter Haug, *Literaturtheorie im deutschen Mittelalter*, *Deutsche Bücher* 19 (1989), pp. 125–6.

Wachinger, Burghart, *Sängerkrieg. Untersuchungen zur Spruchdichtung des zwölften Jahrhunderts* (Münchener Texte und Untersuchungen 42), Munich 1973.

'Zur Rezeption Gottfrieds von Straßburg im 13. Jahrhundert', in Harms and Johnson (eds.), *Deutsche Literatur des späten Mittelalters*, pp. 56–82.

Walde, Ingrid B., 'Untersuchungen zur Literaturkritik und poetischen Kunstanschauung im deutschen Mittelalter', dissertation, University of Innsbruck 1961.

Walliczek, Wolfgang, *Rudolf von Ems: 'Der guote Gêrhart'* (Münchener Texte und Untersuchungen 46), Munich 1973.

Walpole, Ronald N. (ed.), *The Old French Johannes Translation of the Pseudo-Turpin Chronicle*, Berkeley etc. 1976.

Wang, Andreas, *Der 'Miles Christianus' im 16. und 17. Jahrhundert und seine mittelalterliche Tradition* (Mikrokosmos 1), Berne and Frankfurt am Main 1975.

Wapnewski, Peter, *Wolframs Parzival* (Germanische Bibliothek, 3rd series), Heidelberg 1955.

416

Bibliography: secondary literature

'Tristans Abschied. Ein Vergleich der Dichtung Gotfrids von Straßburg mit ihrer Vorlage Thomas', in *Festschrift Jost Trier*, Cologne and Graz 1964, pp. 335–63.

Warning, Rainer, 'Heterogenität des Erzählten – Homogenität des Erzählens. Zur Konstitution des höfischen Romans bei Chrétien de Troyes', *Wolfram-Studien* 5 (1979), pp. 79–95; expanded version 'Formen narrativer Identitätskonstitution im höfischen Roman', in Odo Marquard and Karlheinz Stierle (eds.), *Identität* (Poetik und Hermeneutik 8), Munich 1979, pp. 553–89.

Weber, Gottfried, 'Wolframs von Eschenbach Antwort auf Gotfrids von Straßburg "Tristan". Zur Grundstruktur des 'Willehalm"', *Sitzungsberichte der Wissenschaftlichen Gesellschaft an der Johann-Wolfgang-Goethe-Universität, Frankfurt am Main*, 12/5, Wiesbaden 1975, pp. 177–227.

Wehrli, Max, 'Roman und Legende im deutschen Hochmittelalter', in Gustav Erdmann and Alfons Eichstaedt (eds.), *Worte und Werke. Bruno Markwardt zum 60. Geburtstag*, Berlin 1961, pp. 428–43; repr. in Wehrli, *Formen mittelalterlicher Erzählung*, pp. 155–76.

'Mehrfacher Schriftsinn. Interpretationsprobleme höfischer Dichtung des Mittelalters', *Orbis Litterarum* 19 (1964), pp. 77–89.

'Wigalois', *Der Deutschunterricht* 17 (1965), part 2, pp. 18–35; repr. in Wehrli, *Formen mittelalterlicher Erzählung*, pp. 223–41.

Formen mittelalterlicher Erzählung. Aufsätze, Zurich and Freiburg im Breisgau 1969.

Wolframs 'Titurel' (Rheinisch-Westfälische Akademie der Wissenschaften, Vorträge G 194), Opladen 1974.

Geschichte der deutschen Literatur vom frühen Mittelalter bis zum Ende des 16. Jahrhunderts (Geschichte der deutschen Literatur von den Anfängen bis zur Gegenwart 1; Reclams Universal-Bibliothek 10294), Stuttgart 1980.

'Antike Mythologie im christlichen Mittelalter', *Deutsche Vierteljahrsschrift* 57 (1983), pp. 18–32.

Literatur im deutschen Mittelalter. Eine poetologische Einführung (Reclams Universal-Bibliothek 8038), Stuttgart 1984.

'Literaturtheorie im deutschen Mittelalter. Zu einem Buch von Walter Haug', *Neue Zürcher Zeitung* (13 January 1986), p. 15.

Weinhold, Karl, 'Zu dem deutschen Pilatusgedicht. Text, Sprache und Heimat', *Zeitschrift für deutsche Philologie* 8 (1877), pp. 253–88.

Wenzelburger, Dietmar, *Motivation und Menschenbild der 'Eneide' Heinrichs von Veldeke als Ausdruck der geschichtlichen Kräfte ihrer Zeit* (Göppinger Arbeiten zur Germanistik 135), Göppingen 1974.

Werner, Gisela, *Studien zu Konrads von Würzburg 'Partonopier et Meliur'* (Sprache und Dichtung n.s. 26), Berne and Stuttgart 1977.

Werner, Wilfried, and Heinz Zirnbauer (eds.), *Das 'Rolandslied' des Pfaffen Konrad. Faksimile-Ausgabe des Codex Palatinus Germanicus 112 der Universitätsbibliothek Heidelberg* (Facsimilia Heidelbergensia 1), Wiesbaden 1970.

Wetherbee, Winthrop, *Platonism and Poetry in the Twelfth Century. The Literary Influence of the School of Chartres*, Princeton 1972.

Wiesmann-Wiedemann, Friederike, *Le Roman du 'Willehalm' de Wolfram d'Eschenbach et l'épopée d'Aliscans. Etude de la transformation de l'épopée en roman* (Göppinger Arbeiten zur Germanistik 190), Göppingen 1976.

Bibliography: secondary literature

Wilke, Eckhard L., 'Zur Literaturschau in Gottfrieds von Straßburg "Tristan und Isolde"', *Acta Germanica* 3. *Festgabe Joachim Rosteutscher*, Cape Town 1968, pp. 37–46.

Wilkerson, William Byron, 'Form and Function of the Prologue in Early Middle High German Religious Poetry', dissertation, Pennsylvania State University 1974.

Winkelman, Johan H., 'Die Baummetapher im literarischen Exkurs Gottfrieds von Straßburg', *Amsterdamer Beiträge zur älteren Germanistik* 8 (1975), pp. 85–112.

'*Da ist des lützelen ze vil*. Zur Erkenntnisproblematik in Gottfrieds Tristanroman', *Neophilologus* 64 (1980), pp. 244–61.

'*ze guote und ouch ze rehte verstan*. Über Hartmann, Gottfried und Keiî', *Amsterdamer Beiträge zur älteren Germanistik* 18 (1982), pp. 79–93.

Wisbey, Roy, *Das Alexanderbild Rudolfs von Ems* (Philologische Studien und Quellen 31), Berlin 1966.

Wissmann, Wilhelm, *Skop* (Sitzungsberichte der Deutschen Akademie der Wissenschaften Berlin, Klasse für Sprachen, Literatur und Kunst 1954/2), Berlin 1955.

Woesler, Winfried, 'Heinrich von Veldeke. Der Prolog des "Servatius"', *Leuvense Bijdragen* 56 (1967), pp. 101–19.

Wolf, Alois, *Gregorius bei Hartmann von Aue und Thomas Mann*, Munich 1964.

'Zu Gottfrieds literarischer Technik', in Adolf Haslinger (ed.), *Sprachkunst als Weltgestaltung. Festschrift Herbert Seidler*, Salzburg and Munich 1966, pp. 384–409.

'Erzählkunst und verborgener Schriftsinn', *Sprachkunst* 2 (1971), pp. 1–42.

'*Fol i allai – fol m'en revinc!* Der Roman vom Löwenritter zwischen *mançonge* und *mære*', in Waltraud Fritsch-Rößler and Liselotte Homering (eds.), '*Uf der mâze pfat*'. *Festschrift für Werner Hoffmann zum 60. Geburtstag* (Göppinger Arbeiten zur Germanistik 555), Göppingen 1991, pp. 205–25.

Wolf, Alois (ed.), *Gottfried von Straßburg* (Wege der Forschung 320), Darmstadt 1973.

Wolfzettel, Friedrich (ed.), *Artusroman und Intertextualität. Beiträge der deutschen Sektionstagung der Internationalen Artusgesellschaft vom 16. bis 19. November 1989* (Beiträge zur deutschen Philologie 67), Giessen 1990.

Worstbrock, Franz Josef, 'Translatio artium. Über die Herkunft und Entwicklung einer kulturhistorischen Theorie', *Archiv für Kulturgeschichte* 47 (1965), pp. 1–22.

'Dilatatio materiae. Zur Poetik des "Erec" Hartmanns von Aue', *Frühmittelalterliche Studien* 19 (1985), pp. 1–30.

Wünsch, Marianne, 'Allegorie und Sinnstruktur in "Erec" und "Tristan"', *Deutsche Vierteljahrsschrift* 46 (1972), pp. 513–38.

Wuttke, Dieter, 'Didaktische Dichtung als Problem der Literaturkritik und der literaturwissenschaftlichen Wertung. Ein wissenschaftspolitischer Essay (Friedrich Dürrenmatt, Günter Grass, Der Stricker)', in Dennis Howard Green et al. (eds.), *From Wolfram and Petrarch to Goethe and Günter Grass. Studies in Literature in Honour of Leonard Forster* (Saecula spiritalia 5), Baden-Baden 1982, pp. 603–22.

Wyss, Ulrich, 'Rudolfs von Ems "Barlaam und Josaphat" zwischen Legende und

Roman', in Ganz and Schröder (eds.), *Probleme mittelhochdeutscher Erzähl-formen*, pp. 214–38.

Theorie der mittelhochdeutschen Legendenepik (Erlanger Studien 1), Erlangen 1973.

'Die Wunderketten in der "Crône"', in Alexander Cella and Peter Krämer (eds.), *Die mittelalterliche Literatur in Kärnten. Vorträge des Symposions in St. Georgen/Landsee vom 8. bis 13.9.1980* (Wiener Arbeiten zur germanischen Altertumskunde und Philologie 16), Vienna 1981, pp. 269–91.

Zatloukal, Klaus, 'India – ein idealer Staat im "Jüngeren Titurel"', in Ebenbauer et al. (eds.), *Strukturen und Interpretationen* (Festschrift Blanka Horacek), pp. 401–45.

Zumthor, Paul, 'Le Roman Courtois. Essai de définition', *Etudes Littéraires* 4 (1971), pp. 75–90.

Essai de poétique médiévale, Paris 1972; Engl. trans. by Philip Bennett, *Toward a Medieval Poetics*, Minneapolis and Oxford 1992.

Index

Index

Index

Index

Index

Cambridge Studies in Medieval Literature

General Editor: Professor Alastair Minnis, Professor of Medieval Literature, University of York